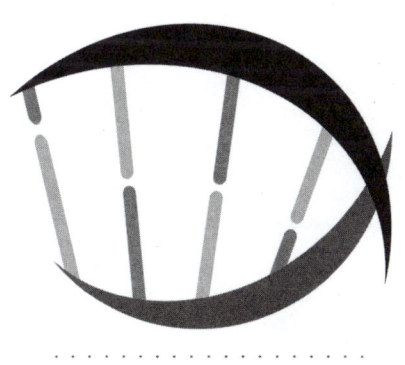

DARWIN DAY
PROGRAM

Darwin Day Collection One:
The Single Best Idea, Ever.

© The Darwin Day Program, 2002

Published Annually by
Tangled Bank Press,
Albuquerque, New Mexico

All rights reserved.
Printed in the United States of America.

Cover design, typography and book design
by Dave Feroe,
graphic designer, web designer, and creator of
Heresy House at www.heresyhouse.com

The portrait of Darwin is by artist Aaron Chesworth
and is a charcoal sketch of Julia Margaret Cameron's
photograph of Darwin, taken in 1881.

The sub-tittle of Darwin Day Collection One:
"The Single Best Idea, Ever" was inspired by Daniel Dennett
and his book *Darwin's Dangerous Idea*.

Library of Congress Cataloging-in-Publication Data

Darwin Day Collection One
edited by Amanda Chesworth. – 1st ed.

ISBN: 0-9723844-0-5

1. Evolution (Biology) – History.
2. Darwin, Charles, 1809-1882.

Darwin Day Collection One

the single best idea, ever.

EDITED BY
*Amanda Chesworth,
Sharon Hill, Kevin Lipovsky,
Eric Snyder, Ward Chesworth*

COVER AND BOOK DESIGN BY
Dave Feroe

published by
TANGLED BANK PRESS

*Contemplate a tangled bank,
clothed with many plants of many kinds,
with birds singing on the bushes,
with various insects flitting about,
and
with worms crawling through the damp earth:
these elaborately constructed forms
have all been produced by laws
acting around us.
Thus, the war of nature,
from famine and death,
the production of higher animals
directly follows.
There is a grandeur in this view of life:
whilst the planet has gone
cycling on according to
the fixed law of gravity,
from so simple a beginning
endless forms most beautiful and
most wonderful have been
and are being
evolved.*

– Charles Darwin

[Phillip Appleman is the poet who reset Darwin's lyrical prose into lines of free verse.]

TO REMEMBER:

William D. Hamilton

Marvin Harris

Stephen Jay Gould

Douglas Adams

CONTENTS

PREFACE

The Darwin Day Program: 1
   An International Celebration of Science and Humanity
   by Robert J. Stephens and Amanda Chesworth

∞

INTRODUCTORY ESSAY

We Are All Scientists 5
   by Thomas H. Huxley

∞

SECTION ONE
IN DARWIN'S FOOTSTEPS: TRIBUTES TO FOUR DEPARTED SCIENTISTS

On W. D. Hamilton (1936-2000) 13
   by Richard Dawkins

Marvin Harris: A Remembrance (1927-2001) 17
   by John R. Cole

Farewell, Fossilface: A Memoir of Stephen Jay Gould (1941-2002) 21
   by Richard Milner

Eulogy for Douglas Adams (1952-2001) 29
   by Richard Dawkins

∞

SPECIAL SECTION: DARWIN COUNTRY

Shrewsbury, Shropshire: Birthplace of Charles Darwin 35
   and Darwin Country, *by Peter D. A. Boyd*

∞

SECTION TWO
DARWIN – THE MAN AND HIS LEGACY

Before the Origin: Commemorating the Darwin Wallace paper 45
   read to the Linnean Society in 1858, *by Richard Dawkins*

About Darwin: Biographies of revolutionary routine 55
   by Frode Skarstein

Book Reviews *by Adrian Barnett* 63
   Alfred Russel Wallace: A Life by Peter Raby
   The Alfred Russel Wallace Reader by Jane R. Camarini

From Scientist or Saint: Does Darwin Deserve a Day? 65
    by Robin McKie

There is a Grandeur in this View of Life 67
    by Charles F. Urbanowicz

Book Review *by Molleen Matsumura* 71
    Darwin – Norton Third Edition edited by Philip Appleman

Celebrating Darwin's Birthday 75
    by Gary L. Bennett

Darwin Before the Penny Dropped 77
    by Hugh Rance

Book Review *by Richard Milner* 81
    Darwin, His Daughter & Evolution by Randal Keynes

An Evolutionary Holiday 85
    by Sharon Hill

The Other Great Emancipator: Charles Darwin's Legacy For Our Lives ... 87
    by Elof Axel Carlson

Book Review *by Mark Ridley* 91
    George Gaylord Simpson by Leo F. Laporte

Happy Birthday Uncle Charlie 95
    by Barry Palevitz

Why Learn About Darwin? 97
    by Léo F. Laporte

Section Three
Natural Selections: Life as We Know It

Where Do We Come From? 103
    We still have few clues to the origin of life, *by Massimo Pigliucci*

Book Review *by Robin McKie* 115
    Y: The Descent of Men by Steve Jones

Book Review *by Wolf Roder* 117
    Strange Creations: Aberrant Ideas of Human Origins from
    Ancient Astronauts to Aquatic Apes by Donna Kossy

Evolution: The Fossils Say YES! 119
    by Warwick Don

As Old as the Hills 123
    by Ian Plimer

Book Reviews *by Ian Tattersall* 125
    The Structure of Evolutionary Theory by Stephen J. Gould
    Genetics, Paleontology, and Macroevolution, 2nd ed. By Jeffrey S. Levinton

Teaching Evolution to the Alienated 131
   by Bill Peddie

Book Review *by Michael Chapman* 137
   Evolution's Workshop by Edward Larson

Darwin Day is here 141
   by Mercutio

But seriously, folks... What's wrong with the Darwin Awards? 145
   by Molleen Matsumura

Book Review *by Vicki Hyde* 151
   Horrible Science: Evolve or Die by Phil Gates

The Natural History Museum marks the anniversary of 153
   Charles Darwin's Birthday, *by Rachel Craddock and Debbie Chapman*

Book Review *by Adrian Barnett* 155
   Stuffed Animals and Pickled Heads: The Culture and
   Evolution of Natural History Museums by Stephen T. Asma

Convincing Men They Are Monkeys 157
   by Sherrie L. Lyons

Book Review *by Diane Swanson* 165
   The Beast in You!: Activities & Questions to Explore Evolution
   by Marc McCutcheon

CSICOP on Creationism 167
   by Kevin Christopher

What Is Darwinian Feminism? 171
   by Nancy L. Easterlin

Does Evolution = Atheism? 181
   by David E. Thomas

Book Reviews *by Robin McKie* 187
   The Future of Life by E.O. Wilson
   What Evolution Is by Ernst Mayr

∞

Special Section:
The Next Generation: Education & Our Future

Challenging Students 193
   by Jon Gonsiewski

Topic: Charles Darwin's Impact Upon Our World
   by Laura Mulcahy 195
   by Owen Jones 197
   by Fern Baldwin 199
   by Dawn VanDerWende 203

Additional Resources 207

Section Four
The Grandeur In This View of Life

Evolving Awareness: Planning your Darwin Day Event 211
   by Rob Beeston and Amanda Chesworth

Darwin Remembers: Recalling a Life's Voyage – A Play in One Act 217
   Excerpt: The Huxley / Wilberforce Debate of 1860
   by Floyd Sandford

Darwin as "Different Drummer" 221
   by Mynga Futrell

Darwin's Gardens 225
   by Joan Treis

Darwin's Ark 229
   by Philip Appleman

Deep Time in the Deep South 237
   by David C. Kopaska-Merkel

Educating the Educators 241
   by Massimo Pigliucci

The Ballad of Charles Darwin 245
   by The Opposums of Truth

Quiz 247
   by Richard Carter

Recipe: Primordial Soup 251
   by Neal Matson

Six Cartoons 253
   by Jeff Swenson

Songs from the Skeptical Choir – Yes, Rhesus Monkey 257
   by Hugh Young

Creationists Announce New Theory of Gravity! 259
   by August Berkshire

A Toast to a Lady 261
   by Langdon Smith

Section Five
In the Beginning Was the Watchmaker: Sighted or Blind?

15 Answers to Creationist Nonsense 267
   by John Rennie

Myths and Conceptions of Darwin: 277
   Refocusing and Refuting Arguments Against Evolution
   by Kieran P. McNulty

Is Creationism Scientific? 287
    by Stephen Law

Book Review *by Glenn Branch* 293
    Intelligent Design Creationism and Its Critics: Philosophical,
    Theological, and Scientific Perspectives, Edited by Robert T. Pennock

The Design Argument 297
    by Elliott Sober

Darwinism and Mendelism-Morganism: 323
    Science As Seen Through Two Ideological Lenses, *by Lawrence S. Lerner*

Rhetorical Legerdemain in Intelligent-Design Literature 327
    by Jason Rosenhouse

Creationism to Universal Darwinism: Evolution and Religion Today 339
    by Taner Edis

Nature's God Tries to Clean up the Mess 345
    by Marie Alena Castle

My Experiences of Evolution in School 347
    by Brandon Seger

Darwin's Day 349
    by Vicki Hyde

SPECIAL SECTION:
PBS PRESENTS EVOLUTION:

Panel Discussion on Evolution 353

SECTION SIX
ABUSING SCIENCE: THE CREATIONIST PHENOMENON

Introduction: Antievolutionism around the world 381
    by Glenn Branch

Creationism in New Zealand 387
    by David Riddell

Book Review *by Bob Merrick* 391
    True North by George Erickson

Antidarwinism in Italy 393
    by Silvano Fuso

Two Worlds in Conflict: Creationism & Evolution in Argentina 399
    by Juan De Gennaro

News from the British Humanist Association 403
    Compiled by Marilyn Mason

Fear of Science in Kansas 407
   by Liz Craig

Creationism in New Mexico 411
   by David E. Thomas

Evolution and Creationism: 415
Why Science and Not Creationism Must Be Taught In Classrooms
   by Gerry Dantone

Harun Yahya and Islamic Creationism 419
   by Taner Edis

Muslim Creationism on the Misinformation Highway 423
   by Lynne Schultz

Section Seven
Science & Society

How The Mind Works 433
   by Steven Pinker

Ecoviews: Pathology and The Meaning of Life 443
   by Ron Brooks

Sustainability and the End of History 445
   by Ward Chesworth

Darwin Day Program Award Winning Essay: 449
How to Increase the Public's Understanding of Science
   by David Aaronson

Why science should warm our hearts 453
   by Colin Tudge

In Conclusion

...So Let's All Be Scientists 461
   by Richard Carter

PREFACE

"It is appropriate to have a special day for the author of one of the most powerful ideas in the history of science and culture, and to press for the global recognition of its importance in the human future."

– E. O. Wilson (2000)

THE DARWIN DAY PROGRAM:
AN INTERNATIONAL CELEBRATION OF SCIENCE AND HUMANITY

by Robert J. Stephens and Amanda Chesworth

The Darwin Day Program celebrates life through one of humanity's great creations, science. Specifically, we base our celebration on the life and work of Charles Darwin, whose discovery of how evolution works through natural selection, not only gave us the framework that makes sense of biology, but a mechanism that reaches into all parts of our existence, as the great Darwinists of today have shown. Indeed, we are lucky that several of those contemporary stars are represented in this volume.

However, if we had confined our book only to the writings of recognized leaders in the field, we would have defeated the objectives of the Darwin Day Program, which is to present science in accessible ways to as many people as possible, and to encourage all who wish, to develop and communicate their own ideas. Developing a real, grass roots understanding of Darwinism is our aim. We all need to be street-smart scientists in the modern world. As Judith Stone, a fine scientific journalist, has said "as voters we're de facto scientific advisers. If we don't get it right, things could go very wrong."

What we succeeded in doing last year, was to encourage and inspire local groups, in both academic and non-academic settings, to celebrate in a number of different ways, the 12th of February, anniversary of Darwin's birthday. Activities appropriate to all age groups and all walks of life were suggested and created, with much feedback between all Darwin day members. As a result, a gratifyingly large cross section of the population became involved. This volume is a record of that wide spectrum of people who offered talks, videos, demonstrations, games and other entertainments, to their fellow citizens. Obviously, everything that went on could not be included, but we think that you will get a real flavor of the celebration from what is to be found between these covers. You will also see the diverse application of the Darwin Day Program and the year-round educational outreach effort the program affords each and every one of us in "evolving awareness" within our global community.

In addition, we have taken the opportunity to include a number of appropriate book reviews and other writings. Many more were submitted than we could find the space to include – but there is always next year.

[ABOUT THE AUTHORS]

Robert J. Stephens holds a Ph.D. in cell biology and is the founder and president of TECHSTAR Industries. He is Co-founder and Chair of the Darwin Day Program.

Amanda Chesworth is Executive Director of the Darwin Day Program and the Educational Director of Committee for the Scientific Investigation of Claims of the Paranormal (CSICOP).

AN INTRODUCTION

WE ARE ALL SCIENTISTS

❝The most wonderful discovery made by scientists is science itself.❞
— Jacob Bronowski in *The Ascent of Man* (1976)

❝All truths are easy to understand once they are discovered; the point is to discover them.❞
— Galileo Galilei (17th Century C.E.)

"We Are All Scientists" is excerpted from Thomas Henry Huxley's collected essays, **Darwiniana***, published in 1893. It is part of "Six Lectures to Working Men On Our Knowledge of the Causes of the Phenomena of Organic Nature," first published in 1863. The essay is a fitting introduction to the primary goal of the Darwin Day Program in improving the public's understanding and involvement in science.*

WE ARE ALL SCIENTISTS
by Thomas H. Huxley

Scientific investigation is not, as many people seem to suppose, some kind of modern black art. You might easily gather this impression from the manner in which many persons speak of scientific inquiry, or talk about inductive and deductive philosophy, or the principles of the "Baconian philosophy." I do protest that, of the vast number of cants in this world, there are none, to my mind, so contemptible as the pseudo-scientific cant which is talked about the "Baconian philosophy."

To hear people talk about the great Chancellor – and a very great man he certainly was, – you would think that it was he who had invented science, and that there was no such thing as sound reasoning before the time of Queen Elizabeth! Of course you say, that cannot possibly be true; you perceive, on a moment's reflection, that such an idea is absurdly wrong...

The method of scientific investigation is nothing but the expression of the necessary mode of working of the human mind. It is simply the mode at which all phenomena are reasoned about, rendered precise and exact. There is no more difference, but there is just the same kind of difference, between the mental operations of a man of science and those of an ordinary person, as there is between the operations and methods of a baker or of a butcher weighing out his goods in common scales, and the operations of a chemist in performing a difficult and complex analysis by means of his balance and finely-graduated weights. It is not that the action of the scales in the one case, and the balance in the other, differ in the principles of their construction or manner of working; but the beam of one is set on an infinitely finer axis than the other, and of course turns by the addition of a much smaller weight.

You will understand this better, perhaps, if I give you some familiar example. You have all heard it repeated, I dare say, that men of science work by means of induction and deduction, and that by the help of these operations, they, in a sort of sense, wring from Nature certain other things, which are called natural laws, and causes, and that out of these, by some cunning skill of their own, they build up hypotheses and theories. And it is imagined by many, that the operations of the common mind can be by no means compared with these processes, and that they have to be acquired by a sort of special apprenticeship to the craft. To hear all these large words, you would think that the mind of a man of science must be constituted differently from that of his fellow men; but if you will not be frightened by terms, you will discover that you are quite wrong, and that all these terrible apparatus are being used by yourselves every day and every hour of your lives.

There is a well-known incident in one of Moliere's plays, where the author makes the hero express unbounded delight on being told that he has been talking prose during the whole of his life. In the same way, I trust, that you will take comfort, and be delighted with yourselves, on the discovery that you have been acting on the principles of inductive and deductive philosophy during the same period. Probably there is not one who has not in the course of the day had occasion to set in motion a complex train of reasoning, of the very same kind, through differing of course in degree, as that which a scientific man goes through in tracing the causes of natural phenomena.

A very trivial circumstance will serve to exemplify this. Suppose you go into a fruiterer's shop, wanting an apple, – you take up one, and, on biting it, you find it is sour; you look at it, and see that it is hard and green. You take up another one, and that too is hard, green, and sour. The shopman offers you a third; but, before biting it, you examine it, and find that it is hard and green, and you immediately say that you will not have it, as it must be sour, like those that you have already tried.

Nothing can be more simple than that, you think; but if you will take the trouble to analyze and trace out into its logical elements what has been done by the mind, you will be greatly surprised. In the first place, you have performed the operation of induction. You found that, in two experiences, hardness and greenness in apples went together with sourness. It was so in the first case, and it was confirmed in the second. True, it is a very small basis, but still it is enough to make an induction from; you generalize the facts, and you expect to find sourness in apples where you get hardness and greenness. You found upon that a general law, that all hard and green apples are sour; and that, so far as it goes, is a perfect induction. Well, having got your natural law in this way, when you are offered another apple which you find is hard and green, you say, "All hard and green apples are sour; this apple is hard and green, therefore this apple is sour." That train of reasoning is what logicians call a syllogism, and has all its various parts and terms – its major premise, its minor premise, and its conclusion. And, by the help of further reasoning, which, if drawn out, would have to be exhibited in two or three other syllogisms, you arrive at your final determination, "I will not have that apple." So that, you see, you have, in the first place, established a law by induction, and upon that you have founded a deduction, and reasoned out the special conclusion of the particular case. Well now, suppose, having got your law, that at some time afterwards, you are discussing the qualities of apples with a friend: you will say to him, "It is a very curious thing, – but I find that all hard and green apples are sour!" Your friend says to you, "But how do you know that?" You at once reply, "Oh, because I have tried them over and over again, and have always found them to be so." Well, if we were talking science instead of common sense, we should call that an experimental verification. And, if still opposed, you go further, and say, "I have heard from the people in Somersetshire and Devonshire, where a large number of apples are grown, that they have observed the same thing. It is also found to be the case in Normandy, and in North America. In short, I find it to be the universal experience of mankind wherever attention has been directed to the subject." Whereupon, your friend, unless he is a very unreasonable man, agrees with you, and is convinced that you are quite right in the conclusion you have drawn. He believes, although perhaps he does not know he believes it, that the more extensive verifications are, – that the more frequently experiments have been made, and results of the same kind arrived at, – that the more varied the conditions under which the same results are attained, the more certain is the ultimate conclusion, and he disputes the question no further. He sees that the experiment has been tried under all sorts of conditions, as to time, place, and people, with the same result; and he says with you, therefore, that the law you have laid down must be a good one, and he must believe it.

In science we do the same thing; – the philosopher exercises precisely the same faculties, though in a much more delicate manner. In scientific inquiry it becomes a matter of duty to expose a supposed law to every possible kind of verification, and to take care, moreover, that this is done intentionally, and not left to mere accident, as in the case of the apples. And in science, as in common life, our confidence in a law is in exact proportion to the absence of variation in the result of our experimental verifications. For instance, if you let go your grasp of an article you may have in your hand, it will immediately fall to the ground. That is a very common verification of one of the best established laws of nature – that of gravitation. The method by which men of science establish the existence of that law is exactly the same as that by which we have established the trivial proposition about the sourness of hard and green apples. But we believe in such an extensive, thorough, and unhesitating manner because the universal experience of mankind verifies it, and we can verify it ourselves at any time; and that is the strongest possible foundation on which any natural law can rest.

So much, then, by way of proof that the method of establishing laws in science is exactly the same as that pursued in common life. Let us now turn to another matter (though really it is but another phase of the same question), and that is, the method by which, from the relations of certain phenomena, we prove that some stand in the position of causes towards the others.

I want to put the case clearly before you, and I will therefore show you what I mean by another familiar example. I will suppose that one of you, on coming down in the morning to the parlour of your house, finds that a tea-pot and some spoons which had been left in the room on the previous evening are gone, – the window is open, and you observe the mark of a dirty hand on the window-frame, and perhaps, in addition to that, you notice the impress of a hob-nailed show on the gravel outside. All these phenomena have struck your attention instantly, and before two seconds have passed you say, "Oh, somebody has broken open the window, entered the room, and run off with the spoons and the teapot!" That speech is out of your mouth in a moment. And you will probably add, "I know there has; I am quite sure of it!" You mean to say exactly what you know; but in reality you are giving expression to what is, in all essential particulars, an hypothesis. You do not know it at all; it is nothing but an hypothesis rapidly framed in your own mind. And it is an hypothesis founded on a long train of inductions and deductions.

What are those inductions and deductions, and how have you got at this hypothesis? You have observed, in the first place, that the window is open; but by a train of reasoning involving many inductions and deductions, you have probably arrived long before at the general law – and a very good one it is – that windows do not open of themselves; and you therefore conclude that something has opened the window. A second general law that you have arrived at in the same way is, that tea-pots and spoons do not go out of a window spontaneously, and you are satisfied that, as they are not now where you left them, they have been removed. In the third place, you look at the marks on the window-sill, and the shoe-marks outside, and you say that in all previous experience the former kind of mark has never been produced by anything else but the hand of a human being; and the same experience shows that no other animal but man at present wears shows with hob-nails in them such as would produce the marks in the gravel. I do not know, even if we could discover any of those "missing links" that are talked about, that they would help us to any other conclusion! At any rate the law which states our present experience is strong enough for my present purpose. You next reach the conclusion, that as these kinds of marks have not been left by any other animals than man, or are liable to be formed in any other way than by a man's hand and show, the marks in question have been formed by a man in that way. You have, further, a general law, founded on observation and experience, and that, too, is, I am sorry to say, a very universal and unimpeachable one, – that some men are thieves; and you assume at once from all these premises – and that is what constitutes your hypothesis – that the man who made the marks outside and on the windowsill, opened the window, got into the room, and stole your teapot and spoons. You have now arrived at a vera causa; – you have assumed a cause which, it is plain, is competent to produce all the phenomena you have observed. You can explain all these phenomena only by the hypothesis of a thief. But that is a hypothetical conclusion, of the justice of which you have no absolute proof at all; it is only rendered highly probable by a series of inductive and deductive reasonings.

I suppose your first action, assuming that you are a man of ordinary common sense, and that you have established this hypothesis to your own satisfaction, will very likely be to go for the police, and set them on the track of the burglar, with the view to the recovery of your property. But just as you are starting with this object, some person comes in, and on learning what you are about, says, "My good friend, you are going on a great deal too fast. How do you know that the man who really made the marks took the spoons? It might have been a monkey that took them, and the man may have merely looked in afterwards." You would probably reply, "Well, that is all very well, but you see it as contrary to all experience of the way teapots and spoons are abstracted; so that, at any rate, your hypothesis is less probable than mine." While you are talking the thing over in this way, another friend arrives. And he might say, "Oh, my dear sire, you are certainly going on a great deal too fast. You are most presumptuous. You admit that all these occurrences took place when you were fast asleep, at a time when you could not possibly have known anything about what was taking place. How do you know that the laws of Nature are not suspended during the night? It may be that there has been some kind of supernatural interference in this case." In point of fact, he declares that your hypothesis is one of which you cannot at all demonstrate the truth and that you are by no means sure that the laws of Nature are the same when you are asleep as when you are awake.

Well, now, you cannot at the moment answer that kind of reasoning. You feel that your worthy friend has you somewhat at a disadvantage. You feel perfectly convinced in your own mind, however, that you are quite right, and you say to him, "My good friend, I can only be guided by the natural possibilities of the case, and if you will be kind enough to stand aside and permit me to pass, I will go and fetch the police." Well, we will suppose that your journey is successful, and that by good luck you meet with a policeman; that eventually the burglar is found with your property on his person, and the marks correspond to his hand and to his boots. Probably any jury would consider those facts a very good experimental verification of your hypothesis, touching the cause of the abnormal phenomena observed in your parlour, and would act accordingly.

Now, in this suppositious case, I have taken phenomena of a very common kind, in order that you might see what are the different steps in an ordinary process of reasoning, if you will only take the trouble to analyse it carefully. All the operations I have described, you will see, are involved in the mind of any man of sense in leading him to a conclusion as to the course he should take in order to make good a robbery and punish the offender. I say that you are led, in that case, to your conclusion by exactly the same train of reasoning as that which a man of science pursues when he is endeavouring to discover the origin and laws of the most occult phenomena. The process is, and always must be, the same; and precisely the same mode of reasoning was employed by Newton and Laplace in their endeavours to discover and define the causes of the movements of the heavenly bodies, as you, with your own common sense, would employ to detect a burglar. The only difference is, that the nature of the inquiry being more abstruse, every step has to be most carefully watched, so that there may not be a single crack or flaw in your hypothesis. A flaw or crack in many of the hypotheses of daily life may be of little or no moment as affecting the general correctness of the conclusions at which we may arrive; but, in a scientific inquiry, a fallacy, great or small, is always of importance, and is sure to be in the long run constantly productive of mischievous, if not fatal results.

Do not allow yourselves to be misled by the common notion that an hypothesis is untrustworthy simply because it is an hypothesis. It is often urged, in respect to some scientific conclusion, that, after all, it is only an hypothesis. But what more have we to guide us in nine-tenths of the most important affairs of daily life than hypotheses, and often very ill-based ones? So that in science, where the evidence of an hypothesis is subjected to the most rigid examination, we may rightly pursue the same course. You may have hypotheses and hypotheses. A man may say, if he likes, that the moon is made of green cheese: that is an hypothesis. But another man, who has devoted a great deal of time and attention to the subject, and availed himself of the most powerful telescopes and the results of the observations of others, declares that in his opinion it is probably composed of materials very similar to those of which our own earth is made up: and that is also only an hypothesis. But I need not tell you that there is an enormous difference in the value of the two hypotheses. That one which is based on sound scientific knowledge is sure to have a corresponding value; and that which is a mere hasty random guess is likely to have but little value. Every great step in our progress in discovering causes has been made in exactly the same way as that which I have detailed to you. A person observing the occurrence of certain facts and phenomena asks, naturally enough, what process, what kind of operation known to occur in Nature applied to the particular case, will unravel and explain the mystery? Hence you have the scientific hypothesis; and its value will be proportionate to the care and completeness with which its basis has been tested and verified. It is in these matters as in the commonest affairs of practical life: the guess of the fool will be folly, while the guess of the wise man will contain wisdom. In all cases, you see that the value of the result depends on the patience and faithfulness with which the investigator applies to his hypothesis every possible kind of verification… ∞

[ABOUT THE AUTHOR]

Thomas Henry Huxley was born on May 4, 1825, and died on June 29, 1895. "In November of 1859, after reading the newly-published *Origin of Species*, he warned Charles Darwin that there would be mischief from anti-evolutionists, and that he himself was sharpening his claws preparing to annihilate these creationist critics. Huxley promoted and defended Darwinism for most of his life, earning the title of Darwin's Bulldog. Huxley also contributed his own work to the scientific community but more importantly, to society at large. His efforts in promoting the public's understanding of science and his thoughts on day-to-day affairs continue to be re-visited and championed within our communities today.

[ADDITIONAL RESOURCES]

The Darwin's Bulldog membership club: http://www.darwinsbulldogs.com
 Darwin's Bulldogs is the official membership club for the Darwin Day Program with its primary aim being to promote and defend science and evolution throughout the world. The name was chosen in honor of Thomas Henry Huxley, Darwin's original Bulldog and a hero for all time.

The Huxley File: http://aleph0.clarku.edu/huxley/
 Created by Charles Blinderman, Professor of English and Adjunct Professor of Biology at Clark University and David Joyce, Associate Professor of Mathematics and Computer Science at Clark University "the Huxley File is a memorial to Thomas H. Huxley's achievements in many fields. Its ambition is to bring forth T. H. Huxley so that we can advance our understanding of Victorian culture, of the contrasting features of superstition and of science, and of our own time; and take pleasure in reading one of the finest writers of any time any where."

SECTION ONE

In Darwin's Footsteps:
Tributes to Four Departed Scientists

❝We are like dwarfs on the shoulders of giants, so that we can see more than they, and things at a great distance, not by virtue of any sight on our part, or any physical distinction, but because we are carried high and raised up by their giant size."

– Bernard of Chartres (12th Century C.E.)

❝If I have seen further it is by standing on the shoulders of Giants ."

– Isaac Newton (17th Century C.E.)

Richard Dawkins' obituary for William D. Hamilton originally appeared in **The Independent** *on March 10, 2000 and is republished here with permission from the author.*

ON W. D. HAMILTON
(1936-2000)
by Richard Dawkins

W. D. Hamilton is a good candidate for the title of most distinguished Darwinian since Darwin. Other candidates would have to include R. A. Fisher, whom Hamilton revered as a young student at Cambridge. Hamilton resembled Fisher in his penetrating biological intuition and his ability to render it in mathematics. But, like Darwin and unlike Fisher, he was also a superb field naturalist and explorer. I suspect that, of all his twentieth century successors, Darwin would most have enjoyed talking to Hamilton. Partly because they could have swapped jungle tales and beetle lore, partly because both were gentle and deep, but mostly because Hamilton the theorist was responsible for clearing up so many of the very problems that had intrigued and tantalised Darwin.

William Donald Hamilton FRS was Royal Society Research Professor in the Department of Zoology at Oxford, and a Professorial Fellow of New College. He was born in 1936, spent a happy childhood botanising and collecting butterflies in Kent, was educated at Tonbridge, then Cambridge where he read Genetics. For his Ph.D. he moved to London where he was jointly enrolled at University College and London School of Economics. He became a Lecturer at Imperial College in 1964, where his teaching skills were not highly rated. After a brief Visiting Professorship at Harvard, he accepted a Museum Professorship at the University of Michigan in 1977. Finally, in 1984 he moved to Oxford at the invitation of Richard Southwood, who had been his Professor at Imperial.

Hamilton was showered with medals and honours by the academies and learned societies of the world. He won the Kyoto Prize, the Fyssen Prize, the Wander Prize, and the Crafoord Prize – instituted by the Swedish Academy because Alfred Nobel unaccountably failed to include non-medical Biology in his list of eligible subjects. But honours and recognition did not come early. The autobiographical chapters of Hamilton's collection of papers, "Narrow Roads of Gene Land", reveal a lonely young man driven to self-doubt by lack of comprehension among his peers and superiors. To epitomise the Cambridge of his undergraduate days, where "many biologists hardly seemed to believe in evolution" he quotes one senior professor: "Insects do not live for themselves alone. Their lives are devoted to the survival of the species…" This is "Group Selection", a solecism which would cause today's biology undergraduates to wince, but they have the advantage of a post-Hamilton education. The young Hamilton felt that in Cambridge he was wincing alone. Only the cantankerous Fisher made sense to him, and he had been advised that Fisher "was good with statistics but knew nothing about biology."

For his doctoral work he proposed a difficult mathematical model with a simple conclusion now known as "Hamilton's Rule." It states that a gene for altruistic self sacrifice will spread through a population if the cost to the altruist is outweighed by the benefit to the recipient devalued by a fraction representing the genetic relatedness between the two. Hamilton's original paper was so difficult and innovative that it almost failed to be published, and was largely ignored for a decade. When finally noticed, its influence spread exponentially until it became one of the most cited papers in all of biology. It is the key to understanding half the altruistic cooperation in nature. The key to the other half – reciprocation among unrelated individuals – is a theory to which Hamilton was later to make a major contribution, in collaboration with the social scientist Robert Axelrod.

The great obsession of his later career was parasites – their evolutionary rather than their medical impact. Over twenty years, Hamilton convinced more and more biologists that parasites are the key to many outstanding problems left by Darwin, including the baffling riddle of the evolution of sex. The sexual shuffling of the genetic pack is an elaborate trick for outrunning parasites in the endless race through evolutionary time. This work led Hamilton into the arcane world of computer simulation, where his models were as richly textured, in their way, as his beloved Brazilian jungle. His spin off theory of sexual selection (how Darwin would have relished it!) was that bird of paradise tails and similar male extravaganzas are driven by the evolution of female diagnostic skills: females are like sceptical doctors, actively seeking parasite-free males to supply genes for their shared posterity. Male advertisement is an honest boast of health.

Hamilton's mathematical models never became arid; they were laced with, and often inspired by, bizarre natural history. Would that every mathematical lump were leavened, as Hamilton's were, by eye-witness accounts of, say, the male mite who copulates with all his sisters and then dies before any of them are born. Or of aphid females who give live birth to their daughters and granddaughters simultaneously.

For most scientists, good ideas are a scarce commodity, to be milked for everything they are worth. Hamilton, by contrast, would bury, in little throwaway asides, ideas for which others would kill. Sometimes he buried them so deeply that he overlooked them himself. Extreme social life in termites poses a particular evolutionary problem not shared by the equally social ants, bees and wasps. An ingenious theory exists, widely attributed to an author whom I shall call X. Hamilton and I were once talking termites, and he spoke favourably of X's theory. "But Bill", I protested, "That isn't X's theory. It's your theory. You thought of it first." He gloomily denied it, so I asked him to wait while I ran to the library. I returned with a bound journal volume and shoved under his nose his own discreetly buried paragraph on termites. Eeyorishly, he conceded that, yes, it did appear to be his own theory after all, but X had explained it much better. In a world where scientists vie for priority, Hamilton was endearingly unique.

Those who loved him saw a Felix with nine lives. Charmingly accident-prone, Bill would always bounce back. A childhood experiment with explosives cost him several finger joints of his right hand. He was frequently knocked off his bicycle, probably because of misjudgements by Oxford motorists who couldn't believe a man of his age with a great shock of white hair could possibly cycle so fast. And he travelled dangerously in wilder and more remote places than Oxford. He hiked through Rwanda at the height of the civil war, and was treated as a spy, so implausible was his (true) story that he was looking for ants. Held up at knife point in Brazil, he made the mistake of fighting back, and was viciously wounded. He jumped into an Amazon tributary when his boat was sinking, in order to plug the hole, like the little Dutch boy, with his thumb (the ferocity of Piranha fish, he explained, is over-rated). Finally, to gather indirect evidence for the theory (of which he was a strong supporter) that the AIDS virus was originally introduced into the human population in an oral polio vaccine tested in Africa in the 1950s, Hamilton went, with two brave companions, to the depths of the Congo jungle in January 2000. He was rushed back to London, apparently with severe malaria, seemed to recover, then collapsed into complications and coma. This time, he didn't bounce back.

He is survived by his wife, Christine, from whom he had been amicably separated for some time, by their three daughters Helen, Ruth and Rowena, and by his devoted companion of recent years, Luisa Bozzi. ∞

[ABOUT THE AUTHOR]

Richard Dawkins is a Fellow of the Royal Society. He is a distinguished evolutionary biologist and the Charles Simonyi Professor For The Public Understanding Of Science at Oxford University; Fellow of New College; recipient of the Cosmos Prize for 1997 and the Kistler Prize for 2001; author of *The Selfish Gene*, *The Extended Phenotype*, *The Blind Watchmaker*, *River Out Of Eden*, *Climbing Mount Improbable*, and *Unweaving The Rainbow* along with countless articles for numerous publications. An anthology of his work will be published in 2003 under the title *A Devil's Chaplain*. Richard Dawkins serves as Honorary President of the Darwin Day Program, wherein his life and work are exemplary of the goals we strive to attain. His work has inspired people the world over, and continues to do so.

[ADDITIONAL RESOURCES]

The Independent: http://www.independent.co.uk/

The Department of Ecology and Evolution at the University of Fribourg, Switzerland Memorial Site for W. D. Hamilton: http://www.unifr.ch/biol/ecology/hamilton/hamilton.html

For a comprehensive resource site entitled, *The World of Richard Dawkins*, created and maintained by John Catalano, visit http://www.world-of-dawkins.com

The author would like to thank Page Stephens and Teresa Kim for their assistance in writing this tribute to Marvin Harris.

MARVIN HARRIS: A REMEMBRANCE (1927-2001)
by John R. Cole

Marvin Harris was a towering and sometimes frustrating figure in anthropology and social science. His work and personality almost always stirred debate, discussion and dissent. His death in October 2001 at age 74, fairly soon after his retirement from the University of Florida where he was Graduate Research Professor Emeritus, silenced a unique, often brilliant voice in the field of cultural evolution – a voice which addressed the public as well as professional colleagues with 17 books and countless articles, speeches and classes. He gained his fame as a Columbia University professor from his 1953 Ph.D. there to his move to Florida in 1981 where his old friend and advisor Charles Wagley had migrated a few years earlier.

I first met Harris when I was an undergraduate at Columbia, but I knew him only by reputation until I returned to Columbia in 1970 to pursue a Ph.D. in anthropology and quickly found myself in his "history of anthropology" class using his classic text, *The Rise of Anthropological Theory* (1968). I jumped in midstream, so to speak, since I had a master's degree from Illinois and all or most other students had been at Columbia and in Harris's orbit – or shadow – for a year or two already. I didn't realize I was supposed to be either intimidated or star-struck, and I simply found the readings, lectures and discussions an exciting, fascinating, heady experience. I was not alone in asking all sorts of questions, but fewer seemed to actually argue with *The Professor*.

When the class was looking at Franz Boas (founder of the Columbia anthropology department and widely considered the founder of academic anthropology in the US), I noticed a strange thing. First, I found myself arguing with Harris about some facts I accidentally knew about Boas (from knowing some of his old students, for example). Harris began taking copious notes on what I was saying. A classmate whispered that I was about to be shot, but instead The Professor started asking me questions to see if I knew what I was talking about. When I seemed to be right and he wrong, Harris seemed really interested. He invited me to his office to talk further – for hours – and he convinced me to write my course research paper on Franz Boas's political life.

We were friends from that point on. He usually knew vastly more than I, of course, and I do not mean to suggest otherwise, but when I *did* happen to know things he did not, he was excited rather than angry.

I specialized in the anthropological subfield of archaeology, but Harris was on my dissertation committee. Being in a field rather removed from his cultural anthropology probably eased our relationship. He was fascinated by archaeology because of what it *could* contribute to theories of cultural evolution, even if it too seldom did so. I thus was asked to kibitz on various Harris publications, such as his textbook, *Culture, Man and Nature; Culture, People, Nature* in later editions, and he asked me to be coauthor of a new textbook on archaeology and physical anthropology. Students and junior colleagues are often asked to "coauthor" textbooks and sometimes are literal ghost writers. By contrast, our book contract called for me to be senior author credit and to get most of the royalties and advance money. To my lifelong regret, this opportunity dissolved when our publisher was absorbed by another company and we were given short notice to turn over a complete manuscript on impossibly short notice, which was of course a successful ploy to kill it (the new company already had competing titles on their list and wanted Harris's general and cultural anthropology titles but not a new Phyzzie book.

In subsequent years we kept in touch, and he often sought my advice (and many others', of course!) on manuscripts and ideas which needed input about archaeology. One of his ideas, developing from the mid-'70s, was the idea that "intensification" was a primary force in cultural evolution – pressure on natural and cultural resources grows with increasing population and/or greater technological exploitation of resources. He argued that cultures essentially fight changes and needed to adapt slowly to new circumstances, and this hastens inventiveness of ways to retain the *old* ways, more and more desperately, until a severe "punctuation" crisis forces change upon cultures – typically collapse of old ways of life and adoption of a radically new one requiring radically new technology and social organization. This was an idea ready-made for archaeological input – and a powerful political idea applicable to contemporary affairs. Can the US or other modern societies learn policy lessons from the failures of the Mayans, for example, to resist change and intensify pressures on resources rather than make painful changes in adaptations?

For several years, Harris wrote a regular column for *Natural History* magazine, and these essays were collected and revised into several popular books – *Cows, Pigs, Wars and Witches* and *Cannibals and Kings* were the most famous, perhaps. He concentrated on "riddles of culture", trying to explain odd-seeming behaviors in the light of "cultural materialistic" interpretations. He almost always related seemingly strange and "foreign" cultural ideas to the Western life of his readers, trying to discover and show universal rules of culture. This column was more or less succeeded by Stephen Jay Gould's long-running column.

In his later years, Harris was clearly one of the most influential members of his profession, but he had never held office in the American Anthropological Association. When I became AAA Nominations Chairman, I managed to get him nominated to the Board of the AAA General Anthropological Division, and he won election and went on to chair the Board. (Madeline Harris chewed me out for adding to his tensions, but I hope she agrees that he loved it – in his own later bio blurbs, he emphasized these honors without noting they were overdue!) ∞

[ABOUT THE AUTHOR]

John R. Cole is a semi-retired anthropologist living in Oakland, CA, and Ph.D. student of Marvin Harris, Ed Lanning, Shirley Gorenstein and others at Columbia University. He has long been active in the creation-evolution "science wars" and is past president of the National Center for Science Education and still on its board of directors. He is a Fellow of the American Anthropological Association (and past officer) and a Fellow of the Committee for the Scientific Investigation of Claims of the Paranormal (CSICOP).

[ADDITIONAL RESOURCES]

Marvin Harris's Cultural Materialism:
http://www.faculty.rsu.edu/~felwell/Theorists/Harris/Index.htm

The Pantheon on Marvin Harris: http://www.users.voicenet.com/~nancymc/marvinharris.html

FAREWELL, FOSSILFACE:
A MEMOIR OF STEPHEN JAY GOULD (1941-2002)
by Richard Milner

> *"The so-called dead are still alive. Our friends are still with us. They guide and strengthen us when owing to absence of proper conditions they cannot make their presence known."*
>
> *– Alfred Russel Wallace (1823-1919)*

I first met Stephen Jay Gould when we were both twelve years old, and about to complete the sixth grade. My family had just moved to Bayside, Queens, a suburb of New York City, from my native Brooklyn. The term was winding down for the summer. Did anyone want to tell the class about their vacation plans or hobbies? Then, as now, I found the prospect of a captive audience irresistible and delivered an impromptu chalk talk on my childhood obsession: dinosaurs. Long-practiced sketches of tyrannosaurs, stegosaurs, and brontosaurs paraded across the blackboard as I expounded on each saurian – when it lived, how much it weighed, what it ate. Because the year was 1953, long before dinomania exploded into popular culture, I thought I was the only kid in the school with a passion for dinosaurs and evolution. I was wrong.

A short, chubby, bright-eyed boy with a broad grin hung on my every word. He approached me, extending his hand in formal greeting. "I'm Steve Gould," he said, "I like dinosaurs, too. I thought I was the only one in this school who did." As we got to know each other over the next few weeks, we discovered other shared interests, including Alfred Hitchcock thrillers and the nineteenth-century musicals of Gilbert and Sullivan. When I went over to visit the Goulds, we hung out in the bedroom he shared with his younger brother, Peter. Before long, we had a literary disagreement about some Gilbert and Sullivan song. "Wait a minute," he said, "I know I have that in my file." Steve went into his closet and consulted a paper accordion-style file, from which he extracted the lyric in question. To this day, he remains the only 12-year-old I have ever seen who kept a filing system. (I tried to emulate his organizational ability over the years, without notable success. Now that I'm an encyclopedist, I'm still trying.)

We continued as classmates at the local junior high, where our geeky interests inevitably resulted in schoolyard nicknames. I became known as "Dino," which I liked, and Gould's moniker was "Fossilface," which he hated but accepted with good humor.

One of our heroes was Charles Darwin, although Steve considered Joe DiMaggio a close second. What did the Sage of Down have in common with Joltin' Joe? To Steve the similarities were obvious: excellence and grace. And the propensity to inspire those ideals in others. On weekends, when he wasn't attending a Yankee baseball game with his father, Steve and I would take bus and subway to Manhattan, to the American Museum of Natural History. There, while still a toddler, Steve had become "imprinted" on the immense Tyrannosaurus rex skeleton. It was mounted standing bolt upright on two gigantic legs, with the tail trailing behind on the ground – a posture since revised to that of a giant, bent-kneed chicken with a cantilevered tail. The great, towering carnosaur had fascinated and terrorized Steve when he was about five, had followed him home and into his dreams. Years before he ever knew the word, Steve decided to become a paleontologist.

I thought that I, too, would become some kind of scientist, or maybe a museum preparator. I learned how to do taxidermy, practicing on carcasses begged from the Bronx Zoo's morgue, and entered my own exhibits in the school science fairs. Whenever we could, Steve and I continued to visit the American Museum of Natural History, enthralled by its world-class collection of dinosaurs, its dioramas of African animals, and the artistry that somehow shoehorned the entire world of life into a single building.

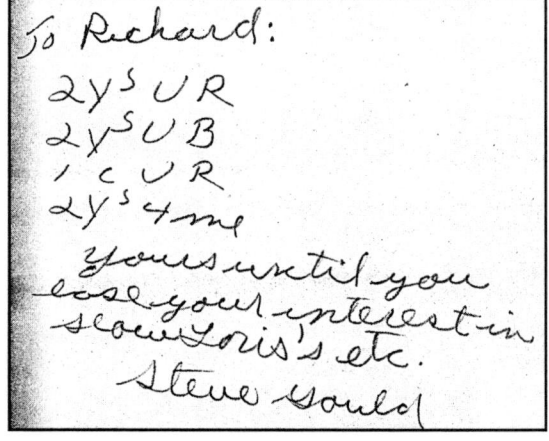

When I turned thirteen, Steve attended my bar mitzvah, the Jewish confirmation celebration. Steve brought me two presents: a set of tie tack and cuff links and a book – "All About Dinosaurs" by Roy Chapman Andrews. How I wish I still had that book, with Steve's congratulatory inscription, but it got away from me over the years. However, I still do have the faux red leather zippered autograph book that we all signed for each other at junior high school graduation, with the page written by Steve. "2 Ys UR / 2 Ys UB / I C UR 2YS for me," he wrote, "Yours until you lose your interest in slow lorises, etc. Steve Gould. "Alas, we went off to separate high schools and different colleges and fell out of touch. He pursued paleontology and became an expert in the evolution of land snails, and I studied anthropology at the University of California. When I returned to New York some years later, with both my marriage and my academic career in tatters, I worked as a writer and editor for newsstand pulp magazines, which were light years away from my childhood interests and ambitions.

One day, in the late 1970s, I discovered that Steve had been writing an extraordinary monthly column in "Natural History," the century-old magazine published at the American Museum of Natural History, and instantly became a fan. He was now a Harvard professor and popular author, whose talents, energies, and interests had taken him far beyond his narrow specialty of land snails. His essays ranged widely over evolutionary theory, history of science, art, literature, and popular culture. The column's title, "This View of Life," refers to Darwin's last sentence in the "Origin of Species": "There is grandeur in this view of life [that] from so simple a beginning endless forms most beautiful and most wonderful have been, and are being, evolved."

Steve and I had not seen or spoken to each other for over twenty-five years. I wrote to him, "You have inherited Thomas Huxley's mantle in explaining evolution to a new generation. Do you remember me?" He replied, "Blood may be thicker than water, but junior high school friendships are thicker than anything." He invited me to have dinner with him next time he visited New York to lecture at the Museum.

We met and instantly resumed our friendship just where we had left off. He reminded me of an exhibit I had made for our junior high school science fair – a series of shoebox dioramas depicting "Life Through the Ages." Along with the miniatures of prehistoric scenes, I had included an actual dinosaur bone, a tail vertebra the size of a steak. Thirteen-year-old Steve had been envious. "Where did you get that dino bone?" he asked. It was a gift from another of our childhood heroes, Dr. Edwin Colbert, curator of dinosaurs at the Museum. All those years ago, I had sent the scientist a handmade Easter card. When you opened it, a paper T. Rex's mouth opened its jaws to reveal a greeting in its cardboard throat: "HAPPY EASTER DOCTOR COLBERT!" To my amazement, Colbert had invited me to the Museum, where he gave me a grand tour of the vertebrate paleontology department, and gifted me with a scrap of bone from a pile of fossil rubble.

At our reunion, Steve had a confession to make. "I never told you this," he said with that infectious grin, "but you inspired me. I made my own card, sent it to Dr. Colbert, he invited me up to the Museum – and he also gave me a dinosaur bone." That bone, and his baseball autographed by DiMaggio, became his two most prized possessions.

When Steve attended graduate school at Columbia, University, Ned Colbert became one of his teachers, and Steve once asked him whether he remembered us and our hand-painted cards. Colbert replied that he had received hundreds of missives from school children over the years and couldn't recall. He had taken thousands of kids on the grand paleo tour. But when Colbert retired and was cleaning out his desk, he called Steve into his office. At the bottom of a drawerful of youngsters' correspondence, he had discovered our cards. We were special, but not any more special than the rest. To Ned Colbert, who died recently at 96, inspiring children was part of his job.

Now it was Steve who inspired me. He insisted that I return to the fold and take up my boyhood interests once again. But where to begin, with no credentials and no umbrella institution? He urged me to pursue the history of science as an independent scholar, to make a pilgrimage to Darwin's home in England, and to buy antiquarian natural history books in the shops around the British Museum. He gave me letters of introduction to librarians and top scholars. I followed his advice and, little by little, I found my way back to the world of research.

In 1982, at age forty, Steve was stricken with abdominal mesothelioma, a rare and "invariably fatal" form of cancer. I went to visit him at Harvard during this period, when many of his colleagues regarded him as doomed and avoided him. He had shrunk to a skeletal ninety pounds, lost his hair, and had to excuse himself every so often to throw up. Nevertheless, he insisted on leading me on a brisk, three-hour walking tour of the campus. We mounted and descended every staircase, and explored every nook and cranny of "his" natural history enclave, the Agassiz Museum. Steve was not ready to leave us. He continued to publish scientific papers during his illness and never missed a month of his column in the magazine. Against great odds, and thanks to a new experimental chemotherapy combined with his fighting spirit, the cancer retreated and seemed to disappear. During the ensuing grace period of twenty years, he accomplished more than most professionals do in a lifetime.

By the mid-1980s, I managed to unearth a few interesting incidents that had almost been lost to history. One was the story of a courtroom trial that took place in 1876: the prosecution of a Spiritualist grifter who summoned departed spirits to answer his client's questions – in writing. As the judge put it, he was running "sort of a post office between this world and the next." (Nowadays, we put such "common rogues," as Darwin called them, on national television with their own shows.) Darwin and Alfred Russel Wallace, the two most brilliant naturalists of the nineteenth century, had taken opposite sides when the supernatural went on trial. Gould was delighted. "I would never have dreamed," he wrote to Scientific American (which published the article in 1996), "that an independent scholar could make fresh discoveries in a field so thoroughly raked over."

Steve also encouraged me to write my "Encyclopedia of Evolution," to which he generously contributed a foreword. Soon after the first edition was published, and at his urging, in 1990 I was hired as a senior editor by Natural History magazine. A few years later, I was assigned to see Steve's column through to press each month. One did not really edit Stephen Jay Gould. You made a hundred suggestions for possible changes, he accepted three, and that was the end of it. Mostly my job was to check for errors (there were mighty few), to help find suitable pictures, and to frame the essay with suitable quotes and captions.

After writing some 300 columns, one a month for twenty-five years, Steve retired from Natural History in the year 2000. It had always been his plan to write them until the millennium. In addition to his teaching, he had other mollusks to fry: A massive 1400-page tome on "The Structure of Evolutionary Theory," which appeared shortly before his death, and two planned books on patterns in evolution and a history of paleontology from the sixteenth through the eighteenth centuries. The last two, unfortunately, were never given to the world. He said they would require another twenty years.

When Steve retired from writing his column, the Skeptic Society in California held an all-day Festschrift celebration at Caltech, featuring speakers who had been inspired by his work. Steve himself spoke (impromptu and brilliantly, for nearly two hours) and I was asked to write and perform a Gilbert and Sullivan-style lyric for the occasion. I chose "My Name is John Wellington Wells (I'm a Dealer in Magic and Spells)" from

"The Sorcerer," to which Steve had introduced me when we were youngsters. With homage to W.S Gilbert, here's the lyric:

STEPHEN JAY GOULD IS MY NAME
Parody lyrics © 2001 R. Milner

Oh! Stephen Jay Gould is my name
And fossils and shells are my game
   Canadian shales
      And Bahamian snails
Have brought me a measure of fame.

If Darwin is your cup of tea
But you don't have a lot of time free
   You don't have to look
      Through his wearisome book
You can learn evolution from me.

I can tell you a tale of a trial
   Where Bryan and Darrow once tangled
A courtroom so laden with bile
   That truth got distorted and mangled.
Fundamentalists shouted defiance,
   "Darwinian textbooks must go,
     The Bible contains all the science
A biology class needs to know!"

I write of cladistics
And baseball statistics
From dodos and mandrills
To friezes and spandrels
With answers provisional
Branches divisional
Watching them practically
Bifurcate fractally, bifurcate fractally

I write
Essays thematical
Always grammatical
Asteroids, sesamoids,
Pestilence tragical
Ratites, stalactites
And home runs DiMaggical

Oh!
If my essays anyone lacks
I've got the back issues in stacks
   You can get them from me
      For a nominal fee
Just drop me a line or a fax!

I can find
>   no cosmic mind behind
Life's eternal mystery
If an ape
>   replayed the tape
He'd see only contingent history.
A plan
>   to make a man
Was not evolution's objective
To believe all the fuss
>   was all about us
Is an anthropocentric perspective!

I write of

Cranial capacity
Owen's mendacity
Huxley's audacity
Galton's urbanity
FitzRoy's insanity
How Ernst Haeckel, without an apology
Faked illustrations about embryology

Marsh's collecting
Butler's objecting
Paley's theology
And teleology
Cope's osteology
And eschatology

But I admit to a preference
For Wallace's deference –
>   for Alfred Wallace's deference!

>   Yes!

My name is Stephen Jay Gould
In science I'm very well schooled
>   So beware adaptationists!
>   Look out, Creationists!
I am not easily fooled.

If my essays anyone lacks
I've got those back issues in stacks
>   You can get them from me
>   For a nominal fee
If you drop me a line or a fax.

(spoken:) Please allow six to eight weeks for delivery.

The second time I performed that song in public was also the last time I saw Steve. It was at a meeting of the American Institute of Biological Sciences in Arlington, Virginia, held in March, 2002. Steve was receiving their Distinguished Scientist award and I was to perform my show, "Charles Darwin: Live & In Concert," immediately afterward. We had been looking forward to appearing together, but I had learned of his diagnosis about two weeks before. Another, even more virulent form of cancer had attacked his brain, liver, and lungs. For the first time, I saw intimations of despair beneath the exuberant, cheerful manner – but the audience had no clue that Steve was dying.

He insisted on personally introducing me to the assembled scientists, and greeted me with a public hug and a kiss on the cheek. During the performance, I saw him sitting in the front row, smiling, staring up at me with the same attention and delight I remembered him showing the very first time we met, at my prepubescent dinosaur lecture. When I came off the stage, he said "Fabulous performance! I see you finally learned the words to my song." We had a wonderful time together, although (and because) we both knew there were not many ticks left in the clock.

A few weeks later, Steve had surgery to remove the brain tumor. Days afterward, he returned to his teaching chores, lecturing as many as five hours a day, and finishing out the Harvard semester. I spoke with him by phone during that time, and diffidently asked him a favor, for which I apologized. "No need to act any differently," he replied. "I know only one way to live – flat out, one day at a time. I'll be happy to do it."

The following week he collapsed, was hospitalized, and died a few weeks later in the antiquarian library of his lavish New York loft apartment, surrounded by the wonderful collection of rare natural history books he loved.

I am in my own library now, and before me is a volume of Steve's essays, "The Lying Stones of Marrakech." He wrote on the title page, "To Dino, from Fossilface. Honoring a lifetime of shared interests. Stephen Jay Gould."

Hail and farewell, Fossilface. You enriched my life and personified the grace and excellence of your childhood heroes. Your friendship was an honor and a privilege – and an inspiration.

[ABOUT THE AUTHOR]

Richard Milner is a Senior Editor of *Natural History* magazine at the American Museum of Natural History. His articles on Darwin have appeared in *Natural History* and *Scientific American*. He is the author of *Encyclopedia of Evolution: Humanity's Search for Its Origins* (a third edition will be published in 2003 under the title *Darwiniana: An Encyclopedia of Evolution*) and *Charles Darwin: Evolution of a Naturalist*. Milner has been highly praised for his performance *Charles Darwin: Live & In Concert* by Stephen Jay Gould, Penn & Teller, Sir David Attenborough, Tony Randall, and many others. CDs of Milner's performance are available through the Darwin Day Program (www.darwinday.org) and information about booking Richard Milner for your event can be obtained through the web site or by contacting Jeannine Frank at frankent1@juno.com tel: 310-476-6735

[ADDITIONAL RESOURCES]

The Stephen Jay Gould Archive at http://www.stephenjaygould.org/

Richard Milner performances: http://www.darwinday.org/art/entertain/

The eulogy was originally presented at the Church of Saint Martin in the Fields, London, 17th September 2001.

Eulogy for Douglas Adams
(1952-2001)
by Richard Dawkins

I believe it falls to me to say something about Douglas's love of science. He once asked my advice. He was contemplating going back to university to read science, I think specifically my own subject of Zoology. I advised against it. He already knew plenty of science. It rings through almost every line he wrote and through the best jokes he made. As a single example, think of the Infinite Improbability Drive. Douglas's ear for science was finely tuned. He thought like a scientist, but was much funnier. It is fair to say that he was a hero to scientists. And technologists, especially in the computer industry.

His unjustified humility in the presence of scientists came out touchingly in a magnificent impromptu speech at a Cambridge conference which I attended in 1998[1]. He was invited as a kind of honorary scientist – a thing that happened to him quite often. Thank goodness somebody switched on a tape recorder, and so we have the whole of this splendid extempore *tour de force*. It certainly ought to be published somewhere. I'm going to read a few disconnected paragraphs. He was a wonderful comedian as well as a brilliant comic writer, and you can hear his voice in every line:

> This was originally billed as a debate only because I was a bit anxious coming here!... in a room full of such luminaries, I thought 'what could I, as an amateur, possibly have to say'? So I thought I would settle for a debate. But after having been here for a couple of days, I realised you're just a bunch of guys!... I thought that what I'd do is stand up and have a debate with myself!... and hope sufficiently to provoke and inflame opinion that there'll be an outburst of chair-throwing at the end.

> Before I embark on what I want to try and tackle, may I warn you that things may get a little bit lost from time to time, because there's a lot of stuff that's just come in from what we've been hearing today, so if I occasionally sort of go... I have a four-year-old daughter and was very, very interested watching her face when she was in her first 2 or 3 weeks of life and suddenly realising what nobody would have realised in previous ages – she was rebooting!

> *I just want to mention one thing, which is completely meaningless, but I am terribly proud of – I was born in Cambridge in 1952 and my initials are D N A!*

These inspired switches of subject are so characteristic of his style – and so endearing.

I remember once, a long time ago, needing a definition of life for a speech I was giving. Assuming there was a simple one and looking around the Internet, I was astonished at how diverse the definitions were and how very, very detailed each one had to be in order to include 'this' but not include 'that'. If you think about it, a collection that includes a fruit fly and Richard Dawkins and the Great Barrier Reef is an awkward set of objects to try and compare.

Douglas laughed at himself, and at his own jokes. It was one of many ingredients of his charm.

There are some oddities in the perspective with which we see the world. The fact that we live at the bottom of a deep gravity well, on the surface of a gas-covered planet going around a nuclear fireball 90 million miles away and think this to be *normal* is obviously some indication of how skewed our perspective tends to be, but we have done various things over intellectual history to slowly correct some of our misapprehensions.

This next paragraph is one of Douglas's set-pieces which will be familiar to some people here. I heard it more than once, and I thought it was more brilliant every time.

> ... *imagine a puddle waking up one morning and thinking, 'This is an interesting world I find myself in-an interesting hole I find myself in-fits me rather neatly, doesn't it? In fact it fits me staggeringly well, must have been made to have me in it!' This is such a powerful idea that as the sun rises in the sky and the air heats up and as, gradually, the puddle gets smaller and smaller, it's still frantically hanging on to the notion that everything's going to be alright, because this world was meant to have him in it, was built to have him in it; so the moment he disappears catches him rather by surprise. I think this may be something we need to be on the watch out for.*

Douglas introduced me to Lalla. They had worked together, years ago, on Dr Who, and it was she who pointed out to me that he had a wonderful childlike capacity to go straight for the wood, and never mind the trees.

If you try and take a cat apart to see how it works, the first thing you have on your hands is a non-working cat. Life is a level of complexity that almost lies outside our vision; it is so far beyond anything we have any means of understanding that we just think of it as a different class of object, a different class of matter; 'life', something that had a mysterious essence about it, was god-given – and that's the only explanation we had. The bombshell comes in 1859 when Darwin publishes '*On the Origin of Species*'. It takes a long time before we really get to grips with this and begin to understand it, because not only does it seem incredible and thoroughly demeaning to us, but it's yet another shock to our system to discover that not only are we not the centre of the Universe and we're not made of anything, but we started out as some kind of slime and got to where we are via being a monkey. It just doesn't read well.

I am happy to say that Douglas's acquaintance with a particular modern book on evolution, which he chanced upon in his early thirties, seems to have been something of a Damascus experience for him:

> It all fell into place. It was a concept of such stunning simplicity, but it gave rise, naturally, to all of the infinite and baffling complexity of life. The awe it inspired in me made the awe that people talk about in respect of religious experience seem, frankly, silly beside it. I'd take the awe of understanding over the awe of ignorance any day.[2]

I once interviewed Douglas on television, for a programme I was making on my own love affair with science. I ended up by asking him, "What is it about science that really gets your blood running?" And here is what he said, again impromptu, and all the more passionate for that.

The world is a thing of utter inordinate complexity and richness and strangeness that is absolutely awesome. I mean the idea that such complexity can arise not only out of such simplicity, but probably absolutely out of nothing, is the most fabulous extraordinary idea. And once you get some kind of inkling of how that might have happened – it's just wonderful. And… the opportunity to spend 70 or 80 years of your life in such a universe is time well spent as far as I am concerned[3].

That last sentence of course has a tragic ring for us now. It has been our privilege to know a man whose capacity to make the best of a full lifespan was as great as was his charm and his humour and his sheer intelligence. If ever a man understood what a magnificent place the world is, it was Douglas. And if ever a man left it a better place for his existence, it was Douglas. It would have been nice if he'd given us the full 70 or 80 years. But by God we got our moneysworth from the forty nine! ∞

[ABOUT THE AUTHOR]

Richard Dawkins is a Fellow of the Royal Society. He is a distinguished evolutionary biologist and the Charles Simonyi Professor For The Public Understanding Of Science at Oxford University; Fellow of New College; recipient of the Cosmos Prize for 1997 and the Kistler Prize for 2001; author of *The Selfish Gene*, *The Extended Phenotype*, *The Blind Watchmaker*, *River Out Of Eden*, *Climbing Mount Improbable*, and *Unweaving The Rainbow* along with countless articles for numerous publications. An anthology of his work will be published in 2003 under the title *A Devil's Chaplain*. Richard Dawkins serves as Honorary President of the Darwin Day Program, wherein his life and work are exemplary of the goals we strive to attain. His work has inspired people the world over, and continues to do so.

[REFERENCES]

(1) The full text of his speech may be seen at http://www.biota.org/people/douglasadams/index.html

(2) http://www.americanatheist.org/win98-99/T2/silverman.html

(3) 'Break the Science Barrier with Richard Dawkins', Channel 4, Equinox Series, 1996

[ADDITIONAL RESOURCES]

The Douglas Adams web site at: http://www.douglasadams.com/

For a comprehensive resource site entitled, *The World of Richard Dawkins*, created and maintained by John Catalano, visit http://www.world-of-dawkins.com

SPECIAL SECTION

Darwin Country

> "He dreamed of going to sea, of visiting exotic lands, of climbing mountains, exploring jungles, and sailing among tropical islands half a world away from the sleepy English countryside he knew so well."
>
> – Richard Milner in
> *Charles Darwin: Evolution of a Naturalist* (1993)

SHREWSBURY, SHROPSHIRE:
BIRTHPLACE OF CHARLES DARWIN AND DARWIN COUNTRY

by Peter D. A. Boyd

Charles Darwin was born in Shrewsbury, the 'County Town' of Shropshire, on 12th February 1809. His birthplace was a house called 'The Mount' built by his father, Robert Darwin, in an elevated position overlooking the town. Charles spent his childhood in Shrewsbury but left it to attend university from 1825-1831 and for his voyage on 'The Beagle' 1831-1836. However, Shrewsbury remained his home and it was Shrewsbury and his family to which he returned between terms from university and after his great voyage. Although he spent most of the rest of his life living in London and Kent, he continued to visit Shrewsbury until his father's death in 1848 and on a memorable occasion in 1869. The town honoured him with a statue in 1897 and a shopping centre named after him in 1989! However, in recent years there has been a growing movement in Shrewsbury to give greater recognition to the town's most famous son through an annual Charles Darwin Memorial Lecture, the Darwin Country website, the formation of a Charles Darwin Birthplace Trust and other initiatives.

THE DARWIN FAMILY IN SHREWSBURY

Charles Darwin was born into a family of intelligent, influential and shrewd people.

Charles Darwin's father was Dr Robert Darwin. In 1786, his father, Erasmus Darwin, took him to Shrewsbury from Derby and left him, with £20 in his pocket, to set up a medical practice in Shrewsbury. From that start as a young doctor of 20, he was to become one of the richest and most influential men in Shropshire and the West Midlands.

In 1796, Robert married Susannah Wedgwood, first child of Josiah Wedgwood I, the pottery manufacturer of Etruria near Stoke. The marriage made the up-and-coming doctor more secure financially and led to an increase in the number of 'useful contacts' as a physician and entrepreneur.

In about 1800, he built the house called The Mount on high ground at Frankwell, overlooking the River Severn and Shrewsbury. The Mount was a large, plain, square, red-brick house, 'of which the most attractive feature [was] the pretty green-house, opening out of the morning room'. Dr Darwin loved his garden, planting it with a wide variety of trees, shrubs and other plants. He and other members of the family maintained a perennial garden diary.

The doctor travelled about his lucrative practice, covering more than three counties, in a yellow chaise. He was a physician to rich and poor alike and much respected. He was also a shrewd businessman and part of his wealth came from his sidelines – property speculation and lending money to the landed gentry. There are some Darwin enthusiasts in Shrewsbury who consider that Robert Darwin was more important than his son!

Dr Robert Darwin (1766-1848) and his wife Susannah (1765-1817) had 6 children:
- Marianne (1798-1858),
- Caroline Sarah (1800-1888),
- Susan Elizabeth (1803-1866),
- Erasmus Alvey (1804-1881),
- Charles Robert (1809-1882),
- Emily Catherine (1810-1866).

Charles's sisters had a great influence on his upbringing and were important correspondents, keeping him in touch with news of Shrewsbury when he was away from it. Susan Darwin lived at The Mount until her death in 1866. She was the last member of the Darwin Family to live there. The sale details of the house and contents provide an insight into the nature of the household and way of life of the Darwins in Shrewsbury.

SHREWSBURY AND THE DARWINS

Shrewsbury is the County Town of Shropshire. Shropshire is England's largest inland county with Wales bordering it on its west side. The historic town centre of Shrewsbury is within a loop of the River Severn. It is well known for its historic buildings including Norman castle, medieval abbey, timber-framed tudor buildings, fine churches and museums. The remains of the Roman town of Viroconium (Uriconium)

Fig 1. Engraving of Shrewsbury 1849 showing the new railway viaduct over the River Severn and part of the castle in the backgound [Shrewsbury Museums Service]

at Wroxeter and the Ironbridge Gorge ('Birthplace of the Industrial Revolution') are nearby.

Shrewsbury is a popular destination for visitors not only because of the interests of the town itself and the nearby heritage sites but also for the wonderful countryside of hills, valleys, rivers, lakes, moors and mountains within easy reach. This was the countryside in which Charles Darwin was brought up and which influenced his lifelong interest in natural history.

Visitors to Shrewsbury can walk the same streets and passage-ways (shuts) that Charles and his family walked. Parts of Shrewsbury are very little changed from his time and many buildings associated with him may be seen (even though the interiors of some are not open to the public).

Among the many places that visitors may see in Shrewsbury include:

- 'The Mount', where CD was born, and some remaining features of its gardens (access limited)

- St Chad's Church, opposite The Quarry Park, where CD was christened

- The Unitarian Chapel on the High Street, attended by CD and his mother (contains an interesting memorial to CD)

- Site of Rev. Case's day school on Claremont Hill attended by CD (private house not open to the public)

- The old Shrewsbury School building near the Castle attended by CD as a boarder (now the public library)

- The Bell-stone in the precincts of the Morris Hall (glacial erratic shown to CD by Mr Cotton – said to be CD's introduction to geology)

- The bronze statue of CD erected in 1897 outside the old Shrewsbury School building

- A bronze statue (erected in 2000) at the present Shrewsbury School site – representing a younger CD

- Shrewsbury Museum and Art Gallery (new Darwin displays planned)

Shrewsbury can also form a base to visit various sites further afield including:

- The grave and memorial of Dr Robert Darwin and Susannah Darwin at Montford Church (a few miles north west of Shrewsbury).

- The Wedgwood Museum, Barlaston, Stoke on Trent – pictures, documents and other items associated with the Darwin and Wedgwood families (see http://www.wedgwoodmuseum.org.uk)

- Lichfield – home of Erasmus Darwin (CD's grandfather) from 1756-1781 (see http://www.lichfield.gov.uk and http://www.erasmus-darwin.org).

The writer plans to create a virtual tour of the Shrewsbury sites on the Darwin Country website at http://www.darwincountry.org. However, real Darwinian visitors to Shrewsbury should make enquiries at the Tourist Information Centre in Shrewsbury for further details (see also Shrewsbury Tourism's website at http://www.shrewsburytourism.co.uk).

Henri Quinn, Robert Darwin enthusiast and local businessman, has carried out research into the Darwins over many years with a band of fellow local researchers. In 1999, Henri published a useful guide to some of the places in Shrewsbury associated with Charles Darwin and the Darwin Family (Quinn, 1999).

The Mount and the Darwin's Garden

Robert Darwin started his garden in about 1800 when he built The Mount on the north side of Shrewsbury. The garden was maintained by members of the Darwin family and their staff until the death of Susan Darwin in 1866 and its arrangement remained similar for many years afterwards. However, in the 1920s, the small housing estate 'Darwin Gardens' was built on about 2.5 acres of the walled kitchen garden and pleasure grounds (about half the total acreage of the garden). Some features of the original garden (e.g. walls, potting shed, ice house) survive in the gardens of these houses (Boyd, 1999 and 2000).

The Mount itself, with its surviving garden, is currently occupied by The Local Valuation Office (Inland Revenue offices responsible for property tax valuation – not local Council offices). It is not open to the public but arrangements can sometimes be made for small parties to visit limited parts of the property.

Robert Darwin, assisted by members of his family, maintained a 'perennial garden diary' recording details of flowerings and fruiting in the kitchen garden, pleasure gardens and glasshouses of The Mount. It seems that Charles Darwin may have sent seeds or plants back to his father in Shrewsbury from his voyage on the *Beagle* 1831-1836. After Robert died in 1848, one of his daughters, Susan, continued the diary until her own death in 1866.

The garden diary is in private hands but the garden history writer, Susan Campbell, is working with the owner of the diary to publish a book based on its contents. Much of the information the diary contains is being kept secret until it has been published!

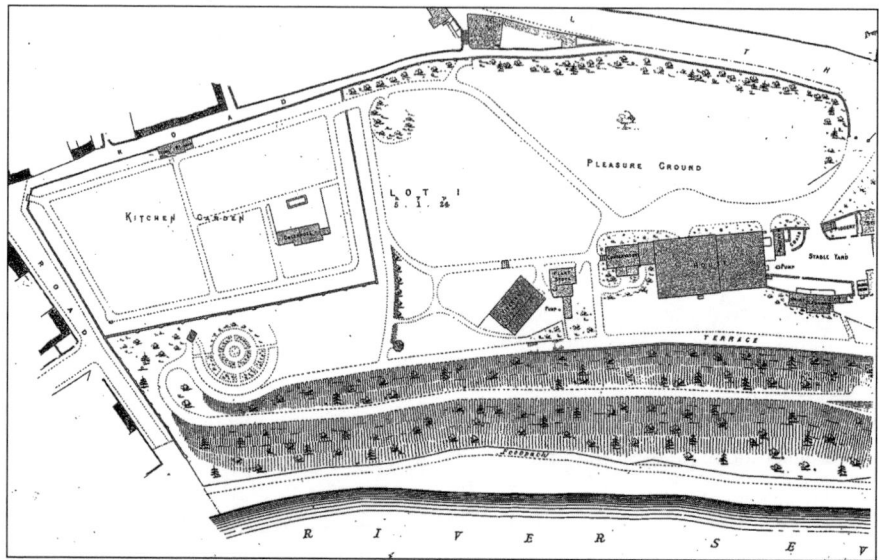

Fig 2. Part of a plan of the gardens of The Mount in 1866. In the 1920s, a small housing estate was built on the kitchen garden and a large part of the pleasure garden (including the site of the vinery in the centre) shown on the left half of the plan [Shrewsbury Museums Service]

However, other information may be culled from the many publications on the life of Charles Darwin, archives kept in the Shropshire Records and Research Centre and other sources. The census returns for 1841, 1851 and 1861 provide details of the household. The 65-page catalogue for the 6-day dispersal sale of the contents of The Mount and garden in 1866 includes a list of potted plants and garden equipment. The plan included in the sale details of The Mount itself in 1867 provides details of the greenhouses and outline plan of the gardens. The 1881 1:500 scale Ordnance Survey map shows the same design. Photographs or other depictions of the garden have been harder to find. Two photographs of the house (of unknown dates) show different versions of the conservatory. The present writer has published some of the results of his research into the history of the garden in the Newsletter of the Shropshire Parks and Gardens Trust and these are available on his website (http://www.peterboyd.com). He has also incorporated some of this information into the Darwin Country website where details of the garden plans may be seen.

Some of the trees, shrubs and other plants growing at the Mount may have been planted in Darwin times. It is difficult to be certain about some until the detailed contents of the garden diaries become available and comparisons between then and now may be made. However, large specimens of *Magnolia acuminata* adjacent to the house are thought to be original Darwin plantings and it is tempting to conjecture that the luxuriant sward of the tender *Selaginella kraussiana* that was, until recently, growing outside close to the house was an escape from one of the Darwins' greenhouses!

SHREWSBURY MUSEUM AND ART GALLERY

The collections of Shrewsbury Museums Service owe their initiation to Darwin's contemporaries, several of whom were his school-fellows and who founded the Shropshire and North Wales Natural History and Antiquarian Society in 1835. Charles Darwin was told of the newly formed society by his sister who wrote to him while he was on the *Beagle*. Charles Darwin became a member of the Society when he returned from his voyage on the *Beagle* and he was made an Honorary Member in 1842.

Shrewsbury Museum and Art Gallery is the headquarters museum of Shrewsbury Museums Service (website at http://www.shrewsburymuseums.com).

The collections of Shrewsbury Museums Service comprise about 166,000 items. Natural Science and Archaeology have remained, numerically, the most important components since those early days with about 112,000 archaeological objects, 18,000 biological specimens and over 5000 geological items currently in the collections. Several of the collections have been judged to be of National importance.

The smaller collections of fine and decorative arts also include component collections of National importance. The collections are rich in Shropshire ceramics (c.2500 items), costume and textiles (c.1500 items), Fine Art (c.1800 items) and photographs (c.3000 items). In addition, the collections include some 1400 miscellaneous items of general social history interest. The museum collections have evolved since 1835 in parallel with scientific, archaeological and social developments.

Shrewsbury Museums Service is responsible for three museum buildings: Shrewsbury Museum and Art Gallery (Rowley's House), Shrewsbury Castle and Coleham Pumping Station. A former museum building, Clive House, was sold in 2001 and the contents transferred to Shrewsbury Museum and Art Gallery. Shrewsbury & Atcham Borough Council has recently given approval for planning to proceed on the redevelopment and enlargement of Shrewsbury Museum and Art Gallery.

The development will include 'new build' to provide up-to-date museum and gallery facilities adjacent to the 17th century Rowley's House as well as work to provide access to new displays and other facilities within the original building. New displays about Charles Darwin, the Darwin Family in Shrewsbury and the development of natural sciences in 19th century Shropshire will be part of the new museum complex.

If the plans, currently being prepared, are approved by Shrewsbury & Atcham Borough Council, grant-aid is obtained from the Heritage Lottery Fund and other necessary funding forthcoming, the redeveloped museum and art gallery should open in late 2007.

THE DARWIN COUNTRY WEBSITE

"Darwin Country" is a website project that was initiated in February 2000. It was grant-aided by the Resource IT Challenge Fund and the West Midlands Regional Museum Council until March 2001 and, with funding for additional digitisation, by WMRMC April 2001- March 2002. The WMRMC has supported further development of the website in 2002-2003. A prime purpose of the website and the funding that it has obtained has been to make images and information about museum collections more accessible. 'Darwin Country' may be found at http://www.darwincountry.org.

The first stage of the project was called "Cradle of Science, Technology and the Better Life!" It was intended to provide an introduction to scientific, technological and social development in part of the West Midlands of England during the 18th and 19th centuries illustrated by the archives, paintings, decorative arts, archaeology and scientific collections of

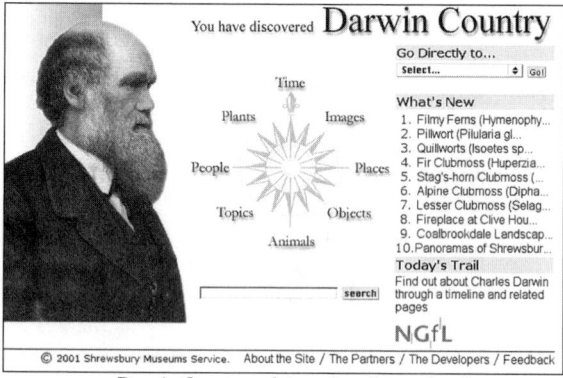

Darwin Country website at http://www.darwincountry.org

the partner museums. The initial partners were Shrewsbury Museums Service (the lead partner), Ironbridge Gorge Museum Trust and the Wedgwood Museum.

After March 2001, the scope of Darwin Country was extended by Shrewsbury Museums Service to include material from other historic, prehistoric and geological periods. By April 2002 the website had about 9000 pages and 6000 images and it will have about 3000 more images by April 2003.

The site provides information about Charles Darwin, the Darwin Family, Shrewsbury and other parts of Shropshire but also much more. It provides access to thousands of images of people, places and museum objects that act as a valuable resource for Lifelong Learning. This has been recognised by its early inclusion in the National Grid for Learning, The People's Network, Curriculum Online (forthcoming) and other portals.

Many of the places depicted on the website are those known by Charles Darwin and the objects depicted made, used or found during his lifetime. His friends and contemporaries initiated the Shrewsbury museum collections in 1835 and continued to contribute items during the following decades.

This database-driven website provides multi-disciplinary content in what the writer has called a 'knowledge-net' environment. The software that runs the site has been developed with Shrewsbury-based software engineers Orangeleaf Systems Ltd. The concepts behind and techniques employed in the creation of the website have been described in detail elsewhere (e.g. Boyd, 2002a and b). Website versions of these papers are accessible at http://www.peterboyd.com.

CHARLES DARWIN MEMORIAL LECTURE AND DARWIN WEEK

Shrewsbury has been looking at ways of increasing interest in Charles Darwin for several years. In 1997, the first phase of new interdisciplinary displays about Charles Darwin and the history of natural history were opened at Clive House Museum and the first annual Charles Darwin Memorial Lecture instigated by the Museums Service. Professor David Bellamy, the well-known naturalist (who was inspired by Charles Darwin) opened the new displays and gave the first lecture to a packed Shrewsbury Music Hall. We have held five more annual lectures plus an extra Millennium Lecture in 1999. They have all been held at the Music Hall on the Sunday closest to Charles Darwin's Birthday. Proceeds have gone to the Friends of Shrewsbury's Borough Museums.

1997 Professor David Bellamy (Naturalist)

1998 David Shepherd (Natural History Artist)

1999 Michael Leach (Natural History Photographer)

1999 Professor Steve Jones (Geneticist and Darwin author) [Millennium Lecture]

2000 Dr. Janet Browne (Biographer of Charles Darwin)

2001 Professor Chris Stringer (Human Palaeontologist)

2002 Randal Keynes (Great Great Grandson of CD and author of 'Annie's Box)

2003 Professor Sir Paul Nurse

These lectures, the Darwin Country website and other activities have helped to raise the level of interest in Charles Darwin in Shrewsbury and February 2003 will see an even wider range of activities.

Jon King is a popular broadcaster on BBC Radio Shropshire with a daily programme of music, local news and interviews. Following a recording with the present writer about the history of the garden at the Mount for his programme and another soon afterwards with Randal Keynes (our 2002 Memorial Lecture speaker), Jon decided it was time for more to be done in Shrewsbury about Charles Darwin! He called together a wide range of individuals with an interest in Darwin to discuss what might be done and this engendered further support not only for the concept of a Charles Darwin Birthplace Trust but for a far wider range of activities around the time of his birthday. As a result, 2003 will see the first of an annual Shrewsbury Darwin Week of events that will grow in future years including lectures, exhibitions and arts events inspired by Darwin or Darwin-related themes.

CHARLES DARWIN BIRTHPLACE TRUST

Perhaps, it is a little surprising that, with the success of the Shakespeare Birthplace Trust in Stratford, the idea of a Charles Darwin Birthplace Trust for Shrewsbury was not discussed until 2001 and not put before the public tentatively as an idea until 2002. A questionnaire on the matter distributed at the 2002 Memorial Lecture received considerable support and support has grown as plans for Darwin Week in 2003 have progressed. At the time of writing, the Trust has not been formally set up but it is hoped that this will happen in the near future.

At least two models for the Trust have been suggested but one model, suggested by the present writer, might be an independent charitable trust supported by public subscription, grants, sponsorship and income from appropriate activities.

The aims of such a Trust might be to:

- collect and disseminate accurate information about Charles Darwin (1809-1882), his family and times in Shrewsbury and its region (c.1786-1866);

- encourage/support appropriate research into Charles Darwin, the Darwin family and their times in Shrewsbury and its region;

- if the property was ever offered for sale, seek to acquire and develop and manage the birthplace and home of Charles Darwin in Shrewsbury (known as The Mount or Mount House) as a museum/visitor facility and study centre;

- if The Mount was ever acquired, seek partnerships with Shrewsbury Museums Service (SABC) and other bodies to support the appropriate interpretation of the buildings and garden, the lives of the Darwin Family and their times;

- if The Mount was ever acquired, seek partnerships and funding to support and sustain the long-term preservation/public use/interpretation of the building and grounds and otherwise support the aims of the Trust;

- provide an annual programme of talks and other events to support the aims of the Trust;

- celebrate the birthday of Charles Darwin each year on or near 12th February through the support of appropriate educational activities;

- plan for and carry out/support an appropriate celebration of the bicentenary of Charles Darwin's birth in 2009;

- carry out such other activities as may support the aims of the Trust and extend public knowledge of Charles Darwin and his family in Shrewsbury.

The Trust would be managed by a specified number of Trustees and a membership that supported the work of the Trust through an annual subscription and fund-raising. It should be noted that:

- the Mount House (the Birthplace building) may or may not become available. The suggested aims provide for such a Trust having a role whether or not the building could ever be acquired as the focus for activities.

- Shrewsbury is the Birthplace town of Charles Darwin. The Trust would have particular interest in the history of Shrewsbury, its people and its natural history from the late 18th century onwards.

- the Trust could start as a society with a committee and membership and then seek charitable status once it had been founded.

If readers of this article would be interested in membership of such a Trust, they

Conclusion

Charles Darwin is Shrewsbury's most famous son and the town has perhaps been a little slow to honour him and his family. However, now (nearly 200 years since his birth) there is a growing movement to honour him and his work. The 'Darwin Country' website, Memorial Lectures, Darwin Week initiatives, plans for new Museum displays and the possible formation of a 'Charles Darwin Birthplace Trust' have all raised awareness and interest in Charles and other members of the Darwin Family in Shrewsbury. Shrewsbury has always been a rather special place and it gave rise to a special man. That man and his links with Shrewsbury and its region have helped to make it even more special!

[References]

Boyd, P.D.A. (in press). 'Darwin Country – a case study in website creation and content management' In Special Content Management issue of *Spectra* (a publication of the Museum Computer Network) Spring 2002, vol. 29, pp20-27. [Available at: http://www.peterboyd.com/spectra2002.htm]

Boyd, P.D.A. 2002. 'Darwin Country – Cradle of Science, Technology and the Better Life!' – a case study In *mda information* vol 5, no5, pp 35-44. Proceedings of the Museum Documentation Association Conference, September 2000: 'Clicks and Mortar – building cultural spaces for the 21st century'. [Available at: http://www.peterboyd.com/mda2000.htm]

Boyd, P.D.A. 2000. Darwin Garden Project – Sale of The Mount in 1866 *Shropshire Parks and Gardens Trust Newsletter* [vailable at http://www.peterboyd.com/darwingard2.htm].

Boyd, P.D.A. 1999. Darwin Garden Project. *Shropshire Parks and Gardens Trust Newsletter* [vailable at http://www.peterboyd.com/darwingard1.htm]

Quinn, H. 1999. 'Charles Darwin: Shrewsbury's Man of the Millennium'. Privately printed. Shrewsbury.

[Additional Resources]

Darwin Country website at http://www.darwincountry.org

Shrewsbury Museums Service Website at http://www.shrewsburymuseums.com

Shrewsbury Tourism website at http://www.shrewsburytourism.co.uk

Shrewsbury and Atcham Borough Council's website at http://www.shrewsbury.gov.uk

Ironbridge Gorge Museums website at http://www.ironbridge.org.uk

Wedgwood Museum website at http://www.wedgwoodmuseum.org.uk

Erasmus Darwin Foundation website at http://www.erasmus-darwin.org

Orangeleaf Systems website at http://www.orangeleaf.com

Peter D. A. Boyd's website at http://www.peterboyd.com

[About the Author]

Peter Boyd is Collections Manager and Darwin Country Project Coordinator for the Shrewsbury Museums Service.

SECTION TWO

DARWIN:
THE MAN AND HIS LEGACY

> "You care for nothing but shooting, dogs, and rat-catching – and you will be a disgrace to yourself and all your family."
>
> – Robert Darwin to his son (1825)

> "Imagine a world without Darwin. Imagine a world in which Charles Darwin and Alfred Russel Wallace had not transformed our understanding of living things. What… would become baffling and puzzling…, in urgent need of explanation? The answer is: practically everything about living things…"
>
> – Helena Cronin in *The Ant and the Peacock* (1993)

On July 1st, 1858 a joint paper by Charles Darwin and Alfred Russel Wallace was presented to the Linnean Society. The paper outlined the new ideas on evolution that would ultimately revolutionize the world of biology and society itself. The area within the old Burlington House where the paper was originally presented became a staircase and toilet in later years. The Royal Academy recently restored this room and re-named it the Reynolds Room. A plaque was placed in the Reynolds Room commemorating the historical presentation of the Darwin-Wallace paper. On November 26th, 2001 the Royal Academy and the Linnean Society marked the occasion with an unveiling and address by Richard Dawkins.

BEFORE THE ORIGIN:
COMMEMORATING THE DARWIN-WALLACE PAPER READ TO THE LINNEAN SOCIETY IN 1858
by Richard Dawkins

Professor King, Sir David Smith, members of the Darwin and Wallace families, ladies and gentlemen.

It is in the nature of scientific truths that they are waiting to be discovered, by whoever has the ability to do so. If two different people independently discover something in science, it will be the same truth. Unlike works of art, scientific truths do not change their nature in response to the individual human beings who discover them. This is both a glory, and a limitation, of science. If Shakespeare had never lived, nobody else would have written Macbeth. If Darwin had never lived, somebody else would have discovered natural selection. In fact, somebody did – Alfred Russel Wallace. And that is why we are here today.

On July 1st 1858, in this very room *(Reynolds Room – part of the Royal Academy buildings)*, was launched upon the world the theory of evolution by natural selection, certainly one of the most powerful and far-reaching ideas ever to occur to a human mind. But it was not just one mind, but two. I shall elaborate on this when we adjourn to the other room *(Meeting Room – part of the Linnean Society buildings)*. Here I just want to note that both Darwin and Wallace distinguished themselves not just for the discovery which they independently made, but for the generosity and humanity with which they resolved their priority in doing so.

Darwin and Wallace seem to me to symbolise not just exceptional brilliance in science but the spirit of amicable cooperation which science, at its best, fosters. It gives me very great pleasure to unveil this plaque, commemorating the reading of the joint Darwin/Wallace papers.

Author's Note: After the unveiling, the meeting adjourned to the lecture room of the Linnean Society, in another part of the building, and I then resumed my remarks:

The philosopher Daniel Dennett has written

> *Let me lay my cards on the table. If I were to give an award for the single best idea anyone has ever had, I'd give it to Darwin, ahead of Newton and Einstein and everyone else*

I have said something similar, although I didn't dare make the comparison with Newton and Einstein explicit.

The idea we were talking about is, of course, evolution by natural selection. Not only is it the all-but-universally-accepted explanation for all the complexity and elegance of life. It is also, I strongly suspect, the only explanation that in principle *could* provide that explanation. But Darwin was not the only person who thought of the idea. When Professor Dennett and I made our remarks, we were – certainly in my case and I suspect that Dennett would agree – using the name Darwin to stand for "Darwin and Wallace". This happens to Wallace quite often, I am afraid. He tends to get a poor deal at the hands of posterity, partly through his own generous nature. It was Wallace himself who coined the word 'Darwinism', he regularly referred to it as Darwin's theory and he referred to himself as 'more Darwinian than Darwin.' The reason we know Darwin's name more than Wallace's is that Darwin went on, a year later, to publish the *Origin of Species*. The *Origin* not only explained and advocated the Darwin/Wallace theory of natural selection as *mechanism* of evolution. It also – and this had to be done at book length – set out the multifarious evidence for the *fact* of evolution itself.

The drama of how Wallace's letter arrived at Downe House on 17th June 1858, casting Darwin into an agony of indecision and worry, is too well known for me to retell it. In my view the whole episode is one of the more creditable and agreeable in the history of scientific priority disputes – precisely because it wasn't a dispute – although it so very easily could have become one. It was resolved amicably, and with heartwarming generosity on both sides, especially on Wallace's. As Darwin later wrote,

> *Early in 1856 Lyell advised me to write out my views pretty fully, and I began at once to do so on a scale three or four times as extensive as that which was afterwards followed in my Origin of Species; yet it was only an abstract of the materials which I had collected, and I got through about half the work on this scale. But my plans were overthrown, for early in the summer of 1858 Mr Wallace, who was then in the Malay archipelago, sent me an essay On the Tendency of Varieties to depart indefinitely from the Original Type; and this essay contained exactly the same theory as mine. Mr Wallace expressed the wish that if I thought well of his essay, I should send it to Lyell for perusal.*

> *The circumstances under which I consented at the request of Lyell and Hooker to allow of an extract from my MS., together with a letter to Asa Gray, dated September 5, 1857, to be published at the same time with Wallace's Essay, are given in the Journal of the Proceedings of the Linnean Society, 1858, p. 45. I was at first very unwilling to consent, as I thought Mr Wallace might consider my doing so unjustifiable, for I did not then know how generous and noble was his disposition. The extract from my MS. and the letter to Asa Gray ... had neither been intended for publication, and were badly written. Mr Wallace's essay, on the other hand, was admirably expressed and quite clear. Nevertheless our joint productions excited very little attention, and the only published notice of*

them which I can remember was by Professor Haughton of Dublin, whose verdict was that all that was new in them was false, and what was true was old. This shows how necessary it is that any new view should be explained at considerable length in order to arouse public attention.

Darwin was over-modest about his own two papers which were read in this room. Both are models of the explainer's art. Wallace's paper is also very clearly argued. His ideas were, indeed, remarkably similar to Darwin's own, and there is no doubt that Wallace arrived at them independently. In my opinion the Wallace paper needs to be read in conjunction with his earlier paper, published in 1855, in the *Annals and Magazine of Natural History*. Darwin read this paper when it came out. Indeed, it led to Wallace joining his large circle of correspondents, and to his engaging Wallace's services as a collector. But, oddly, Darwin did not see in the 1855 paper any warning that Wallace was by then a convinced evolutionist of a very Darwinian stamp. I mean as opposed to the Lamarckian view of evolution which saw modern species as all on a ladder, changing into one another as they moved up the ladder. By contrast Wallace, in 1855, had a clear view of evolution as a branching tree, exactly like Darwin's famous diagram which became the only illustration in *The Origin of Species*. I find it quite hard to understand how Darwin, after reading this paper, could still see Wallace as a creationist. The 1855 paper, however, makes no mention of natural selection or the struggle for existence.

That was left to Wallace's 1858 paper, the one which hit Darwin like a lightning bolt. Here, Wallace even used the phrase 'Struggle for Existence.' Wallace devotes considerable attention to the exponential increase in numbers (another key Darwinian point). Wallace wrote:

> *The greater or less fecundity of an animal is often considered to be one of the chief causes of its abundance or scarcity; but a consideration of the facts will show us that it really has little or nothing to do with the matter. Even the least prolific of animals would increase rapidly if unchecked, whereas it is evident that the animal population of the globe must be stationary, or perhaps ... decreasing.*

Wallace deduced from this that

> *The numbers that die annually must be immense; and as the individual existence of each animal depends upon itself, those that die must be the weakest...*

Wallace's peroration could have been Darwin himself writing:

> *The powerful retractile talons of the falcon- and the cat-tribes have not been produced or increased by the volition of those animals; but among the different varieties which occurred in the earlier and less highly organized forms of these groups, those always survived longest which had the greatest facilities for seizing their prey. Neither did the giraffe acquire its long neck by desiring to reach the foliage of the more lofty shrubs, and constantly stretching its neck for the purpose, but because any varieties which occurred among its antitypes with a longer neck than usual at once secured a fresh range of pasture over the same ground as their shorter-necked companions, and on the first scarcity of food were thereby enabled to outlive them. Even the peculiar colours of many animals, especially insects, so*

closely resembling the soil or the leaves or the trunks on which they habitually reside, are explained on the same principle; for though in the course of ages varieties of many tints may have occurred, yet those races having colours best adapted to concealment from their enemies would inevitably survive the longest. We have also here an acting cause to account for that balance so often observed in nature, – a deficiency in one set of organs always being compensated by an increased development of some others – powerful wings accompanying weak feet, or great velocity making up for the absence of defensive weapons; for it has been shown that all varieties in which an unbalanced deficiency occurred could not long continue their existence. The action of this principle is exactly like that of the centrifugal governor of the steam engine, which checks and corrects any irregularities almost before they become evident.

The image of the steam governor is a powerful one which, I can't help feeling, Darwin might have envied.

Historians of science have raised the suggestion that Wallace's version of natural selection was not quite so Darwinian as Darwin himself believed. Wallace persistently used the word 'variety' as the level of entity at which natural selection acts. You heard an example in the long passage I have just read out. And some have suggested that Wallace, unlike Darwin who clearly saw selection as choosing among *individuals*, was proposing what modern theorists rightly denigrate as 'group selection.' This would be true if, by 'varieties', Wallace meant geographically separated groups or races of individuals. At first I wondered about this myself. But I believe a careful reading of Wallace's paper rules it out. I think that by 'variety' Wallace meant what we would nowadays call 'genetic type', even what a modern writer might mean by a gene. I think that, to Wallace in this paper, variety meant not local race of eagles, for example, but 'that set of individual eagles whose talons were hereditarily sharper than usual.'

If I am right, it is a similar misunderstanding to the one suffered by Darwin, whose use of the word 'race' in the subtitle of *The Origin of Species* is sometimes misread in support of racialism. That subtitle, or alternative title rather, is *The Preservation of Favoured Races in the Struggle for Life*. Once again, Darwin was using 'race' to mean 'that set of individuals who share a particular hereditary characteristic, such as sharp talons, *not* a geographically distinct race such as the Hoodie Crow. If he had meant that, Darwin too would have been guilty of the group selection heresy. I believe that neither Darwin nor Wallace were. And, by the same token, I do not believe that Wallace's conception of natural selection was different from Darwin's.

As for the calumny that Darwin plagiarised Wallace, that is rubbish. The evidence is very clear that Darwin did think of natural selection before Wallace, although he did not publish it. We have his abstract of 1842 and his longer essay of 1844, both of which establish his priority clearly, as did his letter to Asa Gray of 1857 which was read here on the day we are celebrating. Why he delayed so long before publishing is one of the great mysteries of the history of science. Some historians have suggested that he was afraid of the religious implications, others the political ones. Maybe he was just a perfectionist.

When Wallace's letter arrived, Darwin was more surprised than we moderns might think he had any right to be. He wrote to Lyell:

I never saw a more striking coincidence; if Wallace had had my manuscript sketch, written out in 1842, he could not have made a better short abstract of it. Even his terms now stand as Heads of my Chapters.

The coincidence extended to both Darwin and Wallace being inspired by Malthus on Population. Darwin, by his own account (which admittedly can be disputed), was immediately inspired by Malthus's emphasis on overpopulation and competition. He wrote in his autobiography:

> *In October, 1838, that is, fifteen months after I had begun my systematic inquiry, I happened to read for amusement Malthus on population, and being well prepared to appreciate the struggle for existence which everywhere goes on from long continuous observation of the habits of animals and plants, it at once struck me that under these circumstances favourable variations would tend to be preserved and unfavourable ones to be destroyed. The result of this would be the formation of new species. Here, then, I had at last got a theory by which to work.*

Wallace's epiphany was more delayed after his reading of Malthus, but was in a way more dramatic when it came ... to his overheated brain in the midst of a malarial fever, on the island of Ternate in the Moluccas archipelago:

> *I was suffering from a sharp attack of intermittent fever, and every day during the cold and succeeding hot fits had to lie down for several hours, during which time I had nothing to do but to think over any subjects then particularly interesting me...*
>
> *One day something brought to my recollection Malthus's 'Principles of Population.' I thought of his clear exposition of 'the positive checks to increase' – disease, accidents, war, and famine – which keep down the population of savage races to so much lower an average than that of more civilized peoples. It then occurred to me...*

And Wallace proceeds to his own admirably clear exposition of natural selection.

There are other candidates for priority, apart from Darwin and Wallace. I'm not talking about the idea of evolution itself, of course, there are numerous precedents there, including Erasmus Darwin. But for natural selection there are two other Victorians who have been championed – with something like the same zeal as Baconians show when disputing the authorship of Shakespeare. The two are Patrick Matthew, and Edward Blyth; and Darwin himself mentions an even earlier one, W C Wells. Matthew complained that Darwin had overlooked him, and Darwin subsequently did mention him in later editions of the *Origin*. The following is from the Introduction to the Fifth Edition:

> *In 1831 Mr Patrick Matthew published his work on 'Naval Timber and Arboriculture,' in which he gives precisely the same view of the origin of species as that ... propounded by Mr Wallace and myself in the 'Linnean Journal', and as that enlarged in the present volume. Unfortunately the view was given by Mr Matthew very briefly in scattered passages in an Appendix to a work on a different subject, so that it remained unnoticed until Mr Matthew himself drew attention to it in the 'Gardener's Chronicle'...*

As in the case of Edward Blyth, championed by Loren Eiseley, I think it is by no means clear that Matthew really did understand the importance of natural selection. The evidence is compatible with the view that these alleged predecessors of Darwin and Wallace saw natural selection as a purely negative force, weeding out misfits rather than building up the whole evolution of life (this, indeed, is a misconception under which modern creationists can be found labouring). I can't help feeling that, if you really understood that you were sitting on one of the greatest ideas ever to occur to a human mind, you would *not* bury it in scattered passages in an Appendix to a monograph on Naval Timber. Nor subsequently choose the Gardener's Chronicle as the organ in which to claim your priority. That Wallace understood the enormity of what he had discovered, there is no doubt.

Darwin and Wallace did not remain always in total agreement. In old age, Wallace dabbled in spiritualism (in spite of his venerable appearance, Darwin never reached extreme old age), and from earlier times Wallace doubted that natural selection could account for the special abilities of the human mind. But the more important conflict between them came over sexual selection, and it has ramifications to this day, as Helena Cronin has documented in her beautifully-written book, *The Ant and the Peacock*. Wallace once said of himself: "I am more Darwinian than Darwin himself." He saw natural selection as ruthlessly utilitarian and he couldn't stomach Darwin's sexual selection interpretation of bird of paradise tails and similar bright coloration. Darwin's own stomach was not invulnerable. He wrote

The sight of a feather in a peacock's tail, whenever I gaze at it, makes me sick.

Nevertheless, Darwin reconciled himself to sexual selection, and became positively enthusiastic for it. Aesthetic whim, by females choosing among males, was enough to account for the peacock's tale and similar extravagances. Wallace hated this. So did just about everybody at the time except Darwin, sometimes for frankly misogynistic reasons. To quote Helena Cronin:

Several authorities went further, emphasising the notorious fickleness of females. According to Mivart, "Such is the instability of a vicious feminine caprice, that no constancy of coloration could be produced by its selective action." Geddes and Thomson were of the gloomily misogynistic opinion that permanence of female taste was "scarcely verifiable in human experience.

Not for misogynistic reasons, Wallace strongly felt that female whim was not a proper explanation for evolutionary change. And Cronin uses his name for an entire strand of thought which lasts to this day. 'Wallaceans' are biased towards utilitarian explanations of bright coloration while 'Darwinians' accept female whim as an explanation. Modern Wallaceans accept that peacocks' tails and similar bright organs are advertisements to females. But they want the males to be advertising genuine quality. A male with bright coloured tail feathers is showing that he is a high quality male. The Darwinian view of sexual selection, by contrast, is that the bright tail is valued by females for no additional qualities over and above the bright coloration itself. They like it because they like it because they like it. Females who choose attractive males have attractive sons who appeal to females of the next generation. Wallaceans more austerely insist that coloration must mean something useful.

The late W D Hamilton, of Oxford University, was a prime example of a Wallacean in this sense. He believed that sexually selected ornaments were badges of good health, selected for their capacity to advertise the health of a male – bad health as well as good.

One way to express Hamilton's Wallacean idea is to say that selection favours females who become skilled veterinary diagnosticians. At the same time, selection favours males who make it easy for them by, in effect, growing the equivalent of conspicuous thermometers and blood-pressure metres. The long tail of a Bird of Paradise, for Hamilton, is an adaptation to make it easy for females to diagnose the male's health, good or bad. An example of a good general diagnostic is a susceptibility to diarrhoeia. A long dirty tail is a give-away of ill-health. A long clean tail is the opposite. The longer the tail, the more unmistakeable the badge of health, whether good health or poor. Obviously this honesty benefits the particular male only when his health is good. But Hamilton and other neo-Wallaceans have ingenious arguments to the effect that, natural selection favours honest badges in general, even if, in particular cases, honesty has painful consequences. Neo-Wallaceans believe that natural selection favours long tails precisely because they are an effective badge of health. Both good health and (more paradoxically but the theory really does seem to stand up) poor health.

Sexual selectionists of the Darwin school also have their modern champions. Taking their line through R A Fisher in the first half of the twentieth century, modern Darwinian sexual selectionists have developed mathematical models which show that, also paradoxically, sexual selection governed by arbitrary female whim can lead to a runaway process such that the tail – or other sexually selected character – moves far away from its utilitarian optimum. The key to this family of theories is what modern geneticists call 'linkage disequilibrium.' When females choose, say, long-tailed males by whim, offspring of both sexes inherit their mother's whim genes and also their father's tail genes. It doesn't matter how arbitrary is the whim, the joint selection on both sexes can lead (at least if you do the mathematical theory in a certain way) to runaway evolution of longer tails, and of preference for longer tails. So tails can become ludicrously long.

Cronin's elegant historical analysis shows that the Darwin/Wallace opposition, in the field of sexual selection, persisted long after the deaths of the original protagonists, right through the twentieth century to today. It is especially pleasing – and might have amused the two men – that both the Darwinian and the Wallacean strand of sexual selection theory, more particularly in their modern forms, have a strong element of paradox. Both are capable of predicting surprising, even zany, sexual advertisements. Which, indeed, we see in nature. The Peacock's fan is only the most famous example.

I said the idea that occurred to Darwin and Wallace independently was one of the greatest, if not the greatest, ever to occur to a human mind. I want to end by giving this thought a universal spin. The opening words of my first book were:

> *Intelligent life on a planet comes of age when it first works out the reason for its own existence. If superior creatures from space ever visit earth, the first question they will ask, in order to assess the level of our civilization, is: 'Have they discovered evolution yet? Living organisms had existed on earth, without ever knowing why, for over three thousand million years before the truth finally dawned on one of them. His name was Charles Darwin.'*

It would have been fairer, though less dramatic, to have said "two of them" and to have coupled the name of Wallace with Darwin. But let me, in any case, pursue the universal perspective.

I believe the Darwin/Wallace theory of evolution by natural selection is the explanation not just of life on this planet, but of life in general. If life is ever found elsewhere in the universe, I make the strong prediction that, however different it may be in detail, there will be one important principle which it shares with our own form of life. It will have evolved, under the guidance of a mechanism broadly equivalent to the Darwin/Wallace mechanism of natural selection.

I am never quite sure how strongly to put this point. The weak version, of which I am completely confident, is that no workable theory other than natural selection has ever been proposed. The strong form would be that no other workable theory ever *could* be proposed. Today, I think I'll stick with the weak form. It still has startling implications.

The only other theory that a reasonable person could even *suspect* of being workable is the Lamarckian combination of Use and Disuse together with the Inheritance of Acquired Characteristics. It has often been suggested that Lamarck's would be a fine theory if only it didn't conflict with the facts. It is just unfortunate that acquired characteristics are not, as a matter of fact, inherited. I have gone much further than this. I have argued that, even if acquired characteristics were inherited – even if on some distant planet they are inherited – the Lamarckian theory is still, *in principle*, not a powerful enough theory to do the job of explaining the organized and adaptive complexity we call life (see, for example, *The Blind Watchmaker*). Other alleged alternatives, such as Orthogenesis and Mutationism, are so far from being adequate candidates that I find it amazing they have ever been seriously considered.

Natural selection not only explains everything we know about life. It does so with power, elegance, and economy. It is a theory which has evident *stature*, a stature which really measures up to the magnitude of the problem which it sets out to solve.

Darwin and Wallace may not have been the first to get an inkling of the idea. But they were the first to understand the full magnitude of the problem, and the corresponding magnitude of the solution which jointly, and independently, occurred to them. This is the measure of their stature as scientists. The mutual generosity with which they settled the question of priority is the measure of their stature as human beings. It has been a privilege for me to help celebrate their joint achievement today.

[ABOUT THE AUTHOR]

Richard Dawkins is a Fellow of the Royal Society. He is a distinguished evolutionary biologist and the Charles Simonyi Professor For The Public Understanding Of Science at Oxford University; Fellow of New College; recipient of the Cosmos Prize for 1997 and the Kistler Prize for 2001; author of *The Selfish Gene*, *The Extended Phenotype*, *The Blind Watchmaker*, *River Out Of Eden*, *Climbing Mount Improbable*, and *Unweaving The Rainbow* along with countless articles for numerous publications. An anthology of his work will be published in 2003 under the title *A Devil's Chaplain*. Richard Dawkins serves as Honorary President of the Darwin Day Program, wherein his life and work are exemplary of the goals we strive to attain. His work has inspired people the world over, and continues to do so.

[ADDITIONAL RESOURCES]

Details of the Darwin-Wallace paper can be read here:
    http://www.inform.umd.edu/PBIO/darwin/darwindex.html

For a comprehensive resource site entitled, The World of Richard Dawkins, created and maintained by John Catalano, visit http://www.world-of-dawkins.com/

The Linnean Society: http://www.linnean.org/

The Royal Society: http://www.royalsoc.ac.uk/

The Alfred Russel Wallace Page, created and maintained by Charles H. Smith, Associate Professor and Science Librarian at Western Kentucky University: http://www.wku.edu/~smithch/index1.htm

ABOUT DARWIN:
BIOGRAPHIES OF REVOLUTIONARY ROUTINE
by Frode Skarstein
In collaboration with Darwinia Books – http://www.darwinia.com/

Ever since his first publication, Darwin's ideas were received as anything but routine. Throughout the whole of his publishing life, Darwin's work and ideas never ceased to stir the emotions of laymen, clergymen and professional scientists alike. His life, however, must have appeared rather dull on the surface. A mere five years after his return from circumnavigating the globe in the HMS *Beagle*, he was comfortably settled in Downe, Kent, where he lived most days in a daily routine for over forty years until he passed away in 1882. Yet, although every day was neatly divided into sessions of work, family and recreation, this setting enabled the production of the revolutionary ideas that forever changed science and the very way we view ourselves as humans – a static routine that enabled the diligent Darwin to, piece by piece, page by page, compose his evolutionary ideas.

A plethora of biographers have tried to capture this and other apparent paradoxes in Darwin's life and work. The purpose of this chapter is to provide a brief overview of the published biographies of Darwin. New works are continuously added to the already large number of titles dealing with Darwin's life, with a remarkable four new biographical books on Darwin being released this year alone (Aydon 2002; Browne 2002; Keynes 2002; Nicholas and Nicholas 2002), in addition to a new edition of his autobiographical texts (Neve and Messenger 2002).

The sheer number of Darwin biographies out there makes it difficult to obtain a complete overview of all the published works with biographical information on Darwin. Table 1 presents a list of the published Darwin biographies found by searching a range of library databases, including that of the Library of Congress, USA. Figure 1 shows how the frequencies of the included biographies are distributed between the years from Darwin's death and until today. I have focused on those biographies that at the time of publication attempted to provide either new information or novel interpretations of known material. Therefore, I have excluded most titles intended for the educational market, such as for example (Skelton and Robinson 1987), (Anderson

1994) and (Senker 2001), as the purpose of these biographies were not to critically present biographical information, but to popularize and reproduce already accepted ideas. Also excluded from this list are works that only in passing presents biographical information on Darwin (Brackman 1980; Keynes 2001; Keynes 2002). Thus, given these criteria, it is clear that this overview does not purport to be a complete list of all the Darwin biographies out there. Some of these biographies are, I feel, more important today than others. I have selected the ones I believe are the most interesting and present them in a little more detail in the following.

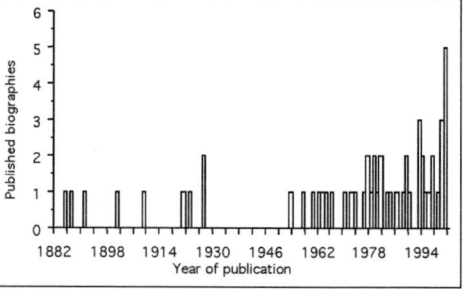

Fig. 1: *Frequency distribution plot of how the published biographies are distributed between 1882 and 2002. See the text for information on how the list is compiled.*

The Autobiography

A good starting point for exploring Darwin is his own autobiography. Written in a simple and straightforward manner, it is easily accessible for anyone. The earliest published transcripts of Darwin's autobiography (first version was published in 1887) had major omissions, which at the time were considered necessary by the family. Mostly these omissions were passages where Darwin stated clearly his religious beliefs or lack of such. The first complete transcript of Darwin's original autobiographical manuscript was published in 1958 by his granddaughter, Nora Barlow (Barlow 1958).

Charles Darwin, *by Grant Allen*

I believe the earliest dedicated Darwin biography is Charles Darwin by Grant Allen, published in 1885 (Allen 1885). Allen was a Canadian born naturalist, trained in Oxford, England, in the 1870s. He published a range of articles on popular science, and in particular on evolutionary thinking. His short study of Darwin was generally admired and still stands up well as a review of Darwin's life and ideas at the time. In his review of Allen's biography in Nature, Darwin's protégé George Romanes praises the study, though gently critical of how it placed Darwin in relation to Herbert Spencer (Romanes 1885).

Charles Darwin: Evolution by natural selection, *by G. De Beer*

As a pioneer in the discovery and publication of Darwin's papers, De Beer presented one of the earliest serious efforts at putting in-depth knowledge of Darwin's own material into a systematic biographical setting. However, De Beer was a biologist, and his limitations as a biographer surface when he tries to explain the development of Darwin's science.

Charles Darwin and his world, *by J. Huxley and Henry BD Kettlewell*

Julian Huxley, the grandchild of "Darwin's bulldog" T. H. Huxley, and the younger geneticists Kettlewell, discoverer of the "Peppered moth" – example of natural selection, worked together on this title. This biography seems to have received little attention at the time of publication, and it is rarely cited in subsequent biographies.

Charles Darwin: a biography, *by J. Bowlby*

In this title, Bowlby, a British child psychiatrist, presents a steady biography with the major novel contribution to be found in the psychological explanations he offers to explain Darwin's debilitating bad health and depression.

Darwin, *by A. Desmond and J. Moore*

A groundbreaking biography in the way it combined and explored the interaction between biographical information and in-depth knowledge of the Victorian social and political setting. In the words of the publisher, "Hailed as the definitive biography, this monumental work explains the character and paradoxes of Charles Darwin and opens up the full panorama of Victorian science, theology, and mores. The authors bring to life Darwin's reckless student days in Cambridge, his epic five-year voyage on the *Beagle*, and his grueling struggle to develop his theory of evolution."

Charles Darwin: Voyaging & The Power of Place, *by J Browne*

With her unparalleled command of the primary Darwin material available, Janet Browne has with her two volume masterpiece presented us with a clearer picture of Darwin as a person than has ever before been published. Through earlier biographies we have been made familiar with the modest, diligent Victorian gentleman who badgered correspondents for information on field observations when he wasn't pottering among experiments at home. But Browne reveals novel details about another Darwin, a remarkable tactician and a dedicated publicist. Darwin well understood that posterity does not necessarily remember the discoverer of an idea but the individual who first convinces the world of its truth. Browne shows a Darwin obsessed over details of publishing, timing, choosing the right translators for foreign editions and closely monitoring book sales. Browne is trained as a biologist, took her Ph.D. in the history of science, and has served as associate editor of *The Correspondence of Charles Darwin*.

[ABOUT THE AUTHOR]

Frode Skarstein is currently working on a post. doc. at the Department of Ecology at the University of Tromsø, Norway, on the subject of evolutionary ecology. Since early graduate days he has nurtured a keen interest in the history of evolutionary thinking and the people behind and involved in the development of the Darwinism we see today. In 1997 he started the online resource Darwinia Books and is still involved in the editorial development of the project.

[REFERENCES]

Allen, G. (1885). *Charles Darwin*. 206 pages. London, Longmans.

Anderson, M. J. (1994). *Charles Darwin: Naturalist*. Enslow Publishers, Inc.

Appleman , P., Ed. (1970 (3rd ed. 2001)). *Darwin: texts, commentary*. Norton Critical Editions. New York, Norton.

Armstrong, P. (1985). *Charles Darwin in Western Australia: a young scientist's perception of an environment*. 80 pages. Nedlands, W.A., University of Western Australia Press.

Aydon, C. (2002). *Charles Darwin: The Naturalist Who Started a Scientific Revolution*. 288 pages., Carroll & Graf.

Barlow, N., Ed. (1958). *The autobiography of Charles Darwin, 1809-1882: with original omissions restored*. London, Collins.

Bettany, G. T. (1887). *Life of Charles Darwin*. 175 pages. London, W. Scott.

Bowlby, J. (1990). *Charles Darwin: a biography*. 511 pages. London, Hutchinson.

Bowler, P. J. (1990). *Charles Darwin: The man and his influence*. 250 pages. Oxford, Blackwell.

Brackman, A. C. (1980). *A delicate arrangement: the strange case of Charles Darwin and Alfred Russel Wallace*. 370 pages. New York, Times Books.

Brent, P. (1981). *Charles Darwin: a man of enlarged curiosity*. 536 pages. London, Heinemann.

Browne, j. (1995). *Charles Darwin: Voyaging*. 662 pages. New York, Knoph.

Browne, J. (2002). *Charles Darwin: The power of place*. 624 pages. New York, Knopf.

Chancellor, J. (1973). *Charles Darwin*. 231 pages. London, Weidenfeld and Nicolson.

Clark, R. W. (1984). *The survival of Charles Darwin: a biography of a man and an idea*. 449 pages. New York, Random House.

Colp, R. (1977). *To be an invalid: the illness of Charles Darwin*. 285 pages. Chicago, Chicago University Press.

De Beer, G. (1963). *Charles Darwin: Evolution by natural selection*. 290 pages. New York, Doubleday.

Desmond, A. and J. Moore (1991). *Darwin*. 808 pages. London, Penguin Books LTD.

Dorsey, G. A. (1927). *The evolution of Charles Darwin*. 300 pages. Garden City, NY., Doubleday, Page & Company.

Farrington, B. (1996). *What Darwin Really Said*. 118 pages., Schocken Books, Incorporated.

Fletcher, F. (1980). *Darwin: an illustrated life of Charles Darwin*, 1809-1882. 48 pages. Aylesbury, Shire.

Freeman, R. (1978). *Charles Darwin: a companion*. 309 pages. Folkestone, Dawson.

Gillespie, N. C. (1979). *Charles Darwin and the problem of creation*. 201 pages. Chicago, University of Chicago Press.

Gribbin, J. and M. Gribbin (1998). *Darwin in 90 Minutes : (1809-1882)*. 80 pages., Constable and Company.

Hands, G. (2001). *Darwin* 96 pages., Headway.

Holder, C. F. (1891). *Charles Darwin*. 279 pages. New York, G.P. Putnam's sons.

Howard, J. (1982). *Darwin*. 101 pages. Oxford, Oxford University Press.

Huxley, J. and H. Kettlewell (1965). *Charles Darwin and his world*. 144 pages. London, Thames and Hudson.

Huxley, L. (1921). *Charles Darwin*. 119 pages. London, Watts & co.

Hyndley, K. (1989). *The voyage of the Beagle*. 32 pages. New York, Bookwright Press.

Johnston, W. W. (1901). *The ill-health of Charles Darwin; its nature and its relation to his work*. 158 pages. New York, G.P. Putnam's sons.

Keynes, R. (2001). *Annie's box: Charles Darwin, his daughter, and human evolution*. 331 pages. London, Fourth Estate.

Keynes, R. (2002). *Fossils, finches and fuegians: Charles Darwin's adventures and discoveries on the Beagle*. 320 pages. London, Harper Collins.

Keynes, R. D., Ed. (1988 (paperback: 2001)). *Charles Darwin's Beagle Diary*. Cambridge, Cambridge University Press.

Markham, E. (1909). *The marvellous year*. 104 pages. New York, B.W. Huebsch.

Marks, R. L. (1991). *Three men of the Beagle*. 256 pages. New York, Avon Books.

Mellersh, H. (1964). *Charles Darwin, pioneer in the theory of evolution*. 120 pages. New York, Praeger.

Miller, J. and B. van Loon (1982). *Darwin for beginners*. 176 pages. New York, Pantheon Books.

Milner, R. (1994). *Charles Darwin: evolution of a naturalist*. 176 pages. New York, Facts on File.

Moore, J. (1994). *The Darwin Legend*. 218 pages. Michigan, Baker Books.

Moore, R. E. (1954). *Charles Darwin, a great life in brief*. 206 pages. New York, Knopf.

Neve, M. and S. Messenger, Eds. (2002). *Autobiographies – by Charles Darwin*, Penguin USA.

Nicholas, F. and J. Nicholas (2002). *Charles Darwin in Australia*. 214 pages. Cambridge, Cambridge University Press.

Olby, R. (1967). *Charles Darwin*. 64 pages. Oxford, Oxford University Press.

Orel, H., Ed. (2000). *Charles Darwin: interviews and recollections*. New York, St. Martin's Press.

Overy, C. (1997). *A teacher's guide to Charles Darwin: his life, journeys and discoveries*. London, English Heritage.

Pearson, K. (1923). *Charles Darwin, 1809-1882*. 27 pages. London, Cambridge University Press.

Pickering, G. (1974). *Creative malady: illness in the lives and minds of Charles Darwin*. 327 pages. New York, Oxford University Press.

Romanes, G. J. (1885). "[Review of] Charles Darwin." *Nature* 33: 147-148.

Senker, C. (2001). *Charles Darwin* 48 pages., Raintree Publishers.

Skelton, R. and J. Robinson (1987). *Charles Darwin and the Theory of Natural Selection*. 119 pages., Barron's Educational Series, Incorporated.

Stefoff, R. (1998). *Charles Darwin and the evolution revolution*. 128 pages. Oxford, Oxford University Press.

Stevens, L. R. (1978). *Charles Darwin*. 159 pages. Boston, Twayne Publishers.

Ward, C. H. (1927). *Charles Darwin; the man and his warfare*. 472 pages. Indianapolis, The Bobbs-Merrill Company.

White, M. and J. Gribbin (1995). *Darwin: A life in science*. 336 pages. New York, Dutton.

Wichler, G. (1961). *Charles Darwin: the founder of the theory of evolution and natural selection*. Oxford, Pergamon Press.

Withers, G. (1971). *Charles Darwin and the theory of evolution*. London, Arnold.

Table 1
An overview of most Darwin biographies published in English from Darwin's death in 1882 up to today. This list does not purport to be a complete overview, but rather a convenient compilation of the biographies which at the time of their publication presented new information or alternative interpretations of known biographical information. The list is based on extensive searches in a range of online library databases, including the Library of Congress, USA. Full citation for all titles can be found in the reference list.

Year	Title	Author(s)
1885	Charles Darwin	Allen
1887	Life of Charles Darwin	Bettany
1891	Charles Darwin	Holder
1901	The ill-health of Charles Darwin; its nature and its relation to his work	Johnston
1909	The marvelous year	Markham
1921	Charles Darwin	Huxley
1923	Charles Darwin, 1809-1882	Pearson

Year	Title	Author
1927	The evolution of Charles Darwin	Dorsey
1927	Charles Darwin; the man and his warfare	Ward
1954	Charles Darwin, a great life in brief	Moore
1958	The autobiography of Charles Darwin, 1809-1882: with original omissions restored	Barlow
1961	Charles Darwin: the founder of the theory of evolution and natural selection	Wichler
1963	Charles Darwin: Evolution by natural selection	De Beer
1964	Charles Darwin, pioneer in the theory of evolution	Mellersh
1965	Charles Darwin and his world	Huxley and Kettlewell
1967	Charles Darwin	Olby
1970	Darwin: texts, commentary (3rd ed. 2001)	Appleman
1971	Charles Darwin and the theory of evolution	Withers
1973	Charles Darwin	Chancellor
1974	Creative malady: illness in the lives and minds of Charles Darwin	Pickering
1977	To be an invalid: the illness of Charles Darwin	Colp
1978	Charles Darwin: a companion	Freeman
1978	Charles Darwin	Stevens
1979	Charles Darwin and the problem of creation	Gillespie
1980	Darwin: an illustrated life of Charles Darwin, 1809-1882	Fletcher
1981	Charles Darwin: a man of enlarged curiosity	Brent
1982	Darwin	Howard
1982	Darwin for beginners	Miller and van Loon
1984	The survival of Charles Darwin: a biography of a man and an idea	Clark
1985	Charles Darwin in Western Australia: a young scientist's perception of an environment	Armstrong
1987	Charles Darwin and the Theory of Natural Selection	Skelton and Robinson
1988	Charles Darwin's Beagle Diary (paperback: 2001)	Keynes
1989	The voyage of the Beagle	Hyndley
1990	Charles Darwin: a biography	Bowlby
1990	Charles Darwin: The man and his influence	Bowler
1991	Darwin	Desmond and Moore
1994	Charles Darwin: Naturalist	Anderson
1994	Charles Darwin: evolution of a naturalist	Milner
1994	The Darwin Legend	Moore
1995	Charles Darwin: Voyaging	Browne
1995	Darwin: A life in science	White and Gribbin
1996	What Darwin Really Said	Farrington
1997	A teacher's guide to Charles Darwin: his life, journeys and discoveries	Overy
1998	Darwin in 90 Minutes: (1809-1882)	Gribbin and Gribbin
1998	Charles Darwin and the evolution revolution	Stefoff
2000	Charles Darwin: interviews and recollections	Orel
2001	Darwin	Hands
2001	Annie's box: Charles Darwin, his daughter, and human evolution	Keynes

2001	Charles Darwin	Senker
2002	Charles Darwin: The Naturalist Who Started a Scientific Revolution	Aydon
2002	Charles Darwin: The power of place	Browne
2002	Fossils, finches and fuegians: Charles Darwin's adventures and discoveries on the Beagle	Keynes
2002	Autobiographies – by Charles Darwin	Neve and Messenger
2002	Charles Darwin in Australia	Nicholas and Nicholas

[ADDITIONAL RESOURCES]

Darwinia Books: http://www.darwinia.com

Adrian Barnett's reviews originally appeared in **California Wild: Natural Sciences for Thinking Animals**, *the science and natural history magazine published by the California Academy of Sciences. The reviews are republished with permission from the author and Academy.*

BOOK REVIEWS:
ALFRED RUSSEL WALLACE: A LIFE
by Peter Raby

THE ALFRED RUSSEL WALLACE READER:
A SELECTION OF WRITINGS FROM THE FIELD
by Jane R. Camarini

Reviews by Adrian Barnett

Imagine journeying to a prize locality with a botanist and a geologist. While the first will interpret what is visible and what might have caused it, the second will focus on the essential underpinning of it all. This very much describes the approach of two current books on the life of Alfred Russel Wallace, the Victorian explorer, biologist and social activist.

In *Alfred Russel Wallace: a life* Peter Raby is our informational botanist, reporting on the skin of events, placing them in the community context of their time and pointing out the odd endemic outcrops of eccentricity. *The Alfred Russel Wallace Reader: a selection of writings from the field* provides an altogether geological perspective, with Jane R. Camarini mining Wallace's writings for nuggets of information and the mother load of perspective. To do this she presents long excerpts from hundreds of popular articles, field notes and 21 books.

Wallace is perhaps most famous as "the man who made Darwin hurry up and get on with *The Origin of Species*." But he was far more than Darwin's intellectual co-voyager and his scientific contribution was far greater than we realize today. Apprenticed as surveyor and with no university degree he was an entirely self-taught naturalist, who also designed and built several of his own houses. A passionate and curious naturalist since childhood, he made money as a surveyor in the British mid-19 century boom in railway building. Then, with friend and fellow beetle-collector Henry Walter Bates, he embarked on the seemingly mad-cap venture of collecting animals for money in the Amazon.

There was also the little matter of answering "the species question".

Sickness, shipwreck, fire and famine all attended his efforts. But so enthusiastic was he that, less than two months after his return from Amazonia, he was planning his trip to Borneo and beyond. As both books show, he was not content to be a simple natural historian, a recorder of events and specimens. Primed by his early surveying career, Wallace sought patterns in nature. As such he was among the elite few responsible for changing the way natural philosophers asked questions, paving the way for modern biological science. He also wrote wonderfully well, using hubris-free language to evoke for his audience the excitement of scientific discovery in remote paces as well as the unconscious grit and determination needed to obtain them.

So, which is the better book? As with many things, the answer depends on your definition. Raby's book is without doubt the more engaging and accessible. There are lovely quotes and the author has gone to great pains to research the information he interprets. Camarini, on the other hand, is more pithy, with wonderfully succinct explanatory commentaries that proceed each carefully chosen excerpt. Raby's analysis edges ahead on breadth, while Camarini's selection succeeds wonderfully in conveying the multi-faceted nature of Wallace's character. The more academically orientated Camarini occasionally assumes knowledge on behalf of the listener, and has chosen to avoid Wallace's powerful interest in mysticism because it has been covered elsewhere. Ruby, in contrast, clearly relishes this part of his subject's life, so seemingly at odds with his extremely rationalistic treatment of most other phenomena.

In synergy, these books work wonderfully to bring the man and his voice to life, and provide a social and political context that allows us to make sense of this complex individual. My, probably unhelpful, suggestion would be to read Raby once, then read it again with Camarini in the other hand as a source of deeper insights to the original quotes.

Complimentary sources for that most complex of topographies, the human life.

[ABOUT THE AUTHOR]

Adrian Barnett is a tropical ecologist with the University of Surrey Roehampton, England and a research associate in the California Academy of Sciences' Anthropology Department.

[ADDITIONAL RESOURCES]

California Academy of Sciences: http://www.calacademy.org/

California Wild Magazine: http://www.calacademy.org/calwild/

The Alfred Russel Wallace Page, created and maintained by Charles H. Smith, Associate Professor and Science Librarian at Western Kentucky University: http://www.wku.edu/~smithch/index1.htm

Robin McKie's article originally appeared in **The Observer**, a leading source for informed news and comment in the United Kingdom. The article is republished with permission from the author.

FROM SCIENTIST TO SAINT: DOES DARWIN DESERVE A DAY?

by Robin McKie, science editor
Sunday January 13, 2002,
The Observer

He was the originator of the most dangerous idea in history. He disenfranchised God as our creator and revealed the animal origins of humanity. Many believe his influence was pernicious and evil.

But now a campaign has been launched to establish an international day of celebration on 12 February: birthday of Charles Darwin, author of the theory of evolution by natural selection.

"Along with Shakespeare and Newton, Darwin is our greatest gift to the world," said Richard Dawkins, honorary president of the Darwin Day Organisation. "He was our greatest thinker. Any campaign to recognise his greatness should have a significant British contribution."

The Darwin campaign was launched by US activists two years ago to resist the anti-evolution campaigning of fundamental Christians. Now the aim is to create global celebrations by 2009, the bicentennial of his birthday.

"We have little chance of getting a national holiday for Darwin in the US – there is far too much anti-science and pseudoscience," said project organiser Amanda Chesworth. "We are more likely to get one established in Europe, particularly in Britain, his birthplace."

Celebrations will include seminars and lectures, and the showing of films and plays on Darwin's life, though other ideas include an atheist giving Radio 4's Thought for the Day, and a lesson on evolution being preached at Westminster Abbey. "I'd do it like a shot," said Dawkins.

Darwin was originally religious. He saw nature's diversity as proof of God's existence. Only a divine creator could be responsible for such marvels, it was then thought. But, after travelling the world in the *Beagle*, and after years of thought and experiment at his Down House home in Kent, he concluded that natural selection offered a better explanation.

Life forms better suited to their environments live longer and so have more offspring, thus triggering an evolution of species moving into new ecological niches. As philosopher Daniel Dennett said, it was 'the single best idea anyone has ever had... ahead of Newton and Einstein and everyone else.'

It is also remarkably simple. "You can explain natural selection to a teenager," said UK biologist John Maynard Smith. "You have difficulty with Newton and little chance with Einstein. Yet Darwin's idea is the most profound. It still haunts us."

Nor is opposition to Darwin confined to religious figures. Sociologists, psychologists and others involved in social policy hate natural selection, said Maynard Smith. "They deny human behaviour is influenced by genes and evolution. They want to believe we are isolated from the animal kingdom. It is damaging, intellectual laziness. That is why we need a Darwin Day."

This point was backed by biologist Steve Jones. "If you look at Africa, US fundamentalism, and the Muslim world, you realise evolution supporters are outnumbered by creationists. Yet these are people who have deliberately chosen to be ignorant. They are flat-Earthers without the sophistication. We need a Darwin Day to counter that ignorance."

[ABOUT THE AUTHOR]

Robin Mckie is science editor for *The Observer*. He has authored several books, including *African Exodus: The Origins of Modern Humanity*, co-written with Chris Stringer; *The Book of Man: The Human Genome Project and the Quest to Discover our Genetic Heritage*, co-written with Walter Bodmer; *Dawn of Man: The Story of Human Evolution*; and *The Genetic Jigsaw: The Story of the New Genetics*.

[ADDITIONAL RESOURCES]

The Observer online: http://www.observer.co.uk/

The Darwin Day Program: http://www.darwinday.org

This paper is an excerpt from a lecture presented to the Humanist Association of the Greater Sacramento Area, Atheists and Other Freethinkers, CSUS Anthropology Department, Sacramento Skeptics, and the Sacramento Organization for Rational Thinking for Darwin Day 2002.

THERE IS A GRANDEUR IN THIS VIEW OF LIFE
by Charles F. Urbanowicz

Perhaps no individual has done as much as Charles Robert Darwin did to help us (at least partially) to understand the question: "why are there so many different kinds of living things?" A decisive event that led to his perspective on the question was when he was chosen by Captain Robert FitzRoy to be the "gentleman naturalist" on board HMS *Beagle* (with no naval duties to perform). Darwin, however, conducted a great deal of research and in April 1832 Robert McCormick (1800-1890), who was the official naturalist on the *Beagle*, was "invalided out" back to England and Darwin was the naturalist for the rest of the voyage.

His observations in the Galápagos are particularly important to the evolution of his own thinking:

> "The natural history of these islands is eminently curious, and well deserves attention... *Hence, both in space and time, we seem to be brought somewhat near to that great fact – that mystery of mysteries – the first appearance of new beings on this earth.*" [stress added]

His remarks on the finches are especially famous:

> "Seeing this gradation and diversity of structure in one small, intimately related group of birds, *one might really fancy that from an original paucity of birds in this archipelago, one species have been taken and modified for different ends.*" [stress added]

Others went to the Galápagos Islands, perhaps most notably Louis Aggasiz of glacial fame and saw the same "things" that Darwin saw, but did not "think" what Darwin thought. We observe behaviors and things through our eyes and interpret what we see according to our theoretical (and philosophical) framework(s). Facts do not speak for themselves. Darwin's interpretation of the facts was tremendously influenced by his readings of Charles Lyell's *Principles of Geology* and of the reverend Thomas Malthus's *An Essay on the Principles of Population*. Malthus:

"argued for population control, since populations increase in geometric ratio and food supply only in arithmetic ratio, *and influenced Charles Darwin's thinking on natural selection as the driving force of evolution.* Malthus saw war, famine, and disease as necessary *checks on population growth.*" [stress added] (Jones, 1996)

Yet people and ideas change over time. Darwin and his ideas changed, and as an examination of the current "Darwin Industry" shows, "Darwin interpretations" change with the times! Just as we view Darwin (in hindsight) as the genius he was, so the famous joint presentation of Darwin's and Wallace's by Charles Lyell at the Linnean Society on July 1, 1858 was viewed as nothing special by at least some of his contemporaries. The President of the Society later reported that "no particularly important papers had been read" in 1858.

Changing views continue, and Gillian Beer (2000) points this out in her most readable *Darwin's Plots*:

"Darwin has grown younger in recent years. He is no longer the authoritative old man with a beard substituting for God. Instead his work and life are again in contention and debate. Sociologists, microbiologists, linguists, sociobiologists, philosophers, feminists, psychologists, biographers, geneticists, novelists, poets, post-colonialists, have their say." [stress added]

The concept of change is definitely vital to an understanding of Darwin, whether you are reading Darwin himself or reading about him. In this context it is important to know that every edition of *Origin* published in Charles Darwin's lifetime is different! He re-wrote every single one and all are different! Various sentences were deleted ("cut"), or re-written, or added for each edition. In everything I write about Darwin I emphasize this by including the following table, based on information in the excellent 1959 publication of Morse Peckham [Editor] entitled The *Origin Of Species By Charles Darwin: A Variorum Text*).

The Various Editions Of "Origin" From 1859-1872

Year	Edition	Copies	Cut	Re-Written	Added	Total	Percent Change
1859	1st	1,250				3,878	-
1860	2nd	3,000	9	483	30	3,899	7%
1861	3rd	2,000	33	617	266	4,132	14%
1866	4th	1,500	36	1,073	435	4,531	21%
1869	5th	2,000	178	1,770	227	4,580	29%
1872	6th	3,000	63	1,669	571	5,088	21-29%

One of the significant changes is demonstrated by a passage that is frequently quoted:

"Thus, from the war of nature, from famine and death, the most exalted object which we are capable of conceiving, namely. the production of the higher animals, directly follows. *There is grandeur in this view of life*, with its several powers, having been originally breathed into a few forms or into one; and that, whilst this planet has gone cycling on according to the fixed law of gravity, from so simple a beginning endless forms most beautiful and most wonderful have been, and are being, evolved." [stress added] (*Origin*, 1st. Edition 1859).

An earlier version from the essay of 1842, is similar:

> "*There is a simple grandeur in the view of life* with its powers of growth, assimilation and reproduction, being originally breathed into matter under one or few forms, and that whilst this our planet has gone circling according to fixed laws, and land and water, in a cycle of change, have gone on replacing each other, that from so simple an origin, through the power of gradual selection of influential changes, endless forms most beautiful and most wonderful have been evolved." [stress added]

The essay of 1844 however introduces "the Creator":

> "My reasons have now been assigned for believing that specific forms are not immutable creations. ... *It accords with what we know of the laws impressed by the Creator* on matter that the production and extinction of forms should, like the birth and death of individuals, be the result of secondary means. It is derogatory that the Creator of countless Universes should have made by individuals His will the myriads of creeping parasites and worms, which since the earliest dawn of life have swarmed over the land and in the depths of the ocean." [stress added]

From 1860 onwards, the Creator appears in the *Origin*:

> "Thus, from the war of nature, from famine and death, the most exalted object of which we are capable of conceiving, namely the production of higher animals directly follows. *There is a grandeur in this view of life, with its several powers, having been originally breathed by the Creator into a few forms or into one*; and that, whilst this planet has gone cycling on according to the fixed law of gravity, from so simple a beginning endless forms most beautiful and most wonderful have been, and are being, evolved." [stress added]

Regarding this interjection, Martin Gardner writes:

> "Darwin himself, as a young biologist aboard H.M.S. *Beagle*, was so thoroughly orthodox that the ship's officers laughed at his propensity for quoting Scripture. Then 'disbelief crept over me at a very slow rate,' he recalled, 'but was at last complete. The rate was so slow that I felt no distress.' *The phrase 'by the creator,' in the final sentence of the selection chosen here, did not appear in the first edition of Origin of Species. It was added to the second edition to conciliate angry clerics.* Darwin later wrote, 'I have long since regretted that I truckled to public opinion and used the Pentateuchal term of creation, by which I really meant 'appeared' by some wholly unknown process.'" [stress added] (Gardner, 1984).

The phrase "Darwin later wrote" by Gardner refers to a letter from Darwin to Joseph Hooker on 29 March 1863. Darwin continued his thoughts with the following sentence: "It is mere rubbish, thinking at present of the origin of life; one might as well think of the origin of matter."

The disbelief that crept over him "at a very slow rate" became complete on the death of his beloved daughter Annie, yet, at the end of his life, the Anglican establishment in England claimed him as one of their own. While visiting a friend in London in December 1881, he suffered a mild heart seizure. On the 12th of February 1882, his 73rd birthday, he wrote to a friend that "my course is nearly run." Darwin had a fatal heart attack on Wednesday April 19, 1882; although he wished to be buried in the village of Downe, Kent, where he and his wife Emma had lived for forty years (1842-1882) it was not to be. On April 24, 1882, as a result of a request by various individuals, Charles Robert Darwin was buried in Westminster Abbey, London. His final place is a few paces away from the resting places of Sir Isaac Newton (1642-1727), Sir Charles Lyell, Michael Faraday (1791-1867), and William Herschel (1792-1871). Darwin's pall bearers included the President of the Royal Society, the American Minister to the British Isles (Robert Lowell), the churchman Cannon Farrar, an earl, two dukes, and the three leading British biologists of the times who were among his closest scientific friends: Thomas Huxley, Sir Joseph Hooker, and Alfred Russel Wallace. Herbert Spencer (1820-1903) thought the occasion of Darwin's internment at the Abbey "worthy enough [to attend] to suspend his objections to religious ceremonies" (Himmelfarb, 1959).

[ABOUT THE AUTHOR]

Charles F. Urbanowicz is a professor of anthropology at the California State University in Chico. He has written several papers on the life and work of Charles Darwin, including one that explores teaching about Darwin and evolution through theatre. Professor Urbanowicz has traveled extensively and maintains a comprehensive website of his studies.

[REFERENCES]

Gillian Beer, 2000, Darwin's Plots: *Evolutionary Narrative In Darwin, George Eliot and Nineteenth-Century Fiction* (Second Edition) (Cambridge University Press).

Charles Darwin, 1845, *The Voyage of the Beagle* [Edited by Leonard Engel, 1962, NY: Doubleday].

Charles R. Darwin, 1859 (as well as): 1860 (2nd edition), 1861 (3rd), 1866 (4th), 1869 (5th), and 1872 (6th), *On The Origin of Species by Means of Natural Selection or the Preservation of Favoured Races in the Struggle for Life*. [Note: Publishers, locations, and introductions vary.]

Gavin De Beer, 1958, *Evolution By Natural Selection: Charles Darwin and Alfred Russel Wallace* (Cambridge University Press).

R.B. Freeman, 1978, *Charles Darwin: A Companion* (Folkestone, Kent, England: Dawson).

Martin Gardner [Ed.], 1984, *The Sacred Beetle And Other Great Essays in Science* (NY: Prometheus Books).

Gerturde Himmelfarb, 1959, *Darwin And The Darwinian Revolution* (NY: W.W. Norton & Co.).

Sarah Jenkins Jones (Editor), 1996, *Random House Webster's Dictionary of Scientists*. (NY: Random House).

Morse Peckham [Editor], 1959, *The Origin Of Species By Charles Darwin: A Variorum Text* (Philadelphia: University of Pennsylvania Press).

[ADDITIONAL RESOURCES]

Charles Urbanowicz' Homepage: http://www.csuchico.edu/~curban/

California State University Sacramento Department of Anthropology: http://www.csus.edu/anth/

Sacramento Freethought: http://www.rthoughtsrfree.org/

Sacramento Organization for Rational Thinking (SORT):
    http://www.quiknet.com/~kitray/index1.html

Molleen Matsumura's review originally appeared on the Secular Web and was later featured on the Darwin Day Program's web site. It is republished here with permission from the author.

BOOK REVIEW:
DARWIN, THIRD EDITION
(NORTON CRITICAL EDITIONS)
by Philip Appleman (Editor)
W W Norton & Co.

Review by Molleen Matsumura

There can be no better celebration of Darwin Day than to learn and teach about Charles Darwin's tremendous contribution to modern life and thought. If you could treat yourself or your best friend to only one book by or about Darwin, the Norton Critical Editions *Darwin* would be the one. Not only that, it is both by and about Darwin!

Darwin is edited by Philip Appleman, who is not only a scholar deeply familiar with the work of Darwin and his contemporaries, but a poet who has made evolution a theme of such works as *Darwin's Ark*. *Darwin* is a labor of love, still vibrant with Appleman's first, youthful discovery of Darwin's work (described in pages 15-17 of the introduction), and informed by thorough scholarship. In this third, greatly expanded edition, Appleman presents generous selections from Darwin's original works, as well as a wide selection of essays and excerpts of other writers' works. We learn about the biographical and scientific background of Darwin's pivotal discovery, as well as its "importance and enduring relevance" not only for science, but for social thought, philosophy and ethics, religious life, and literature.

Appleman understands that *The Origin of Species* and Darwin's other works are valuable not only for what they teach us about the way that the history of life unfolded – as if that weren't enough! – but for their vital contribution to the development of science as a method for understanding the natural world. The process is an exciting, unfinished story, as Appleman tells first through the writing of thinkers like Lyell and Malthus whose work Darwin incorporated in his theory, then through the writing of his contemporary detractors and defenders.

With the achievements and disagreements of those who have built on Darwin's work, incorporating genetics and statistics and refining our understanding of systematics, human evolution, and natural selection, Appleman brings readers up to date and leaves us ready for tomorrow's headlines. *Darwin* offers selections as diverse as an excerpt of *The Woman's Bible*, by pioneering feminist Elizabeth Cady Stanton; discussions of evolutionary medicine and evolutionary ethics; and essays on how the advent of evolutionary thought has changed the meaning of tragedy.

For many of us, it won't be a book we read straight through, but one we dip into at different times. One reader will seek a solid introduction to a particular topic, another will look for provocative insights. You might want to learn more about punctuated equilibrium, or how one poet "put[s] a contemporary gloss on Darwin's theory of sexual selection". Whatever else you read, be sure to read at least one item in each section of "Part VIII: Evolutionary Theory and Religious Theory." In Part VIII, Appleman made a deliberate choice. He might have shown us the theological developments that led to accommodation and even joyful acceptance of scientific knowledge by much of Western religion. This would have been a reasonable addition to the broad intellectual history Darwin offers. Instead, Appleman devotes just over a hundred pages to the problem of "creation science".

The problem is that an essentially religious disagreement over scriptural interpretation has infected our political culture and is undermining scientific literacy. This is not a purely American problem: it is found wherever there are scriptural literalists, particularly among Christian fundamentalists in Canada, Australia and South Africa, but also among Orthodox Jews and Islamic fundamentalists. As Appleman illustrates with selected essays, these last two groups are cooperating with such organizations as the Institute for Creation Research. Some non-western religions have also joined the fray. Perhaps most worrisome is the growing influence of the politically savvy "intelligent design" creationists, whose work is also represented in *Darwin*.

Having worked for over seven years to defend evolution education against continuous assault, I believe Appleman made the right and necessary choice. The history he omitted can be inferred from the examples of "Mainstream Religious Support for Evolution", supplemented by other readings he suggests. But it is hard to find material like this collected with examples of creationism and neocreationism, the scientific rebuttals of that shoddy pseudoscience, and expressions of the broad and deep scientific support for evolution. Read all this, and you will understand the urgency of defending Darwin's precious legacy.

We still have so much to learn, and so much to lose. ∞

[ABOUT THE AUTHOR]

Molleen Matsumura is Executive Director of the American Foundation for Health, which sponsors innovative medical research. Her long-standing interest in public understanding of science led to her work as senior editor at *BASE* and its successor publication *Science21*, magazines showcasing the research of young scientists. For seven years, she was Network Project Director at the National Center for Science Education, where she worked to defend evolution education in public schools, and edited *Voices for Evolution*. She has done considerable public speaking on evolution-creation controversies, and her articles and interviews on the topic have appeared in *Reports of the National Center for Education*, *Free Inquiry*, *Conversations* (a publication of the United Church of Christ), *Humanistic Judaism*, and *Church and State*.

[ADDITIONAL RESOURCES]

National Center for Science Education: http://www.ncseweb.org

The Secular Web: http://www.infidels.org

CELEBRATING DARWIN'S BIRTHDAY

by Gary L. Bennett

On 12 February we celebrate the birthday of possibly the world's greatest scientist: Charles Robert Darwin. Born on that day in Shrewsbury, England, Charles Darwin would belie his early sporting life to write what some have termed the most revolutionary book in science: *The Origin of Species*. After a five-year, 40,000-mile voyage on H.M.S. *Beagle* in which he observed a wide range of natural phenomena (including an earthquake and volcanoes) and in which he collected many specimens, Darwin began to realize that the myths in Genesis did not account for the natural world with its incredible diversity of life.

Just as Darwin and others had observed that the land had undergone great physical changes Darwin began to suspect that organisms would vary too until new species arose. These species would not be independently created but would have descended from other species.

Darwin did not rush to print because he was a careful man. He continued his studies and researches. He contacted experts in many fields to gather information. He raised objections to his own ideas.

After 23 years of work, in 1859 he published *The Origin of Species* in an edition of 1250 copies. The edition sold out that day – and the book continues to sell well today. The book has been called "the most fundamental of all intellectual revolutions in the history of mankind".

Darwin and another English naturalist Alfred Russel Wallace had observed that species vary by location and by time. Today we describe that process by the term "evolution" which means the "change in the hereditary characteristics of groups of organism over the course of generations". Given the fact of evolution Darwin searched for a theory of evolution to explain what he had observed.

Both Darwin and Wallace had read Reverend Thomas R Malthus's essay on population. Malthus had argued that human population would be kept in check by limited resources, diseases, and wars, all of which he lumped into the categories of "vice" and "misery". Clearly something similar was operating in the natural world and that something was what Darwin termed "natural selection".

Evolution as Darwin saw it rested on six points. First, organisms produce more offspring than can survive. Anyone who has tramped through the woods has seen this. Certainly, the annual winter death toll is testimony to this fact.

Second, the offspring have variability that is slight, but meaningful for survival. Anyone who has looked at a litter of puppies or kittens has no doubt been struck by the differences among them. Human siblings also differ from each other.

Third, there is a struggle for existence. Every animal in the wild is in a continuous race to find enough food and adequate shelter. Until the advent of modern civilization we humans were in a similar race (and some in the world still are).

Fourth, those most suited to the conditions in which they live survive and reproduce. This point is almost axiomatic. Obviously we are all descendants of people who lived to reproductive age.

Fifth, favorable traits are passed on to offspring.

And finally the mechanism for evolution is natural selection. There is nothing mysterious about natural selection—it is simply the "greater reproductive success among particular members of a species arising from genetically determined characteristics that confer an advantage in a particular environment".

It cannot be emphasized enough that there is nothing anti-religious in Darwin's theory; in fact, evolution is silent about religion. The major Judeo-Christian-Islamic religious denominations in the U.S. have accepted evolution as the way God works. Creationists sell God short when they insist upon a 6,000-year-old flat Earth with the Sun traveling around it.

There is an almost religious feeling in Darwin's final sentence: "There is a grandeur in this view of life, with its several powers, having been originally breathed into a few forms or into one; and that, whilst this planet has gone cycling on according to the fixed law of gravity, from so simple a beginning endless forms most beautiful and most wonderful have been, and are being, evolved".

[ABOUT THE AUTHOR]

Gary L. Bennett is a consultant who has worked on several major space missions. With a PhD in physics and having done research in nuclear physics he recognizes that creationism is an assault on physics as well as on biology, anthropology, astronomy and geology. In 2000, he received the "Friend of Darwin" Award from the National Center for Science Education.

This paper was presented by Hugh Rance to the Long Island Secular Humanists for Darwin Day 2002.

DARWIN BEFORE THE PENNY DROPPED
by Hugh Rance

The entire process of Creation had taken God the familiar six days recounted in Genesis. A tale tirelessly thundered from the pulpits in the Blessed Isle of Charles Darwin's birth. That occasion was five thousand eight hundred and thirteen years after The Beginning. The time elapsed, even to the day could be reckoned. The doughty Irish prelate James Ussher, while he was Bishop of Armagh, had brought to convincing conclusion the bookish task of backtracking though genealogies and reigns of kings to when God began time. He (the one with a capital), at surely the most gentlemanly hour of 9 a.m., had began the effort of creating the world and all its creatures. The start was on Monday 23, October 4004 BC. A swift sequence of divine machinations ensued. Brooking no argument, God declared done, and all good, before taking time out on the seventh day.

Darwin was born into comfortable circumstances as the fifth child (second son) of Dr. Robert Darwin (his mother, daughter of the wealthy potterer Josiah Wedgwood, had died when he was eight and was remembered with love). His father, a successful physician, Shrewsbury, England, hopeful that Charles could be so too, sent him at age just shy of sixteen to the University of Edinburgh to study medicine (still Hippocratic humoralism, which today is politely called 'alternative' or 'complementary' medicine, of the sort advocated by Benedict Lust – pronounced 'Loost,' his admirers tirelessly insist). Witnessing the surgical removal of limbs, and hearing the screams and cursing of the unananaesthetized in such procedures, persuaded Darwin to a more benign career (Ether, the first modern anaesthetic, was first used in 1842).

He did, though, carry away a skill that he would later use. At the university, he had befriended a taxidermy demonstrator (a black man and ex-slave) who patiently taught him how to properly skin and stuff birds.

What, his father wondered, to do with a callow youth who balked at cutting up people? Charles was slight in build, had thinning, unremarkable, dark blond hair, a blob of a nose (when prominent quizzical noses were fashionable) and a stammer that he did his best to hide. Well, gentlemen could purchase parsonages and in preparation for that his father, though himself an unbeliever and worldly son of the freethinker Erasmus Darwin, transferred Charles to Cambridge University to study theology.

There (at Cambridge), Darwin, from J. S. Henslow (botany) and Adam Sedgwick (geology), received the message (ironic in hindsight) that nature was benign and devoted his time to the pursuit of mostly beetle collecting, occasional horse riding and small game shooting, with others of an outdoorsy bent.

Graduated in 1931, without distinction, Charles felt no calling to Holy Offices. What to do? His only academic passion was for natural history. Apart from his beetle collecting, he had, for a couple of weeks, been field assistant to geologist Sedgwick and had been inordinately pleased by praise received for his skill in taking accurate measurements on the attitudes of strata with compass and plumb bob on a protractor. But the season in Wales had been hot, dry, and midge ridden and they had thoroughly failed to find fossils, which Sedgewick had been so arduously keen to find.

"You are good for nothing save horse riding, shooting birds, and rats." snapped his father. But, with some strings having been pulled by Henslow for this genial (as others saw him) young man, and upon Josiah Wedgwood II's push, addressed to his father: "The pursuit of Natural History, though certainly not professional, is very suitable to a clergyman," he was away, with his father's well wishes, on what would be any naturalist's dream, a trip around the world.

Darwin sailed on second voyage of the H.M.S. *Beagle* captained by Robert FitzRoy descendant of a bastard of Charles II (a fourth great grandson to him), the rakehell king, On the downside, the boat, as a result of its design, was so susceptible to capsizing that the sailors of the Royal Navy called this class of ships 'coffins.' On the upside, with Robert FitzRoy in command. the *Beagle* had already once doubled Cape Horn, fought off the worst of the storms; and had sailed around the Cape of Good Hope and across most of the seas of the world. FitzRoy was on the cutting edge of modern science and his cabin was filled with the latest gadgets, called barometers. One of the secrets of his success was that from the barometers he could tell when a storm was imminent and consequently was never caught by surprise. He was in favor of having more than the usual sadsack H.M.S. assigned naturalist onboard (who were quartered and tolerated no better than the lowest ships boy). However, for Darwin, who would sail as the captain's companion and social equal ashore, a berth and working area was partitioned off for his exclusive use. (Not so for the ships' officially assigned naturalist who quit in disgust on reaching the first port in South America.)

When he sailed, Darwin had no plans to make the century his own. He was to continue the tradition of naturalists of the 18th Century, which was to describe and classify the diversity of life as he came across it. However, his intellectual horizon would be greatly expanded by a bon voyage gift from Henslow. This was volume 1 of the first edition, hot off the press, of Charles Lyell's *Principles of Geology*. Henslow's generosity, and with the certainty that good work was being done, he having seen some of Darwin's first reports home, also had waiting for Darwin at ports in South America, volume 2 of *Principles* at Rio de Janeiro and the third at Valparaiso. These books persuaded that the earth was incredibly much older than 6000 years. In the time before time, sceneries had come and gone. The process of change continues today was Lyell's theme. In time, incremental change adds up. Seen thus, the wondrous rock record can be demystified.

With Principles in mind, Darwin was able to find an easy explanation for marine fossil he found at various elevations high into the Andes. The Andes has been raised slowly out of the sea and in concert the Pacific had sunk. And he could prove that the

Pacific had sunk slowly for islands throughout vast reaches of that ocean there are atolls. Atolls are rings of coral that mark where islands in the Pacific had once stood high. In his model, an atoll begins as a fringing reef to an island. The living reef can grow upward as fast as the island goes down only if the Pacific seafloor on which it rests subsided slowly. His seesaw model of continent up, ocean floor down, is no longer accepted. But proven to be true is that a coral atoll marks where an extinct volcanic island has sunk.

Before setting sail, Darwin had certainly been exposed to idea of organic evolution as this had been famously postulated by the Jean-Baptiste-Pierre-Antoine de Monet, chevalier (citoyen after 1800) de Lamark (1744-1829). However, at the universities he had attended, his mentors had been thoroughgoing Creationists. And now, when the liberating, and momentous, idea of the vastness of geological time should have lead him to further speculations, it did not. "It is idle to dispute about the abstract possibility of the conversion of one species into another when there are known causes, so much more active in their nature, which must always intervene and prevent the actual accomplishment of such conversions," wrote Lyell. But what those known causes are, he neglects to say, and evidently Darwin's own field observations did not alerted him to Lyell's omission and his further (false, though standard for the time) essentialist (stemming from Plato) assumption that "There are fixed limits beyond which the descendants from common parents can never deviate from a certain type."

Collecting in the Galápagos, Darwin had, therefore, no compelling reason why he should not drop the finches from two islands into one bag. "Like Linnaeus, Darwin was well aware", Johnathan Weiner writes in his recent book *The Beak of the Finch*, "that different local conditions can carve a species into local varieties. He and FitzRoy had already seen evidence of that in the foxes of the Falkland Islands, and Darwin thought he saw the same thing in Galápagos rats. But Darwin did not imagine that a species would split into different varieties under the near identical conditions and skies of neighboring islands; even if they had, Darwin did not imagine that such varieties would mean anything all that important."

And that is how it was when The *Beagle* docked in Falmouth in October 1836. In his opinion, the biological specimens he had collected during his voyage were of interest, but of no great significance, and on January 4, 1837, he donated them to the Zoological Society of London after a meeting at which he had shown his Galápagos birds as specimens of "finches, wrens, 'Gross beaks', and blackbirds. These same birds he had taxidermied were then classified according to Linnaean principles by ornithologist John Gould.

For Darwin, approaching thirty years of age, the pressing question was. Should I marry or remain a bachelor? On a large piece of paper he ruled a line down the middle. On the one side he listed all the reasons why the one state would make him happy and on the other side why the other would. Conclusion: Marry, marry, marry. And while his mind was on that pleasant subject news of an additional good subject to contemplate, and act upon, arrived. It was Gould telling him that the Ground Finches, he had collected in the Galápagos, could be formally declared 14 species but their ancestor could only be the one related species that exists in South America. The penny dropped: the series of finches in the Galápagos could be used to question the stability of species. ∞

[ABOUT THE AUTHOR]

Hugh Rance is a professor of geology at Queensborough Community College, has worked as an exploration geologist prospecting in Africa, for coal in Swaziland and diamonds in Tanzania, and in Canada, for nickel in Manitoba and the Northwest Territories, and for gold in Ontario. He is also President of the Secular Humanist Society of NY.

[REFERENCES]

Richard Lee Marks, 1991, *Three Men of the Beagle* (Alfred Knopf, NY)

[ADDITIONAL RESOURCES]

New York Humanist: http://nyhumanist.org/

Long Island Secular Humanists: http://nyhumanist.org/lish.htm

*Richard Milner's review originally appeared in the January 2002 issue of **Scientific American**, a magazine that has been bringing its readers unique insights about developments in science and technology for more than 150 years.*

*Reprinted with permission. Copyright © 2002 by **Scientific American, Inc.** All rights reserved.*

BOOK REVIEW:
CHARLES DARWIN, HIS DAUGHTER, AND HUMAN EVOLUTION
(NORTON CRITICAL EDITIONS)
by Randal Keynes
Riverhead Books

Review by Richard Milner

THE FIRST EVOLUTIONARY PSYCHOLOGIST

Charles Darwin Sought Clues to Human Nature by Studying the Behavior of His Own Children and Other Wild Animals

When descendants of Charles Darwin get together, some still tell the story of a long-ago servant who expressed pity for the family patriarch. The poor man, she said, was so idle that she saw him staring at an ant-heap for a whole hour. Darwin's full-time, self-created job, of course, was to observe every animal creature, from the ants and bees in his garden, to giant tortoises in the Galápagos, to his own family. He even published a monograph on the behavior of his infant children.

Randal Keynes, a great-great-grandson of Charles Darwin (and also a descendant of John Maynard Keynes) has crafted a superb intellectual and social history about Darwin's quiet years (c. 1842-1882) at his country estate, long after his HMS *Beagle* adventures. Charles and Emma Wedgwood Darwin produced 10 children, but lost three – an infant daughter and son, and the bright and charming 10-year old, Annie, whose death plunged her parents into profound bereavement. Annie's fatal tuberculosis (a cogent diagnosis suggested by Keynes, although it was problematic in Darwin's day) was the most wrenching event of the naturalist's middle age.

Among his family's heirlooms, Keynes discovered Annie's writing case, containing her goose-quill pens and stationary, a lock of her hair, and her father's mournful yet objective daily notes on her deteriorating condition. (The British edition of the book is titled "Annie's box".) Initially inspired and affected by these mementos, Keynes came to realize that "Charles's life and his science was all of a piece." With impeccable scholarship, he has woven clips from Victorian magazines, contemporary poems and novels, family letters and keepsakes, and even recollections of living people into a stylish narrative that is both moving and thoroughly documented.

Darwin had often wondered whether his powerful affection for family could be explained in evolutionary terms. His then-radical conclusion: our deepest emotions are rooted in the evolution of primate social organization. If we had descended from bees instead of from apes, he once opined,

> *"there can hardly be a doubt that our unmarried females would, like the worker-bees, think it is a sacred duty to kill their brothers, and mothers would strive to kill their fertile daughters and no one would think of interfering."*

According to Keynes, Darwin was at a loss to understand why most naturalists at the time thought they saw evidence of ubiquitous, benevolent design in a world so full of pain, death, and disease. *"There seems to me,"* he wrote, *"too much misery in the world"* for a loving deity to have designed it that way. He had witnessed genocide of the Indians in Argentina and the torture of slaves in Brazil. He had written of wasps whose larvae devour living caterpillars from within, leaving the beating heart for last. With the slow death of Annie, the misery became personal.

Some contemporary critics painted Darwin as a cold intellect with no place for love in his famous "struggle for existence." Keynes shows he was actually a man of uncommon warmth. While he was "anxious to observe accurately the expression of a crying child," according to his son Francis, he usually found that "his sympathy with the grief spoiled his observation." To comfort his friend Sir Joseph Hooker when the botanist's young son almost died, Darwin drew on his own minute-by-minute deathwatch of Annie: *"Much love, much trial, but what an utter desert is life without love."*

As the first evolutionary psychologist, Darwin was breaking new ground by seeking the roots of human behavior in our species' mammalian history. In the *Origin of Species* (1859), he had predicted that "psychology will be based on a whole new foundation," which he attempted to establish in his 1872 book on *The Expression of the Emotions*. Comparing the behavior of dogs, cats, monkeys, orang-utans, infants, and tribal peoples from all over the world, he argued that human affection, sympathy, parental love, morality, and even religious feelings had gradually developed from a primate base. Such "evil passions" as rage and violence were also part of grandfather Baboon's legacy. Once I had a rare chance to examine Darwin's printers' proofs of this treatise on comparative psychology, which contain his handwritten corrections. The title, as printed, was "*The Expression of the Emotions in Man and the Lower Animals.*" Darwin had emphatically crossed out the word "*Lower.*"

[ABOUT THE AUTHOR]

Richard Milner is a Senior Editor of *Natural History* magazine at the American Museum of Natural History. His articles on Darwin have appeared in *Natural History* and *Scientific American*. He is the author of *Encyclopedia of Evolution: Humanity's Search for Its Origins* (a third edition will be published in 2003 under the title Darwiniana: An Encyclopedia of Evolution) and *Charles Darwin: Evolution of a Naturalist*.

[ADDITIONAL RESOURCES]

Scientific American online: http://www.sciam.com/

Richard Milner performances: http://www.darwinday.org/art/entertain/

Sharon Hill's article originally appeared in Pennsylvania's **Scranton Times Tribune** *on February 12, 2002. It is reprinted here with permission from the author.*

AN EVOLUTIONARY HOLIDAY
by Sharon Calpin Hill

Imagine that your life's work has brought you to a idea that is so profound, so innovative, that when its finally presented to your colleagues, their jaws drop in awe and shock. Imagine that this idea is so revolutionary that facing the public makes you physically ill. So then, imagine yourself as Charles Darwin in nineteenth century England where you have just put out in print *The Origin of Species By Means of Natural Selection*.

That was 1859. Almost 150 years later, people all around the world are celebrating the ideas of Mr. Darwin and general science education in his name.

HAPPY DARWIN DAY.

February 12, 2002 marks the 193rd anniversary of the birth of great scientist Charles Darwin, father of the theory of evolution. But in the US, his name is associated with controversy. Why was Darwin so loathed and yet so honored? Why have a Darwin Day? In fact, why should we bother to learn about evolution? The answers are far more interesting than what you have probably heard about Darwin and evolution.

As a young naturalist, Charles Darwin made his famous sea voyage to South America in which he sowed the seeds for his theory.

Wealthy, but not a man with a desire for public display, he was content in seclusion at his country home in England with his family, studying his specimens – pigeons were a favorite. All the while, he kept secret notebooks detailing his findings.

Darwin was a troubled man in both body and soul – a workaholic who was always in poor health. His brilliant idea was a burden for him. Obviously, his theory would totally change the way people thought about the world and their place in it. Sensitive to the social issues of the time, Darwin was painfully aware that his ideas would clash with religious teachings.

If Mr. Darwin did not flesh out the theory of evolution by natural selection, someone else would have in very short order. In fact, at the same time, another scientist, Alfred Wallace, came to the same general conclusion as Darwin. He almost took the credit because Darwin delayed on presenting his work.

When the book was finally published, it was a sensation.

THE CONTROVERSY BEGAN.

Darwin's fellow colleagues rallied for or against him. His loyal friend, T.H. Huxley gave lectures to the working men who crowded a hall after hours to hear about this new idea. But, Darwin stayed at home, corresponding by mail for news from London and continued to write other books. He lived to an old age.

Today, the topic of evolution is largely misunderstood by the general public and constantly misrepresented. Most students hear barely a mention of evolution in high school. Lately, there has been efforts by non-science groups to remove it altogether.

Science can be difficult going – lots of strange, unknown words and concepts. But it's vital knowledge. Now, more than ever, it's important to know basic science to understand hot topics like bioterrorism, global warming, stem cell research or just to follow what your doctor is saying. We need good science training. Unfortunately, it is lacking. Darwin Day is an opportunity to promote science learning.

Over the past few decades, small groups in Europe, North America and Australia have recognized Darwin and his contributions on the anniversary of his birth or the release of his famous book.

Now, there is a non-profit organization to promote science and humanity within our global community. The Darwin Day Program can be found online at www.darwinday.org

Whether you feel comfortable with the topic or not, its an idea that won't go away. Evolution is an elegant theory that explains so many things. It can't be ignored. Every day, geneticists and fossil hunters find new evidence for evolution. It remains the foundation of biology. Without it, biology doesn't make sense.

Evolution is the reason why antibiotics work and sometimes fail. It's the reason we can see relationships between kinds of animals. It is the key to how experiments with mice, flies and fish can answer question about diseases and help humans live longer and better. It's worth getting to know. Science is our tool kit to understand the world. In science, we have found that life is all connected to each other and to the earth.

Imagine Mr. Darwin could foresee the future some 150 years from his time and find his ideas still debated and denounced. He would find the science of genetics – the progression of his work. And, here are those who would choose him as the rally point for science and humanities – a worthy celebration. ∞

[ABOUT THE AUTHOR]

Sharon Hill is a geologist in the state of Pennsylvania. Sharon is co-director of the Darwin Day Program and also co-creator of the Inquiring Minds Library. Along with various paranormal topics, Sharon's specific areas of interest are paleontology, evolution, geologic hazards, cryptozoology, and anomalous natural phenomena. Sharon's personal objective is to introduce discoveries to the public who may be unaware; to cut through the jargon and preconceptions and help them understand the importance of the scientific process.

[ADDITIONAL RESOURCES]

Scranton Times Tribune online: http://www.scrantontimes.com/

Darwin Day Program: http://www.darwinday.org

Inquiring Minds Program: http://www.inquiringminds.org

This paper was presented by Elof Axel Carlson to the Long Island Secular Humanists for Darwin Day 2002.

THE OTHER GREAT EMANCIPATOR: CHARLES DARWIN'S LEGACY FOR OUR LIVES

by Elof Axel Carlson

Darwin shares more than being a birthday twin with Abraham Lincoln. Both held unpopular views and both gave to the world documents of enduring value. Lincoln provided the Emancipation Proclamation, which destroyed the institution of slavery in the United States. Darwin provided *The Origin of Species*, a work, I hope to show, that liberated humans from a once universal fatalism. Darwin's intent was to seek the laws governing the origin of species. He was motivated to do so by his doubts. In his five-year voyage around the world, from 1831-1836, on the HMS *Beagle*, he encountered contradictions to the beliefs with which he, as a fledgling minister in the Church of England, had anticipated as correct. His initial assumptions were shaped by William Paley's Natural Theology. Paley assumed all creatures were created by God as described in the Book of Genesis; that God's design was seen throughout nature – and that nature was a harmonious whole, designed not only for human happiness, but for all living things. In this fated world, God called the tunes and set forth life's expectations. Darwin had no reason to doubt that he had a soul; that he would be judged; and an afterlife awaited him. He had no reason to doubt that species were fixed in their characteristics and that his role as a naturalist was to describe them, catalogue them, name them, and reveal, as best he could, God's handiwork seen through an inferred bible of nature.

Five years later Darwin knew this view was wrong. He had seen too much. He saw a war of nature in which organisms produced far too many offspring who struggled to survive. He saw what to any human being looked like a massive destruction of life, especially among the newborn. He saw distributions of organisms that did not make sense unless some scientific laws were governing their past history. He saw evidence of extinction when he unearthed the bones of fossilized mammals in Patagonia. He saw past upheavals of ocean floors that were lifted up into the Andes mountains. He saw remarkable adaptations of animals and plants to their surroundings. He became so expert at dissecting barnacles that he could look at a museum specimen and identify its place of origin within fifty miles from any place on South America. When he returned home he was already famous, his letters to his teacher, Henslow, having been privately published without his knowledge and distributed to the leading naturalists of Great Britain. Darwin returned with a secret he could not share. He had lost his faith. He had demoted himself to a Deist, that Unitarian-like penultimate descent to atheism. The word agnostic did not then exist. His secret shaped his career. He was fortunate that he came from the Darwin-Wedgwood family. He was born to wealth and did not have to earn a living to survive. He realized that a university career would be too dangerous because he would not be allowed to teach or publish his views without bringing scandal to his employers.

He chose the life of a private scholar, a role not unknown those days, but rare and still honored. Three years after his return and one year after his having read Malthus's Essay on Population, Darwin had it figured out. The truth of his theory dismayed him. He saw its philosophic and religious implications and realized it would bring denunciations on his name; and, as a young man launching a family, he wanted to protect his wife and children. His 1839 sketch was expanded in 1844. He showed it to his closest friends who shared his secret. By 1857 he had a considerable amount of writing done for a planned series of volumes that he hoped to release *en masse*, like an avalanche of evidence in support of his still secret theory. It was Wallace's letter that changed his plans. His friends Hooker and Lyell assembled some extracts from his 1844 draft and letters he had written to them and had these read with Wallace's manuscript at the Linnaean Society in London in 1858. The following year what Darwin called his abstract (over 350 pages) was published as *The Origin of Species*. That brief narrative tells us something about the way Darwin's secret was finally revealed to the world. What was that secret and why did he fear revealing it more than 20 years?

Darwin argued that life is connected through descent. From microbial beings to giant sequoias, from lice to giant whales, all of life had arisen from ancestors dissimilar from themselves and their ancestry could be traced back through their comparative anatomy. He proposed a theory of evolution with an observable mechanism that he called natural selection. Just as domesticated forms or breeds could be traced back to wild ancestors, the power of natural selection, responding to natural forces, shapes the destinies of populations. Darwin marshaled enormous evidence in support of this theory – he used island biogeography; he compared the fossil ancestors he dug up with the present creatures of the countries he visited; he did experiments on the survival of seeds soaked in brine – he calculated the number of days it would take from branches torn free by storms to float along ocean currents from South America to the Galápagos; he estimated the number of progeny each species produced and how their populations would grow beyond our capacity to count them if they were unchecked by natural forces. He described those natural forces in the lives of the species that were always vulnerable to competition for the space, food, and safety they required to reproduce and leave descendants. He studied vestigial organs. He studied comparative embryology. He related weather, food resources, parasites, competitors, disasters, and other components of the real life of plants and animals and estimated their chances for survival. Darwin was not just a theoretician. He was immersed in the details of life that he studied and without which he would have had neither doubts nor theory. But the science of evolution, as well as science itself, has changed a lot since 1859 and the publication of the *Origin of Species*. Darwin's theory of natural selection still remains solid despite much testing and criticism from scientific critics. The evidence and detailed mechanisms of evolution are impressive.

Here are some of the important additions to our view of the universe:

It is immensely older and bigger than in Darwin's day. Few then would have imagined our sun to be on an outer arm of a spiral galaxy containing one hundred billion stars nor that our galaxy was only a tiny piece of the known universe which consists of hundreds of billions of galaxies. Where does this put earth in cosmic perspective? Nor was it then imagined that the earth was four and half billion years old and our sun a third or fourth generation star, its heavier elements having been recycled from dying ancestor stars. Carl Sagan's perception in *The Cosmic Connection* that we are "star children" did not even exist in mid-nineteenth century imagination.

Geology has changed, especially with the finding that the earth's continents float and move like a glove. Plate tectonics explain much about the past aggregations and breaking up of landmasses and their fossil deposits. It provides a natural explanation for the volcanic activity of the world and formation of mountain chains. Atomic isotopes allow a chronological measurement of the fossil contents independently confirming that dating by index fossils and strata layers. In Darwin's day few fossils were known. Today, hundreds of thousands of fossils of extinct species allow a reconstruction of the evolution of the major phyla and other categories of taxonomic groups.

The universality of biochemical pathways and metabolism in all organisms from bacteria to humans independently supports Darwin's theory of a common descent of all life. The structure of DNA, its universal genetic code, the common set of amino acids in the proteins of all living things, and the rise of the field of comparative genomics supports the line of descent down to the molecular level. The phylogenetic trees constructed in the nineteenth century correspond in their broad features to the phylogenetic trees constructed from comparisons of genomes of and partial genomes of all living things. The rise of classical genetics and population genetics supports evolution by natural selection. The chromosome theory of heredity, the theory of the gene, the analysis of gene and character relations, the analysis of quantitative traits, the mathematical prediction of gene frequencies under changed environmental conditions, and the study of chromosome rearrangements in the evolution of chromosomes all support the Darwinian theory of descent from common ancestors.

What Darwin did not do is articulate in print the philosophic perception of his views. He shared these with his friends and when he attempted to do so with his wife, who adored him, it so horrified her that she wrote him a letter expressing her deep pain. This is what Darwinism meant to Darwin and what it means to us: life probably arose from non-life by natural processes of which he and his generation knew nothing. Once life arose it had a capacity for producing variations. Environments constantly change but there is a reasonable amount of repetition and a range within which life can multiply. Disturbances of this range can lead to selection of those better adapted to surviving these hard times. That is natural selection.

Those that survive pass on their favored hereditary combinations for those adaptations to their progeny. Over long periods of time these accumulated changes can lead to new species and a divergence of body structure and organ systems adapted for new environments. The process of evolution is not progressive. There are no goals or destinies for life. Evolution is not on a trajectory to a foreordained end. Evolution is opportunistic: it makes do with what is there (it has no other choice). The process of evolution is not guided by a creator. There are no detectable signs of a creator's hand at work.

The processes involved are natural and governed largely by chance. From these aspects of evolution by natural selection we can infer some much more troubling consequences for Darwin's generation as well as our own:

If humans accept that they too have evolved, whatever purposes they assign, they do so by their own choice.

This means humans are free of revealed knowledge from a non-existent creator; they are free to make choices; they are obliged to learn and to think. They are responsible for their actions and values.

Darwin gave us a freedom most people are not willing to accept. We have to be ethical without fear of divine punishment. We have to live a life of virtue for its own sake because there is no Heaven awaiting us. We have to accept our mortality and justify the satisfaction of living without the existence of an afterlife. No religion has ever given humans such unrestricted freedom, such a responsibility, and such a task. Darwin's theory of evolution by natural selection gives humans, with their evolved brains, a capacity for self-examination, for wonder, for deeper meaning, and for the nurturing values that sustain us in our relatively short stay in this unbroken journey of life that now extends over three billion years. And that is why Darwin deserves to be called a Great Emancipator.

[ABOUT THE AUTHOR]

Elof Axel Carlson is Distinguished Teaching Professor Emeritus in the Department of Biochemistry and Cell Biology at Stony Brook University and a geneticist and historian of science. He received his BA at NYU and PhD at Indiana University. Prior to coming to Stony Brook in 1968 he had taught at UCLA and Queen's University (Canada). He is the author of *The Gene: A Critical History*; *Genes, Radiation*; also *Society: The Life and Work of H. J. Muller*; and *The Unfit: A History of A Bad Idea*. Carlson has been a visiting professor at the University of Minnesota, the University of Utah, San Diego State University, Tougaloo College, and Semester at Sea. He was a Fellow of the Institute for Advanced Study at Indiana University and he is a Fellow of the American Association for the Advancement of Science (AAAS).

[ADDITIONAL RESOURCES]

Elof Axel Carlson's homepage: http://www.sinc.sunysb.edu/Class/bio101/Elof.htm

Long Island Secular Humanists: http://nyhumanist.org/lish.htm

Mark Ridley's review originally appeared in **The Times Literary Supplement** *(April 20, 2002) and is republished here with permission from the author and TLS.*

Copyright © 2002 by **The Times Literary Supplement**. All Rights Reserved.

BOOK REVIEW:
GEORGE GAYLORD SIMPSON: PALEONTOLOGIST AND EVOLUTIONIST
by Léo F. Laporte
Columbia University Press

Review by Mark Ridley

We can watch evolutionary changes on the small-scale, such as the AIDS virus as it evolves drug-resistance, or the mosquitoes of the London Underground as they evolve into a new species. Evolutionary change on the grand-scale has to be reconstructed from fossils: it is from fossils, for instance, that we know how mammals evolved from reptilian ancestors in many stages over tens of millions of years. Paleontologists call the former, directly observable kinds of change microevolution and the latter, reconstructable kinds of change macroevolution. There is a set-piece debate about the relation between microevolution and macroevolution. Some people think they are driven by different processes, others that they are both driven by the same process – natural selection. In so far as there is an orthodoxy, it is uniformitarian: macroevolution is just microevolution extended over long time periods. The same process that is creating new blood-suckers in the Tube has also created animals and plants from single-celled ancestors, and ultimately all of life. Even those who do not accept this view do accept that it is what they have to argue against. Modern thinkers on evolution are, in this sense, all the intellectual descendants of the American paleontologist G. G. Simpson (1902-1984).

Darwin himself had argued that all evolution, up to the largest scale, is caused by the same set of short-term processes (of which natural selection was the most important). But modern evolutionists who accept this view are historically Simpsonists rather than simply Darwinists. The reason is that in the late nineteenth and early twentieth centuries, Darwin's ideas were thought to be ruled out by fossil evidence. By the 1920s and 1930s, there were a range of views about macroevolution, and Laporte describes them in his intellectual biography of Simpson. The influential American paleontologist, H. F. Osborn, thought that evolution in the long-term was driven by some mysterious internally powered trend: it was one of the "outstanding principles discovered in paleontology...that [life had a] constitutional pre-disposition to speciate in certain predetermined directions which must be inherent in the germ-plasm of ancestral forms." ("Germ-plasm" means the hereditary material, in the gonads; DNA was not then understood.) The influential German paleontologist, O. Schindewolf, thought that macroevolution was driven by big jumps, or macromutations. Others thought that evolution built up a certain momentum, driving it to absurd excesses such as elks with horns that were too big for them to lift their heads. Or that species proceeded through a life cycle, ending in a kind of senescence. What almost no paleontologist seemed to think was that evolution consisted of adaptation to the environment, driven by natural selection on random mutation. After Simpson, the predetermined trends and macromutational jumps were dispersed to the fringes of science, and something like Darwin's view was restored.

But it was not simply a matter of going back to Darwin. The negative case against ideas like Osborn's came mainly from the new science of genetics, which had grown up rapidly since Mendel's work was finally appreciated in 1900. Genetics ruled out that "constitutional pre-disposition", "inherent in the germ-plasm" to evolve in a predetermined direction. Darwin did not know about genetics, and nothing in Darwin's own knowledge of inheritance could rule out the competing ideas. Simpson was the first fossil-expert to master the new genetics, and it was Simpson that did the destructive work. He also knew the fossil evidence that Osborn and others had built up, and reanalysed it, showing that it fitted with Darwinian natural selection. Simpson's main work was in two books – really two editions of the same book – *Tempo and mode in evolution* (1944) and *Major features of evolution* (1953). Laporte gives a good account of the first book, but is less interested in Simpson's changed thinking in the second.

Simpson's main legacy is as one of the architects of neo-Darwinism. However, he ranged across many other topics. Laporte describes how Simpson was spectacularly wrong about continental drift; he was one of its main critics until a belated conversion in 1970. He was also a clear writer, who was interested in the broad implications of evolution. His book *The Meaning of Evolution* sold half a million copies. His travel book *(Attending Marvels)* is still in print, and for good reason. A dry description might say that it is about his first independent fossil-hunting trip, to Argentina in 1930. But it starts with a gun shoot-out in Buenos Aires. So much for dry descriptions of G. G. Simpson.

Simpson was exceptionally clever. He took top grades at school. At Yale he prepared thoroughly for the lectures, and created a summary of the subject in advance. He then ostentatiously ticked off each point as the lecturer reached it: a nasty habit which, not surprisingly, unnerved the lecturer. In the Second World War he joined the Intelligence Corps, and passed in one week a course that was meant to take six. Some of his superiors there also acquired inferiority complexes. But Simpson was not good-looking and had defective eyesight that prevented him from joining in ball games at school. The combination (sharp brain, poor looks, effective exclusion from games) had predictable social effects, and Simpson grew up almost pathologically shy. Laporte has an entertaining section on Simpson's administrative reign at the American Museum of Natural History. Simpson rarely called meetings, avoided decisions whenever possible, and did not tell people his decisions when he did take them. He was inaccessible. When

N. D. Newell found himself criticized for spending too much time with students, he forced a meeting with Simpson. "After ten minutes of total silence following initial explanation of the problem, Newell had to pry out of Simpson just what his responsibilities were." In Laporte's words, "he not only was a difficult person to deal with but he had no interest in dealing with people." Simpson's position as a senior administrator was disastrous, but he resisted all attempts to remove him. Eventually he was moved sideways. He resigned in a huff and went to Harvard.

Laporte is himself a (retired) paleontologist. He has a professional expertise in the fossil material and has spent two decades studying Simpson's writing and interviewing Simpson's surviving colleagues and relatives. He has edited a book of Simpson's letters. The scholarship of this book is therefore top-rate. The book is commendably well produced, particularly relative to its price. The writing itself is not hard to follow. It does not get bogged down in technical details, and it has plenty of personal touches. It does lack the highest literary graces, however, and the expression "Simpson's ongoing marital situation" does seem to have been used unselfconsciously. The book is now the obvious source for anyone who wants to find out about Simpson's scientific work. The readership may be narrow, but those who do read it will be pleased that Laporte has done the work.

[ABOUT THE AUTHOR]

Mark Ridley is a research scientist in the Department of Zoology at Oxford University. Formerly an assistant professor at Emory University, he has also served as a research fellow at St. Catherine's College, Cambridge, and at Linacre, Oriel, and New Colleges in Oxford. Mark Ridley is best known for his highly acclaimed student textbook Evolution (a new edition is planned for 2003 and will be featured within the Darwin Day Program.) Ridley has also authored *The Cooperative Gene: How Mendel's Demon Explains the Evolution of Complex Beings*; *Animal Behavior: An Introduction*; *The Problems of Evolution*; and other texts. He is also the editor of *The Darwin Reader*. Mark Ridley frequently contributes to *The New York Times*, *The Sunday Times*, *Nature*, *New Scientist*, and *The Times Literary Supplement*.

[ADDITIONAL RESOURCES]

Every week, *The Times Literary Supplement* provides intelligent, thoughtful criticism of literature, culture and the visual and performing arts. To take out a subscription to the *TLS*, which will also give you free, exclusive access to our online archive, simply call our credit card hotline on [plus]44 (0) 1858 438 805 or write to *TLS* Subscriptions, Tower House, Sovereign Park, Market Halborough, Leicestershire, LE16 9EF, U.K. http://www.the-tls.co.uk

PBS Evolution Library – George Gaylord Simpson:
  http://www.pbs.org/wgbh/evolution/library/06/2/l_062_02.html

Barry Palevitz' article first appeared in **The Scientist**, the news magazine for life scientists.

©2002 **The Scientist** LLC. All rights reserved. Reproduced with permission.

HAPPY BIRTHDAY, UNCLE CHARLIE
DARWIN DAY CELEBRATIONS
MARK EVOLUTION GURU'S BIRTHDAY
by Barry A. Palevitz

Besides music, Jack Daniels, and the color orange, Tennessee also signifies opposition to evolution in the minds of many people, especially biologists. By banning the teaching of evolution in its schools, the state set the stage for the famous Scopes monkey trial in 1925, which pitted two giants of American history, William Jennings Bryan and Clarence Darrow, in a battle immortalized in books and film. The public controversy over evolution continues to this day, to the consternation of the vast majority of scientists.

It's ironic then that Tuesday, Feb. 12, won't be just any old day in Knoxville, Tenn. Led by evolutionary ecologist Massimo Pigliucci, the University of Tennessee will hold its annual Darwin Day celebration on the old guy's 193rd birthday. Festivities include movies, discussions, information booths, book displays, and a keynote speaker, University of Wisconsin philosopher Elliot Sober. Last year's celebration featured a performance of the play, *Inherit the Wind*. According to Pigliucci, "we usually have a teachers' workshop too. This year it's on using controversial issues to teach about science."

DARWIN DAY ORIGINS, AND EVOLUTION

Pigliucci says Tennessee's Darwin Day started when the state tried to pass more anti-evolution legislation in 1996. "I was discussing it with some students and colleagues, and we asked why don't we do something. I think one of the students suggested we do it on Darwin's birthday." Adds Pigliucci, this year's event "is a broader version of what we started in 1997."

The idea of celebrating Darwin's birthday goes back even farther. Pigliucci thinks it originated at Salem State College in Massachusetts in the 1980s, though the school didn't call it Darwin Day then. That probably started with the Stanford Humanists (now the Humanist Community of California) several years later.

Elizabeth Craig directs the Kansas Citizens for Science, formed in response to the state school board's 1999 decision to remove evolution from the science curriculum.

According to Craig, KCFS will celebrate Darwin Day this year with Science City at Union Station, in Kansas City. Among the many events scheduled, "Harry MacDonald will show clips for teachers from PBS's *Evolution* series," Craig says. "He's one of the lead teachers WGBH selected for the *Evolution* project." Sporting 'Ask a Scientist' buttons, University of Kansas scientists will be on hand to field questions.

The Darwin Day Web site (www.darwinday.org) also offers how-to pointers for neophytes. "We were inspired by Massimo Pigliucci's work," admits Amanda Chesworth, executive director of the Darwin Day site, which counts Oxford evolutionist Richard Dawkins as its honorary president, plus a long list of supporters including Harvard University's E.O. Wilson. She runs the program with monetary support from cell biologist Robert Stephens, owner of TECHSTAR Industries in Redwood City, Calif. Stephens chairs Darwin Day's board of directors. So far, Chesworth knows of about 60 events worldwide, including happenings in the United States, Canada, Britain, Italy, and Argentina.

Why all the hoopla? The group wants to "increase public understanding of Charles Darwin and his contributions to science and humanity," says Chesworth. "Darwin was an exemplary human being – his curiosity about the world, his scientific spirit. He made an enormous difference."

Proud, But Cautious Papa

Pigliucci thinks "it's great that Darwin Day is now international." On the other hand, he worries that the program could become too large and heterogeneous. "I think it's a good trade-off, as long as people don't use it for outrageously stupid things." Chesworth admits, "we have an enormous variety of participants." Pigliucci especially hopes that Darwin Day doesn't become a showcase for other agendas, such as secular humanism. While Chesworth says the Web site does get some logistical support from groups like the Council for Secular Humanism, she insists Darwin Day will always be about science. "We want to show that science isn't just for scientists."

[About the Author]

Barry Palevitz is a Professor of Botany at the University of Georgia in Athens, Georgia. He is a founder and advisor for the student/faculty organization: the Sagan Society, and also works to promote science literacy through other teaching and outreach activities. Barry Palevitz is a regular contributor to *The Scientist*, *BioScience* and *Skeptical Inquirer magazine*.

[Additional Resources]

The Scientist is the news magazine for life scientists. It is available free in print to life science researchers and free to all on the web at www.the-scientist.com.

Barry Palevitz' faculty page at the University of Georgia:
   http://dogwood.botany.uga.edu/~palevitz/palevitz.html

Léo Laporte's article is adapted from his course on Darwin at the University of California at Santa Cruz – to be featured in the Educational Resource Area of the Darwin Day Program web site.

WHY LEARN ABOUT CHARLES DARWIN?

by Leo F. Laporte

Because it's an excellent way to learn about the content and practice of science by examining the life and chief work of a major figure in the history of science. Charles Darwin is especially suitable because his work has had major impact not only on biology and geology, but also on other disciplines such as the social sciences, philosophy, and religion. Moreover, the real – not the apocryphal – Charles Darwin has particular appeal for some young people because he dropped out of the University of Edinburgh, transferred to Cambridge University where he was an indifferent student, was an enigma to his family, and was uncertain about his future career.

One can approach the subject in several ways. First, by focusing on who Darwin was, what he did, and the state of natural history up to the publication of the *Origin of Species*. Begin by reading Darwin's short autobiography to learn something of the environment in which Darwin was raised, get a sense of the kind of person he was, and what he thought he accomplished in life. One also needs to understand the events leading up to the five-year voyage of H.M.S. *Beagle*, the nature and purpose of the voyage itself, and the contemporary views of the immutability of species, the age of the earth, what fossils were thought to signify, and the problem of extinction. One can thus get a broad overview of the context out of which the *Origin* arose and see the sorts of problems that Darwin was to address.

Next, a close reading of the *Origin* in facsimile edition is desirable to reading a primary source to be clear about exactly what Darwin said and didn't say. Also one will see the real (non-idealized) way that scientific discoveries are made and used for theory-building. For example, on some key issues (e.g., the reality and importance of inherited variation) Darwin got it right, while on others (e.g., the source of such variation) he was confused or wrong. It is important to realize that much of science is a kind of back-and-forth questioning and reasoning, and that the so-called "scientific method" as usually presented is not so neat and tidy in real life.

One will see, too, how Darwin was quite aware that he was constructing an argument, a kind of lawyer's brief, in the way he composed the *Origin*. Thus, the first four chapters present the basic theory of "descent with modification" by means of "natural selection." The middle four chapters rebut what Darwin anticipates will be objections to his argument, and in the final five chapters Darwin applies his argument to a wide range of phenomena (e.g., fossils, embryology, biogeography) to show how these are more readily explained by his theory than by other contending theories. Darwin's *Origin* did two things. First, it convinced the scientific world that "descent with modification" (evolution) explained the origin and diversity of animate nature in terms of common ancestry rather than by instantaneous creation. Second, Darwin hypothesized a process, "natural selection," as the cause of "descent with modification." However, Darwin was by no means as successful in convincing his audience about the process of natural selection as he was about the fact of descent with modification. It wasn't until the mid-1930s that natural selection was finally accepted as the cause of biologic evolution, overcoming competing theories of neo-Lamarckianism, vitalism, and mutationism.

After reading the *Origin*, one should think about the "contexts of discovery and of justification," which makes the distinction between the discovery of new evidence and the way in which a new interpretation is justified by that evidence. For example, the discoveries that Darwin made on the *Beagle* voyage were certainly important to his subsequent theory, but equally crucial was how he argued his case around those discoveries. Darwin was fully cognizant that to convince his colleagues of the correctness of his theory he had to follow certain established canons of proper theory-building. In fact, Darwin's obvious attention to creating a sound context of justification within the *Origin* indicates that he was far more than a "lucky collector" who stumbled onto his "descent with modification."

And finally, one can look at post-*Origin* issues, such as Mendel's key contribution to Darwin's evolutionary theory, especially why Mendel's work wasn't appreciated for more than three decades. This provides an excellent example of how a scientist's "answers" are not recognized as such if the answers are to questions no one else is currently asking. (Mendel addressed the causes of discontinuous variation in peas. His contemporaries, on the other hand, were only interested in the sources of continuous variation. It wasn't until the early 20th century that geneticists realized that the source of both kinds of variation is the same.) One needs to learn about our present-day view of evolution, a kind of Darwinian update, and indicate where the hot topics now lie (e.g., extinction, rate of speciation, human origins). And what if anything evolution might say about "an ethics of nature." (Beware the naturalistic fallacy of "is-equals-ought.") It is also useful to see how evolutionists and creationists debate their positions on different wave-lengths, or more properly speaking have different epistemologies, and therefore cannot for that very reason be reconciled to each other's viewpoint.

Of what should the study of Darwin be persuaded? That science involves real people doing real work in a real world; that the history of science is often sanitized and idealized so that it seems lifeless and cold, and that only geniuses (or nerds) need apply; that as new answers emerge, new questions then become possible and therefore the quest is unending; that science often touches our lives in other, non-scientific realms as well and consequently it is important to know something about the scientific enterprise; that even the non-specialist can understand a scientific argument and that perhaps after this effort science may be more appealing than before.

Such a study as this can demonstrate how the history of science is properly pursued: by reading primary sources; by showing that what is done in science at a given moment is contingent upon the contemporary state of knowledge, technology, and methodology available, and therefore one gauges success/failure in the context of that time, not from our own later perspective; and thus that the history of science as presented in science textbooks is usually oversimplified, idealized, and misleading as to how it really happened.

Given the diversity of interests among us, there is always something for everyone in a study of Darwin: people interested in literature may come to see how Darwin influenced authors like Thomas Hardy and Jack London; history buffs recognizing that the history of science has similar methods as does the history of, say, political institutions; and everyone learns that much of what is attributed to "Darwinism" never came from Darwin. And, of course, those interested in biology and geology are delighted to see Darwin-the-biologist and Darwin-the-geologist at work, especially as a young man.

[ABOUT THE AUTHOR]

Léo F. Laporte is Professor Emeritus of Earth Sciences at the University of California, Santa Cruz and is the editor of *Simple Curiosity*, a volume of G. G. Simpson's letters to his family. His other publications include *Ancient Environments* and *Encounter with the Earth*.

[ADDITIONAL RESOURCES]

Léo F. Laporte faculty page: http://people.ucsc.edu/~laporte/

Darwin Day Program Educational Resource Area: http://www.darwinday.org/education/

SECTION THREE

Natural Selections:
Life As We Know It

> "The theory of evolution is outstandingly the most important theory in biology."
>
> – Mark Ridley in *Evolution* (1983)

> "Darwin's theory of common descent does for biology what Galileo did for the planets. It was laid out in a book written for the general reader, the only bestseller to change man's conception of himself. An idea put forward in 1859 is still the cement that binds the marvellous discoveries of today. *The Origin of Species* is, without doubt, the book of the millennium."
>
> – Steve Jones in
> *Almost Like a Whale: The Origin of Species Updated* (2000)

Massimo Pigliucci's article first appeared in **Skeptical Inquirer** *magazine (V23(5); 1999) and is republished here with permission from the author and the Committee for the Scientific Investigation of Claims of the Paranormal (CSICOP).*

WHERE DO WE COME FROM?
WE STILL HAVE FEW CLUES TO THE ORIGIN OF LIFE

by Massimo Pigliucci

"Life has to be given a meaning because of the obvious fact that it has no meaning"
　　　　　　　　　　　　– Henry Miller, The Wisdom of the Heart

Science is about answering our questions about the natural world in a rational manner. One of the fundamentals of the scientific method is the repeatability of the phenomena under investigation. Here lies perhaps the most difficult aspect of the endless quest for the origin of life on Earth. It clearly is a question about the natural world, in fact perhaps one of the ultimate questions (together with the origin of the universe itself). Yet, the events we are attempting to investigate are by definition unique. Life may well have originated multiple times in the universe, including perhaps in our galactic neighborhood. But so far we only have one example to go by. Planet Earth is the only place that we know for certain harbors life as we conceive it.

Before entering into a skeptical evaluation of the heart of the problem, let us answer an even more fundamental question: why do we care? Well, I can come up with three orders of reasons. First, definitely ascertaining that life originated by natural means would certainly have profound implications for any religious belief, further shrinking the role of any god in human affairs. Second, should we arrive at the conclusion that life originated elsewhere in the universe and was then somehow "imported" to Earth, this would automatically imply the existence of life as a widespread phenomenon in the universe, and therefore the fact that living beings are not unique to our planet; it is hard to conceive of a more compelling blow to anthropocentrism since Copernicus and Galileo swept the Earth away from the center of the universe a few centuries ago. Third, and perhaps more relevant, humankind would finally have a decent answer to the question "where did we come from?" which, like it or not, has been vexing our philosophy, art, and science since the beginning of recorded history (and probably much earlier than that). If that doesn't sound to you like enough of a reason to ponder the controversy over the origin of life, the neurons in charge of your sense of curiosity are definitely in need of some repair.

Couldn't We Just Look at the Simplest Organism?

Let me start by clearing the field from one important misconception: there is no such thing as a modern-day "primitive" organism that we can examine to tell what our earliest ancestors looked like. True, there are plenty of "simple" organisms around today, from viruses to bacteria to slime molds. But slime molds are in fact eukaryotes (albeit of taxonomically very uncertain position), i.e. their cellular structure and metabolism are basically not different from those of an animal or a plant (they actually look like fungi, though they are not even closely related to them). Way too complex for our purposes. Bacteria are prokaryotes, i.e. their cells are indeed simpler than most other living beings. Yet, bacteria have been around for more than three billion years, and they have become perfect reproductive machines, characterized by an incredibly efficient metabolism and ability to withstand environmental changes. After all, it is not by chance that they have proliferated for so long. So, no go there either. Finally, viruses are indeed among the simplest living creatures in existence, so simple in fact that some biologists even doubt that they really qualify as "living". However, evolutionarily speaking viruses are late arrivals on the Darwinian stage. Viruses are short pieces of nucleic acids wrapped in a protein, they live only inside cells, they originated from pre-existing cells, and they entirely depend on the host's metabolism to reproduce. Quite obviously, since our problem is to understand how the first living organisms came about, we cannot utilize as a model something that cannot survive outside an already existing cell. No, we are looking for something simple, yes, but self-sufficient, and really primitive. So, without further delay, let the parties enter the scene, and the games begin.

The Alternative Question: What About God?

No serious scientific discussion of any topic should include supernatural explanations, since the basic assumption of science is that the world can be explained entirely in physical terms, without recourse to god-like entities. However, skepticism has the flexibility of going beyond the strict scientific method – even though the two modes of inquiry are tightly connected. After all, as that fictional archetype of rationalism known as Sherlock Holmes said, "when you have eliminated the impossible, whatever remains, however improbable, must be the truth" (it is indeed ironic that Holmes' creator, Conan Doyle, believed in spirits and poltergeists, but that's another story: Polidoro 1998). So, should it turn out that we really do not have a clue about the origin of life, we must entertain other, more esoteric possibilities, however unpleasant they may sound to a skeptical ear.

Furthermore, in the specific case of the origin of life, even some scientists of decent reputation, such as the British astrophysicist Fred Hoyle, have gone on record precisely suggesting a supernatural beginning to all life on Earth. Hoyle, together with his colleague Chandra Wickramasinghe, suggested that a sort of silicon-chip creator actually goes around the universe sprinkling the seeds of life here and there, though for what purpose is not at all clear.

An entirely different, yet congruent, argument is the one advanced by creationists such as Duane Gish (1994). In Gish's case, of course, all we have is the classical God of the bible, who created the universe and humankind with a personal touch, and did so in the span of only six days.

There is one crucial problem with both Hoyle's and Gish's position, of course. There isn't a single shred of evidence supporting them. Furthermore, at least Gish's claims are falsifiable and have been verified to be false: one of the cardinal points of his theory is that the Earth is only a few thousands years old, while geology has long ago demonstrated that the real time frame is measured in billions of years. Hoyle's proposition suffers from the hallmark of all non-scientific statements: it is not disprovable. There isn't a single experiment that could reject the British physicist's hypothesis, which means that it lies by definition outside science's realm.

Should a skeptic then reject outright any possibility of special creation of life? Well, no. As much as it is implausible, it is still possible. There are two points that must be borne in mind, however, before going for a Hoyle-like explanation of the origin of us all. First, it has to be true that we really don't have a clue about how on *Earth* life originated by natural means. As we will see, though the situation is messy, it is not that desperate. Second, the mere fact that we cannot currently (or even ever) explain something does not constitute positive evidence for a supernatural explanation. After all, for a long time we did not know what natural phenomena could cause lightning, but eventually the theory based on Zeus' anger did turn out to be wrong. Consequently, even if we had no better answer, it is still up to the "supernaturalists" to provide at least a shred of *positive* evidence. Without that, the next best position to hold on to would simply be a provisional and salutary "I don't know".

OUT OF THIS WORLD?

The next class of explanations about the ultimate provenance of life is that – as any good old-fashioned science fiction movie or magazine of the 1950s would have proclaimed – it is not of this world. Interestingly, Hoyle and Wickramasinghe have made their contribution in this realm too, by suggesting that life was brought on this planet courtesy of an interstellar cloud of gas and dust, or perhaps by a comet (Hoyle and Wickramasinghe 1978). Yet another British scientist (and also an ex-physicist – but I'm sure this is a coincidence), the Nobel laureate Francis Crick, joined the ranks of the extraterrestrialists. Crick suggested a scenario which envisions extraterrestrials "seeding" the galaxy (Crick 1981), much in the same fashion of Hoyle's silicon-chip creator.

Contrary to the supernatural explanations, the Hoyle-Wickramasinghe theory (but not Crick's, for the same reasons seen above) is at least in principle open to experimental verification, in that it makes some relatively precise predictions. For one thing, we should find plenty of organic compounds in interstellar clouds and/or inside comets. Both these expectations have superficially been verified. I say superficially because the kind of compounds found by astronomers in these media are very simple, much too simple to provide any meaningful "seed" for the origin of carbon-based life forms on Earth. Furthermore, extraterrestrial organic compounds have random chirality, unlike the organic compounds typical of living organisms. Chirality is a property of any chemical structure that deals with the three-dimensional arrangement of its atoms and molecules. All amino acids, for example, the building blocks of proteins, can in theory come in two versions, which are mirror images of each other. These are called "left-" and "right-" handed forms, and they are characterized by exactly the same chemical properties, so that there is no physical-chemical reason for one form to be more abundant than the other. Accordingly, the organic compounds (which is a general term for carbon-based compounds and, contrary to the misleading name, does not necessarily imply the result of an organism's metabolism) found in space or in meteorites come in equal proportions of right and left handed forms.[1] Not so the compounds that are actually used by living organisms on Earth, which are found only in one version. If indeed life had come from space, one would expect to find some sort of chiral asymmetry in space organic matter as well.

A second crucial objection to the life from space hypothesis is the solution of continuity problem. If comets and meteors brought us – literally – to Earth a few billion years ago, why are they not doing it now? Meteors continue to bombard our planet and our neighbors in the solar system on a regular basis, yet so far not a single living organism or complex organic molecule has been found inside any of them. There is no reason to think that the primordial "shower of life" has ceased. Even though the conditions for the persistence of primordial life on our planet do not hold any longer (because of dramatic changes in the composition of the atmosphere, or because of competition from "resident aliens", i.e. from currently living organisms), presumably the space surrounding our solar system has not changed that much, leaving Hoyle, Crick and the like with a major hole in their argument.

Another thought about extraterrestrial theories of life's beginning is that at a minimum they violate one of the most venerable principles of natural philosophy, namely Ockham's razor. This is the idea that if two theories explain equally well a given problem, one should prefer the alternative which assumes the least number of entities (i.e., makes the least gratuitous hypotheses). Since all extraterrestrial theories still rely on organic chemistry, and since they require further assumptions, for example the fact that the "seeds" found a safe passage through the Earth's atmosphere without burning into nothingness as it happens to most meteors, they violate Ockham's rule. On the other hand, there is no real guarantee that the universe behaves as Ockham suggested, so the razor can be invoked only as a provisional way of favoring simpler explanations, not as a definite argument against more complex or less likely alternatives.

Finally, it has to be realized that even if we do admit that life originated outside Earth and was then imported here, we really would not have an answer to how life started. We would have simply shifted the question to a remote and very likely inaccessible location.

The Chicken or the Egg in the Soup?

OK, we are now getting to the meat of the debate. Having excluded – at least temporarily – gods and extraterrestrials, we are left with plain old biochemistry and biology to give us clues to the origin of life on our planet. The history of scientific research in this field is indeed long and fascinating. It started in the 1920s with the Russian Alexander Oparin and his "coacervates", blobs of organic matter (mostly containing sugars and short polypeptides), supposedly the precursors of modern proteins. It was Oparin, together with the British biologist J.B.S. Haldane, who came up with the idea of a 'primordial soup' (Oparin 1938; Haldane 1985) , that is the possibility that the ancient oceans on Earth were filled with organic matter formed by the interaction between the atmospheric gases and energy provided by volcanic eruptions, powerful electric storms, and solar ultraviolet radiation.

We had to wait until the 1950s for Stanley Miller to actually attempt to experimentally reproduce the soup (Miller 1953). Miller started with a reasonable composition of the ancient atmosphere: mostly methane and ammonia, with no oxygen – since atmospheric oxygen, together with the ozone that blocks UV radiation, was in fact produced by the organic process of photosynthesis in blue-green algae much, much later than soup time (which is a fortunate coincidence, given that oxygen attacks and destroys – technically it "oxidizes" – organic compounds at a very fast rate).[2] Miller put the whole thing in a ball, gave it some electric charge, and waited. He did find that amino acids and other fundamental complex organic molecules were accumulating at the bottom of his apparatus. His discovery gave a huge boost to the scientific investigation of the origin of life. Indeed, for some time it seemed like recreation of life in a test tube was within reach of experimental science. Unfortunately, Miller-type experiments have not progressed much further than their original prototype, leaving us with a sour aftertaste from the primordial soup.

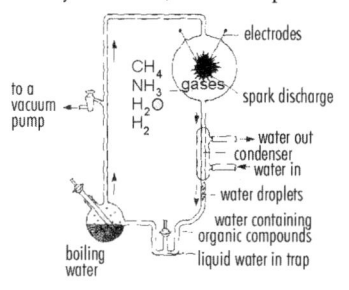

Both Oparin and Miller, as well as other prominent researchers in the field up until the 1960s, thought that the problem was how to explain the appearance of proteins, since they must have caused the initial spark of life. (Another student of the problem who thought along similar lines was Sidney Fox, who discovered the possibility of forming "proteinoids", protein-like structures that can be obtained by heating up mixtures of amino acids in a dry state. All in all, a very distant cousin of actual biological proteins). Now, any student of introductory biology knows that there are two major players inside every living cell: proteins and nucleic acids (such as DNA and RNA). The problem is that the structure of DNA was discovered only in 1953 (in fact, the same year of Miller's experiment), and the nature of DNA as the information carrier of the cell was little appreciated before Watson and Crick unveiled the double-helix nature of this remarkable molecule.

The origin of life debate after the 1950s, however, became decidedly slanted in favor of nucleic acids preceding proteins. The new discipline of molecular biology was making spectacular progress, first uncovering the universal code by which the instructions for making proteins are embedded in the nucleic acids; then by finding ways to actually extract and compare that information from different and distantly related species; and finally with the spin-off of modern genetic engineering and the ability to directly modify the genetic information, thereby transforming the characteristics of species more or less at will. Scientists such as Leslie Orgel, Walter Gilbert and others therefore proposed that the egg, so to speak, came before the chicken. Some sort of primitive nucleic acid had appeared first, followed only later by proteins.

Now, in today's biochemically sophisticated cells, proteins and nucleic acids play very distinct roles. In fact there are four fundamental activities that we need to discuss.

1. The DNA (deoxyribonucleic acid) encodes the information that eventually will give rise to proteins.

2. The 'messenger' RNA (or mRNA, ribonucleic acid, the same as DNA, but with an extra oxygen atom and a few other chemical differences) then carries the information to specialized structures known as ribosomes.

3. Inside the ribosomes (which, by the way, are made of both nucleic acids and

proteins) the message gets translated into proteins by virtue of a second type of RNA, known as 'transfer' RNA (tRNA). The tRNA has the peculiar ability to attach itself to the mRNA on one side, and to amino acids (the blocks which make up proteins) on the other side. This way, you have a chain of mRNA which is paralleled by the forming chain of amino acids, which in turn will eventually result in the final protein.

4. The proteins, most of which (but not all) are enzymes, are actually the "doers" of the cellular world, in that they are both the building blocks of cell structures and membranes, and the builders themselves, in the form of enzymes capable of catalyzing all sorts of chemical reactions, including the replication of DNA and the transcription of its message into RNA – which, of course, closes the circle!

It should be clear from the above extremely concise description of what goes on in a cell that we are indeed facing a classical chicken-egg problem. If the proteins appeared first, so that they could eventually catalyze the formation of nucleic acids, how was the information necessary to produce the proteins themselves coded? On the other hand, if nucleic acids came first, thereby embodying the information necessary to obtain proteins, by which means where the acids replicated and translated into proteins? It seems to me pretty clear that the answer, as much as it is still very much nebulous at the moment, must lie in the proverbial middle (Miller 1997). In fact, the existence of tRNAs points to the distinct possibility of dual structures, containing both RNA and amino acids. On a slightly different take, the discovery by Sydney Altman, Thomas Cech, and others that some RNAs are at least partially self-catalytic (i.e., they can catalyze chemical reactions onto themselves), lends support to the idea of a mixed origin of life in which the original molecules were both replicators and enzymes (Ertem and Ferris 1996), with the two functions slowly diverging through evolutionary time and assigned to distinct classes of molecules. Most importantly, doesn't that appeal to your sense of aesthetics as well?

PRIMORDIAL SOUP OR PRIMORDIAL PIZZA?

There is one major problem with the Haldane-Oparin soup scenario: it could get too watery. Since the organic compounds would be freely bumping into each other within the ocean, unless their concentration was extremely large it is difficult to see how often dense enough pockets of organic molecules could have formed to allow some significant prebiotic chemistry to occur.

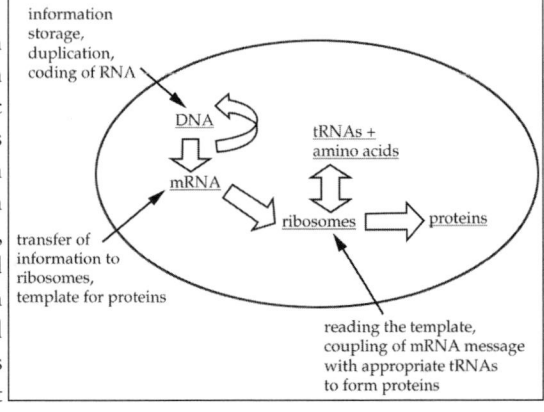

This is more of a problem when we consider the question of the origin of the first metabolic pathways. Metabolism requires proto-enzymes to interact with their substrates so that a given reaction can take place. However, it was unlikely for enzymes and substrates to come close enough together in a three-dimensional space with no enclosing barriers (hence several hypotheses about the formation of proto-cells with a lipid membrane). Furthermore, most of the necessary reactions for prebiotic chemistry, such as the formation of polypeptides by aggregating individual amino acids, produce water. This kind of reaction is difficult to have in an aqueous environment because of thermodynamic considerations (it requires energy, and the products are unstable and can be hydrolyzed back to their component parts).

An alternative to the primordial soup has therefore been proposed, and it has become known as the "primordial pizza" (Maynard-Smith and Szathmary 1995). The idea is that early organic chemistry occurred on dry land, on the surface of minerals with physical properties conducive to accumulating and retaining organic molecules in place. Perhaps the best candidate for such a role is pyrite, fool's gold. On a two-dimensional surface, enzymes and substrates, or even simply different amino acids or nucleotides without enzymes, would find themselves constrained with much less freedom of movement which, of course, would increase the chance of reciprocal encounters. Furthermore, since the pyrite surface would have no water on it, the occurrence of water-producing reactions would be much facilitated. In fact, thermodynamic calculations show that these reactions would increase entropy, and would therefore occur spontaneously.

Very little empirical research has been done on the concept of a primordial pizza, and other candidates are possible as material substrates besides pyrite, but the concept is appealing in its elegant solution of two major problems facing prebiotic chemistry. We should see some progress in this area in the next few years.

And Then What? Hypercycles and Emerging Properties

I suggest that the problem of how complex organic compounds, the building blocks of life as we know it, might have formed on the primordial Earth has been satisfactorily solved by Miller-type experiments or one of their variants. Furthermore, there are good reasons to believe that the initial complex molecules which underwent chemical evolution were some sort of nucleic acid-protein mix such as modern day tRNAs or auto-catalytic RNAs. But what happened after that? There is still a very large gap between a semi-catalytic, semi-replicating nucleo-protein and the first living "organism", whatever that may have been.

Moreover, the uncertainty about what the original organisms looked like is an important part of the problem. What exactly is life? That question was asked precisely in such fashion by physicist Erwin Schrodinger in 1947 (Schrodinger 1947). While Schrodinger's thinking led him to predict some of the properties of DNA as a necessary component of a living organism, we still have a vague notion of the boundary between life and inert matter. And so it should be, if we accept the idea that living organisms are made of inert matter which happens to acquire some "emergent properties" when it is assembled in particular manners. To put it into another fashion, living beings are not separated by the rest of the universe by some mysterious force or vital energy. At least, we have no reason to believe so.

How do we know, then, what is life from what is not? Well, we can come up with a list of attributes, some of which can be properties also of non-living systems, but the ensemble of which defines a living organism. Here is what I could put together:

- Ability to replicate, giving origin to similar kinds (reproduction)
- Ability to react to changes in the environment (behavior, not just limited to the special meaning that the word has in animals)

- Growth (i.e., reduction of internal entropy at the expense of environmental entropy — note that even single cells grow immediately after reproduction, so this is not a property restricted to multicellular life)
- Metabolism (i.e., capacity of maintaining lower internal entropy, including the ability of self-repair)

How did we get from a nucleo-protein to an entity capable of all of the above? And what did this entity (sometimes known as the "progenote") look like? There are very few even tentative answers to these questions, and this — I think — is wherein the real problem of the origin of life lies. The German Manfred Eigen has come up with one possible scenario which invokes what he called "hypercycles". You can think of a hypercycle as a primitive biochemical pathway, made up of self-replicating nucleic acids and semi-catalytic proteins which happen to be found together in pockets within the primordial soup or on the primitive pizza. It is possible to imagine that some of these hypercycles are made of elements that "cooperate" with each other, i.e. the product of a component of the cycle can be the substrate for another one. Different hypercycles could have coexisted before the origin of life, and they would have competed for the ever-decreasing resources within the soup or pizza (the resources were decreasing because the hypercycles were using up some organic compounds at a higher rate than they were formed by comparatively inefficient inorganic processes). Eventually, this competition would have favored more and more efficient hypercycles, where the "efficiency" would be measured by the ability of these entities to survive and reproduce, that is by the parameters of Darwinian evolution. Life as we know it (sort of) would have begun.

Eigen and modern followers of complexity theory also expected these systems to become more complicated by addition of new components to the cycle. From time to time, the addition of one component would modify the whole system dramatically, giving it properties that the previous group did not possess (sort of like adding an atom of oxygen to two of hydrogen and suddenly getting something completely distinct and more complex: water). Complexity theorists such as Stuart Kauffman and Christopher Langton have indeed demonstrated on the basis of mathematical models that some self-replicating systems can display unexpectedly complex patterns of behavior (Farmer et al. 1986; Kauffman 1993). The textbook example of this phenomenon are the so-called cellular automata, mathematical entities first imagined by John von Neumann in 1940 and that can now be studied at leisure by anybody who has a personal computer and a copy of a game aptly called "Life" (Langton 1986).

So, the general path leading to the origination of life seems to have been something like this:

Primordial soup or pizza (simple organic compounds formed by atmospheric gases and various sources of energy)

Nucleo-proteins (similar to modern tRNAs)

Hypercycles (primitive and inefficient biochemical pathways, emergent properties)

Cellular hypercycles (more complex cycles, eventually enclosed in a primitive cell made of lipids)

Progenote (first self-replicating, metabolizing cell, possibly made of RNA and proteins, with DNA entering the picture later on)

How plausible is all this? Oh, it is fairly conceivable, as far as modern biology can tell. The problem is that each step is really difficult to describe in detail from a theoretical standpoint, and so far (with the exception of the formation of organic molecules in the soup and of some simple hypercycles) has proven remarkably elusive from an empirical perspective. It looks like we have several clues, but the puzzle may very well prove one of the most difficult for scientific analysis to solve. The reason for such difficulty could be – as pointed out at the beginning – that after all we only have one example to go by. Or it may simply be that the events in question are so far remote in time that there is very little we can be certain about. Consider that the fossil record shows completely formed, "modern-looking" bacterial cells a few hundreds of million years after the formation of the Earth – i.e., about 3.8 billion years ago. This tells us that whatever happened before that happened fast, but there is no record of it. Finally, it could very well be that we are missing something fundamental here. It may be that the origin of life field has not had its Einstein or Darwin just yet, and that things are going to change just around the corner, or never.

FROM DUST TO DUST...

Apparently, a contemporary discussion of the question of the origin of life cannot be complete without the inclusion of A.G. Cairns-Smith's theory of clay's crystals (Cairn-Smith 1985; Maden 1995). Well, I hope this will not be the case for much longer (except as a footnote of historical value). Don't get me wrong, I am familiar with Cairns-Smith's research and writing, and I find it excellent. But everybody can make a mistake, and I think the clay theory clearly falls within the cracks of Cairns-Smith's career, as much as it is ingenious and at first glance enticing.

Briefly, the idea is that life did not originate with *either* nucleic acids or proteins (and for that matter, neither with a combination of the two). No, the original replicator-catalyzing agents were actually crystals to be found everywhere in the clay that laid around the primitive Earth. The cardinal points of the Cairn-Smith hypothesis are four. First, crystals are structurally much simpler than any biologically relevant organic molecule. Second, crystals grow and reproduce (i.e., they can break because of mechanical forces, and each resulting part continues to "grow"). Third, crystals carry information and this information can be modified. A crystal is a highly regular structure, which tends to propagate itself (therefore it carries information). Furthermore, the crystal can incorporate impurities while growing. These impurities alter the crystal's structure and can be "inherited" when the original piece breaks (hence, the information can be modified). Fourth, crystals have some minimum capacity of catalyzing (i.e., accelerating) chemical reactions.

Cairns-Smith then proposed that these very primitive "organisms" started incorporating short polypeptides (proto-proteins) found in the environment – presumably in the soup or on the pizza – because they enhanced the crystals' catalyzing abilities. The road was then open for a gradual increase in the importance of proteins first, and then eventually of nucleic acids, until these two new arrivals on the evolutionary scene completely supplanted their 'low-tech' progenitor, and became the living organisms that we know today.

What is wrong with this picture? First of all, Cairns-Smith seems to completely ignore what a living organism is to begin with. For one thing, crystals don't really have a metabolism, at least not in a sense even remotely comparable to what we find in actual living organisms. This may have something to do with the fact that not only are crystals structurally much less complex than a protein or a nucleic acid, but also with their non-carbon-based chemistry, recognizably much simpler than the chemistry utilized by living organisms on Earth. The lower complexity and simpler chemistry may be insurmountable "hardware" obstacles to the origination of a true metabolism in clay matter. Secondarily, crystals don't really react to their environment either, another hallmark of every known living creature. Notice that this is a property distinct from metabolism, in that metabolism can be entirely internal, with no reference to the outside (except for some flux of energy that must come into the organism to maintain its metabolism). On the other hand, living organisms universally actively respond to changes in external conditions, for example by seeking sources of energy or by avoiding dangers. Furthermore, an argument can be made that crystals are not actually capable of incorporating new information in their inherited "code", unlike what happens with mutations in living beings. True, they can assimilate impurities from the environment and 'transmit' such 'information' to their 'descendants' for some time; but these impurities do not get replicated, they need continually to be imported from the outside, and they do not become a permanent and heritable part of the crystal. Moreover, impurities do not create new types of crystals, the way mutations give eventually origin to entirely new kinds of animals and plants.

Another colossal hole in the clay theory is – of course – that we have no clue of how the "mutiny" of nucleic acids and proteins actually occurred, and in fact we are given very faint hints about how a crystal could possibly co-opt a polypeptide to enhance its growth (which, by the way, should be something relatively easy to test in a modern biochemistry laboratory). It is true that the competing, more biologically traditional, hypotheses also are at a loss providing detailed scenarios; but in the case of Cairn-Smith's suggestions, we don't simply miss the details, we literally have no idea of how such a transition would come to pass. So, as much as creationists might like the flavor of a theory of the origin of life in which the first living beings came literally from dust (although Cairns-Smith is certainly no creationist), we are still left with ribonucleo-proteins as our best, albeit fuzzy, option. This is one question that skeptics and scientists will be pondering for some time to come. ∞

[ABOUT THE AUTHOR]

Massimo Pigliucci is an Associate Professor at the University of Tennessee in Knoxville, where he teaches ecology and evolutionary biology. He has published 49 technical papers and two books on evolutionary biology: *Phenotypic Evolution* with Carl Schlichting and *Beyond Nature vs. Nurture*. Dr. Pigliucci has received the Oak Ridge National Labs award for excellence in research and the prestigious Dobzhansky Prize from the Society for the Study of Evolution, of which he is now Vice President. Dr. Pigliucci is also widely published within skeptic and freethought journals, and presents lectures and debates throughout the country. A book of his essays entitled *Tales of the Rational: Skeptical Essays About Science and Nature* has been published and his monthly e-column entitled *Rationally Speaking* is hosted on numerous web sites. Massimo Pigliucci is Vice-Chair of the Darwin Day Program.

[FOOTNOTES]

1 This particular statement may need to be modified because of recent research showing that cosmic radiation can in fact cause asymmetric chirality without the intervention of living organisms.

2 Recent research has questioned the notion of complete absence of oxygen from the primordial atmosphere, but the jury is still out on exactly how reducing or oxidizing the primordial conditions were. The alternative to the soup, the pizza proposed in the next section, would solve the problem by making the atmospheric conditions pretty much irrelevant.

[REFERENCES]

Cairn-Smith, A.G. (1985) *Seven clues to the origin of life*. Cambridge University Press, Cambridge, England.

Crick, F. (1981) *Life itself*. Simon and Schuster, New York, New York.

Ertem, G. and Ferris, J.P. (1996) Synthesis of RNA oligomers on heterogeneous templates. Nature 379:238-240.

Farmer, J.D., Kauffman, S.A. and Packard, N.H. (1986) Autocatalytic replication of polymers. Physica 22D:50-67.

Haldane, J.B.S. (1985) The origin of life. In: (eds.) *On being the right size and other essays*, pp. Oxford University Press, Oxford, England.

Hoyle, F. and Wickramasinghe, C. (1978) *Lifecloud*. Harper and Row, New York, New York.

Kauffman, S.A. (1993) *The origins of order*. Oxford University Press, New York.

Langton, C.G. (1986) Studying artificial life with cellular automata. Physica 22D:120-149.

Maden, B.E.H. (1995) No soup for starters? Autotrophy and the origins of metabolism. Trends in Biochemistry 20:337-341.

Maynard-Smith, J. and Szathmary, E. (1995) *The Major Transitions in Evolution*. Oxford University Press, Oxford, England.

Miller, S.L. (1997) Peptide nucleic acids and prebiotic chemistry. Natural Structural Biology 4:167.

Miller, S.L. (1953) A production of amino acids under possible primitive earth conditions. Science 117: 528-529.

Oparin, A.I. (1938) *The origin of life on Earth*. Macmillan, New York, New York.

Polidoro, M. (1998) Houdini and Conan Doyle, the story of a strange friendship. Skeptical Inquirer 22(2):40-46.

Schrodinger, E. (1947) *What is life?* Macmillan, New York, New York.

[ADDITIONAL RESOURCES]

Evolution – International Journal of Organic Evolution: http://lsvl.la.asu.edu/evolution/

Darwin Day at the University of Tennessee, Knoxville: http://fp.bio.utk.edu/darwin/

CSICOP and Skeptical Inquirer: http://www.csicop.org

Massimo's Skeptic & Humanist Web: http://fp.bio.utk.edu/skeptic/

Rationally Speaking (a monthly web column by Massimo Pigliucci):
   http://fp.bio.utk.edu/skeptic/Rationally_Speaking.htm

*Robin McKie's review originally appeared in **The Observer**, a leading source for informed news and comment in the United Kingdom. The review is republished with permission from the author.*

BOOK REVIEW:
Y: THE DESCENT OF MEN
by Steve Jones
Little, Brown

What goes up...

Steve Jones uncovers the battle every man faces to escape the woman within in Y: The Descent of Men

Review by Robin McKie

The sweat of the proletariat and the blood of bourgeoisie are generally credited with driving the Russian revolution – at least according to Karl Marx. Geneticist Steve Jones takes a different view, however. It was all down to testosterone, he says.

Just consider this succession of power: Lenin (bald); Stalin (hairy); Khrushchev (bald); Brezhnev (hairy); Andropov (bald); Chernenko (hairy); Gorbachov (bald); Yeltsin (hairy); and Putin (now thinning on top). Strange things went on inside – and on top of – Politburo minds, it seems.

And note also the details of this presidential sequence: reactionary Soviet leaders were hirsute, reformers were depilated, an observation that has worrying implications for the West, where bald heads of state are now almost extinct. America hasn't had a trichologically challenged leader since Eisenhower and Britain hasn't had a slap-head for PM since Alec Douglas Home. Take note, Mr Duncan Smith. The chemistry of your sex (and a lot more besides) is against you.

It's an intriguing set of observations, to say the least, and shows, as Jones argues in this delightful, witty, insightful analysis of the state of maleness, that being a man can be an uncomfortable, unpredictable business. Once we were viewed as the 'natural sex', the true human prototype. Women were just hormonally insecure, diminished variations, it was argued.

But not any more. Man's comfortable self-elected status has been demolished by science, which has shown that men only retain their maleness through constant chemical interference, a desperate bid to avoid femaleness, the natural state of our species.

This process begins inside the developing foetus when the Y chromosome – the 'most decayed, redundant and parasitic' of all human genetic packages – triggers a biological cascade that marinates the unborn boy 'in a bath of masculinity', an inundation that persists for the rest of his life. As Jones says: 'Biology reveals every man's battle to escape the woman within.'

It's an absorbing argument, though Jones is certainly not concerned merely with assailing our manhoods for the sake of amusing feminists. It is simply time to take an objective, entertaining look at 'the beauty of the world, the paragon of animals' through the lens of modern biology, he says. And Jones certainly succeeds, my only gripe being his section on castration, which told me things I really didn't want to know. (The fact that castrati live 13 years longer than 'unaltered fellows' is particularly unsettling. Balls are bad for you, it seems.)

Apart from that, the book is a delicious romp through the biology of the human male, spattered – if you will pardon the phrase – with some startling ideas and startling visions, beginning with Jones's opening sentence – 'Ejaculate if you are so minded, and equipped, into a glass of chilled Perrier' – and ending with his unsettling conclusion that: 'We are in the midst of an ascent of women matched with an equivalent descent of men.'

In between, the reader is battered with a barrage of weird stories and wonderful statistics. 'Every time a man has sex, he produces enough sperm to fertilise every woman in Europe,' we are told. 'He makes two thousand billion of those potent packages in his lifetime, but for the typical Westerner fewer than two succeed.' And if that doesn't put British men in their place, I don't know what will.

Not that I, as a chap, found the book dispiriting. There is real comfort in learning about all the chemical, hormonal and physiological hindrances that we have had to struggle with all our lives, unappreciated, as we are, by our partners. Those biological handicaps even hold us back when we have sex. 'When it comes to coition, men have a harder time than most,' admits Jones, 'for they depend on hydraulics alone while almost all other mammals have a bone to shore up their most strenuous moments.' It doesn't seem fair, really.

Hard-wired by our chromosomes to spread our DNA and genotypes as widely as possible, we have all become hapless, mindless victims of the urge to procreate. As Robin Williams puts it: 'God gave men a brain and a penis, and only enough blood to run one at a time.' ∞

[ABOUT THE AUTHOR]

Robin Mckie is science editor for The Observer. He has authored several books, including *African Exodus: The Origins of Modern Humanity*, co-written with Chris Stringer; *The Book of Man: The Human Genome Project and the Quest to Discover our Genetic Heritage*, co-written with Walter Bodmer; *Dawn of Man: The Story of Human Evolution*; and *The Genetic Jigsaw: The Story of the New Genetics*.

[ADDITIONAL RESOURCES]

The Observer online: http://www.observer.co.uk

Wolf Roder's review originally appeared in the **Cincinnati Skeptic** *newsletter and is republished here with permission from the author.*

BOOK REVIEW:
STRANGE CREATIONS:
ABERRANT IDEAS OF HUMAN ORIGINS FROM ANCIENT ASTRONAUTS TO AQUATIC APES
by Donna Kossy
Feral House

Review by Wolf Roder

Creationists often want us to believe the only alternative to the theory of evolution is their own insistence on "scientific" i.e. Biblical creationism or its alternative, Intelligent Design. Now here comes Donna Kossy with a book length run down on the wide variety of other explanations of biological history, most of them utter crank. She groups these extraordinary ideas by chapter and source. There are extraterrestrial origins or creation by extraterrestrials. Then there is de-evolution, in the beginning humans were perfect, but they devolved down to this in 72,000 years. Many origin cranks are hung up on race, describing non-whites as having been created before Adam by the devil and not really human. The Church of the Creator and Christian Identity religion belong into this category. The "science" of *eugenics*, and German Nazi philosophy drew generously from the same well. Christian creationism, its propagators and antecedents before Darwin are laid out in some detail. Elaine Morgan's aquatic ape theory is given a chapter. Her ideas accept evolution, but suggest an alternative path to human status. Finally, Kossy examines the *Urantia Book*, and its connection to other cults.

Among the more rational histories is the idea that human evolution went through an aquatic phase, in which our primate ancestors lived and hunted along a lake or ocean shore. The idea was first proposed by a *bona fide* marine biologist, and later taken up by writer Elaine Morgan in her book *Descent of Woman* (1972). The theory takes some aspects that distinguish apes and humans, – the human diving reflex, fat layers inside the skin, upright walk, loss of fur – and explain them as a consequence of a period of evolution of a small population of apes in a wading and shore line habitat.

Unfortunately no evidence for such an evolution or such a population has been found. Moreover, since the book first appeared fossil evidence, e.g. Lucy and the first family have pointed more clearly towards a descent from the trees and a savanna habitat. That has not stopped the cooks from seizing on the aquatic ape theory for their purposes, and turning an originally not unreasonable idea into a ranting pseudo-science.

The weird anthropology of the *Urantia Book* does not fit easily into any one category. The book itself was supposedly dictated or channeled between 1923 and 1955 by a higher intelligence to a bunch of former Seventh Day Adventists. In some thousand pages the book tells a complex cosmology of gravity bodies, super universes, new mankinds, all of which continue to evolve. The *Urantia Book* is understood by its devotees "as an amendment to the Bible, not a replacement for it." (p. 216) Kossy comments that it sounds like "what the Bible would have been like if it had been written by lawyers and businessmen, rather than by priests, prophets and poets." (p. 217)

According to *Urantia* all life, including human life, does not originate spontaneously, it has to be constructed. And, it has to be constructed separately and over again on each world and it is not clear whether these are planets or some imagined spirit worlds. Evolution on each world is then directed by higher beings, eg. Adam and Eve, Moses, Jesus who visit these worlds. Something, however, went wrong on this earth, and the divine powers are struggling to set it right. David Koresh's Branch Davidians of Waco fame, were apparently influenced by these ideas, some of which were taken over from Seventh Day Adventism.

Another group searching for a literal heaven in another world and accessible by UFO were the people looking for "Human Individual Metamorphosis" better known as the Heaven's Gate cult. They wanted to ascend to a higher world above human, which lead to their joint suicide in March 1997. Their leading idea was they would be picked up by a spaceship following in the tail of the comet Hale-Bopp.

Strange Creations is a very useful source on a wide variety of pseudo-science ideas, oddball groups, and their writings. ∞

[ABOUT THE AUTHOR]

Wolf Roder is Professor of Geography at the University of Cincinnati. He is author of papers and books on African subjects, including "Magic, Medicine and Metaphysics in Nigeria" in the *Skeptical Inquirer*. He is the editor of the *Cincinnati Skeptic*, a newsletter of the Association for Rational Thought.

[ADDITIONAL RESOURCES]

Association for Rational Thought (ART): http://www.cincinnatiskeptics.org/

Kooks Museum online: http://home.pacifier.com/~dkossy/kooksmus.html

Book Happy (World of Weird Books): http://home.pacifier.com/~dkossy/

*Warwick Don's article first appeared in the **New Zealand Skeptic** and is republished here with permission from the author and the New Zealand Skeptics.*

EVOLUTION: THE FOSSILS SAY YES!
by Warwick Don

The Old Creationist Claim That There are No Transitional Forms in the Fossil Record is Starting to look a Bit Tired

A perennial contention of creationists opposed to evolution is that transitions or intermediates between the major groups (classes) of vertebrates (animals with backbones) do not exist. The most persistent critic of the part played by the fossil record in providing evidence for evolution is Dr Duane Gish of the Institute for Creation Research in the United States. His arguments are expressed in two books, *Evolution: The Fossils Say No!* and the updated version, *Evolution: The Challenge of the Fossil Record*. The aim of this paper is to show that the above contention is without foundation. A classic example of a transitional form (the ancient bird, *Archaeopteryx lithographica*) will be examined, as well as an example of evolutionary transformation, the evolution of ear bones in vertebrates.

Discovered in 1860, one year after publication of the *Origin*, *Archaeopteryx* is of late Jurassic age. About the size of a magpie, it lived some 150 million years ago. The species is represented by seven skeletons and one isolated feather. Close examination reveals a mixture of reptilian and bird features with many more of the former than the latter. (The table below lists some of the key features). In fact, two specimens in which the feathers were not immediately recognized were initially misidentified as *Compsognathus*, a small bipedal dinosaur. It is often stated that if it were not for its feathers, *Archaeopteryx* would be classified as a small dinosaur. A transitional form between major groups is defined as a fossil which possesses a mixture (or a mosaic) of features usually associated with each of the two groups, one set ancestral ("old"), the other derived ("new"). *Archaeopteryx* fits the bill perfectly. Its reptilian ancestry is patently obvious. *(see Table 1)*

But not according to the creationists. In spite of the evidence outlined above and more fully discussed in advanced textbooks, they continue to proclaim that "a bird, is a bird, is a bird." Thus Dr Morris: "The *Archaeopteryx* is a bird – not a reptile-bird transition." And Dr Gish: "It was not a half-way bird, it was a bird". In this regard it should be emphasized that a fossil does not have to be exactly intermediate in its features in order to be considered transitional. A mixture of definitive features, old and new, is sufficient. The period of transition between bony fish and the first amphibians, for example, is characterized by forms in which the mosaic patterns show varying rates of change of specific features in different genera.

Archaeopteryx hit the headlines a few years ago with the allegation that it was a fraud.

This assertion was made by the astronomer, Sir Fred Hoyle. He claimed that a forger had tampered with the fossilized skeleton of *Compsognathus*, adding impressions of feathers. This prompted scientific testing at the Museum of Natural History in London. Hoyle's view, which must have been welcomed as grist to the anti-evolutionary mill, was proved groundless. The feather impressions were naturally formed. This early bird is still the deluxe example of a transitional form.

Table 1. Characteristics of Archaeopteryx

Bird features
· Feathers (the defining bird feature)
· Feathered wings

Reptilian features
· Long bony tail
· Toothed jaws
· Three functional fingers with grasping claws
· Clavicle (wishbone) boomerang-shaped as in some dinosaurs
· Pelvis more reptilian in shape than in later birds

Now to a classic example of evolutionary transformation, a process whereby a structure becomes modified over time and changes in its primary function. Mammals almost certainly arose from a group of reptiles, aptly named the mammal-like reptiles, some 200 million years ago. The more advanced of these reptiles show trends towards the mammals in a number of features, such as improved locomotion by adopting an upright posture and differentiation of the teeth for the efficient exploitation of food sources. Palaeontologists normally are restricted to skeletal features for classifying a fossil. Soft tissues are seldom fossilized. The lower jaw or mandible in mammals is a single bone (the dentary which carries the teeth), in contrast to that of reptiles which comprises several bones. In addition, the middle ear of mammals contains three ear bones; reptiles have but one, the stapes.

The stapes can be traced to the fish stage of vertebrate evolution. (See fig. 1). The first fishes lacked true jaws. Hence many were filter feeders, extracting food from the stream of water entering the mouth and filling the pharynx. The filtered water then passed out through holes (gill slits) in the wall of the pharynx. The regions between the slits were supported by a basket of linked bones forming the branchial or gill arches. Jaws probably arose from a pair of these arches (another example of transformation). The upper element of the arch immediately behind the jaws eventually became transformed from an unspecialized part of a gill arch into a prop (the hyomandibular) to support the jaws at their region of articulation. It was thus ideally positioned, given its upper attachment to that region of the braincase which housed the organs of balance

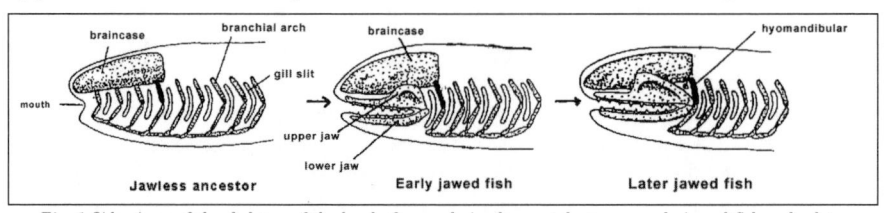

Fig. 1 Side views of the skeleton of the head of an early jawless vertebrate, an early jawed fish and a later fish. Note the hyomandibular which became transformed into the stapes. The predecessors of the hyomandibular (its homologues) are shaded in the jawless and early jawed forms.

and hearing, to become a specialized sound transmitter, a potential realized later in the amphibians. The stapes (the transformed hyomandibular) greatly improved hearing on land.

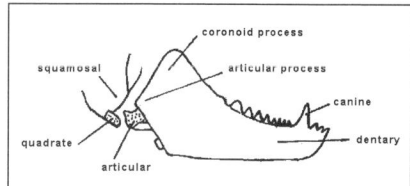

Fig. 2 Lower jaw of Cynognathus, an advanced mammal-like reptile. Note: The expanded dentary for the attachment of powerful jaw muscles, and the different tooth types; the articulating jaw bones – the articular bone (of the lower jaw) and the quadrate bone (of the skull); the articular process of the dentary.

The origin of the other two ear bones in mammals is even more intriguing. During the evolution of the mammal-like reptiles, the dentary bone in the lower jaw expanded greatly in order to provide greater surface area for the attachment of more powerful jaw muscles. At the same time the canines enlarged as efficient instruments for capturing and dismembering prey. Fig. 2 shows the lower jaw of an advanced mammal-like reptile, *Cynognathus*. For the sake of clarity the articular bone of the lower jaw is shown detached from the quadrate bone of the skull. In life these two bones form the jaw joint of reptiles. The expansion of the dentary involved two regions, the ascending coronoid process and the triangular articular *process* at the back (not to be confused with the articular bone).

In some mammal-like reptiles the articular process had grown back to the point where it touched the skull itself. This development created the potential for a new jaw joint formed by the dentary of the lower jaw and the squamosal bone of the skull. In fact, there are several examples of varying degrees of development of the "new" jaw joint, from rudimentary to fully functional, perfect examples of transitional stages, making the classification of such forms (reptile or mammal?) difficult. Should we be concerned? Not at all. Such "tricky" forms are to be expected in evolution. There is a continuity here which negates the creationist thesis of there being no transitional forms in the fossil record.

But the story is not yet over. The "new" mammalian jaw joint, once it became fully functional, rendered the "old" reptilian one superfluous. The bones of the "old" joint now relieved from a jaw articulation function were free to assume a new primary role. In this case it was not strictly a change of function but an enhancement of an existing minor function – sound transmission. The articular and quadrate bones were already somewhat inefficient conductors of sound to the inner ear in the early land vertebrates. The two bones underwent transformation to become ear bones and joined the stapes or stirrup in the middle ear to form a trio of efficient sound transmitters, greatly improving the conduction and amplification of sound waves from the outer to the inner ear. The quadrate became the incus (anvil) and the articular became the malleus (hammer). The improvement in hearing is linked

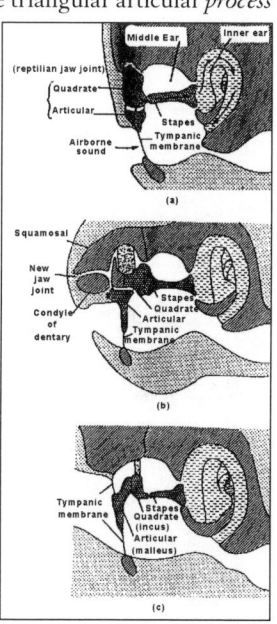

Fig 3. Diagrams of jaw joint and ear regions of (a) a mammal-like reptile; (b) a transitional form between reptiles and mammals, and (c) an early mammal. Points to note: in (a), the reptilian jaw-joint of the quadrate (a skull bone) and articular (a lower jaw bone), and the single ear bones (stapes); in (b), a new mammalian jaw-joint has formed, the reptilian hinge bones are reduced and their migration into the middle ear is iminent. In (c) the migration is completed. After Strickberger 1990.

to the importance of this faculty (along with smell) in promoting the survival of the first mammals as small nocturnal animals in a world dominated by large and aggressive dinosaurs.

What has Gish to say on the subject? He refers to the "unbridged gap between reptile and mammal" and questions how the "intermediates" managed to hear while the changes described above were going on. He seems to have overlooked the fact that the stapes was still present. In addition, as was pointed out above, the "old" jaw joint bones were already sound conductors. He also expresses concern as to how the animals continued to chew while the changes were in progress. But there was never a time when an "intermediate" was without functional jaws. The sequence of change with respect to jaw joints was: Old > Old + New > New.

Diarthrognathus epitomises the transition from reptile to mammal. In this animal, not only was the "old" reptilian joint between a reduced quadrate and articular present, but also a "new" and fully functional mammalian one. To cite a further example, *Probainognathus* also possessed a double articulation between skull and jaw. Furthermore, the quadrate bone, now only loosely joined to the rest of the skull, was intimately articulated with the stapes bone of the middle ear.

On the above evidence I rest my case. Transitional fossils between major groups of vertebrates do exist and lend powerful support to the reality of evolution.

[ABOUT THE AUTHOR]

Warwick Don received his early education in Waihi (Coromandel) and later attended Otago Boys' High School and the University of Otago in Dunedin. He graduated BSc and MSc (First Class Honors in Zoology) and then taught zoology at the same university until retirement in 1997. His main teaching interests were invertebrate zoology, entomology and the vertebrate fossil record and he has published a number of research papers on New Zealand ants. At present he is a volunteer researcher at the Otago Museum in Dunedin and is writing a book on New Zealand ants. He is a past chairman of the New Zealand Skeptics, has written several articles countering creationist attacks on evolution and has participated in numerous newspaper debates on the evolution/creationism issue.

[ADDITIONAL RESOURCES]

The Department of Ecology and Evolution at the University of Fribourg, Switzerland Memorial Site: http://www.unifr.ch/biol/ecology/hamilton/hamilton.html

New Zealand Skeptics: http://skeptics.org.nz/

As Old as The Hills
by Ian Plimer

For millennia, we humans have wondered: How old is the Earth? The first attempt to calculate the age of the Earth (and the Universe) was made by St. Augustine in the fourth century. The 6000-year-old age of the Earth, constructed by St Augustine from the genealogy of the Bible, makes an appearance in Shakespeare's *As You Like It*. This date of creation of the Universe was modified by Johannes Kepler in 1598 A.D. in *Mysterium Cosmographicum* to 11 am, Sunday 27th April 3877 B.C. In 1654 A.D. in *The Annals of the World Deduced from the Origin of Time*, Archbishop James Ussher (1581-1656 A.D.), the Archbishop and Primate of all Ireland, calculated that the Earth was created on 23rd October 4004 B.C. Ussher used the chronology of the Bible and added up all the life spans of the descendents of Adam. Despite the enormous scientific advances over the last 350 years, the Ussherian date of creation is still adhered to as a matter of faith by young Earth creationists.

Ussher's chronology was from the Geneva Bible, just one of the many translations from the Hebrew. There are some doubts about the Alexandrian translators who quoted suspiciously symmetrical sets of ages. Furthermore, the Septuagint version of the Bible has different sets of dates, in agreement with the Samaritan and Josephian versions, and a different age of the Earth can be calculated. For example, the Hales (5411 B.C.), Jewish (3760 B.C.) and Alexandrian (5503 B.C.) ages of the Earth are all different. Just to make these calculations even harder, the Hebrew method of designating numbers by letters of the alphabet is such that all chronology and other numerical notes are liable to errors of transcription. The Hebrew word for day (*yom* or *yohm*) is the same as that for 'a period of time' and hence a literal creation over six 24 hour days is, at best, unreliable. The use of the word 'day' in the Bible can mean many days (Proverbs 25:13; Genesis 30:14), a season (Zachariah 14:8), many years (Matthew 10:15; 11-22-24), a thousand years (Psalm 90:4); 2 Peter 3:8, 10) or, presumably many orders of magnitude higher. A slightly different interpretation of the word yohm could change Ussher's age by millions of years.

The Ussherian date of creation was recalculated by Dr John Lightfoot, a Hebrew scholar and Vice-Chancellor of Cambridge University. The Lightfoot time of creation was 9 am, 23rd October 4004 B.C. This was indeed a convenient date as it was the beginning of the academic year at Cambridge! In the mid 17th Century, the Bible was the principal source of knowledge. Calculation by Ussher followed by a repeated independent calculation by Lightfoot is the methodology of science today and these calculations were the best that could be undertaken in the 17th Century. In the late 18th Century, Hutton showed at Siccar Point (Scotland) that the planet was very old but he was not able to give a figure. In Darwin's time, there was an increasing awareness that the planet was very old and, just before the discovery of radioactivity, attempts to calculate the age of the Earth were made by Jolly in 1899 A.D. based on the salinity of the oceans (99 million years old) and William Thomson (later to become Lord Kelvin) based on the cooling of the Earth (1862 A.D. 20 to 400 million years; 1897 A.D. 20 to 40 million years). With the discovery of radioactivity, an Earth age of billions of years was calculated a few years after the Kelvin date. Since Ussher's time, knowledge has expanded and the age of the Earth calculated by a variety of independent methods is 4550 ± 50 million years.

The Ussherian age was entered as a marginal note in the King James edition of the Bible in 1701 A.D. and there it stayed. Most scholars of the 19th Century, including Charles Darwin, thought that the Ussherian age was part of the original scripture and Darwin was astonished to learn that it was a calculation made 200 years earlier. The enormity of time underpins evolution and the history of Earth and is written in stone for all to see.

[ABOUT THE AUTHOR]

Ian Plimer is the Chair of Geology at The University of Melbourne, Australia.

[ADDITIONAL RESOURCES]

Ian Plimer's faculty page: http://www.earthsci.unimelb.edu.au/people/plimer/

Australian Skeptics: http://www.skeptics.com.au/

Online Resources on Archbishop James Usher:

http://www.pgil-eirdata.org/html/pgil_datasets/authors/u/Ussher,J/life.htm

http://www.go-newfocus.co.uk/articles/archbishopjamesusher.htm

Ian Tattersall's review originally appeared in **Evolutionary Anthropology**, a journal providing a valuable source of current information for classroom teaching and research activities in evolutionary anthropology. The review is republished here with permission from the author.

BOOK REVIEWS:
THE STRUCTURE OF EVOLUTIONARY THEORY
By Stephen Jay Gould
The Belknap Press of Harvard University Press

GENETICS, PALEONTOLOGY, AND MACROEVOLUTION, 2ND ED.
by Jeffrey S. Levinton
Cambridge University Press

Reviews by Ian Tattersall

SELECTION, SPECIES, AND SPANDRELS:
DIVERGING VIEWS OF EVOLUTIONARY THEORY

In his tragically short lifetime, his colleagues gave Stephen Jay Gould grudging credit at best for his achievements. His high public profile, created principally by the books resulting from his astonishing series of articles in Natural History magazine – some 300 columns published monthly without a break over 25 years, despite the toll taken on his energies by a courageous early battle with the cancer that eventually killed him – led lesser spirits to dismiss him as a popularizer who lived off the ideas of others. Unkind critics pointed to the fact that the essential notions which catapulted him to fame, via the 1972 paper on punctuated equilibria that he wrote with Niles Eldredge, had already been expressed the year before by Eldredge alone in a more narrowly-focussed technical paper on trilobites. And attacks in this vein continued relentlessly throughout his career (doubtless fuelled by his spirited, not to say combative, responses). Yet what cannot be disputed is that Gould picked up the evolutionary ball and ran with it as no one else in recent times has been able to do, and that in the process he brought the obscure fields of paleontology and evolutionary theory to a wider audience than ever before. What's more, Gould was aided in this remarkable achievement by an unflaggingly creative mind that ceaselessly bubbled with ideas and new associations. Time and again (doubtless like many others), if I had what I felt was some sort of insight into evolutionary pattern or process, I would discover that Steve had got there first. What's more, if (as was likely) some now-obscure nineteenth-century German biologist had pipped us both to the post, Gould, with his acute sense of history, was much more likely to have known it.

Still, even Gould's most ardent supporter would never claim that brevity stood out among his virtues. Editors at Natural History would tear their hair as yet another column came in hundreds of words overlength – even as, during the early 1980s, they feared that each column would be his last. Prolixity was part of the product, and Gould's virtues were his vices: as far as his columns were concerned, one man's entertaining discursiveness was another's annoying repetitiveness, and what to some was an appealing scientific inquisitiveness and ecumenicism was to others an irritating tendency to digress. The same, it has to be said, is true of some of Gould's scientific writing, and never more so than in the case of his Big Book, published only weeks before his death at the age of 60. The Structure of Evolutionary Theory runs to almost 1500 pages, weighs in at only a hair under 5 pounds, and is something that even the greatest insomniacs among us would be unwise to attempt to read at a sitting – at 15 pages, the Contents list alone is as long as the average scientific paper (and boasts its own abstract!). But while Gould regularly cranked out another book every year or two, this one is far from just one more among many. For although no one could doubt that Gould still had other books in him, this one is very much Steve's personal scientific testament, summarizing the course of his professional career and the development of his scientific interests – both processual and historical – at the same time as it articulates a fairly coherent view of the historical and biological processes that have gone into forming the living world as we think we understand it today. Which makes it rather odd that he apparently didn't consider that it justified a preface. Or perhaps, in an obscure way, the whole thing is intended as an extended preface, to a yet-to-be-realized comprehensive concept of the evolutionary process.

Maybe it's more instructive than is immediately apparent that Gould starts off with a comparison of architectural metaphors for what he, and Darwin before him, had accomplished in their respective lifetimes of cogitation upon the complex mishmash of elements that have entered into the vastness of Life's evolutionary history. A couple of years after the Origin had appeared, the respected paleontologist Hugh Falconer expressed his belief that the sage of Down had "laid the foundations of a great edifice." To which a grateful (and relieved) Darwin replied in a letter that he hoped his "framework would stand." Gould makes much of the distinction between the terms chosen by these two very different biologists, pointing out that while the foundation of an edifice is hidden from view, its framework describes the outlines of its visible structure. What's more, a building's foundation is likely to persist relatively undisturbed through subsequent structural modification, while its outward appearance is susceptible to enormous elaboration and change (Gould's chosen example is Milan's famous Duomo, whose bizarre if captivating appearance is due to the superimposition of an ornate neogothic superstructure upon a neoclassical baroque nucleus). The point seems to be that if Darwin's core notion of evolution as "descent with modification" is taken as the essence of "Darwinism," then the foundation stands unviolated, while there is no doubt that the visible above-ground framework has been subject at the very least to major tinkering between the mid-nineteenth century and today.

Gould points out that, if one is to choose between the two metaphors as they apply to the history of evolutionary theory, it is critical to define Darwinism as a discrete intellectual entity so that its structure can be made apparent. Defining Darwinism is, in fact, much of what this book is about although, as Gould well knew, the task is made enormously difficult by the inconvenient reality that Darwinism means so many different things to so many different people. Indeed, if it is wise to be wary of any religion with an individual's name in its identifier, perhaps it is sensible to even charier of any field of science that is labelled in this way. For, just as every major religious tradition by now seethes with differing interpretations of the True Word, so also does Darwinism. Darwin was, after all, such an extraordinarily fertile and comprehensive thinker and prolific scribe that it is possible with enough diligence to find a justification somewhere in his writings for almost any opinion that one might hold on matters evolutionary. This modest, even diffident, man was horrified by much of the doctrinaire posturing that was committed in his name during his lifetime, and he would certainly be appalled that such presumptions continue unabated more than a century after his death.

For this reason I would personally have preferred it if, in this book above all the others, Gould had forsaken the search for the true Darwinism in favor of a straightforward articulation of his own views on where evolutionary theory (a term so much less loaded than Darwinism; can't we please use it?) stands today. But then again, if he had done so we would have been deprived of the lively historical insights that pepper this book in more senses than one.

In any event, to return to the architectural analogy, Gould claims that the distinction between foundation and framework is a crucial one because, while a foundation can remain essentially unaltered through numerous reconstructions of its framework, the reverse can never be the case. Couple this with his belief that there is a core of Darwinism to which all sensible intellectuals should find themselves able to subscribe, and it is clear why it emerges that Gould's sympathies lie more with Falconer's foundation than with Darwin's framework. But maybe this is too simple, because Gould goes on to describe an intellectual structure in which an intermediate level hovers between foundation and framework, namely the tripodal "essence of Darwinian logic." This consists of the three mutually dependent pillars of agency (natural selection, seen as acting solely on individual organisms), efficacy (of natural selection, never disputed according to Gould, except as an exclusive agent), and scope (extending from microevolutionary change to macroevolution). It is within each of these rubrics that Gould claims common ground (and room for improvement on the original Darwinian formulation) may be found, and in a loose way he organizes the first half of The Structure of Evolutionary Theory around them.

Gould's Chapter 1 ("Defining and Revising the Structure of Evolutionary Theory") serves to introduce his Part I ("The History of Darwinian Logic and Debate," Chapters 2-7), which is a tour de force of historical exposition rivalled only by Ernst Mayr's The Growth of Biological Thought, published in 1986. It is, however, very much less a work of conventional history. Instead, Gould's concern in these 500-odd pages is to expose the intricacies of Darwin's reasoning in the light of both prior and prevailing biological beliefs, and to trace the interpretation of Darwin's thought by succeeding generations of biologists. He doesn't pretend to explore every alley, but rather admits to a degree of "self-serving retrospection" via which he largely bypasses what seem today to be the dead-ends of evolutionary thought, and highlights what he believes to be the main threads leading toward the spectrum of modern views of the processes by which life has evolved. The subtext throughout is to describe the intellectual construct that Darwin (and his successors) created, not simply as a mass of detail but also as a "fully shaped" edifice, whose "walls have developed some cracks and may even be ripe for a breach" (p. 341).

Given that the Origin alone went through six thoroughly revised editions, this is a task worthy of those few who claim to know exactly which words Shakespeare originally wrote (or what he meant by them). Nonetheless, Gould certainly succeeded in convincing me that his rendition of Darwin's (evolving) intent is a largely reliable one. Much of the argument and detail here will be familiar to those who regularly read his columns, but the breadth and depth of Gould's erudition shines through on every page, and a huge variety of observations is integrated here for the first time. Particularly interesting to me was Gould's insistence on the effects on Darwin of the economic arguments propounded by Adam Smith in The Wealth of Nations. Indeed, Gould avers, Darwin's natural selection is "Smith's economics transferred to Nature" (p. 122). Not everyone will instinctively agree with this, but in his occasionally (but not to me, at least, offensively) arch and didactic way Gould makes a typically persuasive case for it.

Having established the flaws as he saw them in the Darwinian structure as it existed at the beginning of his career, a time when the Evolutionary Synthesis reigned supreme, Gould turns his attention in Part II of his book ("Towards a Revised and Expanded Evolutionary Theory") to the post-1970 developments in which he played so conspicuous a role. Reverting to the Three Pillars of Darwinism, he starts with punctuated equilibria (which he rather unsettlingly insists on calling here "punctuated equilibrium"; forgive me if I stay with the established version), which he sees as addressing deficiencies in the Darwinian concept of agency by introducing a hierarchy of levels of action of evolutionary forces. In particular, Gould emphasizes the addition here of species to individual organisms, as subjects of natural triage. Next he tackles efficacy, by pointing out that the addition of his developmental concerns with internal constraints within species or lineages, when added to pure Darwinian natural selection, have enhanced our ability to explain the patterns we see in the fossil record. And he also claims some credit for expanding the scope of Darwinism by the emphasis in his writings on the evolutionary role of catastrophic events and mass extinctions. Throughout, he pays due tribute to his collaborators, foremost among them Niles Eldredge and Elisabeth Vrba, to whom he dedicates this volume. It is virtually impossible to summarize the best part of a thousand pages on those matters of process closest to Gould's heart. Species as individuals cascade by, as do species selection, punctuated equilibria (whose opponents, predictably, get a lively riposte), baseball, time, developmental and structural constraints, adaptation, old movies, homology, exaptation, spandrels, nonadaptive origins, mass extinctions, and much more. All of these are discussed with Gouldian panache and erudition and the odd excursion into jargon (what is one to make, without considerable pondering, of section headings with titles such as "The more radical category of exapted features with truly nonadaptive origins as structural constraints"?); and, in good Darwinian fashion, objectors all receive a lengthy hearing before getting the chop.

Does all this add up to a coherent new framework of evolutionary theory? Some major ingredients are there, it's true; but perhaps it is surprising that Gould, who did so much to raise awareness of the role of contingency in the evolutionary process, so often gives the impression of being in search of a Grand Unified Theory for one of the messier of Nature's phenomena. In the evolution of living things most posited causes turn out to be effects, and most effects to result from multiple potential causes. Speciation, for example, is clearly not a unitary process; it is an outcome, which may occur for a myriad different reasons. All of which makes evolution an intractable subject for those in search of the Big Picture, even those as gifted as Gould. As, of course, Gould himself realized, in suggesting that contingency can usefully be used to fill awkward interstices in the evolutionary framework. Still, evolution isn't all contingency. There is a lot out there that can be understood in terms of predictable forms of interaction, and, whoever you are, it's virtually guaranteed that you'll be a great deal more familiar with the current state of evolutionary explanation when you finish reading this book than when you started. What's more, even the most erudite among us will learn a lot from Gould's musings on the history of evolutionary thought.

So, finally, who is this book written for? This question is above all relevant because this work is, in a sense, an interesting hybrid. In part, it is a technical treatise on evolutionary theory and the history of our understanding of it, and it is probably much too long and detailed for the average lay Gould devotee. Yet it is written in many ways as if for Gould's Natural History audience, especially in its entertaining (or irritating) tendency to follow successive threads of thought wherever they might lead, at whatever length they might demand. In the end, you have to admit that Gould might have served both lay and professional readerships better (and probably have substantially increased both) by exercising a bit more discipline and compressing his arguments into an inevitably hefty book half the length of this one. Of course, if he had submitted to a lengthy editorial process, he might never have lived to see the book published – and perhaps, on some level, he realized this. Still, while this volume is undeniably wordy, repetitive, digressive, and at times meandering, in an odd way this is all part of its charm. And as a final exposition of the strongly-held views and the astonishing erudition of one of the liveliest and – by a wide margin – most productive evolutionary thinkers of his generation, it is a book that should certainly be read or at least consulted by everyone who has enough interest in matters evolutionary even to skim this review. If only because of its sheer length, it is probably better absorbed – and appreciated – by dipping into it than by sustained reading. But whichever method you choose, leave plenty of time.

One of those who presumably won't be doing this is Jeff Levinton, and it seems almost unfair to review the new edition of his Genetics, Paleontology and Macroevolution alongside Gould's magisterial opus. For, by the very nature of things, even an excellent textbook on evolution is likely to pale alongside the vivid personal testament of one of the great scientific writers of the day. Full disclosure also demands my mentioning that Gould fingers Levinton as one of "punctuated equilibrium's harshest critics" (p. 789). It is hardly surprising, then, that his textbook is in a strictly traditionalist mold, with headings bearing slogans such as "Saltation is a Nonproblem in Evolution" and "The Hierarchical Structure of Life Eludes Us as A Successful Framework within Which to Discover Evolutionary Change and Success." Indeed, this second edition is if anything even less forward-looking than Levinton's first, and begins with the emphatic declaration that in the evolutionary arena "models emphasizing species and sorting among species have proven unimportant" (p. xiii). So there.

For all its sloganeering, the book is impressively long and detailed, certainly long and detailed enough to make any student quake at the thought of having to absorb it all. So if you want to know where the Evolutionary Synthesis stood in its "hardened" (Gould's term) and most dogmatic form at the beginning of the 1970s, this is as good a place as any to start, despite the fact that a substantial proportion of the long bibliography is more recent. Even Levinton complains, however, that the founders of the Synthesis largely ignored many of the "foci" (ecology, mass extinctions, continental breakups, etc) that macroevolution must take into account, and he sets out to remedy this deficiency, chiefly by focussing upon the statistical approach used for identifying periods of crisis (presumably ecological) and explosive taxic diversification in the fossil record. For the rest, though, he gives us a pretty standard account of the history of evolutionary thought, the constraining effects of developmental processes, speciation, adaptation and function, allometry, and so forth, all pretty well written and useful if you want to brush up on the basics à la Synthesis. But look in vain for anything but dismissive comments about the role of species, let alone hierarchy, in evolution. Indeed, if Martin Luther's Ninety-Five Theses were revolutionary, then the Ten Theses with which Levinton concludes his new edition are at bottom an attempt to chain evolutionary theory to the past. Even if the last of them is The Unexpected Will Overwhelm Our Preconceived Notions – a sentiment of which, of course, Gould would have approved.

[ABOUT THE AUTHOR]

Ian Tattersall is Curator in the Department of Anthropology of the American Museum of Natural History in New York City. Trained in archaeology and anthropology at Cambridge, and in geology and vertebrate paleontology at Yale, Tattersall has concentrated his research in the analysis of the human fossil record, and the study of the ecology and systematics of the lemurs of Madagascar. Dr. Tattersall has over 200 scientific research publications, as well as more that a dozen trade books to his credit, among them *The Monkey in the Mirror: Essays on the Science of What Makes Us Human*; *Extinct Humans*; and *Becoming Human: Evolution and Human Uniqueness*.

[ADDITIONAL RESOURCES]

Evolutionary Anthropology is an authoritative review journal that focuses on issues of current interest in biological anthropology, paleoanthropology, archaeology, functional morphology, social biology, and bone biology as well as human biology, genetics, and ecology. In addition to lively, well-illustrated articles reviewing contemporary research efforts, this journal also publishes general news of relevant developments in the scientific, social, or political arenas. Visit the journal on the web at: http://www.wiley.com/cda/product/0,,EVAN,00.html

American Museum of Natural History: http://www.amnh.org/

Ian Tattersall's faculty page: http://web.gc.cuny.edu/anthropology/fac_tattersall.html

The Stephen Jay Gould Archive at http://www.stephenjaygould.org/

*Bill Peddie's article first appeared in the **New Zealand Skeptic** and is republished here with permission from the author and the New Zealand Skeptics.*

Teaching Evolution to the Alienated
Presenting the Evidence Just Isn't Enough
by Bill Peddie

In his book *Unpopular Essays*, Bertrand Russell claims that although he was fully aware of the notion that the human is a rational animal, despite years of searching for supporting evidence for that assertion, he could find none. For those hoping to batter the creationist opponents of evolution into submission with logical rational argument, Bertrand Russell's comment should at the very least sound a note of caution.

As a second year student in zoology at Canterbury University, more years ago than I care to remember, I went armed with my genetics evolution notes to a lecture which had the intriguing title Darwin Debunked. The lecturer was the Roman Catholic chaplain and Thomist scholar, Father George Duggan – and his talk even today would stand as a good example of creation science at its thoughtful best. What puzzled me was how, after his talk, despite having the zoologists and geologists in the audience tear his arguments asunder with devastating counter examples, this Rhodes scholar and trained Catholic thinker was totally unmoved.

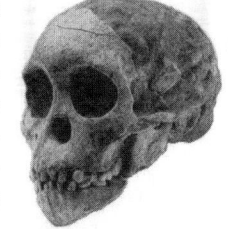

It was much later that I gradually came to realise that where matters of faith and cultural belief are concerned, there is too much at stake for conventional argument to produce a shift in position.

Let me illustrate with three examples.

On several occasions, Jehovah's Witnesses have arrived at my door and unsuspectingly offered me literature which I have previously checked out for myself. The pattern has usually been that sometime later they escape in disarray, I suspect thankfully, promising to return with the answers to the questions raised. They do not return – and yet it is a hollow victory because my visitors can be seen with the same neat little sports jackets, the same briefcases no doubt still containing the same flawed literature; and wearing the same smile of the truly saved, walking up the front paths of houses in the same neighbourhood the very next weekend. One-on-one tutorial teaching does not necessarily lead to total success.

My second example is from a transcript from an interview I had with a seventh form Polynesian pupil. The transcript included the following exchange.

Me: How old do you think the earth is?
Pupil: Six thousand years old.
Me: And the universe?
Pupil: The same.
Me: If someone was to give you very strong evidence that the world was older than that – and that for example there was geological evidence there was no flood of the size that would cover the world – how would you react?
Pupil: Evidence like what?
Me: Annual tree ring data going back seven or eight thousand years for the bristle-cone pine, examples of annual deposits of ice layers which when counted give values into many thousands of years, fossils which from every test appear very ancient and radioactive dating of rocks leading to estimates of not millions but billions of years – those sorts of things for the age of the earth. And then for Noah's flood – the fact that the scientists have calculated that you would need to have three or four times the total amount of water in the sea, atmosphere and under the earth in order to cover the highest mountains like Mount Everest.
Pupil: (there was a pause, then...) Well, I would have to say that God is greater than that. But I am glad you told me about that because if someone had hit me with that on the street – if I was, say witnessing – I would have been stuck dumb. I don't know about that sort of thing. Now I can get ready with an answer.
Me: But it wouldn't change what you think about the age of the Earth.
Pupil: No!

My third example of another attempt to educate those with a built-in resistance, comes from a few years ago by courtesy of physiologist professor Roger Short of Monash University. After discovering 27 percent of his first year medical students held a creationist view, he gave eight lessons on evolution to his class and retested them. Despite having completed an assignment on the subject matter of the lectures he found no change in the creationist views.

What crystallised my thinking on the nature of the problem was an interview I did when I was a few months into my PhD study into the nature of the creation/evolution debate. In the course of this interview a Maori studies lecturer made the comment that the ultimate in alienation would be to be a Maori evolutionist.

When I protested this with the counter example of Rangi Walker's son who is a well known zoologist and one who as far as I know still accepts a concept of evolution my informant's reply was instructive.

"To the extent he believes in evolution he is not a Maori."

GROUP IDENTITY

This reply suggests a way of looking at the debate. For many, the position taken on the debate is more one of identity with a group who are associated with a viewpoint than it is with a rationally constructed, evidence based position. I am not even convinced that this is itself entirely irrational behaviour. After all if your family – your whanau – has a discernible set of characterising beliefs, and you think it is important to identify with that family, that religion, that culture, is it simply a question of logical analysis to cut yourself off from the group by questioning what you believe to be one of its underlying major tenets? In today's politically correct age it is ironic that those who bay for the creationist blood of fundamentalist Christians fall uncomfortably silent when asked to consider the creationism so much part of the thinking of many Maori and Polynesians.

NOT THE DESIRED EFFECT

As already stated, the first surprise for the teacher with creationist pupils of the more extreme sort, is that the usual classroom rehearsing of a few well chosen facts supporting evolution does not have the desired effect on those alienated by their belief system. The second problem is that such is the fervour of the strict creationist camp that their leaders have taken the trouble to assemble the most detailed and documented case which is both technical in flavour and at least superficially plausible. They will, for example, quote figures to cast doubt as to the reliability of radioactive decay figures, talk glibly about astrophysicists' problems with the speed of light, and quote examples where apparently old rocks show signs of recent formation. And they have amongst their number some surprisingly well educated and well qualified supporters. It is true that they have few who are actually doing research or who are specialists in the areas they quote, but criticising them for basing their case on much that is second hand and interpreting science in amateur ways is not the way to deliver the knockout punch.

With some degree of embarrassment, might I dare suggest that familiarity with research and logical analysis may not even always be a central plank of the acquired wisdom of the proevolutionary camp. After all even amongst the Skeptics I am prepared to guess that there are some who would accept the validity of radiochemical dating of rocks – and yet perhaps never have handled a Geiger counter – or without having the faintest idea as to the relative merits, limitations and likely error bars of carbon dating or of Potassium-Argon dating, Uranium Lead dating or fission track analysis. There would be those who accept the idea of pre-hominid ancestors without having seen the fossil collections – or even without having the faintest idea of how the process of identification is made.

METHODS OF STUDY

Let's face it – a huge percentage of our knowledge comes from received, predigested knowledge. The sources of knowledge for the "creation scientist" are admittedly different but the methods of study are proabably sufficiently similar to explain why apparently otherwise well educated people can be found sincerely claiming that the Earth is of the order of six thousand years old. It is important to remember that this hard-won so called knowledge is based on hours of study of a different literature and unquestioning acceptance of the textbook assertions of such worthies as Duane Gish, Henry Morris, Ken Ham or for that matter the apparently authoritative and profusely referenced claims by the anonymous authors of those nicely printed Watchtower publications.

Unfortunately, although in my view science teachers may know their conventional science in their subject disciplines from university they are ill prepared to identify the characteristics or for that matter the dangers of the pseudoscience of creationism as it is sometimes introduced into our schools. For example I received an extraordinary document through the mail the other day entitled "Understanding The Young Earth Model". Yes I have spotted plenty of serious errors and misinterpretations of mainstream science in this publication which incidentally is called a "science teacher resource booklet". But you have to remember I have a relatively recent PhD in the topic. A first encounter with the claims – especially by one unfamiliar with the quoted sources may well produce understandable confusion. Many of our science teachers have no geology in their degrees and it is possible to get right through a university science course without coming up against the raft of evidence which supports such things as an acceptance of the ancient past for the universe and the old Earth.

They are not to know that the PhD in the qualifications cited by an author come from the same university that Ian Plimer once told me had, for the not inconsiderable sum of US$19, inadvertently awarded a Doctor of Divinity to the slobbery blue heeler that belonged to his next door neighbour. Unless they are very well read, nor are the teachers likely to know which of the creationist assertions are founded on thoroughly discredited experiments or total misrepresentations of the literature.

HUMAN AND DINOSAUR FOOTPRINTS

For example a few years ago impressions of human footprints were reported as being found beside dinosaur footprints in the Paluxy River area in Texas. The creation science case was not helped when one of the creation science assistants reported that he had witnessed the Reverend Dr Carl Baugh carving out some new fossil human footprints by torchlight. The Paluxy River findings of human footprints are now considered of no consequence by the paleontologists but they still surface in creationist literature.

In a number of instances I encountered evidence of what is at worst deliberate intellectual dishonesty or at best extremely sloppy and ill-informed research techniques on the part of the leading creationists. In one of his recent lectures in Auckland, John MacKay supported his case by quoting from a book by Derek Ager entitled The New Catastrophism. He underlined the significance of Ager's comments by stressing the authority of the book, posing a rhetorical qustion: "Who of you has had a book published by Oxford University Press?" Unfortunately for Mackay, the copy in the University of Auckland (which incidentally claims to be published by the Cambridge University Press) has a preface. There in bold type is the disclaimer –

> ...*in view of the misuse my words have been put to in the past, I wish to say that nothing in this book should be taken out of context and thought in any way to support the views of the "creationist", who I refuse to call "scientific".*

The existence of creationist influences in our schools raises some fundamental questions about the role of the school as an agent of society. If you are teaching in a comfortable white middle class suburb away from a bible belt enclave or marae the worst you are likely to encounter is a weekend missionary visit offering you a chance for spiritual enlightenment. If you are teaching at the type of school which demands a signature attesting a fundamentalist acceptance of bible literalism as a prerequisite for employment – or you are teaching in an area where the parental customer base represents unquestioning acceptance of Adam and Eve and the Noah flood and the board of trustees is known to have a bible literalist or creationist stance, it is legitimate to question how far you should take heed of in loco parentis. For me with my training in science – and a formal higher degree in science education with a focus on this very debate, there is normally no contest. I am totally convinced in the case for evolution. I personally find the evidence overwhelming as I believe is the case for believing the Earth was created vastly earlier than 6000 years ago. In making room for a discussion of the extreme form of "creation science" it is a little like being asked to condone those wishing to waste my pupils time with a case for the flat Earth, fake cures for cancer or career guidance by astrology, I do however concede that since we have to teach pupils as they are rather than as they should be, the probability they have either already encountered or at least are likely to encounter this set of beliefs make it more reasonable to tackle the problem. Since they have to learn what constitutes pseudoscience as well as good science there is also a case for arguing for creation science as a case study.

I also believe that as a science teacher I have a responsibility to fairly represent mainstream science views and attitudes and not imply a justifiable case where none exists. But when it comes to deciding – as I had to decide a few years ago – whether or not I should share my understanding with four Exclusive Brethren pupils when I knew that the penalty for heresy for them might be being ostracised by their family, I was less confident. The point is that even if the teacher sees "creation science" as being almost devoid of redeeming features, I believe we owe pupils and their families the right to choose their own religion and own place in society. I must also stress that for many teachers the debate is likely to be a non-issue. It is really only in those schools where the contributing community contains a significant number of creationists or vehement creationists intent on spreading their message in the schools that there is likely to be an issue for the teacher.

The regulations governing what happens in schools are of little help. While the education act safeguards the right of university lecturers to raise controversial issues and question cherished beliefs (with the possible exception of revisionist histories of the holocaust) there is no such clear direction for teachers at the secondary level.

What then should the teacher do to deal with someone offering creationist literature to the school or offering to come in and share creationist assertions with his or her pupils.

My main word of advice is that the teachers should make themselves thoroughly familiar with the nature of the literature. I first entered the arena assuming it was just a question of assembling the conventional evidence a la the prescription and thereby overwhelm the counter case. I rapidly discovered that there is a difference between evidence derived from a pseudoscience and that of the more conventional scientific literature. I find it helpful to my students to teach them how to read such evidence critically. The way I now use such material in the classroom is to demonstrate how science can be misrepresented.

I also believe that as teachers we should be sensitive to the fact that we may be dealing here with matters of religious or cultural belief and avoid direct confrontation where it is possible to do so. My personal answer is to introduce some geological and astronomical principles early on to my pupils and leave the evolution of man till much later in the piece. My own preferred strategy is to show a variety of simple methods for establishing the world is very old and inviting the pupils to draw their own conclusions as well as conveying the majority point of view. This might include showing photographs of varves, annual and daily ring formation in coral deposits, speed of light data from distant stars and galaxies and a highly simplified account of radioactive dating.

I give examples of variation in species, then examples of observed speciation. In the senior school I use the examples of new species including the cichlid fishes, *Primula kewensis* and the ring species of the Black-backed Gulls and Herring Gulls.

I find even fifth form pupils are fascinated by skeleton photos of related species and hominid and prehominid fossils.

I also give simplified accounts of protolife experiments such as those of Urey and Miller, and the Fox experiments.

After this I believe the pupils are more ready to make some of their own judgements about evolution when it is formally studied.

I also think that whatever the religious belief of the teacher it does no harm to point out that most mainstream religious believers now accept evolution. If I am asked I make no secret of the fact that I am a lay preacher in the Methodist church and have no problems with reconciling my interpretation of the bible with my scientific understanding of an ancient Earth and processes of evolution.

I think that whatever the constraints of the exam prescription, as science teachers my colleagues and I have an obligation to teach the difference between pseudo science and science. Where creation science is helpful is to highlight for senior pupils how science can be misrepresented.

Finally rather than lament the entanglement of science, education and entrenched world view we might do worse than allow the last word to John C Greene.

"I am convinced that science, ideology and world view will forever be interwined and interacting. As a citizen concerned for the welfare of science and of mankind generally, however, I cannot help but hope that scientists will recognise where science ends and other things begin."

[ABOUT THE AUTHOR]

Bill Peddie is currently teaching as the head of a science department at a South Auckland High School. As a somewhat liberal lay preacher in the Methodist Church and as the writer of a science education PhD entitled Alienated by Evolution, he has a continuing interest in the interface between science and religion. As a member of the New Zealand Skeptics he also confesses to being attracted to the creation evolution debate as an example of a discussion in which the principles of science are sometimes ignored.

[ADDITIONAL RESOURCES]

New Zealand Skeptics: http://skeptics.org.nz/

Michael Chapman's review originally appeared in **Metanexus: The Online Forum on Religion and Science** and was republished in the **National Center for Science Education Reports** 22:1-2, p. 52-3,. It is republished here with permission from the author.

EVOLUTION'S WORKSHOP: GOD AND SCIENCE ON THE GALÁPAGOS ISLANDS
by Edward Larson
Basic Books

Review by Michael Chapman

Evolutionists and clergymen are fallible; they perceive their data or their God as through a glass darkly; yet their pronouncements can change history. The Galápagos Islands have occupied a central position in history of evolutionary thought, but how were these uninhabited islands perceived by the first Christians to visit them? Devout adherents to natural theology, 16th- and 17th-century Pacific explorers dithered over the presence of bizarre giant tortoises, marine iguanas and other animals on the Galápagos Islands; the animals must have traveled there from Noah's ark, but then how to explain their total absence in the Old World? Perhaps the Galápagos were an accursed place, or a purgatory for sinners. But when Charles Darwin visited the islands, he saw nature at work. Based largely on observations during his 1835 *Beagle* voyage, Darwin formulated his theory of evolution by natural selection – and sparked a conceptual revolution like no other, a revolution which shook the foundations of Christianity. And now, as no other historian has done, Edward Larson has delineated the history of the world-famous archipelago in both scientific and religious contexts.

Larson, who currently chairs the history department at the University of Georgia, is the 1998 recipient of the Pulitzer Prize in history. His works on the American creation-evolution controversy is well-known to RNCSE readers; *Evolution's Workshop* is his first work focused outside the continental United States. It is a thoroughly enjoyable read, filled with vivid descriptions of the Galápagos. These truly oceanic islands are volcanic outcroppings several hundred miles off the Ecuadorian coast, inhabited by outlandish creatures such as the famed giant tortoises (Galápagos is Spanish for "tortoises"), marine and land iguanas, and of course Darwin's finches.

The Galápagos tortoises, so far isolated from the mainland yet clearly unable to swim, were difficult to fit into classical European concepts of natural history prior to Darwin's time. William Paley's natural theology, the dominant paradigm of 19th-century European science, described all species as immutable creations of a munificent God, intended for beautification of the earth and for exploitation by man. Certainly the Galápagos, whose only edible fauna consisted of blue-footed boobies and the plug-ugly tortoises, were an embarrassment to God, or perhaps, as Herman Melville portrayed them, a penal colony for fallen souls.

In the chapter entitled "What Darwin Saw", Larson elegantly lays out the central questions posed by the Galápagos and how they led Darwin to his theory of evolution by natural selection. Some such questions are as follows: If all species are immutable, intended for the service of mankind, why should God bother to put multiple varieties of finch, iguana, and so on, on uninhabited islands isolated hundreds of miles out to sea? Why should the many species of Galápagos finch, for example, bear clear anatomical relationships to mainland species, yet occur in a much wider variety of forms than on the mainland? And if Genesis is correct about the Noachian flood, how did the giant tortoises, helpless nonswimmers, ever arrive there? It turns out that the patterns of speciation on the Galápagos are repeated again and again on oceanic islands all over the world; ever since Darwin, considerable study has been devoted to the phenomenon of adaptive radiation in populations of plants and animals isolated on such islands.

In short, Darwin recognized that species are neither immutable nor particularly intended for anything other than propagation of their own offspring and that islands like the Galápagos are ideal places for the evolution of new species from isolated founder populations. On the mainland, there are many genera of birds filling all available niches: woodpeckers, thrushes, snail darters, and other birds compete with finches for food resources and nesting sites. But when an early founder population of finches arrived on the Galápagos, perhaps blown there by a storm, they found an absence of competition from other birds. Hence the finches were free to evolve large nut-cracking beaks, sharp fruit-piercing beaks and tree-, shrub- and ground-nesting habits. The ensuing adaptive radiation led to the remarkable diversity noted by Darwin. Small wonder that on his return, he waited 20 years to publish the dangerous implications of his findings.

The world has never recovered from what Daniel Dennett called *Darwin's Dangerous Idea* and, understandably enough, Darwin's association with the Galápagos has eclipsed all others in the popular imagination. Yet Darwin's work inevitably drew others to the archipelago – David Porter of the United States Navy; Louis Agassiz, premier American naturalist of the 19th century and founder of the Harvard Museum of Natural History; bizarre English plutocrat Lord Walter Rothschild, and multiple expeditions from the California Academy of Sciences (CAS) visited the Galápagos between the mid-19th and early 20th centuries. Larson deftly introduces us to each character in his turn. We learn that Agassiz, an adherent of natural theology, was obsessed with the islands as evidence against Darwin's theory of evolution and returned there on multiple expeditions, undeterred by failing health and mishaps including loss of all his specimens at sea. Rothschild and the CAS competed for the largest, most impressive collection of giant tortoises – the former brought an even gross of them to his estate at Tring Park, and ordered more and more expeditions to fill in "gaps" in his collection on learning of new acquisitions in California. The overall impression one is left with after reading these chapters is one of plunder – the philosophy of manifest destiny inspired the Californians to "stake their claim" in the Galápagos, and like Rothschild, they were determined to "save species for Science" even if it meant driving them to extinction in their native habitats. Accompanying photos document the backbreaking labor it took to move some of the last giant tortoises, many of which weighed a quarter ton, from their inland refuges down to the boats.

Predictably enough, the early 20th century did not bring with it a respite from plunder of the Galápagos fauna. Theodore Roosevelt inspired a generation of young men to adventurism and "taming of the wilderness"; some of these were tycoons such as Vincent Astor, Marshall Field, and Harrison Williams, who built a financial empire in the 1920s on the electrical power boom. Millionaires' yachts were converted to scientific collection vessels such as the Noma, which carried explorer William Beebe on a much-publicized expedition to the Galápagos in 1923. The Noma was equipped with specially heated tanks to house live specimens for the return trip; Beebe's collection went to the New York Zoological Society.

The turning point in human attitude towards the Galápagos seems to have come with World War II. The United States established an airbase there, and bored GIs conducted iguana races and taunted the native goats; of even greater ecological impact were the mainland introduced species such as mice, which overran the island of Baltra. The presence of the military base, with its 1000 personnel, stimulated the economy of the local Ecuadorian colony and swelled the islands' human population; despite the wartime stimulus, however, the desperately poor settlers often needed to slaughter tortoises and other native fauna for food. The burgeoning science of ecology came to the rescue: following the war, ecologists such as Iranäus Eibl-Eibesfeldt and Robert Bowman visited the archipelago and publicly condemned the extinction of native species from Baltra and other islands.

The prominent British evolutionist Julian Huxley soon became involved in efforts to establish a permanent scientific research station on the Galápagos. His efforts within UNESCO (United Nations Educational, Scientific, and Cultural Organization) soon accomplished that goal, and the Charles Darwin Foundation for Galápagos Research was created in 1959, in time for the centennial of the publication of the Origin of Species. Ecuadorian officials had realized the archipelago's value as a tourist commodity and underwrote conservation efforts through the establishment of strict environmental laws in the resident human colony.

The latter half of the 20th century, thankfully, has seen some recovery in populations of endangered species on the larger islands: giant tortoises, for example, still reside in the highlands of Indefatigable, and one can see marine iguanas in the remote bays. Larson traces in detail scientific debates of this more recent period, such as the one between Bowman and ornithologist David Lack on the evolutionary basis for adaptive radiation in Darwin's finches: Lack held that interspecies competition had contributed to speciation, while Bowman stressed differences in food as the only necessary selective force. Canadian finch researchers Rosemary and Peter Grant later published results indicating somewhat of a middle ground: all finch populations exhibited selection for and against specific food types; however, the non-random occurrence of particular combinations of species on certain islands strongly suggested interspecies competition.

Grant quoted geneticist JBS Haldane during a 1977 lecture as follows:

> "There are still a number of people who do not believe in the theory of evolution. Scientists believe in it, not because it is an attractive theory, but because it enables them to make predictions which come true."

Of course creationists still see things differently, even on the Galápagos: Larson quotes a contributor to the Creation Research Society Quarterly as follows:

> "The birds are all still finches, and there is no evidence of change of the magnitude which macroevolution would require."

Christian evolutionists such as David Lack and Alister Hardy labored to reconcile nonscientific believers with their discipline; for them, as Larson quotes Stephen Jay Gould, God and science were "non-overlapping magisteria". Darwin himself is quoted on God:

> "I feel most deeply that the whole subject is too profound for the human intellect. A dog might as well speculate on the mind of Newton. Let each man hope and believe what he can."

While the creation-evolution debate continues into the 21st century, both sides clearly value the archipelago for their own ends. Conservation efforts have been aided immeasurably by Ecuadorian national park status and publicity including visits by journalists Annie Dillard and Richard Atcheson. The present volume itself has helped to raise consciousness about the Galápagos, and preserve their flora and fauna for study by future generations.

In sum, Larson's book is a thorough, meticulously annotated history of what Loren Eiseley has called "actually the most famous islands in the world". This book will also engage the casual reader, particularly those interested in the science-religion dialog on human origins. This evolutionist accords *Evolution's Workshop* his highest recommendation. ∞

[ABOUT THE AUTHOR]

Michael Chapman is an academic evolutionist who has worked with students of all levels, from 6th grade through graduate school. His research interests include non-Darwinian evolution, non-Mendelian inheritance and the evolution of human moral systems. Dr. Chapman teaches in the Biology Department, College of the Holy Cross, Worcester, Massachusetts.

[ADDITIONAL RESOURCES]

Metanexus: The Online Forum on Religion and Science: http://www.metanexus.net

NCSE Reports: http://www.ncseweb.org/newsletter.asp

Edward J. Larson's faculty page: http://www.lawsch.uga.edu/academics/profiles/larson.html

*Mercutio is the pseudonym for David Simpson, a journalist in Zambia, Africa. Simpson's news piece appeared in the **Zambia Post** for Darwin Day 2002.*

News:
Darwin Day Is Here
by Mercutio

Tuesday 12 February is Darwin Day. The event, recently introduced, is intended to lead up to the bicentennial celebration in 2009 of the birth of Charles Darwin on 12 February 1809.

Over one hundred events are scheduled throughout the world, in USA, UK, Canada, New Zealand, with support from South America, China, Japan, Russia, and across Europe.

Events include lectures, exhibitions, scavenger hunts, an evolutionary fashion show, "look-alike" contests and a fish fry! I hope Zambia can participate in the celebrations in some way, so that the importance of this man who changed the thinking of the world can be recognised here.

It's a great opportunity to try to persuade the fundamentalists that their notion of biblical inerrancy is wrong. This is very difficult, because their views are fixed by what they read in the Bible, regardless of how well it accords with scientific observations.

But if they claim to be amenable to reason, let them consider the scientific view, and all the corroborative evidence which has been recorded in the 143 years since the publication of *The Origin of Species*.

Darwin's Theory of Evolution, says Daniel Dennett, is "the single best idea anybody has ever had." Dennett, well-known author and Professor of Philosophy at Tufts University, USA, may be overstating it, but his point is clear.

Fundamentalists dismiss evolution as just a theory. They seem unaware that the word "theory", in scientific use, does not mean some wild assumption, but an idea based on careful observation, and capable of being tested by further experiment and observation.

It can never be the "absolute truth" which the fundamentalists seek. The world does not work that way. It is simply the conclusion which best fits the available evidence.

In fact there is no "absolute truth". The Bible contains a few moral examples, devised by people at a particular time and place. It also includes some ludicrous tales, and many contradictions, written and collated by humans, not by a divine power.

Everything the Bible tells us must be sifted through the net of reason, plausibility, and correspondence with the discoveries of science. Critical analysis is what is needed – not the bullying and ranting of the pastors.

Personal experience of God may appear real to some people of a certain mentality or disposition. But it has no possibility of objective proof, and is probably a psychological aberration.

Darwin was a careful scientist. His theory was based on minute observations of the wildlife he encountered on the voyage of the *Beagle* round South America, and in particular in the Galápagos Islands, where there is a research station named after him.

From the website www.darwinday.org:

> "Darwin Day recognizes and celebrates the achievements of a man who cast a bright, explanatory light on reality, our self-knowledge, and on the world of which we are a part. Charles Darwin contributed to our understanding at the deepest level and forever changed the way we see ourselves in this vast, impersonal universe. He brought about a paradigm shift of epic proportions."

Darwin's birthplace, Down House in Kent, England, has been open as a museum since 1929, and contains over 6,500 items of memorabilia and materials explaining the march of evolution. And London's Natural History Museum opens its Darwin Centre in September 2002.

The Darwin Correspondence project is publishing Darwin's complete letters in 30 volumes. The letters show he was an opponent of slavery and a supporter of local charitable works; a careful investor, and a generous friend and patron.

The Darwin Bulldog membership club commemorates the first "Darwin Bulldog", zoologist Thomas Huxley, who defended evolution against those who sought to ridicule the idea.

Bishop Samuel Wilberforce, in the Oxford Debate of 1860, asked: "Would you prefer to be descended from an ape on the side of your grandfather or your grandmother?"

Huxley replied: "It would not have occurred to me to bring forward such a topic as that for discussion myself, but if the question is put to me, would I rather have a miserable ape for a grandfather, or a man highly endowed by nature and possessed of great means and influence, and yet who employs these faculties and that influence for the mere purpose of introducing ridicule into a grave scientific discussion, I unhesitatingly affirm my preference for the ape."

But let Darwin himself speak: "There is grandeur in this view of life, with its several powers, having been originally breathed into a few forms or into one; and that, whilst this planet has gone cycling on according to the fixed law of gravity, from so simple a beginning endless forms most beautiful and most wonderful have been, and are being, evolved." – *The Origin of Species* (1859)

"Freedom of thought will best be promoted by that gradual enlightening of the human understanding which follows the progress of science. I have therefore always avoided writing about religion and have confined myself to science." – Charles Darwin, 1880, in *The Life and Letters of Charles Darwin* (Francis Darwin, Editor)

Nevertheless Darwin gradually came to accept that, in view of the scientific evidence, the biblical tale of the Creation was no more than a myth, and that the "Creator" himself might not exist. The story that Darwin retracted his scepticism on his deathbed is untrue. His wife spread this tale after his death, fearing the social stigma of having an unbeliever for a husband.

The president of the Darwin Day programme is the well-known biologist Richard Dawkins, who describes the theory of evolution as the "universal solvent", meaning that it pulls together so many strands of scientific knowledge and through them solves many of the puzzles of who we are, where we came from, and where we are going.

The lessons we can learn from Darwin are: observe carefully, record faithfully, analyse accordingly, and when the results contradict received wisdom, have faith in yourself.

[ABOUT THE AUTHOR]

David Simpson, born UK 1934, has been a Zambian citizen since 1965. He has edited various government and private publications and has represented the media on various boards, including notably the Media Institute of Southern Africa, and its Zambian chapter the Zambia Independent Media Association, and the Open Society Initiative in Southern Africa (a wing of the George Soros Foundation). He now works as a freelance writer and contributes a weekly skeptical column (now in its sixth year) to *The Post* under the pseudonym Mercutio.

[ADDITIONAL RESOURCES]

The Post is the only independent daily newspaper in the constitutionally-declared "Christian nation" of Zambia. It began as the Weekly Post in 1991, when it contributed significantly to the campaign to oust the UNIP government under the then president Kenneth Kaunda. Since then it has also become highly critical of the governance record of the ruling Movement for Multiparty Democracy, under Frederick Chiluba and now Levy Mwanawasa. The editor, Fred M'membe, was a founder member of the Media Institute of Southern Africa. He has been imprisoned for his fearless criticism of the Zambian authorities, which has won him several international awards. *The Post* can be accessed online at: http://www.post.co.zm

But seriously, folks...
What's Wrong with the Darwin Awards?

by Molleen Matsumura

One of my all-time favorite cartoons showed a man telling a woman, "Do you know feminists don't have any sense of humor?" She replied, "No, but hum a few bars and I'll fake it." In breaking down barriers to full political and professional participation, feminists had to question a broad range of practices, including grammar, etiquette and humor. Sometimes, as this cartoon illustrates, they had to point out that if a joke was funny at all, the joke was on the teller.

Could this be the case with the Darwin Awards? There are good arguments that folks reading the Awards should think twice (maybe even blush a little) after laughing, if not before; and definitely engage brain before clicking the forward button in their email programs.

In case you've managed not to hear of the Darwin Awards, I'll explain: they are not a prize for advances in evolutionary science. They are a brand of internet story: sometimes taken as truth and always as humor, they are short anecdotes about individuals who are recognized for doing the human species a favor by "removing themselves from the gene pool" through acts of extreme stupidity. An example is the tale of a man who, sleepily reaching for a ringing telephone, took a gun from his night-stand, put it to his ear and shot himself. These aren't just any prize fools; they get the *Darwin* prize because their deaths supposedly demonstrate "evolution in action". At odd times, people get these anecdotes in email, singly or in batches, and then forward them to friends. The Darwin Awards have spawned numerous "official" and unofficial websites, and speculations that they are among the most popular internet chain letters; at any rate, the first Award anthology spent five months on the *New York Times* best seller list.[1]

If you already know about the Darwin Awards, odds are you've laughed at many of them. You've got enough company that you can afford to consider the possibility that sometimes, the joke is on the reader. First ask whether folks can get so busy laughing they forget to exercise due skepticism. The answer is often "yes". It's scientifically proven – at any rate, it's been proven by a scientist. New Mexican scientist Mark Boslough got a list of Awards in his email one day in 1999, and decided to see what would happen if he made up "the most outrageous and twisted death-by-stupidity tale [he] could imagine", added it to the end of the list, and sent it to a few friends. He even made sure the story's characters had names like Baker, Burns, and Cooke that matched the story-line a little too well. The result? Within eight months, the tale was printed in a column in the *Denver Post!* (After hearing from Boslough, the columnist printed a retraction; you can read all about it, and savor Boslough's puns, at http://www.nmsr.org/darwiner.htm.)

Now, some people have questioned some of the stories. Debunkings appear on urban legend websites and in the pages of Award anthologies. Still, many of these tales are swallowed whole, and there's a certain tasty irony at the thought of people laughing at *somebody else's* "stupidity" just when they've taken the bait of an internet legend.

So far, sounds fairly harmless. After all, laughing at yourself can be one of the less painful ways of learning not to believe everything you read. But after the first blush, a more serious question needs to be asked. What do the Darwin Awards mean in a society where public understanding of evolution is poor, and evolution education is continuously under attack? I should explain first that I am passionate concerning this issue. For over seven years my profession was defending the teaching of evolution in public schools. I lost count of how many times the Darwin Awards were emailed to me during those years; my reaction was always, "This doesn't help!" Here's why.

The Darwin Awards are thriving in a climate of ignorance. In the U.S., limited public understanding of science has been documented in the National Science Board's (NSB) biennial *Science and Engineering Indicators*[2]. (This is not to say that there are not problems with scientific literacy elsewhere – as one example below will show – but I am emphasizing evolution understanding *in the U.S.*)

In its 2002 survey, the NSB found, as in earlier years, that, "Most Americans do not know a lot about [science and technology]...," and, "A majority of Americans (about 70 percent) lack a clear understanding of the scientific process..."[3] Where evolution is concerned, the NSB reports that, "For the first time, a majority (53 percent) of NSF survey respondents answered 'true' to the statement 'human beings, as we know them today, developed from earlier species of animals,' bringing the United States more in line with other industrialized countries in response to this question." That's a slim majority, and worse, *when the survey group was asked whether "The earliest humans lived at the same time as the dinosaurs", only 48% answered correctly (down from 51% in the last survey).* These findings are consistent with repeated Gallup poll findings that nearly half [4] of Americans agree that "God created human beings pretty much in their present form at one time within the last 10,000 years or so," and it is likely that a large portion of these answers are due to scientific illiteracy, not religious belief.[5] Also, the NSB noted, "On a 10-question 'pop quiz' on biotechnology, most Americans, Europeans, and Canadians gave the incorrect answer (true) to the statement "ordinary tomatoes do not contain genes, while genetically modified tomatoes do."

The survey also found that Americans get most of their information on recent developments in science and technology by watching television, but when they want answers to *specific* science questions, most people turn to the Internet. Then what do they find? To check this, I visited seven major search engines – such as Yahoo and Google – and searched on the word "Darwin". In every case, references to the Darwin Awards appeared on the first page of links, and on six pages, the top of the screen displayed "meta-links" to sets of links for common topics, including numerous sites about the Darwin Awards. Searching on "evolution" was better, yielding links to sources of accurate and engaging information about evolution; unfortunately, the first page of links for either search also yielded links to creationist sites (where evolution is frequently described as *Darwinism*). Add to these results the likelihood that more people get emails about the Darwin awards than about, say, major fossil discoveries, and the picture that emerges is one in which a common source of "information" about Darwin and evolution is the *misinformation* people get from the Darwin Awards.

The premises of the Darwin Awards match existing misconceptions about evolution. By "premise", I mean the joke's assumptions about reality. Any joke has them, even when the humor depends on stretching them. For example, when a cartoon character steps off a cliff, they may fall and smash into sharp edged bits, fall and bounce like a rubber ball, or flap their arms a bit before falling, but in every case the (true) premise is that people who step off cliffs fall. The joke would fall flat for a viewer who was ignorant of gravity.

There isn't room to discuss all the misconceptions; I'll mention two. The most obvious is that Awardees' genes are removed from the gene pool. Awardees are always adults, who have had plenty of time to reproduce plenty of times. Natural selection depends on people lasting *long enough to reproduce*. It is just this kind of detail that makes it hard to teach and learn about evolution.

The most serious problem is the premise that, "These people deserve to die." I'll admit the most tempting tales are the ones about would-be murderers caught in their own traps. But many (more?) stories are about people who are just trying to have a good time, or to survive. The Darwin Awards promote the idea that "evolution in action" means nothing more than weeding out the "unfit", coupled with over-simplified notions of fitness. They reinforce the perception creationists strenuously cultivate: that evolution is a doctrine of cruelty, and the foundation of racism.[6] A public that isn't well educated about evolution is susceptible to such claims. Witness the legislation introduced in Louisiana in 2001, which would have curtailed the teaching of evolution on grounds that "… the core concepts of Darwinist ideology [are] that certain races and classes of humans are inherently superior to others…"[7]

A related problem is that scientists working to defend evolution are frequently accused of "arrogance". One reason is that they are seen through the lens of popular ideas about evolution. There is a Darwin Award that I believe merits the charge of arrogance; it isn't a far-fetched tale of elaborate machinations gone wrong, but a story of misfortune that actually was reported in newspapers. It is the story of an Egyptian farmer who climbed into a well to retrieve a chicken; he, and those who attempted to save him, were drowned by an unsuspected underground stream. As I write this, in August 2002, some coal miners who survived drilling into a water-filled shaft, and those who worked to save them, are being hailed as heroes. This isn't the first such mining accident, and when miners drown it's called a tragedy. Both the farmer and the miners took miscalculated risks while trying to make a living. The farmer is judged "stupid" because we forget that to a subsistence farmer, a chicken can be a serious economic loss. This comparison reminds us that it is easy to misjudge what is "stupid" or ignorant, rash or heroic.

Scientists from Stephen Jay Gould to Joseph Graves[8] have worked hard to dissociate evolutionary theory from misconceptions about "genetic superiority". Such work is vital to breaking down resistance to evolution education, which in turn is crucial to good public understanding of science. The premise of the Darwin Awards undermines that work.

Many jokes stop being funny precisely when people take them seriously. Possibly the humor of the Darwin Awards would be more innocent, and even funnier, in a world in which evolution is better understood. As it is, I urge people who really honor Darwin's rich legacy to pass along other facts and fantasies. Samples of silly creationist pseudoscience might be a good choice!

[ABOUT THE AUTHOR]

Molleen Matsumura is Executive Director of the American Foundation for Health, which sponsors innovative medical research. Her long-standing interest in public understanding of science led to her work as senior editor at *BASE* and its successor publication *Science21*, magazines showcasing the research of young scientists. For seven years, she was Network Project Director at the National Center for Science Education, where she worked to defend evolution education in public schools, and edited *Voices for Evolution*. She has done considerable public speaking on evolution-creation controversies, and her articles and interviews on the topic have appeared in *Reports of the National Center for Education*, *Free Inquiry*, *Conversations* (a publication of the United Church of Christ), *Humanistic Judaism*, and *Church and State*.

[REFERENCES]

1 Comments in this article are not directed to the Darwin Awards anthologies, though I do refer to them. I realize that, to her credit, the author attempts some serious education in the books and an associated website, but I haven't read them thoroughly and am not reviewing them. I'm discussing the role of the Awards in daily life, as people forward them as email, discuss them with friends, and so forth.

2 National Science Foundation, Division of Science Resources Statistics, *Science and Engineering Indicators–2002*; Arlington, VA (NSB 02-01) [April 2002] Fifteen such surveys have been issued to date. They study many aspects of science and technology, such as workforce, education, and research funding; here I draw on the chapter surveying public attitudes and knowledge concerning science. Internet Links to *Science and Engineering Indicators* (SEI) published from 1993-2002 are at http://www.nsf.gov/sbe/srs/seind/start.htm . A CD ROM containing .pdf files of *SEI 2002* can be requested online at http://www.nsf.gov/sbe/srs/seind02/cdseind.htm, or by email to paperpubs@nsf.gov. Emails should request by both publication number NSB 02-01C and title *Science and Engineering Indicators–2002*

3 The number who could explain in their own words what a molecule is had climbed to 22% – yet strangely, 45% could give an acceptable explanation of DNA, which after all is a molecule. Answers to single survey questions are of limited value, but the entire set of questions and other discussion in the report support these conclusions.

4 An average of 45.5% over four polls

5 Matsumura, Molleen, "Is It Fair to Teach Evolution?" *Reports of the National Center for Science Education*, 19(3): 19-21

6 For example, the Institute for Creation Research's *Impact* series of pamphlets includes titles like *The Ascent Of Racism* (online at http://www.icr.org/pubs/imp/imp-164.htm) and "Evolution and Modern Racism" (http://www.answersingenesis.org/home/area/faq/racism.asp). The Answers In Genesis website lists 15 articles linking evolution and racism, plus cross-references (http://www.answersingenesis.org/home/area/faq/racism.asp). Pictures are especially vivid: When I visited the Institute for Creation Research museum, they displayed a "tree of evolution" bearing evil fruits like racism (plus others you wouldn't agree are evil). A colorful "tree" depicting evolution as equivalent to killing and suffering can be seen online at http://www.answersingenesis.org/home/area/overheads/pages/oh20010316_4.asp, a cartoon setting racism on a foundation of evolution is at http://www.answersingenesis.org/home/area/overheads/pages/oh20010316_2.asp

7 [Anonymous]. Updates. Reports of the National Center for Science Education 2000 Sep/Oct; 20 (5): pp. 9-10.

8 Graves, Joseph L., Jr. *The Emperor's New Clothes: Biological Theories of Race at the Millenium* (New Jersey, Rutgers University Press: 2001); Gould, Stephen Jay, *The Mismeasure of Man* (W J Norton, 1996). The expanded 1996 edition includes a critique of *The Bell Curve*.

[ADDITIONAL RESOURCES]

The Beak of the Finch: A Story of Evolution in Our Time
   by Jonathan Weiner
   This Pulitzer Prize-winning book is a fascinating, highly readable account of Peter and Rosemary Grant's 20-plus years of studying the effects of natural selection among "Darwin's Finches" on an isolated Galapagos isle.

Natural Selection: Domains, Levels, and Challenges
   by George C. Williams
   For those inclined to read a more technical and scholarly treatment of evolution, this volume in the Oxford Series in Evolution and Ecology (published by Oxford University Press) is a masterful treatment of natural selection in evolutionary theory, including discussion of different approaches to different levels of selection.

At the Water's Edge: Fish With Fingers, Whales With Legs, and How Life Came Ashore but Then Went Back to Sea
   by Carl Zimmer
   Drawing on the latest fossil discoveries and breakthrough scientific analysis, Zimmer tells the story of how ocean-dwelling vertebrates adapted to life on dry land, and in some cases returned to a marine way of life. Inevitably, this engaging tale applies and elucidates fundamental principles of evolution.

[AUTHOR'S NOTE]

I would like to thank Dr. Eugenie Scott, Executive Director of the National Center for Science Education, for her assistance in selecting these resources.

BOOK REVIEW:
HORRIBLE SCIENCE: EVOLVE OR DIE
*by Phil Gates,
illustrated by Tony de Saulles
Scholastic Hippo*

Review by Vicki Hyde

"The thing that biology teachers need to remember is that life is a story." So says Phil Gates before plunging into the fascinating, amazing, terrible story of life. He's right about the approach...
Like all the books in the Horrible series, it's a great romp, with a lot of information cleverly hidden within the jokes, cartoons and anecdotes. Gates has got a very good eye for great analogies – I particularly appreciated the one using the differences in American and British English as an analogy of geographic isolation leading to speciation! And I'm definitely going to test out his custard and chips (aka chippies, potato crisps) demo of continental drift next time the kids ask for something interesting to do.

My nine-year-old and seven-year-old sons thoroughly enjoyed the book (sections on petrified poo amused the former clown and intrigued the latter would-be palaeontologist), and it was handy to have around when my mother asked me to explain about evolution after a run-in with a devout neighbour.

Gates doesn't shy away from the controversy associated with evolution, including the famous quotes from the Wilberforce and Huxley debates. His description of human evolution is clear enough for a kid to know that we aren't descended from apes. There are a couple of minor quibbles – I'd argue that hominids now include our hairier close cousins and I think the number of possible species is a tad inflated. That said, he covers a great deal of ground quickly and memorably.

I like the fact that Gates is happy to describe the uncertainty the underlies science, highlights the delight of discovery, and has demonstrable fun in what he calls the "epic adventure" of evolution.

This book deserves to be on your bookshelf or in your school library.

[ABOUT THE AUTHOR]

Vicki Hyde is a science popularizer by choice; a Website development manager by profession. Vicki has been awarded the Science and Technology Medal of New Zealand and has been made a Companion of the Royal Society of New Zealand. The Web-based *SciTech Daily Review* edited by Vicki was a nominee in the Sixth Annual Webby Awards, recognized as one of the top five science sites in the world. Vicki has been Chair-entity of the New Zealand Skeptics for ten years.

[ADDITIONAL RESOURCES]

Sci-Tech Daily: http://www.scitechdaily.com

New Zealand Skeptics: http://skeptics.org.nz/

Royal Society of New Zealand: http://www.rsnz.govt.nz/

This piece is adapted from a press release sent out by the Natural History Museum in London, England for Darwin Day 2002 and reprinted here with permission from the Museum.

THE NATURAL HISTORY MUSEUM MARKS THE ANNIVERSARY OF CHARLES DARWIN'S BIRTHDAY

by Rachel Craddock and Debbie Chapman

Recently voted by the UK public as one of the greatest Britons of all time, Charles Darwin is now the focus of a new international campaign to establish an annual celebration of his birthday, 12 February.

To mark this day, the Natural History Museum in London, England invited photographers to view previously unseen specimens collected by Darwin that will be housed in the new Darwin Centre.

The first phase of the Darwin Centre project, named to reflect and honour Darwin's importance to natural history, opened to the public in September, 2002. The Centre houses 22 million zoological specimens, an important index of the natural world and never before seen by the public. The collection includes many historic specimens including lizards collected by Darwin during his historic HMS *Beagle* expedition.

The Darwin Centre also provides new state-of-the-art facilities for many of the Natural History Museum's scientists and allows visitors an opportunity to find out about the exciting discoveries that these scientists make year upon year. Phase Two of the Darwin Centre is currently in the planning phase and will open to the public in 2007.

The Darwin Day Program aims to create global celebrations on this day building up to 2009, the bicentennial of Darwin's birth. Richard Dawkins FRS, Honorary President of the organisation and Charles Simonyi Professor of Public Understanding of Science at Oxford University, believes that "Along with Newton and Shakespeare, Darwin is Britain's greatest gift to the world. But Darwin is not just a historic figure. His guiding genius hovers over all of modern biology, and this will be excitingly evident in the Darwin Centre of the Natural History Museum."

[ADDITIONAL RESOURCES]

Darwin Center: Inspiring Discovery of the Natural World: http://www.nhm.ac.uk/darwincentre/

The Natural History Museum, London: http://www.nhm.ac.uk/

For further information please contact Rachel Craddock on 020 7942 5881 or Debbie Chapman on 020 7942 5880, or email R.Craddock@nhm.ac.uk or D.Chapman@nhm.ac.uk

Adrian Barnett's review originally appeared in **New Scientist**, *an enchanting and informative mix of the latest science and technology news from around the world. The review is republished here with permission from the author and* **New Scientist**.

Reprinted with permission. Copyright © 2002 by **New Scientist**. *All Rights Reserved.*

BOOK REVIEW:
STUFFED ANIMALS AND PICKLED HEADS: THE CULTURE AND EVOLUTION OF NATURAL HISTORY MUSEUMS

by Stephen T. Asma
Oxford University Press

Review by Adrian Barnett

Charles O'Brien stood 8' 2". Billed as the 'Irish Giant', O'Brien was terrified that his body would be boiled for its highly exhibitable skeleton and made a deathbed arrangement to be leadweighted and buried at sea. But John Hunter, the (in)famous British anatomist, bribed O'Brien's fishermen and boiled the corpse in his Earles Court home. The skeleton stands in the Hunterian Museum to this day.

Hunter may have been extreme in his devotion to obtaining specimens, but he was far from alone in his belief that public exposure to the diversity of the natural word was a good and noble thing. Tracking the history of natural history museums from their earliest curiosity-cabinet beginnings to the magnificence of today's interactive computer displays, Asma shows how such institutions have always been the outward manifestations of the current philosophy of science and the sociology of it's handmaiden, education.

As full of curious facts and mental treats as any museum display, this fascinating book shows there is more behind the museum facade than a covey of busy biologists: there is a whole history of the academic's perception of how their work and discoveries should be presented to the public at large. "After reading this book museum goers will not be able to look at exhibits in the same way again", avows the author. He has every chance of success. ∽

[ABOUT THE AUTHOR]

Adrian Barnett is a tropical ecologist with the University of Surrey Roehampton, England and a research associate in the California Academy of Sciences' Anthropology Department.

[ADDITIONAL RESOURCES]

New Scientist online: http://www.newscientist.com/

Sherrie Lyons' paper was presented at the Center for Inquiry's 2002 Darwin Day event & Fish Fry in Amherst, NY.

Convincing Men They Are Monkeys
Sherrie L. Lyons

Darwin's theory continues to be the most important and unifying theory for the life sciences, having far-reaching applications in diverse fields from biogeography to neurobiology. But I am going to talk about what clearly was in Darwin's time and unfortunately still remains today the most controversial aspect of Darwin's theory – the implications for humans. Now Darwin clearly thought humans were a part of Nature's evolutionary scheme, but *The Origin* did not directly discuss the evolution of man. Instead there was only his cryptic comment: "Light will be thrown on the origin of man and his history."[1] Who immediately saw the light was Thomas Huxley. Unlike Darwin who avoided controversy and did not like being in the public eye, Huxley thrived on conflict. Dubbing himself Darwin's bulldog, he wrote Darwin that he was prepared to go to the stake if necessary in defense of Darwin's bold new theory.

Huxley entered the fray very early on. *The Origin* was published in November of 1859. In a famous encounter with Bishop Samuel Wilberforce at Oxford in 1860 in which the Bishop asked Huxley whether "it was on his grandfather's or his grandmother's side that the ape ancestry comes in."[2] Huxley replied

> ... a man has no reason to be ashamed of having an ape for his grandfather. If there were an ancestor whom I should feel shame in recalling it would rather be a man – a man of restless and versatile intellect – who, not content with an equivocal success in his own sphere of activity, plunges into scientific questions with which he has no real acquaintance, only to obscure them by an aimless rhetoric, and distract the attention of his hearers from the real point at issue by eloquent digressions and skilled appeals to religious prejudice.[3]

Such a reply created an uproar. According to one account ladies fainted.

Huxley correctly perceived that the most threatening aspect of Darwin's theory was its significance for human origins and thus this was where he initially devoted most of his energy. While scientists argued whether natural selection could account for species change, whether change was abrupt or gradual, and a myriad of other aspects of the theory, this was not the fundamental quarrel with *The Origin*. Rather, opponents of

Darwin's theory attacked his book, claiming it was materialistic, atheistic, and worse. Huxley published *Evidence as to Man's Place in Nature*, in 1863, eight years before Darwin published his *Descent of Man*. In his book Huxley argued eloquently and powerfully that humans were no exception to the theory of evolution. Huxley's defense is still timely. Creation science supposedly is attacking Darwin's theory on "scientific grounds," but just as Huxley recognized, the scientific objections in the last analysis boiled down to the question: "Where was God?" This remains true today from the proponents of Creation science. I think we could do well to re-visit and adapt the strategies of Huxley so here I'm going to highlight some of the serious, but also more humorous aspects of "Convincing Men They Are Monkeys," chapter six of my biography of Thomas Henry Huxley.

First of all, people had long been fascinated with the similarity of apes to humans. The exact relationship between humans and other primates had long been a subject of intense debate among taxonomists. Do apes think? Are they moral beings? Do they build societies and social structures? Facts and mythology had intermingled resulting in much confusion over the classification of these animals. Were present day human races derived from distinct species or just varieties of one species? In spite of this great interest in "man's place in nature" most people were deeply opposed to anything which broke down the barrier between humans and the rest of the animal world as this undermined the basic tenets of Christianity. Huxley's approach to the problem was twofold. First he believed that the classification of humans should be determined independently of any theories of origination of species. Such a position removed the question of human ancestry from theological concerns. If he could demonstrate unequivocally the close relationship between apes and humans, he believed this would be the most powerful support for Darwin's theory, because Darwin provided a clear logical explanation for the existence of those relationships. But Huxley recognized that many people would be appalled at the idea of an ape as an ancestor. He argued passionately and articulately that a pithecoid ancestry in no way degraded humankind.

Huxley realized that before he could discuss anatomical and physiological evidence, he had to convince his audience that such a view in no way detracted from the dignity of humankind. Huxley claimed that it didn't matter whether man's origin was distinct from all other animals or whether he was the result of modification from another mammal. "[H]is duties and his aspirations must, I apprehend, remain the same. The proof of his claim to independent parentage will not change the brutishness of man's lower nature nor... will man's pithecoid pedigree one whit diminish man's divine right of kinship over nature."[4] Human dignity, according to Huxley, was not inherited, but rather "to be won by each of us so far as he consciously seeks good and avoids evil, and puts the faculties with which he is endowed to its fittest use."[5] Thus, for Huxley, all aspects of human nature, both "brutishness" and "princely dignity" would have to be accounted for independently of the question of human origins.[6] If he could convince his readers that the highly charged issues concerning man's morals and ethics, questions of good and evil, were not relevant to the question of human origins, the problem of classification could be investigated objectively and dispassionately. Thus, Huxley did not directly address the problem of whether humans were descended from an ape-like ancestor. Instead, he asked how closely related were apes and humans, approaching the question just as a taxonomist would investigate how closely related were the cat and the dog.

How humans had been classified ran the whole gamut from Linnaeus, who classified humans as a primates to Terres, who maintained that humans were so distinctive they should have their own kingdom. Some people even believed that humans should not be thought of zoologically at all.[7] Richard Owen, whom Huxley crossed swords with on many occasions, maintained that *homo sapiens* had a unique structure in the brain called the hippocampus minor. On the basis of that and some other structures including the hallus or big toe, Owen wanted to place *Homo* in a new division, "Archencephala," which was a separate genus that was superior to the others in the mammalian class. It was rumored that Richard Owen may have been the brains behind Bishop Wilberforce's attack on evolutionary theory.

Huxley pointed out that the classification of *Homo sapiens* had been complicated because "passion and prejudice have conferred upon the battle far more importance than, as it seems to me can rationally attach to its issue."[8] Instead, the question should be strictly a scientific one that could be resolved by the facts of comparative anatomy and physiology, "independently of all theoretical views."[9] Darwin's theory, special creation, or any other theory need not even be mentioned in the investigation of the "facts" of anatomy and physiology. After such facts were established, then one could comment on how well a particular theory fit the facts. And Huxley believed the facts were well known. Citing studies in embryology and comparative anatomy, Huxley claimed that all the evidence shows that the differences between humans and the higher apes is no greater than those between the higher and lower apes. Citing numerous authorities he demolished Owen's claim that the hippocampus was a unique structure. If Darwin's hypothesis explained the common ancestry of the latter, then it followed that it also explained the origin of the former.

Not only is there a similarity in anatomical structures, but it was also apparent to Huxley that animals shared certain mental attributes with humans. Huxley appealed to the Victorians' love of their pets to demonstrate the unity of humans with the animal world.

> *The dog, the cat…return love for our love and hatred for our hatred. They are capable of shame and sorrow; and though they may have no logic nor conscious ratiocination, no one who has watched their ways can doubt that they possess that power of rational cerebrations which evolves reasonable acts from the premises furnished by the senses.*[10]

Thus, Huxley claimed a psychical as well as a physical unity existed between man and beast.

Another kind of evidence that argues for the common ancestry between apes and humans is fossils. The first Neanderthal fossils were discovered shortly after the publication of *The Origin*. But after examining the fossils, Huxley concluded that these ancient skulls were not significantly different from modern humans and thus did not represent a missing link that connected humans to apes. Nevertheless, Huxley correctly anticipated that the finds of paleontology would push the origin of humans back to a far earlier epoch than anyone had previously imagined. If humankind is that ancient, clearly this provided evidence against the creation hypothesis. Once again, the Darwinian hypothesis was the only hypothesis that could make sense of these ancient human fossils.

Huxley's presentation of the facts of development and comparative anatomy was superb. It was hard to imagine how any one could deny their ape ancestry after reading his discussion. But Huxley knew beliefs run deep and that many people would still be appalled at the inevitable conclusions to be drawn from his analysis. He knew many would argue that "the belief in the unity of origin of man and brutes involves the brutalization and degradation of the former." [11] But Huxley asked if that was really so. In a passionate entreaty, he claimed that man's dignity did not depend on his physical characteristics or his origins.

> It is not I who seek to base Man's dignity upon his great toe or insinuate that we are lost if an Ape has a hippocampus minor... On the contrary, I have done my best to sweep away this vanity... Is it, indeed, true, that the Poet, or the Philosopher, or the Artist whose genius is the glory of his age, is degraded from his high estate by the undoubted historical probability, not to say certainty, that he is the direct descendant of some naked and bestial savage... Is mother-love vile because a hen shows it, or fidelity base because dogs possess it?[12]

Just because we share admirable traits with the lower animals does not make them less admirable. Furthermore, Huxley argued that man's lowly ancestry was "the best evidence of the splendour of his capacities." Only humans are capable of intelligible and rational speech which made possible the development of culture and civilization. Even if humans *come* from the brutes, they are not *of* them. It is clear that Huxley believed a vast chasm separated us from the rest of the animal world.

Man's Place in Nature was an immediate success. Published in January of 1863, by the middle of February it had sold 2000 copies. By July it was republished in America and was being translated into French and German (*Life* 217). It continued to be reprinted for the next forty years.

The discussions over evolution and human origins had spread far beyond the staid halls of the Royal Society and the Geological Society. The hippocampus debate represented more than some esoteric scientific disagreement over an obscure part of the brain. Rather, "man's place in nature" was at stake. What made humans unique? What was the role of science in answering such a question? How could evolutionary ideas be made compatible with theology?

The personality clash between Richard Owen and Thomas Huxley played a significant role in the popular accounts of the issues. London society reveled in the squabbles between the two men and satirical accounts soon appeared over *the great hippocampus debate*. The fact that their disputes were even the subject of popular satire indicates how deeply the ape-human question had permeated society.

Punch printed a poem supposedly authored by a gorilla from the zoological gardens entitled, "Monkeyana," with a picture of an ape-like creature carrying a sign asking "Am I a Man and a Brother?" The poem was about Darwin's theory, but half of it spoofed the Owen-Huxley clash:

> *Then HUXLEY and OWEN,*
> *With rivalry glowing,*
> *With pen and ink rush to scratch;*
> *'Tis Brain versus Brain*
> *Till one of them's slain;*
> *By Jove! it will be a good match!*

Says OWEN you can see
The brain of Chimpanzee
Is always exceedingly small,
With hindermost "horn"
Of extremity shorn;
And no "Hippocampus" at all.

The Professor then tells 'em,
That man's "cerebellum,"
From a vertical point you can't see;
That each "convolution"
Contains a solution,
Of "Archencephalic" degree

Then apes have no nose.
And thumbs for great toes,
And a pelvis both narrow and slight;
They can't stand upright,
Unless to show fight,
With "Du Chaillu," that chivalrous knight!

Next HUXLEY replies,
That OWEN he lies,
And garbles his Latin quotation;
That his facts are not new,
His mistakes not a few,
Detrimental to his reputation,

"To twice slay the slain,"
By dint of the Brain,
(Thus HUXLEY concludes his review)
Is but labour in vain,
Unproductive of gain,
And so I shall bid you "Adieu!"
(18 May, 1861, 206)

This poem reveals that the debates over human ancestry also had implications for the relationship between the races. The United States was immersed in a civil war over the issue of slavery. Are not Negroes our brothers? Certainly if a gorilla is claiming to be related to humans, what does this say about all of humankind?

In 1863 George Pycroft anonymously printed a pamphlet entitled "A Sad Case". It described the imaginary courtroom proceedings of Owen and Huxley, who had been charged with disturbing the peace. The two men had been about to come to blows when the police arrived. Huxley had called Owen a "lying Orthognathous Brachcephalic Bimaneous Pithecus," while Owen had accused Huxley of being "nothing else but a thorough Archencephalic Primate"[3]. As the trial proceeded, it was apparent that the dispute was not just about whether apes had a hippocampus minor. Owen was outraged that he was being told in public that he was physically, morally, and intellectually only a little better than a gorilla[6]. But the problem went deeper than that. Huxley claimed that everything was fine, "as long as Dick Owen was top sawyer, and could keep over my head, and throw his dust down in my eyes. There was only two or three in our trade, and it was not very profitable; but that was no reason why I should be called a liar by an improved gorilla, like that fellow"[6]. The disagreements between the two men reflect the fighting for power and prestige that is occurring within the scientific community as a whole. Are Darwinian ideas going to prevail?

The most famous account of the feud between Huxley and Owen is undoubtedly by Charles Kingsley who immortalized the dispute in his satirical fairy tale *The Waterbabies*, sparing neither man in his commentary. In the first part of the book Huxley and Owen were mentioned as experts who could help evaluate whether waterbabies really existed. Later in the book, the two men appeared as caricatures of themselves. The empiricist Huxley was portrayed as the great naturalist Professor Pttmilnsprts of Necrobioneopaleonthydrochthoanthropopithekology. He held the view that "no man was forced to believe anything to be true, but what he could see, hear, taste, or handle." Furthermore, "he had even got up once at the British Association and declared that apes had hippopotamus majors in their brains just as men have" (107-09). But clearly, Kingsley was on Huxley's side. Ridiculing Owen's view, the narrator pointed out that to claim that apes had hippopotamus majors

> *was a shocking thing to say; for if it were so what would become of the faith, hope, and charity of immortal millions? You may think that there are other more important differences between you and an ape, such as being able to speak and make machines, and know right from wrong, and say your prayers, and other little matters of that kind: but that is a child's fancy my dear. Nothing is to be depended on but the great hippopotamus test. If you have a hippopotamus major in your brain, you are no ape, though you had four hands, no feet, and were more apish than the apes of all aperies. But if a hippopotamus major is ever discovered in one single ape's brain, nothing will save your great-great-great great-great-great-great-great-great-great-great-great-greater-greatest grandmother from having been an ape too. (109-10)*

This passage not only lampooned the debate over the hippocampus, but also made light of the Wilberforce-Huxley clash. (which you can read all about in Floyd Sandford's play *Darwin Remembers*)

In closing, I think there are two important and somewhat contradictory lessons we can take from Huxley's defense of Darwin that are just as relevant today. Huxley was a great empiricist. He honestly and sincerely believed that by educating people of the facts of anatomy and physiology, that the truth of evolutionary theory would become apparent. I would be the last one to deny the importance of education but Huxley was naive in his belief that a clear distinction could be made between "facts" and their interpretation. The facts do not speak for themselves. The history of science demonstrates this time and time again. In the debate over the hippocampus, the structures of the brain could not be as easily identified as either Huxley or Owen would have us believe. Even Huxley's good friend Kingsley ridiculed Huxley's extreme empiricism in his portrayal of Professor Pttmilnsprts in *The Waterbabies*.

Huxley was naive in one way, but in another way he was quite sophisticated. He understood very well the deep revulsion and fear many people felt over the possibility of an ape ancestry. He did not dismiss the anxiety people felt as stupid or silly. Instead he brought all of his considerable rhetorical skills and passion to allay those fears which would then enable him to "convince men they were monkeys."

[ABOUT THE AUTHOR]

Sherrie Lyons has her PHD from the University of Chicago. She is the author of *Thomas Henry Huxley, the Evolution of a Scientist*. Her most recent manuscript examines three cases of marginal science: spiritualism, phrenology, and sea serpent investigations in the context of evolutionary theory in the Victorian period.

[REFERENCES]

1. C. Darwin, *The Origin of Species* (London: John Murray, 1859, New York: Avenel, 1979), 458.

2. Quoted by Rev. W.H. Freemantle, "Account of the Oxford Meeting," 1892, *LLTHH* 1, p. 200.

3. T. Huxley, 1860, Quoted by John Green in a letter to Boyd Dawkins. Reprinted in *LLTHH* 1, p. 199. Oddly enough, no totally reliable version of what transpired at Oxford exists. Huxley, in a letter to Francis Darwin claimed that Freemantle's account of the whole day was essentially correct, while Green had the substance of his speech most accurately, although he claimed that he definitely did not use the word "equivocal." While the accounts might differ in detail, in substance they are in agreement. Leonard Huxley has reprinted most of the different accounts of what happened including Thomas Huxley's own comments on the various versions. See *LLTHH* l, pp. 193-204.

4. T. Huxley, "On the Zoological Relations of Man with the Lower Animals," *The Natural History Review*, 1861, pp. 67-84, *SMTHH* 2, pp. 471-492, 472.

5. Ibid.

6. In this regard, Huxley differed significantly from Darwin. A full discussion of Huxley's views on ethics is beyond the scope of this paper. In his 1893 lecture on evolution and ethics, Huxley discussed why he did not think the doctrine of evolution could give us an ethics to live by. "The propounders of what are called the "ethics of evolution," when the "evolution of ethics" would usually better express the object of their speculations, adduce a number of more or less interesting facts and more or less sound arguments in favor of the origin of the moral sentiments, in the same way as other natural phenomena, by a process of evolution. . . . But as the immoral sentiments have no less been evolved, there is so far, as much natural sanction for the one as the other. The thief and the murderer follow nature just as much as the philanthropist. Cosmic evolution may teach us how the good and the evil tendencies of man may have come about; but, in itself, it is incompetent to furnish any better reason why what we call good is preferable to what we call evil than we had before." T. Huxley, 1893, "Evolution and Ethics," *Selections from the Essays of T.H. Huxley*, ed. A Castell (New York: Appleton & Croft, 1948), 106-107.

7. T. Huxley, "On the Zoological Relations of Man with the Lower Animals," 474.

8. Ibid., 471-472.

9. Ibid., 475.

10. Ibid.,473.

11. T. Huxley, 1863, *Man's Place in Nature* (New York: D. Appleton & Co., 1898), 103.

12. Ibid., 152-154.

[ADDITIONAL RESOURCES]

The Center for Inquiry: http://www.centerforinquiry.net

The Huxley Files: http://aleph0.clarku.edu/huxley/

BOOK REVIEW:
DISCOVERING THE BEAST IN YOU
by Marc McCutcheon, Michael P. Kline (Illustrator)
Williamson Publishing

Review by Diane Swanson

I first came across science writer and lexicographer Marc McCutcheon when I picked up a copy of his Roget's Super Thesaurus, which has since taken up permanent residence next to my computer. Then I discovered *The Compass in your Nose & Other Astonishing Facts about Humans* – a truly fun and informative read. But I was most impressed by his contribution to a series of books called *Kaleidoscope Kids*, published by Williamson Publishing for "kids ages 7-14 & their families and friends." In *The Beast in You: Activities & Questions to Explore Evolution* (1999), McCutcheon has tackled an especially important subject that's both complex and – sad to say – controversial, and his approach is first-rate.

Speaking directly to his readers, McCutcheon makes evolution particularly relevant by directing them to spot the "beast" inside themselves – finding vestigial parts, such as canine teeth, goose bumps, and the divot below the nose. He uses humor – "We don't walk on all fours anymore. Nor do we bite (baby brothers and sisters excluded)" and language that talks to kids – "In the old days, supermarkets and McDonald's didn't exist. Food had to be found or hunted."

In 96 pages, McCutcheon explores basic principles of evolution, such as natural selection and variation, in a way that is clear, direct, and entertaining. Throughout the book, "Evolution Solution" sidebars address questions such as "Are you evolving?," and "Think about It" sidebars ask the reader to do just that – think: "Could it be that Bigfoot isn't extinct? Or is he simply alive and well in our imaginations?" McCutcheon also involves his readers in the subject by encouraging them to perform simple experiments, such as spending a "prehistoric day" (bathing in cold water without soap – or rubber duckies – going to the bathroom in the woods, walking everywhere, and sleeping on the floor, close to siblings).

For extra value, McCutcheon has included an annotated time line ("From Ape

People to Humans"), a list of museums where the reader can learn more about evolution, a bibliography, and an index. *The Beast in You* is a job well done – a book that is especially welcome during these days of misguided attacks on evolution. Let's hope the whole family reads it! ∞

[ABOUT THE AUTHOR]

Diane Swanson is a children's author, having made a career of writing fun and informative non-fiction books for kids. She credits the astonishing natural world as the inspiration behind her writing. Diane has published over 50 books for children. Her most recent titles include *The Dentist & You* (2002), *Nibbling on Einstein's Brain* (2001), and *The Doctor & You* (2001), all with Annick Press. She has been recognized for her work with several awards, including the B.C. Award, the Orbis Pictus Award for Outstanding Nonfiction for Children, the Mr. Christie's Award, the B.C. Book Prize, the Red Cedar Award, the Silver Birch Award, and many more.

[ADDITIONAL RESOURCES]

Diane Swanson's author page on Annick Press: http://www.annickpress.com/ai/swanson.html

Nibbling on Einstein's Brain Book Page:
    http://www.annickpress.com/catalog/nibblingoneinsteinsbrain.html

Inquiring Minds Program: http://www.youngskeptics.org

CSICOP ON CREATIONISM
by Kevin Christopher

In 1859 Darwin published his groundbreaking thesis that genetic variation in a population could be selected by the natural environment, causing genetic change in the population over time, and that such changes accumulated over time drove the evolution of new species. Ever since, Biblical literalists and others who see evolution as a challenge to a traditional worldview have attacked Darwin and his ideas through various tactics.

One tactic involves the concoction of "theories" consistent to varying degrees with Biblical and church dogmas. The two main theories proposed have been creationism and intelligent design (ID). Note that the term "theories," from a scientific perspective is misapplied in this context. Creationism and intelligent design should be considered merely claims. Neither of these claims have any evidence in their support, nor do they appear in peer-reviewed scientific journals.

Creationism is the belief that nature shows evidence demonstrating the factuality of the creation account in the Biblical Book of Genesis. ID proposes that the complexities exhibited in many biological mechanisms are beyond the power of evolution and natural selection to explain: therefore the only "reasonable" explanation is that an "intelligence" (left to the individual proponent to interpret as "God") created such intricate phenomena in life. Both alleged theories exhibit all of the classic hallmarks of pseudoscience. Therefore they are subjects of interest to skeptics: especially because this brand of pseudoscience is being actively pushed on school boards and teachers around the United States.

WHAT MAKES CREATIONISM AND ID UNSCIENTIFIC?

Both claims are argued from ignorance (the logical fallacy often denoted by the Latin phrase *argumentum ad ignorantiam*). Even a casual reading of the "literature" shows that authors devote their arguments to alleging that evolution fails to explain diversity and complexity in living things and that therefore creationism or ID must be true. In sum, arguments for creationism and ID are based on alleged anomalies, rather than a body of evidence in their favor.

Both claims rest on an assertion that is either untestable or begs the very question of where a complex living phenomenon like intelligence comes from. The assertion is that an intelligence (divine or otherwise) exists that is in control of the universe and its phenomena. If such an intelligence were indeed part of nature, that fact would only beg the question of what the natural cause of the force behind the complexity and diversity of life is; if this intelligence is not part of nature, then it is by definition supernatural and therefore at best an untestable religious belief and, at worst, nonsensical.

Creationists and ID proponents like to argue that scientists prefer evolution because they have an anti-religion agenda. This allegation is only a distraction from the real issue: namely, which claim has the evidence to support it? Scientists do not dispute creationismism and intelligent design because these claims are religious, they dispute them because they are logically flawed and lack any evidence to support them. The evolving scientific account of the universe has often been in conflict with sacred texts and dogmas. In an open and democratic society, people are entitled to their beliefs--even if the conflict with science. However, they are either deluded or dishonest when they claim that their beliefs are scientific when they are not.

The Committee for the Investigation of Claims of the Paranormal (CSICOP), its flagship journal, *Skeptical Inquirer*, and its newsletter for associate members, *Skeptical Briefs* have several articles and resources available both on- and off-line to Internet researchers.

Online resources include the following:

Skeptical Inquirer, September-October 2001
Design Yes, Intelligent No:
A Critique of Intelligent Design Theory and Neocreationism
 by Massimo Pigliucci
"The claims by Behe, Dembski, and other 'intelligent design' creationists that science should be opened to supernatural explanations and that these should be allowed in academic as well as public school curricula are unfounded and based on a misunderstanding of both design in nature and of what the neo-Darwinian theory of evolution is all about...."
 http://www.csicop.org/si/2001-09/design.html

Skeptical Inquirer, March-April 2002
Darwin in Mind: 'Intelligent Design' Meets Artificial Intelligence
What's Wrong with the Information Argument Against Evolution?
 by Taner Edis
"Proponents of 'Intelligent Design' claim information theory refutes Darwinian evolution. Modern physics and artificial intelligence research turns their arguments on their head...."
 http://www.csicop.org/si/2001-03/intelligent-design.html

Skeptical Briefs, December 2002
"Reality Check":
The Emperor's New Designer Clothes
by Victor J. Stenger
"Intelligent Design is the latest buzzword in the so-called dialogue between science and religion. The claim is made that scientific data cannot be understood naturally, that is, without gods or spirits, but require the additional element of divine purpose. In the minds of at least some of the proponents of Intelligent Design, the evidence in support of their position has become so strong that they demand, in the name of fairness, that it should become part of science texts and taught in the K-12 science curriculum. Scientists who raise objections are denigrated as 'dogmatic' preachers of the religion of 'scientism.'..."
http://www.csicop.org/sb/2000-12/reality-check.html

In addition, Senior Research Fellow Joe Nickell has created an online Skeptiseum displaying artifacts and information on paranormal and skeptic-related subject matter. A feature exhibit on creationism can be found at http://www.csicop.org/skeptiseum
Items currently on display include: The Bible, Dinosaurs, Fossils, and Noah's Ark.

[ABOUT THE AUTHOR]

Kevin Christopher is Public Relations Director of the Committee for the Scientific Investigation of Claims of the Paranormal (CSICOP) and its official publication, *Skeptical Inquirer* magazine. He earned his bachelor degrees in Classics and Linguistics at the State University of New York at Buffalo in 1992.

[ADDITIONAL RESOURCES]

CSICOP web site: http://www.csicop.org

Skeptical Inquirer magazine: http://www.csicop.org/si/

Skeptiseum: http://www.csicop.org/skeptiseum

Nancy Easterlin's paper was presented at the University of New Orleans Third Annual Darwin Day.

WHAT IS DARWINIAN FEMINISM?
by Nancy Easterlin

A week before I was scheduled to present this talk for Darwin Day, I was running some errands and listening to *Car Talk* on the radio. A female caller with the unforgettable name "Flap" posed another in the series of sex difference questions that are regularly offered up to these gurus of the automotive world. The exchange went something like this: "When my husband and I are going someplace in the car together, he always asks me which way I would go. And I respond by saying, 'If I were driving, I would go this way.' When I'm finished talking, he pulls out of the driveway and goes off in *exactly the opposite direction*. Why is that?" One of the Tappit brothers responded, "We could write a book on this. Well, maybe just a paragraph. But I've learned. If my wife and I have five errands to run, I just get in the car and wait, and when she says, 'Go this way, Stupid,' I do. She can even leave out the 'Stupid' part, and I still do it." The other Tappit brother jumped in with, "Why is that? We all KNOW men are better at linear thinking, and this is just strictly question of 'What's the most direct route between A and B?' – of linear reasoning. It's a strictly linear question."

Of course, what the rest of this conversation determined was that, well, how to order the five errands most efficiently is not a strictly linear question – the wife was factoring in other relevant information, such as when school lets out in a certain part of town, and that sort of thing. Click and Clack couldn't really answer the caller's question, but Flap said she was looking forward to their pamphlet on sex differences.

Most of us enjoy this kind of men vs. women humor when it's well done, and most of those who enjoy it would admit to enjoying it. But the actual issues underlying such humor – 1) why we perceive general differences in patterns of behavior between men and women; 2) what the sources of these differences are; and 3) what the implications of sex or gender differences are for feminism and for a positive, progressive relationship between the sexes – are by no means simple, and certainly not funny. The main purpose of this paper is to argue that feminism needs to concern itself with contemporary research on sex differences, a body of research that is growing and is consistent (or *consilient*, to use E.O. Wilson's word) with evolutionary explanations of adaptation and behavior (Wilson, 1998). The first part of this paper will review the state of contemporary feminist theory. The second portion of this paper will survey some of the research on sex differences and suggest the implications of such research for feminist thought and practice.

I.

The entry of women in significant numbers into the workplace since the 1970s, including the academic workplace, has helped to direct attention to the condition of women in American and other societies. It has produced crucial, practical initiatives aimed at remedying social injustices; and has propelled a reconsideration within the academy of the extent to which received concepts of truth and knowledge may be biased toward male models of thought. There are those who argue that women are now fully liberated and that we are in a postfeminist phase of development. But if you gather statistics on the lives of American women about, for example, job and career advancement opportunities, or if you live as a working woman in America for upwards of forty or fifty years, you will not be inclined to accept the view that women currently enjoy equal rights and opportunities with men. With regard to the pace of progress for the women's movement, on the positive side, we need to remember that thirty-odd years is not a very long time. On the negative side, we need to ask why current feminist theory is so far removed from the apparent physical realities of human experience that it obfuscates rather than clarifies the issues at stake.

Today, most academic feminist thought falls under the category of "constructionism," the theoretical position that differences between men and women are *constructed* – that is, created by a sociocultural reality that does not reflect underlying biological differences. Recent constructionist thinking within the humanities has been influenced by those theorists who have likewise influenced postmodernist and poststructuralist thought, including (but not limited to) the social theorist Michel Foucault, the Marxist philosopher Louis Althusser, and the psychoanalyst Jacques Lacan. These influential thinkers stress the enormous power of social and political culture in shaping the individual, whether through the power of ideology or the power of *discourse* – language structures that direct persons to their *subject positions* (what we might call in common parlance their social roles) and control human behavior.

While constructionist philosophy importantly reminds us of the profound degree to which we, wittingly or unwittingly, conform to and are controlled by the social status quo, it poses logical and practical problems, not least because of the extreme determinism inherent in its most extreme articulations. Even when constructionism may not have determinist implications, its power to explain is quite limited. For example, let's go back to the *Car Talk* episode: If one adopts the stance that linear reasoning is socially constructed as a male mode of cognition – that men are, so to speak, shaped by their societies and cultures to think in linear, logical terms – such a stance begs the question of why male cognition would be constructed *in that particular way*. Indeed, the notion of construction itself implies materials to build with, yet constructionism is strangely silent about what those might be (N. Easterlin, 1999).

Why has feminist theory opted, by and large, to pitch its tent in the constructionist camp, and why is there a general unwillingness to discuss biological sex differences? Part of the problem is due to the way the issue is framed. As Diana Fuss explains in her 1989 book *Essentially Speaking*, feminists generally conceive of the debate in binary terms, opposing *essentialism* to *constructionism*. "Essentialism", as Fuss puts it, "is most commonly understood as a belief in the real, true, essence of things, the invariable and fixed properties which define the 'whatness' of a given entity. In feminist theory, the idea that men and women, for example, are identified as such on the basis of transhistorical, eternal, and immutable essences has been unequivocally rejected by many anti-essentialist poststructuralists feminists concerned with resisting any attempts to naturalize human nature" (Fuss, xi). Again, as Fuss elaborates a few pages later, "Essentialism is classically defined as a belief in true essence – [in] that which is most irreducible, unchanging, and therefore constitutive of a given person or thing. This definition represents the traditional Aristotelian understanding of essence, the definition with the greatest amount of currency in the history of Western metaphysics" (Fuss, 2).

Fuss's definition and placement of the term within the Western metaphysical tradition usefully clarifies what might be problematic to a feminist or, for that matter, to a Darwinian with the alternative to constructionism. If we take up our *Car Talk* example from the essentialist stance as here defined, we would be led to conclude that linear thinking is part of the static, unchanging essence of things male, whereas some other static, unchanging mode of cognition (intuitive? experientially based?) inheres in the static, unchanging essence of things female. Framing the issue in terms of transcendent, eternal qualities logically implies, then, that these modes of thought are inevitably constitutive of *all* men and *all* women for all time, and thus cancels out the degree to which such qualities might vary from individual to individual and might, as well, be subject to historical contingencies. The opposition of *constructionism* to *essentialism*, then, is yet another way of framing the age-old nature-nurture debate.

How this debate is framed – *constructionism* versus *essentialism*, within the metaphysical tradition – signals the disturbing degree to which feminist thought is out of sync with the intellectual paradigm shift produced by the Enlightenment and, ironically, instrumental in its collapse. As many poststructuralist feminists have themselves pointed out, such two-term (binary) thinking and argument seems to go hand-in-hand with the rise of patriarchal power and the concurrent disempowerment of women. So, from the perspective of feminist values and goals, it is a puzzle – and a particularly disturbing one – that this specific paradigm should be placed at the center of and fundamentally shape feminist debate. Even more importantly, from the perspective of the intellectual history of the past several hundred years, in which belief in a timeless, static, unchanging universe has been giving way to an awareness that the order of life emerges from complex, dynamic processes that produce change over vast periods of time, this model of Western metaphysics is anachronistic. If not utterly epistemologically obsolete, the model is of decidedly limited value.

Given a framework in which the alternative to constructionism is essentialism, in other words, the attribution of generalized, timeless, diametrically opposed qualities – like linear versus intuitive thinking, rationality versus emotionality, strong versus weak – to all men and women, and given the attendant assumptions that such qualities are not only preordained but invariant from individual to individual, it is no wonder that feminists have refused to discuss – even sought to deny – biological differences. Yet constructionism is crippling to feminism, in part because it forestalls causal explanation. An understanding of the *causes* of inequality, which may have something to do with a culture's intentional as well as unintentional manipulation of the differences between men and women, is, arguably, vital to finding accurate solutions to problems of inequality.

II.

To be candid, feminism's loyalty to the constructionist theoretical position is not just due to the binary framing of the argument against essentialism. As the biological anthropologist Sarah Blaffer Hrdy explains in *Mother Nature: A History of Mothers, Infants, and Natural Selection*, hypotheses about male and female abilities and behavior in nineteenth-century evolutionary thought and in early sociobiology and ethology in the mid-twentieth century were hardly free of a male-biased perspective. Herbert Spencer, a Victorian-era theorist whose particular notion of evolution strongly reflected his culture's positivism, the view that material and spiritual progress for humans inheres in evolutionary process, is father to a number of theories, including those about women, that have become somewhat tarnished with the passage of time. As Hrdy puts it, "The supreme function of women, Spencer believed, was childbearing, and toward that great eugenic end women should be beautiful so as to keep the species physically up to snuff. Because mammalian females are the ones that ovulate, gestate, bear young, and lactate ... Spencer assumed that the diversion of so much energy into reproduction had inevitably to lead to 'an earlier arrest of individual evolution in women' than in men – a dubious extension. Not only were men and women different, but Spencer's females were mired in maternity ... [Spencer argued that] the costs of reproduction constrained mental development in women and imposed narrow bounds on how much any one female could vary from another in terns of intellect ... [Indeed], Spencer reasoned that there was too little variation among females for proper selection to occur, precluding the evolution in women of higher 'intellectual and emotional' faculties, which are the 'latest products of human evolution'" (Hrdy, 14). In short, Spencer and other evolutionists of his day imported many of their culture's attitudes about men and women – that the cultural division of labor was preordained by physiology, that women had not evolved 'the power of abstract reasoning and the most abstract of emotions, the sentiment of justice' (Hrdy, 15), that smaller-than-average brain mass correlates with lower intelligence for women – into evolutionary theory, and used evolution to validate those attitudes.

Indeed, Darwin himself was not free of the view that the capacity for reproduction necessitated *incapacity* in other arenas: in his words, "'whether requiring deep thought, reason, or imagination, or merely the use of the sense of hands, [man will attain] a higher eminence ... than can woman.'" As Hrdy points out, "Like Spencer, Darwin convinced himself that because females were especially equipped to nurture, males excelled at everything else. No wonder women turned away from biology" (Hrdy, 19).

Hindsight reveals that many of these attitudes were still robust nearly a hundred years later. In the 1960s, many animal researchers studied maternal behavior out of its natural context, focusing on the dyadic unit without observing how relations with the larger group and features of the physical environment are fundamental to a mother's *decision* to nurture. One thing these empirical research programs reveal is a failure to grasp the implications of Darwinian thinking that fluctuating and, over time, changing features of the environment are central to evolution, which in turn implies that behavior gauged to promote survival will vary significantly depending on environmental conditions. Recognition that researchers needed to look at a more complicated picture emerged with a growing awareness that natural selection doesn't function at the level of the group: individual behavior must function to perpetuate *inclusive fitness*, the survival of that individual's genes. Mothers who focus solely on producing and nurturing young without taking account of changes in the social group and of the viability of the natural environment – in other words, mothers who are *essentially* passive except with respect to their young – are unlikely to survive for very long, much less produce viable offspring. In short, animal researchers became aware that a picture in which males compete for access to females and females reproduce and nurture young was highly simplified, and research in the past thirty years has focused on *female choice* about when conditions are favorable for raising young to maturity. As Hrdy relates "pregnant monkeys ... whose social groups have been recently usurped by a new male have been reported to spontaneously abort" (Hrdy, 90).

The studies Hrdy documents in the first chapters of *Mother Nature* make it impossible, in my assessment, to see women or their mammalian relatives as *essentially* nurturing reproducers in the Aristotelian sense; given the right set of conditions in a natural habitat, a chimpanzee, for example, will choose to bear and raise its offspring to maturity. Given the right set of circumstances in the environment of evolutionary adaptation (the Pleistocene era, 1.6 million years ago), ancestral women would choose to do the same. Today, however, things are quite different. In the late nineteenth century, after the development of germ theory and the institution of sanitation regulations in the modern city, human life expectancy increased and, especially, infant mortality declined. Corresponding to these developments and probably as a result of them, women began to consciously control the number of offspring they produced. The modern demographic transition suggests that not only the survival of children is more important than the total number of children produced but that, in effect, women have discovered an array of activities that substitute for a lifetime preoccupation with childbearing (R. Easterlin; Hrdy). Humans have altered their environment radically and, in response, people born and raised in that environment make reproductive and life choice decisions our ancestors could never have imagined.

III.

My last remarks might seem to bring the argument full circle to suggest that environmental factors are so overwhelmingly influential in the direction of a woman's life takes that there is, *in essence*, no meaningful conjunction of the terms "Darwinian" and "feminism". If women can choose to control their fertility – choose not to be mothers – they are, so the argument might go, choosing to override the game plan of evolution.

But to limit the discussion to a matter of reproductive choice or to anatomical differences between men and women, as some feminist arguments do, is to take a part for the whole, to forget that biological differences might be expected to correspond to average psychological differences. This is really the crux of the matter for Darwinian feminism. If men and women are, *on average*, different in some psychological respects that manifest themselves in differences in behavior under particular conditions, how do we ensure conditions of equality in a society in which men wield disproportionate power? My answer to this question is that if we direct attention to the normative psychological and cognitive differences between men and women, our findings will reveal the biases of our social structure, and only then can we work to correct these biases.

Empirical studies demonstrate that men and women differ in a range of physiological and cognitive ways that are logically interrelated and, from a Darwinian point of view, that these characteristics and their logical interrelationship make sense in light of their capacity to aid the reproductive success of individuals in the ancestral environment. In simple terms, the goal of individual members of a species is to produce viable offspring, and therefore Darwinians study physical characteristics as well as behaviors to assess how they function to assist the individual's survival and production of offspring who themselves survive to reproduce. However, in nearly all species, including humans, males and females will have distinct reproductive strategies, because the two sexes have rather different roles in the reproductive process. Human beings are a decidedly good example of how reproductive roles differ between the sexes. For women, as for most mammalian females, reproduction is *expensive*; fertilization of an egg entails a long and physically taxing pregnancy. Not only is the human infant notoriously helpless, demanding a great deal of attention, but the developmental span of a human being is extremely long compared to that of other species. Since all evidence drawn from traditional societies and ethology as well as modern societies indicates that women are overwhelmingly responsible for the nurture and protection of the young, they have a very high degree of *parental investment*. By contrast, for men, sex and reproduction are not costly: as compared to women, who have a limited supply of eggs, sperm are abundant; men do not have physiological costs associated with pregnancy; and their parental investment in young is typically a fraction of what women invest. Given this scenario, Darwinians argue that males will seek out sex more often than females and will compete with other males for access to females, whereas females will be more selective in mate choice, prizing males who can provide protection and resource – the counterpart to their high parental investment in young.

The research on reproductive strategies suggests a number of things, but I would just like to look at one important part of this picture – the likelihood that women will be less directly competitive and more predisposed to nurture than men and, correspondingly, that men will be more competitive and aggressive. Does this hold true for contemporary humans? There are in fact such a wide range of studies supporting these normative generalizations that it is hard to distill them into a brief summary, but I'd like to present some striking examples from the research on child's play, because, as David Geary, author of *Male/Female: The Evolution of Human Sex Differences*, puts it, "play provides a pattern of early experiences that results in the fine-tuning of a number of social and physical competencies associated with survival and reproduction in adulthood" (Geary, 224).

Not only are sex differences a universal feature of child's play (Geary, 224), but these differences occur *more* frequently in child-initiated rather than adult-initiated play. Both sexes engage in rough-and-tumble play, for instance, but it is far more frequent in boys than girls. As Geary documents, "In situations where play activities are not monitored by adults and in context in which their activities are not otherwise restricted ... groups of boys engage in various forms of rough-and-tumble play – including playful physical assaults and wrestling – three to six times more frequently than girls ... Research in the United States indicates that the sex difference in playful physical assaults and other forms of rough-and-tumble play begins to emerge about 3 years of age, and the same general pattern is found in other industrial, as well an many preindustrial, societies, though the magnitude of the sex difference in this form of play varies across these cultures." Likewise, studies of older children (10-11 years) indicate that boys are much more likely than girls to participate in competitive activities in large groups and to display in these activities a more marked degree of role differentiation than girls do in their games. This preference has been connected to prenatal exposure to androgens (male sex hormones). Boys also engage in more gross locomotor play (such as running) than girls, an activity that increases the size of the play range and is related to cognitive developments such as the ability to position landmarks, an ability which enhances the capacity to represent the local environment and is related to mapping skills.

Darwinians attribute preferences and abilities in play exhibited by boys to specific selection pressures in the ancestral environment. Activities that develop physical strength and skill are important to individuals who compete for access to females, and who also serve an indispensable role in protecting the group. Similarly, the development of dominance hierarchies, which mirror the dominance hierarchies of chimpanzees and are evident in the preference for competitive group sports, strengthened male coalitions which served to protect the group. Likewise, the ability to generate accurate mental representations of unfamiliar territory would have benefited ancestral men: "Across preindustrial societies, men travel farther from the home village than women, on average, for a number of reasons, including finding mates, developing alliances with the men of neighboring villages, hunting, and participating in intergroup warfare" (Geary, 233). In sum, there are distinct parallels between the skills conducive to survival and reproduction in the ancestral environment and the competences boys are motivated to hone through play.

In contrast to the preferences of boys, play parenting occurs with greater frequency in girls. As Geary summarizes the research, "a sex difference in play parenting ... is found in both industrial and preindustrial societies and, in fact, many other species of primate ... For children, this sex difference is related, in part, to the fact that child-care responsibilities are assigned more frequently to girls than boys throughout the world ... But even in the absence of assigned roles, girls engage in play parenting much more frequently than boys do, a pattern that is a precursor of the later sex difference in the level of parental investment" (Geary, 236). Ethological research supports the relationship between play and evolutionary function, for studies of a variety of primate species suggest that play parenting improves the survival rate of firstborn offspring.

Overall, the tendency of boys and girls to self-segregate into same-sex play groups is explained by differences in social style and behavior: "The social relationships that develop among girls are more consistently communal – manifesting greater empathy, more concern for the well-being of other girls, more nurturing, intimacy, social-emotional support, and so forth – than the relationships that develop among boys; whereas relationships among boys are more concerned with establishment of dominance, control of group activities, task orientation, and risk-taking" (Geary, 242).

IV.

These studies on child's play, which provide a small sampling of the available research on sex differences, cohere with an overall pattern of evolutionarily advantageous behaviors. These provide *ultimate* explanations – in other words, evolutionary explanations about the source of normative psychological differences between men and women and the adaptive function of those predispositions, but they do not imply that human *behaviors or roles* are essentially pre-established. If we are concerned with establishing not only equal opportunity but also a balanced society, they do prompt us to ask this question: How do we establish a social environment that is conducive to the average social styles of both sexes? I think this is an urgent question, because the present orientation toward male styles is now at a point where is threatens the survival of all.

For the Darwinian, there can be no Rousseauean past golden age. But there was, arguably, a time when the roles of men and women did not diverge as sharply as they do now. As E.O. Wilson explains, small average differences between men and women are apparent in traditional societies, but what seems to happen as human groups move from hunting and gathering to settled communities is that, with alarming swiftness, the roles of men and women become much more distinct and circumscribed. This shift, which began for us about 10,000 years ago, seems to have served the development of culture, although it now threatens to undo the world it has helped to create. Wilson coins the word "hypertrophy" to refer to the extreme growth of pre-existing structures, such as, for example, the slight differences in the roles of men and women in hunter-gatherer culture that have become more pronounced and resulted in male dominance as culture has progressed (Wilson, 1978, 89-92).

Industrialization and modernization, even as they brought with them democracy and, eventually, the women's suffrage movement, exacerbated a situation in which the distribution of power between men and women became increasingly imbalanced simultaneously with the development of gender roles increasingly divorced from one another. In the movement from an agricultural to an industrial economy, work and the family livelihood no longer revolved around the home and adjacent land, and cottage labor declined. Whereas husband and wife had both formerly been productive in providing family resources, middle class husbands went out to managerial jobs in factories and women stayed home to raise and nurture children. With the dramatic expansion of the middle class in the nineteenth century, women became disengaged from the modern equivalent of resource-gathering, labor outside the home to provide for the livelihood of the household. What is usually emphasized about the state of affairs in modern culture is that the assignment of economic pursuits to men goes hand-in-hand with male dominance and the disempowerment and denigration of women; what is less fully analyzed is the belittling attitude toward women *and their primary activity, nurturing the young*, as well as the psychological and social styles that evolved because they facilitate species survival.

From an evolutionary perspective, any attitude that sees parental nurture as something less than an activity of fundamental importance is, quite frankly, completely bizarre. If the motivation to gather resources stems from the will to survive, evolutionary theory explains the desire to sustain the self as a component of the overarching motivation to maximize *inclusive fitness*, that is, the perpetuation of one's genetic matter. Reproduction alone only results in offspring, but does not ensure that those offspring will themselves survive to reproduce, and nurture plays a vital role in ensuring that survival. Especially in humans, who are born so helpless, the emotional bond that develops between mother and young was in the ancestral environment (and still is) instrumental in keeping the infant close to the mother and, therefore, under her protection. The attachment of mother and infant is of primary importance, not a feature of a secondary drive, as Sigmund Freud and twentieth-century learning theorists would have it, not simply an effect of feeding, as John Bowlby and subsequent attachment theorists have explained (Bowlby). Much to the contrary, the first relationship and attachment to the primary caregiver, usually the mother, provides an essential foundation for the impetus to orient toward the external environment, the development of social relationships, and the acquisition of language (Stern).

The purpose of this foray into developmental research is not to claim, of course, that women have a social and psychological predisposition that is best realized in caretaking, but rather to argue that the social competences more typically observable in women than in men have been vastly underrated, to the detriment of individual women, relationships between the sexes, and of modern society as a whole. Not only is nurture a foundation of species survival and later abilities but, in the larger picture, the normative psychological attributes of women – communality, cooperation, caretaking, and the like – serve to benefit our species in relationships with all others, not just with small children.

It would be nice to argue that Darwinian feminism simply needs to teach people love and cooperation, but I am not an idealist, and I believe such argument is generally futile. How do we encourage greater cooperation and curb the competitiveness and aggression prevalent in our culture? Clearly, women need to be in the workplace, but the presence alone of women in the workplace is not enough. Since the issue at hand is altering the dominant institutional structures and modifying the styles that have shaped these institutions, the institutions are only likely to change unless there are a great number of women in relation to men in places of power and importance. In fact, the biological anthropologist Melvin Konner and others have argued that the future well-being of our society depends upon an influx of women into such positions. I believe this view, which anticipates work and other environments more conducive to equal opportunities for individual women at the same time it suggests improvement for our culture as a whole, should be central to Darwinian feminism. Potentially, what would emerge from such a social realignment is a culture in which everyone enjoys the advantage of broadened abilities through exposure to a more enriched social environment.

The *Car Talk* anecdote I began with, perhaps, provides a good example of what might emerge. Are men superior at linear thinking? Interestingly, the results of mapping studies with children indicated that under natural play conditions boys developed more accurate mental representations than girls, but when the children were given supports, such as maps of tours of the route, that girls could model the environment equally well. The study suggests how specific environmental factors can have a pronounced effect on the development of cognitive abilities normally perceived as the strength of the other sex. By the same token, if men participate in caretaking, if they drop their children off and pick them up from school with some regularity, they will be less inclined to organize this activity by an abstract mapping procedure alone. Women can encourage men to become attuned to human-related concerns, and to the recognition that nothing in this world is ever a matter of a straight line from A to B. And if they can just resist calling our husbands and male friends "stupid" while they're providing this sensitivity training, we'll all be a lot better off.

[ABOUT THE AUTHOR]

Nancy Easterlin is Professor of English and Associate Director of Women's Studies at the University of New Orleans, and Associate Editor of *Philosophy and Literature*. She is the author of *Wordsworth and the Question of "Romantic Religion"* and of numerous articles on literature and literary theory, as well as co-editor, with Barbara Riebling, of *After Poststructuralism: Interdisciplinarity and Literary Theory*. All of her scholarship stresses the importance of a Darwinian understanding of human psychology for literary interpretation, literary theory, and women's studies.

[REFERENCES]

Althusser, Louis (Rpt. 1998). "Ideology and Ideological State Apparatuses." In *Literary Theory: An Anthology*. Ed. Julie Rivkin and Michael Ryan. Oxford: Blackwell Publishing.

Bowlby, John (1969). *Attachment*. New York: Basic Books.

Easterlin, Nancy (1999). "Making Knowledge: Bioepistemology and the Foundations of Literary Theory." *Mosaic* 32.1: 131-47.

Easterlin, Richard A. (1996). *Growth Triumphant: The Twenty-first Century in Historical Perspective*. Ann Arbor: University of Michigan Press.

Fuss, Diana (1989). *Essentially Speaking: Feminism, Nature & Difference*. London: Routledge.

Foucault, Michel (1979). *Discipline and Punish: The Birth of the Prison*. Trans. Alan Sheridan. New York: Pantheon Books.

Geary, David C. (1998). *Male/Female: The Evolution of Human Sex Differences*. Washington, D.C.: American Psychological Association.

Konner, Melvin (1983). *The Tangled Wing: Biological Constraints on the Human Spirit*. New York: Harper Trade.

Lacan, Jacques (1977). *Ecrits*. Trans. Alan Sheridan. New York: W.W. Norton.

Stern, Daniel N. (1985). *The Interpersonal World of the Infant: A View from Psychoanalysis and Developmental Psychology*. New York: Basic Books.

Wilson, E. O. (1978). *On Human Nature*. Cambridge: Harvard University Press.

Wilson, E. O. (1998). *Consilience: The Unity of Knowledge*. New York: Random House.

[ADDITIONAL RESOURCE]

New Orleans Secular Humanist Association: http://nosha.secularhumanism.net/

*David Thomas' article first appeared in the monthly newsletter of **New Mexicans for Science and Reason** and is republished here with permission from the author.*

DOES EVOLUTION = ATHEISM?

by David E. Thomas

Paul Gammill is an Intelligent Design advocate who lives in Albuquerque, New Mexico. For six years, he has sent one anti-evolution letter after another to NMSR, the New Mexicans for Science and Reason. I have responded with dozens of letters to him, in which I have tried to explain the merits of evolutionary theory, and to point out problems with his supposed "refutations" of evolution. To this day, however, he is so wound up in his "Design" world that he cannot even acknowledge the simple fact that the great similarity between chimpanzee and human DNA does in fact support the hypothesis that we're actually related.

It's become apparent that no amount of logic and reason will ever sway Paul Gammill on any topic concerning evidence for evolution. And that is because he Knows that evolution is a False Theory. How does Gammill know this? It's related to the way he Knows anyone who supports evolutionary theory is really an Atheist. To really understand Paul Gammill, and the Intelligent Design movement at large, one must move above mere things like fossils, DNA, natural selection, and the rest. The only logical explanation for Gammill's world view is Religion, pure and simple.

Gammill has long insisted that evolution is an atheistic belief. I challenged this assertion in the June 2001 issue of NMSR's monthly newsletter, NMSR Reports:

> THOMAS: You consistently claim that evolution is inherently atheistic, ignoring the very large and significant fraction of religious people who believe that evolution is simply God's method of Creation. In my last letter, I laid out the plain logic of the situation, showing clearly where the position you are ignoring, theistic evolution, belongs. My question to you: why do you advocate a theory that can exist only by suppressing the facts – in this case, suppressing the fact that a great many of the world's religions do not consider evolution to be incompatible with God? – *June 2001 NMSR Reports, Vol. 7, No. 6.*

Here is Gammill's "answer," from his letter of June 29, 2001. It provides much insight into the deeper sources of Gammill's world view.

GAMMILL: Answer: The fact that **some religious people** believe that the BWH [Blind Watchmaker Hypothesis] is God's method has nothing to do with the facts of biological origins. I do not ignore or suppress the fact of their belief. I do understand the rationale, though. **They trust "science"** in general, based on its technological successes in particular. **These people don't realize** that the metaphysical BWH piggy-backs on real science. **They don't realize** that it's a metaphysical construct. **They've bought off** on science's indoctrination. **These people haven't researched** the problem like I have. **They don't realize** that there's a paradigm crisis in origins theory. **They don't realize** that the BWH is built on a foundation of impossible chance processes, philosophical dogma, and indoctrination. **They don't know** about the information problem, or the irreducible complexity problem, or all the other problems I've cited here and in other letters to you. **Design and chance are antithetical, diametrically opposed, and mutually exclusive. Intelligent design cannot rely on chance. Chance, on the face of it, precludes design. No designer of complex algorithms or machines would put his designs in the hands of chance processes.** The <u>real leaders</u> in the BW establishment would never concede that God had anything to do with the BWH of mutation and natural selection leading to "macroevolution" from yeasts and bacteria to mankind. They'd laugh that idea to scorn. They consistently make that position publicly. I could and probably have, at some time, given you some quotations on that from Gould, Eldredge, Dawkins, Provine, Dennett, Ridley, Miller, Scott, Ruse, Alberts, etc. There are the leaders that you rely on, along with New Mexico academicians and scientists, etc. *[Original emphasis underlined; boldface emphases not in original.]*

Gammill repeats these themes again and again. In fact, on June 27, 2002, Gammill called all NMSR members atheists, writing *"I certainly failed to persuade you folks to open your minds that night [Jan. 13th, 1999]. But that's all right. In the long run, you'll come around to the democratic/republican view, the American way. People indoctrinated into a religious (atheistic) belief set over a life time don't change their minds overnight. Speaking of atheism: Isn't that true? That is, aren't all of you on the NMSR Board of the atheistic persuasion? You certainly never use the 'A' word. But isn't that true? And aren't all of you NMSR members committed atheists? Isn't Darwinism just another subset of atheism for you? NMSR zealotry for evolution is understandable in view of an atheistic worldview."*

I became curious: how does this happen? How does the simple support of evolutionary science turn someone, even professing Christians like Kenneth Miller, into a "zealous atheist" in Gammill's mind?

I have re-read several of Gammill's letters, and a clear pattern has emerged. Gammill reads the works of Intelligent Design (ID) writers incessantly, and has done us a favor by consolidating their arguments down to their basics. These basics are a small set of axioms, assumptions, things Gammill regards as obviously true to all concerned. His six axioms form the premises for a logical argument, which is carried out *perfectly* according to the formal rules of Logic. And the final results are: **Intelligent Design is True, God is True, Evolution is False, and Evolution is Atheism**. From my reading, it's apparent that Paul Gammill has indeed adopted this peculiar logical argument. And it might even turn out to be the core of the modern ID movement. It's a tidy package, and once someone has bought into the premises, there's no use discussing "evidence" like fossils or DNA. If evolution is False, then any supporting evidence must also be False. End of story. All you need to do is present some arguments that show it is False. If the arguments are rebutted, they can still be used again. And again. After all, if Evolution is False, then Anti-Evolution arguments must be True. (This sure explains why Gammill keeps coming back with the same lame defenses of Denton's invalid arguments against sequence comparisons!) An ID theorist doesn't have to be right; simply responding to his critics is sufficient to show they are "wrong."

So, what are the premises, the axioms, the statements of "obvious facts" that are the basis of Gammill's World? I submit that they are...

Premise 1) Life Exists, Life is True, L = T.
Premise 2) Life is Designed, If Life Then Design, L → D.
Premise 3) Design requires Intelligence,
If Design Then Intelligence, D → I.
Premise 4) The Creative Intelligence is God,
If Intelligence Then God, I → G. *[This premise is rarely, if ever, stated publicly, but it's required for the Conclusion, as will be seen.]*
Premise 5) Chance and Design are Incompatible, If Chance Then NOT (Design), If Design Then NOT (Chance), C AND D = F,
C → NOT (D), D → NOT(C).
Premise 6) Evolution requires Chance, If Evolution Then Chance, E → C. This is the same as If NOT(Chance) Then NOT (Evol.), NOT (C) → NOT (E).

Well, those are the premises. Some of them don't sound unreasonable, others are more questionable. But, if you accept them as is, here are the bits of formal logic that quickly yield Gammill's desired conclusions:

From Premise 1, "Life Exists (L=T)," and Premise 2, "Life is Designed (L → D)," we derive **Conclusion 1**: "Design Exists, Design is True (D=T)."

Adding Premise 3, "Design requires Intelligence (D → I)," to Conclusion 1, "Design is True (D=T)," we logically arrive at **Conclusion 2**: "Intelligence Exists, Intelligence is True (I=T)."

Given I=T, and adding Premise 4, "If Intelligence Then God (I → G)," we deduce **Conclusion 3**: "God Exists, God is True (G=T)."

Backtracking to Conclusion 1, "Design is True (D=T)," and adding Premise 5, "If Design Then NOT(Chance) (D → NOT(C))," we arrive at **Conclusion 4**: "NOT(Chance) is True, so Chance is False (C=F)."

With Conclusion 4, "Chance is False (C=F)," and adding Premise 6, "If NOT(Chance) Then NOT(Evolution) (NOT(C) → NOT(E))," we deduce **Conclusion 5**: "NOT(E)=T, or E=F, or Evolution is False."

We're almost there. This last bit is the payoff. By simply combining Conclusion 3, "God is True (G=T)," and Conclusion 5, "Evolution is False (E=F)," we deduce that Evolution and God cannot **both** be true (it's kind of obvious when it's "known" that Evolution is False anyway). This translates into **Conclusion 6**: "Evolution AND God = False, E AND G = F," or equivalently, "If Evolution Then NOT(God), E → NOT(G)," i.e. "**Evolution is Atheism.**"

And there you have it. If you accept the six premises, the conclusions "Intelligent Design is True," "God is True," "Evolution is False," and "Evolution is Atheism" immediately follow, and all by the formal rules of Logic.

This hypothesis explains a *lot*. For one, it explains why Gammill continually states the equivalent of *"Design and Chance are Incompatible"* as often as he can. He's trying to establish Premise 5 as "obvious." Do you see the spot (emphasized in bold face) in the June 29, 2001 answer, where Gammill asserts Design and Chance are mutually exclusive *four times in a row?* And of course, if Evolution is False, then any evidence claimed to support it must also be False, *independent of any merits it may have*. Gammill unwittingly revealed this core assumption in his latest (July 25th 2002) letter: "If, by the term 'molecular evolution,' you mean naturalistic, undirected macroevolution by means of mutation and natural selection, yes, **we observe that that is a false theory**. We **then** attempt to show by **reason, argument and debate** that it's false and that Design theory offers the best explanation for biological origins."

Amazing, isn't it? And Gammill's six premises are science-free. No messy natural selection, fossils, genetic comparisons, or any of that "data" stuff. No, just pure ideas, simple axioms existing in the realm of abstract thought, which immediately prove Intelligent Design (God) is True, but that Evolution (Atheism) is False.

There's a problem with this logical argument, however. The logic is fine, *given the premises*. But if the premises are wrong, then the conclusions don't follow. And some of these premises are most certainly *False*.

Premise 1 is quite reasonable: "Life exists." The few who would disagree with this axiom don't give a hoot about design or evolution anyway.

Premise 2, "Life is Designed," is also not unreasonable. The talon of an eagle, or the sonar apparatus of a bat, have all the appearances of design. Evolution theorists don't deny the appearance of design; instead, they propose and test scientific explanations for this apparent design.

Premise 3, "Design requires Intelligence," is a fundamental tenet of the Intelligent Design movement. Nowadays it goes by the seductive name "Irreducible Complexity," popularized by biochemist Michael Behe. But this premise is just Paley's watch all over again. It's sometimes stated as *"Because the Designed Objects we see [such as watches] required intelligence in their formation, **All** Designed Objects require Intelligence for their formation."* But, this is really the supposed conclusion of "Intelligent Design" – it's hardly fair to try and slip it in as a premise. That logical fallacy is known as "begging the question." When stated a little more accurately, this premise no longer seems obviously true: *"Because the **Artificial** Designed Objects we see [such as watches] required intelligence in their formation, All Designed Objects (both Artificial and **Natural**) require Intelligence for their formation."* Clearly, this "axiom" isn't valid. The fact that artificial objects need designers doesn't prove natural objects need designers, because natural objects aren't artificial. They simply aren't the same thing. The analogy doesn't work. *(And, there is a counterexample. It's called evolution.)*

Premise 4, "The Creative Intelligence is God," is rarely, if ever, publicly stated by Gammill or other "ID theorists." This is a "stealth" premise. But it **must** be part of Gammill's and ID's worldview, because they couldn't arrive at Conclusion 6, "Evolution is Atheism," *without it*. After all, the leaders of ID often say the Designer doesn't have to be God, but could be a super-smart Alien, for example. Why is it, then, that anyone who suggests that perhaps these smart Aliens used mutations to help them with their designs – who suggests that perhaps the Aliens even used evolution to design things for them – is criticized for their *"atheism?"* Why aren't they criticized for being anti-*alien*? If the Intelligent Design choir is *promoting* it, it doesn't have to be God – it could be an Alien. But if anyone *criticizes* ID, that critic is an "atheist," pure and simple. There's no doubt about it – ID is based on religion. The Designer is God. Period. And if you don't believe in the peculiar, specific incarnation of God that these people believe in, then they declare that you don't believe in God at all.

Premise 5, "Design is incompatible with Chance," is stated by Gammill at every opportunity, yet this "axiom" isn't obvious at all. Nonetheless, this concept is taking hold in the ID movement under the guise of *"specified complexity."* In the following statement from "card-carrying design theorist" William Dembski, Dembski defines "specified complexity" with the use of an analogy in his article *"The Chance of the Gaps"* (2001, www3.baylor.edu/~William_Dembski/articles.htm):

"Imagine it is January 1971 and you are at Orchestra Hall in Chicago listening to Arthur Rubenstein perform. ... you think to yourself, 'I know the man I'm listening to right now is a wonderful musician. But there's an outside possibility that he doesn't know the first thing about music and is just banging away at the piano haphazardly. ... How, then, do you know that you are listening to Arthur Rubenstein the musical genius and not Arthur Rubenstein the lucky poseur? ... a necessary condition for recognizing Rubenstein's musical skill (i.e., *design*) is that he was following a pre-specified concert program, and in this instance that he was playing Liszt's 'Hungarian Rhapsody' note for note ... In other words, you recognized that Rubenstein's performance exhibited *specified complexity*. ... without that recognition there would have been no way to attribute Rubenstein's playing to *design* rather than *chance*." [emphasis not in original] In effect, Dembski here assumes design is the antithesis of chance – just like Gammill does.

I wonder if Paul has heard of Charles Goodyear's *accidental* discovery of vulcanized rubber in 1839? (After all, vulcanized rubber is an important part of the design of many wheels). Or how about Thomas A. Edison's assistants, who tried out one light-bulb design after another, until they *chanced* on the right one? Or how about the jet engines and new medicines that are designed with genetic algorithms, which use random number generators (*"chance"*) to work? Premise 5, "Design and Chance are Incompatible," and its equivalent, "Specified Complexity Requires Design (Not Chance)," are simply not valid "axioms."

And that brings us to **Premise 6**, "Evolution requires Chance." This is true, of course, but evolution also requires heredity, natural selection, environment, physically determinate processes (e.g., laws that allow $2H+O \rightarrow H2O$), and any number of other things. *These simply aren't necessary* in Paul's disproof of evolution, in which evolution **IS** "chance," but they are necessary, of course, in any *scientific* discussion of evolution.

In summary, Paul Gammill has apparently collected a small set of core beliefs, six premises, which can be used to quickly prove that Intelligent Design (and God) are True, that Evolution is Chance, that Evolution is False, and that Evolution is Atheism. But, the argument collapses because some of the premises are not true, or simply religious, or unproven. Omitting the untrue, religious and unproven axioms, we can only conclude that Life Exists, and that Life appears Designed.

Evolution is not atheism. As I've told Gammill many times, quite a few people accept that "In the Beginning, God Created Evolution." But this obvious reality has absolutely no impact on Gammill. After this little logic analysis, I think I know why. Indeed, this analysis might just help explain the intractibility of the entire Intelligent Design movement. It also demonstrates, with the rules of formal logic, that Intelligent Design is really all about Religion; all about God. If your image of God doesn't match the ID theorists' concept of Deity, namely One who would never stoop to using Chance (=Evolution), they will say that you are an Atheist! It's really that simple. And it's wrong.

[ABOUT THE AUTHOR]

David E. Thomas is a physicist and mathematician, employed at a small high-tech testing firm in Albuquerque, NM. Dave is president of the science group, New Mexicans for Science and Reason as well as a Fellow of the Committee for Scientific Investigation of Claims of the Paranormal (CSICOP), publishers of *Skeptical Inquirer* magazine. He has published several articles in *Skeptical Inquirer* on the Roswell and Aztec UFO Incidents, as well as on the Bible Code. He received the National Center for Science Education's Friend of Darwin Award in 2000.

[ADDITIONAL RESOURCES]

New Mexicans for Science and Reason (NMSR): http://www.nmsr.org

Coalition for Excellence in Science and Math Education: http://www.cesame-nm.org/

CSICOP & Skeptical Inquirer magazine: http://www.csicop.org

National Center for Science Education: http://www.ncseweb.org

*Robin McKie's reviews originally appeared in **The Observer**, a leading source for informed news and comment in the United Kingdom. The article is republished by permission of the author.*

Book Reviews:
The Future of Life
by Edward O Wilson
Knopf

What Evolution Is
by Ernst Mayr
Basic Books

Reviews by Robin McKie

The end of the world is nigh...

Robin McKie on Edward O Wilson's lament for a dying planet and the first book for the general reader from the godfather of modern biology, Ernst Mayr.

Small but perfectly formed, South America's dart frogs are some of evolution's strangest by-products. They come in a vivid array of reds, oranges and greens and are so tiny they could perch on a fingernail.

Yet these little popinjays are the rainforest's most feared denizens, for each secretes poisons that can flatten even the largest predator. Take Colombia's wonderfully named Phyllobates horribilis. Each one has enough toxin to kill 10 men, a fact exploited by Choco tribesmen who rub their blow-gun darts (very carefully) over phyllobates when preparing for battle.

Then there is Equador's Epipedobates tricolor which exudes a cocktail of different chemicals, including one that medical researchers John Daly and Charles Myers discovered was a powerful, opium-like painkiller, but which seemed to lack addictive side effects.

And thereby hangs a tale. Having stumbled on this exceptional amphibian emission, Daly and Myers needed more samples to develop their research. So they returned to the little frogs' homeland glade, only to find it had been turned into a banana plantation. Thus a pharmacological miracle seemed to have perished forever at the hands of the fruit farmer. Only the subsequent discovery of a separate, distant epipedobates' lair saved the day.

The world was lucky, but it has not been in thousands, possibly millions, of other cases when we have bulldozed, cemented, flooded, dynamited, or burned unique environment after unique environment, taking each one's remarkable, but usually unstudied, occupants with it. As Wilson says: 'We are chipping away at the miracles around us.'

Ecological horror stories are ten-a-penny, of course, and their capacity to alarm was long ago neutralised by overuse. This is 'the litany' that is disparaged by Danish statistician Bjorn Lomborg in his anti-green diatribe, The Sceptical Environmentalist, which so delighted right-wing commentators last year. For a few months, they nearly had us believing everything was tickety-boo on planet Earth.

The appearance of *The Future of Life*, is, therefore, timely, for it is not the work of desk-bound pedants who spend their days analysing and finding flaws in UN statistics but of the greatest natural history expert of our age, a double Pulitzer Prize winner, a distinguished Harvard professor and a renowned naturalist who has spent his life grubbing through the forest floor in search of novel wildlife.

And he can see absolutely no grounds for dismissing the warnings of the doommongers. 'An Armageddon is approaching,' he says. 'Not the cosmic war and fiery collapse of mankind foretold in scripture. It is the wreckage of the planet by an exuberantly plentiful and ingenious humanity.' We are back in eco-horror land, in other words, though never has it been so vividly and disturbingly described.

Consider the book's first sentence: 'The totality of life, known as the biosphere to scientists and creation to theologians, is a membrane of organisms wrapped around Earth so thin it cannot be seen edgewise from a space shuttle, yet is so internally complex that most species composing it remain undiscovered.'

It is a majestic start from which Wilson proceeds lovingly to assemble a picture of the delicate interrelatedness of the 10 million species with which we share that biosphere – 'the Sumatran rhinoceros, flat-spined, three-toothed land snail, furbish lousewort' and all the other plants and animals that we are now eradicating at a stunning rate.

The trouble, Wilson says, is that human population growth has become 'more bacterial than primate', creating a biomass (the combined weight of all six billion humans alive today) that is now 100 times that of any other large animal that has ever existed. We already consume 40 per cent of Earth's green plants to feed our swelling numbers and will gorge ourselves on even more in the centuries ahead. The planet simply cannot take any more, no matter how much economists quibble over statistics, dispute extinction estimates and argue about agricultural production rates.

Only 'Palaeolithic obstinacy' stops us realising the danger, Wilson argues. We are descendants of Stone Age men and women who were hard-wired to commit themselves 'to a small piece of geography, a limited band of kinsmen, two or three generations into the future', and not much else. Hence we miss the global overview and end up as eco-deniers. The boys at *the Economist* must love being described this way.

In short, this is a brilliantly constructed analysis of our planetary woes, a much needed response to those who think our environments are safe and secure from global degradation. It is only when Wilson comes to solutions that he is on less sure ground. Some of his suggestions are eminently sensible – protect our last remaining great forests, cease all logging in ancient woodlands, increase our capacity to breed endangered species and support all population planning projects. These may well help to slow down the slaughter, but they will not stop it. His other proposals – calls to encourage biophilia (the love of living things) and urges to adopt a 'global land ethic' – will do absolutely nothing.

The trouble is that having outlined our global crisis so starkly, and having convincingly depicted life on a planet denuded of all variety or ecological interest, he clearly feels compelled to offer some salvation. Thus he states in the book's concluding sentence: 'A civilisation able to envision God and to embark on the colonisation of space will surely find the way to save the integrity of this planet and the magnificent life it harbours.' Compared to Wilson's opening sentence, these closing words are limp and inane and belied by everything else he has written. As he states earlier in the book: 'The conservation ethic, whether expressed as taboo, totemism or science, has generally come too late to save the most vulnerable of life forms. A paradise found is a paradise lost.' Not much room for hope there. In short, as a call to environmental arms, *The Future of Life* must be rated an honest failure. By contrast, as a swan song for our dying planet, it is a magnificent success.

Certainly we can see that the handiwork of millions of years of natural selection faces destruction in the twinkling of an evolutionary eye. Yet we have only just come to understand that process itself, one of the great intellectual triumphs of the past 150 years, and the basis of *What Evolution Is*, the first book that the godfather of modern biology, Ernst Mayr, has written for the public. Given that the venerated Harvard scientist is now 97 years old (and still carrying out research), this delay may seem tardy. It is a pleasure to say the wait was worth it, nevertheless.

'Evolution is a fact,' says Mayr. 'It has taken place ever since the origin of life', the end result being the improbable menagerie of life on Earth, from the ant to the doubting creationist, to whom Mayr pays special attention, mainly by demolishing all objections they can mount about natural selection's ability to explain the wonders of the living world. The only tragedy is that we now face losing most of those marvels in a single lifetime. ∞

[ABOUT THE AUTHOR]

Robin Mckie is science editor for *The Observer*. He has authored several books, including *African Exodus: The Origins of Modern Humanity*, co-written with Chris Stringer; *The Book of Man: The Human Genome Project and the Quest to Discover our Genetic Heritage*, co-written with Walter Bodmer; *Dawn of Man: The Story of Human Evolution*; and *The Genetic Jigsaw: The Story of the New Genetics*.

[ADDITIONAL RESOURCES]

The Observer online: http://www.observer.co.uk

SPECIAL SECTION

The Next Generation:
Education & Our Future

> " The ability to use scientific knowledge and ways of thinking depends to a considerable extent on the education that people receive from kindergarten through high school. Yet the teaching of science in the nation's public schools often is marred by a serious omission. Many students receive little or no exposure to the most important concept in modern biology, a concept essential to understanding key aspects of living things – biological evolution."
>
> – National Academy of Sciences,
> *Teaching About Evolution and the Nature of Science* (1998)

CHALLENGING STUDENTS

By Jon Gonsiewski

Sitting at my desk after school one day, I began reflecting on the day's lesson. In the 1920s unit that I was covering in AP US History, the class period revolved around the major trials that occurred during the emerging decade. One particular trial, The Scopes Monkey Trial seemed to have the students in an uproar. "How could people think like this?" "Obviously, Scopes will be found not guilty!" were just some of the comments the class shouted out before we read over the transcripts. To their shock and dismay, the students realized two amazing truths. One, Scopes was found guilty, although to a lesser charge that he never paid. Two, although set in 1925, this issue is still very much alive today. The country is still fighting the issue of what information should be covered in biology classes.

Pondering these realizations, it gave me a strong sense of Charles Darwin's impact on the world. It is not just a science issue, or even a social studies concern. For all educators, Darwin created the most important concept that students need to use in the classroom. He gave us the power to think. Students need to question the information they receive; test it out for themselves. Darwin didn't take the common belief of Creationism as the whole truth and tried to find out more on his own. This intrigue and desire to know more is what teachers should see from all their students.

Darwin is a true role model for students today to take their education seriously. When I found this essay contest on the internet, I couldn't resist giving my students this wonderful challenge. Now in my third year using this tool, I have found that students love putting their minds to the task and thinking for themselves. Wouldn't Darwin be so proud! ∞

[ABOUT THE AUTHOR]

Jon Gonsiewski is a teacher at New Hope-Solebury High School in Pennsylvania.

Charles Darwin's Impact Upon Our World

by Laura Mulcahy
New Hope Solebury High School

There are few great thinkers that have left a truly fundamental and astounding impact on the world, and Charles Darwin is one of them. Darwin was born in 1809 and until around 1830 he planned to become a clergyman of the Church of England. While at the University of Cambridge, as he was preparing to become a clergyman, he met Adam Sedgwick, a geologist, and John Stevens Henslow, a naturalist. Both of these associates sparked Darwin's first interest in the sciences. In 1831 Darwin boarded the English ship HMS *Beagle* to be an unpaid naturalist on a scientific expedition that would go around the world. It was on this journey that the first sparks of Darwin's revolutionary idea were lit. Darwin's influence on the world was vast and his concepts included exemplified applied rational thinking to the natural world resulting in his groundbreaking theory of evolution and natural selection. In a larger sense he opened people's horizons and stimulated a new way of thinking without the compulsion to integrate beliefs into their observations of the natural world.

On Darwin's journey aboard the *Beagle* he observed different living organisms and fossils that were found on numerous islands and continents. Darwin was struck by how natural forces played a part in shaping the earth's surface. He also noticed a variety of different examples that contributed to his theory of evolution, such as the fact that certain fossils of species thought to be extinct were very similar to organisms that were currently living. While visiting the Galápagos Islands, Darwin made the observation that played the most important role in the development of his theory. Each of the numerous islands had animals that were slightly different from those on the other islands. Although closely related, there were slight differences such as body structure or eating habits. From this observation, Darwin realized that there could be a connection between distinctive yet similar species. The concept that was accepted at the time, the catastrophist theory, had many holes, yet instead of exploring the inconsistencies scientists accepted the conventional ideas. Darwin provided a new way of thinking when he rationally compared different observations of the natural world to create a sound hypothesis.

Darwin's most widely recognized influence on the world is his theory of evolution by natural selection. As soon as he returned to England in 1836 he began to record all of his observations in his *Notebooks on the Transmutation of Species*. His ideas came together much better after he read *An Essay on the Principle of Population* by Thomas Malthus, which discussed how human populations remained in balance. The work stated that the food supply, which increased arithmetically, could not support the the growth of a logarithmically increasing population. Since the available food supply was inadequate the fittest in the population were the most likely to survive based on competition for limited resources. In 1838, after applying this concept to animals and plants, Darwin came up with a theory of evolution through natural selection. This theory states that each species competes against other species with only those most appropriately adapted to their environments surviving to propagate their population. Darwin's theory wasn't announced until 1858 and wasn't published until 1859 in *On the Origin of Species*, which sold out on the first day. Darwin's theory was proven to be true in the early 20th Century with the birth of modern genetics and is widely known and accepted today.

Darwin's theory of evolution opened horizons in allowing people to explore a world of thinking unencumbered by religious beliefs, which restricted their ability to see the truth from a forced need to marry religion into science. Before Darwin, the most accepted theory of evolution was the catastrophist theory, which states that species become extinct due to sudden catastrophes. According to this theory Noah's flood was the latest disaster that destroyed all species except those on the ark, with fossils being all that remain of the extinct fauna. This theory was religiously accepted since the concept was backed up by evidence stated in the Bible. For the most part people felt that it should be accepted without any question because of this. When Darwin's theory was published there was a large amount of intellectual resistance because people did not want to go against what they assumed the Bible stated.

Even through the 1920's there was still resistance to Darwin's theory of evolution. A famous example is a Tennessee court case, the Scopes Trial of 1925. John Scopes, a high school biology teacher who taught evolutionary theory, was accused of violating the Butler Act. This act was a state law forbidding the teaching of the theory of evolution because it went against the story of creation in the Bible. This was a landmark trial which highlighted the fact that the theory was forcing people to think outside their religious confinements. Even so, Scopes did break the law, was found guilty and forced to pay the one hundred dollar fine. The state supreme court later reversed the verdict, but the Butler Act stayed on the books until 1967. This trial has since been fought out numerous times since Scope's time and the issue is still being argued today.

In the later years of his life Darwin wrote many additional books expanding upon his ideas expressed in the *Origin*. He worked out slight problems he found in his first book in such works as *The Variation of Animals and Plants Under Domestication*, *The Descent of Man* and *The Expression of the Emotions in Man and Animals*. These books contributed to Darwin's theory becoming a widely accepted concept, more so as people learned to overcome their religious beliefs which commonly restricted their thinking in regard to the natural world. Darwin's theory of evolution not only changed the way people thought of the natural world, but his rational approach profoundly influenced future scientific endeavors for generations to come.

Charles Darwin's Impact Upon Our World

by Owen Jones
New Hope Solebury High School

Of all the influential people in our world's history, few have raised as much controversy as Charles Darwin. Darwin, the father of the theory of evolution, has inspired both respect and revulsion through his theories of natural selection. Darwin was born in 1809 during a period when few people could comprehend his modern ideas yet still managed to influence evolutionary theory for years to come. After Darwin published his *Origin of Species*, late Victorian society witnessed the "very foundations of human thought" being rearranged and Darwin's Theory of Natural Selection affect "the entire intellectual life of our Western civilization." Clearly Darwin is one of the most influential thinkers of all time – a man who revolutionized people's basic understanding of the world.

Despite being raised to enter the Church, Darwin would later go against many of the Church's basic teachings. Charles Darwin first "discovered" his Theory of Evolution in the Galápagos Island. Traveling on the H.M.S. *Beagle*, Darwin witnessed and classified hundreds of new organisms living on the islands. It wasn't until Darwin returned to England, however, that he would state his Theory of Evolution. In the Galápagos, Darwin catalogued many different varieties of finches, which were all uniquely suited to the island's environment that they inhabited. He later turned these records into his theory of Natural Selection, stating that the organisms better suited to their environment are the ones that survive and pass on their genes to subsequent generations. It wasn't until the 1859 however, that Darwin published his theory in his book *Origin of Species* – twenty years after his voyage on the H.M.S. *Beagle*.

Darwin's claim, that man was like any other animal and had evolved from the same ancestor as the ape, shocked society's entire belief system. The response was immediate, even though Darwin didn't directly confront human evolution until *The Descent of Man* in 1871. Both those offering praise and those displaying contempt were strongly attracted to the radical ideas put forth by Darwin. Perhaps more important than Darwin's theory, was the effect it had upon society. Many scientists began to publish more theories such as Darwin's – theories that went against the teachings of the church. Darwin's publications ushered in a new era of modern science in which scientists were free from the constraints previously place on them by the church. Without Darwin's publications, the development of science may have stagnated much longer in the fundamentalist quagmire in which it was stuck.

It wasn't until the 20th century that Darwin achieved household recognition. In Dayton, Tennessee in 1925, the Scopes Monkey Trial sought to test the Constitutionality of the "Butler Law." The Law prohibited the teaching of evolutionary theory in any Tennessee classroom. Newspapers carried reports of the trial and the theory began to be debated throughout the world. Although at first it appeared that John Scopes was a criminal, Clarence Darrow, his defense attorney, showed how insensible William Jennings Bryan's absolute belief in a literal interpretation of the Bible, was. The judge handed out the most lenient sentence to John Scopes – a fine of one hundred dollars. Although the trial determined that it was illegal to teach darwinism in Tennessee, the trial also served to open the minds of the public in the same way Darwin's publications did almost a hundred years before the Trial.

These two events, the Scopes Monkey Trial and Darwin's publications *The Origin of Species* and *The Descent of Man*, are both responsible for a scientific revolution that would change the face of the planet.

Without such bold thinkers as Charles Darwin, scientific thought would have stagnated under the oppressive rules of the Church. With his controversial ideas, Darwin beat down the door that was keeping scientific thought under restraint. His effect on the world is evident – one hundred and fifty years after Darwin's publications, he is still influencing the way people think and the way science is done.

CHARLES DARWIN'S IMPACT UPON OUR WORLD

by Fern Baldwin
New Hope Solebury High School

Throughout history, as scientific philosophy and theory developed, a merging as well as a conflict of religion and science began to take place. Most likely the deep-rooted conflict between religion and science is due to the fact that science is based on the observation of nature, while religion is based on faith. The peak of this merge, and a definite beginning of tension between the two realms, occurred in the mid-nineteenth century when Charles Darwin presented his findings on the evolution of life.

1859 was not the beginning of evolutionary ideas, however. Facts and theories on evolution have been traced back as early as the Greeks, who had a philosophical notion of descent with modification. Aristotle suggested a transition between the living and the nonliving and believed that in all things there is a constant desire to move from the lower to the higher, eventually becoming divine.

Medieval theories of evolution were scarce due to the domination of the Christian idea of special creation, which argued that all living things came into existence in unchanging forms due to divine will. The idea of spontaneous generation also existed, suggesting living things can appear from inorganic matter (example: maggots from rotting meat.) In the mid- to late-eighth century, the proposition of existence from a common ancestor formed, although the idea was held back by the contradiction it posed to strong Christian views. Scientists such as Linnaeus, Lamarck, and Malthus, influenced Darwin's thinking.

As Darwin's ideas rapidly spread, his influence became evident. Today, observing the application of his ideas, as well as the significant Scopes Monkey Trial of 1825, his immense influence on history and science is clear.

Charles Robert Darwin was born in 1809 in Shrewsbury, England. He began to follow in his father's footsteps to become a doctor but after studying medicine at Edinburgh and later theology at Cambridge, he realized neither profession was of great interest. While Darwin was studying at Cambridge he became friends with the biology professor John Henslow and his interest in zoology and geology grew. Through his friendship with Henslow he was given the opportunity to take a five-year voyage upon the H.M.S. *Beagle*, The voyage of the *Beagle* started Darwin on a career of accumulating and assimilating data that resulted in the formation of his mechanism for evolution, natural selection. Darwin visited many areas of the world on his voyage; the Galápagos Islands trip being among the most well-known. He returned to England and spent the remainder of his life working over the information from his notes of the voyage and researching other available data. The introduction of Darwin's evolutionary ideas within society, in 1859, not only made a great impact on science but also altered the thinking of the common man.

Up until the time of Darwin, people were able to think of religion and science as two separate ideas. When Darwin championed the theory that the earth was much older than previously thought, as Charles Lyell and other geologists had shown, the conflict with the Bible's teachings became clear. At first the idea seemed impossible and the public turned to ridicule. By the time of his death there was still a large contingent of anti-evolutionists.

His books, including the most well-known – *The Origin of Species* – began circulating more widely. His theory of evolution by natural selection became widely accepted within the scientific community and though doubt still existed among the public, more evidence was being gathered to show its validity. One real display of the conflict Darwin's ideas posed to religion was in the Scopes Monkey Trial of the 1920s.

In 1921 Fundamentalist Protestants, led largely by William Jennings Bryan, began to push for a campaign that would prohibit the teaching of evolution in school classrooms. A belief in the literal account of creation as described in the Bible was extremely popular in the South during this time. The goal of the campaigners was achieved when in 1925 the Tennessee legislature passed the Butler Law, forbidding teachers in state schools and colleges to teach evolution. That same year, the American Civil Liberties Union (ACLU) found the young biology teacher John Thomas Scopes who was willing to bring a test case to trial by breaking the Butler Law.

In July 1925, Scopes was tried in Dayton, Tennessee, defended by Clarence Darrow and prosecuted by William Jennings Bryan. The small trial got an immense amount of attention by the media especially since the judge refused to allow expert testimony. The trial became a battle between Darrow and Bryan.

The outcome of the trial was that John Scopes was convicted of breaking the Butler Law and thereby fined one hundred dollars. Not only was this trial proof of the increasing merge of religion and science and the increasing tension within the United States, but it also had a lasting effect on education and the public's mindset towards such. This small trial in Tennessee acted as a breakthrough in science and education.

As a result of Darwin's example, more scientists showed confidence in proclaiming new ideas. In schools, especially the science classroom, the teaching of evolution became more prevalent and accepted by officials and independent thinking was encouraged instead of punished. Darwin not only had a lasting effect on scientific research but his theories and way of thinking changed the way of teaching and learning within education.

The fact and theory of evolution eventually began to penetrate the minds of the entire human population. Due to the contradictions evolution posed to a literal interpretation of biblical creation, not only was the world of science changed, but the world of religion was changed as well. Darwin sparked a tension between science and religion unintentionally and this tension was made famous in the Scopes Monkey Trial. It can be seen today among anti-evolution crusaders across the world – most notably in the United States.

Today, Darwin's ideas are used throughout science and are widely accepted. It is impossible to deny the colossal influence that Darwin has had on science, religion, and society.

CHARLES DARWIN'S IMPACT UPON OUR WORLD

by Dawn VanDerWende
New Hope Solebury High School

The 1920s was a decade of change and exploration. American society witnessed a sudden change in society's norms and values. There was a constant clash between people who believed in tradition, and those who encouraged change. A whole turn-around occurred within religion. People began to "think outside the box" (or the triangle in this case) and question the long cemented Christian beliefs.

A movement that helped bring about the freedom from religion was the increasing popularity and acceptance of science. Like many elements of the twenties, science was relatively new and exciting to eager minds. Science brought about theories that held more truth than religion. One of these theories was called Darwinism. Darwinism posed a direct challenge to creationism – a religious belief that promoted a literal interpretation of the Biblical account of life's creation. Darwinism, by contrast, stated that life evolved. Most offensive to creationists was the claim that man evolved from the same evolutionary lineage as apes and monkeys. Man and all other living organisms, along with the planet Earth, were not simply created in a matter of days by a little wave of God's magic wand, but from millions – often billions – of years of change. For life, this biological change through time is termed evolution. The theory of evolution proved to be a direct attack on religious belief and also impacted the realm of morality. To the average Christian of the twenties, the theory of evolution posed great turmoil to their belief system. In this respect, Darwinism changed the face of the nation – of the entire world.

Darwinism created controversy among groups of people that still exists today. A prime example of this controversy can be seen in the Scopes Monkey Trial of the 1920s. In a trial over John T. Scopes teaching evolution in biology class, the relationship between science and religion became a battleground. The theory of evolution altered history by dramatically influencing religion, science, and education.

When Darwinism was introduced to American culture, religion would never be the same. Many Christians were already altering their beliefs with the findings of science and this continues today. In the Scopes Monkey Trial, fundamentalism (a strict interpretation of the Bible), was put to the test. Defending the fundamentalist position was William Jennings Bryan. Bryan was a devout Christian as well as a former presidential candidate, politician and lawyer. He was prosecuting John T. Scopes for teaching evolutionary theory in the science classroom – something that was not allowed in Tennessee because of the Butler Law. Defending Scopes was the famous lawyer Clarence Darrow. It was during this trial that many strict believers in the Bible became uncomfortable in their beliefs. Darrow grilled Bryan, a professed expert of the Bible, on the stand about every story found in the Book. People began to realize how ridiculous a literal interpretation of the Bible was. It became apparent that man was probably not created from Adam and Eve, and that many other claims could not be taken as scientific fact. Darrow challenged Bryan about the 6-day creation story. The story states that God had created the whole planet and all its life within a mere six days. Through Darrow's interrogation, Bryan was made a fool because he refused to accept anything other than what the Bible stated. Because of the widespread publicity of the Scopes Trial and the uproar it caused within America, religion was forever changed. Because of the Scopes Monkey Trial, Christianity was no longer the only word of reason. Darwinism helped to show that science was a more reasonable approach to understanding our physical and biological reality.

The scientific community was another area greatly impacted by Darwinism. Evolution, in its direct applicability to life, helped make science popular among the public.

Darwinism was first theorized around 1838 and made public in 1859. Charles Darwin, a British scientist, became an influential leader within his field of naturalism, by defining his theory of evolution by natural selection. Other scientific advances that were made in this time period, carrying on through the early 20th century, were in health care and nutrition. Life expectancy grew because of the discoveries of science. In medicine, new thinking led to less illness and disease. Darwinism played an important role in these advancements. By understanding life, and its evolution, more valid information could be gathered and a greater understanding of ourselves could be reached. Darwinism caused a revolution in science. People found the ideas proposed within the evolutionary sciences intriguing. Curiosity soared.

Darwin and his ideas, however, continued to receive a lot of criticism from fundamentalists since the moment it was released to the public in 1859. Fortunately, the criticism could not stop the inquiring minds. The Scopes Monkey Trial helped make science and Darwinism more popular among the public. People began to inquire, search, and ultimately – understand. The defense and promotion of teaching evolution became more prevalent among educators and concerned citizens and is, in the 21st century, a global movement.

Reform and change were brought about in education by Darwinism. The teaching of evolution was actually banned in three southern states called "The Bible Belt South". If schools were changing socially in the twenties, what they taught had to change as well. There was a much greater number of students required to stay in school longer and therefore, there was a larger student population to educate. John Dewey's "learning by doing" approach shows his agreement with experimentation and this became an important aspect of the new reform in education. No discipline is more "in tune" with experimentation than the scientific and so greater emphasis was placed on science education. With the greater emphasis, came greater public attention. This public attention was what fueled the fundamentalist movement against the teaching of evolution in the science classroom.

The laws in Tennessee did not allow for evolution to be taught in the science classroom, after a successful claim to ban it, by the creationists. John T. Scopes, however, rebelled against the law. He harmlessly taught evolution in his high school biology class. However, he was breaking the law. Even though Scopes was found guilty of breaking the law and on the surface it looked like a victory for creationism, education was forever changed. Evolution became a recognizable necessity in science education and more and more schools began to adapt to this need. This change can still be seen today thanks to science advocates such as Clarence Darrow and John T. Scopes.

The most influential changes are the long-lasting ones. The theory of evolution is certainly one of these. Backed by a mountain of evidence, evolutionary science offers an explanation for life and the biological change through time that is clear from an observation of the facts. The validity of evolution helped others to open their minds to new ideas and not be so constrained by religious belief. Science became more appreciated and understood. Darwinism gained increasing respect among the general population. Though it altered people's religious belief, many found a way to harmonize their belief with the understanding provided by science. Students received a better education – one more applicable to the reality in which they were a part.

Charles Darwin's Impact Upon Our World
Additional Resources

National Academy of Sciences – Teaching About Evolution and the Nature of Science:
http://www.nap.edu/readingroom/books/evolution98/

National Academy of Sciences – Science and Creationism:
http://search.nap.edu/readingroom/books/creationism/

American Association for the Advancement of Science – Educational Resources:
http://www.aaas.org/spp/dser/evolution/education/default.htm

The Royal Society – Education: http://www.royalsoc.ac.uk/education/

Evolution and the Nature of Science Institutes: http://www.indiana.edu/~ensiweb/

Darwin Center at the Natural Museum of History:
http://www.nhm.ac.uk/darwincentre/index.html

National Center for Science Education – http://www.ncseweb.org/

Darwin Day Program Educational Resource Area – http://www.darwinday.org/education/

National Science Foundation – National Science Education Standards
http://books.nap.edu/html/nses/html/index.html

PBS Evolution Project: http://www.pbs.org/wgbh/evolution/

BBC Education – Evolution Web Site: http://www.bbc.co.uk/education/darwin/index.shtml

Institute of Human Origins: http://www.asu.edu/clas/iho/

Understanding Evolution: http://evolution.berkeley.edu/

Lawrence Lerner's Good Science, Bad Science:
http://www.fordhamfoundation.org/library/lerner/gsbsteits.html

Inquiring Minds Program & Educational Resource Area: http://www.youngskeptics.org/education/

The Talk.Origins Archive: http://www.talkorigins.org/

Access Excellence – Resource Center: http://www.accessexcellence.org/RC/

About Darwin: http://www.aboutdarwin.com/

SECTION FOUR

THE GRANDEUR –

In This View of Life

> "One ought, every day at least, to hear a little song, read a good poem, see a fine picture, and if it were possible, to speak a few reasonable words."
>
> – Johann Wolfgang von Goethe (1811)

> "Every day you may make progress. Every step may be fruitful. Yet there will stretch out before you an ever-lengthening, ever-ascending, ever-improving path. You know you will never get to the end of the journey. But this, so far from discouraging, only adds to the joy and glory of the climb."
>
> – Sir Winston Churchill (1940)

Evolving Awareness: Planning Your Darwin Day Event

by Rob Beeston and Amanda Chesworth

Celebrating Darwin Day within your community offers you an opportunity to make a difference. Here is a useful guide to help in the coordination of your Darwin Day event.

First let's consider the focus and goals of an event:

- Public Education – A large segment of the public has only a rudimentary knowledge of Darwin and evolution. Increasing public interest and understanding in the diversity of life and the contributions of one individual who changed the way we look at ourselves is a worthwhile focus for an event.

- Interactivity – Hands-on learning where participants will be able to interact with activities has been shown to successfully improve understanding. It creates more lasting memories of the event, and allows people to be directly involved in the line-up of events.

- Raising Awareness – Along with educational aspects, you also want to promote the day itself, attracting local media attention and other groups and individuals who are interested in supporting your efforts.

- Having Fun – Science is fun, and that's what will keep bringing people back year after year. Through events and activities, you are able to show first-hand that an interest in science is a rewarding endeavor. You are able to celebrate the curious minds that have explored and discovered, investigated and experimented, imagined and realized a great many things about our world and ourselves.

Available Resources

What resources are available for your event? Are there science professionals willing to volunteer their time? Do you have access to convenient locations? What are your budgetary constraints?

Make a few phone calls, visit educational outlets and gather interest within your community. You may be surprised by your success in finding resources and helpful volunteers.

Once you create a preliminary list of available resources you can start developing realistic event ideas.

Tailoring Your Message

Who is your target audience? Do you want a program for the general public, students, families, teachers, colleagues or community leaders? What age groups do you want to reach?

Answers to these questions impact the type of event you plan, and whether it will be a success.

Dealing with Controversy

You may be asked how your event impacts religious feelings within your community or what position it takes with respect to creationism. Decide early on how you will handle this issue.

Our recommendation is to be inclusive – acceptance of evolution does not require an individual to reject religion, and people with religious beliefs of all flavors are a part of our community – whether it be the scientific community or society at large.

Creationism on the other hand, flies in the face of scientific understanding and logic. Yet, instead of playing the role of antagonist, we recommend that your event focus on science and the celebration of our shared humanity. Darwin Day is a positive celebration where the public's understanding of science is promoted and, where possible, improved. Debating with a group of people who have an incompatible epistemology is futile. All it will do is dilute your message and spread further confusion and misunderstanding. Yes, help others to correct of the misinformation that proliferates but only if you are able to do so in a thoughtful manner, where understanding can indeed be reached.

If the media bring up the topic of creationism as part of an interview, and this is a common occurrence in America, explain that the day is about celebrating science and humanity, not about challenging faith or bashing religion. Creationism does unfortunately require concerned citizens to react – especially in educating the young – but there exist competent organizations with this as their focus and it is best to leave this unfortunate task to the experts. Consult the National Center for Science Education for guidance in how to effectively tackle creationism.

We suggest using the Darwin Day celebration as a time to discuss Darwin's life and work, and the life and work of many great thinkers before and after Charles Darwin. Show your audience how the discovery of evolution by natural selection has shaped later discoveries, and that even though there has been nearly 150 years of research since then, Darwin's original theory has stood the test of time, with only minor modifications and the continued gathering of evidence in support of evolution by natural selection. Evolution has impacted every aspect of the scientific community and, in many respects, society at large. Explore the diverse applications of evolution to our world and the myriad of disciplines that have been inspired by our improved understanding of life on earth. Darwin has helped us to understand ourselves and other life forms on Earth, and in addition has helped humanity to prosper and excel in many directions. The subjects explored through the Darwin Day Program are of great fascination to us and through events and celebrations we can foster an excitement for science and our role in discovery.

Engaging Other Organizations

Part of your event should be geared towards attracting others to join in with future events. Schools, conservation boards, museums, zoos and local science clubs should be urged to follow suit with their own programs and events, or become involved in a community-wide celebration. Local businesses, informal educational programs and other potential participants can be found within your area. Attempt to create a community-wide celebration of science and humanity, each and every February.

Activity Ideas

Once you've tackled the above considerations, it's time to decide your line-up of activities.

Be Creative!

On the Darwin Day Program's website, ideas and activity suggestions are being added all the time. (Check them out: www.darwinday.org/events)

Here are a few popular choices:

Information Distribution – Hand out brochures, fliers, awareness ribbons, fact cards (discussed later), and other informative items. Make it fun and attention getting. Don't just stand behind a table with the information laid out in front of you, dress up as Darwin, rent a gorilla suit, be outrageous.

Birthday Parties – Throw a theme party with cake, ribbons and balloons! This can be a memorable event for the work, home or school environments. Be sure to offer an explanation alongside the fun so that participants can understand the significance of the party.

Banquet – Banquets require a lot of preparation and should be planned well in advance. Banquets can include a variety of activities and mix several worthwhile elements within any given event or celebration: intellectual stimuli, social interaction, entertainment, an interesting menu, and more. Banquets also allow a diverse group of people of all ages and interests to gather together and enjoy themselves.

Awards & Award Ceremonies – We find plenty of time to moan and complain about the individuals and groups who threaten to send civilization into another dark and confusing age, but we rarely take time to recognize, encourage and offer tribute to the many men, women and children who are doing the very opposite – helping to promote learning and understanding, working to reduce the amount of misinformation in society, and contributing in many ways to our lives. Darwin Day celebrations offer us an opportunity to show gratitude to the groups and individuals who share our commitment to science and humanity and who are helping our communities to move forward and tackle the challenges of our 21st Century civilization head on! They are the real heroes and heroines of our times.

Evolving Awareness Ribbons – The Evolving Awareness ribbons are distributed and worn by the many people within our communities who support, who support and help us to improve the public's understanding of science. They are also well designed and make an interesting conversation piece. They can be purchased for a nominal fee through the Darwin Day Program at www.darwinday.org or via mail at PO Box 92762, Albuquerque, NM 87106 USA.

The Annual Darwin Day Lecture – The annual lecture to commemorate Darwin day has become popular with faculty and university departments, as well as larger community groups. With speakers available in many different disciplines and with the hot topics of today, an event featuring a speaker or group of speakers can bring in a large audience and work well in promoting science and understanding.

Film Festivals – Film festivals, either live or on video, can be a fun for participants. Entertaining performers are surprisingly common within the scientific community and are good at illuminating difficult aspects of science, as well as the often obscure lives of the scientists themselves. Movie marathons with videos like those offered by the BBC and PBS are excellent, but don't forget tongue in cheek presentations of movies such as the 'Planet of the Apes' series and even Tarzan, they're bound to stir up lively discussions about what is and is not possible. A list of entertainers, films and popular movies is available on the Darwin Day site at www.dawrinday.org

Fact cookies/cards – A take-off on fortune cookies, fact cookies are an idea that should go over well with event participants and can be included quite easily in other activities. A recipe for fact cookies, along with a selection of facts to include, can be found at http://www.darwinday.org/events/facts.html Fact cards have similar content as cookies but are put on sheets of paper the size of a playing card and distributed throughout the community or to event participants.

Teachers' workshop – Lectures and discussion on teaching evolution in schools, informing teachers of the latest discoveries, and addressing public concerns are all worthy events, but they must be planned well in advance with qualified staff. Reaching out to the teachers within the community is a very important endeavor – especially in America where our educational institutions are under attack by the forces of pseudoscience. Massimo Pigliucci, a professor at the University of Tennessee in Knoxville and Vice-Chair of the Darwin Day Program has planned successful Teachers' Workshops as part of a week-long Darwin Day celebration in TN. He is available to discuss and help in the planning of such an event for those interested in considering this activity.

Scavenger Hunts – Scavenger hunts are fun and an easy way to educate children, families, and students. They can also be designed to work with whatever resources are available. A zoo may apply the scavenger hunt to animal adaptations, whereas a botanical center would do the same for plants. If you're hosting a local party at your home, it could be a combination of plants, insects, birds, or other backyard flora and fauna. Scavenger hunts can also be based on answering questions through research or exploring one's community to see just how significant science is within society. Online scavenger hunts have also proved popular and can easily be planned by teachers, parents and other interested individuals.

Darwin Road Show – A wonderful concept was created by the California Academy of Sciences for Darwin Day 2002, to give the public an opportunity to meet and greet experts working in several scientific disciplines. The Darwin Road Show invited the public to bring in feathers, bugs, fossils, bones, leaves, rocks or anything from the natural environment that they had questions about and the experts would try to identify the specimens and provide useful information to the participants. Academy experts from the fields of Anthropology, Botany, Entomology, Geology, Herpetology, Ichthyology, Invertebrate Zoology, Mammalogy and Ornithology were on hand to answer questions.

What a fabulous idea to popularize throughout the nation. Think how well it would go down on TV!

Planning for Future Events

It is a good idea to start planning at least a year in advance for your event, especially if you need to reserve a location, bring in speakers, get permits and/or insurance, and organize a complex budget.

If you plan on selling items, these should also be ordered in advance. If you are unsure how large your attendance will be, start small, then in following years you can build your event based on prior experience.

Don't try to do it all yourself. Get a small group of volunteers together to focus on specific tasks, and encourage other local organizations to cooperate or plan complementary events. Museums, zoos, science clubs, universities and schools may have great ideas and resources. Working together will benefit the entire community and individual events can be coordinated together and cross-promoted.

Register Your Event!

Last but not least, register your event on the Darwin Day Program web site (www.darwinday.org) Not only does this allow the program to reach its goal of a global celebration but it also helps people within your community find your event. On February 12, 2002, the Darwin Day Program web site received 700,000 individual visitors to the site. The Events Calendar was one of the more popular pages visited by Internet surfers. We expect this number to continue to rise and the number of events throughout our international community to increase accordingly.

We invite you to join us! ∽

[ABOUT THE AUTHORS]

Rob Beeston is a Co-director of the Darwin Day Program and Director of the Iowa Community Science Initiative, a community based science education resource based in Des Moines, Iowa. Rob is currently involved in projects and books to develop a love and interest in science among children while helping adults understand the necessity for science literacy.

Amanda Chesworth is co-founder and director of the Darwin Day Program and also director of CSICOP's Inquiring Minds program. After running an errand for her father which involved transporting fragile Neanderthal bones on the London "Tube", her interest in the evolutionary sciences soared. She was educated in Canada in interdisciplinary sciences, science communication and education and had the pleasure of attending the Charles Lyell / James Hutton bi-centennial conference in 1997.

[ADDITIONAL RESOURCES]

This article compiles ideas, resources and materials available on the Darwin Day Program web site in the Events area: http://www.darwinday.org/events/

The SkepticWeb: http://www.skepticweb.com

Inquiring Minds: http://www.youngskeptics.org

The Iowa Community Science Initiative: www.iowacsi.com

The excerpt below is from Floyd Sandford's play entitled **Darwin Remembers: Recalling a Life's Voyage**. *It is a re-enactment of the infamous battle between Thomas Henry Huxley and Samuel "Soapy Sam" Wilberforce in 1860 at Oxford. The complete script for Darwin Remembers will be published by Tangled Bank Press for Darwin Day, 2004.*

DARWIN REMEMBERS: RECALLING A LIFE'S VOYAGE

A PLAY IN ONE ACT
(A LIVING HISTORY RE-ENACTMENT FOR ONE ACTOR)
EXCERPT: THE HUXLEY/WILBERFORCE DEBATE OF 1860

by Floyd Sandford

In June of 1860 *The Origin* was publicly debated at the British Association meeting in Oxford. I was too ill to attend. It is providential that I was absent given the nature of the attacks on me and my ideas by Richard Owen, FitzRoy, and the Bishop Samuel Wilberforce.

I don't think I could have borne to confront the Bishop or the sight of FitzRoy holding the Bible aloft and yelling "The book, The book". *(moves to armchair ... and sits)*. Sadly, years later, FitzRoy was dead by his own hand. ... What a mixed character of a man!! *(sets book down on tea table)*.

Discouraged as I was by the attacks against me I was immensely cheered when I heard the news that Hooker and Huxley had so ably defended my views at the debate. What a scene it was! *(Darwin rises. As he speaks he puts on a black robe hanging on side of a room screen, stage right)*. The meeting room was packed to suffocation with 700 people. On the platform sat my good friend Prof. Henslow, who chaired the meeting. The clergy, who shouted lustily for Wilberforce, were in the middle of the room, and behind them a cluster of undergraduates. After several opening speakers the moment of expected confrontation occurred. Ah – *(Darwin pausing/reflecting)* – much has been made of that meeting and of what was actually said at its conclusion by Wilberforce and my champion Huxley. Wilberforce was the first to speak *(actor disappears behind the room screen)* **

** **Note:** *In the following imaginary re-creation of a small part of the historic Wilberforce – Huxley debate, it is recommended that the actor use a high-*

pitched, unctuous voice for Wilberforce and a low stentorial voice for Huxley.

[Before actor appears from behind screen (i) 30-40 seconds of crowd noises could be played for sound effect or (ii) audience could be encouraged to make anticipatory "crowd noises"]

[Stage lights dim ... single red or orange spotlight at front of screen. Actor appears from behind screen wearing a bishops alb over the black robe and a black hood that covers bald patch and beard. Actor is wearing a Wilberforce face mask, and steps into spotlight]

Wilberforce: Mr. Chairman, ladies and gentlemen ... *(with emphasis)* ... fellow human beings. I am sure I speak for nearly all those here, and those unable to attend, when I indicate the disquietude I feel at seeing an ape in a zoo and being told it is my ancestor.

My good friends, there is nothing to this pernicious idea of evolution *(pronounced as "evil-ution")*. Are we to give up the glorious message of the 6-day creation in order to embrace the grotesque godlessness of some cosmic accident? Are we to abandon a long tradition of Christian teaching for this new creed of Darwinism? Good friends ... I can assure you that rock-pigeons are the rock-pigeons that they have always been.

According to Mr. Darwin all forms of life are derived from some common ancestor. Think of it ladies and gentlemen – the delicate dragonfly, the lovely lily, the graceful swan, the cows and sheep grazing in the Kent countryside, and man himself – all descended from some lowly worm lanquishing beneath a rock – or some miraculous mushroom or other fungus flourishing in the darkness of the dank and damp!

Mr. Darwin tells us of finding the fossils of giant beasts from Patagonia who he says are the ancestors of smaller forms he encountered in the jungles of the Amazon. Does he not realize that these are merely antideluvian creatures that perished in the great flood because their large size prevented them from entering the doorway of the Ark?

(Taking a grave tone) Good Christian people, hold firm to your faith, and know that Mr. Darwin's views are contrary to the revelation of God in the Scriptures.

And so ... to you ... my dear Huxley, *(in an oily manner)* about to tear me to pieces once I have sat down – I put to you the question: Is it through your grandfather or your grandmother that you claim descent from a monkey? *(pronounced as "mawnk-kee")*

(Actor leaves and goes behind screen)

[Begin either (i) taped recording of agitated crowd noises, etc. lasting about 30 seconds or (ii) audiance prompted to hiss, catcall, applaud etc. according to their emotion/point of view]

(Actor re-appears from behind screen, wearing black robe and Huxley face mask]

Huxley: Mister chairman, ladies and gentlemen, your lord Bishop. Good friends, I have appreciated – as have all fair men here assembled – the admonishments of the chair, Prof. Henslow, who has demanded of the earlier speakers that the discussion here today should rest on *scientific* grounds only.

Would that the Bishop had been listening!! And would that he had taken the time to read the book being discussed here today before he elected to speak. Conflict between religious doctrine and new scientific discovery is nothing new. When Galileo presumed to question the notion that our Earth was the center of the universe he was thrown into prison. Had Mr. Darwin written this book 400 years ago he would likewise have been imprisoned, tortured, or burned at the stake – all in the name of religion.

But hopefully we live in more enlightened times. Mr. Darwin has written a book. It was long in the writing. Mr. Darwin spent many years making careful observations, he carried out experiments, he gathered massive amounts of evidence, and, after much careful thought and rational consideration, he proposed a theory to help explain what exists in the natural world – for any of those who have the eyes willing to see and the brain willing to reason. And in putting forth his scientific views Mr. Darwin did so without spewing forth disparaging remarks about the Bible or anyone's personal religious faith.

I came here today only in the interests of science, and I have not yet heard anything which could prejudice the case of Mr. Darwin.

The Bishop implies that the idea of Natural Selection drives out the Creator, and then he asserts that he was made by God; and yet you know, do you not, that you yourself were originally a little piece of matter, no bigger than a not-quite-visible speck. Consider your transformation from a microscopic bit of matter to the man you are today. Is that so different from new forms arising over the eons of time?

Finally, good sir, in regards your question of my ancestry. Would I rather have a miserable ape for a grandfather or a man highly endowed by nature and possessed of great means and influence for the mere purpose of introducing ridicule into grave scientific discussion – why then, sir, I would unhesitatingly affirm my preference for the Ape!!

I should feel no shame to have arisen from such an origin. For I sir would rather be the offspring of two apes than be a man who is eloquent in the service of prejudice and falsehood, and who is afraid to face the truth!!
(actor disappears behind screen)

[Either (i) taped recording for about 30 seconds of angry crowd, commotion, etc., or (ii) audience prompted to respond as their emotions or intellectual positions dictate]

(Spotlight off, stage lights come back on, and actor appears from behind screen as Darwin)

I found the Bishop generally free of malice. But as for Huxley – well – his dislike of the man lasted until many years later when, sadly, Wilberforce was thrown from his horse and his head struck a stone. At hearing the news Huxley wrote "for once the Bishop's brains and reality came into contact ... And the result was fatal". *(spoken in deep, Huxley voice)*.

[ABOUT THE AUTHOR]

A native New Yorker, Floyd Sandford has lived in Iowa and taught Biology at Coe College, a small private liberal arts college in Cedar Rapids, since 1971. A former Peace Corps Volunteer in Nigeria, he is an environmentalist who enjoys gardening, hiking, and international travel. Long an admirer of Darwin, he wrote "Darwin Remembers" to help shed more light on the nature of the man and the significance of his scientific accomplishments.

[ADDITIONAL RESOURCES]

Note: Tangled Bank Press will be publishing the full play Darwin Remembers in 2004.

Darwin as "Different Drummer"

by Mynga Futrell

In the *Different Drummers: Nonconforming Thinkers in History* teaching materials, there is a lesson featuring Charles Darwin. It is for good reason that he figures among the assortment of persons highlighted in this supplemental curriculum module. Centering as it does on the topic of *free and independent thought in historical context*, this educational package focuses on thinking that has deviated from the ordinary. Thus, it's no surprise to find Darwin included.

As the introduction to the module states:

> Not always, but not surprisingly either, a society's resounding ideas frequently emerge from people who tend to "look at things" ... well ... differently. In fact, in every era there seem to live people who think freely and independently and do not conform to the mainstream. They are, so to speak, the "different drummers" of their times. These nonconforming thinkers make for an interesting and worthwhile topic of study.

The story lesson on Darwin, aimed at middle school youngsters, is entitled, "The Hungry Learner's Big Picture." The children who read that short two-page story cannot fail to see that Darwin's desire to learn, and his ability to put diverse pieces of information together and draw conclusions, was exceptional!

The story begins with the notion of how a well-educated family saw in young Charles a lazy boy. It quotes the father's memorable rebuke about Charles's caring for nothing but shooting and dogs and rat-catching:

> In reality, though, Charles was busy all the time. He just preferred a different way of learning than most people. Young Charles liked best to collect things. He collected shells, birds' eggs, and coins. He was very curious. He examined closely. He watched birds and insects. He helped his brother make chemical experiments at home. He said in later years these activities were the best part of his education (much better than school!).

Later, the story further emphasizes the contrast with others' notions of learning, noting the young man's empirical bent, along with how much he looked forward with anticipation to his job as naturalist for the sailing ship HMS *Beagle*, which he approached in hopes he would be able to examine things he found to his heart's content.

> Now this was the kind of studying Charles loved to do. "Lazy" would be the wrong word to describe a Charles Darwin, Naturalist. "Hungry" would be much better – hungry to learn. And hungry to learn **directly, from Nature**.

Final portions of the Darwin story allude to how he "thought through' and made use of the information he had gathered on his trip to create a "universal explanation" that deviated from the assorted creation stories and cultural explanations of his times.

> He had acquired more information to think about than any other naturalist of his day had. All the travel and study had given him a "big picture" about life on our planet. ... Darwin could explain how life developed to everybody because (his explanation) was based on the totality of his big picture... **and** his different way of learning. He had learned from Nature by examining Nature directly. He learned by observing, not by reading books or listening to stories. And, he had examined very carefully. ... His idea explained those many observations.

In *Different Drummers*, Darwin is but one in a long lineup of individuals who have made their mark in large part because their ideas departed from what was anticipated within their society. Much such "different thinking" has had important consequence. Often, it has spurred societal changes within the individual's lifetime. In many cases, such as Darwin's, the changes extend far beyond the person's own times and the society within which she or he lived. The *Different Drummers* materials seek to ensure that students of social studies are made aware of such individuals.

The teaching module, which consists of 300 pages of lessons, stories, activities, and supplementary items, such as "baseball cards" of some notable free and independent thinkers, has a clear purpose. Here is how the module states its goals for the teacher:

(1) To cultivate your students' respect for the freedom of people to think freely or to hold unfamiliar or dissimilar philosophic and religious beliefs,

(2) To increase your students' awareness of the vast diversity of human thought, and

(3) To foster your students' commitment to safeguarding within society individual conviction and independence of thought.

The module, in addition to offering examples of different thinkers, helps to focus students' attention on the attributes of people whose "habits of mind" depart from the conventional. *Curiosity, skepticism, and divergent thinking* (the tendency to come up with "way out in left field" sorts of notions) receive special attention.

What it means *to conform* or *not to conform* is also an important topic, as are the varied consequences of "different thinking" for the individual and for society. The intent is to foster in students an open-mindedness toward (rather than disapproval of) non-conformity. Such an attitude serves to buffer immediate judgment made without basis (rather than a surface response, judgment of "that which is different" can be *reasoned*). Likewise, there is also a hope to nurture students' appreciation that a different drummer's actions or views may be of benefit in the long run. Attention is also given to cultivating in students a sense that those who think "too differently" may be vulnerable and in need of legal protection.

To come forth with ideas that directly challenge prevailing thinking is generally "no picnic" for the person. Is it just fortuitous that a Mark Twain could become renowned for his creative irreverence whereas others have met bitter ends for less? Society can lash back forcefully against those whose thinking departs from strongly held societal beliefs. Yet, are we not fortunate that there still exist people whose ideas leap beyond the bounds of convention?

In *Different Drummers*, students analyze historical situations in which free and independent thought changed the course of history and resulted in social progress. They also analyze historical situations in which dramatically nonconforming thought meets up with strongly held societal norms. In the hands of the imaginative and committed teacher, they can grow to understand the relevance of our country's constitutional protections for religious freedom to its free and independent thinkers.

The teacher's manual suggests:

> As part of guiding your students in their study of the past, you can help them see how some of the concepts they hold in high regard today were once disparaged or condemned. You can help students to appreciate their own freedom to reason independently and to see things differently than their peers. And you can shepherd your students' indulgence of those who happen to reach conclusions or hold convictions unlike their own. After all, a different drummer's idea sometimes changes history!

Indeed, the course of history has seen civilization advance via many different avenues. There is no single thoroughfare by which humans have reaped the world's greatest ideas. The *Different Drummers* module explores the pathway of free and independent thinking. As the Charles Darwin example evidences, it has proved particularly fruitful.

> The Different Drummers teaching materials are available direct from the publisher (at cost of printing, approx. $25). Order at the www.trafford.com web site. Teachers can, if they prefer, download any portions of interest from the Different Drummers web site [www.teachingaboutreligion.com] and then duplicate the materials free for use in their classes.

∞

[ABOUT THE AUTHOR]

Mynga Futrell is schooled in science and curriculum development from Eastern Kentucky University and the University of Wyoming, where she earned her Ph.D. She is a founding members and current president of Sacramento's Atheists and Other Freethinkers, a board member of the Atheist Alliance, an officer in Americans United, and a counselor at Camp Quest. Mynga is "institution free" having run her own computer training school and now is a full-time freelance writer and curriculum developer. She co-authored *Teachers, Computers, and Curriculum* (a college text for teachers), *Different Drummers: Nonconforming Thinkers in History* (freethought materials for teaching about religion), and the Teaching About Religion web site for educators.

[ADDITIONAL RESOURCES]

Teaching about Religion: http://www.teachingaboutreligion.org

The English Garden of the Victorian era is well known for its aesthetic beauty and vibrant fragrances. Charles and Emma Darwin spent much time and effort creating the gardens and orchard at Down House. Here, Joan Treis shares her research and ongoing quest to create a replica of Darwin's Gardens in Woodmere, Missouri and invites others to do the same in celebration of Darwin Day.

DARWIN'S GARDENS
by Joan Treis

On September 15 in 1835, the HMS *Beagle* anchored on the Galápagos Islands. Charles Darwin, only 26 at the time, stepped ashore and cut his shoes on the sharp edged lava rocks. His life on the ship was wretched: cramped quarters, terrible food combined with seasickness day after day.

Darwin had little space for his specimens, his notebooks or his instruments, yet he still found himself amassing great collections from the natural world and enjoying deep thought and investigation into all that he encountered: coral reefs, volcanic isles, finches and other fascinating organic and inorganic treasures of our world.

It was once said that destiny is seldom recognized until it has changed its name to history. Charles Darwin's voyage on the H.M.S. *Beagle* is an exciting part of the history of all people... of all life. His revolutionary voyage captures the story of a brilliant idea... "the single best idea anyone has ever had" wrote Daniel Dennett in *Darwin's Dangerous Idea*.

Darwin gave us the first reasonable glimpse into the origin of species. What was unknown to preceeding generations, has now become a foundation of knowledge and understanding: man is a fellow voyager with other creatures in the grand odyssey of evolution. Our understanding allows us a sense of kinship with all animals and a wonderous excitement for life.

In nature Darwin knew that nothing is insignificant, there is no boredom or tedious repetition to be found in the study of life and earth process. At his private country home in Downe, Kent, Charles Darwin and his wife Emma offered a tribute to nature by nurturing the gardens at Down House. Charles and Emma grew Virginia Creeper, Clematis, Wisteria, Victorian Climbing Roses, Creeping Gloxinia, Hyacinth Bean, Morning Glories, Painted Lady Runner Beans and much more.

My research into Darwin's Gardens led to my own, similar creation at our property in Missouri, USA. Correspondence with curators at Down House, as well as collecting information in Darwin letters, memoirs and books written by family members, led me on a journey to the gardens at Down. As though I was looking over the shoulder of Charles and his dear Emma I captured the science and beauty they applied to their labor of love – laying out the plans for the gardens, choosing a rich assortment of trees, flowers and shrubs with great care and aesthetic appeal, tending to their creations for many years to follow. Gardening is an artform in Britain and we are fortunate that the descendents and curators of Down House have preserved the gardens for future generations.

Down House is a remarkable place – home to the greatest of modern naturalists.

In a letter to their son William, Emma lamented the rainy weather. This bit of correspondence led me to her notes on the variety of roses she grew at Down. Notebooks and texts on Victorian gardening practices along with Richard Mabey's *Frampton Flora* all aided in my research. Further study led to an homage to Emma, for it was her devoted care and influence that created and maintained this fine and private place. Her elegance is captured in the beauty of Darwin's Gardens.

To gather material for his work on the fertilization of orchids, Darwin would hike slowly up a hillside near a sloping pasture near his house and patiently stand there, waiting for the bees to arrive and perform their progenitive rites. He called it his "orchis meadow", because of the thickly grown but delicate flowers of the genus "Orchis" to be found there. This image of Darwin, the rural sage, stuck with me through my reading and research.

My list of the flora found in the gardens at Down fills dozens of pages. With this botanical list one can see the progress of seasons in a gardener's year and the succession of colors and scents from the first flowers of spring through the last wild rose of autumn. Each Down garden plant was selected with care and admired for its individuality of character, as if looked at and studied with a hand lens.

My family and I live in mid Missouri on 23 acres called "Woodmere" by previous owners.

"Woodmere" is a Scottish name meaning wooded lake and refer to the 8 acres of tree lined lake that are part of the setting. A well developed forest community can be found here and is characterized by oaks, maples, dogwood, pine, willow and elm trees. The seasonal flora can be quite spectacular with large masses of asters, goldenrods, multiflora rose, touch me nots, day lily, bluebells, phlox and elderberries to name only a few. Other wildflowers seemed grouped by natural habitats. The collection includes an awesome variety of plant species (mosses and lichen) which grow on limestone rocky hills in pinetums, woodland and wetland communities as well as plants that thrive in the clay soil. The diverse and brilliant display of wildflowers in the woods and surrounding the lakes changes dramatically with the seasons. Many of the woodland plants growing at Down are also part of the setting at Woodmere. Surrounding the lake area is a 'sandwalk' path akin to Darwin's thinking path, of the same name at Down.

Our aim at Woodmere is to create a self sustaining population of native species while taking into account aesthetic considerations and to have the hand of nature and the hand of horticulture so intertwined that you can't tell where one stops and the other begins. "Survival of the fittest" will be the guiding principle. A decaying tree stump will be as much a part of the landscape as an elegant birdbath and the baby birds that gather around.

The gardens at Woodmere are dedicated to Charles and Emma Darwin. Their own gardens were a source for inspiration, study and experiment, and peace of mind. The creation and research of a garden such as my own, pays homage to Darwin's work, and helps one understand how different parts of the natural world enhance, depend, and play off one another. This concept also helps to describe Charles and Emma's life together, for Charles called Emma "his greatest blessing." In other words, science and the life of scientists, are not devoid of love but are instead guided continuously by such.

An unfortunate reality about gardens is that they often do not survive their gardeners, or can quickly fall to ruin without proper care. The story of Charles and Emma's garden however, has a happy ending. Plans are underway to restore and faithfully maintain the integrity of the gardens at Down House. The house is now fully restored and the restoration of the garden and surrounding meadows and woodlands is due to be completed in 2002. Charles and Emma would be most happy to learn that generations of enthusiasts have the opportunity to walk through the Kentish fields and along the sandwalk to see what one Victorian flower album from the 1860s calls "… the floral gems glistening on the verdant face of nature."

Last week while walking our own 'sandwalk' path around the lake I noticed some brightly colored flowers on the hillside near the farmland adjacent to ours. Viola tricolor. Common names for Viola tricolor are "love in idleness", and "heartsease." By any name this enchanting flower (a Victorian favorite) symbolizes the peace and serenity a garden can offer. A garden can have many harvests, the most important being the one that awakens our spirit each and every day. A fitting tribute to the life and work of Charles Darwin and in celebration of Darwin Day is to create your own garden in the special area of the world you call home. ∞

[ABOUT THE AUTHOR]

Joan Treis lives on a 23 acre property near the historic town of Hermann, Missouri. It is here where she runs a Bed & Breakfast named Cabin At Woodmere. Joan is an avid gardener, collecting native Missouri wildflower species and conducting research into the plants, insects and wildlife that live in the wooded surroundings. Her property also contains a Darwin's Garden, complete with a Sandwalk. Joan continues to do research into the life of Charles and Emma Darwin and contributes to the Darwin Day Program regularly.

[ADDITIONAL ONLINE RESOURCES]

Darwin's Gardens by Joan Treis: http://www.darwinday.org/features/gardens.html

Cabin at Woodmere: http://www.ktis.net/~woodmere/

Darwin Country: http://www.darwincountry.org/

Darwin's Ark is republished with permission from the author.

DARWIN'S ARK
by Philip Appleman

        Queasy again, and feeling
        as wintry as Methuselah,
        Darwin begins to drowse, and thinks,
        as he always does, of animals, all
        those animals, and remembers
        his leafy days at Cambridge, chasing beetles
        and cramming for the Ministry: the Testament
        in Greek, the classy proofs
        of God's design – and in that jungle
        of memories, he drifts off, and dreams
        that he is Noah, seed of Methuselah, already
        six hundred years old, more than a little tired
        from all that virtuous living – and then (just
        his luck) a finger out of the clouds
        pokes down at him, and a voice
        like a celestial sergeant commands:
        "Make thee an ark of gopher wood…"
        The details follow, in that same
        platoon-leader's voice: the boat shall be
        four hundred fifty feet long,
        seventy-five feet wide, three decks,
        one window, one door.

                And then
                the voice tells him why.

His sons, Shem, Ham, and Japheth, just
cannot handle this news:
"He's going to drown them *all*?" Japheth whispers,
"Every last woman and child? But why?"
Noah's mind isn't what it used to be; lately
it strays like a lost lamb: "Uh –
wickedness, I believe
that's what He said – yes, wickedness."
Too vague for Japheth: "But wicked *how*? I mean,
what are the charges, exactly?"
The old brow wrinkles again: "Evil, that's
what He said. Corruption. Violence."
"*Violence*? What do you call
this killer flood – this program – this Final
Solution of His? He's going to deep-six
the lot of them, just
for making a few mistakes? For being – *human*?"
Now Japheth was really riled; being the youngest,
he still had a lot of drinking buddies out there –
Enos and Jared, and raunchy Adah
and his pretty young neighbor,
Zillah – together they'd put away
many a goatskin of red wine
under the big desert stars. Besides,
being a kid, a mere ninety years old,
he still enjoyed stumping his father
with embarrassing questions: "Listen,
Dad, I thought you said He
was omniscient – well, then,
wouldn't He have foreseen all this? And if He did,
then why did He make us the way we are,
in the first place? Just think of all this
useless trouble, the waste,
the genocide!"

"Ours not to reason why," says Shem (the first-born,
and something of a prig), "Ours but to build the ark."
"And that's another thing," Japheth scowls,
"what is an *ark*, exactly? I mean,
we're desert people, right? – nomads,
living out here in this miserable dry scrub
with our smelly goats and camels –
I never saw a boat in my life."
"Well I saw one once," Noah quavers,
"but I don't remember it very well,"
that was four hundred years ago –
or was it five, let's see…"

"Concentrate, Dad," says Ham,
always the practical one, "Look,
it can't be that hard, and ordinary boat,
we'll mock one up, no problem – a keel,
that's it, you begin with a keel of gopher wood,
and the rest is easy: ribs, then planks,
pitch, decking – listen,
just give me a crew of hard-hats, say a hundred
of those wretched condemned sinners out there,
and I'll handle it."

So finally they had themselves an ark,
and God says, "OK, Noah,
get the animals – clean breasts, seven of a kind,
unclean, just two, but make sure
they're male and female, you got that straight?
Now hurry it up, I'm itching to get
the drowning started."
Noah had thought that this
would be the easy part, but Japheth,
of course, knows better: "Dad,
did you say *every* animal?"
"Every animal," Noah repeats,
quoting Authority: " 'Every living thing
of all flesh' – fowl,
cattle, creeping things, the works.
Plus food enough for a year."

Well, just imagine: you're living out there
in that abominable desert, and all of a sudden
you're supposed to come up with two elephants.
Or is it more? "Shem – Shem, is the elephant
a clean of an unclean animal –
if it's clean, that means seven of them,
and the ark is in trouble. And how
about rhinos? hippos? And what do we do
about the dinosaurs? How do we get a brontosaurus
up the gangplank?" Japheth, of course,
loved raising problems that Noah
hadn't thought of at all: "Pandas – kids
love pandas, we can't let them drown,
but how do we get two of them here
in a hurry, all the way from China?
And, of, by the way, Dad,
how are we going to keep the lions
away from the lambs?"

Let's face it, it was a nightmare:
the apes and monkeys were bad enough –
gibbons, orangutans, gorillas, chimps,
howler monkeys, spider monkeys, squirrel monkeys,
capuchins, mandrills, baboons, marmosets –
just think of poor Ham, after all of his angst
and sweat, getting the ark assembled, and then
having to schlepp off to the Congo, the Amazon,
to bring 'em back alive, all those tricky
long-tailed leapers, up in the jungle greenery.

And Shem, dutiful Shem, in charge
of the other mammals – the giraffes,
the horses, zebras, quaggas, tapirs, bison,
the pumas, bears, raccoons, weasels,
skunks, mink, badgers, otters, hyenas,
the rats, mice, squirrels, gophers, beavers,
porcupines, rabbits, hares, bats,
sloths, anteaters, moles, shrews – thousands
of species of mammals.

And Japheth out there on the cliffs and treetops
trying to snare the birds: the eagles,
condors, hawks, buzzards, vultures, and every
winged beauty in the Field Guides, and bring then back,
chattering, twittering, fluttering around
on the top deck – thousands on thousands
of hyperkinetic birds.

> Two by two
> they come strolling through:
> antelope, buffalo, camel, dog,
> egret, ferret, gopher, frog,
> quail and bunny, sheep and goose,
> turtle, nuthatch, ostrich, moose,
> ibex, jackal, kiwi, lark,
> two by two they board the ark.

Well, it's pretty clear, isn't it,
that we've got a space problem here: a boat
only four hundred fifty feet long, already buzzing
and bleating and squeaking and mooing
and grunting and mewing and hissing and cooing
and trumpeting and growling and roaring and snarling
and chirping and peeping and clucking and croaking –
and the crocodiles aren't back from the Nile
yet, or the iguanas from the islands,

or the kangaroos and koalas, or
the pythons or boas or cotton-mouthed moccasins
or the thirty different species of rattlesnake
or the tortoises, salamanders, centipedes, toads...

It took some doing, all that,
but Ham came back with them,
and wouldn't you know,
it's Japheth who opens up, so to speak,
the can of worms: "Worms, Dad! There are thirty-two
thousand species of worms – who's
going digging for *them*? And oh, yes –
how about the insects?"
"Insects!" Shem, old Goody-Two-Shoes, rebels
at last. "Dad, do we have to save *insects*?" Noah,
faithful servant, quotes the Word:
"every living thing." "But Dad, the cockroaches?"
Noah has all the best instincts
of a minor bureaucrat: he
is only following orders; the roaches
go aboard.

But it turns out, the insects almost
break up the team, because
this is not just anybody's dream,
this is Darwin's dream, so of course
Japheth knows too much. "Look, Dad,
we've got dragonflies, damselflies, locusts, and aphids,
grasshoppers, mantises, crickets, and termites...
Wait a minute – termites?
You're going to save termites – in a wooden boat?"
But Japheth knows that arguing with Noah
is like driving a nail into chicken soup – he shrugs
and ticks away at his clipboard:
"We've got lice, beetles, God knows
(pardon the expression) how many beetles;
we've got bedbugs, cooties, gnats, and midges,
horseflies, sawflies, bottleflies, fireflies,
we've got ants, bees, wasps, hornets –
can you imagine what it's going to be like
locked in with *them* for a whole year?
But listen, Dad, we haven't scratched the surface –
there are nine hundred thousand species
of insects out there, did you happen to know that
when you took this job?
Even if we unload all the other animals,
the insects alone will sink the ark!"

Ah, but the ark was not floating on fact,
it was floating on faith: that is to say,
on fiction – and in fiction, the insects
went aboard, all nine hundred thousand
buzzing, stinging, chittering, biting species,
and a year's supply
of hay for the elephants, a year's bananas
for the monkeys – "OK," Japheth says,
"But you still haven't answered my question –
what will the meat-eaters eat?"
"We'll cross that bridge when we come to it,"
Noah replies, in history's
least appropriate trope. "Come on,
all aboard; it's starting
to sprinkle."

    The east wind, full of broth,
    bullies the bay windows, and Darwin
    stirs in his sleep, losing the ark
    for a moment, seeing Brazil again,
    the rain forests, the insects, blue-
    green, vermilion, saffron – all
    those beautiful insects...

Well, the fountains of the great deep
were broken up, and the windows of heaven opened,
and the rain was upon the earth
forty days and forty nights,
and the ark was lifted up
and went upon the face of the waters,
and the floundering began outside, the running
for the hills. Noah knew it was happening,
and so did Shem and Ham, snug
as a bug on A deck; but
it was hard-boiled Japheth who howled and keened
for Eros and Jared, still out there
somewhere, and Adah and beautiful Zillah,
so he was the first to break and run
for the one small window; and yes,
there it was, just the way fear
had been painting it on his eyelids ever since
that divine command: the fighting
for high ground, crazed beasts goring
and gnashing, serpents dangling from trees.
Then Shem and Ham and finally Noah
and the four nameless wives
couldn't resist; they ran for the window

and watched their friends and neighbors
hugging in love and panic until
they all went under. Japheth caught
one final glimpse, and of course it had to be Zillah,
holding her baby over her head
till the water rolled over her
and she sank, and the baby
sank, splashing a little, and then
there was silence upon the waters,
and God was well pleased.
They all turned away from the window, Noah
and his boys, and their weeping wives,
and no one in the ark would look
at anyone else for many days.

So, for a solid year that strange menagerie
lived in the ark, the sixteen thousand hungry birds
lusting for the eighteen hundred thousand insects,
and the twelve thousand snakes and lizards
nipping at the seven thousand mammals,
and everyone slipping and sliding around
on the sixty-four thousand worms
and the one hundred thousand spiders –
and Noah driving everyone buggy, repeating
every morning, as if he'd just thought of it:
"Well, we're all in the same boat."

> (Oh, in case you're wondering, Noah
> conveniently
> forgot about the dinosaurs:
> even in miracles, enough
> is enough.)

It was a long, long year. Imagine,
if you will, the trouble
for those washed-out men and their bedraggled wives,
feeding the gerbils and hamsters, cleaning
the thousands of cages, keeping the jaguars
away from the gazelles, the grizzlies away
from the cottontails – everything aboard, after all,
was an endangered species.
And imagine those seven clean elk,
clashing antlers at mating time,
and imagine Noah, with his brittle bones, trying
to dodge all those rattlers and copperheads
and vipers and cobras and scorpions and
black widows and tarantulas: and imagine – oh, imagine

cleaning up after the elephants
for a whole year, swabbing those
unspeakable decks...

But enough –
our sleeper is stirring.

Darwin starts out of his bad dream, sweating,
and lies there thinking of Noah.
Darwin knows all about death, and extinction, and so
he understands
the sinking heart of poor old Noah,
after the waters subsided,
and the dove fluttered off and never returned,
and the gangplank slid to Ararat,
and the animals scampered out to the muddy,
corpse-ridden earth – Noah,
burning a lamb on his altar
under that relentless rainbow, remembering
that he rescued the spiders and roaches, but
he let Enoch and Jubal
and Caiman and Lamech and
their wives and innocent children
go to a soggy grave – and Darwin knows
that Noah knows, in his tired bones,
that now he will have to be fruitful once more,
and multiply, and replenish the earth
with a pure new race of people who
would never, never sin again,
for if they did,
all that killing would be
for nothing, a terrible
embarrassment to God. And Noah knows
that just like his grandpa, Methuselah,
he will be obliged to live
with his strangling memories
for another three hundred years.

[ABOUT THE AUTHOR]

Philip Appleman is Distinguished Professor Emeritus at Indiana University, where he was a founding editor of *Victorian Studies*, national committee chairman for English Section II of the Modern Language Association, and member of the national council of the American Association of University Professors. He is the author of a book on overpopulation, *The Silent Explosion*; coeditor of *1859: Entering an Age of Crisis*; editor of Thomas Malthus's *An Essay on the Principle of Population*; Charles Darwin's *Origin of Species*; *Darwin: A Norton Critical Edition*; and author of several award-winning volumes of poetry, including *Darwin's Ark* and *New and Selected Poems: 1956-1996*, as well as three novels, including *Apes and Angels*.

DEEP TIME IN THE DEEP SOUTH

by David C. Kopaska-Merkel

Alabama is a study in contrasts. It is a state that is more diverse geologically than most other areas of comparable size, yet earth science classes are taught in only a handful of schools around the state while the public debate about evolution continues in full force.

As a consequence of the paucity of earth science instruction, knowledge of geology among Alabamians is minimal, yet the state geological survey is one of the largest, oldest, and most active in the United States. I work for the Geological Survey of Alabama (GSA), and one of my tasks is to provide geological information to teachers, children, and citizens of the state.

An important aspect of our educational program is the publication of scientific findings and research uncovered in the daily activities and projects of the GSA. These diverse educational publications have been produced since the second decade of the 20th Century. The complete List of Publications is accessible on the Survey web site www.gsa.state.al.us. Paleontological publications include handbooks for collectors at various levels of sophistication (Copeland, 1963; Toulmin, 1977; Burdick and Strimple, 1982) and a guidebook to fossils of northwest Alabama that was written specifically for K-12 teachers (Kopaska-Merkel and others, 2001). Excluded from the List are no-charge publications including brochures (topics range from landslides to radon to ground water), posters, calendars, fact sheets and post cards, which can be requested by teachers or picked up in person. The Survey budget pays for the publication program, but not for any other educational outreach activities.

Other educational-outreach activities of the Survey are funded by an annual golf tournament that is run by staff members of the Survey and its sister agency the Alabama State Oil and Gas Board. Thus to a large extent the ingenuity and energy of individual employees define the nature and scope of educational outreach activities at the Survey. Outreach activities include field workshops, fossil kits and more.

A field workshop series for K-12 teachers was initiated in 1997. Current offerings consist of an annual one-day workshop in Sumter County, in which we focus on the Cretaceous (144 - 65 million years ago) marine faunas of Alabama's Black Belt. A similar workshop in Mississippian (360 - 320 million years ago) strata of northwest Alabama is run on an irregular schedule. About 30 teachers attend each workshop. We collaborate with local universities on these projects (the University of West Alabama and the University of North Alabama), and our local contacts in both cases are earth-science faculty members. This collaboration is absolutely critical, because it provides no-cost or inexpensive laboratory and classroom space, vehicles, local geological expertise, and in some cases additional funds donated by the universities. The workshops are popular, the teachers have fun and learn a lot, they earn continuing-education credit that they can report to their schools and we get feedback from them which is used to improve the workshops. At first it was difficult to attract sufficient teachers to fill up our roster, but after 5 years of workshops we now usually have to turn people away, most attracted to the event by word of mouth. We send notices directly to former participants and to organizations that publish newsletters targeting K-12 science teachers (Alabama Science Teachers Association, other Alabama institutions such as the Alabama Geological Society, the Tennessee science-teacher association, and the southeastern section of the National Association of Geoscience Teachers). Most high-school science teachers in Alabama are biologists and they have never "done geology" in the field before their experience at our workshop.

Survey staff members attend teachers' professional meetings, such as the annual meeting of the Alabama Science Teachers Association. At these meetings we staff booths in the exhibit halls, giving away free publications and fossils, and sometimes run workshops. We have also held workshops at other meetings, such as those of the League of Municipalities and other groups that have a professional interest in earth science but whose members are neither earth scientists nor teachers. Generally at these meetings we make a few contacts with teachers who get in touch with us later requesting assistance in the classroom or specialized information.

Many of our outreach efforts are aimed at the classroom. Staff members frequently visit schools to speak or conduct demonstrations on geological topics ranging from using a GPS unit to basic paleoecology. The subject matter is tailored to the participating schools' course of study. Similar visits are also made to social groups such as girl-scout troops. Survey staff members have constructed several fossil kits which are lent to schools and day-care centers anywhere in the state. The fossil kits contain 37 different Alabama fossils, an activity book and other materials. We pay to send the kits via UPS and ask schools to pay for their return. This arrangement has caused package return problems in a few cases because the kits are large and heavy and thus expensive to ship. To remedy this situation, the GSA has developed a small rock and mineral kit that is sold for $5 to the general public (and sometimes given to teachers). We would like to develop similar fossil kits that we might offer for sale, but the time has not been available for mass production of such kits. The Survey participates in the Adopt-a-School program, and is a partner of two Tuscaloosa schools. The Survey also donates many labeled fossil specimens to schools all over the state, generally when we meet teachers at workshops and meetings so that we can save the cost of shipping. Most of the fossil specimens are provided by a tireless fossil collector in north Alabama, Mr. Don Williams. Mr. Williams provides the fossils, and the Survey gets the fossils into the hands of teachers who will be able to use them. This demonstrates once again the influence of individual action in relation to a low-cost educational program, and also the great service that can be provided to earth-science education by private citizens.

An activity strictly for children is a fossil dig, which is held in conjunction with

Tuscaloosa's annual CityFest. The fossil dig takes advantage of children's fascination with fossils to let us teach them and their parents a little about geology. The dig is the most popular children's activity at CityFest, and garners excellent publicity for the agency. Some K-12 science teachers visit the fossil dig with their children and then later contact the Survey for assistance in the classroom.

The Survey also provides advice and assistance to other educational institutions, thus indirectly reaching many more students than the agency could contact directly. The Survey is currently helping the University of Alabama Arboretum develop a set of earth-science activities and has in the past provided advice, assistance and materials to the Turtle Point Science Center, Legacy (the state environmental-education organization), Tuscaloosa Children's Hands-On Museum and the Alabama Historical Commission. In addition, the Survey redistributes (at no charge) publications of the U.S. Geological Survey, the American Geological Institute, and other professional geological organizations.

Other GSA outreach activities include a partnership with an amateur organization (the Birmingham Paleontological Society) and the Alabama Museum of Natural History to salvage trace fossils from a coal mine in Walker County. This project has an internationally recognized scientific value as well as an educational component. One result of the salvage operation will be an illustrated monograph to which the Survey is contributing editing expertise as well as several chapters. The potential readership of the monograph will include both professional geologists and amateur fossil collectors. However, the heavily illustrated book will provide a nontechnical summary of one of Alabama's greatest geologic treasures and should therefore be useful to earth-science teachers at the high school and undergraduate levels.

Other services provided by the Survey include tours of the GSA facilities, science-fair judging, job shadowing by students and internships for students and K-12 teachers. Educational information is available on the Survey web site at www.gsa.state.al.us/ under the heading "Programs."

How does all of this educational activity affect the general public's understanding of evolution? Many Survey educational publications concern paleontology. Children generally find fossils fascinating and nontechnical publications provide good opportunities to introduce deep time, which is virtually unavoidable in anything having to do with fossils or stratigraphy. Other educational activities provide similar opportunities. For example, one of the most popular activities in elementary classrooms is to pass around and talk about fossils. Any such discussion involves the great age of the Earth, but, more importantly, ancient environments. Why do we find marine shells in almost every part of the state? What does the distribution of fossil shells show about the ancient world? Implicit in questions like these is the concept of great age.

Educational programs can be surprisingly effective and yet inexpensive, if people are willing to donate time and effort to the job. It helps if supervisors allow people to volunteer, design and implement their own tasks. The reward is seeing the children and teachers benefit. ∞

[ABOUT THE AUTHOR]

David Kopaska-Merkel is Head of the Ground Water Section at the Geological Survey of Alabama, where he has worked since 1989. Kopaska-Merkel holds a Ph.D. in geology from the University of Kansas, and his published research ranges from petroleum geology to systematics. Current endeavors focus on earth-science education, hydrogeology, and coastal sedimentology.

Kopaska-Merkel improves concision by writing poetry during lunch.

[REFERENCES]

Copeland, C. W., 1963, Curious creatures in Alabama rocks: Alabama Geological Survey Circular 19, 45 p.

Toulmin, L. D., 1977, Stratigraphic distribution of Paleocene and Eocene fossils in the eastern Gulf Coast region: Alabama Geological Survey Monograph 13, 602 p.

Burdick, D. W., and Strimple, H. L., 1982, Genevievian and Chesterian crinoids of Alabama: Alabama Geological Survey Bulletin 121, 277 p.

Kopaska-Merkel, D. C., Rindsberg, A. K., Logue, Terence, Puckett, T. M., and Vick, Christa, 2001, Mississippian of north Alabama: A hands-on fossil workshop for teachers: Alabama Geological Survey Educational Series 13, 57 p.

[ADDITIONAL RESOURCES]

Geological Survey of Alabama: http://www.gsa.state.al.us

EDUCATING THE EDUCATORS
by Massimo Pigliucci

In 1859 the world got a piece of shocking news: it seems that not only is the earth *not* the center of the universe, as Copernicus and Galileo had amply demonstrated, but that human beings are not the pinnacle of creation after all. This devastating blow to our self-esteem (as Freud called it) – the second in three centuries – was dealt by Charles Darwin, a quiet Englishman who had made his lifelong activity the understanding of the natural variation of living organisms. As is well known, the publication of his *On the Origin of Species* caused quite a stir in academic circles and among the general public. The first kind of controversy (the scientific one) lasted only a few decades: by the turn of the 20th century the theory of descent with modification (as Darwin called it), or evolution (as we now refer to it), was as solidly established as general relativity or the theory of gases.

Not so for the second sort of controversy: while the general public in most European countries does not consider the notion that we are closely related to chimps and monkeys particularly outrageous anymore, a vocal minority in the United States refuses the very idea on ideological grounds: it's not in the Bible, so it can't be.

How can this bizarre state of affairs persist into the 21st century?

To a scientist, this seems as incredible as somebody seriously defending the theory that the earth is flat (which a few people belonging to the Flat Earth Society in California actually do!). Scientists are not in the business of questioning people's religious beliefs, but they are also paid to teach the best of what we have good reasons to think we know, leaving individuals to make decisions on how to reconcile the discoveries of science with their own religious views.

It is this disconnect – between what scientists accept as established beyond reasonable doubt and what a sizable portion of the American public believes – that has prompted the annual celebration of "Darwin Day" at the University of Tennessee at Knoxville.

Darwin Day got started in Tennessee in 1996 as the result of a reaction to the silliness of a bill then being considered by the state legislature and which would have curtailed the teaching of evolution in Tennessee's public schools. A group of students and faculty of the then recently created Department of Ecology and Evolutionary Biology at the University in Knoxville was discussing the situation over a beer (at a several-times-since-defunct brewery on Gay Street in Knoxville, TN) and decided to create a group whose mission would be to dispel the so many myths and misunderstandings about evolution and Darwinism that periodically fuel such misguided legislative attempts as the 1996 Tennessee Senate bill n. 3229. (The bill fortunately died in committee, although it generated enough negative publicity that the BBC did a special show on the controversy). So was born the Tennessee Darwin Coalition.

The Tennessee Darwin Coalition served as inspiration behind the international Darwin Day Program. The Darwin Day Program works to encourage the public to learn about evolutionary biology and to prompt scientists to get out of their ivory towers for at least a few hours and talk to the people who, after all, pay their salaries and research grants. Surely this sort of communication between experts and lay people can't be a bad idea. Bridging the gap between science and society is what the Darwin Day Program is all about.

Just in case you'd like to start your own Darwin Day celebrations, let me tell you what we did in Tennessee this year.

The events started on February 11 with a workshop for local junior and high school teachers on how to use evolution as an example of critical thinking. Imagine! The idea is that it would be much better for students to learn about the process of science and how certain conclusions (e.g., that we did evolve from a common ancestor shared with currently living chimps) are actually reached instead of just learning facts that they have to take on faith.

On February 12 there was a whole array of events, starting with an all-day information booth at the student union where faculty and graduate students will answer questions about evolution, and continuing with a documentary festival in which videos were followed by a discussion of the main ideas presented. Darwin Day 2002 in Tennessee concluded with a special lecture by philosopher Elliott Sober (of the University of Wisconsin-Madison), who nicely showed why intelligent design theory is actually no theory at all (see his paper in this anthology.)

Now, you don't have to do all this to have a Darwin Day next year, but make sure to take advantage of your local colleges and univerisities - work with the community of which you are a part.

While it is astounding to see that the state of science education in this country is so poor that people proudly "reject" well established scientific theories simply because they don't fit with their preconceptions, there is a bright side to almost everything, and the evolution-creation controversy is no exception. After my rude awakening to the realities of creationism when I moved to Tennessee, I started to study the problem and its roots. In so doing I learned quite a bit about why people believe what they believe, and what shortcomings of science education are contributing to cause the problem. The result has been a better awareness of the situation and a renewed willingness to do something about it (and a new idea or two to try out). The feeling is spreading throughout the nation: the Society for the Study of Evolution (the premiere professional society of evolutionary biologists) now has a permanent committee dealing with creationism and many of its members are starting to wake up from the torpor of their shielded academic lives to get back into the classrooms and in the public arena.

The reason this is excellent news for everybody, creationists included, is because it goes far beyond the scope of this particular controversy. It means that scientists-shaken by attacks on their discipline from as varied sources as the religious right and the academic left-may be finally starting to realize that they have a moral obligation to come to the public and explain what they are doing, why and how. This, as the final words of Casablanca famously went, may be the beginning of a beautiful friendship. The result could be a better informed and critically thinking public, the true guarantors of a democracy... and a civlization. ∞

[ABOUT THE AUTHOR]

Massimo Pigliucci is an Associate Professor at the University of Tennessee in Knoxville, where he teaches ecology and evolutionary biology. He has published 49 technical papers and two books on evolutionary biology: *Phenotypic Evolution* with Carl Schlichting and *Beyond Nature vs. Nurture*. Dr. Pigliucci has received the Oak Ridge National Labs award for excellence in research and the prestigious Dobzhansky Prize from the Society for the Study of Evolution, of which he is now Vice President. Dr. Pigliucci is also widely published within skeptic and freethought journals, and presents lectures and debates throughout the country. A book of his essays entitled *Tales of the Rational: Skeptical Essays About Science and Nature* has been published and his monthly e-column entitled *Rationally Speaking* is hosted on numerous web sites. Massimo Pigliucci is Vice-Chair of the Darwin Day Program.

[ADDITIONAL RESOURCES]

Darwin Day at the University of Tennessee, Knoxville: http://fp.bio.utk.edu/darwin/

Massimo's Skeptic & Humanist Web: http://fp.bio.utk.edu/skeptic/

*The Ballad of Charles Darwin is available on the Scientific Gospel's **Ain't Gonna Be No Judgment Day** CD. Lyrics are published here with permission from Stephen Baird and the Opossums of Truth.*

THE BALLAD OF CHARLIE DARWIN

by Stephen Baird and The Opossums of Truth
Scientific Gospel.com
©2000 Stephen Baird

We were mired in mystery, whose mists obscured our view.
Mythology told everyone what we should say and do.
Then Darwin's parents made him diploid back in eighteen eight,
And when their son began to shine the darkness would abate.

> Charlie went to Cambridge for his bachelor's degree.
> Though most folks haven't heard he got it in theology.
> He set sail on the Beagle after he turned twenty-two,
> And nothing would remain the same when Darwin's trip was through.

>> CHORUS:
>> It was Charlie Darwin who gave sight to our eyes,
>> Who showed, with Alfred Wallace, how species did arise.
>> It was Charlie Darwin who showed there was no plan -
>> Just mutation and selection, in The Descent of Man.

>>> He used his own money, for there were not any grants.
>>> He studied variation both of animals and plants.
>>> He found when variation puts a species to the test,
>>> Although it happens gradually, selection finds the best.

>>>> *CHORUS*

>>>>> Darwin wrote his origin and everyone said, "Great!"
>>>>> Well, maybe not exactly, for it kindled some debate.
>>>>> But evidence has mounted, so there's no remaining doubt
>>>>> That evolution made us all unless you are devout.

>>>>>> *CHORUS*

[ABOUT THE AUTHORS]

Scientific Gospel is a unique musical genre created by Dr. Stephen Baird to impart scientific knowledge, discuss social and political issues, and argue for rational inquiry and thought. Evolution, gravity, water, heat, time, sexually transmitted diseases, false gods, and heroes of science all are worthy and appropriate subjects for Scientific Gospel. Dr. Baird's aim is to combine Man's intelligence with the majesty of the universe as he champions science and rational thought through musical enlightenment.

[ADDITIONAL RESOURCES]

Scientific Gospel: http://www.scientificgospel.com/

Unnatural Selections

by Richard Carter

A multiple-choice Darwinian trivia quiz for people who really should get out more.

1. Which other famous person was born on exactly the same day as Darwin (12th February, 1809)?
   a) Charles Dickens
   b) Abraham Lincoln
   c) George Eliot
   d) Charles Babbage

2. Which other famous person was accepted into the Athenaeum Club on exactly the same day as Darwin?
   a) Charles Babbage
   b) Charles Dickens
   c) Isambard Kingdom Brunel
   d) General Gordon

3. The writing of which author did Darwin confess finding "so intolerably dull that it nauseated me"?
   a) Charles Dickens
   b) George Eliot
   c) William Wordsworth
   d) William Shakespeare

4. In his youth, Darwin delighted in eating unusual meals. Which of these choice titbits did he not sample?
    a) Darwin's rhea
    b) Echidna
    c) Puma's foetus
    d) Owl

5. What was the name of Darwin's pet dog while he was at Cambridge University?
    a) Jake
    b) Sappho
    c) Polly
    d) Rex

6. Which of the following was not the nickname of any of the Fuegans returned to their homeland on HMS *Beagle*?
    a) York Minster
    b) Fuega Basket
    c) Plymouth Sound
    d) Jemmy Button

7. What was the last drink to pass Darwin's lips?
    a) Tea
    b) Port
    c) Brandy
    d) Whisky

8. To celebrate Darwin's 25th birthday, Captain FitzRoy named something in his honour. What was it?
    a) Darwin Sound
    b) Darwin Bay
    c) Mount Darwin
    d) River Darwin

9. What was the name of Darwin's butler at Down House?
    a) Parker
    b) Parslow
    c) Partington
    d) Partridge

10. On the day that Origin of Species was first published, where was Darwin staying, undergoing the so-called water-cure?
a) Buxton
b) Great Malvern
c) Ilkley
d) Isle of White

Answers: 1 b), 2 b), 3 d), 4 b), 5 b), 6 c), 7 d), 8 c), 9 b), 10 c)

[ABOUT THE AUTHOR]

Richard Carter, FCD, was born in England 57,027 days after Charles Darwin. He was one of the founders of The Friends of Charles Darwin, who successfully campaigned to have their hero celebrated on a Bank of England bank note. Despite possessing a complex brain evolved over several million years of natural selection, he is fighting a losing battle of wits against the molluscs in his garden.

The Friends of Charles Darwin were originally founded to campaign for the depiction of their hero, Charles Darwin, on a Bank of England bank note.

On 7th November 2000, the Bank of England finally released its new £10 note featuring a certain Charles Robert Darwin (and some woman wearing a crown). An image of the note can be viewed on the Bank of England's website.

Although we've got exactly what we wanted we're still taking on new members. Membership is free, so if you can truly say "Charlie is my Darwin", and you'd like to be able to write the letters FCD after your name, why not join us*?

[ADDITIONAL RESOURCES]

You can join The Friends of Charles Darwin at www.gruts.demon.co.uk/darwin/

Friends of Darwin: The Campaign: http://www.gruts.demon.co.uk/darwin/campaign/index.htm

Friends of Darwin: Bank of England Press Release:
http://www.gruts.demon.co.uk/darwin/articles/2000/boe-pr-2000-044/index.htm

Friends of Darwin: Ballad: "Charlie is my Darwin":
http://www.gruts.demon.co.uk/darwin/articles/2000/ballads/my-darwin.htm

Friends of Darwin: Join: http://www.gruts.demon.co.uk/darwin/join.htm

Bank of England web site: http://www.bankofengland.co.uk/banknotes/newten/index.htm

The Primordial Soup recipe is served for and by the Science Club in Anchorage, Alaska.

PRIMORDIAL SOUP
by Neal Matson

1) slow cook some bones, usually beef, for several hours to make the stock.

2) add whatever veggies or grains you like

3) keep on slow cooking for several hours, salting and peppering to taste
   * mung bean sprouts resemble prokaryote cells so add those for visual effect

4) finally, add some store-bought alphabet soup at the very end
   (so as not to overcook it) in order to get all the nucleotides
   (including the G, A, C, T, of our DNA)

[ABOUT THE AUTHOR]

Neal Matson is a retired geologist, member of the Science Club in Alaska, the founder of two congregations in the Bush, and currently an evangelist with the Progressive Church of Christ.

Six Cartoons by Jeff Swenson

A MILLIONAIRE PAYS TO LAUNCH THE FLAT EARTH SOCIETY INTO SPACE.

MAKEOUT POINT, 1798

SOMEHOW THE CREATIONISTS HAD OBTAINED A TIME MACHINE, BUT THE FIRST TRIP RESULTED IN CONFUSION.

CREATIONIST ZOMBIES

[ABOUT THE ARTIST]

Jeff Swenson began his cartooning career after graduating from The Art Institute of Seattle with an associate degree in Visual Communications. His first contract job was to perform digital ink and paint duties at Humongous Entertainment on the children's software game "Spyfox". From there he took on graphic design responsibilities for a small design studio, including print production, layout, storyboards, illustrations, and digital coloring. After leaving the studio, he decided it was time to venture off in pursuit of his real passion – cartooning. Working a fulltime job at a printery and cartooning on the side, Jeff was eventually able to start a freelance business developing comic strip features for the web and wireless markets as well as animating e-cards in Flash and creating logos and illustrations for a variety of clients. Currently the artist is working on several animated cartoons to be shown on the web, including exclusive items for the Darwin Day Program.

[ADDITIONAL RESOURCES]

Swenson Funnies: http://www.swensonfunnies.com/

SONGS FROM THE SKEPTICAL CHOIR
YES, RHESUS MONKEY
by Hugh Young

(Tune: "Yes, Jesus Loves Me")

Rhesus monkey, this I know,
that the Bible Belt must go.
Trusting to authority
must give way to "test and see".

Yes, rhesus monkey,
Yes, rhesus monkey,
Yes, rhesus monkey,
The Bible Belt must go.

Rhesus monkeys in the jung-
-gle think Darwin's work was bung-
-gled, for evolution'ry
progress seems delusion'ry.

Yes, rhesus monkey, (x3)
The Bible Belt must go.

Rhesus monkey, don't get madder;
evolution is no ladder.
It's a bush and we are twigs --
you of dates, and we of figs.

Yes, rhesus monkey, (x3)
The Bible Belt must go.

Rhesus monkeys in the lab
wonder who picks up the tab;
ask, Who put man at the top,
Who says we must get the chop?

Yes, rhesus monkey, (x3)
The Bible Belt must go.

Rhesus monkey, give us time,
Homo sap. has far to climb,
Evolutionists are giants
compared with creation "science".

Yes, rhesus monkey, (x3)
The Bible Belt must go.

Ah-monkeys!

[ABOUT THE AUTHOR]

Hugh Young was born in Christchurch, New Zealand. He graduated in zoology and worked as a journalist and broadcaster in Christchurch, Auckland, Whangarei, Honiara (Solomon Islands), Gisborne, Napier and Wellington. A man of many talents, Hugh Young is an active member of the New Zealand Skeptics and contributes his time and work to a number of on and off-line programs.

[ADDITIONAL RESOURCES]

New Zealand Skeptics: http://skeptics.org.nz/

Hugh Young's homepage: http://www.geocities.com/WestHollywood/Park/7712/index.html

CREATIONISTS ANNOUNCE NEW THEORY OF GRAVITY!

by August Berkshire

Today a spokesman for the Institute for Creative Research (I.C.R.), located in Fault Line, California, announced a new theory of gravity that contradicts traditional scientific explanations.

Dwayne Wish, head of the I.C.R., stated, "This is one of the most glorious days in the 6,000 year history of our universe. Finally, we have a theory of gravity that is just as sound as our theory of creation."

Wish went on to explain, "Most scientists think all forces – such as gravity, electricity and magnetism – originally came from a single, common force. They're currently searching in vain for a Grand Unification Theory. But there is no evidence of a common origin! They have never discovered any transitional forces! Where are the missing links?!

"Many scientists also believe gravity is caused by warped space or gravitons," Wish continued. "Has any scientist actually seen this? Was any scientist there when gravity first occurred? And yet they have the gall to claim gravity is part of nature! It is intellectually arrogant to assume gravity is a naturally occurring, rather than a supernaturally occurring phenomenon."

Asked what alternative the I.C.R. proposed, Wish smiled and said, "We're offering a much more plausible explanation for gravity: the Theory of Angelic Pressure. It should be obvious to any rational person that the universe is filled with invisible, undetectable angels who constantly push objects towards the Earth – objects that would otherwise drift away!

"There is plenty of evidence for our theory," he continued. "For example, in spaceships objects float about randomly. They don't go toward each other unless at least one of them is pushed by an astronaut. This demonstrates that gravity works by design, not 'random chance'."

Asked what research the I.C.R. had done, Wish stated, "In Revelation 8:10 of the Holy Bible it says, 'And the third angel sounded, and there fell a great star from heaven…' This is a clear reference to the fact that angels are responsible for gravity! In addition, many pagan books, such as the *Koran* and the *Book of Mormon*, are also filled with references to angels."

Wish went on to explain that although the Theory of Angelic Pressure is supported by the Bible, it is in no way based on it. "That's just a coincidence," he declared.

"Our theory of gravity cannot be disproven, so it should be taught in public schools," Wish continued. "Not to teach it is tantamount to censorship! Moreover, forcing students to believe a secular model of gravity is a violation of academic freedom and freedom of religion! Traditional scientists blithely ignore the axiom that all theories are equally valid."

When it was suggested there might be other equally valid theories, perhaps from other religions, that would explain gravity, Wish vehemently responded, "We have already discredited the 'other model' of gravity. It's obvious our Theory of Angelic Pressure is the only possible alternative.

"In fairness, students should be allowed equal time to hear our theory. Both models of gravity should be presented, then students can make up their own minds. At the very least, someone should take a public opinion poll to see if our theory is popular."

Wish explained that the I.C.R. was establishing a special division to further investigate their theory of gravity. "It's going to be called the Center for Research on Angelic Pressure, " he said. "C.R.A.P."

[ABOUT THE AUTHOR]

August Berkshire co-founded the Twin Cities (Minnesota) Chapter of American Atheists in 1984, which became Minnesota Atheists in 1991. Berkshire is currently president of Minnesota Atheists and international liaison for Atheist Alliance International. He has spoken about atheism to high school and community college comparative religion classes since 1985.

[ADDITIONAL RESOURCES]

This pamphlet is available on-line at: www.mnatheists.org/august/creationist_gravity.html

Langdon Smith's poem **A Toast to a Lady** *first appeared in the periodical* **The Scrap Book** *in April, 1906. It later appeared in several anthologies, including* **A Treasury of the Familiar** *and* **The Pocket Book of Popular Verse.** *The poem was featured in an article by Martin Gardner for* **Antioch Review** *(Fall 1962) later reprinted in Gardner's* **Order and Surprise.** *A Toast to a Lady is also known under the title "Evolution" and "A Tadpole and A Fish." The poem has been translated into many languages including a Swedish translation by retired Botany Professor, Lars Olof Bjorn.*

A Toast to a Lady
by Langdon Smith (1858-1908)

When you were a tadpole and I was a fish
    In the Paleozoic time,
And side by side on the ebbing tide
    We sprawled through the ooze and slime,
Or skittered with many a caudal flip
    Through the depths of the Cambrian fen,
My heart was rife with the joy of life,
    For I loved you even then.

Mindless we lived and mindless we loved
    And mindless at last we died;
And deep in the rift of the Caradoc drift
    We slumbered side by side.
The world turned on in the lathe of time,
    The hot lands heaved amain,
Till we caught our breath from the womb of death
    And crept into light again.

We were amphibians, scaled and tailed,
    And drab as a dead man's hand;
We coiled at ease 'neath the dripping trees
    Or trailed through the mud and sand.
Croaking and blind, with our three-clawed feet
    Writing a language dumb,
With never a spark in the empty dark
    To hint at a life to come.

Yet happy we lived and happy we loved,
    And happy we died once more;
Our forms were rolled in the clinging mold
    Of a Neocomian shore.
The eons came and the eons fled
    And the sleep that wrapped us fast
Was riven away in a newer day
    And the night of death was past.

Then light and swift through the jungle trees
    We swung in our airy flights,
Or breathed in the balms of the fronded palms
    In the hush of the moonless nights;
And, oh! what beautiful years were there
    When our hearts clung each to each;
When life was filled and our senses thrilled
    In the first faint dawn of speech.

Thus life by life and love by love
    We passed through the cycles strange,
And breath by breath and death by death
    We followed the chain of change.
Till there came a time in the law of life
    When over the nursing side
The shadows broke and soul awoke
    In a strange, dim dream of God.

I was thewed like an Auruch bull
    And tusked like the great cave bear;
And you, my sweet, from head to feet
    Were gowned in your glorious hair.
Deep in the gloom of a fireless cave,
    When the night fell o'er the plain
And the moon hung red o'er the river bed
    We mumbled the bones of the slain.

I flaked a flint to a cutting edge
    And shaped it with brutish craft;
I broke a shank from the woodland lank
    And fitted it, head and haft;
Then I hid me close to the reedy tarn,
    Where the mammoth came to drink;
Through the brawn and bone I drove the stone
    And slew him upon the brink.

Loud I howled through the moonlit wastes,
    Loud answered our kith and kin;
From west and east to the crimson feast
    The clan came tramping in.
O'er joint and gristle and padded hoof
    We fought and clawed and tore,
And check by jowl with many a growl
    We talked the marvel o'er.

I carved that fight on a reindeer bone
    With rude and hairy hand;
I pictured his fall on the cavern wall
    That men might understand.
For we lived by blood and the right of might
    Ere human laws were drawn,
And the age of sin did not begin
    Till our brutal tush were gone.

And that was a million years ago
    In a time that no man knows;
Yet here tonight in the mellow light
    We sit at Delmonico's.
Your eyes are deep as the Devon springs,
    Your hair is dark as jet,
Your years are few, your life is new,
    Your soul untried, and yet -

Our trail is on the Kimmeridge clay
    And the scarp of the Purbeck flags;
We have left our bones in the Bagshot stones
    And deep in the Coralline crags;
Our love is old, our lives are old,
    And death shall come amain;
Should it come today, what man may say
    We shall not live again?

God wrought our souls from the Tremadoc beds
    And furnished them wings to fly;
We sowed our spawn in the world's dim dawn,
    And I know that it shall not die,
Though cities have sprung above the graves
    Where the crook-bone men make war
And the oxwain creaks o'er the buried caves
    Where the mummied mammoths are.

> Then as we linger at luncheon here
>   O'er many a dainty dish,
> Let us drink anew to the time when you
>   Were a tadpole and I was a fish.

[ABOUT THE AUTHOR]

Langdon Smith was an American journalist born in Kentucky in 1858. He served in the Comanche and Apache wars as a trooper and reported these campaigns for the *New York Herald*. In addition to the poem, A Toast to a Lady, Smith is known to have penned the novel *On the Pan Handle*.

[ADDITIONAL RESOURCES]

The Darwin Day Program would like to thank *The Wondering Minstrels* – a poetry-by-email service run by Abraham Thomas and Martin DeMello on the Internet. The site offers poetry, discussion forums, personal commentary, critical analyses, historical and biographical information, and much more. The site is maintained by Sitaram Iyer and hosted on the Rice University site. Visit the site at: http://www.cs.rice.edu/~ssiyer/minstrels/

SECTION FIVE

IN THE BEGINNING WAS THE WATCHMAKER:

SIGHTED OR BLIND?

> "In the struggle for survival, the fittest win out at the expense of their rivals because they succeed in adapting themselves best to their environment."
> – Charles Darwin in *The Origin of Species* (1859)

> "Your theory is crazy, but it's not crazy enough to be true."
> – Niels Bohr (1942)

John Rennie's article originally appeared in the July 2002 issue of **Scientific American**, *a magazine that has been bringing its readers unique insights about developments in science and technology for more than 150 years.*

Reprinted with permission. Copyright © 2002 by **Scientific American**, Inc. All Rights Reserved.

15 Answers to Creationist Nonsense

Opponents of evolution want to make a place for creationism in the classroom by tearing down real science, but their arguments don't hold up

by John Rennie

When Charles Darwin introduced the theory of evolution through natural selection 143 years ago, scientists of the day argued over it fiercely, but the massing evidence from paleontology, genetics, zoology, molecular biology and other fields gradually established evolution's truth beyond reasonable doubt. Today that battle has been won everywhere – except in the public imagination.

Embarrassingly, in the 21st century, in the most scientifically advanced nation the world has ever known, creationists can still persuade politicians, judges and ordinary citizens that evolution is a flawed, poorly supported fantasy. They lobby for creationist ideas such as "intelligent design" to be taught as alternatives to evolution in science classrooms. As this article goes to press, the Ohio Board of Education is debating whether to mandate such a change. Some antievolutionists, such as Philip E. Johnson, a law professor at the University of California at Berkeley and author of *Darwin on Trial*, admit that they intend for intelligent-design theory to serve as a "wedge" for reopening science classrooms to discussions of God.

Besieged teachers and others may increasingly find themselves on the spot to defend evolution and refute creationism. The arguments that creationists use are typically specious and based on misunderstandings of (or outright lies about) evolution, but the number and diversity of the objections can put even well-informed people at a disadvantage.

To help with answering them, the following list rebuts some of the most common "scientific" arguments raised against evolution. It also directs readers to further sources for information and explains why creation science has no place in the classroom.

1. Evolution is only a theory. It is not a fact or a scientific law.

Many people learned in elementary school that a theory falls in the middle of a hierarchy of certainty – above a mere hypothesis but below a law. Scientists do not use the terms that way, however. According to the National Academy of Sciences (NAS), a scientific theory is "a well-substantiated explanation of some aspect of the natural world that can incorporate facts, laws, inferences, and tested hypotheses." No amount of validation changes a theory into a law, which is a descriptive generalization about nature. So when scientists talk about the theory of evolution – or the atomic theory or the theory of relativity, for that matter – they are not expressing reservations about its truth.

In addition to the *theory* of evolution, meaning the idea of descent with modification, one may also speak of the *fact* of evolution. The NAS defines a fact as "an observation that has been repeatedly confirmed and for all practical purposes is accepted as 'true.'" The fossil record and abundant other evidence testify that organisms have evolved through time. Although no one observed those transformations, the indirect evidence is clear, unambiguous and compelling.

All sciences frequently rely on indirect evidence. Physicists cannot see subatomic particles directly, for instance, so they verify their existence by watching for telltale tracks that the particles leave in cloud chambers. The absence of direct observation does not make physicists' conclusions less certain.

2. Natural selection is based on circular reasoning: the fittest are those who survive, and those who survive are deemed fittest.

"Survival of the fittest" is a conversational way to describe natural selection, but a more technical description speaks of differential rates of survival and reproduction. That is, rather than labeling species as more or less fit, one can describe how many offspring they are likely to leave under given circumstances. Drop a fast-breeding pair of small-beaked finches and a slower-breeding pair of large-beaked finches onto an island full of food seeds. Within a few generations the fast breeders may control more of the food resources. Yet if large beaks more easily crush seeds, the advantage may tip to the slow breeders. In a pioneering study of finches on the Galápagos Islands, Peter R. Grant of Princeton University observed these kinds of population shifts in the wild [see his article "Natural Selection and Darwin's Finches"; *Scientific American*, October 1991].

The key is that adaptive fitness can be defined without reference to survival: large beaks are better adapted for crushing seeds, irrespective of whether that trait has survival value under the circumstances.

3. Evolution is unscientific, because it is not testable or falsifiable. It makes claims about events that were not observed and can never be re-created.

This blanket dismissal of evolution ignores important distinctions that divide the field into at least two broad areas: microevolution and macroevolution. Microevolution looks at changes within species over time – changes that may be preludes to speciation, the origin of new species. Macroevolution studies how taxonomic groups above the level of species change. Its evidence draws frequently from the fossil record and DNA comparisons to reconstruct how various organisms may be related.

These days even most creationists acknowledge that microevolution has been upheld by tests in the laboratory (as in studies of cells, plants and fruit flies) and in the field (as in Grant's studies of evolving beak shapes among Galápagos finches). Natural selection and other mechanisms – such as chromosomal changes, symbiosis and hybridization – can drive profound changes in populations over time.

The historical nature of macroevolutionary study involves inference from fossils and DNA rather than direct observation. Yet in the historical sciences (which include astronomy, geology and archaeology, as well as evolutionary biology), hypotheses can still be tested by checking whether they accord with physical evidence and whether they lead to verifiable predictions about future discoveries. For instance, evolution implies that between the earliest-known ancestors of humans (roughly five million years old) and the appearance of modern humans (about 100,000 years ago), one should find a succession of hominid creatures with features progressively less apelike and more modern, which is indeed what the fossil record shows. But one should not – and does not – find modern human fossils embedded in strata from the Jurassic period (144 million years ago). Evolutionary biology routinely makes predictions far more refined and precise than this, and researchers test them constantly.

Evolution could be disproved in other ways, too. If we could document the spontaneous generation of just one complex life-form from inanimate matter, then at least a few creatures seen in the fossil record might have originated this way. If superintelligent aliens appeared and claimed credit for creating life on earth (or even particular species), the purely evolutionary explanation would be cast in doubt. But no one has yet produced such evidence.

It should be noted that the idea of falsifiability as the defining characteristic of science originated with philosopher Karl Popper in the 1930s. More recent elaborations on his thinking have expanded the narrowest interpretation of his principle precisely because it would eliminate too many branches of clearly scientific endeavor.

4. Increasingly, scientists doubt the truth of evolution.

No evidence suggests that evolution is losing adherents. Pick up any issue of a peer-reviewed biological journal, and you will find articles that support and extend evolutionary studies or that embrace evolution as a fundamental concept.

Conversely, serious scientific publications disputing evolution are all but nonexistent. In the mid-1990s George W. Gilchrist of the University of Washington surveyed thousands of journals in the primary literature, seeking articles on intelligent design or creation science. Among those hundreds of thousands of scientific reports, he found none. In the past two years, surveys done independently by Barbara Forrest of Southeastern Louisiana University and Lawrence M. Krauss of Case Western Reserve University have been similarly fruitless.

Creationists retort that a closed-minded scientific community rejects their evidence. Yet according to the editors of *Nature*, *Science* and other leading journals, few antievolution manuscripts are even submitted. Some antievolution authors have published papers in serious journals. Those papers, however, rarely attack evolution directly or advance creationist arguments; at best, they identify certain evolutionary problems as unsolved and difficult (which no one disputes). In short, creationists are not giving the scientific world good reason to take them seriously.

5. The disagreements among even evolutionary biologists show how little solid science supports evolution.

Evolutionary biologists passionately debate diverse topics: how speciation happens, the rates of evolutionary change, the ancestral relations of birds and dinosaurs, whether Neandertals were a species apart from modern humans, and much more. These disputes are like those found in all other branches of science. Acceptance of evolution as a factual occurrence and a guiding principle is nonetheless universal in biology.

Unfortunately, dishonest creationists have shown a willingness to take scientists' comments out of context to exaggerate and distort the disagreements. Anyone acquainted with the works of paleontologist Stephen Jay Gould of Harvard University knows that in addition to co-authoring the punctuated equilibrium model, Gould was one of the most eloquent defenders and articulators of evolution. (Punctuated equilibrium explains patterns in the fossil record by suggesting that most evolutionary changes occur within geologically brief intervals – which may nonetheless amount to hundreds of generations.) Yet creationists delight in dissecting out phrases from Gould's voluminous prose to make him sound as though he had doubted evolution, and they present punctuated equilibrium as though it allows new species to materialize overnight or birds to be born from reptile eggs.

When confronted with a quotation from a scientific authority that seems to question evolution, insist on seeing the statement in context. Almost invariably, the attack on evolution will prove illusory.

6. If humans descended from monkeys, why are there still monkeys?

This surprisingly common argument reflects several levels of ignorance about evolution. The first mistake is that evolution does not teach that humans descended from monkeys; it states that both have a common ancestor.

The deeper error is that this objection is tantamount to asking, "If children descended from adults, why are there still adults?" New species evolve by splintering off from established ones, when populations of organisms become isolated from the main branch of their family and acquire sufficient differences to remain forever distinct. The parent species may survive indefinitely thereafter, or it may become extinct.

7. Evolution cannot explain how life first appeared on earth.

The origin of life remains very much a mystery, but biochemists have learned about how primitive nucleic acids, amino acids and other building blocks of life could have formed and organized themselves into self-replicating, self-sustaining units, laying the foundation for cellular biochemistry. Astrochemical analyses hint that quantities of these compounds might have originated in space and fallen to earth in comets, a scenario that may solve the problem of how those constituents arose under the conditions that prevailed when our planet was young.

Creationists sometimes try to invalidate all of evolution by pointing to science's current inability to explain the origin of life. But even if life on earth turned out to have a nonevolutionary origin (for instance, if aliens introduced the first cells billions of years ago), evolution since then would be robustly confirmed by countless microevolutionary and macroevolutionary studies.

8. Mathematically, it is inconceivable that anything as complex as a protein, let alone a living cell or a human, could spring up by chance.

Chance plays a part in evolution (for example, in the random mutations that can give rise to new traits), but evolution does not depend on chance to create organisms, proteins or other entities. Quite the opposite: natural selection, the principal known mechanism of evolution, harnesses nonrandom change by preserving "desirable" (adaptive) features and eliminating "undesirable" (nonadaptive) ones. As long as the forces of selection stay constant, natural selection can push evolution in one direction and produce sophisticated structures in surprisingly short times.

As an analogy, consider the 13-letter sequence "TOBEORNOTTOBE." Those hypothetical million monkeys, each pecking out one phrase a second, could take as long as 78,800 years to find it among the 26[13] sequences of that length. But in the 1980s Richard Hardison of Glendale College wrote a computer program that generated phrases randomly while preserving the positions of individual letters that happened to be correctly placed (in effect, selecting for phrases more like Hamlet's). On average, the program re-created the phrase in just 336 iterations, less than 90 seconds. Even more amazing, it could reconstruct Shakespeare's entire play in just four and a half days.

9. The Second Law of Thermodynamics says that systems must become more disordered over time. Living cells therefore could not have evolved from inanimate chemicals, and multicellular life could not have evolved from protozoa.

This argument derives from a misunderstanding of the Second Law. If it were valid, mineral crystals and snowflakes would also be impossible, because they, too, are complex structures that form spontaneously from disordered parts.

The Second Law actually states that the total entropy of a closed system (one that no energy or matter leaves or enters) cannot decrease. Entropy is a physical concept often casually described as disorder, but it differs significantly from the conversational use of the word.

More important, however, the Second Law permits parts of a system to decrease in entropy as long as other parts experience an offsetting increase. Thus, our planet as a whole can grow more complex because the sun pours heat and light onto it, and the greater entropy associated with the sun's nuclear fusion more than rebalances the scales. Simple organisms can fuel their rise toward complexity by consuming other forms of life and nonliving materials.

10. Mutations are essential to evolution theory, but mutations can only eliminate traits. They cannot produce new features.

On the contrary, biology has catalogued many traits produced by point mutations (changes at precise positions in an organism's DNA) – bacterial resistance to antibiotics, for example.

Mutations that arise in the homeobox (*Hox*) family of development-regulating genes in animals can also have complex effects. *Hox* genes direct where legs, wings, antennae and body segments should grow. In fruit flies, for instance, the mutation called *Antennapedia* causes legs to sprout where antennae should grow. These abnormal limbs are not functional, but their existence demonstrates that genetic mistakes can produce complex structures, which natural selection can then test for possible uses.

Moreover, molecular biology has discovered mechanisms for genetic change that go beyond point mutations, and these expand the ways in which new traits can appear. Functional modules within genes can be spliced together in novel ways. Whole genes can be accidentally duplicated in an organism's DNA, and the duplicates are free to mutate into genes for new, complex features. Comparisons of the DNA from a wide variety of organisms indicate that this is how the globin family of blood proteins evolved over millions of years.

11. **Natural selection might explain microevolution, but it cannot explain the origin of new species and higher orders of life.**

Evolutionary biologists have written extensively about how natural selection could produce new species. For instance, in the model called allopatry, developed by Ernst Mayr of Harvard University, if a population of organisms were isolated from the rest of its species by geographical boundaries, it might be subjected to different selective pressures. Changes would accumulate in the isolated population. If those changes became so significant that the splinter group could not – or routinely would not – breed with the original stock, then the splinter group would be *reproductively isolated* and on its way toward becoming a new species.

Natural selection is the best studied of the evolutionary mechanisms, but biologists are open to other possibilities as well. Biologists are constantly assessing the potential of unusual genetic mechanisms for causing speciation or for producing complex features in organisms. Lynn Margulis of the University of Massachusetts at Amherst and others have persuasively argued that some cellular organelles, such as the energy-generating mitochondria, evolved through the symbiotic merger of ancient organisms. Thus, science welcomes the possibility of evolution resulting from forces beyond natural selection. Yet those forces must be natural; they cannot be attributed to the actions of mysterious creative intelligences whose existence, in scientific terms, is unproved.

12. **Nobody has ever seen a new species evolve.**

Speciation is probably fairly rare and in many cases might take centuries. Furthermore, recognizing a new species during a formative stage can be difficult, because biologists sometimes disagree about how best to define a species. The most widely used definition, Mayr's Biological Species Concept, recognizes a species as a distinct community of reproductively isolated populations – sets of organisms that normally do not or cannot breed outside their community. In practice, this standard can be difficult to apply to organisms isolated by distance or terrain or to plants (and, of course, fossils do not breed). Biologists therefore usually use organisms' physical and behavioral traits as clues to their species membership.

Nevertheless, the scientific literature does contain reports of apparent speciation events in plants, insects and worms. In most of these experiments, researchers subjected organisms to various types of selection – for anatomical differences, mating behaviors, habitat preferences and other traits – and found that they had created populations of organisms that did not breed with outsiders. For example, William R. Rice of the University of New Mexico and George W. Salt of the University of California at Davis demonstrated that if they sorted a group of fruit flies by their preference for certain environments and bred those flies separately over 35 generations, the resulting flies would refuse to breed with those from a very different environment.

13. **Evolutionists cannot point to any transitional fossils – creatures that are half reptile and half bird, for instance.**

Actually, paleontologists know of many detailed examples of fossils intermediate in form between various taxonomic groups. One of the most famous fossils of all time is *Archaeopteryx*, which combines feathers and skeletal structures peculiar to birds with features of dinosaurs. A flock's worth of other feathered fossil species, some more avian and some less, has also been found. A sequence of fossils spans the evolution of modern horses from the tiny *Eohippus*. Whales had four-legged ancestors that walked on land, and creatures known as *Ambulocetus* and *Rodhocetus* helped to make that transition [see "The Mammals That Conquered the Seas," by Kate Wong; *Scientific American*, May 2002]. Fossil seashells trace the evolution of various mollusks through millions of years. Perhaps 20 or more hominids (not all of them our ancestors) fill the gap between Lucy the australopithecine and modern humans.

Creationists, though, dismiss these fossil studies. They argue that *Archaeopteryx* is not a missing link between reptiles and birds – it is just an extinct bird with reptilian features. They want evolutionists to produce a weird, chimeric monster that cannot be classified as belonging to any known group. Even if a creationist does accept a fossil as transitional between two species, he or she may then insist on seeing other fossils intermediate between it and the first two. These frustrating requests can proceed ad infinitum and place an unreasonable burden on the always incomplete fossil record.

Nevertheless, evolutionists can cite further supportive evidence from molecular biology. All organisms share most of the same genes, but as evolution predicts, the structures of these genes and their products diverge among species, in keeping with their evolutionary relationships. Geneticists speak of the "molecular clock" that records the passage of time. These molecular data also show how various organisms are transitional within evolution.

14. Living things have fantastically intricate features – at the anatomical, cellular and molecular levels – that could not function if they were any less complex or sophisticated. The only prudent conclusion is that they are the products of intelligent design, not evolution.

This "argument from design" is the backbone of most recent attacks on evolution, but it is also one of the oldest. In 1802 theologian William Paley wrote that if one finds a pocket watch in a field, the most reasonable conclusion is that someone dropped it, not that natural forces created it there. By analogy, Paley argued, the complex structures of living things must be the handiwork of direct, divine invention. Darwin wrote *On the Origin of Species* as an answer to Paley: he explained how natural forces of selection, acting on inherited features, could gradually shape the evolution of ornate organic structures.

Generations of creationists have tried to counter Darwin by citing the example of the eye as a structure that could not have evolved. The eye's ability to provide vision depends on the perfect arrangement of its parts, these critics say. Natural selection could thus never favor the transitional forms needed during the eye's evolution – what good is half an eye? Anticipating this criticism, Darwin suggested that even "incomplete" eyes might confer benefits (such as helping creatures orient toward light) and thereby survive for further evolutionary refinement. Biology has vindicated Darwin: researchers have identified primitive eyes and light-sensing organs throughout the animal kingdom and have even tracked the evolutionary history of eyes through comparative genetics. (It now appears that in various families of organisms, eyes have evolved independently.)

Today's intelligent-design advocates are more sophisticated than their predecessors, but their arguments and goals are not fundamentally different. They criticize evolution by trying to demonstrate that it could not account for life as we know it and then insist that the only tenable alternative is that life was designed by an unidentified intelligence.

15. Recent discoveries prove that even at the microscopic level, life has a quality of complexity that could not have come about through evolution.

"Irreducible complexity" is the battle cry of Michael J. Behe of Lehigh University, author of *Darwin's Black Box: The Biochemical Challenge to Evolution*. As a household example of irreducible complexity, Behe chooses the mousetrap – a machine that could not function if any of its pieces were missing and whose pieces have no value except as parts of the whole. What is true of the mousetrap, he says, is even truer of the bacterial flagellum, a whiplike cellular organelle used for propulsion that operates like an outboard motor. The proteins that make up a flagellum are uncannily arranged into motor components, a universal joint and other structures like those that a human engineer might specify. The possibility that this intricate array could have arisen through evolutionary modification is virtually nil, Behe argues, and that bespeaks intelligent design. He makes similar points about the blood's clotting mechanism and other molecular systems.

Yet evolutionary biologists have answers to these objections. First, there exist flagellae with forms simpler than the one that Behe cites, so it is not necessary for all those components to be present for a flagellum to work. The sophisticated components of this flagellum all have precedents elsewhere in nature, as described by Kenneth R. Miller of Brown University and others. In fact, the entire flagellum assembly is extremely similar to an organelle that *Yersinia pestis*, the bubonic plague bacterium, uses to inject toxins into cells.

The key is that the flagellum's component structures, which Behe suggests have no value apart from their role in propulsion, can serve multiple functions that would have helped favor their evolution. The final evolution of the flagellum might then have involved only the novel recombination of sophisticated parts that initially evolved for other purposes. Similarly, the blood-clotting system seems to involve the modification and elaboration of proteins that were originally used in digestion, according to studies by Russell F. Doolittle of the University of California at San Diego. So some of the complexity that Behe calls proof of intelligent design is not irreducible at all.

Complexity of a different kind – "specified complexity" – is the cornerstone of the intelligent-design arguments of William A. Dembski of Baylor University in his books *The Design Inference* and *No Free Lunch*. Essentially his argument is that living things are complex in a way that undirected, random processes could never produce. The only logical conclusion, Dembski asserts, in an echo of Paley 200 years ago, is that some superhuman intelligence created and shaped life.

Dembski's argument contains several holes. It is wrong to insinuate that the field of explanations consists only of random processes or designing intelligences. Researchers into nonlinear systems and cellular automata at the Santa Fe Institute and elsewhere have demonstrated that simple, undirected processes can yield extraordinarily complex patterns. Some of the complexity seen in organisms may therefore emerge through natural phenomena that we as yet barely understand. But that is far different from saying that the complexity could not have arisen naturally.

"Creation science" is a contradiction in terms. A central tenet of modern science is methodological naturalism – it seeks to explain the universe purely in terms of observed or testable natural mechanisms. Thus, physics describes the atomic nucleus with specific concepts governing matter and energy, and it tests those descriptions experimentally.

Physicists introduce new particles, such as quarks, to flesh out their theories only when data show that the previous descriptions cannot adequately explain observed phenomena. The new particles do not have arbitrary properties, moreover – their definitions are tightly constrained, because the new particles must fit within the existing framework of physics.

In contrast, intelligent-design theorists invoke shadowy entities that conveniently have whatever unconstrained abilities are needed to solve the mystery at hand. Rather than expanding scientific inquiry, such answers shut it down. (How does one disprove the existence of omnipotent intelligences?)

Intelligent design offers few answers. For instance, when and how did a designing intelligence intervene in life's history? By creating the first DNA? The first cell? The first human? Was every species designed, or just a few early ones? Proponents of intelligent-design theory frequently decline to be pinned down on these points. They do not even make real attempts to reconcile their disparate ideas about intelligent design. Instead they pursue argument by exclusion – that is, they belittle evolutionary explanations as far-fetched or incomplete and then imply that only design-based alternatives remain.

Logically, this is misleading: even if one naturalistic explanation is flawed, it does not mean that all are. Moreover, it does not make one intelligent-design theory more reasonable than another. Listeners are essentially left to fill in the blanks for themselves, and some will undoubtedly do so by substituting their religious beliefs for scientific ideas.

Time and again, science has shown that methodological naturalism can push back ignorance, finding increasingly detailed and informative answers to mysteries that once seemed impenetrable: the nature of light, the causes of disease, how the brain works. Evolution is doing the same with the riddle of how the living world took shape. Creationism, by any name, adds nothing of intellectual value to the effort. ∞

[ABOUT THE AUTHOR]

John Rennie is editor in chief of *Scientific American*.

[ADDITIONAL RESOURCES]

Scientific American online: http://www.sciam.com/

National Center for Science Education: http://www.ncseweb.org

This paper was presented by Kieran P. McNulty to the Long Island Secular Humanists for Darwin Day 2002.

Myths and Conceptions of Darwin:
Refocusing and Refuting Arguments Against Evolution
by Kieran P. McNulty

This address focuses on the misconceptions perpetuating debate about Darwinian evolution and ensuring that agreement will never be reached. I do not believe that perfect concordance among evolutionists and creationists is ever possible. Certainly it is not the goal of this work to review the preponderance of evidence supporting evolutionary theory – a semester-long class is barely enough time for that. Nor is my purpose to indulge in the typical "creation bashing." Rather, I hope to parse Darwinian evolution into its component theories, showing areas where agreement actually can be reached – and where it cannot. Then I will tackle some of the criticisms leveled at Darwinism, showing them to result in large part from general misconceptions about the relevant science. Finally, I will touch briefly on the distinction between the belief in creation and creation "science." This treatise will not end arguments over Darwinian evolution, but perhaps it will help to inform and focus future debates.

Defining Evolution

The most fundamental problem with arguments over evolution lies in the fact that evolution is generally not well taught nor well understood:

> "The Creationists wrongly believe that their understanding of evolution is what the theory of evolution really says, and declare evolution banished... (The situation isn't helped by poor science education generally. Even most beginning college biology students don't understand the theory of evolution.)" (Isaak, 1995).

> "Evolutionists wrongly believe that their views are validated by persuasive presentations invoking scientific terminology and allusions to a presumed monopoly of scientific knowledge and understanding on their part... (The situation isn't helped by poor science education generally. Even advanced college biology students often understand little more than the dogma of evolutionary theory, and few have the time [or the guts] to question its scientific validity)" (Wallace, 2001).

In rare agreement, both an evolutionist and a creationist (respectively) cite a poor understanding of evolutionary theory as a common ailment. Indeed, it is impossible to have meaningful debate over an issue that neither side fully understands. Such arguments pattern after the Indian parable of six blind men describing an elephant: each associates "elephant" with whichever part of the elephant's body he can feel (trunk, tail, tusk, etc.). Without a reasonable understanding of the whole beast, namely evolutionary theory, there can be no meaningful debate: evolutionists and creationists simply talk past each other.

Correlated to this is the problem that evolution is not a term that is easily defined. One can search both dictionaries and text books without finding a single good definition. Many texts do not even bother to define it. Population geneticists define evolution as a change in allele frequencies in a population over time. The main problem with this definition (and there are other theoretical problem as well) is that it is not readily accessible to the general public – one needs to study the fundamentals of population genetics to figure out its meaning. Futuyma (1986) provides a less precise, but more useful definition:

> *"In the broadest sense, evolution is merely change... Biological evolution ... is change in the properties of populations of organisms that transcend the lifetime of a single individual... The changes in populations that are considered evolutionary are those that are inheritable via the genetic material from one generation to the next."*

Evolution, then, only means change. It is not the bugbear from which so many people cringe. In biological terms, it is a specific type of change: namely, changes in population characteristics over generations.

New York City, once settled by the Dutch, is now home to the most diverse population in the world. The properties of this population have changed since its colonization because of migration and admixture. Is such change anti-religious or anti-Christian? Can anyone actually propose that this change did not really happen? And yet, *that is evolutionary change*. It is not enough for creationists to argue that *that* type of evolution is not what they are opposed to, nor for evolutionists to say that because this example is true then every example must be true. The thesis of this address is that evolution as such need not be debated. As I have just shown, it can be simple change, with no religious implications. The controversy should be focused on specific issues within the evolutionary rubric, not on evolution itself.

Darwin's Five Theories Regarding Evolution

While scientists and religious alike continue to argue over Darwin's theory of evolution, astute readers will note that he did not propose a *single* theory. In *On the Origin of Species by Means of Natural Selection* (Darwin, 1859), Darwin outlined several theories regarding the evolution of organisms. Although we tend to group them as a single concept for the sake of convenience, this amalgamation perpetuates misunderstanding by framing debates in such ambiguous terms. Five major theories regarding evolution can be distilled from the *Origin of Species*. In understanding these separate but related propositions, one can precisely define the axes along which the evolutionist/creationist debate should align.

1. **Species are not immutable.** This is the most basic of the theories, suggesting only that species can change... evolution does indeed happen. As in the above example of New York City, we can talk about evolutionary change without invoking large-scale alterations in form. The changes that have occurred in the domesticated dog, *Canis familiaris*, are a more conspicuous example. It is well documented that species can change, and indeed "even most creationists recognize that evolution at this level is a fact." (Wallace, 2001) Thus, there is little room for controversy over this basic tenet of Darwin's.

2. **Evolution is gradual.** This is another basic proposition stating that changes in populations or species happen in stages or grades. Many, including prominent evolutionary theorists (e.g. Eldredge & Gould, 1972), misinterpret gradualism as meaning that evolution is slow. Darwin's assertion that evolution is driven by interactions with nature (see below) should make it obvious that evolution will not proceed at a constant pace, slow or otherwise. Gradual evolution means, for example, that the domestication of the dog did not, in a single generation, transform a wolf into a Dachshund. There were intervening stages through which the features of primitive dogs progressed toward those of modern ones. Again, if both evolutionists and creationists can accept that small-scale evolutionary change happens naturally, then there should be no disagreement that it happens in gradual stages.

3. **Evolution is driven by Natural Selection.** This is perhaps the most important component of Darwinian evolution – the one for which he is alternately hailed and reviled. Natural selection is a simple logical construction that leads to changes in populations. Understanding natural selection begins with the observation that all species are variable; no two individuals are alike. If there is variability among individuals, then under certain circumstances some individuals will have a better chance of survival than others. Think of a population of rabbits: some are faster, others slower. If there are predators around, the faster rabbits will have a better chance of escape and survival. Now, if this variation can be inherited, then those who survive will pass on their advantageous traits to their offspring. Those without the advantageous features will be less successful, and fewer will pass on their genes. Returning to the rabbits, a faster rabbit will survive to produce many offspring and those offspring with inherit its successful (and other) traits. A slower rabbit will have a smaller chance of survival, and so those genes will be much less frequent in the next generation. In that manner, rabbits will tend toward speed with each generation (and indeed they are quite quick) as long as the selection factors remain the same. It is through this mechanism that Darwin proposed evolution occurred: traits that increase the chance of survival will be passed on more frequently than deleterious ones.

Natural selection is a logical process that rests upon three assumptions: populations are variable, some variation leads to better survival, and some variation can be passed on genetically. If these assumptions hold true then selection will naturally result. Conversely, to invalidate the process of selection, one needs to demonstrate that one or more assumption is false. Which of them is arguable? We know that individuals are variable and that traits are passed from parent to offspring. Is it really inconceivable that faster rabbits survive more often than slower ones? that a white bird would live longer on the snowy tundra than a brown one? This intuitive simplicity was summed up by one of my students far better than any words of mine could: "that isn't natural selection. That's just a logical outcome." Indeed, that *is* natural selection.

The creationists' rejection of natural selection is based on its connection to the rest of Darwin's theories (see below), rather than on its own merits. Indeed, many creationists actually praise the work of Edward Blyth, who discussed the elements of natural selection (in a religious framework) years before Darwin's publication (see Eisley, 1979). This is a tacit acceptance of the tenets of natural selection under the guise of creationist naturalism. There is nothing inherently anti-religious about natural selection, variation, or inheritability. Clearly Edward Blyth recognized this, as do his proponents. It is the connections that Darwin drew between selection, speciation, and common ancestry that upset the faithful. Thus, natural selection should *not* be the focus of evolutionary debate. It is a simple, logical process that is provable theoretically and empirically. Arguments about Darwinian evolution should be reserved for his last two theories.

4. **Evolution leads to speciation.** While some creation advocates are willing to accept the role of natural selection in affecting small changes, it is large-scale change that stirs contention. To put it another way, many accept microevolution (changes in specific features of organisms) as valid, while rejecting macroevolution (evolution leading to new species and higher-level taxa). This was the main thesis of Darwin's work, as indicated by the title, *On the Origin of Species by Means of Natural Selection* (1859). It is this connection between speciation and selection that mistakenly draws fire to the latter concept, rather than the former. Darwin suggested that species originated from other species; creationists believe that species originated from God. *This* is the conflict – species origins – without regard to natural selection. Consider global warming. You might argue that industrial byproducts being released into the air will lead to elevated world temperatures. Alternatively, one could say that there is no scientific proof that these chemicals will have any significant impact on the global environment. *No one*, however, is trying to argue that these byproducts are not released into the air.

This is not to suggest that there is a lack of evidence supporting speciation. Indeed, the evidence is ample and far beyond the scope (and purpose) of this address. One of the best examples, however, can be seen in the so-called "ring species." For simplicity's sake, imagine a species of animal that is distributed throughout continental Europe. Now, imagine the onset of an ice age, when glaciers advance southward from the arctic. As the ice sheet penetrates Europe, the species will continue to live around its edges, but abandon the ice regions. Thus, we now have a species distributed in roughly a U-shape around the glacial border. Each population of this species can interbreed with adjacent populations because they belong to the same species. Now, imagine the ice age ending thousands of years later and the glaciers receding. The populations at either end of the U-shaped distribution can now re-colonize the lands liberated from ice. As these endpoint populations meet in the middle, the species is now distributed in a roughly circular shape (thus the appellation ring species). In many such instances, we find that these endpoints – reunited after thousands of years – can no longer interbreed! Genetic continuity is maintained through a chain of interbreeding around the "U." But, variability between the groups at the ends, developed through long separation, has reached a level equivalent with speciation. This is the very process of speciation taking place: small amounts of variation accumulate over time to the point when two populations of the same species can no longer interbreed. There are many documented examples of this in nature and I refer the reader to any decent evolutionary biology text for specifics.

5. **All living organisms share a single, common ancestry.** Even speciation is not a point of contention for some creationists. One needs only to look at species of North American warblers, for example, to see that the many different varieties still share a common body plan. For these, it is the common ancestry of all organisms that causes problems. In other words, I may be related to neaderthals, but I am not a monkey's uncle. The theory of common ancestry is the ultimate extrapolation of natural selection and speciation: that all living things are related by a single evolutionary history. This theory, then, contradicts literal interpretations of creation stories from every culture.

Common ancestry is supported by evidence from neontological, paleontological, embryological, and genetic studies. For example, comparing the forearm of frogs, lizards, birds, cats, apes, and humans, one finds that all share exactly the same set of bones. Each is somewhat modified for different functions, but homologous bones are clearly recognizable in each forearm. I am not about to suggest that God was incapable of coming up with more than one body plan. Why, then, do we see such commonalities? In the genome, some of our most basic structural genes are shared with mice, fish, even fruit flies. This is strong evidence that, hundreds of millions of years ago, we all shared a common ancestor.

To summarize, there is little value in debating the whole of Darwinian evolution as if it were a monolithic construct. *The Origin of Species* posed not one, but several theories relating to the process of evolution. As demonstrated above, three of Darwin's five theories should be acceptable – in reference to small-scale change – to creationists and evolutionists alike. In particular, the logic behind natural selection is unimpeachable; it can be proven on theoretical and empirical bases. Therefore, let us end the tiresome debates over natural selection and evolution. In matters of small-scale change they are simple, observable, and provable concepts – not the spectral minions of atheism.

Instead, we must focus the debate on speciation and common ancestry. It is these ideas that potentially conflict with religious teachings. Several forests (not to mention endless gigabytes) have been wasted by people arguing disparate issues under the general label of Darwinism. Such debates have all the appeal of a football game in which the opposing teams are on different fields. By defining the true areas of contention, perhaps we can establish a meaningful dialogue over the roles that these ontologies should play in our society.

OTHER MISCONCEPTIONS ABOUT DARWINIAN EVOLUTION

Having distilled Darwinian evolution into its several components, I will now address other common misunderstandings about evolution. As in the previous section, my goal is not to convince creationists that they are wrong. Rather, it is to demonstrate that many of the typical attacks on evolution are misinformed. I would like to retire these ragged soldiers so that more meaningful debate can arise.

Darwinian evolution is intimately tied to abiogenesis. Just as many people conflate natural selection and speciation, so often do they include abiogenesis: the origin of life out of non-life. In his *Origin of Species*, Darwin did not discuss the origin of life, either divine or spontaneous, in any specific terms. Rather, he wrote of "breathing life" into "a few forms or one" (p. 459). Regardless of his (public or private) beliefs on the subject, it is clear is that his theories exist apart from theories about life's beginning. Whether God or chance created the first reproducing organic structures has no bearing on their subsequent evolution. In fact, if we define evolution as change in a population over time, and we agree that there were no biological populations *before* life began (i.e. there were no populations of living organisms before there were living organisms), then the origin of life *cannot be an evolutionary phenomenon*. Even if one rejects this definition and still considers the origin of life to be evolutionary, it is properly ascribed to the force of mutation, *not* natural selection. In either case, abiogenesis is not logically tied to Darwin's theories, although many scientists subscribe to both concepts.

Evolution has never been observed. Classic examples documenting natural selection's effects on populations (e.g. peppered moths, Darwin's finches) can be found in most biology texts. I will not dwell on them here because I hope that we can now agree that evolution has been observed. Recall that evolution means only changes in populations over time. As discussed above, the population in New York City has changed over time; the species of *Canis familiaris* has changed over time. This is evolution. It is observable. Creation advocates should be arguing that speciation or higher-level macroevolution has never been observed (although speciation has been documented in the laboratory and can arguably be seen in ring species). Macroevolutionary arguments can document only *effects* of evolution, not macroevolution itself. Let us bear in mind, however, that gravity has never been observed either – only its effect on other objects.

Evolution violates the 2nd law of thermodynamics. This is a horse that just refuses to die. A general ignorance among scientists (excepting chemists and physicists) and laypersons alike has allowed this mythical beast to keep drawing breath. The second law of thermodynamics states that no process is possible in which the sole result is a transfer of energy from a cooler to a hotter body. Put another way, the entropy in a *closed system* cannot decrease. What does this have to do with evolution? According to the perpetrators of this idea, the increased organization of life through evolution represents a decrease in entropy, thus violating the 2nd law. Wallace (2001) argues that the 2nd law is universal, allowing no exceptions – including evolution. Thus, by his reasoning, evolution is impossible. One must similarly conclude, then, that he and his followers do not plan to have children. For, the growth of a child from zygote to infant (and beyond) violates the 2nd law of thermodynamics as much as (and in similar fashion to) evolution. Of course, a developing embryo is not a closed system; it receives energy and nourishment from its mother. Neither, however, is the Earth a closed system, receiving intense energy from the sun. As the University of Vermont Department of Chemistry explains, "The earth... receives large amounts of low-entropy energy from the sun and radiates it back as high-entropy heat. We may be more highly organized (lower entropy) than slime molds, but the universe increased in entropy as humans evolved" (http://learn.chem.vt.edu). Thus, evolution represents, not a decrease in entropy, but an increase in the entropy of the only true closed system: the universe.

Evolution is only a theory, not fact. Thus far I have only discussed evolution in terms of natural selection. As shown above, natural selection rests on the three basic assumptions that populations are variable, some variation helps organisms succeed, and successful traits can be inherited. Each of these assumptions is easily proven empirically. And, as with any logical construction, the conclusion follows from the assumptions. Because the assumptions are true, then the theory holds as well. Natural selection is, in fact, as provable as any scientific theory (gravity, inertia, thermodynamics) can be. Subsequent to Darwin's publication, however, the field of genetics has revealed other forces that contribute to evolution. Forces like mutation and gene flow are easily documented in life – provable beyond argument. The fourth evolutionary mechanism, genetic drift, is actually a statistical phenomenon. Thus, evolution via genetic drift is *provable mathematically*. All of these forces contribute to changes in populations over time.

Darwinian evolution cannot account for molecular complexity. Perhaps the only serious scientific attack of Darwinian evolution (yes, I'm discounting the 2nd law of thermodynamics) has been from proponents of the intelligent design theory. Coming from the field of biochemistry, this theory suggests that the complex molecular inter-relationships within the cell are irreducible. In other words, components of these systems could not have gradually arisen over time – they are too interdependent. Since Darwinian evolution has yet to address such issues, design advocates conclude that intelligence underlies sub-cellular complexity. Without going into the details of the arguments, I must agree that Darwinian evolution has *not* adequately dealt with complexity theory. Advances in biochemistry over the last few decades have opened up an entire new world of biology… one that is staggering in its complexity.

Unfortunately, advocates of intelligent design have climbed to this incredible molecular vista and leapt back into the darkness. To quote one of the movement's founders, "One branch of science was not invited to the [Modern Synthesis] meetings, and for good reason: it did not exist" (Behe, 1996: 24). It is hardly surprising that the framers of Neo-Darwinian evolutionary theory were unable to anticipate and refute evidence from a field that hadn't been invented. Biochemistry offers great new approaches and challenges to understanding the fundamental processes of life. I respectfully submit, however, that the mysteries of a field in its scientific infancy are not ready to be declared unsolvable. Just because Darwinian evolution does not easily explain cellular complexity does not mean that it *cannot*. Where would science be if nature's secrets were all abandoned as being beyond comprehension? Rumor has it that the theory of gravity was knocked into Newton's head by a falling apple. Then, Einstein came along and updated gravitational theory to include relativistic concepts. The newer field of quantum physics has produced theories that we cannot, as of yet, reconcile with our understanding of gravitation. Should we decide, then, that there is no gravity? that Einstein was wrong? It seems reasonable that Einstein's formulation of gravity will someday be reconciled or updated to encompass quantum physics. Similarly, new advances in biochemistry offer chances to expand our understanding of how Darwinian evolution works at the very foundation of life.

CREATION VERSUS CREATION SCIENCE

Having parsed the scientific perspective into specific components, I will finish with a differentiation of the creationist ideology. Typically, the evolutionist attitude toward creationists mirrors the creationist attitude toward evolutionists. This is largely unnecessary, as science and religion are in contention as much as a figure skater competes with a baseball team. Science is an epistemological system of exploring the universe. Religion is a system of beliefs. One is about proof, the other faith. Neither system really has much to offer about the other. As a Kenyan colleague of mine put it, "You have lots of Religion professors in America who do not believe in God, why should I not believe in God and still study evolution?" Why not, indeed? The beliefs that people subscribe to in their households and their churches are not relevant to scientific inquiry, just as the axioms of science have no bearing on peoples' faith.

The real problem is the hybrid called Creation "Science." This hopeful monster is somehow concerned with scientifically proving the creation story of Genesis. In reality, creation scientists settle for raising objections to evolutionary theory. The problem with this hybrid is easily illustrated in the work of Wallace (2001). He claims that evolution violates the 2nd law of thermodynamics (see above). Since this law is universal, there are no exceptions. Therefore, evolution of complex organisms cannot be true. One must note, however, that complex organisms do in fact exist. How is this possible? God. Therefore, we go from having no exceptions to the 2nd law to allowing God to make exceptions. Could we also let evolution be an exception, then? In fact, one can always claim that things are the way they are because God made them that way. While strong of faith, that approach will do nothing to advance science.

The problems with creation science are not just in supplanting the scientific method with faith. Creation science undermines the ideals of faith with science! Indeed, one must ask how strong can faith be, if it must be continually proven. Trying to prove a belief is the antithesis of faith. Creationists are welcome to their belief. Creation "science," however, is a deplorable subversion of science and a fundamental corruption of faith. To quote a figure that even creationists respect – Christ: "Have you come to believe because you have seen me? Blessed are those who have not seen and have believed" (John, 20:29; New American Bible, 1987).

Acknowledgements

This address was not intended as a comprehensive literature review and was not researched and presented as such. Rather, it represents some of my thoughts regarding Darwinian evolution, natural selection, and creation "science." I have no doubt that many of the ideas presented herein have been written elsewhere (and more eloquently) by other authors. Those sources that I consulted directly in preparing this presentation are duly cited below. Of the myriad influences that shaped my education over the years, I can only say a general "thank you." Having said that, I will make two exceptions. First, much of my theoretical musings are based on lectures and discussion with Dr. Frederick Szalay of Hunter College. Fred is one of the great evolutionary theorists of our time and often under-appreciated by North American scholars. Second, my view of the relationships between science and religion was heavily shaped by Frank Herbert. Rather than writing books, Mr. Herbert created intellectual landscapes within with the reader can interact with a world of ideas.

[ABOUT THE AUTHOR]

Like many children, Kieran McNulty was afflicted with fossil-fever at a young age due to prolonged exposure to dinosaur texts and coloring books. Sadly, his case was untreatable. A minor mutation in this condition led him to pursue a B.A. in anthropology at Dartmouth College, focusing on human evolution. Disregarding the advice of specialists, he went on to earn an M.A. in anthropology from Hunter College and an M.Phil. in anthropology from the City University of New York. Currently, Kieran is finishing his Ph.D. at the latter and pursuing his research at the American Museum of Natural History. Though his dissertation (geometric morphometric analyses of extant and fossil apes) occupies most of his time, he occasionally sneaks off to participate in paleoanthropological field projects.

[WORKS CITED]

Behe, M. J. (1996). *Darwin's Black Box*. New York: The Free Press.

Darwin, C. R. (1859). *On the Origin of Species by Means of Natural Selection*. London: J. Murray.

Eiseley, L. (1979). *Darwin and the Mysterious Mr. X*. New York: E.P. Dutton.

Eldredge, N. & Gould, S.J. (1972). Punctuated equilibria: an alternative to phyletic gradualism. In (T.J.M Schopf, Ed.) *Models in Paleobiology*. San Francisco: Freeman, Cooper & Co. p. 82-115.

Futuyma, D.J. (1986) *Evolutionary Biology*. Sinauer Associates

Isaak, M. (1995). Five major misconceptions about evolution. *The Talk.Origins Archive*. http://www.talkorigins.org/faqs/faq-misconceptions.html

New American Bible (1987). Wichita: Devore & Sons, Inc.

Wallace, T. (2001). Five major evolutionist misconceptions about evolution. *The True.Origin Archive*. http://www.trueorigin.org/isakrbtl.asp

[ADDITIONAL RESOURCES]

Long Island Secular Humanists: http://nyhumanist.org/lish.htm

American Museum of Natural History: http://www.amnh.org/

This article was first commissioned and published by The British Humanist Association and is reprinted here with permission from the author and the BHA.

Is Creationism Scientific?

by Stephen Law

A state-funded UK school in Gateshead is teaching children that creationism is scientifically respectable. Other schools plan to follow suit. Some think that there is no educational harm in this. But are they correct?

No. To teach children that creationism is scientifically respectable is to teach children to think in ways that are, quite literally, close to lunacy. To understand why the teaching of creationism in schools may do real educational harm, we need first to be clear about exactly what creationism is.

What is Creationism?

Creationism, as the term is usually used, is not simply the view that God created the universe. Many reputable scientists are prepared to accept that. Rather, those who call themselves creationists typically believe that the account of creation in Genesis is literally true. The universe was produced over a six-day period. All living creatures were created at that time.

Creationism entails that:

(i) The universe is just a few thousand years old (in fact creationists typically say less than 10,000 years old – their calculation is based on the number of generations since Adam listed in the Bible).

(ii) Modern scientific cosmologies on which the universe is many billions of years old and began with a Big Bang are thus fundamentally wrong

(iii) No new species has ever evolved. They were all created in the same week just a few thousand years ago. So dinosaurs (creationists don't deny they existed) walked the Earth with mankind at that time.

Teaching creationism involves teaching children that all these things are true.

Almost all creationists also believe that creationism is at least as well supported by the available empirical evidence is the Big Bang/evolution alternative. The Gateshead school is teaching children that creationism is scientifically respectable.

Evidence Of A Very Old Universe

Yet there appears to be overwhelming evidence that we inhabit a very old universe with life having evolved only comparatively recently (though still many millions of years ago). Here are five examples of such evidence:

(i) Astronomers have observed objects from which it would take light many billions of years to reach us.

(ii) Look at the moon and you will see thousands of craters. These craters are produced by impacts that occur very infrequently. In order for the moon to have that many craters, it would have to be very old indeed.

(iii) The surface of the Earth is made up of continental plates that drift. For example, Africa and South America were once physically connected. The very slow rate at which the plates drift means that many millions of years must have elapsed since Africa and America were linked.

(iv) The surface of the Earth is made up of rock strata. Given the rate at which strata are laid down, it would take many millions of years for that depth of strata to form.

(v) The rock strata contain fossils. These fossils are ordered in a way that shows evolutionary progression. For example, they show that man evolved from earlier primates. But if creationism were true, and if the rock strata were produced in only the last few thousand years or so, one would expect to find creatures fossilized in a fairly random way throughout the strata. For example, one would expect to find fossils of mammals distributed fairly evenly throughout the layers. Yet even today, after many millions of fossils have been discovered, not one single well documented example of an out of place fossil has been found (e.g. not one single mammal fossil has been found in the dinosaur layers).

Countless other examples of counter-evidence to creationism can be drawn from almost every branch of science.

The Popularity Of Creationism

Yet creationists have succeeded in persuading many that their theory is at least as scientifically respectable as the Big Bang/evolution alternative.

In fact recent Gallup polls indicate that

> 45% of US citizens believe God created human beings "pretty much in (their) present form at one time or another within the last 10,000 years."

Even college graduates are drawn to creationism. A Tennessee academic who recently surveyed his own students writes that scientists are having to fight the battles of the Enlightenment all over again. Medieval ideas that were killed stone dead by the rise of science three to four hundred years ago are not merely twitching; they are alive and well in our schools, colleges and universities.

Doesn't the fact that so many intelligent people been persuaded of the truth of creationism show there must be something to it? No. What is true is that what creationists practice strongly resembles good science in certain respects. That is why so many have been duped.

The Core Creationist Strategy

The central creationist argumentative strategy is to try to deal with the evidence by showing that it is consistent with creationism after all.

Take the fossil record, for example. Creationists maintain that the layering in the fossil record can be explained by reference to the Biblical Flood. The rains that caused the Flood were responsible for producing huge mud deposits that then metamorphosed into the rock strata we find beneath our feet.

Creationists insist that the ordering of the life-forms within these layers can also be accounted for on their theory. For example, some suggest the reason one finds dinosaurs below mammals is that dinosaurs are slow, cumbersome and relatively unintelligent creatures that are likely to have been buried as the faster, more intelligent mammals ran to higher ground.

A similar strategy is used to deal with other evidence. Take the craters on the Moon. Given the craters are produced so infrequently, why does the Moon have so many? A creationist could suggest that, at the time the Moon was formed, there was far more debris in space. This debris was quickly drawn to bodies like the moon, producing many craters over a short period of time. Now most of the debris has gone, which is why impacts are currently rare.

How Creationism Can Be Made To Look "Scientific"

We have seen that creationists defend their core theory by developing and adding to it in various ways so that it continues to fit the available evidence. Each time another piece of apparently solid counter-evidence to creationism is produced, the creationist adds a bit more to their core theory to protect it. In short:

> *Creationists have developed a theory of increasing complexity and ingenuity to fit the empirical data.*

And isn't this exactly how good scientific theories are developed?

Well, it looks like a little like science. That's one reason why so many are convinced that creationism is properly "scientific".

But, despite the superficial similarity to genuine science, the central creationist strategy is thoroughly unscientific. The easiest way to see why is by means of an analogy.

Are Cats Martian Secret Agents?

Suppose I claim that cats are Martian secret agents. You might think my theory easily disproved. After all, cats are pretty stupid creatures, obviously incapable of such treachery. We don't find transmitters hidden about our houses by which they might transmit their secret reports. And Mars is uninhabited. Everything points to my theory being false, surely.

But what if, in reply, I suggest that cat brains are particularly efficient, and that cats merely hide their intelligence from us. And their transmitters are embedded in their brains, which is why we don't discover them. And Mars is inhabited, but the Martians live in underground secret bunkers.

Now my theory fits the data again.

In reply, you might point out that an X-ray of a cat's head reveals no transmitter, and that we can detect no transmissions coming from it.

To which I might reply that the transmitters are organic and made to look like brain tissue. That's why we haven't discovered them. And cats transmit by means of a medium we Earthlings do not yet understand and cannot yet detect.

Again, I have made my theory fit the evidence.

You can see how this game might continue forever. Any theory, no matter how utterly absurd, can be protected from falsification and made to fit the available data if one is prepared to keep on modifying and adding to it in this way.

This is the main reason why what creationists practice is unscientific. While reputable scientists do sometimes defend their theories by making such "ad hoc" moves, one shouldn't make a habit of it. Once almost all ones energies are expended on protecting ones core theory from being falsified, it is no longer being approached as a scientific theory but as an item of faith - to be defended come what may.

Notice that creationist "scientists" expend almost all their energies on devising exactly such moves. We would rightly consider someone who defended the cat's-are-Martian-secret-agents theory in this way to be suffering from sort of mental illness. In fact, this sort of twisted reasoning is fairly common in schizophrenics. It is, quite literally, close to lunacy.

Yet this sort of reasoning constitutes the creationist's core intellectual strategy.

DEALING WITH CREATIONIST CLAIMS

It's tempting, when faced with creationist claims, simply to wheel out contrary evidence: the fossil record, for example. The problem with this strategy is that creationists soon tie their opponents up in knots. Just like a defender of my cats-are-Martian-secret-agents theory, they confound and infuriate their critics by constantly amending or adding to their core theory in order to protect it from being falsified.

In order to deal more effectively with creationist claims and arguments one needs to take a step back and look at their method. Whatever it is, it isn't science.

ISN'T THE BIG BANG/EVOLUTION HYPOTHESIS EQUALLY A "FAITH POSITION"?

In their defence, creationists often point out that, if any theory can be protected from falsification come what may, then no theory can be conclusively falsified. But then it follows that the Big Bang/evolution theory cannot be conclusively falsified either.

In addition, a creationist can point out, nor is any scientific theory ever conclusively proved. Any theory necessarily goes beyond what we have observed. As such, it must involve an element of speculation.

So, concludes the creationist, creationism and the Big Bang/evolution theory are equally "faith positions". They are intellectually on par.

This is muddled thinking. Just because no theory can be conclusively falsified or proved doesn't mean that all theories are equally good.

Notice that theories aren't just falsified, they are also confirmed. The fact is that, while any theory is open to some degree of doubt, some are confirmed to the extent that they are beyond any reasonable doubt. For example, it is now beyond any reasonable doubt that the Earth moves and that there are no such things as fairies.

Now the fact is that the Big Bang/evolution theory is overwhelmingly confirmed by the empirical evidence. Scientists may argue over the details, such as over exactly how evolution took place. But the basic framework theory – that the universe is very old and that species evolution has taken place – is beyond any reasonable doubt.

That's Not True of Creationism.

Notice that if the "they're both faith positions" move is allowed, then we will also have to allow that the "theories" that fairies exist, that the Sun goes round the Earth and that the universe was created by a huge yellow banana called "Ted" are all just as scientifically respectable as our leading scientific theories about the universe.

The Perils of Teaching Creationism

Creationism is not, as some have suggested, a harmless "extra" that faith schools should be free to teach in addition to the national curriculum.

The real problem is not that we are letting those in positions of power and authority over young minds teach them ludicrous falsehoods, though that is bad enough. The problem is that the only way children can be taught that creationism is true and supported by the available evidence is by instilling in them such twisted conceptions of logic and evidential support that they are likely to remain gullible idiots for the rest of their lives.

As I say, teaching that creationism is respectable science means teaching children to think in ways that are, literally, close to lunacy.

The "Parental Choice" Argument

But what of parental choice? Whether or not creationism is "scientific", surely parents should be free to choose how their children are educated. After all, the belief that Jesus literally rose from the dead is hardly "scientific", is it? (It's not well supported by the empirical data.) Yet we allow it to be taught in the classroom. If we ban the teaching of creationism on the grounds that it's unscientific, won't we have to ban all religious education?

This is to misunderstand my objection. I am not arguing that we shouldn't teach things that are unscientific. That's fine, as long as it's acknowledged that they are unscientific.

But the Gateshead creationists, like many schools in the US, are teaching that creationism is good science. Teaching that creationism is good science involves teaching children to reason in ways that are likely to do real educational harm. Children are likely to leave school with a profoundly mistaken conception of what science actually is.

That is not true of standard religious education.

When teaching does real educational harm it should be stopped. We don't allow parents the freedom to send their children to schools where racist teaching goes on. Nor would we allow schools to teach children that alchemy and extispicy (the reading of entrails) are "good science". This is because it would be educationally harmful. Teaching children that creationism is good science also does real educational harm. That's why it should be stopped.

[ABOUT THE AUTHOR]

Stephen Law is Lecturer in Philosophy at Heythrop College, University of London. He is the editor of the Royal Institute of Philosophy's new journal of philosophy for everyone: *Think*. He is also the author of the children's introduction to philosophy *Philosophy Rocks!* and the adult introduction *The Philosophy Gym: 25 Short Adventures in Thinking*.

[ADDITIONAL RESOURCES]

The Royal Institute of Philosophy's *Think* is a unique publication – a popular philosophy journal aimed at a wide, non-specialist audience. Think contains work by leading philosophers on topics that have broad appeal. It can be accessed online at: http://www.royalinstitutephilosophy.org/think.htm

This review first appeared in the **National Center for Science Education Reports** and is reprinted here with permission from the author.

BOOK REVIEW:
INTELLIGENT DESIGN CREATIONISM AND ITS CRITICS:
PHILOSOPHICAL, THEOLOGICAL, AND SCIENTIFIC PERSPECTIVES
Edited by Robert T. Pennock
The MIT Press

Review by Glenn Branch

The reaction of the Duke of Gloucester to the second volume of Gibbon's *The Decline and Fall of the Roman Empire* springs irresistibly to mind: "Another damned, thick, square, book!" Pennock's hefty anthology, divided into nine sections – Intelligent Design Creationism's "Wedge Strategy"; Johnson's Critique of Evolutionary Naturalism; A Theological Conflict? Evolution vs. the Bible; Intelligent Design's Scientific Claims; Plantinga's Critique of Naturalism and Evolution; Intelligent Design Creationism vs. Theistic Evolutionism; Intelligent Design and Information; Intelligent Design Theorists Turn the Tables; Creationism and Education – contains no fewer than thirty-seven essays that together comprehensively address the phenomenon of the intelligent design movement from (as the subtitle promises) philosophical, theological, and scientific perspectives.

Intelligent design, defined as uncontentiously as possible, is the view that there is scientific evidence for the handiwork of a personal designer – possibly but not necessarily supernatural – in the biological world. As such, it is arguably the descendant of the Bridgewater Treatises (1833-1840), Paley's *Natural Theology* (1802), Ray's *Wisdom of God Manifested in the Works of the Creation* (1691), and so on back to Diogenes of Apollonia, but its contemporary ur-texts are Thaxton, Bradley, and Olsen's *The Mystery of Life's Origin* (1984), Davis and Kenyon's *Of Pandas and People* (1989; second edition 1993), and Johnson's *Darwin on Trial* (1991). Thus the intellectual ancestry of intelligent design is principally in creationism, whence the noun in *Intelligent Design Creationism and Its Critics*. Although Pennock traces the ancestry of intelligent design in his previous book *Tower of Babel* (1999), there is no essay in the present anthology that covers the same ground – which is regrettable, especially in light of William Dembski's public complaint that its very title is tendentious. Still, any qualm about the title is likely to be assuaged by the realization that intelligent design's eschewal of scientific research in favor of political activism and educational propaganda is parallel to creationism's, as Barbara Forrest details in her exhaustive description of the wedge strategy for promoting intelligent design, devised by Phillip Johnson and implemented by the Discovery Institute's Center for the Renewal of Science and Culture.

With the exception of the philosopher Alvin Plantinga, the proponents of intelligent design represented in Pennock's anthology are associated with the Center for the Renewal of Science and Culture: in addition to Johnson, the Center's advisor, there are Michael Behe, Paul Nelson, and William Dembski, all Senior Fellows of the Center. Also prominent in the activities of the Center is Jonathan Wells, but since Wells's contribution to intelligent design consists in *Icons of Evolution* (2000), a screed reminiscent of the worst excesses of the Institute for Creation Research (see reviews by Coyne [2001], Scott [2001], and Padian and Gishlick [2002]), his absence from the book is no loss. Despite the scientific pretensions of the Center, the proponents of intelligent design have not managed to produce any relevant scientific articles in the peer-reviewed scientific literature; as Forrest trenchantly remarks, "the wedge strategy is failing miserably in its most important goal: the production of scientific research data to support intelligent design creationism and the publication of such data in scientific journals."

If there is a scientific component to intelligent design, it is due mainly to Behe, the only working scientist among the proponents of intelligent design represented here, and, significantly, the least extreme in his distance from the evolutionary mainstream. Behe's contribution to intelligent design is the concept of irreducible complexity, introduced in his popular work *Darwin's Black Box* (1996) and reiterated thereafter, with negligible changes, in a series of articles in popular publications; Behe argues that certain complex structures at the cellular level could not have arisen through random mutation and natural selection. His microminiaturization of Paley was roundly criticized in the scientific literature on its initial appearance, and the discussions by Philip Kitcher and by Matthew J. Brauer and Daniel R. Brumbaugh, although worthy, add little to the conversation. It is surprising that Pennock includes no contribution by Kenneth R. Miller, the Brown University biologist who regularly debates Behe and whose *Finding Darwin's God* (1999) devotes a chapter to refuting him.

Still, as Johnson wrote elsewhere, "This isn't really, and never has been, a debate about science. It's about religion and philosophy." For Johnson, the project is clear: to argue that evolution "is based not upon any incontrovertible empirical evidence, but upon a highly controversial philosophical presupposition" – which, of course, he rejects on theological grounds. Unfortunately for his project, Johnson appears to be as poorly equipped for philosophical disputation as he is for scientific inquiry. Reading through his exchanges with Pennock on methodological naturalism and with Richard Dawkins and George C. Williams on genetic information, it is difficult to decide in which area he exhibits less acumen. Less lively but still interesting are the theological critiques of Johnson offered by Nancey Murphy and Howard J. van Till, whose poignant assessment of intelligent design's presumption that evolution threatens Christianity deserves quotation: "a tragedy of major proportions for the Christian witness to a scientifically literate world." In the same section of the book, although not addressing Johnson specifically, is Arthur Peacocke's Idreos Lecture "Welcoming the 'Disguised Friend'

– Darwinism and Divinity" (1997) – itself a welcome contribution.

Unlike Johnson, Plantinga is undeniably possessed of philosophical acuity, which he deploys here against methodological naturalism – crudely, the view that science is able to investigate only the natural world – at a level of philosophical sophistication beyond Johnson's reach. In "Methodological Naturalism?" he argues, on the basis of his celebrated view about the proper basicality of Christian belief, that Christian believers are not obligated to practice science as methodological naturalists. In his response, Michael Ruse justly castigates Plantinga for "a deliberate ignorance of work that is going on today in science" that encourages him to underestimate the value of methodological naturalism. Ruse also remarks that Plantinga's rejection of methodological naturalism is premised on "his prior commitment to his own version of Christian theism"; in their exchanges with Plantinga reprinted from the obscure *Christian Scholar's Review*, van Till and Ernan McMullin demonstrate that not all Christians share Plantinga's repugnance for methodological naturalism.

Plantinga's rejection of methodological naturalism is bolstered by his argument (reminiscent of C. S. Lewis's) that philosophical naturalism – crudely, the view that the natural is all that there is – is self-defeating. Pennock fails to explain that the argument is not aimed against evolution per se: as Plantinga himself notes, a theist who accepts the argument "may indeed endorse some form of evolution; but if he does, it will be a form of evolution guided and orchestrated by God" (*Warrant and Proper Function* [1993]). But, as his "When Faith and Reason Clash" suggests, Plantinga thinks that the untenability of naturalism clears the way for the creationist: "The believer in God, unlike her naturalistic counterpart, is free to look at the evidence for the Grand Evolutionary Scheme, and follow it where it leads, rejecting that scheme if the evidence is insufficient" – as he evidently supposes that it is. So it is, after all, appropriate that Pennock includes a pair of excellent, if technical, articles (by Evan Fales and by Brandon Fitelson and Elliott Sober) criticizing Plantinga's argument; those interested in the debate should consult ch. 7 of Plantinga's *Warranted Christian Belief* (2000) and *Naturalism Defeated?* (2002), ed. James Beilby, for the latest developments.

Finally, in the last section of the anthology, Plantinga and Pennock philosophically spar about whether it is appropriate to teach creationism in the public schools. It is not at all surprising that the science writer for the Columbus, Ohio, *Dispatch* publicly recommended the exchange (as well as Forrest's contribution) to members of the Ohio Board of Education, who are presently beset by creationists eager for intelligent design to be included in the state science standards. Pennock, whose response includes a brilliant refutation of a specious appeal by Plantinga to Rawls's theory of justice, is the clear winner here; it is to be hoped that the Ohio Board of Education prefers his vision of science education to Plantinga's.

Compared to Plantinga's, Nelson's and Dembski's contributions are philosophically nugatory. (It is unfortunate that Pennock includes nothing by Del Ratzsch, a philosopher of science influenced by Plantinga; his work, which is sympathetic to, if not quite so invested in, intelligent design [see his *Nature, Design, and Science* (2001)], is of substantially higher philosophical quality.) Nelson is a young-earth creationist – he comes by it honestly; his grandfather Byron C. Nelson was a prominent anti-evolutionary pamphleteer of the 1930s – but there is no trace of it in his essay here, in which he soberly argues that evolutionary biologists are prone to make theological assumptions that are not only unjustifiable but inconsistent with their professions of methodological naturalism. To Kelly C. Smith's withering response, it is necessary only to add that the texts that Nelson examines are popular works and introductory textbooks, not the sort of writing that evolutionary biologists professionally produce.

And then there is Dembski, who is rapidly consolidating a reputation as the *enfant terrible* of intelligent design – not so much on account of his youth as of his combativeness, his ceaseless self-promotion, and his tendency to put his foot in his mouth (as when he told *The Chronicle of Higher Education* that he prefers publishing popular books to scholarly articles because "I get a royalty. And the material gets read more"). In "Intelligent Design as a Theory of Information" (1997; reprinted with revisions as ch. 7 of *Intelligent Design: The Bridge Between Science and Theology* [1999]; reprinted in part with revisions as ch. 3 of *No Free Lunch* [2002]), Dembski argues that "information is not reducible to natural causes," a claim that Peter Godfrey-Smith exposes as a restatement of the antediluvian creationist canard about the improbability of evolution. Dembski's so-called explanatory filter is the main topic of Branden Fitelson, Christopher Stephens, and Elliott Sober's review of *The Design Inference* (1998); it is unfortunate that Pennock includes no explanation by Dembski himself of the filter. Finally, in "Who's Got the Magic?" Dembski argues that evolutionary biology relies in effect on appeals to magic ("getting something for nothing"); it is noteworthy that, when it was reprinted as the final section of *No Free Lunch*, Dembski failed to respond to "The Wizards of ID," also reprinted here, in which Pennock convincingly replies that it is, on the contrary, intelligent design that relies on magic.

Pennock, whose *Tower of Babel* remains the most important philosophical evaluation of the intelligent design movement available, provides a brief preface to each of the sections as well as to the book itself; while not disguising his intellectual antipathy to the intelligent design movement, Pennock admirably manages to provide a balanced (if not equal) selection of essays that is essential reading for anyone interested in investigating the relationship between science and theology. For, as *Intelligent Design Creationism and Its Critics* shows, the intelligent design movement conceives of the relationship in a particularly counterproductive – and even disastrous – way.

[ABOUT THE AUTHOR]

Glenn Branch is Deputy Director of the National Center for Science Education, a nonprofit organization that defends the teaching of evolution in the (U.S.) public schools.

[ADDITIONAL RESOURCES]

National Center for Science Education: http://www.ncseweb.org

This paper was presented by Elliott Sober to the Darwin Coalition of Tennessee for Darwin Day 2002. It is published in **The Blackwell Guide to Philosophy of Religion** *and reprinted here with permission from the author.*

THE DESIGN ARGUMENT
by Elliott Sober[1]

The design argument is one of three main arguments for the existence of God; the others are the ontological argument and the cosmological argument. Unlike the ontological argument, the design argument and the cosmological argument are *a posteriori*. And whereas the cosmological argument can focus on any present event to get the ball rolling (arguing that it must trace back to a first cause, namely God), design theorists are usually more selective.

Design arguments have typically been of two types – *organismic* and *cosmic*. Organismic design arguments start with the observation that organisms have features that adapt them to the environments in which they live and that exhibit a kind of *delicacy*. Consider, for example, the vertebrate eye. This organ helps organisms survive by permitting them to perceive objects in their environment. And were the parts of the eye even slightly different in their shape and assembly, the resulting organ would not allow us to see. Cosmic design arguments begin with an observation concerning features of the entire cosmos – the universe obeys simple laws, it has a kind of stability, its physical features permit life and intelligent life to exist. However, not all design arguments fit into these two neat compartments. Kepler, for example, thought that the face we see when we look at the moon requires explanation in terms of intelligent design. Still, the common thread is that design theorists describe some empirical feature of the world and argue that this feature points towards an explanation in terms of God's intentional planning and away from an explanation in terms of mindless natural processes.

The design argument raises epistemological questions that go beyond its traditional theological context. As William Paley (1802) observed, when we find a watch while walking across a heath, we unhesitatingly infer that it was produced by an intelligent designer. No such inference forces itself upon us when we observe a stone. Why is explanation in terms of intelligent design so compelling in the one case, but not in the other? Similarly, when we observe the behavior of our fellow human beings, we find it irresistible to think that they have minds that are filled with beliefs and desires. And when we observe nonhuman organisms, the impulse to invoke mentalistic explanations is often very strong, especially when they look a lot like us. When does the behavior of an organism – human or not – warrant this mentalistic interpretation? The same question can be posed about machines. Few of us feel tempted to attribute beliefs and desires to hand calculators. We use calculators to help us add, but they don't literally figure out sums; in this respect, calculators are like the pieces of paper on which we scribble calculations. There is an important difference between a device that *we* use to help us think and a device that *itself* thinks. However, when a computer plays a decent game of chess, we may find it useful to explain and predict its behavior by thinking of it as having goals and deploying strategies (Dennett 1987b). Is this merely a useful fiction, or does the machine really have a mind? And if we think that present day chess-playing computers are, strictly speaking, mindless, what would it take for a machine to pass the test? Surely, as Turing (1950) observed, it needn't look like us. In all these contexts, we face *the problem of other minds* (Sober 2000a). If we understood the ground rules in this general epistemological problem, that would help us think about the design argument for the existence of God. And conversely – if we could get clear on the theological design argument, that might throw light on epistemological problems that are not theological in character.

What is the Design Argument?

The design argument, like the ontological argument, raises subtle questions concerning what the logical structure of the argument really is. My main concern here will not be to describe how various thinkers have presented the design argument, but to find the soundest formulation that the argument can be given.

The best version of the design argument, in my opinion, uses an inferential idea that probabilists call *the Likelihood Principle*. This can be illustrated by way of Paley's (1802) example of the watch on the heath. Paley describes an observation that he claims discriminates between two hypotheses:

(W) O1: the watch has features G1 ... Gn.
W1: the watch was created by an intelligent designer.
W2: the watch was produced by a mindless chance process.

Paley's idea is that O1 would be unsurprising if W1 were true, but would be very surprising if W2 were true. This is supposed to show that O1 *favors* W1 over W2; O1 supports W1 more than it supports W2. Surprise is a matter of degree; it can be captured by the concept of conditional probability. The probability of O given H – Pr(O * H) – represents how unsurprising O would be if H were true. The Likelihood Principle says that comparing such conditional probabilities is the way to decide what the direction is in which the evidence points:

(LP) Observation O supports hypothesis H1 more than it supports hypothesis H2 if and only if Pr(O * H1) > Pr(O * H2).

There is a lot to say on the question of why the likelihood principle should be accepted (Hacking 1965, Edwards 1972, Royall 1997, Forster and Sober 2003; Sober 2002); for the purposes of this essay, I will take it as a given.

We now can describe the likelihood version of the design argument for the existence of God, again taking our lead from one of Paley's favorite examples of a delicate adaptation. The basic format is to compare two hypotheses as possible explanations of a single observation:

(E) O2: the vertebrate eye has features F1 ... Fn.
E1: the vertebrate eye was created by an intelligent designer.
E2: the vertebrate eye was produced by a mindless chance process.

We do not hesitate to conclude that the observations strongly favor Design over Chance in the case of argument (W); Paley claims that precisely the same conclusion should be drawn in the case of the propositions assembled in (E).[2]

Clarifications

Several points of clarification are needed here concerning likelihood in general and the likelihood version of the design argument in particular. First, I use the term "likelihood" in a technical sense. Likelihood is not the same as probability. To say that H has a high likelihood, given observation O, is to comment on the value of Pr(O * H), not on the value of Pr(H * O); the latter is H's *posterior probability*. It is perfectly possible for a hypothesis to have a high likelihood and a low posterior probability. When you hear noises in your attic, this confers a high likelihood on the hypothesis that there are gremlins up there bowling, but few of us would conclude that this hypothesis is probably true.

Although the likelihood of H (given O) and the probability of H (given O) are different quantities, they are related. The relationship is given by Bayes' theorem:

Pr(H * O) = Pr(O * H)Pr(H)/Pr(O).

Pr(H) is the hypothesis' *prior probability* – the probability that H has before we take the observation O into account. From Bayes's theorem we can deduce the following:

Pr(H1 * O) > Pr(H2 * O) if and only if Pr(O * H1)Pr(H1) > Pr(O * H2)Pr(H2).

Which hypothesis has the higher posterior probability depends on how their likelihoods are related, but also on how their prior probabilities are related. This explains why the likelihood version of the design argument does not show that Design is more probable than Chance. To draw this further conclusion, we'd have to say something about the prior probabilities of the two hypotheses. It is here that I wish to demur (and this is what separates me from card-carrying Bayesians). Each of us perhaps has some subjective degree of belief, before we consider the design argument, in each of the two hypotheses (E1) and (E2). However, I see no way to understand the idea that the two hypotheses have *objective* prior probabilities. Since I would like to restrict the design argument as much as possible to matters that are objective, I will not represent it as an argument concerning which hypothesis is more probable.[3] However, those who have prior degrees of belief in (E1) and (E2) should use the likelihood argument to update their subjective probabilities. The likelihood version of the design argument says that the observation O2 should lead you to increase your degree of belief in (E1) and reduce your degree of belief in (E2).

My restriction of the design argument to an assessment of likelihoods, not probabilities, reflects a more general point of view. Scientific theories often have implications about which observations are probable (and which are improbable), but it rarely makes sense to describe them as having objective probabilities. Newton's law of gravitation (along with suitable background assumptions) says that the return of Haley's comet was to be expected, but what is the probability that Newton's law is true? Hypotheses have objective probabilities when they describe possible outcomes of a chance process. But as far as anyone knows, the laws that govern our universe were not the result of a chance process. Bayesians think that *all* hypotheses have probabilities; the position I am advocating sees this as a special feature of *some* hypotheses.[4]

Just as likelihood considerations leave open what probabilities one should assign to the competing hypotheses, they also don't tell you which hypothesis you should *believe*. I take it that belief is a dichotomous concept – you either believe a proposition or you do not. Consistent with this is the idea that there are three attitudes one might take to a statement – you can believe it true, believe it false, or withhold judgment. However, there is no simple connection of the matter-of-degree concept of probability to the dichotomous (or trichotomous) concept of belief. This is the lesson I extract from the lottery paradox (Kyburg 1961). Suppose 100,000 tickets are sold in a fair lottery; one ticket will win and each has the same chance of winning. It follows that each ticket has a very high probability of not winning. If you adopt the policy of believing a proposition when it has a high probability, you will believe of each ticket that it will not win. However, this conclusion contradicts the assumption that the lottery is fair. What this shows is that high probability does not suffice for belief (and low probability does not suffice for disbelief). It is for this reason that many Bayesians prefer to say that individuals have degrees of belief. The rules for the dichotomous concept are unclear; the matter-of-degree concept at least has the advantage of being anchored to the probability calculus.

In summary, likelihood arguments have rather modest pretensions. They don't tell you which hypotheses to believe; in fact, they don't even tell you which hypotheses are probably true. Rather, they evaluate how the observations at hand discriminate among the hypotheses under consideration.

I now turn to some details concerning the likelihood version of the design argument. The first concerns the meaning of the intelligent design hypothesis. This hypothesis occurs in (W1) in connection with the watch and in (E1) in connection with the vertebrate eye. In the case of the watch, Paley did not dream that he was offering an argument for the existence of *God*. However, in the case of the eye, Paley thought that the intelligent designer under discussion was God himself. Why are these cases different? The bare bones of the likelihood arguments (W) and (E) do not say. What Paley had in mind is that building the vertebrate eye and the other adaptive features that organisms exhibit requires an intelligence far greater than anything that human beings could muster. This is a point that we will revisit at the end of this essay.

It also is important to understand the nature of the hypothesis with which the intelligent design hypothesis competes. I have used the term "chance" to express this alternative hypothesis. In large measure, this is because design theorists often think of chance as the alternative to design. Paley is again exemplary. *Natural Theology* is filled with examples like that of the vertebrate eye. Paley was not content to describe a few cases of delicate adaptations; he wanted to make sure that even if he got a few details wrong, the weight of evidence would still be overwhelming. For example, in Chapter 15 he considers the fact that our eyes point in the same direction as our feet; this has the convenient consequence that we can see where we are going. The obvious explanation, Paley (1802, p. 179) says, is intelligent design. This is because the alternative is that the direction of our eyes and the direction of our gait were determined by chance, which would mean that there was only a 1/4 probability that our eyes would be able to scan the quadrant into which we are about to step.

I construe the idea of chance in a particular way. To say that an outcome is the result of a *uniform chance process* means that it was one of a number of *equiprobable* outcomes. Examples in the real world that come close to being uniform chance processes may be found in gambling devices – spinning a roulette wheel, drawing from a deck of cards, tossing a coin. The term "random" becomes more and more appropriate as real world systems approximate uniform chance processes. However, as R.A. Fisher once pointed out, it is not a "matter of chance" that casinos turn a profit each year, nor should this be regarded as a "random" event. The financial bottom line at a casino is the result of a large number of chance events, but the rules of the game make it enormously probable (though not certain) that casinos end each year in the black All uniform chance processes are probabilistic, but not all probabilistic outcomes are "due to chance."

It follows that the two hypotheses considered in my likelihood rendition of the design argument are not exhaustive. Mindless uniform chance is one alternative to intelligent design, but it is not the only one. This point has an important bearing on the dramatic change in fortunes that the design argument experienced with the advent of Darwin's (1859) theory of evolution. The process of evolution by natural selection is *not* a uniform chance process. The process has two parts. Novel traits arise in individual organisms "by chance;" however, whether they then disappear from the population or increase in frequency and eventually reach 100% representation is anything but a "matter of chance." The central idea of natural selection is that traits that help organisms survive and reproduce have a better chance of becoming common than traits that hurt. The essence of natural selection is that evolutionary outcomes have *un*equal probabilities. Paley and other design theorists writing before Darwin did not and could not cover all possible mindless natural processes. Paley addressed the alternative of uniform chance, not the alternative of natural selection.[5]

Just to nail down this point, I want to describe a version of the design argument formulated by John Arbuthnot. Arbuthnot (1710) carefully tabulated birth records in London over 82 years and noticed that in each year, slightly more sons than daughters were born. Realizing that boys die in greater numbers than girls, he saw that this slight bias in the sex ratio at birth gradually subsides until there are equal numbers of males and females at the age of marriage. Arbuthnot took this to be evidence of intelligent design; God, in his benevolence, wanted each man to have a wife and each woman to have a husband. To draw this conclusion, Arbuthnot considered what he took to be the relevant competing hypothesis – that the sex ratio at birth is determined by a uniform chance process. He was able to show that if the probability is ½ that a baby will be a boy and ½ that it will be a girl, then it is enormously improbable that the sex ratio should be skewed in favor of males in each and every of the years he surveyed (Stigler 1986, pp. 225-226).

Arbuthnot could not have known that R.A. Fisher (1930) would bring sex ratio within the purview of the theory of natural selection. Fisher's insight was to see that a mother's mix of sons and daughters affects the number of *grand*offspring she will have. Fisher demonstrated that when there is random mating in a large population, the sex ratio strategy that evolves is one in which a mother invests equally in sons and daughters (Sober 1993, p. 17). A mother will put half her reproductive resources into producing sons and half into producing daughters. This equal division means that she should have more sons than daughters, if sons tend to die sooner. Fisher's model therefore predicts the slightly uneven sex ratio at birth that Arbuthnot observed.[6]

My point in describing Fisher's idea is not to fault Arbuthnot for living in the 18th century. Rather, the thing to notice is that what Arbuthnot meant by "chance" was very different from what Fisher was talking about when he described how a selection process might shape the sex ratio found in a population. Arbuthnot was right that the probability of there being more males than females at birth in each of 82 years is extremely low, if each birth has the same chance of producing a male as it does of producing a female. However, a male-biased sex ratio in the population is extremely probable, if Fisher's hypothesized process is doing the work. Showing that Design is more likely than Chance leaves it open that some third, mindless, process might still have a higher likelihood than Design. This is not a defect in the design argument, so long as the conclusion of that argument is not over-stated. Here the modesty of the likelihood version of the design argument is a point in its favor. To draw a stronger conclusion – that the Design hypothesis is more likely than *any* hypothesis involving mindless natural processes – one would have to attend to more alternatives than just Design and (uniform) Chance.[7]

I now want to draw the reader's attention to some features of the likelihood version of the design argument (E) concerning how the observation and the competing hypotheses are formulated. First, notice that I have kept the observation (O2) conceptually separate from the two hypotheses (E1) and (E2). If the observation were simply that "the vertebrate eye exists," then since (E1) and (E2) both entail this proposition, each would have a likelihood of unity. According to the Likelihood Principle, this observation does not favor Design over Chance. Better to formulate the question in terms of explaining the properties of the vertebrate eye, not explaining why the eye exists. Notice also that I have not formulated the design hypothesis as the claim that God exists; this existence claim says nothing about the putative designer's involvement in the creation of the vertebrate eye. Finally, I should point out that it would do no harm to have the design hypothesis say that God created the vertebrate eye; this possible reformulation is something I'll return to later.

OTHER FORMULATIONS OF THE DESIGN ARGUMENT, AND THEIR DEFECTS

Given the various provisos that govern probability arguments, it would be nice if the design argument could be formulated deductively. For example, if the hypothesis of mindless chance processes entailed that it is *impossible* that organisms exhibit delicate adaptations, then a quick application of *modus tollens* would sweep that hypothesis from the field. How ever much design theorists might yearn for an argument of this kind, there apparently are none to be had. As the story about monkeys and typewriters illustrates, it is *not* impossible that mindless chance processes should produce delicate adaptations; it is merely very *improbable* that they should do so.

If *modus tollens* cannot be pressed into service, perhaps there is a probabilistic version of *modus tollens* that can achieve the same result. Is there a Law of Improbability that begins with the premiss that Pr(O * H) is very low and concludes that H should be rejected? There is no such principle (Royall 1997, ch. 3). The fact that you won the lottery does not, by itself, show that there is something wrong with the conjunctive hypothesis that the lottery was fair and a million tickets were sold and you bought just one ticket. And if we randomly drop a very sharp pin onto a line that is 1000 miles long, the probability of its landing where it does is negligible; however, that outcome does not falsify the hypothesis that the pin was dropped at random.

The fact that there is no probabilistic *modus tollens* has great significance for understanding the design argument. The logic of this problem is essentially comparative. To evaluate the design hypothesis, we must know what it predicts and compare this with the predictions made by other hypotheses. The design hypothesis cannot win by default. The fact that an observation would be very improbable if it arose by chance is not enough to refute the chance hypothesis. One must show that the design hypothesis confers on the observation a higher probability, and even then the conclusion will merely be that the observation *favors* the design hypothesis, not that that hypothesis *must be true*.[5]

In the continuing conflict (in the United States) between evolutionary biology and creationism, creationists attack evolutionary theory, but never take even the first step in developing a positive theory of their own. The three-word slogan "God did it" seems to satisfy whatever craving for explanation they may have. Is the sterility of this intellectual tradition a mere accident? Could intelligent design theory be turned into a scientific research program? I am doubtful, but the present point concerns the logic of the design argument, not its future prospects. Creationists sometimes assert that evolutionary theory "cannot explain" this or that finding (e.g., Behe 1996). What they mean is that certain outcomes are *very improbable* according to the evolutionary hypothesis. Even this more modest claim needs to be scrutinized. However, if it were true, what would follow about the plausibility of creationism? In a word – *nothing*.

It isn't just defenders of the design hypothesis who have fallen into the trap of supposing that there is a probabilistic version of *modus tollens*. For example, the biologist Richard Dawkins (1986, pp. 144-146) takes up the question of how one should evaluate hypotheses that attempt to explain the origin of life by appeal to strictly mindless natural processes. He says that an acceptable theory of this sort can say that the origin of life on Earth was somewhat improbable, but it must not go too far. If there are N planets in the universe that are "suitable" locales for life to originate, then an acceptable theory of the origin of life on Earth must say that that event had a probability of at least 1/N. Theories that say that terrestrial life was less probable than this should be rejected. How does Dawkins obtain this lower bound? Why is the number of planets relevant? Perhaps he is thinking that if * is the actual frequency of life-bearing planets among "suitable" planets (i.e., planets on which it is possible for life to evolve), then the true probability of life's evolving on earth must also be *. There is a mistake here, which we can uncover by examining how actual frequency and probability are related. With small sample size, it is perfectly possible for these quantities to have very different values (consider a fair coin that is tossed three times and then destroyed). However, Dawkins is obviously thinking that the sample size is very large, and here he is right that the actual frequency provides a good estimate of the true probability. It is interesting that Dawkins tells us to reject a theory if the probability it assigns is *too* low, but why doesn't he also say that it should be rejected if the probability it assigns is *too* high? The reason, presumably, is that we cannot rule out the possibility that the earth was not just *suitable* but was *highly conducive* to the evolution of life. However, this point cuts both ways. Although * is the *average* probability of a suitable planet's having life evolve, it still is possible that different suitable planets might have different probabilities – some may have values greater than * while others may have values that are lower.

Dawkins' lower bound assumes that the earth was above average; this is a mistake that might be termed the "Lake Woebegone Fallacy."

Some of Hume's (1779) criticisms of the design argument in his *Dialogues Concerning Natural Religion* depend on formulating the argument as something other than a likelihood inference. For example, Hume at one point has Philo say that the design argument is an argument from analogy, and that the conclusion of the argument is supported only very weakly by its premises. His point can be formulated by thinking of the design argument as follows:

> Watches are produced by intelligent design.
> Organisms are similar to watches to degree p.
> p[================================
> Organisms were produced by intelligent design.

Notice that the letter "p" appears twice in this argument. It represents the degree of similarity of organisms and watches, and it represents the probability that the premisses confer on the conclusion. Think of similarity as the proportion of shared characteristics. Things that are 0% similar have no traits in common; things that are 100% similar have all traits in common. The analogy argument says that the more similar watches and organisms are, the more probable it is that organisms were produced by intelligent design.

Let us grant the Humean point that watches and organisms have relatively few characteristics in common (it is doubtful that there is a well-defined totality consisting of all the traits of each, but let that pass). After all, watches are made of metal and glass and go "tick tock"; organisms metabolize and reproduce and go "oink" and "bow wow." This is all true, but entirely irrelevant, if the design argument is a likelihood inference. It doesn't matter how overall similar watches and organisms are. With respect to argument (W), what matters is how one should explain the fact that watches are well adapted for the task of telling time; with respect to (E), what matters is how one should explain the fact that organisms are well adapted to their environments. Paley's analogy between watches and organisms is merely heuristic. The likelihood argument about organisms stands on its own (Sober 1993).

Hume also has Philo construe the design argument as an inductive argument, and then complain that the inductive evidence is weak. Philo suggests that for us to have good reason to think that our world was produced by an intelligent designer, we'd have to visit other worlds and observe that all or most of them were produced by intelligent design. But how many other worlds have we visited? The answer is – not even one. Apparently, the design argument is an inductive argument that could not be weaker; its sample size is zero. This objection dissolves once we move from the model of inductive sampling to that of likelihood. You don't have to observe the processes of intelligent design and chance at work in different worlds to maintain that the two hypotheses confer different probabilities on your observations.

THREE POSSIBLE OBJECTIONS TO THE LIKELIHOOD ARGUMENT

There is another objection that Hume makes to the design argument, one that apparently pertains to the likelihood version of the argument that I have formulated and that many philosophers think is devastating. Hume points out that the design argument does not establish the attributes of the designer. The argument does not show that the designer who made the universe, or who made organisms, is morally perfect, or all-knowing, or all-powerful, or that there is just one such being. Perhaps this undercuts some versions of the design argument, but it does not touch the likelihood argument we are considering. Paley, perhaps responding to this Humean point, makes it clear that his design argument aims to establish the *existence* of the designer, and that the question of the designer's *characteristics* must be addressed separately.[9] My own rendition of the argument follows Paley in this regard. Does this limitation of the argument render it trivial? Not at all – it is *not* trivial to claim that the adaptive contrivances of organisms are due to intelligent design, even when details about this designer are not supplied. This supposed "triviality" would be *big* news to evolutionary biologists.

The likelihood version of the design argument consists of two premises – Pr(O * Chance) is very low and Pr(O * Design) is higher. Here O describes some observation of the features of organisms or some feature of the entire cosmos. The first of these claims is sometimes rejected by appeal to a theory that Hume describes under the heading of the Epicurean hypothesis. This is the monkeys-and-typewriters idea that if there are a finite number of particles that have a finite number of possible states, then, if they swarm about at random, they eventually will visit all possible configurations, including configurations of great order.[10] Thus, the order we see in our universe, and the delicate adaptations we observe in organisms, in fact had a high probability of eventually coming into being, according to the hypothesis of chance. Van Inwagen (1993, p. 144) gives voice to this objection and explains it by way of an analogy: Suppose you toss a coin twenty times and it lands heads every time. You should not be surprised at this outcome if you are one among millions of people who toss a fair coin twenty times. After all, with so many people tossing, it is all but inevitable that some people should get twenty heads. The outcome you obtained, therefore, was not improbable, according to the chance hypothesis.

There is a fallacy in this criticism of the design argument, which Hacking (1987) calls "the inverse gambler's fallacy." He illustrates his idea by describing a gambler who walks into a casino and immediately observes two dice being rolled that land double-6. The gambler considers whether this result favors the hypothesis that the dice had been rolled many times before the roll he just observed or the hypothesis that this was the first roll of the evening. The gambler reasons that the outcome of double-six would be more probable under the first hypothesis:

Pr(double-6 on this roll * there were many rolls) >
Pr(double-6 on this roll * there was just one roll).

In fact, the gambler's assessment of the likelihoods is erroneous. Rolls of dice have the *Markov property*; the probability of double-six on this roll is the same (1/36), regardless of what may have happened in the past. What is true is that the probability that a double-six will occur *at some time or other* increases as the number of trials is increased:

Pr(a double-6 occurs sometime * there were many rolls) >
Pr(a double-6 occurs sometime * there was just one roll).

However, the *principle of total evidence* says that we should assess hypotheses by considering *all* the evidence we have. This means that the relevant observation is that *this* roll landed double-6; we should not focus on the logically weaker proposition that a double-6 occurred *sometime*. Relative to the stronger description of the observations, the hypotheses have identical likelihoods.

Applying this point to the criticism of the design argument we are presently considering, we must conclude that the criticism is mistaken. It *is* highly probable (let us suppose), according to the chance hypothesis, that the universe will contain order and adaptation somewhere and at some time. However, the relevant observation is more specific – *our* corner of the universe is orderly and the organisms now on earth are well-adapted. These events *do* have very low probability, according to the chance hypothesis, and the fact that a weaker description of the observations has high probability on the chance hypothesis is not relevant (see also White 2000).[11]

If the first premiss in the likelihood formulation of the design argument – that Pr(O * Chance) is very low – is correct, then the only question that remains is whether Pr(O * Design) is higher. This, I believe, is the Achilles heel of the design argument. The problem is to say how probable it is, for example, that the vertebrate eye would have features F1 ... Fn, if the eye were produced by an intelligent designer. What is required is not the specification of a single probability value, or even a precisely delimited range of values. All that is needed is an argument that shows that this probability is indeed higher than the probability that Chance confers on the observation.

The problem is that the design hypothesis confers a probability on the observation only when it is supplemented with further assumptions about what the designer's goals and abilities would be if he existed. Perhaps the designer would never build the vertebrate eye with features F1 .... Fn, either because he would lack the goals or because he would lack the ability. If so, the likelihood of the design hypothesis is zero. On the other hand, perhaps the designer would want above all to build the eye with features F1 ... Fn and would be entirely competent to bring this plan to fruition. If so, the likelihood of the design hypothesis is unity. There are as many likelihoods as there are suppositions concerning the goals and abilities of the putative designer. Which of these, or which class of these, should we take seriously?

It is no good answering this question by assuming that the eye was built by an intelligent designer and then inferring that he must have wanted to give the eye features F1 ... Fn and that he must have had the ability to do so since, after all, these are the features we observe. For one thing, this pattern of argument is question-begging. One needs *independent* evidence as to what the designer's plans and abilities would be if he existed; one can't obtain this evidence by *assuming* that the design hypothesis is true (Sober 1999). Furthermore, even if we assume that the eye was built by an intelligent designer, we can't tell from this what the probability is that the eye would have the features we observe. Designers sometimes bring about outcomes that are not very probable given the plans they have in mind.

This objection to the design argument is an old one; it was presented by Keynes (1921) and before him by Venn (1866). In fact, the basic idea was formulated by Hume. When we behold the watch on the heath, we know that the watch's features are not particularly improbable on the hypothesis that the watch was produced by a designer who has the sorts of *human* goals and abilities with which we are familiar. This is the deep disanalogy between the watchmaker and the putative maker of organisms and universes. We are invited, in the latter case, to imagine a designer who is radically different from the human craftsmen with whom we are familiar. But if this designer is so different, why are we so sure that he would build the vertebrate eye in the form in which we find it?

This challenge is not turned back by pointing out that we often infer the existence of intelligent designers when we have no clue as to what they were trying to achieve. The biologist John Maynard Smith tells the story of a job he had during World War II inspecting a warehouse filled with German war materiel. He and his coworkers often came across machines whose functions were entirely opaque to them. Yet, they had no trouble seeing that these objects were built by intelligent designers. Similar stories can be told about archaeologists who work in museums; they often have objects in their collections that they know are artefacts, although they have no idea what the makers of these artefacts had in mind.

My claim is not that design theorists must have independent evidence that singles out a specification of the exact goals and abilities of the putative intelligent designer. They may be uncertain as to which of the goal-ability pairs GA-1, GA-2, ..., GA-n is correct. However, since

$$\Pr(\text{the eye has F1 ... Fn} * \text{Design}) =$$
$$*_i \Pr(\text{the eye has F1 ... Fn} * \text{Design \& GA-i}) \Pr(\text{GA-i}*\text{Design}),$$

they do have to show that

$$*_i \Pr(\text{the eye has F1 ... Fn} * \text{Design \& GA-i}) \Pr(\text{GA-i}*\text{Design}) >$$
$$\Pr(\text{the eye has F1 ... Fn} * \text{Chance}).$$

I think that Maynard Smith in his warehouse and archaeologists in their museums are able to do this. They aren't sure exactly what the intelligent designer was trying to achieve (e.g., they aren't certain that GA-1 is true and that all the other GA pairs are false), but they are able to see that it is not terribly improbable that the object should have the features one observes if it were made by a human intelligent designer. After all, the items in Maynard Smith's warehouse were symmetrical and smooth metal containers that had what appeared to be switches, dials, and gauges on them. And the "artefacts of unknown function" in anthropology museums likewise bear signs of human handiwork.

It is interesting in this connection to consider the epistemological problem of how one would go about detecting intelligent life elsewhere in the universe (if it exists). The SETI (Search for Extraterrestrial Intelligence) project, funded until 1993 by the US National Aeronautics and Space Administration and now supported privately, dealt with this problem in two ways (Dick 1996). First, the scientists wanted to send a message into deep space that would allow any intelligent extraterrestrials who received it to figure out that it was produced by intelligent designers (namely, us). Second, they scan the night sky hoping to detect signs of intelligent life elsewhere.

The message, transmitted in 1974 from the Arecibo Observatory, was a simple picture of our solar system, a representation of oxygen and carbon, a picture of a double helix representing DNA, a stick figure of a human being, and a picture of the Arecibo telescope. How sure are we that if intelligent aliens find these clues, that they will realize that they were produced by intelligent designers? The hope is that this message will strike the aliens who receive it as evidence favoring the hypothesis of intelligent design over the hypothesis that some mindless physical process (not necessarily one involving uniform chance) was responsible. It is hard to see how the SETI engineers could have done any better, but still one cannot dismiss the possibility that they will fail. If extraterrestrial minds are very different from our own – either because they have different beliefs and desires or process information in different ways – it may turn out that their interpretation of the evidence will differ profoundly from the interpretation that human beings would arrive at, were they on the receiving end. To say anything more precise about this, we'd have to be able provide specifics about the aliens' mental characteristics. If we are uncertain as to how the mind of an extraterrestrial will interpret this evidence, how can we be so sure that God, if he were to build the vertebrate eye, would endow it with the features we find it to have?

When SETI engineers search for signs of intelligent life elsewhere in the universe, what are they looking for? The answer is surprisingly simple. They look for narrowband radio emissions. This is because human beings have built machines that produce these signals and, as far as we know, such emissions are not produced by mindless natural processes. The SETI engineers search for this signal, not because it is "complex" or fulfills some *a priori* criterion that would make it a "sign of intelligence," but simply because they think they know what sorts of mechanisms are needed to produce it.[12] This strategy may not work, but it is hard to see how the scientists could do any better. Our judgments about what counts as a sign of intelligent design must be based on empirical information about what designers often do and what they rarely do. As of now, these judgments are based on our knowledge of *human* intelligence. The more our hypotheses about intelligent designers depart from the human case, the more in the dark we are as to what the ground rules are for inferring intelligent design. It is imaginable that these limitations will subside as human beings learn more about the cosmos. But for now, we are rather limited.

I have been emphasizing the fallibility of two assumptions – that we know what counts as a sign of extraterrestrial intelligence and that we know how extraterrestrials will interpret the signals we send. My point has been to shake a complacent assumption that figures in the design argument. However, I suspect that SETI engineers are on much firmer ground than theologians. If extraterrestrials evolved by the same type of evolutionary process that produced human intelligence, that may provide useful constraints on conjectures about the minds they have. No theologian, to my knowledge, thinks that God is the result of biological processes. Indeed God is usually thought of as a *super*natural being who is radically different from the things we observe *in* nature. The problem of extraterrestrial intelligence is therefore an intermediate case; it lies between the watch found on the heath and the God who purportedly built the universe and shaped the vertebrate eye, but is much closer to the first. The upshot of this point for Paley's design argument is this: *Design arguments for the existence of human (and human-like) watchmakers are often unproblematic; it is design arguments for the existence of God that leave us at sea.*

I began by formulating the design hypothesis in argument (E) as the claim that an intelligent designer made the vertebrate eye. Yet, I have sometimes discussed the hypothesis as if it asserted that *God* is the designer in question. I don't think this difference makes a difference with respect to the objection I have described. To say that some designer or other made the eye is to state a disjunctive hypothesis. To figure out the likelihood of this disjunction, one needs to address the question of what each putative designer's goals and intentions would be.[13] The theological formulation shifts the problem from the evaluation of a disjunction to the evaluation of a disjunct, but the problem remains the same. Even supposing that God is omniscient, omnipotent, and perfectly benevolent, what is the probability that the eye would have features F1 ... Fn, if God set his hand to making it? He *could* have produced those results if he had wanted. But why think that this is what he *would* have wanted to do? The assumption that God can do anything is part of the problem, not the solution. An engineer who is more limited would be more predictable.

There is another reply to my criticism of the design argument that should be considered. I have complained that we have no way to evaluate the likelihood of the design hypothesis, since we don't know which auxiliary assumptions about goal/ability pairs we should use. But why not change the subject? Instead of evaluating the likelihood of Design, why not evaluate the likelihood of various conjunctions – (Design & GA-1), (Design & GA-2), etc? Some of these will have high likelihoods, others will have low, but it will no longer be a mystery what likelihoods these hypotheses possess. There are two problems with this tactic. First, it is a game that two can play. Consider the hypothesis that the vertebrate eye was created by the mindless process of electricity. If I simply get to *invent* auxiliary hypotheses without having to *justify* them independently, I can just stipulate the following assumption – if electricity created the vertebrate eye, the eye must have features F1 ... Fn. The electricity hypothesis now is a conjunct in a conjunction that has maximum likelihood, just like the design hypothesis. This is a dead end. My second objection is that it is an important part of scientific practice that conjunctions be broken apart (when possible), and their conjuncts scrutinized (Sober 1999, 2000). If your doctor runs a test to see whether you have tuberculosis, you will not be satisfied if she reports that the likelihood of the conjunction "you have tuberculosis & auxiliary assumption 1" is high while the likelihood of the conjunction "you have tuberculosis & auxiliary assumption 2" is low. You want your doctor to address the first *conjunct*, not just the various *conjunctions*. And you want her to do this by using a test procedure that is *independently* known to have small error probabilities. Demand no less of your theologian.

My formulation of the design argument as a likelihood inference, and my criticism of it, have implications concerning the problem of evil (see essay X in this volume). It is a mistake to try to *deduce* the nonexistence of God from the fact that so much evil exists. Even supposing that God is all-powerful, all-knowing, and entirely benevolent, there is no contradiction in the hypothesis that God allows various evils to exist because they are necessary correlates of greater goods, where we don't understand in any detail what these correlations are or why they must obtain (Plantinga 1974). The status of the problem changes, however, when we think of it as *nondeductive* in character (Madden and Hare 1968; Rowe 1979; Plantinga 1979). Within the framework of likelihood inference, there are two quantities we must evaluate: What is the probability that there would be as much evil as there is, if the universe were produced by an all-powerful, all-knowing, and entirely benevolent God? And what is the probability of that much evil's existing, if the universe were produced by mindless natural processes? The logical observation that saves theism from the attempt to deduce the nonexistence of God comes back to haunt the theistic hypothesis in this new context. If the ways of God are so mysterious, we have no way to evaluate the first of these likelihoods. The theistic hypothesis is saved from disconfirmation by the fact that it is untestable.

The Relationship of the Organismic Design Argument to Darwinism

Philosophers who criticize the organismic design argument often believe that the argument was dealt its death blow by Hume. True, Paley wrote after Hume, and the many Bridgewater Treatises elaborating the design argument appeared after Hume's *Dialogues* were published posthumously. Nonetheless, for these philosophers, the design argument after Hume was merely a corpse that could be propped up and paraded. Hume had taken the life out of it.

Biologists often take a different view. Dawkins (1986, p. 4) puts the point provocatively by saying that it was not until Darwin that it was possible to be an intellectually fulfilled atheist. The thought here is that Hume's skeptical attack was not the decisive moment; rather, it was Darwin's development and confirmation of a substantive scientific explanation of the adaptive features of organisms that really undermined the design argument (at least in its organismic formulation). Philosophers who believe that theories can't be rejected until a better theory is developed to take its place often sympathize with this point of view.

My own interpretation coincides with neither of these. As indicated above, I think that Hume's criticisms largely derive from an empiricist epistemology that is too narrow. However, seeing the design argument's fatal flaw does not depend on seeing the merits of Darwinian theory. The Likelihood Principle, it is true, says that theories must be evaluated comparatively, not on their own. But for this to be possible, each theory must make predictions. It is at this fundamental level that I think the design argument is defective.

Biologists often present two criticisms of creationism. First, they argue that the design hypothesis is untestable. Second, they contend that there is plenty of evidence that the hypothesis is false. Obviously, these two lines of argument are in conflict.[14] I have already endorsed the first criticism, but I want to say a little about the second. A useful example is Stephen Jay Gould's (1980) widely read article about the Panda's thumb. Pandas are vegetarian bears who have a spur of bone (a "thumb") protruding from their wrists. They use this device to strip bamboo, which is the main thing they eat. Gould says that the hypothesis of intelligent design predicts that pandas should not have this inefficient device. A benevolent, powerful, and intelligent engineer could and would have done a lot better. Evolutionary theory, on the other hand, says that the panda's thumb is what we should expect. The thumb is a modification of the wrist bones found in the common ancestor that pandas share with carnivorous bears. Evolution by natural selection is a tinkerer; it does not design adaptations from scratch, but modifies pre-existing features, with the result that adaptations are often imperfect.

Gould's argument, I hope it is clear, is a likelihood argument. I agree with what he says about evolutionary theory, but I think his discussion of the design hypothesis leads him into the same trap that ensnared Paley. Gould thinks he knows what God would do if he built pandas, just as Paley thought he knew what God would do if he built the vertebrate eye. But neither of them knows this. Both help themselves to *assumptions* about God's goals and abilities. However, it is not enough to make assumptions about these matters; one needs independent evidence that these auxiliary assumptions are true. Paley's problem is also Gould's.

ANTHROPIC REASONING AND COSMIC DESIGN ARGUMENTS

Evolutionary theory seeks to explain the adaptive features of organisms; it has nothing to say about the origin of the universe as a whole. For this reason, evolutionary theory conflicts with the organismic design hypothesis, but not with the cosmic design hypothesis. Still, the main criticism I presented of the first type of design argument also applies to the second. I now want to examine a further problem that cosmic design arguments sometimes encounter.[15]

Suppose I catch 50 fish from a lake, and you want to use my observations O to test two hypotheses:

> O: All the fish I caught were more than 10 inches long.
> F1: All the fish in the lake are more than 10 inches long.
> F2: Only half the fish in the lake are more than 10 inches long.

You might think that the Likelihood Principle says that F1 is better supported, since

(1) $Pr(O^* F1) > Pr(O * F2)$.

However, you then discover how I caught my fish:

(A1)   I caught the fish by using a net that (because of the size of its holes) can't catch fish smaller than 10 inches, and I left the net in the lake until there were 50 fish in it.

This leads you to replace the analysis provided by (1) with the following:

(2) $Pr(O^* F1 \& A1) = Pr(O * F2 \& A1) = 1.0$.

Furthermore, you now realize that your first assessment, (1), was based on the erroneous assumption that

(A0)   The fish I caught were a random sample from the fish in the lake.

Instead of (1), you should have written

$Pr(O^* F1 \& A0) > Pr(O * F2 \& A0)$.

This inequality is true; the problem, however, is that (A0) is false.

This example, from Eddington (1938), illustrates the idea of an *observational selection effect* (an OSE). When a hypothesis is said to render a set of observations probable (or improbable), ask yourself what assumptions allow the hypothesis to have this implication. The point illustrated here is that the procedure you use to obtain your observations can be relevant to assessing likelihoods.[16]

One version of the cosmic design argument begins with the observation that our universe is "fine-tuned." That is, the values of various physical constants are such as to permit life to exist, but if they had been even slightly different, life would have been impossible. McMullin (1993, p. 378) summarizes some of the relevant facts as follows:

> If the strong nuclear force were to have been as little as 2% stronger (relative to the other forces), all hydrogen would have been converted into helium. If it were 5% weaker, no helium at all would have formed and there would be nothing but hydrogen. If the weak nuclear force were a little stronger, supernovas could not

occur, and heavy elements could not have formed. If it were slightly weaker, only helium might have formed. If the electromagnetic forces were stronger, all stars would be red dwarfs, and there would be no planets. If it were a little weaker, all stars would be very hot and short-lived. If the electron charge were ever so slightly different, there would be no chemistry as we know it. Carbon (^{12}C) only just managed to form in the primal nucleosynthesis. And so on.

I'll abbreviate the fact that the values of these physical constants fall within the narrow limits specified by saying that "the constants are right." A design argument can now be constructed, one that claims that the constants' being right should be explained by postulating the existence of an intelligent designer, one who wanted life to exist and who arranged the universe so that this could occur (Swinburne 1990a). As with Paley's organismic design argument, we can represent the reasoning in this cosmic design argument as the assertion of a likelihood inequality:

(3) Pr(constants are right * Design) > Pr(constants are right * Chance).

However, there is a problem with (3) that resembles the problem with (1). Consider the fact that

(A3) We exist, and if we exist the constants must be right.

We need to take (A3) into account; instead of (3), we should have said:

(4) Pr(constants are right * Design & A3) = Pr(constants are right * Chance & A3) = 1.0.

That is, given (A3), the constants must be right, regardless of whether the universe was produced by intelligent design or by chance.

Proposition (4) reflects the fact that our observation that the constants are right is subject to an OSE. Recognizing this OSE is in accordance with a *weak anthropic principle* – "what we can expect to observe must be restricted by the conditions necessary for our presence as observers" (Carter 1974). The argument involves no commitment to *strong anthropic principles*. For example, there is no assertion that the correct cosmology must entail that the existence of observers such as ourselves was inevitable, nor is it claimed that our existence *explains* why the physical constants are right (Barrow 1988, Earman 1987, McMullin 1993).[17]

Although this point about OSEs undermines the version of the design argument that cites the fact that the physical constants are right, it does not touch other versions. For example, when Paley concludes that the vertebrate eye was produced by an intelligent designer, his argument cannot be refuted by claiming that:

(A4) We exist, and if we exist vertebrates must have eyes with features F1 ... Fn.

If (A4) were true, the likelihood inequality that Paley asserted would have to be replaced with an equality, just as (1) had to be replaced by (2) and (3) had to be replaced by (4). But fortunately for Paley, (A4) is false. However, matters change if we think of Paley as seeking to explain the modest fact that organisms have at least one adaptive contrivance. If this were false, we would not be able to make observations; indeed, we would not exist. Paley was right to focus on the details; the more minimal description of what we observe does not sustain the argument he wanted to endorse.

The issue of OSEs can be raised in connection with other cosmic versions of the design argument. Swinburne (1990b, p. 191) writes that "the hypothesis of theism is that the universe exists because there is a God who keeps it in being and that laws of nature operate because there is a God who brings it about that they do." Let us separate the *explananda*. The fact that the universe exists does not favor Design over Chance; after all, if the universe did not exist, we would not exist and so would not be able to observe that it does.[18] The same point holds with respect to the fact that the universe is law-governed. Even supposing that lawlessness is possible, could we exist and make observations if there were no laws? If not, then the lawful character of the universe does not discriminate between Design and Chance. Finally, we may consider the fact that our universe is governed by one set of laws, rather than another. Swinburne (1968) argues that the fact that our universe obeys *simple* laws is better explained by the hypothesis of Design than by the hypothesis of Chance. Whether this observation also is subject to an OSE depends on whether we could exist in a universe obeying alternative laws.

Before taking up an objection to this analysis of the argument from fine-tuning, I want to summarize what it has in common with the fishing example. In the fishing example, the source of the OSE is obvious – it is located in a device outside of ourselves. The net with big holes insures that the observer will make a certain observation, regardless of which of two hypotheses is true. But where is the device that induces an OSE in the fine-tuning example? There is none; rather, it is the observer's own existence that does the work. Nonetheless, the effect is the same. Owing to the fact that we exist, we are bound to observe that the constants are right, regardless of whether our universe was produced by chance or by design.[19]

This structural similarity between fishing and fine-tuning may seem to be undermined by a disanalogy. In the latter case, we know that proposition (3) is correct – the probability that the constants will be right if the universe is created by a powerful deity bent on having life exist is greater than it would be if the values of the constants were set by a uniform chance process. This inequality seems to hold, regardless of how or whether we make our observations. The fishing example looks different; here we know that proposition (1) is false. There is no saying whether a likelihood inequality obtains until we specify the procedure used to obtain the observations; once we do this, there is no likelihood inequality. Thus, in fine-tuning, we have an inequality that is true because it reflects the metaphysical facts; in fishing, we have an inequality that is false for epistemic reasons. My response is that I agree that this point of difference exists, but that it does nothing to save the argument from fine-tuning. Although proposition (3) is true, we are bound to observe that the constants are right, regardless of whether our universe arose by chance or by design. My objection to proposition (3) is not that it is false, but that it should not be used to interpret the observations; (4) is the relevant proposition to which we should attend.

To visualize this point, imagine that a deity creates a million universes and that a chance process does the same for another million. Let's assume that the proportion of universes in which the constants are right is greater in the former case. Doesn't it follow that if we observe that the constants are right in our universe, that this observation favors the hypothesis that our universe arose by design? In fact, this does not follow. It *would* follow if we had the same probability of observing any of the first million universes if the Design hypothesis were true, and had the same probability of observing any of the second million universes if the Chance hypothesis were true. But this is not the case — our probability of observing a universe in which the constants are right is unity in each case.

What this means is that a full understanding of the workings of OSEs must acknowledge that there are two stages at which a bias can be introduced. There is first the process by which the system described by the hypotheses under test generates some state of the world that we are able to observe. Second, there is the process by which we come to observe that state of the world. This two-step process occurs in fishing and fine-tuning as follows:

Composition of the Lake * Contents of the net * We observe the contents of the net

Origin of the Universe * Constants are right * We observe that the constants are right

The OSE in the fishing example arises in step 1; the OSE in fine-tuning crops up in step 2.

Leslie (1989, pp. 13-14, 107-108), Swinburne (1990a, p. 171), and Van Inwagen (1993, p. 135,144) all defend the fine-tuning argument against the criticism I have just described. Each mounts his defense by describing an analogy with a mundane example. Here is Swinburne's rendition of an example that Leslie presents:

> On a certain occasion the firing squad aim their rifles at the prisoner to be executed. There are twelve expert marksmen in the firing squad, and they fire twelve rounds each. However, on this occasion all 144 shots miss. The prisoner laughs and comments that the event is not something requiring any explanation because if the marksmen had not missed, he would not be here to observe them having done so. But of course, the prisoner's comment is absurd; the marksmen all having missed is indeed something requiring explanation; and so too is what goes with it — the prisoner's being alive to observe it. And the explanation will be either that it was an accident (a most unusual chance event) or that it was planned (e.g., all the marksmen had been bribed to miss). Any interpretation of the anthropic principle which suggests that the evolution of observers is something which requires no explanation in terms of boundary conditions and laws being a certain way (either inexplicably or through choice) is false.

First a preliminary clarification — the issue isn't whether the prisoner's survival "requires explanation" but whether this observation provides evidence as to whether the marksmen intended to spare the prisoner or shot at random.[20]

My response takes the form of a dilemma. I'll argue, first, that if the firing squad example is analyzed in terms of the Likelihood Principle, the prisoner is right and Swinburne is wrong — the prisoner's survival does not allow him to conclude that Design is more likely than Chance. However, there is a different analysis of the prisoner's situation, in terms of the *probabilities* of hypotheses, not their *likelihoods*. This second analysis says that the prisoner is mistaken; however, it has the consequence that the prisoner's inference differs fundamentally from the design argument that appeals to fine-tuning. Each horn of this dilemma supports the conclusion that the firing squad example does nothing to save this version of the design argument.

So let us begin. If we understand Swinburne's claim in terms of the Likelihood Principle, we should read him as saying that

(L1)   Pr(the prisoner survived * the marksmen intended to miss) >
       Pr(the prisoner survived * the marksmen fired at random).

He thinks that the anthropic principle requires us to replace this claim with the following irrelevancy:

(L2)   Pr(the prisoner survived * the marksmen intended to miss & the
       prisoner survived) =
       Pr(the prisoner survived * the marksmen fired at random & the
       prisoner survived) = 1.0.

This equality would lead us to conclude (Swinburne thinks mistakenly) that the prisoner's survival does not discriminate between the hypotheses of Design and Chance.

To assess the claim that the prisoner has made a mistake, it is useful to compare the prisoner's reasoning with that of a bystander who witnesses the prisoner survive the firing squad. The prisoner reasons as follows: "given that I now am able to make observations, I must be alive, whether my survival was due to intelligent design or chance." The bystander says the following: "given that I now am able to make observations, the fact that the prisoner is now alive is made more probable by the design hypothesis than it is by the chance hypothesis." The prisoner is claiming that he is subject to an OSE, while the bystander says that he, the bystander, is not. Both, I submit, are correct.[21]

I suggest that part of the intuitive attractiveness of the claim that the prisoner has made a mistake derives from a shift between the prisoner's point of view and the bystander's. The bystander is right to use (L1) to interpret his observations; however, the prisoner has no business using (L1) to interpret his observations since he, the prisoner, is subject to an OSE. The prisoner needs to replace (L1) with (L2). My hunch is that Swinburne thinks the prisoner errs in his assessment of likelihoods because we bystanders would be making a mistake it we reasoned as he does.[22]

The basic idea of an OSE is that we must take account of the procedures used to obtain the observations when we assess the likelihoods of hypotheses. This much was clear from the fishing example. What may seem strange about my reading of the firing squad story is my claim that the prisoner and the bystander are in different epistemic situations, even though their observation reports differ by a mere pronoun. After the marksmen fire, the prisoner thinks "I exist" while the bystander thinks "he exists;" the bystander, but not the prisoner, is able to use his observation to say that Design is more likely than Chance, or so I say. If this seems odd, it may be useful to reflect on Sorensen's (1988) concept of *blindspots*. A proposition p is a blindspot for an individual S just in case, if p were true, S would not be able to know that p is true. Although some propositions (e.g., "nothing exists," "the constants are wrong") are blindspots for everyone, other propositions are blindspots for some people but not for others. Blindspots give rise to OSEs; if p is a blindspot for S, then if S makes an observation to determine the truth value of p, the outcome must be that not-p is observed. The prisoner, but not the bystander, has "the prisoner does not exist" as a blindspot. This is why "the prisoner exists" has an evidential significance for the bystander that it cannot have for the prisoner.[23]

To bolster my claim that the prisoner is right to think that likelihood does not distinguish between chance and design, I want to describe a slightly different problem.

Suppose that a firing squad always subjects its victims to the same probabilistic process, which has the result that the prisoner either survives or is killed. A thousand prisoners who have one by one each survived the firing squad are assembled and are asked to pool their knowledge and estimate the value of an unknown probability. What is the probability that a prisoner will survive if the firing squad fires? The standard methodology here is *maximum likelihood estimation*; one finds the value of the parameter of interest that maximizes the probability of the observations. This is why, if a coin lands heads 512 out of a thousand tosses, the "best" estimate of the probability that the coin will land heads when it is tossed is 0.512. Those who believe that the single prisoner has evidence about his firing squad's intentions are obliged to conclude that the best estimate in this new problem is that the probability is unity. However, those persuaded that the single prisoner is subject to an OSE will want to maintain that the thousand prisoners are in the same boat. These skeptics will deny that the observations provide a basis for estimation. Isn't it *obvious* that testimony limited to survivors provides no evidence on which to base an estimate of the probability that someone will survive the firing squad's shooting? And if this is true of a *thousand* survivors, how can a *single* survivor be said to know that design is more likely than chance?

I now turn to a different analysis of the prisoner's situation. The prisoner, like the rest of us, knows how firing squads work. They always or almost always follow the orders they receive, which is almost always to execute someone. Occasionally, they produce fake executions. They almost never fire at random. What is more, firing squads have firm control over outcomes; if they want to kill (or spare) someone, they always or almost always succeed. This and related items of background knowledge support the following *probability* claim:

(Pf) Pr(the marksmen intended to spare the prisoner * the prisoner survived) >
 Pr(the marksmen intended to spare the prisoner).

Firing squads rarely intend to spare their victims, but the survival of the prisoner makes it very probable that his firing squad had precisely that intention. The likelihood analysis led to the conclusion that the prisoner and the bystander are in different epistemic situations; the bystander should evaluate the hypotheses by using (L1), but the prisoner is obliged to use (L2). However, from the point of view of probabilities, the prisoner and the bystander can say the same thing; both can cite (Pf).[24]

What does this tell us about the fine-tuning version of the design argument? I construed that argument as a claim about likelihoods. As such, it is subject to an OSE; given that we exist, the constants must be right, regardless of whether our universe was produced by Chance or by Design. However, we now need to consider whether the fine-tuning argument can be formulated as a claim about probabilities. Can we assert that

(Pu) Pr(the universe was created by an intelligent designer* the
 constants are right) >
 Pr(the universe was created by an intelligent designer)?

I don't think so. In the case of firing squads, we have frequency data and our general knowledge of human behavior on which to ground the probability statement (Pf). But we have neither data nor theory to ground (Pu). And we cannot defend (Pu) by saying that an intelligent designer would ensure that the constants are right, because this takes us back to the likelihood considerations we have already discussed. The prisoner's conclusion that he can say nothing about Chance and Design is mistaken if he is making a claim about probabilities. But the argument from fine-tuning can't be defended as a claim about probabilities.

The rabbit/duck quality of this problem merits review. I have discussed three examples – fishing, fine-tuning, and the firing squad. If we compare fine-tuning with fishing, they seem similar. This makes it intuitive to conclude that the design argument based on fine-tuning is wrong. However, if we compare fine-tuning with the firing squad, *they* seem similar. Since the prisoner apparently has evidence that favors Design over Chance, we are led to the conclusion that the fine-tuning argument must be right. This shifting gestalt can be stabilized by imposing a formalism. The first point is that OSEs are to be understood by comparing the *likelihoods* of hypotheses, not their *probabilities*. The second is that it is perfectly true that the prisoner can assert the *probability* claim (Pf). The question, then, is whether the design argument from fine-tuning is a likelihood argument or a probability argument. If the former, it is flawed because it fails to take account of the fact that there is an OSE. If the latter, it is flawed, but for a different reason – it makes claims about probabilities that we have no reason to accept; indeed, we cannot even *understand* them as objective claims.[25]

A Prediction

It was obvious to Paley and to other purveyors of the organismic design argument that if an intelligent designer built organisms, that designer would have to be far more intelligent than any human being could ever be. This is why the organismic design argument was for them an argument for the existence of *God*. I predict that it will eventually become clear that the organismic design argument should never have been understood in this way. This is because I expect that human beings will eventually build organisms from nonliving materials. This achievement will not close down the question of whether the organisms we observe were created by intelligent design or by mindless natural processes; on the contrary, it will give that question a practical meaning, since the organisms we will see around us will be of both kinds.[26] However, it will be abundantly clear that the fact of organismic adaptation has nothing to do with whether God exists. When the Spanish conquistadors arrived in the New World, several indigenous peoples thought these intruders were gods, so powerful was the technology that the intruders possessed. Alas, the locals were mistaken; they did not realize that these beings with guns and horses were merely *human* beings. The organismic design argument for the existence of God embodies the same mistake. Human beings in the future will be the conquistadors, and Paley will be our Montezuma.

[About the Author]

Elliott Sober is the Hans Reichenbach Professor and William F. Vilas Research Professor at the University of Wisconsin, Madison and currently serves as President of the Philosophy of Science Association. Dr. Sober has received numerous awards and fellowships for his work and has written extensively on the philosophy of science and evolution. Among Dr. Sober's books are *Unto Others: The Evolution and Psychology of Unselfish Behavior*, with David S. Wilson (2000); *From a Biological Point of View: Essays in Evolutionary Philosophy* (1994); and *The Nature of Selection: Evolutionary Theory in Philosophical Focus* (1993, 2nd Edition).

[REFERENCES]

Arbuthnot, J. (1710): "An Argument for Divine Providence, taken from the Constant Regularity Observ'd in the Births of both Sexes." *Philosophical Transactions of the Royal Society of London* 27: 186-190.

Barrow, J. (1988): *The World Within the World*. Oxford: Clarendon Press.

Behe, M. (1996): *Darwin's Black Box*. New York: Free Press.

Carter, B. (1974): "Large Number Coincidences and the Anthropic Principle in Cosmology." In M.S. Longair (ed.), *Confrontation of Cosmological Theories with Observational Data*. Dordrecht: Reidel, pp. 291-298.

Darwin, C. (1859): *On the Origin of Species*. Cambridge, MA: Harvard University Press, 1964.

Dawkins, R. (1986): *The Blind Watchmaker*. New York: Norton.

Dembski, W. (1998): *The Design Inference*. Cambridge: Cambridge University Press.

Dennett, D. (1987a): "Intentional Systems in Cognitive Ethology – the 'Panglossian Paradigm' Defended." In *The Intentional Stance*. Cambridge: MIT Press, pp. 237-286.

Dennett, D. (1987b): "True Believers." In *The Intentional Stance*. Cambridge: MIT Press, pp. 13-42.

Dick, S. (1996): *The Biological Universe – the Twentieth-Century Extraterrestrial Life Debate and the Limits of Science*. Cambridge: Cambridge University Press.

Earman, J. (1987): "The SAP Also Rises – a Critical Examination of the Anthropic Principle." *American Philosophical Quarterly* 24: 307-317.

Eddington, A. (1939): *The Philosophy of Physical Science*. Cambridge: Cambridge University Press.

Edwards, A. (1972): *Likelihood*. Cambridge: Cambridge University Press.

Fisher, R. (1930). *The Genetical Theory of Natural Selection*. New York: Dover, 2nd edition, 1957.

Fitelson, B., Stephens, C., and Sober, E. (1999): "How not to Detect Design – a Review of W. Dembski's *The Design Inference*." *Philosophy of Science* 66: 472-488. Also available at the following URL: http://philosophy.wisc.edu/sober.

Forster, M. and Sober, E. (2003): "Why Likelihood?" In M. Taper and S. Lee (eds.), *The Nature of Scientific Evidence*. Chicago: University of Chicago Press. Also available at the following URL: http://philosophy.wisc.edu/forster.

Gould, S. (1980): *The Panda's Thumb*. New York: Norton.

Hacking, I. (1965): *The Logic of Statistical Inference*. Cambridge: Cambridge University Press.

Hacking, I. (1987): "The Inverse Gambler's Fallacy: The Argument from Design. The Anthropic Principle Applied to Wheeler Universes." *Mind* 96: 331-340.

Hempel, C. (1965): "Studies in the Logic of Confirmation." *In Aspects of Scientific Explanation and Other Essays in the Philosophy of Science*. New York: Free Press.

Hume, D. (1779): *Dialogues Concerning Natural Religion*. London: Penguin. 1990.

Keynes, J. (1921): *A Treatise on Probability*. London: Macmillan.

Kyburg, H. (1961): *Probability and the Logic of Rational Belief*. Middletown, CT: Wesleyan University Press.

Leslie, J. (1989): *Universes*. London: Routledge.

Madden, E. and Hare, P. (1968): *Evil and the Concept of God*. Springfield: Charles Thomas.

McMullin, (1993): "Indifference Principle and Anthropic Principle in Cosmology." *Studies in the History and Philosophy of Science* 24: 359-389.

Paley, W. (1802): *Natural Theology, or, Evidences of the Existence and Attributes of the Deity, Collected from the Appearances of Nature*. London: Rivington.

Plantinga, A. (1974): *The Nature of Necessity*. New York: Oxford.

Plantinga, A. (1979): "The Probabilistic Argument from Evil." *Philosophical Studies* 35: 1-53.

Rowe, W. (1979): "The Problem of Evil and Some Varieties of Atheism." *American Philosophical Quarterly* 16: 335-341.

Royall, R. (1997): *Statistical Evidence – a Likelihood Paradigm*. London: Chapman and Hall.

Sober, E. (1993): *Philosophy of Biology*. Boulder, Co.: Westview Press.

Sober, E. (1999): "Testability." *Proceedings and Addresses of the American Philosophical Association* 73: 47-76. Also available at the following URL: http://philosophy.wisc.edu/sober.

Sober, E., (2000a): "Evolution and the Problem of Other Minds." *Journal of Philosophy* 97: 365-386.

Sober, E. (2000b): "Quine's Two Dogmas." *Proceedings of the Aristotlean Society*, Supplementary Volume 74: 237-280.

Sober, E. (2002): "Bayesianism – Its Scope and Limits." In R. Swinburne (ed.), *Bayesianism*. London: British Academy. Also available at the following URL: http://philosophy.wisc.edu/sober.

Sorensen, R. (1988): *Blindspots*. Oxford: Oxford University Press.

Stigler, S. (1986): *The History of Statistics*. Cambridge: Harvard University Press.

Swinburne, R. (1968): "The Argument from Design." *Philosophy* 43: 199-212.

Swinburne, R. (1990a): "Argument from the Fine-Tuning of the Universe." In. J. Leslie (ed.), *Physical Cosmology and Philosophy*. New York: Macmillan, pp. 160-179.

Swinburne, R. (1990b): "The Limits of Explanation." In D. Knowles (ed.), Explanation and Its Limits. Cambridge: Cambridge University Press, pp. 177-193.

Turing, A. (1950): "Computing Machinery and Intelligence." *Mind* 59: 433-460.

Van Inwagen, P. (1993): *Metaphysics*. Boulder, Co.: Westview Press.

Venn, J. (1866): *The Logic of Chance*. New York: Chelsea.

White, R. (2000): "Fine-Tuning and Multiple Universes." *Nous* 34: 260-276.

[Notes]

1. I am grateful to Martin Barrett, Nick Bostrom, David Christensen, Ellery Eells, Branden Fitelson, Malcolm Forster, Alan Hajek, Daniel Hausman, Stephen Leeds, Williams Mann, Lydia McGrew, Derk Pereboom, Roy Sorensen, and Richard Swinburne for useful comments. I have used portions of this chapter in seminars I've given in a large number of philosophy departments, too numerous to list here. My thanks to participants for their stimulating and productive discussion.

2. Does this construal of the design argument conflict with the idea that the argument is an *inference to the best explanation*? Not if one's theory of inference to the best explanation says that observations influence the assessment of explanations in this instance via the vehicle of likelihoods.

3. Another reason to restrict the design argument to likelihood considerations is that it is supposed to be an *empirical* argument. To invoke prior probabilities is to bring in considerations *besides* the observations at hand.

4. In light of the fact that it is possible for a hypothesis to have an objective likelihood without also having an objective probability, one should understand Bayes' theorem as specifying how the quantities it mentions are related to each other, *if all are well-defined*. And just as hypotheses can have likelihoods without having (objective) probabilities, it also is possible for the reverse situation to obtain. Suppose I draw a card from a deck of unknown composition. I observe (O) that the card is the four of diamonds. I now consider the hypothesis (H) that the card is a four. The value of $Pr(H * O)$ is well-defined, but the value of $Pr(O * H)$ is not.

5. Actually, Paley (1802) *does* consider a "selective retention" process, but only very briefly. In Chapter 5 (pp. 49-51) he explores the hypothesis that a random process once generated a huge range of variation, and that this variation was then culled, with only stable configurations surviving. Paley argues against this hypothesis by saying that we should see unicorns and mermaids if it were true. He also says that it mistakenly predicts that organisms should fail to form a taxonomic hierarchy. It is ironic that Darwin claimed that his own theory *predicts* hierarchy. In fact, Paley and Darwin are both right. Darwin's theory includes the idea that all living things have common ancestors, while the selection hypothesis that Paley considers does not.

6. More precisely, Fisher said that a mother should have a son with probability p and a daughter with probability (1-p), where the effect of this is that the expected expenditures on the two sexes are the same; the argument is not undermined by the fact that some mothers have all sons while others have all daughters.

7. Dawkins (1986) makes the point that evolution by natural selection is not a uniform chance process by way of an analogy with a combination lock. This is discussed in Sober (1993, pp. 36-39).

8. Dembski (1998) construes design inference as allowing one to argue in favor of the design hypothesis, and "sweep from the field" all alternatives, without the design hypothesis' ever having to make a prediction. For criticisms of Dembski's framework, see Fitelson *et al.* (1999).

9. Paley (1802) argues in Chapter 16 that the benevolence of the deity is demonstrated by the fact that organisms experience more pleasure than they need to (p. 295). He also argues that pain is useful (p. 320) and that few diseases are fatal; he defends the latter conclusion by citing statistics on the cure rate at a London hospital (p. 321).

10. For it to be certain that all configurations will be visited, there must be infinite time. The shorter the time frame, the lower the probability that a given configuration will occur. This means that the estimated age of the universe may entail that it is very *im*probable that a given configuration will occur. I set this objection aside in what follows.

11. It is a standard feature of likelihood comparisons that O_w sometimes fails to discriminate between a pair of hypotheses, even though O_s is able to do so, when O_s entails O_w. You are the cook in a restaurant. The waiter brings an order into the kitchen – someone ordered bacon and eggs. You wonder whether this information discriminates between the hypothesis that your friend Smith ordered the meal and the hypothesis that your friend Jones did. You know the eating habits of each. Here's the probability of the order's being for ±bacon and ±eggs, conditional on the order's coming from Smith and conditional on the order's coming from Jones:

Pr(– * Smith)	Pr(– * Jones)
Eggs + - + 0.4 0.1 Bacon - 0.2 0.3	Eggs + - + 0.1 0.4 Bacon - 0.5 0

The fact that the customer ordered bacon does not discriminate between the two hypotheses (since 0.5 = 0.5). And the fact that the customer ordered eggs doesn't help either (since 0.6 > 0.6). However, the fact that the customer ordered bacon *and* eggs favors Smith over Jones (since 0.4 > 0.1).

12. The example of the SETI project throws light on Paley's question as to why we think that watches must be the result of intelligent design, but don't think this when we observe a stone. It is tempting to answer this question by saying that watches are "complicated" while stones are not. However, there are many complicated natural processes (like the turbulent flow of water coming from a faucet) that don't cry out for explanation in terms of intelligent design. Similarly, narrow-band radio emissions may be physically "simple" but that doesn't mean that the SETI engineers were wrong to search for them.

13. Assessing the likelihood of a disjunction involves an additional problem. Even if the values of Pr(O * D1) and Pr(O * D2) are known, what is the value of Pr(O * D1 or D2)? The answer is that it must be somewhere in between. But exactly where depends on further considerations, since Pr(O * D1 or D2) = Pr(O * D1)Pr(D1 * D1 or D2) + Pr(O * D2)Pr(D2 * D1 or D2). If either God or a superintelligent

extraterrestrial built the vertebrate eye, what is the probability that it was God who did so?

14. The statement "p is both false and untestable" is logically consistent (assuming that the verificationist theory of meaning is mistaken). However, the *assertion* of this conjunction is paradoxical, akin to Moore's paradoxical statement "p is true but I don't believe it." Both conjunctions embody pragmatic, not semantic, paradoxes.

15. To isolate this new problem from the one already identified, I'll assume in what follows that the design hypothesis and the chance hypothesis with which it competes have built into them auxiliary assumptions that suffice for their likelihoods to be well-defined.

16. This general point surfaces in simple inference problems like the ravens paradox (Hempel 1965). Does the fact that the object before you is a black raven confirm the generalization that all ravens are black? That depends on how you gathered your data. Perhaps you sampled at random from the set of ravens; alternatively, you may have sampled at random from the set of *black ravens*. In the first case, your observation confirms the generalization, but in the second it does not. In the second case, notice that you were bound to observe that the object before you is a black raven, regardless of whether all ravens are black.

17. Although weak and strong anthropic principles differ, they have something in common. For example, the causal structure implicitly assumed in the weak anthropic principle is that of two effects of a common cause:

                                    we exist now
                                         *
(WAP)   origin of universe
                                         *
                              constants now are right

In contrast, one of the strong anthropic principles assumes the following causal arrangement:

(SAP)   we exist now * origin of the universe * constants now are right

Even though (WAP) is true and (SAP) is false, both entail a *correlation* between our existence and the constants' now having the values they do. To deal with the resulting OSEs, we must decide how to take these correlations into account in assessing likelihoods.

18. Similarly, the fact that there is something rather than nothing does not discriminate between Chance and Design.

19. The fishing and fine-tuning examples involve *extreme* OSEs. More modest OSEs are possible. If C describes the circumstances in which we make our observational determination as to whether proposition O is true, and we use the outcome of this determination to decide whether H1 or H2 is more likely, then a *quantitative* OSE is present precisely when

$$Pr(O * H1 \& C) * Pr(O * H1) \text{ or}$$
$$Pr(O * H2 \& C) * Pr(O * H2).$$

A *qualitative* OSE occurs when taking account of C alters the likelihood ordering:

$$Pr(O * H1 \& C) > Pr(O * H2 \& C) \text{ and } Pr(O * H1) * Pr(O * H2) \text{ or}$$
$$Pr(O * H1 \& C) = Pr(O * H2 \& C) \text{ and } Pr(O * H1) * Pr(O * H2).$$

Understood in this way, an OSE is just an example of *sampling bias*.

20. There is a third possibility – that the marksmen intended to kill the prisoner – but for the sake of simplicity (and also to make the firing squad argument more parallel with the argument from fine-tuning), I'll ignore this possibility.

21. The issue, thus, is not whether (L1) or (L2) are true (both are), but which an agent should use in interpreting the bearing of observations on the likelihoods of hypotheses. In this respect the injunction of the weak anthropic principle is like the principle of total evidence – it is a pragmatic principle, concerning which statements should be used for which purposes.

22. In order to replicate in the fine-tuning argument the difference between the prisoner's and the bystander's points of view, imagine that we observe through a telescope another universe in which the constants are right. We bystanders can use this observation in a way that the inhabitants of that universe cannot.

23. Notice that "I exist" when thought by the prisoner, is *a priori*, whereas "the prisoner exists," when thought by the bystander, is *a posteriori*. Is it so surprising that an *a priori* statement should have a different evidential significance than an *a posteriori* statement?

I also should note that my claim is that the proposition "I am alive" does not permit the prisoner to conclude that Design is more likely than Chance. I do not say that there is no proposition he can cite after the marksmen fire that discriminates between the two hypotheses. Consider, for example, the observation that "no bullets hit me." This favors Design over Chance, even after the prisoner conditionalizes on the fact that he is alive. Notice also that if the prisoner were alive but riddled with bullets, it is not so clear that Design would be more likely than Chance.

24. I have argued that the prisoner should assign the same likelihoods to Chance and Design, but that he is entitled to think that his survival lowers the probability of Chance and raises the probability of Design. On its face, this contradicts the following consequence of Bayes' Theorem:

$$\frac{\Pr(\text{Chance} * \text{I survive})}{\Pr(\text{Design} * \text{I survive})} = \frac{\Pr(\text{I survive} * \text{Chance})}{\Pr(\text{I survive} * \text{Design})} \times \frac{\Pr(\text{Chance})}{\Pr(\text{Design})}.$$

If the ratio of posterior probabilities is greater than the ratio of priors, this must be because the two likelihoods have different values.

The reason my argument implies no such contradiction is that I have argued, first, that the relevant likelihoods are *not* the ones displayed above, but are ones that take account of the presence of an OSE. I further imagined that the prisoner possesses knowledge (inferred from frequencies) that the two posterior probabilities displayed above are, respectively, low and high. This inference might be called "direct" since it proceeds without the prisoner's having to assign values to likelihoods. Bayes's theorem describes how various quantities are related when each is well-defined; it does not entail that all of them are well-defined in every situation (Sober 2002). It is a familiar point made by critics of Bayesianism that likelihoods can be well-defined even when prior and posterior probabilities are not. This severing of the connection between likelihoods and probabilities, or something like it, arises in the firing squad problem. The prisoner can know that Chance is improbable and that Design is highly probable, given his observation after the firing squad fires that he exists, even though his evaluation of likelihoods should focus on likelihoods that are identical in value.

25. The hypothesis that our universe is one among many has been introduced as a possible explanation of the fact that the constants (in our universe) are right. A universe is here understood to be a region of space-time that is causally closed. See Leslie (1989) for discussion. If the point of the multiverse hypothesis is to challenge the design hypothesis, on the assumption that the design hypothesis has already vanquished the hypothesis of chance, then the multiverse hypothesis is not needed. Furthermore, in comparing the multiverse hypothesis and the design hypothesis, one needs to attend to the inverse gambler's fallacy discussed earlier. This is not to deny that there may be other evidence for the multiverse hypothesis; however, the mere fact that the constants are right in our universe does not favor that hypothesis.

26. As Dennett (1987a, pp. 284-285) observes, human beings have been modifying the characteristics of animals and plants by *artificial selection* for thousands of years. However, the organisms thus modified were not *created* by human beings. If the design argument endorses a hypothesis about how organisms were brought into being, then the work of plant and animal breeders, *per se*, does not show that the design argument should be stripped of its theological trappings.

[ADDITIONAL RESOURCES]

Elliott Sober's Faculty Page: http://philosophy.wisc.edu/sober/

Darwin Day at the University of Tennessee at Knoxville: http://fp.bio.utk.edu/darwin/

Darwinism and Mendelism-Morganism:
Science As Seen Through Two Ideological Lenses
by Lawrence S. Lerner

I have for quite some time been annoyed by the constant misuse by intelligent-design creationists (IDCs) of the term "Darwinism" for the body of knowledge that scientists call evolution. This misuse is doubtless rooted in the desire of IDCs to persuade their audiences that evolution is nothing more than the ideology of a 19th-century guru named Charles Darwin – an ideology that has been eagerly adopted by his followers. Audiences so persuaded will infer that evolution is a static set of beliefs rather than the dynamic, ever-expanding scientific endeavor it really is.

The unprejudiced observer would certainly lift an eyebrow if the parallel effort were made – perhaps by some geocentrist concerned with the implications of the motion of "God's footstool"[1] – to refer consistently to physics as "Newtonism," or for some phlogistonist to repeatedly call modern chemistry "Lavoisierism." But although Newton's contributions to physics are its foundations, it would be folly to insist that the modern physicist is no more than a disciple sitting at the feet of Newton and absorbing his wisdom *ad infinitum*. Indeed, although I am a very ordinary physicist, only a fraction as smart as Newton, I can do much more physics much better than Newton, precisely because I am "standing on the shoulders of giants," Newton predominant among them. The same may be said of Lavoisier and the modern chemist. Likewise, the modern biologist has far more explanatory power at his fingertips than Darwin ever did, thanks to Darwin himself and thousands of his successors.

Is this mischaracterization of modern biology as Darwinism unique? I used to think so, until it occurred to me that there is a recent parallel in the crackpot theories of the Soviet agronomist Trofim Lysenko. Just as the present-day IDCs have dusted off the long-discarded views of the early 19th-century theologian William Paley, Lysenko dusted off the long-discarded views of Paley's approximate French contemporary Lamarck. In order to discredit the evolutionary views universally accepted among working biologists, Lysenko brushed them away with the epithet "Morganism-Mendelism."

Like the IDCs, Lysenko had a nonscientific – one is tempted to say theological – end in view. Evolution through genetic variation and natural selection appeared to conflict with fundamental Marxist-Leninist views – specifically, the view that human nature was purely the product of political-economic environment and not constrained by inherited properties. For, if man were not infinitely malleable by social influences, how could socialism produce the "new Soviet man," who would march triumphantly to the inevitable goal of communism? And how could the nonteleological "aimlessness" of evolution be squared with the eschatological Newtonian determinism of the Marxist sequence of social systems terminating in communism and utopia?

The IDCs have a parallel problem. Though they paper it over when addressing certain audiences (while trumpeting it to others) they are bound by an eschatology. An Intelligent Designer, whether he be God or an extraterrestrial visitor[2], clearly has an end in view. The mere creation of a planetary zoo is only one possibility and not the most congenial one at that. One is bound to suspect that the real IDC vision (which is more evident in their approach to sympathetic church groups than to public education forums) is salvation in the conservative Christian sense. Ascended Man takes the place of Soviet Man, but the parallels are obvious.

In this world view, evolution can have no place because evolution is not eschatological – it is not even teleological. It must therefore be abandoned at all costs. For persons not thus committed, however, the costs are of interest. Here again, Lysenkoism provides a historical parallel.

With the endorsement of Stalin (and later Khrushchev) the Soviets adopted Lysenkoism as the basis for all biology and agronomy. Distinguished biologists who protested – or even simply kept quiet – lost their positions and very often were dispatched to the gulag or worse. Under pressure to produce results, Lysenko and his followers reported spectacular improvements in various crops. But when these "improvements" were put into practice, the result was disaster. Most notable was Khrushchev's New Lands program. Based on Lysenko's promise that his grain seeds had attained unprecedented heights of drought- and cold-resistance, hundreds of thousands of agricultural workers were moved eastward into arid regions to plant and cultivate them. Within a few years, the project collapsed as the crops failed disastrously, resulting in a nation-wide food shortage, to say nothing of the desperate state of the unfortunate peasants who had been moved. These failures led to the fall of Lysenko and were a major contributor to Khrushchev's fall as well. But the damage to biology and agronomy has not been fully repaired in the successor states of the Soviet Union even today.

Of course, state boards of education have nothing like the all-encompassing power of Soviet dictators. Were such a board to adopt intelligent-design creationism (or any other species of creationism) the immediate damage would be confined to the K-12 school system. But the K-12 school system feeds into almost all of the productive segments of the society. A child nurtured in creationist nonsense is less likely to become a biologist, but very few children end up as biologists. More significantly, such children will grow into adults who have gross misconceptions of the nature and processes of science, to the detriment of their effectiveness as citizens and their ability to understand the natural world around them.

There are shorter-term effects as well. We have the example of Kansas, which briefly adopted creationist-generated science standards. In the short time before that action was reversed, Kansas lost several high-tech companies to other states and had to endure world-wide ridicule. Fortunately, short-term effects usually respond to simple cures.

I would argue that the main damage done by ideologically driven pseudosciences runs deeper. The scientific approach to nature involves a healthy humility. Nature is as it is, our value judgments notwithstanding. We learn as much as we can of Nature's ways and, if possible, bend them to our will and our needs. It has been healthy for humans to learn, in historic succession, that

- The local group is not God's chosen people
- The earth is not the center of the universe
- The solar system is a pretty small place
- Human history is a very small part of the history of the universe
- The universe would not be a very different place if we were not here at all

In spite of these humbling insights, we can still take pride that, small as we are, we can understand quite a lot about Nature, and we can expect that we will learn still more in the future. These views may not sit well with a belief that the end is near, but they are essential to the practice and progress of science. Eschatology has its uses, but it is folly to govern public-school curricula on the basis of the eschatological beliefs of a small segment of society. Science works best when the goals of the society that sustains it are open-ended.

[Footnotes]

1 Gerardus Bouw typifies this school of thought. For a long time, he published a journal titled *The Biblical Astronomer*, devoted to the proposition that modern astronomy could be based on a geocentric position that preserved the stasis of the footstool.

2 As part of the strategy of presenting intelligent-design creationism as purely scientific and secular, IDCs often present God and some unspecified extraterrestrial on the same footing, as possible creators of life on Earth. I do not think that anyone takes this tactic at face value; all or nearly all IDCs are situated in that part of the Christian spectrum that places great stress on the supernatural and nonmaterial fate of humans.

[About the Author]

Lawrence Lerner is Professor Emeritus in Physics and Astronomy at California State University, Long Beach. His areas of expertise include condensed-matter physics; history of science; science education (college level and K-12); science and the humanities; science and religion; K-12 science textbooks and the evaluation of K-12 science standards. Dr. Lerner's books include two college-level calculus-based physics texts; translation of Giordano Bruno, *The Ash Wednesday Supper* (1584), *An Appraisal of Science Standards in 36 States* (1998), and numerous articles and papers on the subjects listed above.

[Additional Resources]

Good Science, Bad Science: Teaching Evolution in the States:
   http://www.edexcellence.net/library/lerner/gsbsteits.html

This paper was presented by Jason Rosenhouse to Individuals for Freethought at the University of Kansas for Darwin Day 2002.

RHETORICAL LEGERDEMAIN IN INTELLIGENT-DESIGN LITERATURE
by Jason Rosenhouse

Charles Darwin presented his theory of evolution to a scientific community overwhelmingly creationist in temperament. Biology as an organized discipline was in its infancy and consisted of little more than raw descriptions of nature's oddities. The origin of species was not considered an appropriate topic for scientific investigation. Indeed, evolution was hardly original to Darwin; Jean Baptiste de Lamarck and Robert Chambers, among others, had beaten him to it; but scientists wanted nothing to do with the concept. The argument from design, presented by William Paley in his *Natural Theology*, seemed convincing to nearly everyone.

So if Darwin convinced the thinking world of both the reality of evolution and the plausibility of a naturalistic explanation for that reality, it was not because he was preaching to a choir of militant atheists. Darwin achieved his intellectual revolution by presenting compelling evidence, culled from numerous scientific disciplines. The century since has seen his theory confirmed by new data from branches of science he never dreamed of, genetics and molecular biology in particular.

Evolution's critics remain unimpressed, and they offer an endless supply of books, magazines, and religious tracts in defense of their view. For most of the twentieth century, organized anti-evolutionism has been associated with religious fundamentalism. The scientific arguments they raised were amateurish to say the least, causing scientifically knowledgeable readers to dismiss them with amusement. Less amusing was their dishonest use of rhetoric, their penchant for removing quotations from their proper context, and their rank distortions of modern scientific thought.

That school of anti-evolutionism still exists, but several hostile court decisions have reduced it to the level of background noise. Nowadays anti-evolutionism is controlled by a group of eloquent, well-educated academics. The term creationism being rather debased, they prefer the title "Intelligent-Design Theory" (ID). Their placid tone and skillful writing have convinced many that there is now serious, scholarly criticism of evolutionary theory. Press accounts are careful to distinguish ID theorists from the creationists of old.

In part this distinction is appropriate. The scientific arguments ID's raise are quite sophisticated, and require a considerable education to refute. Furthermore, their attacks on science are narrowly focused. Whereas creationists tended to dismiss everything from biology to astronomy to geology, ID aims solely at the explanatory sufficiency of natural selection.

But in another, more important, sense this distinction is not appropriate. In terms of their dishonesty ID's are no improvement over their creationist forebears. Their scientific arguments have been decisively refuted elsewhere. Here I will analyze the rhetorical tricks they use to convert slipshod science into persuasive prose.

What Is Neo-Darwinism?

Many critics of evolution learn their science solely from popular-level, often hostile, treatments of the subject. This allows ID's to present a caricatured version of the theory. By knocking over a straw-man they make biologists look foolish and doctrinaire. Understanding what modern evolutionary theory really says is essential for penetrating the fog they disperse.

The modern view of evolution is often called the Neo-Darwinian synthesis, or simply Neo-Darwinism. It is called a synthesis because it unifies the work of several disparate branches of science. As such, it is not a single theory.

The major ideas of Neo-Darwinism can be summed up roughly as follows:

1. The history of life on Earth reveals a pattern of descent with modification. Thus, any two species alive today had a common ancestor in the past.

2. Organisms produce more offspring than can survive given the limited resources of natural environments. Organisms also show heritable variation. Some organisms possess variations making them more successful at reproduction.

3. As a result, favorable variants will accumulate over time, leading to evolutionary change. In particular, complex organs like eyes or wings arise by gradual accretion.

4. Evolutionary change is nearly always gradual. Large-scale reorganizations of the genome do not occur in a single generation.

5. Macroevolutionary change is the result of numerous microevolutionary events. There is no need to invoke new mechanisms to explain such change.

Statement one is referred to as the hypothesis of common descent. Statement two is a simple empirical fact. The process described in statement three is known as natural selection. Evolution/creation disputes revolve entirely around claims one and three, and when scientists describe evolution as entirely uncontroversial it is these claims they have in mind. Claims four and five, by contrast, generate substantial controversy, a fact IDs seize upon.

Most biologists would not recognize their theory in ID presentations. Consider:

> It is sheer dumb luck that alters the genetic message so that, from infernal nonsense, meaning for a moment emerges; and sheer dumb luck again that endows life with its *opportunities*, the space of possibilities over which natural selection plays, sheer dumb luck creating the mammalian eye and the marsupial pouch, sheer dumb luck again endowing the elephant's sensi-

tive nose with nerves and the orchid's translucent petal with blush. – David Berlinski, *"The Deniable Darwin"*

Berlinski acknowledges the existence of natural selection, but completely overlooks its role in crafting complexity. Genetic variation is random, but selection is not. Selection's sieving action preserves the incipient stages of new organs, making it possible for complexity to arise gradually. This statement is typical of ID literature, which seeks to dismiss evolution by presenting it as a theory of chance. Consider that evolutionary biology is the source of thousands of pages of professional journal articles every year. If sheer dumb luck is the sum total of evolutionary theorizing, one wonders what all the verbiage is for.

ID's frequently, and wrongly, present evolution as a theory regarding the origin of life:

> In fact, Justice Scalia used the general term "evolution" exactly as scientists use it – to include not only biological evolution but also prebiological or chemical evolution, which seeks to explain how life first evolved from non-living chemicals. – Phillip Johnson, *Darwin on Trial*

> The task of evolutionary biology is to explain the origin and development of life. – William Dembski, *Intelligent Design*

Johnson is commenting on the dissenting opinion in the 1987 Supreme Court case Edwards v. Aguillard, hence the reference to Justice Scalia. Johnson and Dembski are mistaken; the question of life's origin is logically and empirically separate from its subsequent evolution. This is obvious when one considers the lines of evidence cited on evolution's behalf, which take for granted the existence of some life form equipped with the full complement of known genetic mechanisms. Evolution explains how biological complexity arises from biological simplicity. It is silent on the origin of biological simplicity.

Of course, the two topics are often discussed together. Accepting Neo-Darwinism makes it natural to wonder about life's origin. Many of the theories in this regard bear similarities to Darwinian explanations of evolution, hence the phrase "chemical evolution". But the fact remains that it is a different theory that is being described.

The fossil record is completely consistent with the hypothesis of common descent; a powerful source of evidence in Darwin's favor. However, tracing specific lines of descent through a collection of fossils is difficult, if not impossible. ID's deliberately confuse these two points:

> The horse sequence has proved vexing to everyone who looks at it, and the term of choice is that it's an astonishingly bushy sequence... We have dozens and dozens of species entering the record suddenly and departing from the record just as abruptly as they entered. We don't really know whether the modern horse has ancestral patterns with the dozens of other species that we find in the fossil record. – David Berlinski, "Firing Line" Debate

Any fossil species is a snapshot into deep time. It tells us that an animal showing certain morphological features existed at a particular time in natural history. It does not come with labels announcing its proper place relative to other fossil species, and it is generally impossible to say with certainty that this pile of bones *over here* is a direct ancestor to that pile of bones *over there*.

From this sensible point Berlinski wishes to conclude that "bushy" fossil sequences can not be used as powerful evidence for evolution, but this conclusion is unwarranted. Evolution makes definite predictions about what sorts of fossils should be found and not found in rocks of a given age. When paleontologists repeatedly confirm these predictions, it constitutes evidence for the theory.

The extant collections of fossil horses may form a bushy sequence, but it is not a chaotic one. There is a clear pattern of morphological change that coincides nicely with what selection would have preserved given the environmental changes going on at that time. It therefore supports evolution.

Evolutionists often cite the patterns of embryological development as indicative of common descent. ID's challenge this by observing that the once popular theory of "ontogeny recapitulates phylogeny" has turned out to be false:

> Since Darwin's theory is affirmed regardless of the evidence, and "ontogeny recapitulates phylogeny" is a logical deduction from that theory biology textbooks continue to teach it – though they usually attach von Baer's name to it. – Jonathan Wells, *Icons of Evolution*

Ontogeny refers to the process of embryological development of an organism between conception and birth. Phylogeny refers to evolutionary history. Even before Darwin scientists noticed that the embryological development of wildly different organisms often passed through similar early stages. Von Baer was among the first to observe this pattern, which explains why his name arises in this context.

Ontogeny recapitulates phylogeny was a specific theory developed to explain these observations. It was the brainchild of Ernst Haeckel and was in no way a logical deduction from Darwin's theory. It is also distinct from Von Baer's ideas. Haeckel argued that early stages of embryological development were similar because they recapitulated the shared evolutionary history of the organisms in question. This theory was based in part on the idea that programs of development could be modified only by adding new stages to the end of the program, an idea that is now discredited. Wells wishes to conclude that since Haeckel's theory is mistaken, there must be no relation between ontogeny and phylogeny. This conclusion is absurd.

Now consider the rhetorical impact of these misconceptions. Presenting evolution as a theory of chance, or as a theory of life's origins, allows ID's to set-up a caricatured evolutionist. No one would explain life's manifold complexity via chance alone, but by presenting this straw-man ID's can look clever when knocking it down. Similarly, ID's capitalize on current ignorance regarding life's origins to imply that evolutionists leave an explanatory hole at the start of their theory. This allows them to appear open-minded, frankly admitting the existence of open questions, unlike arrogant Darwinists who presume to cover up such things.

They also permit ID's to imply skullduggery among scientists. By presenting discredited ideas as if they represent modern thought they strive to make evolutionists appear blinkered and dishonest.

DISTORTIONS OF SCIENTISTS' WORK

The fourth and fifth claims of Neo-Darwinism are the source of considerable controversy. Consider three examples:

1. Stephen Jay Gould / Niles Eldredge: Punctuated Equilibrium

2. Stuart Kauffman: Self-Organizing Systems

3. Jerry Coyne / H. Allen Orr: The role of mutations of large effect in adaptation.

All three theories have been misrepresented in the ID literature. None of them has anything to do with the validity of common descent or the ability of natural selection to craft complex adaptations. Kauffman's argument is that complex systems can order themselves spontaneously, offering a source of biological order not mediated by natural selection. It is a challenge to claim five. Coyne and Orr argue that mutations of large effect play a greater role in adaptation than Neo-Darwinism generally acknowledges. Thus, it is a challenge to claim four.

To IDs, these are the sorts of gaping theoretical holes scientists are at pains to conceal. They make their point by distorting the nature of these theories, and often lift quotations out of context to support their view. For example:

> Jerry Coyne, of the Department of Ecology and Evolution at the University of Chicago, arrives at an unanticipated verdict: 'We conclude – unexpectedly – that there is little evidence for the Neo-Darwinian view: it's theoretical foundations and the experimental evidence supporting it are weak.' – Michael Behe, *Darwin's Black Box*

Sounds bad, doesn't it? Now consider what was actually written:

> Although a few biologists have suggested an evolutionary role for mutations of large effect, the Neo-Darwinian view has largely triumphed, and the genetic basis of adaptation now receives little attention. Indeed, the question is considered so dead that few may know the evidence responsible for its demise. Here we review this evidence. We conclude – unexpectedly – that there is little evidence for the Neo-Darwinian view: its theoretical foundations and the experimental evidence supporting it are weak, and there is no doubt that mutations of large effect are sometimes important in adaptation. – Jerry Coyne and H. Allen Orr, *"The Genetics of Adaptation: A Reassessment"*

Gives a rather different impression. Note that Behe altered the quotation to give the impression that an esoteric comment about adaptation was actually a searing indictment of all of Neo-Darwinism.

Behe similarly exaggerates the challenge posed by Kauffman's theories:

> Kauffman is one of the leading lights in a group of scientists exploring complexity theory – roughly, the idea that complex systems can organize themselves – explicitly as an alternative to natural selection. – Michael Behe, "Fatuous Filmmaking"

Actually, Kauffman's intent is to supplement natural selection, not replace it. Indeed, his work is far more threatening to IDs, since it implies that complex order arises naturally, almost inevitably, without any need for the action of an intelligent agent.

The Gould/Eldedge theory of punctuated equilibrium comes in for particular abuse, largely because Stephen Jay Gould was an especially prominent evolutionist. To hear an ID theorist tell it, punctuated equilibrium exists solely as an ad hoc explanation for the absence of transitional forms in the fossil record. It is commonly said to be an assault on the efficacy of natural selection, or that it is a return to saltationist theories of evolution. Consider just two examples:

> Are transitional forms conspicuously lacking at certain points in the fossil record? Punctuated equilibrium comes forward to account for the gap: it happened too fast (only thirty million years or so) to leave enough to be noticed. – Huston Smith, *Why Religion Matters*

> Unlike Martin Gardener, I do believe that punctuated equilibrium damages the Darwinian viewpoint; so does everyone else. By compressing the time available for speciation, Stephen Jay Gould has eliminated an accretion of small changes as its mechanism. – David Berlinski, Response to Martin Gardner

Both of these quotations are serious distortions of the theory. Punctuated equilibrium was an attempt to connect modern theories of speciation with the findings of paleontology. Starting in the forties, biologist Ernst Mayr developed, based on countless field studies, the allopatric model of speciation. In this model speciation occurs when small "founder" populations become isolated from their ancestral stock. Within such populations, gene frequencies can change quickly. In a 1954 paper, Mayr suggested this would lead to a pattern of stasis interrupted by sudden changes in the fossil record. Gould and Eldredge developed this idea into a workable model for paleontologists, and punctuated equilibrium was born.

We can now see why the quotations above are so misleading. In the fossil record ransitional forms at the species level are rare, but they exist in large numbers at higher taxonomic levels. That this should be so is a consequence of punctuated equilibrium, not the reason for its development. Smith's comment about "thirty million years" is truly pathetic; it is a number he simply made up.

David Berlinski is mistaken in both of his major claims, and it is worth noting that Gould himself rejected them unambiguosuly. First, punctuated equilibrium addresses the tempo and mode of evolution. It says nothing about mechanisms. By itself it poses no threat to classical Neo-Darwinian ideas regarding natural selection. The "punctuations" referred to in the theory are rapid only relative to the much longer periods of stasis. They are plenty long enough for selection to account for the observed changes.

Darwin believed that paleontologists should confirm evolution by finding series of insensibly graded fossil forms. The record generally does not document such change, a fact he had to address. He argued that the absence of transitional forms was an artifact of the extreme imperfection of the fossil record, a sound answer that would be endorsed by many evolutionists today.

Not necessarily the correct answer, however. Gould and Eldredge argue that Darwin was mistaken in believing that insensibly graded fossil series were the logical conclusion of his theory. Darwin erred because he had no sound estimate of the age of the Earth, no working model of speciation, no knowledge of the physical basis of heredity, and no information regarding the extent to which paleontologists could resolve the ages of fossils. He was also at pains to stress the gradualism of his model as a contrast to the dominant catastrophism of his day.

All three challenges discussed here remain controversial, but even if thy are right in every particular the resulting theory would still be Darwinism. They are interesting for another reason, however. Anti-evolutionists are fond of claiming the professional journals are closed to them because of editorial bias against work critical of Neo-Darwinism. Yet these theories, along with countless others, have all been hashed out in academic journals. Contrary to ID protestations, journal editors thrive on controversy; it brings much needed attention to the journals they edit. They simply require the heretic to have something other than ignorance and obfuscation to offer in defense of his theory.

Distortions of Scientific Methodology

If IDs wish respectability to be conferred upon their ideas, the test they must pass is simple: Go discover something. Show how your methods and theories lead to the discovery of useful insights about nature. This is a test evolution has passed for more than a century.

Such success will elude ID, because its scientific arguments are a smoke-screen. In reality it is the intellectual foundation for a movement that wishes to have supernatural explanations be considered a part of science. Berkeley law professor Phillip Johnson is particularly passionate on this point. The following quotations are representative:

> On the other hand, modernists also identify science with naturalistic philosophy. In that case science is committed to finding materialistic explanations for every phenomenon – regardless of the facts. – *The Wedge of Truth*

> By skillful manipulation of categories and definitions, the Darwinists have established philosophical naturalism as educational orthodoxy in a nation in which the overwhelming majority of people express some form of theistic belief inconsistent with naturalism. – "Evolution as Dogma"

> Darwinists know that the mutation-selection mechanism can produce wings, eyes, and brains not because the mechanism can be observed to do anything of the kind, but because their guiding philosophy assures them that no other power is available to do the job. The absence from the cosmos of any Creator is therefore the essential staring point for Darwinism. – *Darwin on Trial*

Johnson would have you believe all the field studies, laboratory experiments, professional journals, conferences, books, magazine articles, and countless hours of toil spent by dedicated researchers in the tedium of day to day scientific work are all just planks in a grand scheme to promote atheism to the world at large. The scope of his attack is truly breathtaking. First he blithely accuses scientists of allowing their philosophical presumptions to blind them to the facts. Then we learn that a monolithic band of Darwinists has, merely by playing semantic games, managed to thwart the will of the American public. The deal is sealed by claiming that scientists have rejected creationism a priori, despite the countless books and articles scientists have devoted to the subject.

Johnson is wrong because he fundamentally misunderstands the nature of science. It is true that scientists reject supernatural explanations when doing their work. This is for entirely pragmatic reasons; there is no reliable means for testing supernatural explanations against data, making them useless for practical purposes. This is referred to as methodological naturalism. It makes no assumption about how the world actually is. Metaphysical naturalism, by contrast, is the explicit statement that natural forces can account for everything. Were a poltergeist to invade a laboratory and perform miracles in defiance of all physical explanation, metaphysical naturalism would be utterly defeated. Methodological naturalism would shrug its shoulders.

A commitment to naturalistic explanations does not mandate acceptance of the first theory to come down the road. Admissions of ignorance are perfectly acceptable. Theories abound for the origin of life, but no scientist describes the problem as solved. Neo-Darwinism is accepted because if it were false, it should be easy to disprove. That a century's worth of research has failed to do so surely counts for something.

What is really going on here is rather more insidious. In modern society a statement is true to the extent that it is scientific. Thus, every two-bit demagogue and snake-oil salesman must don scientific raiment to persuade others of the correctness of his view. Johnson, for reasons having nothing to do with science, wishes to convince people of the truth of his religious views. If that means misrepresenting science to a public eager to believe his message, so be it.

OVERSIMPLIFICATIONS OF BIOLOGICAL RESEARCH

Though ID theorists pretend to be at the cutting edge of biological research, much of their *modus operandi* involves presenting simplistic versions of difficult scientific ideas. We consider a typical example.

Jonathan Wells and Paul Nelson wish to persuade us that homologies, those peculiar anatomical similarities that strongly suggest common descent, are on their way out as a source of evidence for Darwinism. They write:

> In a recent commentary on the troubled state of the concept [of homology], David Cannatella, of the Department of Zoology at the university of Texas wrote: 'Wake (1994) offered that homology is the central concept of all biology. If this is true, then a large group of comparative biologists lacks a guiding principle. One does not have to look far to see that homology ... is not understood by many biologists.' – Jonathan Wells and Paul Nelson, "Homology: A Concept in Crisis"

The trouble begins when we note that Cannatella was not lamenting the troubled state of homology. He was writing a favorable review of two books on the subject, books which were themselves celebrating the glut of recent work in the area. It continues when we consider the remainder of Cannatella's statement:

> Wake (1994) offered that homology is the central concept of all biology. If this is true, then a large group of comparative biologists lacks a guiding principle. One does not have to look far to see that homology ... is not understood by many biologists. For example, Quiring et al (1994) isolated the Drosophila homolog of the Pax-6 gene, which is very similar to the Pax-6 of mice, quail, humans, and zebrafish. They concluded that 'because Pax-

6 is involved in the genetic control of eye morphogenesis in both mammals and insects the traditional view ... that the vertebrate eye and the compound eye of insects evolved independently has to be reconsidered'. Here the faulty logic lies in equating different hierarchical levels, the beginnings and ends (genes and eyes) of the developmental cascade. The presence of the Pax-6 gene is probably a synapomorphy of a large group of metazoans and thus the Pax-6 genes are homologous. But the distribution of the character state 'eyes present' on the phylogeny of metazoans requires homoplasy, and the eyes of insects and vertebrates are independently evolved.
– David Cannatella, Book Review

Cannatella is criticizing the idea that a gene playing similar roles in different classes of organisms must have arisen by descent from a single common ancestor. The issue is not whether homology is a useful concept for comparative biologists. Rather, the logic of its application can be subtle in real-life cases, and sometimes even professionals are led astray.

It is commonly believed that the findings of modern biology hold deep theological significance. As a result, everyone feels qualified to discuss them. But the fact is that biology, like any other mature science, is subtle and complex at its frontiers. Some humility is in order when considering popular-level treatments of this material.

OUTRAGEOUS CHARGES

I have been reading ID literature for several years now and have developed a thick skin as a result. I can read dozens of pages of nonsense in one sitting, without once coming up for air. I can identify the proper context of a scientific quotation solely on the basis of how it is misrepresented by ID's.

But every once in a while I come across something so outrageous, dishonest, or just flat ignorant that I am stopped dead in my tracks. For example:

> [Douglas Futuyma] writes, 'The gradual transition from therapsid reptiles to mammals is so abundantly documented by scores of species in every stage of transition that it is impossible to tell which therapsid species were the actual ancestors of modern mammals.' But large numbers of eligible candidates are a plus only to the extent that they can be placed in a single line of descent that could conceivably lead from a particular reptile species to a particular early mammal descendant. The presence of similarities do not necessarily imply ancestry. The notion that mammals-in-general evolved from reptiles-in-general through a broad clump of diverse therapsid lines is not Darwinism. Darwinian transformation requires a single line of ancestral descent. – Phillip Johnson, *Darwin on Trial*

Truly extraordinary! The theory that modern mammals descended from ancient reptiles mandates that creatures exhibiting certain bizarre, transitional characteristics must have existed at a particular time in natural history. The fossil record documents the existence of many such animals. Johnson thinks this is a problem for evolution?

Consider also that Darwinists do not claim that similarities imply ancestry; actually they claim precisely the opposite. Hypotheses of common descent mandate anatomical similarities; when those similarities are documented in the fossil record it's called evidence. And surely Johnson understands that the question of whether mammals descended from reptiles is independent of our ability to pick out the precise line of descent from a thicket of fossil candidates.

> There is no publication in the scientific literature – in prestigious journals, specialty journals, or books – that describes how molecular evolution of any real, complex, biochemical system either did occur or even might have occurred. – Michael Behe, *Darwin's Black Box*

Ahem. There are *hundreds* of journal articles addressing the evolution of irreducibly complex machines, a fact pointed out by numerous biologists since the publication of Behe's book. But who outside a handful of professional biologists is likely to know this?

> If the evolutionary scientists were better informed or more scientific in their thinking, they would be asking about the origin of information. The materialists know this at some level, but they suppress their knowledge to protect their assumptions. – Phillip Johnson, *The Wedge of Truth*

The picture of professional biologists needing a law professor to point them in fruitful investigative directions is almost too amusing to contemplate, but note Johnson's willingness to impugn the integrity of large groups of scientists. Also note how the evolutionary biologists of the first sentence morphed into the materialists of the second. Johnson complains bitterly when ID's are tarred as religious extremists, but presenting evolutionists as atheists is just fine. Finally, there is the simple point that *plenty* of scientists are seeking the origin of information. Whole books get written on the subject. The origin of life is one of the hottest open problems in biology today.

> It is now 140 years since the publication of Darwin's book. Since then, there have been many disputes about Darwinism, to the degree that Darwinists have had to modify their arguments into new Darwinism, thus creating the sect of Neo-Darwinists. – David Foster, "Proving God Exists"

This will come as news to biologists. Neo-Darwinism is the vindication of Darwin's theories, not a desperate attempt to prop them up. It is the marriage of Darwin's original ideas to modern views of genetics. Also, don't overlook Foster's use of the incendiary word "sect" in describing evolutionists.

Examples like this could be multiplied endlessly, but surely the point is made. Anti-evolutionists are not above simply making stuff up to support their case.

Does Evolution Equal Atheism?

If you still think the evolution/ID schism is primarily about rival interpretations of scientific data, consider the following statements:

> Now [the dispute over God's existence] takes an inferential form over whether life on Earth could have arisen and developed by chance, or (alternatively) whether it could have arisen and been developed through intel-

ligent design and conscious application. The former case is maintained by the atheists and their devotion to neo-Darwinism, while the latter case is for the believers and their need for a creative God. – David Foster, "Proving God Exists"

The problem with allowing God a role in the history of life is not that science would cease but rather that scientists would have to acknowledge the existence of something important that is outside the boundaries of natural science. For scientists who want to be able to explain everything – and "theories of everything" are now openly anticipated in the scientific literature – this is an intolerable possibility. – Phillip Johnson, *Objections Sustained*

These are just two examples of many such laments, and they reveal the true concern of ID theorists. Foster, after first committing the fallacy of describing evolution as a theory of chance, explicitly identifies Neo-Darwinism as an ideology for atheists. Johnson believes God-talk causes such dissonance in the minds of biologists, they will glom on to any theory that will protect their assumptions. (Incidentally, "theory of everything" is a term from physics referring to hypotheses for uniting the four fundamental forces of nature into one grand framework. It has nothing to do with metaphysical naturalism.)

Ours is a very religious society, and charges of atheism are serious business. As rhetoric the charge works very well; in the minds of many, atheists are inherently unworthy of trust. The ubiquity of this charge in ID literature speaks volumes regarding their motives and intentions.

The equation of evolution with atheism is false and deeply offensive to countless religious scientists. Darwinism is no more atheistic than any other scientific theory. When astronomers develop theories for the motions of the planets, no one accuses them of atheism for not mentioning God's role in the process. Why, then, is it atheistic to offer naturalistic explanations for life's development through natural history?

Conclusion

So what are we to make of all this? The specific scientific claims of the ID theorists have been decisively refuted. Their use of rhetoric and propaganda has shown they have little interest in open and honest debate. They take quotations out of context, distort evidence, misrepresent whole scientific disciplines, oversimplify difficult ideas, and impugn the integrity of scientists. All the while they claim God's blessing for their project and invoke conspiracy theories against those who disagree. And when they are done with all of that, they turn around and accuse scientists of arrogance.

Where I come from we call that chutzpah.

Let us tell it like it is. Intelligent-design theory is nonsense both as science and philosophy. It has contributed nothing to our understanding of biology, and never will. The only proper response to their faulty arguments, sleazy rhetoric, and distorted science is contempt.

[ABOUT THE AUTHOR]

Jason Rosenhouse received his PhD in mathematics from Dartmouth College in 2000. Currently he is a post-doc at Kansas State University. He has written about evolution and creationism in "The Mathematical Intelligencer", "Evolution", "Skeptic", and "Free Inquiry". He can be reached at jasonr@math.ksu.edu.

[SOURCES OF ID QUOTATIONS]

Michael Behe, *Darwin's Black Box*, The Free Press, 1996.

William Dembski, *Intelligent Design*, InterVarsity Press, 1999.

Phillip Johnson, *Darwin on Trial*, Regnery Gateway, 1991.

Phillip Johnson, *Objections Sustained*, InterVarsity Press, 1998.

Phillip Johnson, *The Wedge of Truth*, InterVarsity Press, 2000.

Huston Smith, *Why Religion Matters*, Harper Collins, 2001.

Jonathan Wells, *Icons of Evolution*, Regnery, 2000.

David Berlinski, "The Deniable Darwin" and "David Berlinski and Critics", *Commentary*, June 1996 and September 1996.

David Foster, "Proving God Exists, Parts I and II", *The Saturday Evening Post*, Nov-Dec 1999 and Jan-Feb 2000.

Phillip Johnson, "Evolution as Dogma: The Establishment of Naturalism", *First Things*, 1990 #6.

Jonathan Wells and Paul Nelson, "Homology: A Concept in Crisis", *Origins and Design*, Fall 1997.

Transcript of the "Firing Line" Debate "Resolved: The Evolutionists Should Acknowledge Creation" held on December 4, 1997. Michael Behe's quotation regarding Stuart Kauffman's ideas was posted at the website www.arn.org in an article entitled, "Fatuous Filmmaking." The reference is to the PBS documentary series "Evolution".

[ADDITIONAL RESOURCES]

Individuals for Freethought: http://www.k-state.edu/freethought/splash.html

There are many excellent books available for the reader interested in learning more about the basics of evolutionary biology. The best presentation of the evidence of evolution remains Douglas Futuyma's *Science on Trial: The Case for Evolution*, Pantheon, 1983. A somewhat more technical but still accessible treatment is given by Ernst Mayr in *What Evolution Is*, Basic Books, 2001.

For discussions on how natural selection makes it possible for complexity to arise gradually consult the two books by Richard Dawkins: *The Blind Watchmaker*, 2nd Ed., Norton 1996 and *Climbing Mount Improbable*, Norton 1996. Stephen Jay Gould's magisterial *The Structure of Evolutionary Theory*, Harvard University Press, 2002, is also an excellent source for approachable discussions of many of the issues discussed here. Finally, for a clear exposition of Stuart Kauffman's ideas consider his book *Investigations*, Oxford University Press, 2001.

For books dealing specifically with Evolution and ID see Kenneth Miller, *Finding Darwin's God*, Harper Collins 1999, and the two books by Robert Pennock – *Tower of Babel*, MIT Press, 1999 and *Intelligent-Design Creationism and its Critics*, MIT Press 2000.

Finally, two other articles quoted in this essay are:

Jerry Coyne and H. Allen Orr, "The Genetics of Adaptation: A Reassessment", *American Naturalist*, Vol. 140, 1992.

David Cannatella, Review of Homology, ed. by B.K. Hall, and Homoplasy, ed. by M. Sanderson and L. Hufford, *Systematic Biology*, Vol. 46, 1997.

This paper was presented by Taner Edis to the Freethinkers Society at Truman State University for Darwin Day 2002.

CREATIONISM TO UNIVERSAL DARWINISM: EVOLUTION AND RELIGION TODAY
by Taner Edis

Thus sayeth the polls

Today, more than a century after Darwin convinced biologists that life had evolved, we still see a raging controversy over creation and evolution. Together with this, we have a large range of ideas about what evolution means for religion.

Since we live in poll-driven times, let us start by looking at public opinion. We find that in the United States,

- 45% are creationists; often of the young-earth variety. When pollsters ask whether humans were created in a form much as they are today, within the last ten thousand years, they say yes.

- 45% believe in a progressive evolutionary process guided by a divine force, typically identified with the traditional God. This is the common liberal Christian option, though it is also strong in New Age circles.

- 5-10% accept naturalistic evolution with no explicit divine involvement, though a God may still be lurking behind the scenes.

This poll data has remained fairly consistent since at least 1980. And unsurprisingly, it reflects the religious make-up of the country. The United States is unusual among industrialized Western countries in its intense religiosity, and certainly in its large religiously conservative population.

The polls also demonstrate the thinness of public support for *Darwinian* evolution in the US. A strong minority completely reject evolution, if we take evolution to mean no more than descent with modification over long ages of time. However, if we emphasize the naturalism of modern evolutionary theory, where the history of life is shaped by blind mechanisms, we see that full-blown Darwinians are the smallest minority.

Creationism and "Intelligent Design"

Outright creationism, including its recently evolved cousin, "Intelligent Design" (ID), are the most religiously orthodox options. However, it is important not to caricaturize rejection of evolution as a byproduct of a mindless Bible-thumping mentality. In Darwin's day, editorial cartoonists would depict evolutionists as monkeys; today every time a state such as Kansas or Ohio flirts with anti-evolutionary ideas in their school boards, cartoons with ape-like creationists show up. But there is more to creationism than scriptural literalism. ID proponents in particular can be rather sophisticated, and from within a religious perspective, there are serious reasons to resist evolution.

ID'ers strongly object to the Darwinian mechanism of evolution, precisely because it ties life to a *mechanism*, as opposed to a creative purpose imposing itself on an otherwise formless and lifeless material world. Their central concern is design; they demand that complex functional order such as that we see in biology must be a direct product of a mind. This claim is not confined to biology; in fact, it might be more clearly understood as a claim about the nature of intelligence. Intelligence must not be reducible to material processes; it must impose order from outside the material world. This means ID resonates with the convictions of many people who are not fixated on Genesis.

So it is no surprise creationists and ID proponents attack evolution with a particular vehemence. They perceive that materialism has gained ground, in our intellectual culture if not in everyday beliefs. They also see evolution as a prime example of removing creativity from God and relocating it in the natural world. So denying that evolution can account for true creative novelty makes sense: they block materialism by refusing it a foothold in the first place.

Guided Evolution

Religious liberals try to defuse the Darwinian challenge, first of all by confining it to biology. If creationists tend to see biological evolution as a particularly nasty manifestation of a larger materialist threat, liberals treat it as a theory about the history of life only, a fact which calls for some reinterpretation of doctrine but not much more.

Moreover, liberals are not just defensive about evolution – they can be quite positive about it. The salvation history in scripture may no longer be literally believable these days, but liberals displace the cosmic purpose and meaning expressed in the old stories onto the history of life in the universe. They see evolution as an intrinsically progressive unfolding, an ascent towards higher and higher levels of complexity, consciousness, spirituality, and morality. And of course, there must be a transcendent driving force behind this process. Evolution becomes God's way of creation.

Though this is not a Darwinian vision, liberals do not object to Darwin. Since they see evolution as descent with modification only, they have no problem with Darwin as an important scientific figure. And after all, Darwin did leave room for God as a somewhat remote First Cause, so there's room for a happy coexistence between science and religion.

In fact, this is a common liberal theme. There can be no conflict between science and religion since, if done properly, they address entirely different concerns. Religion has no business pontificating about the fossil record, and science has no business pronouncing on ultimate matters like purpose in the universe. Science and religion have separate spheres, end of story.

Religion-free Evolution

Many, however, would emphasize the separation of science and religion more strongly. After all, guided evolution still brings them together, since it uses evolutionary progress to support a spiritual view of the history of life. Most biologists would point out that evolution is not quite so progressive, and would like the wall between science and religion to be higher.

Natural selection, most importantly, is a mechanism with no intrinsic direction. Evolution is blind – it has no foresight to choose a path of progress and follow it. Of course, there are trends like the existence of increasingly complex and brainy forms of life as we get close to the present. However, this "progress" is just an artifact, due to the fact that life started out simple and stupid. From this starting point, Darwinian evolution explores a diversity of ways of life, and among these, some just happen to be more complex options.

Most biologists will further argue that blind natural selection is the source of creativity in evolution. Other pieces of the puzzle such as genetic drift, phenotypic plasticity, mass extinctions and so forth are also very important in shaping the particular history the fossils record. However, creative novelty is due to Darwinian variation-and-selection.

Modern biology, in other words, presents a thoroughly naturalistic picture of life; not one which requires any God. But many biologists would add that this does not mean evolution opposes religion. Biology, they might say, is naturalistic because any science *must* operate that way. This only means that we must seek God elsewhere, not that science has anything negative to say about God.

Godless Evolution

All very well, but this backing up and declaring no intention to poach on religious territory sounds a bit suspicious. Critics of religion have generally not been so reticent, arguing that there is much about evolution that makes it very dubious that a God is running the universe.

To begin with, the old, robust concept of scriptural revelation seems to be crippled after Darwin. And this is no small thing. Though there is much liberal handwaving and reinterpretation going on, there is something unconvincing about the effort. Ernest Gellner, when comparing the conviction inspired by Islam to the anemic religiosity in Britain, described Christianity as "a religion bowdlerized by its own theologians." At a certain point, a religion which keeps backing off and accommodating to naturalistic science becomes hard to take seriously.

Evolution is, in fact, a good illustration of the religious danger of making God an unnecessary hypothesis. We might be tempted to declare that God works through evolution, even if saying this adds nothing to our understanding of biology. But this God is like a Santa Claus to the Christmas of Darwinian evolution. We do not, after learning the ugly truth, insist that Santa Claus is still real, that he is the moving spirit behind the holiday season, and that he works through parents placing gifts under trees.

On top of all this, Darwinian evolution seems to go very well with a classic reason to doubt the existence of a God: The Problem of Evil. Evolution is an inefficient process which requires much suffering – it is an implausible instrument for an infinitely competent and benevolent force trying to achieve any humanly intelligible end.

Of course, all this does not mean that evolution disproves God in any strict sense.

Any discussion of the implications of evolution for religion must be part of a much broader argument. Nevertheless, evolution does have a place in the debate over religion – this cannot be avoided by invoking separate spheres. And it would appear that Darwinian evolution throws its weight on the side of the infidels.

Universal Darwinism

All of the preceding ideas were, in various primitive forms, part of the early debate over evolution and religion. In the last couple of decades, however, a new species has arrived on the scene: Universal Darwinism.

The basic thrust here is that Darwinian evolution is not only one of the most profound theories our sciences have come up with, but that it applies beyond biology. The Darwinian process underlies all creativity; it is central to achieving *all* complex functional order.

Some of the ideas in this fold are rather speculative. For example, Lee Smolin proposes a "Darwinian cosmology" to explain certain features of our universe. He takes current ideas about a multiplicity of universes, and how the formation of a black hole might create another universe – one, perhaps, where the laws of physics are similar to that of the parent but slightly mutated. In that case, we can bring Darwinian population thinking to bear on cosmology, and find that the most common universes will be those which produce lots of black holes and hence offspring. Such as our universe.

Another speculative idea applies Darwinism to human culture. Richard Dawkins and Susan Blackmore speak of "memes" as units of culture which reproduce via human brains, copied by imitation. The notions of memes and meme complexes still needs much development; they appear to encompass anything from a catchy advertising jingle to a complex scientific theory, even religions. Still, ideas do, in some sense, reproduce and are subject to selection. So "memetics" does show some promise at least.

A more solid example of universal Darwinism, however, is perhaps the most significant. Much recent research in machine intelligence concerns using Darwinian processes to move computers beyond pre-programmed responses, having them produce genuine creative novelty, even if only in narrow contexts so far. Indeed, there are very good reasons to believe that ultimately *our own* intelligence and creativity relies on Darwinian processes in the brain!

Darwin vs. God?

Today, with Darwin's ideas spilling over far beyond biology, the Darwinian challenge to religion is much broader than it once was. Our religions have typically imputed creativity to minds standing apart from mere nature, claiming that spiritual realities shape the material world. If we universalize Darwinism, however, we do much more than chase God out of biology. Whether in the physics of complexity, brain sciences, or the cultural role of religion, the Darwinian approach substitutes naturalistic explanations where the devout were wont to see the hand of God.

The challenge today's Darwinism presents to religion is also deeper. Back in the nineteenth century, evolutionary ideas emerged as an alternative explanation to intelligent design. Evolutionary thinkers set aside the products of design, and said that life was not so similar to these artifacts, that a mindless process was in fact responsible for their origin. But if our own creativity is rooted in Darwinian variation-and-selection, this sharp division comes into question again. For then, if life is a direct result of

Darwinian evolution, our artifacts are indirectly also Darwinian products. In that case, religion is in deep trouble. Traditionally, divine creativity has been conceived of analogously to human creativity, leading to the classical design argument. Now, this analogy cannot even get started, because our own minds appear to be completely rooted in the randomness and mindless mechanisms of the material world.

In other words, it is no accident skeptics about religion are usually such great fans of Darwin. His ideas are, in fact, central to a thoroughgoingly naturalistic picture of the world.

Unfortunately, it also no surprise that opposition to evolution so consistently appeals to religious people. Though creationists are masters of the bad argument, their basic intuition that modern evolutionary theory has a corrosive effect on religion is correct. Liberal assurances that Darwin's ideas are no threat to spirituality are at best evasive. So anti-evolutionary reactions are not about to go away; we can expect creationism to flare up with regularity in deeply religious cultures like the US and the Islamic world.

[ABOUT THE AUTHOR]

Taner Edis is Assistant Professor of Physics at Truman State Univeristy in Kirksville Missouri. He is the author of numerous articles on physics, philosophy, artificial intelligence, and anti-evolutionary thought.

[ADDITIONAL RESOURCES]

All of this is very interesting, but it is only a short taste of a long argument. In finding out more about evolution and religion, particularly the implications of Universal Darwinism, the following may be helpful:

www2.truman.edu/~edis

Taner Edis, *The Ghost in the Universe: God in Light of Modern Science* (Amherst: Prometheus, 2002).

Daniel C. Dennett, *Darwin's Dangerous Idea: Evolution and the Meanings of Life* (New York: Simon and Schuster, 1995).

Nature's God Tries to Clean up the Mess

by Marie Alena Castle

Evolution is basically an evil process, although not without a major redeeming feature-after all, we're here. Its major defect is that it works off of high birth and death rates, a method guaranteed to maximize misery. Its profligacy and random genetic tinkering managed to produce a biosphere filled to every last nook and cranny. A lot of those fillers we could do without... do we really need ticks, mosquitoes and cockroaches? Most life forms inflict incredible torment on each other. They cause disease. They sting, poison, claw, bite, club and shoot each other. Some eat other sentient life forms alive, slowly.

The system also has serious quality control problems, some of which hit where it really counts-us. When an offshoot of the primates evolved an upright posture sufficient for improved survival, the adjustments needed to prevent back problems and sinuses that drain the wrong way were left out. When it evolved a brain large enough to give a truly major survival advantage, its pelvic structure barely kept up with the cranial size, making birth difficult, painful and dangerous. Par for the evolutionary course.

At some point, this primate offshoot's brain became complex enough to produce self awareness, and the optimistically named *homo sapiens* arrived on the scene.

For better or worse it could, unlike all other life forms, contemplate the mindlessly sadistic mess evolution had created. *Homo sapiens* was sapiens enough to see that nature's idea of life-nasty, brutish and short-was a poor one and to start thinking up ways to introduce a few upgrades. An impressive breakthrough! A brain that could learn to take nature's power for its own.

Nature had created its own god!

As is typical of the evolutionary process, it was a barely adequate god, not much deserving of evolution's *Best of the Bunch* award, although it certainly thought it was deserving of such.

Its brain, for all the advantages it offered, had an ongoing problem-a tendency to think that what it imagined was real. While its imagination could be enormously useful in practical ways such as making fire and discovering DNA, it kept getting sidetracked by imagining the world is controlled by a capricious spirit realm of gods, ghosts, angels, demons and whatnot.

Against overwhelming evidence to the contrary, it even imagined that life continued after death and dreamed up all manner of happy-ever-after scenarios, along with some miserable ones to keep in line those who might have a few doubts about all this.

Over the millennia it wasted an awful lot of time and resources catering to, defending and promoting the supernatural products of its imagination. In a total failure of the *sapiens sapiens* part of *homo*, it managed to inflict more human misery over the course of history with this spirit-world idea than with any other.

Despite this, progress was made as nature's newly evolved god set to work trying to fix a few million years' accumulation of design deficiencies.

- It redesigned plants and animals to improve its food supply and even created some nice dogs and cats for companions.
- It redesigned biology to help control diseases, birth defects, and manage procreation.
- It redesigned chemicals to create materials of better quality than evolution supplied. Now it is working at redesigning life itself through genetic manipulation.
- In a growing part of the world, nature's assorted torments are kept at bay with an impressive array of medical, industrial and chemical technology.

Not that all of this has always and everywhere turned out as well as expected. The law of unintended consequences remains in full force and *homo sapiens sapiens* seems determined to move at least one step backward for every two steps forward. And it doesn't always know which way is forward.

Whether nature's god can improve on itself in terms of its erratic mental functioning remains to be seen. It clearly needs a lot of work. It is still driven by primitive impulses that once had survival value but now cause it to do incredibly cruel and stupid things.

Supernatural imaginings still get in the way of making improvements. Magical thinking, though notoriously ineffective, is still popular.

We need to get a grip on reality if we are to succeed in making nature our benefactor instead of our tormentor. Imaginary deities are at best useless and at worst destructive. Besides, they all disagree with each other (just ask their followers). The only god available is good ol' *homo sapiens sapiens*, warts and all. We just have to make the best of it.

[ABOUT THE AUTHOR]

Marie Alena Castle has been a leader in the atheist movement locally and nationally since the 1980s. She is the immediate past president of Atheist Alliance International. Currently she is the communications director for Atheists for Human Rights, a national activists' network that offers a secular moral balance to the religious right's inhumane social agenda. AHR's Moral HighRoad Fund provides scholarships for gay/lesbian atheist students and funding for impoverished women in need of an abortion. Ms. Castle welcomes comments at mac@mtn.org.

[ADDITIONAL RESOURCES]

Atheist Alliance International: http://www.atheistalliance.org

This article is adapted from the Darwin Day Program's award-winning essay of 2001 and appeared in **The National Center for Science Education Reports** *2001 Jan/Apr; 21(1-2): 37-8. It is reprinted with permission from the author.*

MY EXPERIENCES OF EVOLUTION IN SCHOOL
by Brandon Seger

After school had started last fall, I knew that there would be the momentous day later in the year when the biology class would consider evolution. In my Southern California community, there are many religious students at my school, and I anticipated some problems when students who opposed evolution for religious reasons came to class in the week the evolution unit would be presented. Early in the year I spoke with my biology teacher. At first I was concerned that we might not be doing the evolution unit, since a couple of the other biology classes were not going to.

"So after the second semester, we will get into more of the animal chapters?"

"Yes, like the chordates and the invertebrates," replied my teacher.

"As well as evolution?"

My teacher smiled and told me, "Yes, we will be getting into that as well."

A few weeks after, I brought up the issue again. Since I knew that some of the students in the class bitterly rejected the theory of evolution, I asked him about some of his experiences in earlier years of teaching. He informed me that the previous year, when he was teaching the evolution chapter, one girl came up to him after class and presented him with the admonition, "You're going to hell!"

A few months passed, and I had no more conversations with my teacher about the issue. However, about a week before the beginning of March, the teacher showed us his schedule. I saw on the calendar that the following week would be spent studying the evolution chapter. After he presented the schedule, I came up to speak with him more about the following week's plans for teaching the evolution chapter and to learn more about his past experiences. In this conversation, my biology teacher informed me that the chronology of events is the same each year: the first day, the students are very quiet, and then the next day, the students come back outraged. He assumes that the students go home to their parents and then return the next day, fortified by their parents' opposition to the chapter, but this year it was to be a little different.

On the first day of the evolution unit, I walked to my biology class early and sat down at my desk. I watched as the students came in and grabbed the evolution chapter packet, piled in a stack near the entrance door. Only one student class growled in displeasure as she picked up the packet and glanced at the bold, black title "Evolution".

After the bell rang, the teacher walked to the center of the room, and before doing the lecture, he presented a "disclaimer", as he called it. In this disclaimer, he told the class that everyone has a right to his or her personal beliefs, that the purpose of the day's presentation was not to change anyone's beliefs, but that it is state law to teach the chapter. All the students sat quietly and listened to the teacher's speech. The first day ran more smoothly than I had anticipated, but it was what the teacher had experienced in the past.

On the following day, our teacher showed a section of the Carl Sagan video "Cosmos" in class. In this particular video clip, Sagan discussed the origin of life and commented on evolution. At one point in the video, there was an animated scene that traced the path of life on the earth, showing animals evolving from primitive organisms to modern ones. Just as this video was finishing, a burst of laughter came from a couple of students from the opposite side of the room. They were apparently laughing because they found the material to be unbelievable

For the rest of the unit, we completed the worksheets in the study packet, as well as a myriad of labs (on topics such as divergent evolution and variations in a population). Through it all, rather than passionate outbursts from the students opposed to evolution, as I had originally expected, these students simply made fun of evolution. On the day of the variations lab, a group of students was laughing and ridiculing evolution ("Hey teacher, since we have long fingers, does that mean we evolved from ducks?" and "If evolution is true, why don't I look changed in the morning?"). Later on, as the bell rang and the students left the room, I was headed out when I heard my teacher say with vexation, "Man, they don't pay attention. They're expecting to be wolves in the morning. It doesn't work that way."

The other notable event of the evolution unit was the test made up of 66 multiple-choice questions and an essay. For the essay, the students had to write about either the differences between Lamarck's and Darwin's evolutionary theories or the evidence for evolution. I chose to write on the evidence, so I could summarize the evidence and provide some of my own commentary.

I asked the teacher about the results, and he informed me that there were some students who doodled in their study packets (such as drawing the face of the devil), as well as a few students who wrote their entire essay explaining why they thought evolution is false.

These were my unfortunate experiences of learning evolution in school. I hope that supporters of evolution can improve the situation by promoting a better public understanding of evolution, and science in general for that matter. The willful rejection of evolution by students is more tragic because they never learned what evolution really is. They just retreated into their ignorance and ridiculed ideas that they did not understand. ∞

[ABOUT THE AUTHOR]

Brandon Seger is a high school student residing in Bakersfield, California. His interests include reading, writing, internet browsing, music, theater, arts, and school. For career interests, he wants to enter a field that involves helping others. His life motto is "Let reason be our guide, and let love be our inspiration."

Darwin's Day was first presented for the Sunday Supplement opinion programme on the National Radio station in New Zealand for Darwin Day 2002.

DARWIN'S DAY

by Vicki Hyde

It's an author's dream – you work on your book for twenty years and when it finally hits the shops, it sells out in one day flat. No, not *Harry Potter*, but a book that far fewer have read but which has had, and will continue to have, a much greater impact on society than any fantasy frolic.

The book? Charles Darwin's *Origin of Species*.

And why should we be interested in a book published almost 150 years ago? Well, February 12th is Darwin Day, celebrated internationally to honour Darwin's ideas which are still hotly debated, even called dangerous.

We may snigger at American fundamentalists trying to have the seven days of Creation, the 6,000-year-old Earth and Noah's Flood taught in science classrooms, but it happens here in New Zealand too, and at some of our best state schools. Even those teachers confident of their grounding in science tread warily when challenged by religiously motivated pupils – it is not acceptable to look as if you might be questioning a strongly held belief, even if does contradict the curriculum.

I don't have a problem with creation stories as metaphors for what some would see as a Divine Creator at work, but I object when these are pushed in the science classroom in an attempt to use the mantle of science to cloak personal beliefs. Even more so when they flat-out contradict things we do know for a fact. And by any measurement, the claims of young-Earth creationists are on the same intellectual plane as those of flat-Earthers.

I guess half the problem is that we always hear about the "theory" of evolution, which for most of us suggests that it's just an idea we're not sure about. But Darwin's theory is a lot more solid than the general use of the term would have us realise.

Darwin made two major propositions. The first is that evolution has occurred; the second concerns how it happened. Darwin saw it as a process of natural selection, more popularly and less accurately referred to as "survival of the fittest".

It is this process which is still being debated as part of the challenge that any theory meets in science, but that does not detract from the powerful nature of Darwin's concept of evolution, nor from its underpinning foundation of fact after fact after fact.

Evolution is a scientific "fact", in the sense that Stephen Jay Gould uses the word "fact" – something confirmed to such a degree that it would be perverse to withhold provisional assent.

And perverse creationists are, twisting and bending almost every aspect of science to shoehorn God and His Creation into their rigidly defined box. As we learn more and more about the history of our planet, it becomes clearer and clearer just how perverse is the reasoning involved in dogmatic young-Earth creationism.

We find layer after layer of glacial sediments, and are told these were laid down by Noah's Flood, even if it implies glaciers motoring along at over 10 kilometres an hour to do so. We discover link after link in the chain of life, and infinitely more are demanded. We see vast ages open up in the form of fossils and quasars, and are told this is a cosmic test by God of our faith.

Science is all about this sort of discovery, evidence, facts. So-called creation science has none of these.

I think one of the most perverse things about creationists is the vast intellectual dishonesty that is involved. One of the best science toy stores in Christchurch, NZ stocks a large range of creationist books. These tomes claim Earth to be 6,000 years old, state that every type of living thing was created by God all at once in immutable form, and even have drawings of stegosaurs inside Noah's Ark. And these sit alongside displays of dinosaur skeletons, real million-year-old fossils and posters of stars being born. Where's the honesty in that?

I'm comfortable sitting on the fence with regard to the ultimate questions of creation, and I enjoy looking over the sides and seeing the various explanations people have come up with, medieval or modern, religious or scientific, to explain how we arrived where we are today.

But I have to agree with philosophy professor Michael Ruse, when he says that would-be "scientific" creationism is a grotesque parody of human thought and a downright misuse of human intelligence. In short, to the believer, it is an insult to God."

Darwin, who once studied for the clergy, would no doubt agree. ∞

[ABOUT THE AUTHOR]

Vicki Hyde is a science popularizer by choice; a Website development manager by profession. Vicki has been awarded the Science and Technology Medal of New Zealand and has been made a Companion of the Royal Society of New Zealand. The Web-based *SciTech Daily Review* edited by Vicki was a nominee in the Sixth Annual Webby Awards, recognized as one of the top five science sites in the world. Vicki has been Chair-entity of the New Zealand Skeptics for ten years.

[ADDITIONAL RESOURCES]

Sci-Tech Daily: http://www.scitechdaily.com

New Zealand Skeptics: http://skeptics.org.nz/

Royal Society of New Zealand: http://www.rsnz.govt.nz/

SPECIAL SECTION

PBS presents Evolution:
A Journey Into Where We're From and Where We're Going

evolution

PANEL DISCUSSION ON EVOLUTION

NSTA Annual Conference,
San Diego, CA

March 27, 2002

Bill Jersey
(producer of Evolution's seventh episode, What About God?)

Carl Zimmer
(award-winning science journalist and author)

Dr. Kenneth Miller
(cell biologist)

Dr. Eugenie Scott
(executive director of National Center for Science Education)

Roger Bybee,
Founder of BSCS, presider

Julie Benyo,
Education Director of the Evolution Project, presider

(This transcript has been edited for clarity. Some information has been added to illustrate video or powerpoint slides used in the presentation.)

Roger Bybee: I don't need to tell you that we've had long and continuing struggles with teaching evolution in our schools. You should know that the individuals you're going to hear are the advocates for you, the science teachers. They're out there doing the good work of making sure that you have the right to teach biological evolution in your courses. This afternoon, they have selected "Capturing Billions of Years of Life on Screen, on the Web, and in Print." I'm going to turn this over to Julie Benyo from WGBH, who will introduce the panel.

Julie Benyo: Welcome, everyone. We're glad you could make it. Almost three years ago, WGBH, the Nova Science Unit in Boston, and Clear Blue Sky Productions, a Seattle-based production company, began the development of a multimedia project that resulted in Evolution. In September 2001, the seven-part, eight-hour series premiered on PBS.

Evolution is a topic, as we all know, that can generate a lot of interest, and also a lot of controversy, across a wide spectrum of activities, from the ongoing educational standards battles that are occurring in states like Ohio, to forming the basis of a good or sometimes not-so-good movie like Jurassic Park or Planet of the Apes. Our version of evolution aims to entertain, inform, and educate general viewers, but especially teachers and students, about the scientific theory of evolution, the evidence, the processes, and what we still don't know.

Evolution provides a multimedia way to explore the topic. In addition to the broadcast series, there is an extensive Web site, a digital library that provides access to over 800 resources on evolution, online professional development that's free, and aims to improve content knowledge, teaching methodologies, and strategies for dealing with the controversy that can sometimes occur. There are teacher methodology videos that show real teachers in classrooms across the country, teaching evolution. There are classroom videos, and these are just short, four-to-seven minute videos that you can use as discussion starters; online student lessons, where they can explore various concepts in evolution; a 40-page teacher's guide; and 25 teachers that are around the country, working to help other teachers – their colleagues – become better prepared to teach evolution. All of these resources are free, available through our Web site. There's also a companion book to the series, and you'll hear more about that today.

Today's panelists will be talking to you about various aspects of the project. Bill Jersey is the producer of Evolution's seventh episode, "What About God?" Producer, cameraman, and director, Bill Jersey founded Quest Productions, a leading producer of documentary films, series, and specials for PBS, cable, and major television networks, over 35 years ago. Jersey's body of work exemplifies a lifelong commitment to the exploration of important social issues on American television. He's currently completing a four-hour documentary series, "The Rise and Fall of Jim Crow," for PBS.

Carl Zimmer is an award-winning science journalist and author. His first book, *At the Water's Edge*, followed scientists involved with solving two intriguing evolutionary puzzles: how fish walked ashore, and how whales returned to the sea. It was followed in 2000 with *Parasite Rex*, which explored the bizarre world of nature's most successful life forms. His latest book, *Evolution: The Triumph of an Idea*, is a companion volume to this PBS television series. From 1994 to '99, he was senior editor at Discovery. He currently writes for magazines including National Geographic, Science, Audubon, and Natural History, where he regularly contributes a column on evolution. He's currently working on a book about the dawn of neurology.

Dr. Ken Miller is a cell biologist and professor of biology at Brown University. He received his Ph.D. in cell biology from the University of Colorado, and then served as a lecturer and assistant professor at Harvard University. He's been with Brown University since 1980. His research focuses on the structure and function of biological membranes. He's also co-author, with Joe Levine, of several widely-used high school and college biology textbooks. Professor Miller's interest in evolution came about when he was approached by a group of students who encouraged him to debate Henry Morris, a well-known creationist. In 1997, he appeared on "Firing Line," in a "Firing Line" debate on evolution, and recently completed the book, *Finding Darwin's God*.

Finally, Dr. Eugenie Scott is the executive director for the National Center for Science Education, and she's been in that role since 1987. We encourage all of you to join this great organization. The Center is a pro-evolution, nonprofit science education organization with members in every state. She holds a Ph.D. in biological anthropology from the University of Missouri, and has taught at the University of Kentucky and the University of Colorado, and in the California state university system. She's nationally recognized as a proponent of church/state separation, and has served on the executive committee of the National Coalition for Public Education and Religious Liberty. She frequently is called upon by radio, print, and television media as a spokesperson for the scientific view when conflicts arise between scientific and pseudoscientific explanations.

We welcome them all, and I'm sure you'll hear some wonderful information from them. We will open the floor to questions afterwards. Thank you.

Bill Jersey: It took Charles Darwin 21 years to go from the onset of an idea to the publication of it. Now, I assume that there were many reasons for it. I assume one reason was the concern over the dangerousness of his idea, which continues to be dangerous today. I also think he probably knew intuitively or cognitively that an idea is only as good as its telling, that great ideas frequently languish because they're not told well. And if we do anything well, or try to do anything well, we try to tell good stories. We try to explicate ideas in interesting ways.

It certainly was what I intended to do when I was hired by WGBH and Clear Blue Sky Productions to do the last program in the series, which was then called "Evolution Wars." And we went through the process of getting ideas and submitting them, and everything went well, and our advisors were helpful, and everybody was helpful. And I did what we call a rough cut. And the rough cut is basically the story as you understand it, with all the main characters, all the main ideas, narration, a little music thrown in to keep people awake and interested. And I took it to WGBH in Boston. Now, a lot of things were said after the screening, but the thing I remembered most was our chief science advisor said, "You don't know how terrible those people are." And I thought to myself, oh boy, my assignment is to make the greatest meatloaf ever, and deliver it to a conference of vegetarians.

Well, fortunately, it wasn't that bad, as it turns out, since it was neither a meatloaf nor a conference of vegetarians. But it did remind me that I had a problem. And

I realized that the problem was not that I didn't know how terrible they were. The problem was that I knew too much, and I assumed my audience was on the same page as I was on, and they weren't. I grew up a fundamentalist, so I knew about their arrogance and anger, but I also knew about their fear and ignorance. I remember when Richard Dawkins, who cannot be accused of being too friendly to religion, came to the United States. He said the surprise was not the hostility that met him, but the ignorance. And I think that probably was the motivation for doing this series by the Clear Blue Sky folks, and WGBH. The issue is really not so much the hostility – though there is a fair amount of that – but the ignorance.

And you know, of course, that evolution is so important, and why it's important. It's important if we're going to understand the consequences of the genetic revolution, if we're going to understand the consequences of drugs and so forth, you all know better than I the importance of these things. And so we started off writing, and this notebook is what we came up with. [ed.note: He's holding up a notebook to the audience.] It's interesting what they called this. They called it The Evolution Bible. And the reason they called it The Evolution Bible is because it is a guide that gives a sense of where we fit in the total picture. This is a series, and a series has to have connective tissues. Otherwise it's not a series, it's just a collection of disparate elements. So they worked a long time on this, and then we went to evolution school. For those of us who were art majors, a lot of this was very new. And the eminent Dr. Miller, among others, told us more than we could absorb. But it was all interesting.

And I'd like to show you clips from the series, especially those of you who haven't seen it. But we don't have time to show too many clips, so I thought I'd show, as the first clip, the question that's probably on all of your minds right now, which is, "Why sex?" Roll the tape, please.

[The audience viewed Segment 2 from the "Why Sex?" episode. For more details, go to the Evolution series index found on page 38 of the Evolution teacher's guide (and which is available online at www.pbs.org/wgbh/evolution/educators/teachstuds/tguide.html).]

So after seven hours of entertainment and enlightenment, we come to the question, "What about God?" Well, it was both, as I think John Foster Dulles first said, in my hearing, an embarrassment of riches, and a tyranny of large numbers. There were so many issues to address, some on a very sophisticated level, and some on a pretty primitive level. But we decided that we'd look for the area in which it seemed to make the most difference to us collectively, corporately, in America. And we felt that there were three areas we wanted to go into. One was the area with people like Ken Ham, who are biblical literalists, and adamantly opposed to evolution in any form. And the second was schools, where the confrontation was outside of the church, and maybe not biblical literalism, but might involve things like the so-called intelligent design movement.

But I also wanted to find a group of people who were struggling personally. So the first sequence in "What about God?" is Ken Ham. I'm going to jump over that, since I presume you know the position of the biblical literalists – how the development of life happened so quickly and efficiently – and move onto the situation that some of you may be well familiar with too, which is the conflict in the schools. And we're going to show a piece from Jefferson High School in Indiana.

[The audience viewed Segment 9 from the "What About God?" episode.]

So for Clare McKinney, it was clear. She'd gone through the process of looking at religion, and looking at science, and came out feeling comfortable with both. But I wasn't happy with this sequence as the total story, because it seemed to me that we didn't get a sense of what it was really like, what life was like for those kids. And it seems to me that if you're going to tell a story, you're going to create a drama, and drama requires conflict. So you're looking for a place where the conflict was personal. It was not just community conflict, as this was in Indiana. We found a young man at Wheaton College in Wheaton, Illinois, an evangelical school. His relationship with his parents gave us a better understanding of what the experience was like to grow up believing in a God who created this world in a few days, 10,000 or so years ago. So I want you to listen to Nathan Baird and his family. Nathan Baird is the college student. He comes home to visit with his parents, and he raises the question of what his parents think, or particularly his father thinks about evolution, and wants them to understand about what he thinks about what he's learned at Wheaton College.

[The audience viewed Segment 4 from the "What About God?" episode.]

The key for me is always access, that I'm not interested in telling you what they think. I'm very interested in bringing you into their world, so hopefully you can experience what they think. And while I suppose many of you might think, well, but he's just a fool, I hope you saw also in that sequence that that was a father who was willing to listen to his son. Will he ever be converted? Well, probably not. Because those who are absolutist in their thinking don't leave a lot of room for dialogue. But there was a caring and a loving there, and I hope that came through too. And ultimately, we'll see one little piece at the end, which I think we'll have time for. You'll see the conclusion that Nathan came to after his experience in the science department.

But one always gets criticism, when one makes any kind of a television program, about what you don't put in. And of course, I got some very angry notes from intelligent design folks. But I have to tell you that they were invited, at Wheaton College, at a symposium on the age of the earth, which we filmed. I met an editor of their magazine, and I liked him a lot. We discussed his participation. He was very happy to participate, to be on the panel at Wheaton College, along with Dr. Miller from Kansas, who was going to present his support of evolution. And then one day I got a phone call, and he said, "I'm not going to be on your program." And I said, "Golly, can you tell me why?" He said, "Call Discovery Institute." So I called them, and they said, "He's not going to be on the program because this is a fraud. Seven hours on evolution, and then just one hour on alternate ideas." I think it was Phillip Johnson who said to me, "We only get one hour?" I said, "No, Phil, you don't get one hour. If you get five minutes you'll be lucky."

But they were offended that so little time was given to their theory. But they were given the opportunity. They refused it and, I must say, were very angry with me that I didn't include them. And I said, "You had a chance to, and you weren't part of it." So we can only include what we have access to. And I think the key word is gaining access. It's letting people know that you care about who they are. You care about their struggle, and ultimately I hope you'll see the whole series, so you can see that there's struggle from the beginning to end, that Darwin's struggle is replicated today in many homes, in many parts of the world. We hope that there will be some empathetic understanding of the religious impulse. I think it was you, Ken Miller, who had said something about science not making itself the oracle for all wisdom? Am I misquoting you?

Ken Miller: I wish I had said that.

Bill Jersey: Well, okay. You now can. And you don't even have to attribute it to me, and I won't accuse you of plagiarism. But I think that's where I come from, and I think the statement we tried to make in the last show, is that the religious impulse has a place in most people's lives, and we want to affirm that. We don't want, however, people to feel that a belief system that gains us access to a certain sort of wisdom will therefore gain us access to all wisdom. Although as Ken Ham reminded us when we did his program, if you can't trust the bible in science, you can't trust it in ethics. Well, Ken, I have to tell you, I don't agree with you. It's two different domains, and to understand what each brings, I think, is to understand the best of all possible worlds.

Let's see what Nathan concluded at the end of his year at Wheaton, after visiting with his parents and hearing the presentation of Dr. Miller from Kansas at Wheaton College. He finally concluded the following.

[The audience viewed the end of Segment 9 from the "What About God?" episode.]

Carl Zimmer: There was a joke that I heard more than once among the producers at WGBH – that they had eight hours to cover 4 billion years. I had a bit more luxury. I had about 320 or 330 pages. But still, it was a pretty tall order. And it was really quite an extraordinary experience, from the very beginning. I basically got a call out of the blue, at the end of 1999, saying, "We're working on this evolution project, and there's going to be a TV series. And we were hoping that you would write a book that would go along with it. And basically, it would cover all of evolutionary biology from Aristotle to the Human Genome Project." And I said yes. And then it didn't take too long for me to realize I had about a year to do it. So, basically I cleared out my entire life and went to work.

We agreed that this would not be a summary of the series. That really wouldn't even be possible, because television and publishing work on different schedules. They hadn't even really started shooting yet when I started writing the book. They knew the areas that they were going to cover, and they wanted me to write a book that generally addressed the same areas, and going into more detail, things that they couldn't possibly get into. For example, there is an episode called "What About God?" I have a chapter of the same name, where I talk about some of these issues. There's an episode called "Why Sex?" and I have a chapter as well, about sex and evolution. But I also had the luxury of going into detail about things that I think are very important for people to understand in order to get an idea of how the science of evolution really hangs together. So for example, I think the figure is about 45% of

Americans think that the Earth is 10,000 years old or less. So I felt it was important to write about how that's not true, how geologists know that the Earth is 4.5 billion years old, and how they know that life is probably at least 3.8 billion years old.

And I went about it as the science journalist that I am. I went to the scientific literature to see what was the major research going on, the major findings. And then I called up a lot of the leading scientists to find out, what were the important things that were going on. What are the unresolved debates that are going on in science? And hopefully, what I came up with is something that reflects what I've felt in writing about evolution for some years now, which is that, really, evolution is an exceptional science. Because it's a kind of science that brings together all sorts of different kinds of sciences under one sort of big tent, as it were. I mean, evolution has applications in medicine. Computer programmers are very interested in evolution to help them solve their problems. It's this wonderful kind of meeting place for different sorts of scientists. And right now, we really are in a golden age of evolutionary biology.

So just to give you an example of this wonderful sort of coming together of sciences, I wanted to pick out one example which draws on some of the things I talk about in the book. So, what do geology and germs have in common? One of the most interesting realizations that I had in working on this book was that Darwin really started out in life, or in his career, as a geologist. We think of him as the quintessential biologist, but that's not true at all. In fact, when he went out on his voyage of the Beagle, it was really to look at mountains and coral reefs and so on, to look at a lot of geological structures that he was most excited about.

At the time, as he was traveling on the Beagle, he was reading a book that would prove to be the fundamental influence on him, called *The Principles of Geology*, by Charles Lyell. This image [projected on the screen, which also appears on pg. 17 of Zimmer's book, *Evolution: The Triumph of an Idea*] is from the frontispiece. It's the ruins of a temple that really impressed Charles Lyell because you could actually see that the sea level had risen to the tops of the pillars after they had been built, and then had fallen back down again. The reason you could tell was that there are marks left at the top of the pillars where, I believe, bivalves had attached themselves. The point of this picture, and Lyell's whole book, was that slow, gradual tiny processes that we can actually see in front of us, like erosion by rain, or tiny rises in sea level, or even earthquakes, could, if they had enough time, gradually build up to produce large differences. And Darwin was so inspired by Lyell that he basically tried to apply it everywhere he could. He looked at the Andes, and tried to figure out, if he could understand how the Andes formed by thinking about Lyell, and it turned out that he could.

Now, along the way, Darwin did a little bit of zoology. He gathered lots and lots of dead animals and plants and so on, including some birds. He was a bit of a dilettante when he gathered these birds, which come from the Galápagos Islands. He didn't really even take careful notes about where they were from. But when he got back to England, as he was being recognized as a really promising young geologist, he got very puzzled by the birds. They didn't fit into the standard way that people thought about how species were created because they were very different looking birds. You've got these birds with these very different kinds of beaks. But they turn out to be all finches, and they're living on islands right next to each other. So how could you explain having such different kinds of birds, unique to these islands, looking so different, and yet having these underlying similarities? Darwin started to think that maybe these ideas that Lyell had been proposing about rocks could apply to life, that maybe slow changes could change one species into another.

This next image is of pigeons [image appears on pg. 47 of Zimmer's book]. It's a nice old print of pigeons. Darwin was really impressed by how pigeon breeders could breed all sorts of amazing breeds just by choosing which pigeons in each generation would get to reproduce. So they would favor certain pigeons with certain traits, and then over time, they could produce really dramatic differences. So Darwin thought, well, this is what happens when a person is controlling the reproduction of pigeons. What happens in nature? Because obviously some animals get to reproduce more than others, and there's variation in nature as well. What happens? Well, Darwin suggested that maybe in nature you could get even more dramatic changes, because you had so much time in which to do it. Because geologists, influenced by Lyell, began to realize the Earth probably wasn't just a few thousand years old. It might have been a lot of time. And you could produce lots of changes.

So for example, you might be able to, in the process, even create new species. This image [found on page 26 of Zimmer's book] is a tree that he sketched out in one of his private notebooks many years before he wrote *The Origin of Species*. And he published another tree in *The Origin of Species* in 1859. Trees really have become a fundamentally important way in which biologists look at life. And today, scientists can get a real good look at natural selection happening by studying trees. And one of the best places to look at it are in viruses and bacteria, things that make us sick.

You have influenza virus, for example. You have to bear in mind, Darwin wrote *The Origin of Species* a few years before Louis Pasteur came up with his experiments that helped to bring together the germ theory of disease. But viruses and bacteria reproduce. They mutate very quickly, and they then compete with each other, and experience natural selection. And that has a lot to do with why we get sick. So for example, the influenza virus. I believe about 20,000 people die of influenza every year. It's a big public health issue. How do scientists study influenza to understand ways to fight it? They study its evolution.

This next image is kind of a modern twist on that tree that I showed you before. This came out a couple years ago, in the journal Science. [No image available.] Scientists took the DNA of influenza viruses from 1983 to 1997. They were able to reconstruct how they had evolved, how they had split off in different branches. Some branches hit a dead end. Other branches gave rise to the next year's virus. It turns out that by studying the evolution of these viruses, you can actually start to get an idea of how to predict which strains are going to give rise to next year's flu season. This is a big problem in designing flu vaccines, because scientists often don't know what's coming next. It might be possible, by studying these trees, that you might be able to say, "Okay, this is the strain that's going to be hitting us next year."

HIV is another virus that's perhaps even more devastating today. I believe about 35 million people are infected by it. Unlike the flu and other diseases, HIV is pretty new. There aren't records of people suffering from AIDS 100 or 200 years ago. So the question is, where did it come from? This is also an important aspect of studying medicine. Where do diseases come from? How can we be on our guard for new diseases emerging? Again, you have to study the evolution of these diseases to figure that out. And again, an evolutionary tree, in Darwin's tradition, is exactly where you need to go.

This image also appears on pg. 220 of my book. Basically, scientists were able to build a tree of all of the strains of HIV on Earth. They then found that they actually emerged from a deeper tree, a tree of viruses that infect another species altogether. The closest relatives of HIV live in chimps. And it turns out that the virus has jumped from chimps – and actually, I should say, another species of primate called a mangabey – as many as six or seven times in less than 100 years. And then it turns out that if you look at those primate viruses, you can figure out where they came from. They came from big cats, like lions, for example. So this virus, this group of viruses, has been jumping over millions of years from one host to the next, and we are just its latest victim. If you didn't know about evolution, you'd have no way of knowing about the incredible history that this virus has had, and you might not be able to find these sorts of clues to know how to deal with the disease.

Now, I've been talking about viruses. Bacteria are a bit different, just in the sense that they're more like us. They're more alive, in a sense. They have membranes. They have their own DNA. They don't have to hijack our DNA to reproduce. But bacteria also evolve quickly, much like viruses do. And the crisis that we have these days with antibiotics is an evolutionary crisis. The evolution of bacterial resistance happens in two different ways. One way is through what you could call standard evolution. In other words, you have one bacterium. It divides. You have two new copies of DNA. One of those copies might mutate in the process. You have a new kind of DNA, a new gene. And that particular bacterium may do better than other bacteria, take off, and basically come to dominate the species. If that gene happens to be something that helps them resist antibiotics even a little, it can become very common. Given that bacteria can breed very quickly in some circumstances, you can get bacterial resistance to happen pretty fast.

But it can happen even faster, because in the single-celled world, heredity is kind of a funny thing. You have to imagine, what would happen if you shook someone's hand and immediately some of their genes penetrated your skin and became incorporated into every cell of your body – maybe turned your brown eyes blue, or made you gain 50 pounds, or something like that. It's a weird thought, but that's kind of what happens with bacteria. They trade genes, and they trade genes a lot. It can happen in a lot of different ways. This slide on the projection screen shows a few different ways. [No image available.] Viruses can actually jump from one bacterium to another, and carry genes along with them, and paste them into their new bacterial home. Bacteria can just sort of join up together and trade genes that way. Bacteria can die, and other bacteria can just slurp up the DNA that's in the environment. So if they pick up a gene that gives them some sort of advantage – for example, antibiotic resistance – boom, evolution is going to happen again, and resistance is going to spread.

The study of the evolution of antibiotic resistance is a very big field. I'll show you just a couple of headlines, to give you a sense that when medical researchers study this, they are studying an evolutionary phenomenon. But what's really interesting is that this brings medicine back around to geology. Now, how is that the case? Well, scientists have been able to compare the DNA of lots and lots of species, and to start to put together a really big tree of life, to figure out the question of how all the species on Earth are related. The standard tree they've come up with shows you the diversity of life, how different a particular stretch of DNA is in these different organisms. So you can see [on page 102 of Zimmner's book] that we are way off in this little corner or branch of the tree – animals in the upper right hand corner. There's very little distance between us and oak trees when you look at the whole tree of life. So it's really a microbial world. And this is a really important insight that scientists have had.

This is based on the very sound assumption that genes are generally carried down from one generation to the next. Certainly that's how we do it. But it turns out that sometimes genes can hop back and forth. So they can spread from one species to another, and then evolution can make that gene that was in one species become very prevalent in the other one. In fact, it can completely take over the species. There have been some of these sort of genetic trades over time. As you get down to the base of the tree of life, to our presumable common ancestor, you find that the trading was happening a lot. And this may give us a glimpse of what life was like on the early Earth. I'll just show you a very schematic picture of what that might look like [page 107 of Zimmer's book].

So you have a few trades going on recently in the history of life. And at the bottom, you had this kind of genetic orgy going on all over the world, genes just flying all over the place, being traded between microbes 3 or 4 billion years ago. This is an insight that really came from medicine but helps us understand the history of life. And it's particularly important because fossils are very, very, very rare, if you go back to 2 or 3 billion years ago. In a sense geology, through Charles Darwin, gave medicine this incredible gift of understanding how pathogens evolved. And now medicine is able to return the favor by giving a glimpse of what early Earth might have been like. And what unites them is evolution. I think that's what makes evolution such an amazing field.

Kenneth Miller: I thought I would bring you a report from the front. I was privileged, just a couple weeks ago, to speak in Cleveland in front of a huge crowd of 2,500 people, the crowd drawn not by me but by a certain name in the center, Stephen J. Gould. And I was pleased to see that the "Answers in Genesis" Web site wrote this up. They described it as theatrics, and they talked about whether or not Ohio would become the first state of the United States to teach intelligent design theory.

What I talked about in Cleveland – and this is sort of the title for my talk – is entitled "Looking for God in All the Wrong Places: Do the Details of Life Reveal Design or Evolution?" The crowd that we had was, as I say, around 2,500 people in Cleveland, and the reason they were interested in this is because just a week later, in front of the Ohio Board of Education, I and Lawrence Krauss, who is a physicist at Case Western Reserve, defended evolution in front of the Ohio Board of Education, and we were opposed by Jonathan Wells and Stephen Meyer from the Discovery Institute in Seattle, who argued in favor of intelligent design. The debate was widely reported and written up in Time magazine, New York Times, Associated Press, that sort of stuff.

This story is not over, because the Board of Education simply has not decided where they're going to go with this. However, lest you not be from Ohio or Kansas or one of the other states, and lest you think this is some sort of a geographical, regional phenomenon, I would direct you towards this map, which appeared last month [February] in Scientific American. [No image available.] The states in red, which are all over the country, including my own region of New England, are those states in which the science education standards either don't mention evolution, or mention it in a useless or misleading way. As you can see, those states run the gamut from Alaska, Maine, Illinois, Montana, all the way down to Florida and Georgia. So having evolution not presented properly in state science education standards is nothing new. It's nothing regional. And in fact, it's a nationwide problem.

These days, attacks against evolution come under the banner of something very frequently called intelligent design, or intelligent design theory. The fellow in the picture there is Michael Behe, a biochemist at Lehigh University who wrote a book called *Darwin's Black Box*. I put up a couple of other books by Jonathan Wells and by Phillip Johnson that also come under the heading of intelligent design theory. And the intelligent design theory is sort of spearheaded by a single institution called the Discovery Institute, which is based in Seattle, Washington. They have several senior fellows. Among them, the people that we debated in Ohio, Stephen Meyer and Jonathan Wells. There's also Michael Behe, of whom you've probably heard. Another is Phillip Johnson, who is sort of the leader of the movement. Nancy Pearcey is a former speech writer for Pat Buchanan, and another is William Dembski.

They had a wonderful logo. They had a logo at their Web site based on the work of Michaelangelo. It showed God creating what you would recognize as a DNA molecule. I thought that both this piece of art and the name of the subcommittee of the institute, the Center for the Renewal of Science and Culture, are significant, first of all because it shows what they think natural history was like, and secondly, because the notion that science is somehow moribund and needs to be renewed is an extraordinary notion. I don't know about you, but I have a heck of a time keeping up with science, because it's moving so quickly. And I don't get the idea that those of us in biology are stifled by some sort of lack of progress. If anything, things are moving so quickly that quite the opposite is true.

Now, the interesting thing about this logo, which I rather liked for its artistic content, and its theological accuracy, was that just prior to the broadcast of the PBS Evolution series, they changed the logo. The logo that appears now, it seems to me, first of all, artistically it doesn't rise to quite as high a level. Aesthetically, it looks kind of scary. There's a big eye staring down at us from space. But it avoided, I think, the theological content of the previous one, and therefore, that is the logo that currently appears at the Discovery Institute. I think they did this just prior to the PBS series, because in effect they were girding themselves for battle, and they were preparing for battle against the very sort of videos that Bill Jersey showed.

What they essentially argue is that there are a series of scientific objections to evolution – that there are lots of them. I won't go through all of these, but I'll give you one. My own personal point of view is that where there's a specific objection against evolution, the best way to answer it always is with a specific scientific response. So an example would be the issue of mechanism. Phillip Johnson says that science knows of no mechanism capable of accomplishing the enormous changes in form and function required to complete the Darwinist scenario. And I think the easiest way to answer that is simply to cite papers in which we show what those mechanisms are, how we understand that they can create and carry out the changes in form and function. In this case, a paper talking about the remodeling of two proteins, and in another case, a paper talking about the way in which mutations, which we can sort of characterize as being purposeful, can carry out large scale transformations to produce major changes in phenotype.

The famous sticker that was stuck inside of textbooks in Alabama asked students to ask their teachers – to ask you – why do major groups of plants and animals have no transitional forms in the fossil record? And the simplest answer, the simplest response to that, is to say the statement is false. There is a quotation from a report from the National Academy of Sciences which simply says that there are so many intermediate forms that have been discovered between fish and amphibian, amphibians and reptiles, reptiles and primates, and within the primate line of descent, that it is often difficult to identify categorically where the transition occurs from one to another particular species. Far from there being no transitional forms, in many cases, we have an embarrassment of riches.

The charge is frequently made, well, microevolution can be observed, but no one's ever observed macroevolution. Well, it turns out that every study that's every been carried out in nature, basically assessing the rate at which microevolutionary changes take place shows that the rate of change that can be observed in nature in response to environmental stress or environmental changes exceeds the amount that would be necessary to carry out even the most rapid examples of evolutionary change in the fossil record by three to four orders of magnitude. And what that means is that these so-called microevolutionary changes are more than sufficient to drive what we see happening in the fossil record.

One of the charges that we heard in Ohio, and you will hear in your state – I can pretty much guarantee it – is that the scientific community is closed to an idea like intelligent design, because the scientific community is under the control of a sort of Darwinist oligopoly that suppresses novel ideas.

Novel claims come into science all the time. The people who advance those claims usually try to back them up with research, and they subject it to peer review. Now, peer review doesn't mean you write off a paper, and then if somebody rejects it, you go "Oh darn," and you decide to go into economics or history or something like that. Peer review means that you engage in what an economist would call the scientific marketplace of ideas, the give and take of the scientific process. The people advocating intelligent design say, "Well, we've written papers, but they've been rejected." Well, I could paper my wall with the rejection notices that I have had from various scientific journals, and for that matter granting agencies. That's part of the scientific process.

But the important point is, you show up, you carry your idea, you fight hard. And even if people are against you originally, if you can develop the evidence and the experimentation, you will not only get a hearing, you may begin to convince people. And if you do that, you will eventually emerge as part of the scientific consensus, either about what is right and true, or at least about what is possible. And this happens very often for competing theories. And then at that point, automatically, without doing anything else, you begin to wind up in college courses and classrooms and textbooks and so forth and so on.

Now, what about an idea like intelligent design theory? The people behind it argue that they have a very good scientific alternative to evolution. Maybe they do. I would be thrilled if they would simply do what everybody else does in science, which is to engage in this entire process. Their idea, however, of how intelligent design theory should be received, is not this. It's this. [No images available.] They would like to skip all that nasty stuff in between, and they would like to do things like, in Ohio, have an agency of government inject them directly into classroom and textbook. What that turns out to be, I think, is a very poor object lesson for the children of Ohio in how science is done. Because it essentially tells them is that what you do if you have a new scientific idea is you petition the state legislature to pass an act to put it in the classroom, or the board of education, or something along those lines.

Because I have an audience of teachers from around the country today, I want to make an important point. A number of people in Ohio and other states have argued that the "No Child Left Behind" education act, which was signed into law by President Bush on January 8, requires the teaching of intelligent design as an alternative theory to evolution. One provision didn't receive a lot of coverage. It is called the Santorum amendment. The Santorum amendment basically states that because of quality science education preparing students to distinguish data and testable theories from religious or philosophical claims, where topics are taught that may generate controversy, such as biological evolution, the curriculum should help students to understand the full range of scientific views that exist, why such topics may generate controversy, and how scientific discoveries can profoundly affect society.

I would still argue, even if this was law, that this doesn't say anything about intelligent design, because intelligent design is not a scientific theory. It's a philosophical idea. However – and this is the important point – this statement right here [no image available] didn't receive a lot of coverage for a very simple reason. That is, Congress struck it from the bill, and it wasn't in the bill that was passed. Now, this contention that this is the law, and you as teachers in your states and local districts are required to do this, was made at the Ohio debate. And being sort of a corny and theatrical guy, I ran up to the podium with my PowerBook, I plugged it in, and I pointed out that on my computer I happened to have a copy of the education bill which I had downloaded from the Congressional Web site. And very theatrically, I typed in the words of the so-called Santorum amendment, and I did a search in Adobe Acrobat through all 670 pages, looking for an occurrence of the language. And at the end of it, the Adobe Acrobat program, God bless it, comes up and says, "Words not found." And it indicated very clearly that it wasn't in the bill.

So what is the fact? The fact is the so-called Santorum language was struck from the bill in December of 2001. The conference committee would not reinsert it. It was not in the final version of the bill as passed by Congress, and it was not signed into law by President Bush. So where is this language? It turns out that this language survives in what is known as the joint explanatory statement of the conference committee. Senator Santorum inserted this into this language. This was accepted by both houses of Congress. So one might be able to say, technically, that this is attached to or is a provision of law, but the important thing, in terms of reality, is if you look up – and you can do this on the Congressional Web site – public law 110-107, that language is not there, and that language simply does not have the force of law.

Professor Dennis Hirsch of the Capital University Law School, wrote the following opinion. And this is very important to understand. "The decision to remove an amendment from the text of the bill has a very specific legal meaning. It demonstrates that Congress considered the language, and then rejected it." The leading legal textbook on this point, which is the Sutherland book on statutory construction, has this to say: "The rejection of an amendment indicates that the legislature does not intend the bill to include the provisions embodied in the rejected amendment. " Congress deleted the Santorum amendment. This leads to the unavoidable conclusion that it rejected it, and those who would assert otherwise are wrong as a matter of law. I've put up stuff on Web sites and things like this to make this clear, and if you hear someone saying "The education act requires the teaching of intelligent design. It's not an opinion. It's a fact," they are wrong as a matter of law.

I am here not to rant and rave about Ohio, or any of this, but to talk about evolution. And a very interesting thing happened when the Evolution series premiered. And those of you who read the science section of The New York Times may have noticed this. For two weeks prior to the airing of the series, this was the banner headline that appeared at the top of the Science Times. This is one of these things that you buy. And that banner morphed, as you were watching the page, from this into that, the magnum opus of a dying theory. This doesn't sound like something PBS would put out. And then it said, "Get our viewer's guide." I'm watching this, and I'm thinking, wow, this is funny. PBS's Evolution, magnum opus of a dying theory. Get our viewer's guide. And there's a leaf there.

Now, I'm in a room of biologists. I'll bet you that most of you would look at that leaf, and you would know what it's from. It's a gingko leaf. And what is the gingko? The gingko is the only surviving species of a division, a phylum of plants that is otherwise extinct. And that was the symbolism. Well, if you clicked on this, where did you go? You went to a Web site that certainly sounds like it's PBS. It was PBSEvolution.org. Get a viewer's guide. This is great. Must be some of the free stuff that goes along with this. Well, it turns out it wasn't. What you were seeing was a dirty trick of the Discovery Institute. They had registered a Web site that deceptively sounded like PBS's, and what you were getting was a critique of this series from their point of view.

They called it "Getting the Facts Straight," and they offered to sell you this. It was 100- or 150-page booklet arguing with just about everything that is in the series as being unfair, wrong, or misleading. I'll give you an example. They wrote, "Viewers of this series will be told that all living things share the same genetic code. They will be assured that the universality of the genetic code provides, 'powerful evidence that living things evolved in a single tree of life.' What viewers will not be told is that this so-called fact is not true. The supposed fact of the universal genetic code is based on outdated research, says biochemist Michael Behe, professor of biological sciences of Lehigh University, and a Discovery Institute senior fellow." So if you've been telling your students that all organisms share a common genetic code, you have been lying to them.

Now, what's the reason for that? Most of you I'm sure know the answer. And that is, we now know, from studying, for example, the universal genetic code has UGA as the stop codon, and has certain codons coding for three amino acids. It turns out that mitochondrial DNA in mammals and yeast has a number of exceptions to the universal code. For example, AGA functions in our mitochondria as a stop codon, but in the cytoplasm, it's an argenine codon. So these are exceptions to the universal genetic code. They aren't the only one. This is a chart showing the variance in the universal genetic code. Almost all of these are in mitochondrial DNA, but a few of them are in nuclear DNA. But it's also worth pointing out, the standard code is the code that we have and all animals have and, in fact, all plants have in their cytoplasm.

This diagram appeared in a paper by Laura Landwebber of Princeton University in Nature Reviews Genetics in 2001. She talked about the evolvability of the genetic code. This paper was actually cited by the anti-evolution people in the Discovery Institute, saying "the first hard evidence we are given for Darwin's tree of life turns out to be false." Well, I ask you the following question: Is it false because of the variations of the code, that all living things share a common genetic code? And I'll propose an analogy. And that is, let's suppose that last night you watched a PBS history special, and it noted that America and Canada share a common tongue with their colonial ruler, Britain, and that language we share with that country is called English. The next morning, a critic attacked the program as filled with historical misstatements, errors, and omissions – that's what the Discovery Institute said – and the evidence was, the full statement that we share a common language. In Canada, he points out, the word "colour" is spelled with as C-O-L-O-U-R, and in Britain, they call trucks lorries, and this shows that the language is not common, because some words are spelled differently.

As it turns out, that is exactly the case in the genetic code. As it turns out, 48 of the 64 possible codons are identical – identical – in all living organisms, and only 16 of them vary. Moreover, these slight variations actually do something that the Discovery Institute wouldn't even dare to hint at. And that is that they document the evolution of the code itself from a common ancestor. That's how Laurie Landwebber and her associates were able to produce the diagram. That's a process that Darwin called dissent with modification.

Well, being a bit of a trickster myself, what I did was I contacted Professor Landwebber, and I read her the Discovery Institute take on her research as invalidating the notion of a universal genetic code. What she emailed me back was to say that "what you have just read to me is a horrible misrepresentation of the facts. Because it is true, particularly in the tree in our paper and many others, that each nonstandard code is a subtle derivative of the standard genetic code, and that all genetic codes are derived from it." Her associate who did this work, who's now moved from Princeton, was a little blunter than that. "Variation in the code and subsequent adaptation of the code is an exact molecular simile for the variation in finch beak morphology that Darwin famously drew from in order to derive his theory. The slight coding differences we see today hint at an evolutionary plasticity that can accumulate over time into significant change, just as slight variation can lead to different species of birds."

When you see challenges like this, where do you find the answers? Here is a list of answers to all of the objections that have been raised against the PBS series. It is at an outfit called the National Center for Science Education. This is the Web site of the National Center for Science Education [NCSEWeb.org], and this is a plug for Eugenie Scott, who is the executive director of this institute. I wrote three of these rebuttals, but some other absolutely splendid people wrote them as well, and the gist of what I've just told you is there. And when they produce more critical press releases in response to any rebroadcast, you will have more responses at this Web site. It's a fantastic resource, and I would encourage you to go ahead and look at it.

What I'm going to do is I'm going to skip over some points about the nature of the religious conflict with evolution. I'll just show two of them quickly. People who are religious often have several objections to evolution as being too unpredictable, too cruel, and too indirect. I think those objections, as a religious person myself, are illusory. Because the unpredictability of evolution results from the contingency of any historical process. The cruelty of evolution is not a special thing about evolution. It is a fact that every organism that has ever lived will eventually die. I remember a wonderful phrase – Thou art dust and into dust thou shalt return. I don't think it was Charles Darwin who wrote that. But that provides the essential nature of the cruelty of evolution. Is evolution too indirect? If it is, then history in all its forms is also too indirect to be compatible with divine plan and purpose. I don't think it is.

I made this point on the air in the very first episode of the Evolution series. And I wanted to make it a point of priority. And that is that I, and we who did the Evolution series, are not exactly the first people to argue that evolution and religion are compatible. This guy did it first. And what he wrote is he saw no reason why the views given in this volume should shock the religious feelings of anyone, and that person of course was Charles Darwin. And Darwin went on to make the point that it's just as noble of you to believe the deity created a few original forms capable of self-development into other forms, as to believe that he required a fresh act of creation to supply the voids caused by the actions of his laws, and I certainly agree.

We are here because of the PBS Evolution series. And lastly, I wanted to close by pointing something out that has been pointed out elsewhere at these meetings. If you are a teacher, and if you teach evolution, the Evolution Web site at PBS.org/evolution is by far the richest source of teaching material, ancillaries, handouts, exercises, simulations on the teaching of this subject that exists on the Web. There is nothing else that is even in the ballpark of this particular resource. There are things like sex, which always grab student interest. In this case, sex and guppies, and in this particular case, more information than you've ever cared for about the sex life of these guppies, and how we can use them to follow sex and sexual selection. Are we in the midst of a mass extinction? There's a whole series of roundtable discussions here, and you can use this as a point/counterpoint for your students to examine, and to think about critically.

The Evolution Web site has a wonderful series of resources on Darwin as a reluctant revolutionary. It has biological examples galore. It has beautiful graphics and videos. And it even has Charles Darwin's diary. And it's set up in such a way that you can actually watch the development of Darwin's ideas. It's an exceptional resource. I hope you'll all make use of it. I hope that you will all watch the program whether you see it on air or have it on videotape to use again and again.

Eugenie Scott: Needless to say, the anti-evolutionists did not ignore the PBS Evolution program. As Ken pointed out, there was quite a bit of material from various anti-evolution groups opposing the showing of it, the content of it, anything you could possibly think of. Answers in Genesis proclaimed that PBS now stands for "pushing bad science." That gives you a little bit of the tone here.

Well, because this is an educational organization, let me start with just a little bit of background information. Let me give you a quick taxonomy of the anti-evolution movement. The most familiar anti-evolutionists are, of course, the bible-based anti-evolutionists. Young earth creationism, the proponents of creation science. These are the Genesis literalist creationists. And they're very familiar. The second kind is the design-based creationists, who tend not to be biblical literalists so much, but rather tap into a more generalized American cultural uncomfortableness with the idea of a special creator not being actively involved in the natural world, particularly in a creative fashion, the idea of design being very important to these people.

Let's start with the old creationists, the creation science movement. Henry Morris is, hands down, the most important anti-evolutionist of the 20th century. If you thought William Jennings Bryan was important, forget it. Henry Morris is much more important. Henry Morris, until recently, was the director of the Institute for Creation Research, and he is the major proponent of something called scientific creationism. I want to stress "scientific" because that is the claim. The claim is that an essentially biblical literalist view can be made scientific. Using the facts and theories and observations of science, you can prove that the Earth was created in its present form and a very short time ago, approximately 10,000 years. And people like Duane Gish, Henry Morris, and Ken Ham, who of course was featured in Bill Jersey's "What about God?" program, are typical and familiar proponents of this view. There is a great deal of literature of this creation science type, some of which many of you I suspect are familiar with.

The more recent form of creationism, intelligent design, as Ken mentioned, is being promoted right now in Ohio. And some of the people that Ken showed you are Michael Behe, Phillip Johnson, Steve Meyer, William Dembski, and Jonathan Wells. They have also been active in producing quite a literature of anti-evolutionist and pro-intelligent design books and also videotapes.

I want to point out, unfortunately, this last book, Intelligent Design, by William Dembski. The subtitle is, The Bridge Between Science and Theology. I think it's important to realize that the intelligent design movement, which is a major critic of the Evolution program, does have two orientations or concentrations. One attempts to deal only with scientific and philosophical issues. Here we have Michael Behe's concept of irreducible complexity, and William Dembski's concept of the design inference. The second concentration is this cultural renewal component, which I won't detail, because Ken has very kindly pointed out the name of the major intelligent design think tank is the Center for Renewal of Science and Culture. The cultural renewal component is I think illustrated by the subtitle of Dembski's book. This is the bridge. Intelligent design is the bridge between science and theology. So in many respects, the intelligent design anti-evolutionists are not terribly dissimilar from their ancestral creation science forebears.

If I were to summarize intelligent design creationism briefly for people, I would argue that it is a religious movement to promote theism over materialism. It attacks the methodological materialism of science as being indistinguishable and promoting and producing philosophical materialism, and evolution is an example of materialism. It's not that their anti-evolutionism is just because they believe evolution is bad science. They have a much larger goal. These are people who believe that American society is too secular. It is too materialist in the philosophical sense. Not materialist in the sense that we all want new stereos, but materialist in the philosophical sense of denying God. And they want to change this. They want to bring especially Christianity, Christian religion, into the body politic, and into our daily lives to a much higher degree, and into our public institutions like education and science.

And in order to get the attention of the public, they seize upon evolution as the aspect of science for which the methodological materialist assumptions of science do have philosophical or religious implications. When you think about it, evolution is no more philosophically materialist than cell division, but cell division doesn't have the existential and religious implications of evolution, so they focus in on evolution as part of this larger religious movement.

The evidence for my perspective here can be found if you look carefully at the Web site of the Center for Renewal of Science and Culture, where they write their goals are "to defeat scientific materialism and its destructive moral, cultural, and political legacies, to replace materialistic explanations with the theistic understanding that nature and human beings are created by God." This is a specifically religious effort, even though they try to present to the general public that it is a fully scientific perspective.

I want to call your attention to this particular phrase – scientific materialism. That is an odd phrase. I want to spend just a tiny bit of time on this, because I think it's important in understanding one of the major objections to evolution that teachers run into quite regularly. The word materialism refers to matter and energy. Matter, energy, and their interactions. We have in science something called methodological materialism, which is simply the way we do science. In science, we're trying to understand the natural world by using matter, energy, and their interactions – by using material cause. We limit ourselves in science to explaining the natural world using natural cause. This is very different from another kind of use of the term materialism, which is philosophical materialism. A philosophical materialism is a philosophical view that there is no God. The universe consists only of matter and energy. It is not a scientific view. It is a philosophical view. Many people look at the evidence of science and may come to that conclusion, but it is not compelled by science. After all, there are many people who are scientists and who are theists. There are many scientists who are non-theists who are philosophical materialists. Science itself does not compel you to one view or the other. They are not the same.

The intelligent design creationists work very hard to confuse methodological with philosophical materialism in their efforts to confuse the public about evolution and whether evolution should be taught to students in schools. The anti-PBS Evolution movement was, of course, mentioned in more detail by Ken. The Discovery Institute presents its diatribe against the PBS Evolution program at ReviewEvolution.com. And as Ken mentioned, if you go to NCSEWeb.org, our Web site, go to the resources section of our page, and look at PBS Evolution. You will find what he very kindly showed you as a number of sources of refutation for this.

Let me just talk about a couple of the critiques. I may skip over a couple of these because Ken dealt with them in more detail. The Discovery Institute claims that the PBS Evolution series is scientifically inaccurate, claiming that it doesn't present the scientific problems with the evidence for Darwinian evolution. Of course, the inaccuracies are not especially accurate. Again, our Web page resources deal with these in more detail. I want to just give you a couple of quick examples.

The Discovery Institute, as the example Ken gave, the genetic code is based on outdated science that has been invalidated by more recent research. Well, we've talked not only to Ken, but we've talked to Norman Pace who actually does research in this area. And he points out the same point that Ken made, that all of the – and Laura Landwebber – that the variants are actually evolved forms of the code that we are most familiar with.

The Discovery Institute criticizes the series for omitting disagreement. "The systematic omission of disagreements among evolutionary biologists themselves about central claims in this series, and the complete failure to report the view of scientists who dispute Darwinism at its roots." Well, again, Ken talked about this a little bit more, so I'll just skip through it. For example, they say, "Consider Stuart Kauffman." Kauffman is one of the leading lights in a group of scientists exploring complexity theory – roughly, the idea that complex systems can organize themselves explicitly as an alternative to natural selection. "No mention is made of Kauffman or his colleagues in the seven-hour series." So Stuart Kauffman is presented as somebody who disagrees that Darwinian processes can produce evolution. We thought this was rather odd, being a little bit familiar with Kauffman's work, and as we did with a number of these scientists quoted in the Discovery Institute critique of the Evolution series, we asked these people whether their views were being properly represented.

Stuart Kauffman pointed out in no uncertain terms, "My own work in self organization suggests that spontaneous order in complex systems may offer a second source of order in biology, in addition to natural selection," which is rather different from saying that natural selection doesn't work. "My argument does not entail that Darwinian descent with modification into the branching tree of life is invalid, nor does it entail that natural selection is not a critical process in evolution."

I think it's worthwhile pointing out here, at least briefly, that this confusion between pattern and process, or between a phenomenon and mechanism, is something that's very, very common, not only with the intelligent design anti-evolutionists, but also with traditional creation science. There is a great deal of confusion out there in the literature that I would like to have you think about when students bring it to you in the classroom. Look very carefully to see whether evolution itself is being critiqued, or whether a mechanism or process of evolution is being critiqued. Because after all, evolution is a phenomenon. It is the inference of common ancestry, that living things have descended with modification from earlier forms. The mechanisms or processes of evolution include natural selection, but also nonselective factors and so forth.

There's a large number of biological mechanisms by which evolution takes place. Evolution is something that happened. This is different from how something happened. Don't let people get away with saying, "So-and-so scientist says natural selection doesn't have this effect or that effect. Therefore, evolution didn't take place." They are making a categorical error. It's extremely common in the scientific literature. We don't argue about whether evolution took place. We do argue about the pattern of evolution, and the role of various mechanisms. We argue about who is descended from what, and we argue about how important natural selection versus other mechanisms are in producing this change.

I'd like to talk about one intelligent design critique of the PBS program that I think is worthwhile calling your attention to because many of you might have seen a full-page advertisement that was taken out in The New York Review of Books and The New Republic and also in the Washington DC area newspaper called The Weekly Standard. It was published by the Discovery Institute. It purports to be a statement signed by over 100 scientists – we'll just call it, for shorthand, the 100 scientist statement – that questioned evolution, that critiqued the idea that was presented in the PBS Evolution series.

The first thing I want to point out about this full-page ad is a rather odd statement at the bottom in the fine print. What it says is, "scientists listed by doctoral degree or current position." This made us curious. And being fairly compulsive at the National Center for Science Education, we got a little database together, and we looked all 104 of these characters up, and found out where they worked, what they did, what their degrees were, and just a little bit more about these folks. If they had Web pages, what kinds of things were they writing, and so forth. We found a most fascinating pattern about the 100 scientists listed here and their affiliations. We found that anybody who worked for, say, Probe Ministries, or the Institute for Creation Research, or any obvious anti-evolution organization was listed by where they got their degree. I'm sure it was just purely luck of the draw. I'm sure that didn't have anything to do with this.

But let's take a look at the introductory paragraph for this 100 scientist statement. It says, "public TV programs" – couldn't imagine what that would be – "educational policies, statements, and science textbooks have asserted that Darwin's theory of evolution fully explains the complexity of living things." The public has been assured, most recently by spokespersons for PBS Evolution series, that, "all known scientific evidence supports [Darwinian] evolution," as does, "virtually every reputable scientist in the world."

We were curious about the brackets around the word Darwinian, and we wondered why the brackets had to be added here. We emailed the PR guy for Discovery and said, "Hey, Mark, where did the quote come from." He said, "I'll get right back to you." That was October 2001. But it just so happens that since I was an advisor to the PBS Evolution series, I had some literature from WGBH from which this quote was taken. It was a briefing book that was sent to PBS stations around the country. It was an in-house document. It wasn't a public document. It was just sent to the various PBS stations around the country to give them an idea about the content of the program, what was going to be in them, and give them some ideas for how they could help promote the shows, and just understand the reasoning behind the project, and a little bit of advice for if you get flak, here's where you can go for help.

And in fact, this was indeed the source for this introductory paragraph quotation in the 100 scientist ad, because the Discovery Institute itself published excerpts from that in-house memo. Obviously, some PBS station person had given it to them, and they went to town with it. So I think even though the PR director of Discovery didn't get back to me on this specifically, I think I can be pretty confident that the statement, "all known scientific evidence supports [Darwinian] evolution" comes from the PBS memo.

And you know something? The word "Darwinian" isn't in there, nor does the word Darwinian help explain the paragraph from which this quote comes, because the paragraph from which the quote comes talks about a variety of mechanisms and processes that affect the common ancestry, the idea of evolution itself, and does not rely upon Darwinism, the hypothesis of natural selection – I would say the law of natural selection – as being the only explanatory mechanism. Now, ladies and gentlemen, when your students insert incorrect information in the term papers they write for you, I suspect you consider this an incorrect quote, and it's a sort of odd kind of inverse plagiarism, in a sense, isn't it? You'd probably give that student a D.

For reasons which we don't have time to go into, the intelligent design people are especially hung up on the Darwinian principle of natural selection. This seems to be the thing that gets their knickers in a twitch more than anything else. "Virtually every reputable scientist in the world..." There's a quote from me. I'm so honored. And I also was not talking about Darwinism. I was talking about evolution. Darwinism is a mechanism. Evolution is the phenomenon. This is that category of error that I was talking about.

The document continues, "The following scientists dispute the first claim, and stand in living testimony and contradiction to the second. There is scientific dissent to Darwinism. It deserves to be heard." Well, here's the statement that the men and women signed. "We are skeptical of claims for the ability of random mutation in natural selection" – which is what natural selection is all about – "to account for the complexity of life. Careful examination of the evidence for Darwinian theory should be encouraged." Well, yeah. I mean, fine. The 100 scientists signed a statement about natural selection as a mechanism. They didn't sign a statement saying evolution didn't happen, or the PBS Evolution program is a bunch of bunk because it talks about evolution, and evolution is a bad scientific idea. No, no, no! These guys and ladies signed a statement about natural selection, which is a mechanism.

I think Stephen J. Gould could sign this statement. I could sign this statement. So what we did is we sent an email out to the scientists on this list, saying, "Hi, we're from the NCSE. We're curious about this ad. Would you mind just answering a couple of quick questions for us? 1. Do you think living things descended with modification from common ancestors? 2. Do you think humans and apes had a common ancestor?" We got back a couple of answers from, incidentally, some very prominent members, people who would be recognized, not the people working out at funny little creationist institutions, but real scientists from real secular institutions, who wrote back saying, "Oh, evolution is fine." One guy said, "I just don't think the origin of life is ..." Somebody said, "Well, I just don't think natural selection is all that important." So at least some of the 100 scientists signing this document were expressing a suspicion of the Darwinian mechanisms as the be-all-and-end-all of evolutionary change. But the way this document is being used is as a club for the concept of evolution itself. The confusion between the phenomenon and the mechanism is repeated over and over.

Just a quick point: We don't argue about whether evolution occurred. We argue about the patterns and processes. I want to give you one example. It's one that Ken has used in some of his talks as well. And it is so annoying to me as a physical anthropologist that I will share it, although I won't go into detail here. Again, along the lines that the PBS series ignores the disagreement over evolution from scientists. Henry Gee, chief science writer for Nature, has pointed out that all the evidence for human evolution between about 10 and 5 million years ago can be fitted into a small box. And that is absolutely true. Note the dates. Between 10 and 5 million years ago. What about the evidence for human evolution between 5 and 1 million years ago? Could you fit that in a small box? No, you sure as heck couldn't. You couldn't fit it on that table. You couldn't fit it on five tables. You could fit the Homo erectus material maybe on several tables. And if you saw the PBS Evolution program, what time period are they talking about? They're not talking about 10 to 5 million years ago. They're talking about a time period between about 800,000 to 50,000 years ago. That is the focus of the PBS Evolution program. This is a red herring. I you go to our Web site [ncseweb.org] you can download a rather thick "Setting the Record Straight" document of ours in which you will find an awful lot of these red herrings.

One of the things that you find in creationist literature, whether it's intelligent design or traditional, is a lot of what we call quote mining. They sift through the literature and they pull out a quotation from a real scientist, and they pretend as if this is a criticism of either evolution or the mechanism itself. They criticize the religious bias of the show, alleged religious bias, extensive and biased focus. Well, of course, there is only one show out of eight hours that deals with religion, so that's rather foolish.

The intelligent design creationists did go into quite a bit of detail about why the PBS Evolution program was rather bad. There are ways of countering their claims. But also, Ken Ham's "Answers in Genesis" also criticized the program. On his Web page you can find an analysis that repeats a lot of the same stuff that you find elsewhere. Let me just give you a quick survey of the kind of general things that you will find criticizing evolution, not just the PBS program, but just across the board. Virtually any letter to the editor that you find in your local newspaper, the literature your students bring in to you, the positions presented at board of education meetings in your community, will take one of three forms. I call them the big three. They will argue that evolution is a theory in crisis. Certainly the critiques of the PBS program were very clear about that. They'll argue that evolution and religion are incompatible. And they will argue that it's only fair to teach creationism with evolution.

Ken has already gone over some of the very typical reasons why evolution is bad science. Micro/macro, young earth, and so forth. You can find, at TalkOrigins.org and the NCSE Web site, a lot of refutations of these specific ideas. In the notion that evolution and religion are incompatible, of course, what this breaks down into is the notion that you have to choose between one or the other, that there are these two warring camps, and you're either a good guy or a bad guy, and it's pretty easy to see who the good guys and bad guys are. Something that many teachers have found to be extremely useful in diffusing this dichotomous view is the creation/evolution continuum, where you basically walk your kids through a continuum – not a dichotomy – of creation and evolution, including flat earthers, geocentrists, young earthers, old earthers, theistic evolutionists, and materialists. You can find information on that on our Web page. I've got an article with a blackline master you can download, and also descriptions of the difference between day age creationists and progressive creationists and all the rest of them.

The fairness argument, though, is the most powerful thing they have going for them. And this is something that Ken is running into a lot, we are running into a lot in Ohio – the argument that it's only fair to present these alternatives to evolution, whether it's creation science, intelligent design, or just the evidence against evolution. Unfortunately, many teachers have been sucked into this idea that you can use this as a critical thinking kind of exercise, that it will improve the students' critical thinking abilities by having them judge creation and evolution. But I want you to think about this a little bit.

But just as a point here, think about what your goals of a critical thinking exercise are. Your goals really are to help students understand the process of critical thinking. So you want them to collect information, evaluate it, present it in a systematic way that allows the testing of alternate views. And the sides should be approximately scientifically equivalent. There should be a genuine scientific controversy, obviously. And there should be approximately the same scientific support for each side. I want you to think about whether that's true in the creation and evolution controversy. It is wrong on all three issues. There should be approximately the same amount of information on each side to be fair to the students. That's an important part of fairness, too. You are burdening your evolution side students unfairly by making them have to wade through this enormous amount of scientific information to try to find the particularly relevant aspects.

And another consideration, especially for younger kids, is that scientific issues should be predominating, not the ethical and moral ones. Otherwise, your discussion falls into the 'oughts' versus the 'shoulds,' and that is not really how you teach kids critical thinking, especially younger kids who really don't have a lot of objectivity, shall we say, about issues around which they have a great deal of emotion. If you want to find out more about dealing with the big three, go to NCSEWeb.org/resources and to Teaching Evolution at pbs.org/evolution You may be interested in some legal cans and can'ts. The same places offer these resources. And when all else fails, there's the National Center for Science Education. That's what we're here for. Call us when you need help.

In the April issue of Natural History there is a series of articles on intelligent design in which you have an intelligent design proponent and an opponent telling you, of course, the reason why these ideas are terrible. Ken and I both have articles here. You might want to take a look at that.

Julie Benyo: We'd like to open up the floor to questions now. We have about 15 minutes left. Anyone on the panel I'm sure will be welcome to answering your questions.

Question #1: What is the response of other countries, cultures, and religious traditions to evolution?

Kenneth Miller: Some of my British friends think that the anti-evolutionism movement in the United States is a particular and peculiarly American phenomenon, and then they make deprecating comments about American society, American culture, television, and the American educational apparatus. But the interesting thing is that there is now a growing anti-evolution movement in Britain. There is an anti-evolution movement in Russia. And recently, because I have Web sites up on evolution, I've been getting emails from Turkey and from other countries in the Middle East, talking about an anti-evolution movement within Islam.

So it turns out that evolution being, as the first episode of this series said, a dangerous idea, is dangerous I think to lots of traditional ways of thinking and lots of traditional cultures. And there are many cultures that have difficulty accommodating this idea. So as it turns out, evolution being such a powerful idea stirs a broad and wide response around the world.

Question #2: I've been reading reports like the House of Lords report to gain an understanding of world wide acceptance of science and evolution. Could you comment on statistics that have been circulating about the public's misconceptions about evolution in the US and where that puts Americans in respect to global science literacy. I mean, even folks who claim to agree with evolution even surprise me in that they too have misconceptions that need to be addressed.

Carl Zimmer: I think I'd have to agree, just as a journalist who observes the scene. The statistics about how many people think the Earth is less than 10,000 years is one example. What I find interesting sometimes is even people who claim to understand or even accept evolution bring to it all sorts of strange ideas that I have a hard time figuring out where they come from. So for example, someone who was a little skeptical about some aspects of evolution was emailing me, and he just couldn't figure out how it was that whales go into the water, because obviously evolution is all about progress, and so therefore life could only have evolved from water onto land, and not from land back to water. I tried to email him back saying, "Look, it's not about progress, it's about local adaptation." It just didn't work. So it's not an issue just of particular opponents of evolution. It's a very broad thing.

Eugenie Scott: There's a researcher named Jonathan Miller – no relation to Ken – who has done a lot of surveys of public understanding of science, both in the US, as well as cooperating with colleagues internationally, using the same questions translated, and so forth. We're not talking about students here. We're talking about grown-ups – random, stratified samples of American adults and British adults and Japanese adults, etc. He finds that Americans don't do all that poorly. We're sort of in the middle of the pack. There are some nations in which the general public science literacy is better than ours, but quite a few where it's poorer than us. He asks about actual content knowledge. Do you understand what a molecule is, and things like that.

But what he does find is that the concept of evolution is especially poorly understood in the United States, probably Canada too, because they have similar patterns. And of course, the reasons for this are myriad. But one of them does have to do with the teaching of evolution in the public schools, which is your job, and which a lot of your colleagues routinely do not do. If evolution is not taught, and hopefully taught well, and coherently, and as part of a bigger scientific endeavor – science as a way of knowing – then obviously we are not going to understand it. There's some things that science journalists can do, and movie and video people too. Television has a tremendous cultural effect. But a great deal of it depends on what kids learn in school. Not that I'm blaming teachers. That's only part of the overall picture. It's a very complex problem.

Kenneth Miller: I'll just say one thing. You referred to the House of Lords report, and you wondered if one of the reasons why Americans in general have accepted or at least expressed less resistance to things like genetically modified organisms than Europeans have, maybe that's because Americans don't know what they're getting, and Europeans do. Well, it depends on what you think about these things. I would put a slightly different spin on it, and that is that the entire history of this country has been one of what I would characterize as technological optimism. It's one of the reasons why this country has been such fertile ground for science and scientific development, which is that Americans, regardless of their political point of view, their religious point of view, or their feelings about evolution, Americans generally embrace technological change. And Europeans, if I had to make a generalization, are somewhat fearful of it.

Whatever the merits of genetically modified organisms, the fact of the matter is that Americans in general don't have an instinctive fear of the new, to the extent that many of my European friends and colleagues do, and I think that's the principal reason, not poor or good teaching in the schools.

Question #3: During the final program, Ken Ham is shown giving his reasons for why dinosaurs are extinct. Did anyone in the audience question his reasoning?

Bill Jersey: They didn't hear that particular remark until they saw the television program, because it was made in the hall, and it was made for our benefit, to enlighten us. He didn't include that in his lectures. We did spend two days with him, one day as he made a presentation to children, and one day with his presentation to adults.

Continuation of Question #3: Were his explanations ever questioned by his audiences?

Bill Jersey: The answers were never questioned, because he carefully justified everything he said with a biblical reference, and after all, you would not be arguing with Ken Ham, you'd be arguing with God, and that's a tough thing to do. His sort of summation, if you saw the program, and apparently you did, his summation to all the issues whenever any evolutionist approaches you, or any scientist, I presume also, about the origins of life, that you simply say to them, "Were you there?"

Question #4: Can you tell us more about the 100 scientists statement?

Eugenie Scott: Well, like I said, we sent a little questionnaire out to see whether they knew what they were signing, so to speak, or knew how it was going to be used. We did get back a couple of answers from these scientists, which indicated at least some of them are not anti-evolutionists. They are merely disputing the strength of the natural selection – "Darwinian mechanism." What happened of course was that as soon as our email went out – I suspect within a matter of hours – Mark, the PR guy at Discovery, would have sent out an email to everybody saying, "Whatever you do, don't talk to those people," devils incarnate that we are. So we didn't get a full response. We certainly don't have a random sample. But the fact that we got at least some responses from among those 100 scientists, which were of the sort, "Oh, yeah, evolution is fine with me. It's just the mechanism that we're fussing with," means that I think I'm quite justified in pointing out that what was actually signed is not necessarily how this document is being used. And it's being used as a club for evolution.

And I do want to thank those of you – teachers and citizens – with whom we're working in Ohio. You've hung the moon, as far as I'm concerned. Basically, what I at NCSE, and my staff – and Ken as a fellow outside agitator/resource – can provide is information. We can provide some advice. But if people in the communities, in the states, are not willing to step up to the plate and make a difference, and say "No, this is wrong. My colleagues shouldn't be doing this. This is not good education for our kids," then nothing important happens.

I just want to underscore how critically important it is for you to pay attention to what's going on in your districts, and what your colleagues are doing. If you really want the kids in your district to have a good science education, they need to be taught evolution, they need to be taught it in a straightforward way that does not denigrate it or qualify it or present it as just a theory. And they deserve to be taught what the consensus feels science is, which is that evolution is the underpinning of all biology.

Julie Benyo: I'm afraid that's all we have time for today. Thank you for coming. Be sure to check out the Evolution Web site at pbs.org/evolution. We hope you'll find these resources useful in your teaching.

The Darwin Day Program would like to thank Susan Buckey, Evolution Outreach Coordinator for PBS for her assistance and generosity in providing this piece.

[ADDITIONAL RESOURCES]

PBS Online: http://www.pbs.org/

SECTION SIX

ABUSING SCIENCE:
THE CREATIONIST PHENOMENON

> "If any choose to maintain, as many do, that species were gradually brought to their maturity from humbler forms ... he is welcome to his hypothesis, but I have nothing to do with it."
>
> – Philip Henry Gosse (1857)

> "Reality is that which, when you stop believing in it, doesn't go away."
>
> – Philip K. Dick in *I Hope I Shall Arrive Soon* (1987)

The National Center for Science Education
Defending the Teaching of Evolution in the Public Schools

As a supporter of Darwin Day, you already know that because evolution is central to biology, learning about evolution is essential to a sound science education. But did you know that now — over seventy-five years after the Scopes trial — there is still religiously motivated opposition to the teaching of evolution? NCSE works with civil liberties, scientific, religious, and educational organizations to defend the teaching of evolution. But we can't do it without your help.

"The National Center for Science Education — frontline defenders of quality science education in America."
— Niles Eldredge

For a complimentary copy of Reports of the NCSE, or to subscribe at the special Darwin Day rate of $25 for six issues, write to NCSE, PO Box 9477, Berkeley CA 94709-0477, call 1-800-290-6006, or send e-mail to ncse@ncseweb.org. Be sure to mention that you saw our advertisement in the Darwin Day collection!

ANTIEVOLUTIONISM AROUND THE WORLD
by Glenn Branch

Darwin's argument for evolution – descent with modification – was accepted quickly by the scientific community. His identification of natural selection as the process that is largely responsible not only for evolution but also for the "adaptation of means to ends" that impressed the practitioners of natural theology such as William Paley (Paley 1802) was controversial, however; it was not fully accepted until the neo-Darwinian synthesis of the 1930s and 1940s, when Mendelian genetics and Darwinian natural selection were united in a comprehensive system (Bowler 1989, chs. 7, 9, and 11). Evolutionary biology has of course progressed since the neo-Darwinian synthesis, incorporating such insights as endosymbiosis (Margulis 1970), punctuated equilibrium (Eldredge and Gould 1972), and evolutionary developmental biology (Raff 1996). Still, among scientists, there is no serious doubt about the fact of evolution; as Niles Eldredge writes, "Evolution is triumphant in the intellectual realm" (Eldredge 2000: 18).

Yet evolution is widely regarded as in conflict with various ideologies, religious and non-religious: it is in that sense, and that sense alone, that evolution remains controversial. The most notorious instance of non-religious ideological opposition to evolution – primarily to the Mendelian component of the neo-Darwinian synthesis – was the Soviet institutionalization of Trofim Lysenko's revival of Lamarck. The results were disastrous not only for Soviet biology but also for Soviet agriculture (Medvedev 1969). (For a useful survey of the varieties of ideological resistance to evolution, see John Wilkins's "So you want to be an anti-Darwinian" [Wilkins 1998].)

But the bulk of ideological resistance to evolution is religious in nature. Primarily it is adherents of the Abrahamic religions – Judaism, Christianity, and Islam – who reject evolution because they regard it as antithetical to their religious beliefs (although there is a growing body of Hindu antievolutionism, e.g., Cremo and Thompson [1993]; for commentary, see Brass [2002] and Brown [2002]). To be sure, it is not the case that all, or even most, Jews, Christians, and Muslims reject evolution on religious grounds. According to Pope John Paul II, "new knowledge has led to the recognition [that evolution is more than a hypothesis]. It is indeed remarkable that this theory has been progressively accepted by researchers, following a series of discoveries in various fields of knowledge. The convergence, neither sought nor fabricated, of the results of work that was conducted independently is in itself a significant argument in favour of this theory" (John Paul II 1997: 382; a mistranslation from the original French is corrected in brackets). Likewise, most mainline Protestant denominations in the United States have no trouble with evolution (Matsumura 1995, 1998), and the same is true of most Jewish congregations, with the exception of certain strands of ultra-Orthodoxy (Nussbaum 2002).

In Darwin's own day and country, there were bumps in the road as the clergy reconciled itself to accepting evolution: the exchange between Thomas Henry Huxley and Bishop Samuel Wilberforce is widely known (and widely misrepresented: Gould 1991), as is the perhaps apocryphal lament, "Oh my dear, let us hope that what Mr. Darwin says is not true. But if it is true, let us hope that it will not become generally known!" But the Church of England quickly made its peace with Darwin (Moore 1979; Bowler 1989, ch. 8), and across the Atlantic, the reaction from the religious community in the United States was neither immediately nor uniformly hostile (Moore 1979; Roberts 1988; Numbers 1998).

What happened, then? How is it that the United States became the bastion of religiously motivated opposition to evolutionary biology? Sociologists and historians cite a variety of possible reasons: the lack of any established church in the United States, the strong Protestant tradition of independent thought in religious matters, the tendency to regard evolution as part and parcel of modernity's desacralization of the world, and so forth (Eve and Harrold 1991; Marsden 1991, ch. 6; Numbers 1992; Toumey 1994). Whatever the cause, religiously motivated opposition to evolutionary biology – creationism – is primarily based in the United States, home to the Institute for Creation Research (in Santee, California), Answers in Genesis (in Florence, Kentucky), and the Discovery Institute's Center for Science and Culture (in Seattle, Washington), to name only the three most conspicuous creationist organizations. It is from such bases that creationism spreads across the globe.

The National Center for Science Education works to defend the teaching of evolution in the public schools of the United States; consequently, most of its requests for information and assistance come from the United States, with a significant percentage of its foreign requests coming from English-speaking countries such as Canada, the United Kingdom, and Australia. Yet from everywhere – from Belgium to Cameroon, from the Ivory Coast to Jamaica, from Switzerland to Turkey – reports of creationist attacks on evolution education pour in. Creationism is thus a worldwide phenomenon, in which antievolutionary material produced by the centers of creationism in the United States are exported overseas.

Creationism assumes two forms for export. First, it is viewed as a useful tool for proselytizing by many creationists, particularly those who, as evangelical Christians, regard themselves as obliged to fulfill the Great Commission (Matthew 28:19-20) by spreading the gospel. A case in point is Answers in Genesis (AIG), whose United States president Ken Ham writes, *"In an increasing number of instances, it is apparent that before we can effectively proclaim the message of Christ we must establish the creation foundation upon which the rest of the Gospel can be built"* (Ham 1987: 101-102, emphasis in original; see also Morris 1991). Hence in its publications in English as well as in Afrikaans, Albanian, Chinese, Czech, French, German, Italian, Japanese, Polish, Portuguese, Romanian, Russian, and Spanish, AIG uncompromisingly insists on the absolute accuracy and authority of Genesis. In the United Kingdom, as Marilyn Mason describes in her article, AIG's message was heeded by Emmanuel College, thereby unleashing a storm of protest and concern. Creationist evangelizing occurs elsewhere, if not always so publicly or successfully, as attested to by the following articles about creationism in Argentina, Italy, and New Zealand.

Second, creationist material originating in the United States is frequently borrowed and adapted by overseas creationists who may not necessarily agree with the particular religious views of its originators. The most astonishing example involves overseas creationists who are not even Christians. In Turkey, Bilim Arastirma Vakfi (BAV; the name translates as Science Research Foundation) worked with the Institute for Creation Research (ICR) to hold a series of creationist "conferences" in the major cities of Turkey (Edis 1999: 31). And BAV produces a series of slick creationist books, supposedly authored by the pseudonymous Harun Yahya, that rely heavily on the products of the ICR, such as *The Evolution Deceit* (Yahya 1999). Understandably, BAV is selective in its borrowings from the ICR: since the Qur'an and Islamic tradition insist on neither the young age of the earth nor the global extent of Noah's Flood, these elements of the ICR's belief system are absent from its literature. Yet BAV evidently finds the rest of the ICR's material useful in its attack on Turkey's tradition of secularism (Edis 1999; Shapiro 2000), and thus employs it, with ICR's blessing.

Although the United States remains the bastion of creationism, it is not as though its creationist organizations drive all the rest of the world's antievolutionary activity: there is plenty of back and forth. As creationism increasingly becomes a global phenomenon, creationists overseas become major players in their own right and then are welcomed by the legions of creationists in the United States (see Numbers 1992, ch. 10, for a decade-old but still useful summary). As David Riddell notes in his article on creationism in New Zealand, the Australian Michael Denton was a darling of the "intelligent design" creationists of the Discovery Institute (although his star is apparently waning among them; see the discussion of his *Nature's Destiny* [Behe *et al.* 1999]). The German creationist Siegfried Scherer is a Fellow of the Discovery Institute's Center for Science and Culture; his compatriot Werner Gitt works closely with Answers in Genesis (Kutschera 2001, ch. 10). Harun Yahya's condemnations of evolution have been reproduced with approval on traditional young-earth creationist web sites, such as True.Origins (Yahya 2001). Perhaps most significantly, Answers in Genesis, now the largest creationist organization in the United States, is run by a cadre of Australian creationists, including its president Ken Ham, Carl Wieland, and Jonathan Sarfati.

The science of evolutionary biology that Darwin inaugurated is, to its enduring credit, an international endeavor. Unfortunately, it appears as though religiously motivated opposition is, and will remain, an international threat to it. ∞

[ABOUT THE AUTHOR]

Glenn Branch is Deputy Director of the National Center for Science Education, a nonprofit organization that defends the teaching of evolution in the (U.S.) public schools.

[REFERENCES]

Behe, Michael, Dembski, William, Johnson, Phillip, Meyer, Stephen, Wells, Jonathan, and Nelson, Paul. A roundtable on Nature's Destiny. Origins & Design Winter 1999; vol. 19, no. 2, pp. 26-32.

Bowler, Peter J. *Evolution: The History of an Idea*, revised edition. Berkeley: University of California Press, 1989.

Brass, Michael. *The Antiquity of Man: Artifactual, Fossil and Gene Records Explored*. Baltimore: America Press, 2002.

Brown, C. Mackenzie. *Hindu and Christian creationism: "transposed passages" in the geological book of life*. Zygon 2002 March, vol. 37, no. 1, 95-114.

Cremo, Michael A., and Thompson, Richard L. *Forbidden Archaeology*. San Diego: Bhaktivedanta Institute, 1993.

Edis, Taner. *Cloning Creationism in Turkey*. Reports of the National Center for Science Education November-December 1999, vol. 19, no. 6, pp. 30-35.

Eldredge, Niles. *The Triumph of Evolution and the Failure of Creationism*. New York: W. H. Freeman, 2000.

Eldredge, Niles, and Gould, Stephen Jay. Punctuated Equilibria: An alternative to phyletic gradualism. In Models in Paleobiology, ed. T. J. Schopf, pp. 82-115. San Francisco: Freeman and Cooper, 1972.

Eve, Raymond A., and Harrold, Francis B. The Creationist Movement in Modern America. Boston: Twayne Publishers, 1991.

Gould, Stephen Jay. Knight takes bishop? In Stephen Jay Gould, Bully for Brontosaurus, pp. 385-401. New York: W. W. Norton, 1991.

Ham, Kenneth A. The Lie: Evolution. El Cajon (CA): Creation-Life Publishers, 1987.

John Paul II. Message to the Pontifical Academy of Sciences. The Quarterly Review of Biology December 1997, vol. 72, no. 4, pp. 381-3.

Kutschera, Ulrich. Evolutionsbiologie: Eine allgemeine Einf̦hrung. Berlin: Paley Buchverlag, 2001.

Margulis, Lynn. The Origin of Eukaryotic Cells. New Haven: Yale University Press, 1970.

Marsden, George M. Understanding Fundamentalism and Evangelicalism. Grand Rapids (MI): William B. Eerdmans Publishing, 1991.

Matsumura, Molleen. What do Christians really believe about evolution? Reports of the National Center for Science Education March-April 1998, vol. 18, no. 3, pp. 8-9.

Matsumura, Molleen, ed. Voices for Evolution, second edition. Berkeley: The National Center for Science Education, 1995.

Medvedev, Zhores. The Rise and Fall of T. D. Lysenko. New York: Columbia University Press, 1969.

Moore, James R. The Post-Darwinian Controversies: A Study of the Protestant Struggle to Come to Terms with Darwin in Great Britain and America 1870-1900. Cambridge: Cambridge University Press, 1979.

Morris, Henry M. The importance of creation in foreign missions. Creation ex Nihilo September-November 1991, vol. 13, no. 4, pp. 16-18.

Numbers, Ronald L. The Creationists: The Evolution of Scientific Creationism. Berkeley: University of California Press, 1992.

Numbers, Ronald L. Darwinism Comes to America. Cambridge (MA): Harvard University Press, 1998.

Nussbaum, Alexander. Creationism and geocentrism among Orthodox Jewish scientists. Reports of the National Center for Science Education January-April 2002; vol. 22, no. 1-2, pp. 38-43.

Paley, William. Natural Theology: Or Evidences of the Existence and Attributes of the Deity Collected from the Appearances of Nature. London: Printed for R. Faulder by Wilks and Taylor, 1802.

Raff, Rudolf A. The Shape of Life: Genes, Development, and the Evolution of Animal Form. Chicago: University of Chicago Press, 1996.

Roberts, Jon H. Darwinism and the Divine in America: Protestant Intellectuals and Organic Evolution 1859-1900. Madison: University of Wisconsin Press, 1988.

Shapiro, Arthur M. Fundamentalist bedfellows: Political creationism in Turkey. The New Leader March-April 2000; vol. 83, no. 1, pp. 13-18.

Toumey, Christopher P. God's Own Scientists: Creationists in a Secular World. New Brunswick (NJ): Rutgers University Press, 1994.

Wilkins, John. So you want to be an anti-Darwinian: Varieties of opposition to Darwinism. http://www.talkorigins.org/faqs/anti-darwin.html, 1998. Spotted September 12, 2002.

Yahya, Harun [pseudonym]. The Evolution Deceit: The Scientific Collapse of Darwinism and Its Ideological Background. Istanbul: Okur Publications, 1999.

Yahya, Harun [pseudonym]. A whale fantasy from National Geographic. http://www.trueorigins.org/ng_whales01.asp, 2001. Spotted September 12, 2002.

[ADDITIONAL RESOURCES]

National Center for Science Education: http://www.ncseweb.org

CREATIONISM IN NEW ZEALAND
by David Riddell

Creationism is on the move in New Zealand. While this country has had visits from international creationist speakers for many years (e.g. Duane Gish in 1975, Richard Bliss in 1980, AE Wilder Smith in 1986), such visits have in more recent times increased dramatically in frequency, particularly with the growth of creationism in Australia, and we now have a few home-grown speakers on the circuit.

Few outside of the movement are probably aware of just how much activity there is, as they have eschewed the frontal attacks on the scientific and educational establishment which have characterised operations in the US. Instead, there has been an explicit policy of reaching out to the already converted, establishing a firm grass-roots support base from which to operate, and then supplying these ground forces with resource material to be distributed, on a one-to-one basis, to the general populace. The policy, known as "Linking and Feeding", was spelled out on the Creation Science Foundation (CSF) website in 1997 by CEO Carl Wieland. A similar message was delivered by the CSF's Peter Sparrow at a meeting I attended in Hamilton in 1995.

Occasionally, a creationist will adopt a higher profile. Such a one was the late Ron Wyatt ("probably the best known archaeologist in the world"), who toured the country claiming to have discovered Noah's Ark in 1998. But these are the exceptions.

In late 1997, the CSF changed its name to the Answers in Genesis Ministries (AiG). While the abandonment of any pretense of scientific objectivity was hailed by the Australian Skeptics as a victory, this move was simply a matter of tapping in to the post-modern notion that science has no monopoly on the truth. It certainly doesn't seem to have done the organisation any harm; they now have branches in six countries, including New Zealand.

The local office, in Howick, Auckland, opened back in CSF days, in 1997, with a staff of three. They now produce a quarterly newsletter, *Answers Prayer News*, available in PDF format via email. The April-June 2002 issue announced the addition of a new "ministry coordinator", Jennifer Baker, to the staff. It also offered for sale, as it does each issue, numerous attractively presented books and videos, and the AiG magazine, *Creation ex Nihilo*. It also advertised a "Homeschool Conference", and a creation seminar, both held in Howick. The former featured Adrian Bates, a former fireman, lawyer, and drug and alcohol education officer, now CEO of AiG-NZ. The latter was held by Dr Don Batten, an Australian agricultural scientist, who speaks regularly for AiG in his home country.

The AiG website (www.answersingenesis.org) lists a great many more events, however. Adrian Bates alone has 18 presentations scheduled nationwide between July and October, all at churches and Christian schools.

In July, Wellington was the scene of two "Weekends of Ministry" (six events in total) featuring Dr Jonathan Sarfati. Sarfati was born in Australia, then raised in New Zealand (where he made a name for himself as a chess player), before returning to Australia in 1996 to take up a position as a "research scientist and editorial consultant" with CSF. He is the author or co-author of several creationist books and articles (e.g. *Refuting Evolution*, *The Answers Book*), recently contributing a response to the *Scientific American* article, *15 Answers to Creationist Nonsense*, on the AiG website. Sarfati visits New Zealand regularly; he participated in an AiG "Creation Camp" at Rotorua in January, which around 85 people attended, and he returns in September for another weekend of ministry in Hamilton. Visits from other Australian AiG speakers, such as Peter Sparrow (who has twice done extensive tours in his "Creation Bus"), are frequent.

Loosely allied to AiG is the somewhat misleadingly named Alpha-6 Educational Services, Inc., a registered non-profit charitable trust based in Hamilton. Alpha-6 have to date produced two rather crude booklets, *Understanding the Young Earth Model* and *Bible Chronology – His Story*. No author is credited on either publication, but they are apparently the work of Hamilton high school science teacher Peter Dennis, who also led a geological field trip examining Rotorua's "post-flood" volcanic activity on the AiG creation camp. Dennis has a sizeable collection of overhead transparencies and occasionally gives creationist presentations.

Answers in Genesis are not the only players on the New Zealand creationist scene. Queenslander John Mackay founded the Creation Research Institute (now known simply as Creation Research, and not to be confused with the American-based Institute for Creation Research and Creation Research Society) as a splinter group from CSF, and now has branches in many countries, including New Zealand. The four local staff don't seem to be particularly active, apparently preferring to supply resources for anyone who may wish to organise an event themselves. Mackay himself is a regular visitor here, and led one of his trademark field trips to Waikato Heads in early July 2002. In July 1999 he debated against me and two other members of the NZ Skeptics (John Riddell and Alastair Brickell) in Thames; though he claims victory on his website (www.creationresearch.org), it is telling that the video which was made of the evening is not available among his extensive product list.

Although not a creationist organisation per se, the Christian-oriented Family Television Network, a local Auckland channel, regularly screens creationist "documentaries". The Radio Rhema network has two regular weekly creationist slots: on Sundays at 4.30pm, Chris O'Brien presents *Science, Scripture and Salvation*, courtesy of AiG (who else?), where you can find out whether the Bible is "truly inspired and actually able to stand up to whatever the evolutionary community throws at it". And on Wednesday afternoons at 4.20 Lew Meyer presents *Science Report*. Meyer has been sending out brochures to schools for several years offering creationist seminars, and gets about half a dozen takers each year (Philp, 2000).

Mention should also be made of Dr Michael Denton, who is a senior research fellow in human molecular genetics at the University of Otago. Though he claims not to be a creationist, at least of the Young Earth variety, his presentation of the molecular evidence is misleading to say the least. His books *Evolution: A Theory in Crisis* (1993) and *Nature's Destiny: How the Laws of Biology Reveal Purpose in the Universe* (1998) are staples of the Intelligent Design movement, and are widely quoted by the likes of Phillip Johnson in his book *Darwin on Trial*, and elsewhere.

New Zealand is still one of the most secular societies on Earth, with those claiming to have no religion comprising more than a quarter of citizens in the 1996 census. Those identifying themselves as Christian have declined to 60.6% of the population (non-Christian religions account for only a couple of percent), with the mainstream denominations accounting for most of the fall. Fundamentalist denominations, however, are holding steady at around 9%, or even gaining slightly, with the Pentecostals showing a dramatic increase of 55% since the previous census, though their overall numbers (39,228 or 1.14% of the population) are still small (US State Dept, 2001).

While there is an active creationist home schooling movement, and creationism is taught is some private church-run schools, creationism's impact on the state education system remains minor (Philp, 2001). But with AiG and others reporting big turnouts to their meetings and huge interest in their message, it's a fair bet that, in the short term at least, the creationist star in New Zealand will continue to rise.

[ABOUT THE AUTHOR]

David Riddell has been fascinated by animals since early childhood, but only became interested in creationists after meeting some Jehovah's Witnesses at the age of 13. After receiving his master's degree in zoology at Auckland University in 1982 he has had a varied career which has included refurbishing the university's invertebrate museum, dairy farming, journalism, surveying birds and trapping stoats in New Zealand's wild south-west, and proofreading documents translated from Japanese. He currently works for an environmental consultancy company and assists his wife, Annette Taylor, with the production of the *New Zealand Skeptic*.

[REFERENCES]

Philp, M. 2000. God's Classroom. New Zealand Listener, April 22-28, pp. 16-21.

US State Dept, 2001. International Religious Freedom Report.
http://www.state.gov/g/drl/rls/irf/2001/5677.htm. Released by the Bureau of Democracy, Human Rights, and Labor

[ADDITIONAL RESOURCES]

New Zealand Skeptics: http://skeptics.org.nz/

BOOK REVIEW:
TRUE NORTH: EXPLORING THE GREAT WILDERNESS BY BUSH PLANE

by George Erickson
The Lyons Press

Review by Bob Merrick of *Canadian Flight* magazine
Republished with permission

Starting from Ely, Minnesota..., George Erickson relates his journey in a fascinating book called *True North*. And what a book it is. Is it a mere travelogue? Lord, no. It's an entertaining romp through the north, through history, through science, through astronomy, through exploration, through many interests and activities; a romp with something for everyone.

Erickson's interests are broad, and this was not his first trip north. Thus he tells stories not only from this voyage, but from earlier travels as well. And he does it with skill, style and panache... Is it all sociological or historical essays with nothing of flying? Far from it. The odyssey is, above all, a celebration of the new horizons that can be attained with an airplane ... At one point he says, "The sun returns, bathing the Cub in golden light as the tundra unrolls a carpet of ochre and green around lakes rimmed with orange lichens and butterscotch sand. Deepening, their waters shift from clear to aquamarine, and then to black as the Cub drones through indolent air above the deep, cold waters of Nueltin Lake..." A page or two later, he introduces Evangellista Torricelli and Blaise Pascal. Who are they, you say? They are the people whose pioneering work resulted in the barometer, the grandfather of the altimeter that graces [aircraft] instrument panels...

A few pages later, he mesmerizes an entire campsite by replicating an experiment first conducted by Eratosthenes to measure the earth's circumference. Before leaving Ely, Erickson measured the length of a shadow cast by the sun on a right-angle wire.

At Chantrey, he used the same wire to measure the shadow again. His findings provide new respect for that long-ago geometer who helped pushed back the frontiers of our knowledge of our world...

A skilled photographer – 17 superb color plates attest to that – Erickson likes to capture wildlife on film by landing nearby and stalking them. Sometimes, that gets boring. "By the time the Cub passes the tiny cabin at Lookout Point I'm weary of searching for game, so I push the nose down until I'm 20 feet above the river, pour on the fuel and roll from side to side as I bank through the Thelon's turns. As the shoreline flashes past, waves of goose bumps wash up and down my spine. I am Walter Mitty, come to the rescue in my Spitfire, or perhaps in a Wart Hog – the ugly, low-level fighter-bomber of the Gulf War. Darting up the Thelon at all of Mach .13, I hold my heading when the river turns, pull up abruptly to clear the trees, then shove the nose down again as the river rounds the bend."

The book is full of such vignettes, for it is, first and foremost, a celebration of life. It is also a celebration of flight, for without flight, the book could not have been written. The Tundra Cub is the vehicle that takes us to each of the outposts, campsites and remote lakes Erickson visited on his superb voyage. But it's also a tribute to an unassuming, capable, pilot and author who undertook a solo journey that most of us will only ever dream of... Perhaps Erickson's philosophy is best summed up by poet Robert Bums, who wrote, "If there be life after death, he lies in bliss; If not, he made the most of this."

True North is the story of a man and an airplane who combined to "make the most of this." It is a joyous voyage of discovery through time and space, providing fascinating glimpses of Canada and Alaska, aeronautics, exploration and science and social history all wrapped up in one entertaining, readable book written with humility and humor by a pilot with the capacity to dream, and the ability to make the dream come true. *True North* should be in every pilot's library *and in every school library as well.*

> *True North is available online and in bookstores. However, for those who purchase True North for $22.00 incl. postage from the author at 2300 17th St NW, New Brighton, MN 55112, the author will donate $8.00 per book to the Darwin Day program You must mention Darwin Day with your order.*

∞

ANTIDARWINISM IN ITALY

by Silvano Fuso
CICAP (Comitato Italiano per il Controllo delle Affermazioni sul Paranormale)[*]

In Italy the currents of Antidarwinist thought are quite limited, luckily. The Catholic Church, which has a considerable influence on Italian culture, has taken an open position towards the theory of evolution, even if the following quotation from the encyclical *Fides et ratio* of John Paul II appears somewhat ambiguous:

> Later, in his Encyclical Letter Humani Generis, Pope Pius XII warned against mistaken interpretations linked to evolutionism, existentialism and historicism. He made it clear that these theories had not been proposed and developed by theologians, but had their origins "outside the sheepfold of Christ". He added, however, that errors of this kind should not simply be rejected but should be examined critically: "Catholic theologians and philosophers, whose grave duty it is to defend natural and supernatural truth and instill it in human hearts, cannot afford to ignore these more or less erroneous opinions. Rather they must come to understand these theories well, not only because diseases are properly treated only if rightly diagnosed and because even in these false theories some truth is found at times, but because in the end these theories provoke a more discriminating discussion and evaluation of philosophical and theological truths"[1].

Namely: it is necessary to know better the theory of evolution in order to defend the Divine Truth.

Apart from this, however, the currents openly Antidarwinist are surely a minority.

As for the academic field, Darwinism is largely approved. The only prominent exceptions are represented by Prof. Giuseppe Sermonti and Prof. Antonino Zichichi.

Born in Rome in 1925, graduate in agronomy and biology, Sermonti has taught at the University of Palermo and Perugia. He has developed researches in the field of genetics and he has had important roles in some scientific institutions. He has written numerous scientific books and some texts of critical reflection on modern science. Moreover, he is the author of works devoted to a naturalistic analysis of the fables and of some "table comedies" (that are recited from interpreters sat around a table).

The criticism of Sermonti to Darwinism starts in 1970 and reaches its extreme peak claiming that:

> *The idea of a gradual evolutionary development of our species from creatures like the australopithecus, through the pithecanthropus, the sinanthropus and the neanderthaliano, must be considered totally ground-less and it must be rejected with decision. The man is not the most recent ring of a long evolutionary chain but, contrarily, it represent a taxon that exists substantially unchanged at least since the dawns of the Quaternary Era [...] On the morphological and anatomo-comparative plan, the most primitive – or less evolved – between all the ominidis results to be really the man of modern type! [...] Are certainly less distant from truth those people that [...] sustain the opposite hypothesis, and that is that Australopiteci, Arcanthropi and Paleoanthropi are all forms derived by the man of modern type!*[2]

In his recent book *Dimenticare Darwin* (1999 – Forget Darwin), Sermonti turns his criticisms towards the modern molecular interpretations of Darwinian thought by saying that:

> *The molecular revolution has consisted just in the abandonment of the naturalistic observations, with explicit indifference for the forms.*[3]

On the contrary, the author vindicates the importance of the study of the "form" at different levels and of the organism in his integrity.

Also, on an epistemological plain, Sermonti manifests an evident antiscientific attitude, as it is clearly expressed by the following passages:

> *I remember an evening, I wandered between the benches of the empty classroom and I asked myself: "Why do I teach Genetics? Why do I teach the Science? I teach something to which I don't believe, rather I teach the contrary one of this to which I believe". The science doesn't help us there to know the reality, rather it is employed to teach us that the reality count nothing, only some abstract principles, that the man of the road can not understand, are worth. The science is not even useful. It pours his products on the society, it creates artificial necessity that coincide with what it knows how to produce.*[4]

> *[...] the whole care contained in the foundation of the Technique and the contemporary Science has consisted in depriving the human work of every meaning, that is deritualizing it. The meaning is a exigence that limits the efficiency, forcing the operator to a quantity of formal fulfillments that distract it to pursue directly the point of arrival. The big progress realized by the technique have been simply the result of abolition of every sacredness from the human operations: this has made, as for enchantment, marvelously efficient the human practices, this have allowed to set every thing in commerce, to develop from every operation an industry. To one price only, just: what everything renounced his meaning. But the nature withstands to the desecration.*[5]

Regarding the experimental method, pillar of the modern science, he claims:

> *The experimental method compares technical activity to that cognitive, inaugurating so a fatal misunderstanding for the science.*[6]

The heterodox quotation of Sermonti could continue, but it appears now clear that his ideas possess little rigor and scientific objectivity. They appear speculations of an individual that, dissatisfied by the inevitable limits that science imposes, tries to overcome them giving free reign to his own personal opinions and his own personal vision of the world.

Antonino Zichichi, born in Trapani in 1929, is professor of superior physics at the University of Bologna. He has had important roles in scientific institutions and has founded a "Center of scientific culture Ettore Majorana" in Erice, Sicily, which he directs since 1963. He has published various books on popular science and he doesn't miss a chance to state and defend his unshakable Catholic faith.

In his book *Perché io credo in Colui che ha fatto il mondo* (1999 – *Why I believe in He who created the World*), he writes:

> *Dominant culture has set the theme of the biological evolution of the human species on the pedestal of a great scientific truth in total contrast with the Faith. [...]*
>
> *Arrived to the Homo Sapiens Neaderthalensis (one hundred thousand years ago around) with a brain of superior volume to ours, the Theory of the Biological evolution of the human species says us that, forty thousand years ago around, the Homo Sapiens Neaderthalensis is extinguished in inexplicable way. And it appears finally, in way as much inexplicable, twenty thousand years ago around, the Homo Sapiens Sapiens. That is us. A theory with lacking rings, miraculous developments, inexplicable extinctions, sudden disappearances is not galilean science. [...] How can an application of the electromagnetism, still very defective and lacunose – what is the theory of the human evolution – to pretend to deny the existence of God? Yet the man of the road is convinced that Charles R. Darwin has shown our direct descent from the monkeys: for dominant culture not believing to the evolutionistic theory of the human species is fit of serious obscurantism, comparable to persist in believing that is the Sun to turn around, with the firm Earth to the center of the world. True is the exact contrary.*
>
> *The oscurantistis are those people that pretend to consider scientific truth a theory deprived of one elementary structure mathematics and without some experimental proof of galilean kind. [...] We know with certainty that the biological evolution of the human species is firm from at least ten thousand years (from the dawn of civilization) [...] moment from which we are able to study with certainty the properties of this form of living matter said man. During ten thousand years this form of living matter has remained exactly identical to itself. Biological evolution: zero.*[7]

By saying this Prof. Zichichi shows to own a very personal concept of galilean science and to ignore a big portion of the proofs that confer value to the evolutionistic theory.

Outside the academic world, we find that in Italy there exists a Centro Studi

Creazionismo (http://www.creazionismo.org). It is an association that sets forth:

- To spread knowledge by whatever means of what the Bible teaches about the creation of the world;
- To make known the studies that have been and continue to be done in Italy and other countries on the subject of creationism as a viable alternative to evolutionism and any other theory that denies the idea of a Creator God;
- To promote dialog through all available means with creationists, evolutionists and all those who wish to understand the biblical message regarding the great issues of human existence;
- To form in the area of public opinion an awareness that evolution is only a hypothesis and that it is necessary to know the biblical message of creationism, today more relevant than ever;
- To sponsor studies, lectures and conferences on the subject of creationism;
- To introduce into both public and private schools the biblical message of creationism and the scientific studies that confirm it;
- To create a library in which to collect whatever Italian and foreign books and periodicals are needed to spread the creationist message.

The Center publishes a journal, *Eco creazionista*, that contains articles and reviews of theological and antievolutionistic matters. Contrarily to the creationists from other countries, the Italians appear to be less aggressive and, at least on paper, more open to dialogue. On their Web pages that illustratesthe nature of the Center we read in fact:

> The "Centro Studi Creazionismo" (CSC) is a voluntary association of like-minded people who, while respecting modern culture and science, aim to promote a dialog open to all about the relationship between science and faith and between the biblical message and human knowledge.
>
> In particular, without being narrow-minded, it aims to point out that evolutionistic theories cannot be considered as undisputed scientific fact without considering the alternatives.
>
> Both in Italian schools and in the wider community, for example, criticisms of evolutionistic theories should not be ignored, nor should the validity of the creationist alternative be discounted.
>
> We are convinced that the Biblical account of creation and the laws of nature are not in conflict with each other but, on the contrary, are convergent.
>
> In short, the aim is to make available to Italian-speaking people more balanced information, so that young people and other open-minded inquirers can make an informed choice between the evolutionistic world-view and that based on the Bible.
>
> According to the Word of God, physical matter and life are not the product of chance but of design, the work of the Supreme Programmer.

[ABOUT THE AUTHOR]

Silvano Fuso is teacher of chemistry in high schools and attends to didactic of the sciences and to epistemological problems. He collaborates with some magazines of didactic and popular science and is the author of some books like which *Realtà o illusione? Scienza, pseudoscienza e paranormale* (1999).

[ACKNOWLEDGEMENTS]

The author is grateful to Massimo Polidoro for his contributions to this article.

[FOOTNOTES]

1 The complete text of the encyclical is available on the site: http://www.vatican.va/holy_father/john_paul_ii/encyclicals/documents/hf_jp-ii_enc_15101998_fides-et-ratio_en.html

2 Sermonti G., Fondi R. 1980. Dopo Darwin. *Critica all'evoluzionismo*. Milano: Rusconi, pages. 285-287.

3 Sermonti G. 1999. *Dimenticare Darwin*. Milano: Rusconi: 1999, page 151.

4 Sermonti G. 1981. *Intervento* 49.

5 Sermonti G. 1982. *L'anima scientifica*. Roma: Dino Editori, pages 51-52.

6 Sermonti G. 1998. *Miseria dello sperimentalismo*, in AA.VV., *Goethe scienziato*. Torino: Einaudi, page 531.

7 Zichichi A. 1999. *Perché io credo in Colui che ha fatto il mondo*. Milano: Il Saggiatore, page 91.

[ADDITIONAL RESOURCES]

CICAP (Italian Committee for the Control of the Claims on the Paranormal) is a scientific and educational organization that promotes a scientific and critical investigation on claims of the paranormal and the spreading of a rational mentality. For more information: http://www.cicap.org

Two Worlds in Conflict:
Creationism & Evolution in Argentina
by Juan De Gennaro

"*Descended from apes! My dear, let us hope it is not so; but if it is, let us hope that it does not become generally known.*"
— Wife of the Bishop of Worcerster [1]

"*When on board H.M.S. 'Beagle', as naturalist, I was much struck with certain facts in the distribution of the organic beings inhabiting South America, and in the geological relations of the present to the past inhabitants of that continent. These facts, as will be seen in the latter chapters of this volume, seemed to throw some light on the origin of species —that mystery of mysteries, as it has been called by one of our greatest philosophers.*"
— Charles Darwin, The Origin of Species. [2]

The Preamble to the Argentine Constitution calls upon "God's protection" – with God being described as "[the] source of all reason and justice" – and, Article 2 establishes the inseparability of the Catholic Church and the State: "El Gobierno Federal sostiene el culto católico apostólico romano".[3]

According to a recent *Gallup Argentina* poll, 83 % of Argentine nationals claim to be religious (among these, 84% said to be Catholics), 12 % claim to be non religious (they believe in something) and 4 % declared to be staunch atheists.[4]

Thus, we could say that Argentina is a "Catholic" nation.

However, since the years of our Independence in the early 19th Century, two conflicting worlds strive to build a Nation according to their respective beliefs: on the one hand, the religious, i.e., Catholic world, and, on the other, the liberal, i.e., rationalist world – empiricist, positivistic and evolutionist. This conflict is perceived most clearly and plainly in the field of education, particularly during two key periods of Argentine history: first, in the 19th century, in the 1880's and 1890's and, second, in the 1990's.

The conflicts in the first period stemmed from three major events: the creation of the *National Board of Education*, the meetings of the *Pedagogy Conference* and the debate about the *Common Education Law*, from two opposite views with respect to education: the Catholic position, that wanted no innovation whatsoever as regards religion, based on the purported moral evils that would arise from such innovations, and the liberal or naturalistic position, which supported a secularist project where religion was excluded as an educational element. The latter, liberal position, finally prevailed both in the field of philosophy and of educational policy.[5]

At this point, it is most important to point out that the philosophical *substratum* of local liberalism is none other than the so-called "Argentine positivism", characterized by scientificism, a naturalistic conception of the world, and (Darwinian) evolutionism:

> "Estas teorías [las paleontológicas] evidenciaban algunas veces una clara significación socio-política. Este es el caso, por ejemplo, de uno de sus primeros trabajos científicos [la referencia es a Florentino Ameghino] donde el transformismo es esgrimido contra la teología y el clericalismo. Confrontando las afirmaciones bíblicas con los descubrimientos paleontológicos, Ameghino suscita un conflicto entre la ciencia y la religión: entre las ciencias naturales y la revelación. El alcance de esta manera de plantear el problema es de una extraordinaria importancia si se tiene en cuenta la lucha que se desarrollaba entonces entre el laicismo de la generación de 1880 y las fuerzas católicas tradicionalistas." [6]

A similar confrontation took place in the mid 1990's, on account of changes introduced in the *Common Basic Contents* – the content of the curricula for child and teenage students – under the *Federal Education Act*. Among these changes were: the elimination of any reference to sex education, substitution of the concept of "gender" for the concept of "sex" and exclusion of the names Lamarck and Darwin along with a toning down of the theory of the evolution of species. Thus, the original basic content (*Natural Science*, p. 122) that read: "Introduction to the theory of evolution. Presentation of the positions of Lamarck and Darwin, the natural selection mechanism and the process of species extinction, establishing a connection between the contributions made by natural science and other contributions afforded by social science to allow understanding how individuals participate both in the extinction and preservation of species", was replaced by the following: "Presentation of the mechanisms of species evolution, the theories that explain them and the process of species extinction, in relation to the scientific contributions of different fields of science to understand human participation as part of the ecosystem, in the processes of species extinction, conservation and preservation".[7]

Those changes were introduced as a result of "suggestions" made by the Catholic Church and led to the resignation of quite a number of specialists who had worked in preparing said contents[8]. One of the resigning experts said: "As they cannot remove the theory of evolution altogether, they add subtle changes, they eliminate these names [Lamarck and Darwin] because they are symbolic."[9]

Now then, it is not only the political influence of the Catholic Church that should be taken into account when examining the factors that threaten the evolutionist perspective. Indeed, the nearly absent Government support of scientific activity in Argentina[10], the powerful onslaught and growth of fundamentalist Christian groups and destructive cults, the proliferation of pseudo-scientific practices enveloped in the New Age paradigm, the massive and non-critical propagation in the media of the occult and paranormal, the profound and unprecedented social and economic crisis running rampant in the region and the ensuing increase of magic thinking, all of the above combine to delay the development of a model of society based on rational parameters where, of course, the theory of evolution holds an extremely important position.

Anyway, news reporting paleontologic and paleoanthropological finds in Argentina and other parts of the world are frequently published in local newspapers[11] and articles on Darwin and the theory of evolution appear in those same media[12]. Furthermore, a book by Argentine scientists has been published recently, addressing the non academic readers interested in the current status of Darwin's theory[13], while different Argentine museums of natural science persist in their scientific and educational task on really diminished budgets.

Lastly, *Darwin Day Program* was mentioned in a fundamentalist Christian publication[14] and in the *Education Supplement of Clarín*, one of the most important newspapers of the country[15]. These articles point out, in the light of a study published by *Scientific American*, the escalating diffusion and expansion of creationism in the US population and the American educational system, and briefly set out a few opinions of the *Darwin Day Program* with respect to said expansion and the tactics implemented by creationists to promote their doctrine, for example, the notion of "intelligent design".

Actually, the creation-evolution controversy is a matter of global proportions and significance. Florentino Ameghino, honoring Charles Darwin, in 1884, although rather overstating the matter, wrote:

> "Todos vosotros sabéis sin duda que Darwin puede considerarse como uno de nuestros sabios, pues el descubrimiento de su teoría está ligado a la historia de nuestro progreso científico, por ser aquí, entre nosotros, donde recogió los materiales de ella y tuvo su primer idea. Y, por una coincidencia bien extraordinaria, por cierto, es aquí, sólo aquí en la Pampa , donde ella puede encontrar su más evidente comprobación, y eso por razones que están al alcance de todos". [16]

[ABOUT THE AUTHOR]

Juan De Gennaro is the founder and director of Argentina Skeptics (AS) and editor of *Argentina Skeptics Newsletter*. He was a researcher in the philosophy department of the University of Buenos Aires. He speaks and writes on skeptical and philosophical topics from a rational and scientific perspective. He is a former New Ager.

[REFERENCES]

1) Quoted in Pennock, R.T. (2000). *Tower of Babel. The Evidence against the New Creationism*. Cambridge, MA: The MIT Press, 43.

2) Darwin, Ch. (1991). *The Origin of Species by Means of Natural Selection*. Amherst, NY: Prometheus Books, Introduction, 1.

3) [The Federal Government upholds the Roman Apostolic Catholic religion]. *Constitución de la Nación Argentina* (1995). Buenos Aires: Biblioteca del Congreso de la Nación. Preámbulo; Primera Parte, Capítulo Primero, Artículo 2°.

4) Gallup Argentina / Universidad Católica Argentina. *Clarín*, December 2, 2001, 47.

5) Auza, N. T. (1981). *Católicos y liberales en la generación del ochenta*. Buenos Aires: Ediciones Culturales Argentinas, I, V, VI, X.

6) [These [paleontologic] theories sometimes evidence an obvious socio-political significance. This is the case, for instance, of one of his early scientific works [reference to Florentino Ameghino], where transformism is wielded against theology and clericalism. Confronting the Bible's assertions with paleontologic finds, Ameghino stirs up a dispute between science and religion: between natural sciences and revelation. The scope of this way of presenting the problem is extremely significant, bearing in mind the struggle that was taking place at that time between the secularism upheld by the 1880 generation and the forces of traditional Catholicism]. Soler, R. (1979). *El positivismo argentino. Pensamiento filosófico y sociológico*. México D.F.: Universidad Nacional Autónoma de México, 55. AMEGHINO, Florentino (1854-1911), an outstanding Argentinian naturalist.

7) Gelderen, Alfredo M. (1996). *La Ley Federal de Educación de la República Argentina*. Buenos Aires: Academia Nacional de Educación, 81-87. Página 12 (1995), July 7, 11. Also see, July 8, 10-11; July 11, 10-11; July 12, 6-7; July 13, 10; July 14, 6; July 15, 10.

8) *Página 12* (1995), July 7, 11.

9) *Página 12* (1995), July 8, 10-11, esp. 11. Pope John Paul II (1996). *Message to Pontifical Academy of Sciences*. Vatican, "Evolution and the Church's Magisterium", §§ 4-6. Stenger, V.J., "Are Christianity and Darwinism Compatible?", Skeptical Briefs 12, 2 (June 2002), 13-14, esp. 13.

10) Kaiser, J., "Economic Crash Brings Ill Winds for Science", *Science* 295, 2356 (29 March 2002).

11) See, for example, Ríos, S. A. (2002), "Primera huella de los mamíferos americanos", *La Nación*, March 15, 12; Rauhut, O. W. M., Martin, T., Ortiz-Jaureguizar, E., Puerta, P., "A Jurassic Mammal from South America", *Nature* 416, 165-168 (14 March 2002).

12) Juárez, F. N. (2001). "Recorridos de un naturalista inquieto", *La Nación*, December 9 (it provides information about Darwin-related sites in South America); Piattelli Palmarini, M. (2001). "¿Los norteamericanos aún no han evolucionado?", *La Nación*, September 2; Kookson, C. (2001). "Annie, el eslabón perdido", *La Nación*, July 15; Wilford, J.N. (2001). "Ancient fossils stir human origin debate", *Buenos Aires Herald*, April 22; (2001), "Las islas inspiraron los estudios de Darwin", *Publimetro*, January 30; Canaletti, R.V. (2000). "El juicio del mono", *Clarín*, July 23 (an article commemorating the Scopes Monkey Trial in Dayton, TN); Brown, A. (2000). "Children of the evolution", *Buenos Aires Herald*, January 2; *Fast Company* (1999). "¿Sólo los paranoicos sobreviven?", *Clarín*, November 7; Kettle, M. (1999). "Darwin's pride: the biblical creationists are evolving", *Buenos Aires Herald*, September 15; Roman, V. (1999). "Un antepasado del hombre y del mono echa luz sobre la evolución", *Clarín*, September 4; Wade, N. (1999). "Comprueban la teoría de la evolución", *La Nación*, May 15; Gentil, A. (1999). "La evolución de las especies fue muy lenta y gradual", *Clarín*, April 24.

13) Scheinsohn, V., et al. (2001). *La evolución y las ciencias*. Buenos Aires: Emecé, 160 pp., softcover.

14) "Darwin en crisis", *La corriente del Espíritu* 5, 67 (Abril 2002), 5.

15) "Prohibido enseñar Darwin", *Clarín, Education Supplement,* March 3, 2002, 18.

16) [You all know, undoubtedly, that Darwin can be regarded as one of our wise men of learning, because the discovery of his theory is linked to the history of our scientific development, as it was here, among us, where he gathered the materials for his theory and had his first idea. And, by an extraordinary coincidence, indeed, it is here, and only here, in the Pampas, where said theory can be accurately and evidently proved, for the reasons that here are for us all to see]. Ameghino, F. (1915). *Filogenia*. Buenos Aires: La Cultura Argentina, "Un recuerdo a la memoria de Darwin", 56; Scheinsohn, V., et al., 76-79. *The Pampas*: an extensive and fertile plain in the central region of Argentina that has few trees and is covered in grass.

News from the British Humanist Assocation

British MPS Back Early Day Motion on Darwin Day

In January 2002 Ashok Kumar MP tabled the following Early Day Motion (EDM 706), which has so far (July 2002) attracted 45 signatures:

"That this House notes the scientific achievements of Charles Darwin in the face of centuries of religious dogma; welcomes proposals for the creation of a 'Charles Darwin Day' in recognition of the ground-breaking work of the British scientist responsible for the theory of evolution by natural selection; and calls for Darwin's birthday, 12th February, to be designated a public holiday, in honour of one of the fathers of modern science."

British Humanist Association Includes Darwin Day Holiday In Education Policy

As part of its education policy aimed at creating schools that include and accommodate pupils of all faiths and none, the British Humanist Association is campaigning for more school and public holidays for non-Christians, including Darwin Day for humanists. The *Times Educational Supplement* of 19 April 2002 couldn't resist featuring this aspect of BHA policy under the headline *Darwin day makes natural holiday selection*.

The British Humanist Association invites distinguished supporters and academics in Britain to add their signatures to the following joint letter, to be sent to the Prime Minister, the Home Secretary, The Times and other media, just before February 12th 2003:

We, the undersigned, support proposals for the creation of a new public holiday, Darwin Day, on February 12th. This is the birthday of Charles Darwin, one of the greatest British scientists and thinkers that ever lived. At a time when creationism appears to be gaining ground in English schools, the public celebration of Charles Darwin's contribution to modern science could send out a clear message of support for scientific thinking.

It will be the 200th anniversary of his birth in 2009, and we very much hope that this new public holiday will be in place by then.

Professor Simon Blackburn
Sir Hermann Bondi
Sir Roy Calne FRS
Dr Malcolm Cass
Michael Clark
Sir Kenneth Clucas
Professor Francis Crick FRS
Dr Helena Cronin
Professor Richard Dawkins
Professor Robin Dunbar FBA
Dr Steven French
Professor Hugh Huxley MBE, FRS
Professor Sir Hans Kornberg
   MA, DSc., ScD, FRS
Dr Brendan Larvor

Dr Stephen Law
Professor John Maynard Smith FRS
Professor David Papineau
Sir Roger Penrose FRS
Dr Janet Radcliffe Richards
Jonathan Rée
Dr Ben Rogers
Professor Sir Joseph Rotblat FRS
Professor Peter Simons
Sir David Smith FRS
Professor Sir Kenneth Stuart FRS
Professor Sir David Weatherall FRS
Dr Nigel Warburton
Professor Lewis Wolpert CBE FRS

Creationism In British Schools

The British Humanist Association was very active in bringing the activities of creationist teachers at Gateshead City Technology College in the North of England to the attention of the media early in 2002, and keeping it there – in fact it was we who first alerted the *Times Educational Supplement* to the story back in January, when a member of the public in Gateshead contacted us with his concerns about what was going on at a local school. Although the TES published the story, the other media were slow to take it up and things remained quiet until (with the assistance of the Darwin Day program) *The Guardian* took up the story in March, shortly followed by *Channel 4 News*, Radio 4's *Today* programme and numerous newspapers.

Throughout March and April creationism remained a prominent issue in the British media, which featured critical interviews, letters, articles and comment from scientists (Richard Dawkins was much in demand), philosophers, humanists (including BHA staff), and even bishops. We were delighted when Jenny Tonge MP challenged the Prime Minister on it in the House of Commons on 14th March, though less delighted with the PM's weak response, which attempted to justify what was going on by arguing for diversity and choice in education. Gateshead school has since been cited frequently in the continuing debate in Britain about religion in schools and religious schools, one issue emerging from the media coverage being that other state-funded and independent religious schools in Britain also teach creationism.

BHA organised a joint letter demanding changes to the English National Curriculum Science syllabus, as creationist science teachers appeared to be exploiting the wording of Key Stage 4 Science (aimed at 14-16 year olds) in the National Curriculum, which refers to pupils learning "how scientific controversies can arise from different ways of interpreting empirical evidence (for example Darwin's theory of evolution)." The letter called for: a tightening up of the legal requirements in National Curriculum Science to prevent creation stories being taught as anything other than religious myths; clear guidance from public examination boards to teachers and pupils that creationism is not a scientific hypothesis; and reform of the Science curriculum to enable teaching about Darwinian evolution well before secondary school. It was signed by over 40 eminent scientists and philosophers, and sent at the end of March to the Prime Minister, and various other ministers and regulatory bodies involved in education. The letter attracted a lot of media interest and featured in articles in *The Guardian*, *The Independent on Sunday*, *The Sunday Telegraph*, *The Times Educational Supplement*, and the *Times Higher Education Supplement*.

BHA also separately sent a letter to the Prime Minister and to education ministers, on the teaching of creationism in schools, requesting clarification and action. We asked whether ministers approved of this kind of teaching and what could be done to stop fundamentalists taking over other faith-based schools. We also wrote to the chair of the Qualifications and Curriculum Authority requesting action, and to the Chief Inspector of Schools, requesting that Emmanuel College be re-inspected and that future school inspections consider the treatment of creationism when inspecting Science departments. Responses to these letters came in slowly, and were not entirely reassuring, tending to focus on the good academic results of the Gateshead school and consequent parental satisfaction. But at the very least, those who decide such matters have been made aware of the issue and have registered widespread concern at the arrival on these shores of a problem that we had hitherto imagined confined to the USA.

BHA is using its website www.humanism.org.uk and newsletters to raise awareness and disseminate information on where to find the evidence and arguments to counter creationists. Humanist Philosophers' Group member Stephen Law wrote an article on the subject for the website (published in this anthology.)

We will continue to monitor the situation, keep the public and those in schools informed, and contribute actively to the debate. Future projects include a publication on creationism from the Humanist Philosophers' Group and the Humanist Scientists' Group.

[ADDITIONAL RESOUCES]

News from the British Humanist Association was written and compiled by Marilyn Mason, Educational Officer, and Madeleine Pym, Policy Officer. You may contact the BHA at:

British Humanist Association
47 Theobalds Rd
London WC1X 8SP

Tel: 020 7430 0908
Fax: 020 7430 1272
Website: http://www.humanism.org.uk

FEAR OF SCIENCE IN KANSAS
by Liz Craig

In 1632, Galileo had the impudence to publish a book that said the sun, not the earth, as the Bible suggested, was the center of our planetary system. The church at Rome banned Galileo's book. After recanting at the order of the Inquisition, he lived out the rest of his days under house arrest.

When Ben Franklin invented the lightning rod, some people called it the work of Satan. They were afraid such a device might thwart the will of a lightning-bolt-hurling God.

In 1923, some people branded Einstein's new theory of relativity as evil. "Relativity" must mean there is no absolute moral code, they thought. If that were so, then what was to prevent humanity from turning into a herd of murderous, promiscuous beasts?

Today, the majority of people have no problem accepting that the planets orbit the Sun, that lightning rods are useful in preventing fires, and that the theory of relativity has helped us understand the universe better. Most of us now realize that none of those discoveries threatened morality or God. But there still is one scientific discovery that inspires fear and loathing in some religious circles. That is Darwin's theory of evolution.

What Darwin saw during his five-year voyage on the H.M.S. *Beagle* suggested to him that species change over time to adapt to their environments, because individuals which exhibited better adaptations were more likely to survive to reproduce. Darwin also saw that there was an interrelatedness of living things. In "Origins," he speculated that all life on earth derived from one or a few original organisms. And that's where the trouble began. Darwin's views flatly contradicted the Genesis creation story. The controversy simmered on a low flame during Darwin's time, but it came to a full, rolling boil in the early 20th century.

In the 1920s, the encroachment of "modernism," the liberal interpretation of Scripture, which academic theologians embraced, sent fundamentalists into a frenzy. Evolutionary theory became the battleground in a broader cultural war whose opposing camps were clearly defined in the 1925 Scopes Trial.

Evolutionary theory said modern humans probably had descended from apes. If that theory was correct, then man was not the special creation of God, but only another animal in a long succession of other animals. Even more troubling, if the Genesis story was wrong, then the entire Bible was thrown into question. If the Bible was not a reliable spiritual authority, then what was the basis for morality? Was there no absolute moral code? The more fundamentalists thought about it, the more their worries compounded.

These doubts were new and difficult to deal with. In early America, Christianity had been infused into public life and public education. It was common practice to read Bible verses in class and have regular prayer times. However, in the 1920s, as more public schools were built and the general level of education increased, and as graduates of secular universities gained influence, religion's role in education and government began to wane. The notion of America as a Christian nation gave way to that of a nation of diverse beliefs, all deserving of respect. Thus began the war of conservative Christians versus secularism that continues today. It is occurring in politics, in religious institutions, and in public schools. In regard to public schools, witness the current antievolution efforts across America, carried out by Young-Earth Creationists and promoters of so-called "intelligent design," which Kansas University's Leonard Krishtalka has memorably referred to as "creationism in a cheap tuxedo."

Anti-evolutionism is the last bastion of Biblical literalism, or fundamentalism. Even though most Americans would not call themselves fundamentalists, about half believe creation happened the way Genesis tells it. It should not be a surprise, then, that at the same time scientists are unlocking the secrets of the human genome, staking claims to more and more "unknown" territory where mystery, superstition and faith once found a home, creationists are determined to stop it from encroaching any farther. In recent years, anti-evolutionists have launched vigorous new assaults in the public education arena. The most well-publicized of these – after the Scopes Trial – took place in Kansas in 1999.

State Boards of Education generally pursue their duties in relative obscurity. We assume they're taking care of administrative details of K-12 education, and we imagine everything is going along smoothly unless we hear otherwise. However, in August of 1999, the Kansas Board of Education made front-page headlines across the nation and the globe. What had everybody in a tizzy was that against the recommendations of educators and scientists, the "social conservative" majority on the BOE voted to adopt a set of public school science standards from which certain scientific ideas were missing: the geological age of the earth, the Big Bang, global warming, and macroevolution. Kansans, who have long prided themselves on their excellent public education system, were taken aback by the BOE's apparent contempt for modern scientific knowledge. Over the course of 14 months, a BOE-appointed 26-member writing team of educators, scientists and curriculum experts had produced science standards which integrated evolutionary theory more thoroughly into the K-12 science education. They used model standards drafted by the National Research Council, part of the National Academy of Sciences, as their starting point. The goal was to bring Kansas' standards into line with currently accepted methods of teaching about evolution and its role in producing the diversity of life on earth.

When the creationists on the Board of Education saw the changes, they were outraged. One of them, Dr. Steve Abrams, a veterinarian from Arkansas City, presented a different set of standards to the BOE. Those standards, it turned out, had been authored by a Missouri Young-Earth Creationist group, the Creation Science Association of

Mid-America. The document Abrams presented was riddled with illogic, inconsistencies and misstatements of science. After consideration, the Board decided not to adopt the CSAMA standards, but by a 6-4 vote, they adopted a "compromise" version of the standards – part writing team content, part CSAMA content – which had been cobbled together by three BOE members: two creationists and one malleable moderate. The conservative Fordham Foundation examined the new standards and gave them a grade of "F-minus." Who knew there was a grade lower than "F?"

In the ensuing media firestorm, Kansans were severely embarrassed by ridicule from every quarter, some far-flung – even BBC-TV, a Japanese TV crew, a Swedish film team, and a French reporter flew in to report on Kansas' amazing devolution. Cars sported bumper stickers reading "Kansas: Where Evolution Is Outlawed and the Monkeys Are In Charge." When Kansans told out-of-staters where they were from, they were subjected either to snickers or outright laughter. "Kansas? You're from KANSAS??"

Scientists and academics were first stunned, then spurred to action. A new organization formed: Kansas Citizens For Science (www.kcfs.org). KCFS was composed of citizens, educators and scientists who favored adoption of the original writing team's science standards, which the Fordham Foundation said would have rated a solid "A." The pro-science campaign mounted by KCFS focused on education of the general public. Moderate political organizations focused on getting the creationists off the Board.

Half of the ten-member Kansas Board of Education is up for election every two years. Normally, there isn't much campaigning. But with seats held by four creationists and one pro-science moderate up for grabs, and the science standards riding on the outcome, the 2000 Board of Education race was the hottest thing going. The creationist Chair of the BOE, conservative Republican Linda Holloway, spent $90,000 on her primary campaign against moderate Republican Sue Gamble, the most that had ever been spent in a Board race. She even bought TV spots. Yard signs for Gamble or Holloway popped up all over Johnson County. Both candidates were interviewed on national news shows.

The MAINstream Coalition's political action committee and the Kansas NEA PAC supported Gamble and the other moderate candidates. Get-out-the-vote efforts in the Holloway-Gamble race were especially intense. The Republican primary would determine the winner, because in Kansas general elections, most voters simply go down the list and check all the boxes marked "R." In Kansas, a Democrat is roughly equivalent to a Wobbly: quaint and irrelevant.

In the primary, Kansas voters delivered an unmistakable message. Two of the three incumbent creationists were defeated. The fourth creationist had moved out of state, leaving an empty seat. The one incumbent moderate retained his seat. When the dust settled, the balance of power had shifted to 7-3 in favor of the moderates. They took office in January of 2000. On Valentine's Day, they delivered a sweet victory to science education, overturning the "F-minus" standards in favor of the writing team's "A" standards. Hosannas rang out across the state. Then the matter was quickly forgotten, except for the lingering sting of humiliation. But now, 2002 brings another election and another shake-up on the Board of Education.

In the August 6 Republican primary, two pro-science BOE members were defeated by creationists. One incumbent creationist retained his seat. A pro-voucher conservative took the seat vacated by a retiring BOE member. In the November general election, only one conservative has a Democratic challenger. That race will determine whether the Board returns to a 5-5 moderate-conservative deadlock configuration or a 6-4 pro-science majority.

Creationists on the BOE have said they want to revisit the science standards. Like other states, Kansas is in the grip of a severe educational budget squeeze, so we can only hope the Board won't have time or energy to rehash the evolution issue. At least not right now. But as long as there are people who think science is a threat to religion, the evolution issue will keep bobbing up, like a rubber ducky in a Jacuzzi. We are not defenseless, however. Everywhere anti-science activists surface, groups like Kansas Citizens For Science pop up, too. They include Michigan Citizens For Science, the Burlington-Edison Committee for Science Education (Washington State), Coalition for Excellence in Science and Math Education (CESE) (New Mexico), Nebraska Religious Coalition for Science Education, and most recently, Ohio Citizens For Science.

Recently, Kansas "intelligent design" proponents have been traveling to Ohio, where they are making their case before that state's Board of Education. Will ID promoters get their philosophy taught as science in Ohio public schools? If not, will they sue the Board of Education? The Discovery Institute, home of "intelligent design," is swarming with attorneys who have written articles purporting to show that it's legal to teach ID in public school science classes. They have been rattling their litigation swords for some time. Some observers think soon, the IDers will tire of trying unsuccessfully to convince school boards and Boards of Education their religiously based philosophy is science and resort to lawsuits to force it into science classes. It's unclear what the grounds would be, but in this cultural war, the stakes are high, and if the law seems likely to offer a remedy, the ID people are likely to try it.

Mr. Darwin, you would be surprised to see all that science has learned and accomplished in the past couple of centuries, based on your theory. And you would be astounded to see how the strategies of anti-evolutionists have evolved, though their basic arguments have not. It becomes ever more obvious that in the biotechnical, biomedical, bio-everything future, science will adapt, survive, and thrive. It is constantly growing in sophistication, identifying cures for once-hopeless diseases, solving pressing environmental and resource problems around the world, and giving us ever-clearer visions of how the physical universe works. We've moved past fear of the heliocentric model, the lightning rod, and the theory of relativity. Will we someday move past the fear of science? For the sake of our children's education, I devoutly hope so. ∞

[ABOUT THE AUTHOR]

Liz Craig is President of Kansas Citizens for Science. She first became a pro-science activist in 1999, when the Kansas Board of Education attempted to remove macroevolution and other generally accepted scientific ideas from the state's science standards. She is a free-lance writer living in Roeland Park, Kansas.

[ADDITIONAL RESOURCES]

Kansas Citizens for Science: http://www.kcfs.org/

Talk.Origins Online Resource: http://www.talkorigins.org/

Talk.Design Online Resource: http://www.talkdesign.org

CREATIONISM IN NEW MEXICO
by David E. Thomas

The history of creationism in New Mexico is typical of many rural states. It has long followed national teaching trends, with occasional punctuations like the "Evolution is just a theory" disclaimer pasted on school biology books by the State Board of Education in the 70's.

But things really heated up in the summer of 1996. In spring of that year, a committee of teachers and scientists had finished draft science standards for public schools, which included (of course!) evolution and the age of the earth. But these standards were unacceptable to a Governor appointed Board member, Roger X. Lenard, of Sandia Laboratories. He took on the task of opposing them, and was joined in his new quest by Board member Millie Pogna. In the version of the standards released to the public on the day before the acceptance vote, August 21, 1996, Lenard's and Pogna's work was finally revealed. Evolution and the age of the earth were completely omitted, replaced by the vague "various theories of origin." On August 22nd, 1996, dubbed "Black Thursday" by many New Mexican scientists, the State Board of Education, swayed by Lenard's persuasive anti-Darwinian rhetoric, passed the set of Content Standards with Benchmarks for Science. Several academic, science religious and other groups vigorously opposed these changes. Groups stating opposition to the gutting of science from the standards included New Mexicans for Science and Reason, the New Mexico Academy of Science, the National Center for Science Education, several University of New Mexico Departments (Faculty and Students: Physics, Biology, Earth and Planetary Science; Faculty: History, Anthropology, Psychology), individuals/faculty from New Mexico State University and from the New Mexico Institute of Mining and Technology, individuals from the New Mexico Senate and House of Representatives, members and the Rabbi of Temple Albert, The Albuquerque Journal, The Albuquerque Tribune, The Santa Fe New Mexican, The United Church of Santa Fe, Christ Unity Church, and many other groups.

Even with these numerous protests, efforts to change the newly-adopted creationism-friendly standards were making little progress. So, State Senator Pauline Eisenstadt (D-Corrales) introduced Senate Bill 155 to the New Mexico state legislature on Jan. 28th 1997. The Bill said simply "In determining public school curriculum policy or prescribing courses of instruction for public schools, the state board shall adopt curriculum standards for life sciences and earth and space sciences that conform with the national academy of sciences' national science education standards for life sciences and earth and space sciences." Since the National Standards included evolution (of course! Chemistry was included too!), the bill would get evolution back into New Mexico standards, if only in an indirect way. The Bill narrowly passed the Senate Education committee by 4 to 3, and went to the full Senate on Feb. 17th. During a lengthy debate, Sen. Leonard Lee Rawson of Las Cruces waved a stuffed ape he called "Uncle Harry" as he denounced evolution. Ex-UNM Biology chair Jim Findley and I provided Sen. Eisenstadt with answers to questions during the hearing on the bill. I was honored to be the scientist standing on the floor of the State Senate that day to affirm that the best modern science really does show that the age of the Earth is four and a half billion years. The Senate passed the bill 24 to 17, in a strongly partisan vote (Democrats for, Republicans against).

Meanwhile, a counter-offensive was launched in the House. House Bill 1321 said, among other things, that "no fossil or any other evidence exists for this common ancestor and noted evolutionists have described the extreme scarcity of transitional forms as the 'trade secret of paleontology.'"

On Tuesday, March 11th, 1997, the bill came before the House Business and Industry Committee. After much discussion, including passage of an amendment calling for "balanced treatment," the bill was tabled by a 10 to 2 vote. Three days later, Rep. Tim Macko tabled his creationism bill (HB 1321). SB 155 still had one last gasp of activity. On March 15th, the Business and Industry suddenly un-tabled the bill, and passed it without recommendation to the House Education Committee. The bill came up the morning of Friday, March 21st, the day before the end of the session. Sen. Eisenstadt presented four speakers, including Nobel laureate Murray Gell-Mann. After testimony from board and department of education members against legislating standards, a roll call vote to table the bill passed 6 to 5. And that was the end of Senate Bill 155.

In the meantime, members of several of the opposition groups banded together to form CESE, the Coalition for Excellence in Science Education. CESE drafted a set of suggested changes to the standards, and the Department of Education appeared to be considering them seriously. A survey was carried out on the suggested changes. What happened after that was "rather disturbing," in the words of UNM science history professor Tim Moy. In a September 1997 radio interview, Moy said that the State Board spent tens of thousands of dollars of taxpayer money to do the survey, sending it to hundreds of scientists, and engineers, teachers, and parents. It listed the changes that the CESE had proposed on how to fix the standards. When the results were returned and tallied, the CESE recommendations passed by overwhelming margins – 60 to 70 percent for each of these recommendations. The State Board reviewed these results and announced that they were not going to make any of the changes.

With no results from efforts with the Legislature and with the State Department of Education, concerned citizens turned their attention to politics. Lenard's appointed position ended in the upcoming election cycle (1998), and creationist incumbent Millie Pogna was running for re-election. At first, the dubious task of defeating a 20-year incumbent in a primary election seemed difficult indeed. But CESE founder Marshall Berman accepted the challenge as a candidate in the Republican primary. Berman built up a tremendous grass-roots effort staffed by dozens of volunteers, including many of the scientists and teachers who had opposed the new standards. Near the end of the campaign, on May 27th, 1998, several noted community leaders took the unusual step of holding a press conference to endorse a candidate for the board of education. The dignitaries included Sen. Harrison "Jack" Schmitt, the last man to walk on the moon.

On Tuesday, June 2nd, District 2 handed Marshall Berman a two-to-one margin of victory. His primary opponent, Millie Pogna, lost her 20-year position on the board, getting just 33 percent of the vote. Berman faced no opposition in the general election in November. During the campaign, Pogna tried to claim that she also opposed creationism in the science classroom. Perhaps voters remembered statements like one from the October 9th, 1996 Albuquerque Journal, where Pogna said "The only thing the standards do is it kind of opens the door to a discussion of creationism."

On August 11th, 1999, the Kansas State Board of Education voted 6-4 to remove evolution from school standards and testing requirements. As happened in New Mexico, a diverse group of teachers, parents and scientists worked hard to develop accurate and complete science standards, modeled on national standards developed by groups like the National Academy of Sciences or the American Association for the Advancement of Science. And, just as in New Mexico, a few members of the school board threw out the work of the committee, and introduced their own standards – heavily biased against evolution.

Marshall Berman advanced quickly in the State Board, and was soon leading a number of innovative efforts. But the board consensus at that time was that it was too soon to re-visit the science standards. Once Kansas was in the spotlight, however, and with New Mexico receiving renewed attention for its own anti-evolution standards, the Board decided to revisit the science standards quickly. And so they did. At 1:06 PM Mountain Standard Time on October 8th, 1999, the New Mexico State Board of Education voted 13-to-1 in favor of a proposal to revise state science teaching standards to include evolution and related concepts, such as the age of the earth. And so the fuzzy language in New Mexico's standards, which encouraged creationists and anti-evolutionists for three years, officially became history. Both major newspapers in the state strongly endorsed the action. The Albuquerque Tribune wrote on Oct. 14th "How odd that public officials should draw praise for doing perfectly sensible things. But given the state of teaching standards for science classes across the nation these days, the New Mexico Board of Education has earned its accolades." The state's largest paper, the Albuquerque Journal, said on Oct. 17th that "The religious beliefs of students and their parents must be respected – but the beliefs of some must not be allowed to curtail the science education of all." Even Archbishop Michael J. Sheehan of the Diocese of Santa Fe weighed in, saying in two state newspapers that "I don't believe there is any real contradiction between the theory of evolution and the creation of the world by God. The church has no problem accepting the theory of evolution, provided that it is understood that God infuses a human soul at a certain point in the evolutionary process and that, in fact, God is the force behind the evolution process." (Albuquerque Journal, Santa Fe New Mexican, Oct. 15th 1999).

The board member who sponsored the new proposal, Sandia physicist /CESE founder/NMSR member Marshall Berman, was interviewed in the Oct. 22nd '99 Science (page 659), as was CESE member Kim Johnson. Berman's efforts were also discussed in "Speaking up for Science" in the November '99 issue of Scientific American.

The creationists, and their new incarnation ("Intelligent Design") continue their efforts to remove evolution from New Mexico schools. On February 15, 2000, the Senate Education Committee gave Sen. Rod Adair's "Creation Theory" Bill a "DO PASS" recommendation, by a vote of 9-0. The bill, Senate Joint Memorial 47, was titled "Requesting The State Board Of Education To Allow The Use Of Materials In The Classroom For The Study Of Creation Theory." It never got to the full Senate. Adair is now the Republican candidate for Lieutenant Governor.

Signs are looming that New Mexico is the next target of anti-evolutionists, who have been most active recently in Kansas and Ohio. There has been an ongoing Intelligent Design Blitz at New Mexico universities (UNM, NM Tech) and state science labs (Sandia, Los Alamos). Several of the most prominent ID theorists have recently visited New Mexico. Phillip Johnson stumped the state in February of 2001 (http://www.nmsr.org/johnson.htm), William Dembski in November of 2001 (http://www.nmsr.org/dembski.htm), and Michael Behe in March of 2002 (http://www.nmsr.org/behe.htm). A Christian activist group, the New Mexico Family Council (NMFC), claimed credit for sending out hundreds of copies of Michael Behe's book on Intelligent Design to science teachers around the state, but the name on the cover letter only stated the author's affiliation with the University of New Mexico (http://www.nmsr.org/omdahl.htm). The formation of a New Mexico chapter of the Intelligent Design Network (IDNet) was announced on July 23rd, 2002 (http://www.intelligentdesignnetwork.org/PressReleaseNewMexico.htm).

Members of NMSR (http://www.nmsr.org) and CESE (http://www.cesame-nm.org) have long participated in the never-ending struggle to keep real science in science classrooms. We were there in Santa Fe in 1996 as the science standards were being gutted, and we were on the Senate floor as teaching evolution was being debated. We were there in 1998 when the State Board overturned the anti-science standards. We were there on the editorial pages, and in the university halls giving pro-science talks to balance ID rhetoric. And we are there on the Internet, defending and explaining science, and debating creationists from New Mexico to Minnesota.

Seeing the clouds on the horizon, we in New Mexico know it's only a matter of time before creationism rears its ugly head once again. But next time won't be like 1996.

Next time, we'll be *ready*. ∞

[ABOUT THE AUTHOR]

David E. Thomas is a physicist and mathematician, employed at a small high-tech testing firm in Albuquerque, NM. Dave is president of the science group, New Mexicans for Science and Reason as well as a Fellow of the Committee for Scientific Investigation of Claims of the Paranormal (CSICOP), publishers of *Skeptical Inquirer* magazine. He has published several articles in *Skeptical Inquirer* on the Roswell and Aztec UFO Incidents, as well as on the Bible Code. He received the National Center for Science Education's Friend of Darwin Award in 2000.

[ADDITIONAL RESOURCES]

New Mexicans for Science and Reason (NMSR): http://www.nmsr.org

Coalition for Excellence in Science and Math Education: http://www.cesame-nm.org/

This paper was presented by Gerry Dantone to the Long Island Secular Humanists for Darwin Day 2002.

EVOLUTION AND CREATIONISM:
WHY SCIENCE AND NOT CREATIONISM MUST BE TAUGHT IN CLASSROOMS, AND THREATS TO GOOD SCIENCE EDUCATION
by Gerry Dantone

The Creation Research Society, established to promote and fund "scientific" creation research, publishes a journal called the *Creation Research Society Quarterly*. It is one of the only journals where creationists are able or have even tried to publish their work. Prominent creationists such as Duane Gish, Henry Morris, Thomas Barnes, and Harold Slusher have all served on its board of directors at one time or another. The society and journal require that all members adhere to the following statement of belief. Here it is:

Statement of Belief:

The Bible is the written Word of God, and because it is inspired throughout, all its assertions are historically and scientifically true in the original autographs. To the student of nature this means that the account of origins in Genesis is a factual presentation of simple historical truths.

All basic types of living things, including man, were made by direct creative acts of God during the Creation Week described in Genesis. Whatever biological changes have occurred since Creation Week have been accomplished only changes within the original created kinds.

The great flood described in Genesis, commonly referred to as the Noachian Flood, was an historic event worldwide in its extent and effect.

We are an organization of Christian men and women of science who accept Jesus Christ as our Lord and Savior. The account of the special creation of Adam and Eve as one man and one woman and their subsequent fall into sin is the basis for our belief in the necessity of a Savior for all mankind. Therefore, salvation can come only through accepting Jesus Christ as our Savior.

Whatever the above is, it is not scientific. If science is anything, it is NOT assuming the conclusion and looking for ways to rationalize what is preferable to you. It is going where the evidence leads, period, not twisting the evidence or omitting evidence that does not suit you.

Sir Isaac Newton is famous for his discovery of the laws of gravity. However, even he was not totally satisfied with his own theories. He worried that perturbations in the planetary orbits would lead to the long-term instability of the solar system. He assumed that divine intervention was needed to ensure stability; perhaps we could call it "intelligent guidance." His admitted ignorance led him to this supernatural assumption. No one in his day could disprove "intelligent guidance" with a complete natural explanation. Eventually marquis de Pierre-Simon Laplace came along and proposed a hypothesis, which led to a theory, that the solar system was formed from rotating gas. It was so complete that Newton's concerns were explained away very admirably. Napoleon, informed of this theory, complained to Laplace possibly in a teasing manner that Laplace had left God out of his system of the planets to which Laplace replied, "I have no need of that hypothesis."

If Laplace had accepted "intelligent guidance" as an explanation, what possible motivation would he have had for going any further? A magical, supernatural explanation is a science stopper – it ends all inquiry. By NOT accepting "intelligent guidance," Laplace found a deeper explanation that did not require a supernatural hypothesis. It did not require a "God of the gaps" of human ignorance. For us to accept such a God now, in Creationism or Intelligent Design, would also be to end inquiry in the area we are pursuing. Accepting a supernatural explanation is the end of thought. It is the opposite of science.

Creationism starts with the bible, not observations. All data either conforms or is rejected, period. Henry Morris, President of the Institute for Creation Research says, "There is no observational fact imaginable which cannot, one way or another, **be made** to fit the creation model." Then, one must ask, why bother with facts at all? If facts directly opposite of each work for the model, who needs any observations at all?

This is not science, and real science is important to the well being of humanity, increasing life spans by leaps and bounds around the world. That is why science, the inquiring kind of science that is not simply rote memorization of facts, but instead the kind that provokes thought and further inquiry, needs to be in public schools.

What are the Threats to Science Education:

There are always new laws and resolutions being proposed that threaten science education in Public Schools;

1) State Sen. Hochstatter of Washington has proposed an act (Senate Bill 6500, year 2002) banning the teaching of evolution in schools. The article states that, "The legislature finds that the theory of evolution in the common schools of the state of Washington is repugnant to the principles of the Declaration of Independence and thereby unconstitutional and unlawful." Yes, the bill actually says that evolution is unconstitutional because it contradicts the Declaration of Independence! It goes on to ban all textbooks that teach it and that Creationism replaces it. It's unlikely to pass, but consider he got elected somehow!

2) The Ohio Board of Education held a panel discussion featuring both advocates and opponents of including intelligent design (ID) in the newly drafted statewide science standards at its March meeting. The decision to hold the discussion came after a contentious meeting on Sunday, January 14th, at which lawyer John Calvert, of the Kansas based Intelligent Design Network, made the case for inclusion of the controversial field in the standards. Opponents of ID were not allowed to speak at the meeting at that meeting. Summary: Intelligent Design is on the table in Ohio.

3) The Alabama State Board of Education voted on November 8, 2001 to require that a statement referring to evolution as controversial be inserted in science textbooks. Since 1995 an evolution disclaimer has been pasted in Alabama's state-approved texts.

4) Louisiana HCR 74 Amended and Adopted House Concurrent Resolution 74 was introduced in the legislature in April 2001, and referred to the Education Committee. As introduced, this resolution opposed racism. It then asserted that Charles Darwin and his books promoted the justification of racism, and that Adolf Hitler ultimately exploited these same views to justify killing millions of people. In addition, the resolution deplored and rejected "... the core concepts of Darwinist ideology that certain races and classes of humans are inherently superior to others..."

5) On June 13, 2001, the US Senate adopted a "Sense of the Senate" amendment to the Elementary and Secondary Education Act Authorization bill, S.1, currently under consideration. The resolution (Amendment #799) read: "It is the sense of the Senate that (1) good science education should prepare students to distinguish the data or testable theories of science from philosophical or religious claims that are made in the name of science; and (2)where biological evolution is taught, the curriculum should help students to understand why the subject generates so much continuing controversy, and should prepare the students to be informed participants in public discussions regarding the subject." The amendment was proposed by Senator Santorum of Pennsylvania. Ultimately this was deleted but not until an in intense effort by pro-science activists. But consider that it easily passed the first time around.

These are not nearly all of the threats to science education – not by a long shot. This is NOT a matter of forcing a dogma on unsuspecting children – it's all about REMOVING dogma from the classroom and letting evidence speak for itself. It's about evidence instead of magic and faith. School is a place to investigate and a place to ask questions, not simply accept. Now it's true that science is often taught by rote, but that once again is the result of poor science education in the first place. The technologically dangerous world we live in demands that we understand the real world in terms of the real world. We cannot afford to do less. ∞

[ABOUT THE AUTHOR]

Gerry Dantone is President of Long Island Secular Humanists, has a B.S. in Chemical Engineering and an M.B.A. in Finance.

[ADDITIONAL RESOURCES]

Long Island Secular Humanists: http://nyhumanist.org/lish.htm

HARUN YAHYA AND ISLAMIC CREATIONISM
by Taner Edis

"Darwin Day" could probably only be thought of in the United States. After all, among industrialized nations, the US is the only one with a strong creationist movement, causing endless battles over school curricula. Other countries have their anti-evolutionary moments, but the American market for creationism is the largest. Ken Ham might present his "Answers in Genesis" (www.answersingenesis.org) with an Australian accent, but he found it best to move to the US.

Of course, Americans are not the only people who have a strong streak of old-time religion in their culture, and who perceive the strain modern science puts on the old verities. In this time of religious revival around the globe, the Islamic world is perhaps the most striking in its attachment to a scripturally literalist faith. However, until recently, "creation-science" was not very visible in Muslim lands. Ironically, this was mainly because Darwinian evolution rarely appeared in education or in intellectual life.

In 1873, in the days of the Ottoman Empire, Mithat Efendi mentioned Darwin's theory in one of his writings. The religious scholars put out a fatwa declaring him an apostate. In the twentieth century, the scholars lost their traditional power in many countries, and Western ideas increased in influence. Still, Muslim thinkers took it for granted that either evolution did not occur, or that any development in life happened under direct divine guidance. The Quran, after all, declares special creation, particularly of humans. The blind naturalistic process modern science has come to accept obviously had to be wrong; the Darwinian view of nature was but another indication of Western degeneration in religion and morals. However, Muslim apologists rarely felt a need to elaborate their dismissal of Darwin.

In the US, creationism appeals to a religiously conservative population who have become upwardly mobile, joining professional classes where technical knowledge is highly valued. They are concerned both to affirm their traditional, morality-infused view of nature and at the same time, respect science and technology. Creation-science promises to accomplish this without compromise. Interestingly, a similar situation has developed in the Islamic world. Particularly in Turkey, long the most modernized among Muslim nations, the last few decades has been a time of both religious revival, and of the growing power of a religiously conservative segment of society who operates in a global capitalist economy. And so, perhaps unsurprisingly, creationism has recently erupted in Turkey, and influenced other Muslim countries. Muslim immigrant communities in the West – also caught between old-time religion and the modern world – have also been increasingly exposed to creationism, often imported from Turkey.

One name dominates Turkish creationism: *Harun Yahya*. Supposedly this is the pen name of Adnan Oktar, the leader of a religious order. But Yahya is credited with so many books, articles, videos, and web pages (www.hyahya.org) that it is hard to believe this is a one-man industry. Plus the intellectual prowess of leaders of religious orders are commonly exaggerated – tales of incredible intellectual productivity serve as a kind of modern miracle story, bolstering the stature of charismatic teachers. So Yahya is not really a person but the flag under which the most prominent Turkish creationist activities set sail.

What is immediately striking about Yahya's productions is how modern and media-conscious they are. Before the Yahya era, expressions of creationist sentiment in Turkey were generally confined to religious intellectual circles; these writings rarely went beyond throwaway references to the obvious intelligent design in biology, and denunciations of evolution generally occupied a few passages in books concentrating on larger religious themes. Some religious orders striving to create an Islamic version of modernity attacked evolution in their "science magazines," but these had limited effect – a well-heeled and media-savvy creationism, with great production values, continually harping on the evils of evolution, was unheard of. In contrast, Yahya's material is in full color, printed on glossy paper, copiously illustrated, popular in orientation (it uses few Arabic terms, unlike much religious literature), and available in all sorts of modern media. These publications are ubiquitous, found not just in bookstores but even in supermarket chains owned by the new breed of "Islamic corporations."

It is clear that Yahya's project commands an immense amount of resources. It is doubtful that Yahya's lavishly produced materials support themselves – they are priced to be affordable, and even obtaining them for free takes no great effort. The August 2002 issue of *Mercek*, his "monthly scientific and cultural magazine" sold for about $1.80, including two VCD's (video CD-ROM's), and the only ad for non-Yahya merchandise it contained was for a series of materials to learn English (important for the upwardly mobile). Yahya's web sites make most of his books available online, in a wide variety of languages – at no charge. Turkish creationism has gone international, and Yahya's books are as easily found and as prominently displayed in Islamic bookstores in London as in Istanbul. And the organization behind all of this, and the sources of its finances, are virtually unknown. The Turkish state, notoriously unable to bring the underground economy under control, or even collect taxes from most businesses, is also unable to enforce regulations on religious foundations.

Another striking aspect of Yahya's material is how much of it is taken, with minimal changes, from Western creationist literature such as that associated with the Institute for Creation Research (ICR). Since the Quran is not as specific as the Genesis story, Islamic creationists usually allow an old earth, so Yahya discards flood-geology and is noncommittal about the age of the earth. But the rest is there, flavored with quotations from some "Intelligent Design" figures, and all set in a matrix of traditional Islamic apologetics hammering on how obvious it is that there is a designing intelligence behind all the wonders of nature. ICR-style creationism, which we tend to think of as a sectarian, evangelical Protestant peculiarity, turns out to be pre-adapted to an Islamic environment.

Yahya also promotes other beliefs far from mainstream science and scholarship, besides creationism. These tend to be his versions of conspiratorial ideas popular in the Muslim world, such as Masonic plots and holocaust denial. But even when indulging these politically-colored fantasies, Yahya has a way of getting back to denouncing evolution. *Fascism: The Bloody Ideology of Darwinism* (Istanbul: Kultur, 2002) begins with a "To The Reader" section, where Yahya explains that evolution is at the root of evil today:

> *The reason why a special chapter is assigned to the collapse of the theory of evolution is that this theory constitutes the basis of all anti-spiritual philosophies. Since Darwinism rejects the fact of creation, and therefore the existence of God, during the last 140 years it has caused many people to abandon their faith or fall into doubt. Therefore, showing that this theory is a deception is a very important duty, which is strongly related to the religion. It is imperative that this important service be rendered to everyone. Some of our readers may find the chance to read only one of our books. Therefore, we think it appropriate to spare a chapter for a summary of this subject.*

The same preface and the same anti-evolutionary chapter, "The Misconception of Evolution" (with different illustrations) appear in *Islam Denounces Terrorism* (3rd edition, Bristol: Amal Press, 2002). In this book, Yahya treats the reader not only to standard apologetics about Islam being a religion of peace, but in his chapter "The Real Roots of Terrorism: Darwinism and Materialism" exposes the true culprit behind events like September 11: evolution. Apparently, "the way to stop acts of terrorism is to put an end to Darwinist-materialist education, to educate young people in accord with a curricula [sic] based on true scientific findings and to instil in them the fear of God and the desire to act wisely and scrupulously." (p. 147)

What then, of opposition to Yahya, particularly in Turkey, where his name is known best? Unfortunately, this is weak. Turkey is a "developing country," a polite term to describe a place which is economically a colony administered by the IMF, politically unstable, and poor. The Turkish scientific community is weak, unable to find even a unified voice in fighting the creationists, let alone muster comparable resources. Occasionally, political secularists complain about Yahya, but secularists can do little else lately but wring hands and hope against hope that the European Community will let Turkey become a member, and maybe then everything will be all right. At the time of writing, Turkey was poised for elections at the end of 2002, and an Islamist party was expected to come out with the largest share of the vote.

Still, friends of Darwin can find a few reasons to be optimistic. After all, creationism is a reaction, and the very fact that a Harun Yahya exists is evidence that evolutionary ideas have penetrated far enough into Turkish culture that religious conservatives feel a need to take action. And Yahya becoming known throughout the Islamic world might mean that evolution is making inroads there as well.

On the other hand, there are even more reasons to be pessimistic. Yahya seems successful in grabbing public attention, with little opposition. As the degree of conservatism of Turkish governments fluctuates, the degree of creationism in high school biology texts also goes up and down, but evolution, if present, will inevitably be relegated to the last chapter the class will not have time to cover. And the notion that the complexities of life and the universe can only result from divine design runs very deep in Islamic apologetics. Muslims will, by and large, to continue to see Darwinian evolution as obviously false, and maybe even evil, for a long time to come. With Harun Yahya, we have a phenomenon which we in the Western world we should carefully watch and learn from as we celebrate "Darwin Day." For here we have a creationism which threatens to be successful in its ambitions to drive evolution out of the culture.

[ABOUT THE AUTHOR]

Taner Edis is Assistant Professor of Physics at Truman State Univeristy in Kirksville Missouri. He is the author of numerous articles on physics, philosophy, artificial intelligence, and anti-evolutionary thought.

[ADDITIONAL RESOURCES]

A number of papers on Islamic creationism are available at www2.truman.edu/~edis/.

MUSLIM CREATIONISM ON THE MISINFORMATION HIGHWAY

by Lynne H. Schultz

If cyberspace is any indication, creationism is quite prevalent among Muslims. Muslim websites, especially the more popular ones, typically include an attack on some aspect of the theory of evolution. About half of these sites adopt an Intelligent Design sort of creationism while the other half resembles Old Earth creationism. Ironically, almost all express the view that Islam is a very "scientific" religion, and that the Quran is miraculous because it predicted discoveries that were not made by scientists until thousands of years later. These arguments, as might be expected, are quite deficient in their science and history. It would seem then that Islamic Creationism is like the Christian creation "science," in that with few exceptions it prefers to say that it is scientific and that the theory of evolution is not, rather than attacking science per se.

Nearly all the Muslim sites I surveyed promote some version of the Quran's six-day creation story, although none supported six literal days. Some Muslims use Quran 70: 4, *"The angels ascend to Him in a day, the measure of which is fifty thousand years,"* to claim that to Allah a day is equal to 50,000 years, which would mean that the earth was created in 300,000 years. Others accept the scientific view that the earth is about 4.5 billion years old, and that the universe itself is much older.

I only found one Muslim website, The Islamic Homepage , that appears to support evolution   (http://members.tripod.com/aaltinkaya/islam_and_modern_science.htm). The author, an undergraduate history student in Turkey, does not defend evolution, but rather briefly expresses concern about the spread of creationism in his home country, saying there is "very serious propaganda in this direction" and "some people are trying to discard the Evolution Theory or Darwinism…"

According to fatwa-online.com, the Permanent Committee for Islaamic Research and Fataawa, which is Saudi Arabia's highest religious authority and is headed by Shaykh 'Abdul-'Azeez Aal ash-Shaykh, banned Pokemon because it resembles gambling. They also warned that the concept of the characters in the game appeared to be based on Charles Darwin's theory of evolution. The irony is that Pokemon "evolution" is a metamorphosis that individual Pokemon may either undergo or refuse at will, and bears no resemblance to evolution by natural selection.

According to *Human Rights Watch*, a man named Dr. Farouk el Nur, arrested for his left-wing political views in 1989 in the Sudan, was tortured in an attempt to get him to recant his favorable views on evolution. His torturers were convinced that evolution conflicts with Islam. (http://www.thefileroom.org/FileRoom/documents/Cases/318darwin.html)

An online Book called "Nature's Holism," written by a Muslim, promises that it "provides an ecological model as an alternative to the 'competitive' theory of evolution." (http://www.ecotao.com/holism/3_RELIGION.htm) In other words, it rejects the idea that the theory of evolution must compete with religion. Holism, as defined in "Nature's Holism", seeks to reconcile the two, or so it seems. However, upon further examination, it seems that the site is really promoting the notion of Intelligent Design, although it doesn't use that phrase. This is from the section on creationism:

> "…we can reject the comments of philosophers such as Dennett who observe: 'The existence of a universe obeying a set of laws as elegant as … the laws of our own physics does not **logically** require an intelligent Lawgiver.'"

The same section has a very odd argument about mutations. The author says that mutations can't be random if they are caused by something. Since we know the causes of some mutations, they all have to have a cause; therefore, God could be causing some of them.

Very few Muslim sites use the phrase "Intelligent Design" or "Intelligent Designer" but the concept is expressed in many other Muslim websites, such as Tara's World of Islam (http://www.angelfire.com/mo2/scarves/evolution.html), which claims that "evolution" and "creation" are two different words for the same thing. However, instead of natural selection, it promotes the notion of "Allah selection."

> "What is the firing power of evolution? Is it random selection? No! It is Allah. He changes climates and selects the fittest or weakest to survive and produces creation after creation for a just end."

Notice that the author used the words "random" selection instead of natural selection. Like many of their Christian counterparts, Muslim creationists do not understand that the selection process is not random.

Islam For Today (http://www.islamfortoday.com/emerick16.htm) is another site that promotes a kind of Muslim Intelligent Design notion, and that also confuses natural selection with "mere chance." Attempting to speak for all Muslims, the author advocates a middle ground between evolutionists and Christian creationists. This view is that yes, living things adapt to their environments and have developed slowly from other species, but that the process was directed by God.

Another site on Islam (http://web.fares.net/w/.ee7f33a) again confuses natural processes with mere chance, and repeats the tired arguments concerning the second law of thermodynamics, irreducible complexity, and the supposed lack of transitional fossils. It also confuses metamorphosis with evolution in butterflies, and mistakenly promotes the view that the theory of evolution is a theory of competition only and does not allow for symbiotic relationships.

Islam101.com says nothing about evolution, but refers to Allah creating the world in six "periods." In many Muslim websites such as this one, creationism in one form or another is such a built in assumption that they make no attempt to defend it, or to attack evolution specifically.

ViewIslam.com insists that the theory of evolution is objectionable to Muslims because it "elevates 'chance' to the level of a deity." Science4Islam.com says, "science leads to Islam," yet provides perhaps the largest collection of misinformation about science on the Internet, and says nothing about evolution.

About half of the popular Muslim sites, however, are closer to Old Earth Creationism, although some of them accept the evolution of plants and other animals, but not that of humans.

AskIslam.com features Hazrat Mirza Tahir Ahmad, a Muslim scholar who answers questions. Although he says that the Christian creationists are wrong, he rejects the idea that humans evolved. Ahmad claims that the Quran is ahead of the scientists, and so it is the Quran where we should look for answers. He is what we might call an old earth Muslim creationist. Ahmad believes that God created the universe in six "days," but since time is relative, Allah's six days seem like billions of years to us.

Dr. Tahir ul Qadri, in his article "Creation & Evolution of the Universe" (*Western Views International*, Issue 1. Online: http://www.westernviews.com/issue1/creation.htm), says that although similarities between animals and humans exist,

> "...the Quran does not agree with the inference drawn from these similarities, nor do all the scientists agree on this. Also, they could not prove their theory conclusively. They acknowledge the lack of continuity in their theory. This discontinuity is called missing links. Due to many such missing links, there are several contending and contradicting interpretations, of the theory of evolution and no single unified theory has been put forward..."

Of course, like every scientific idea, evolution is never proven conclusively. It is instead supported by a network of interwoven strands of evidence from various fields of science that are obtained independently of one another. Other mechanisms of evolution (mutation, genetic drift, etc.) work alongside natural selection, and do not contradict it. Evolution is a unified theory; the disagreements among scientists have to do with the mode and tempo of evolution. Qadri echoes the mindset of those Muslims who are creationists and yet still call Islam scientific, and claim the Quran is a great scientific miracle:

> "We would say here that whichever aspects of the scientific research are inline with the Quranic concepts will smoothly reach their conclusion in a natural way. On the other hand, any idea or research which contradicts the Quran will never get out of the cobweb of confusion and doubts."

Answering-christianity.com says evolution has no place in Islam, because it is against what the Quran says. The authors also argue that since verse 20:55 of the Quran says Allah created every living thing from earth/dust, of course there would be similarities. They claim that we have co-existed with animals for thousands of years and "they have not changed a bit. In fact, many of them have already been extinct." Actually, we know that most animals have in fact changed quite a bit *if* they needed to change in order to adapt to a changing environment. That is why horses changed more dramatically than sharks. In addition, this site claims that Allah breathed his spirit into people, but not animals. It actually includes "Darwinism" among the "cults" listed on their answering the Pagan Religions page (http://www.answering-christianity.com/answering_pagans.htm).

Islamweb.net has a message board upon which the Webmaster answers questions. The answer to a question about human evolution is titled "Proving the falsity of Darwinian theory." Their first argument is that many scientists have disproved evolution. Supposedly, Dr. Surial, author of Collapse of Darwin's Theory, Dallas, and Huxley did, along with someone named "another scientist" and "a third scientist." First of all, Huxley was the strongest supporter of Darwin's ideas, being even more outspoken about them than Darwin himself. Second, Dr. Surial uses a typical, and ignorable, "missing links" argument. Who is Dallas? An Internet search on Dallas and evolution eventually led to creationist Dallas Willard. Willard is *not* a scientist. His doctorate is in philosophy, with a minor in the *history of* science. He is a philosophy professor and an author of books on Christianity (http://www.dwillard.org/biography/).

Other arguments on that same page were even worse: confusion about the meaning of the word "theory"; the idea that evolution and sexual reproduction are somehow mutually exclusive; a confusion of natural selection with survival of the strongest or "best," leading to the argument that evolution and death are mutually exclusive; and a confusion of natural selection with mere chance leading to the argument that living things cannot create themselves. They also say:

> "Then, ability of animals to accommodation is borne [sic] not gained or developed as claimed by Darwin and his followers. For example, a chameleon can change its colors according to its backgrounds. Other animals can not do that, since they have no such an ability. Then, we don't find such an ability in stones and other solid bodies."

This is massive confusion at best. Lastly:

> "Honoring the human being is contradictory to Darwin's theory which degrades the human being's rank to that of an ape."

It is not the job of science to tell us who or what to honor; science and ethics are two different things. The theory of common descent does not inevitably lead every individual to feel that human beings are now degraded; that is only one possible emotional reaction to common descent. An alternative reaction would be to continue to honor human beings, and have a greater sympathy for apes than in times past.

Islamicity.com does not say much about evolution, but it does advertise a book by Harun Yahya, the star of the Muslim creationists. Harun Yahya is said to be the pen name of Adnan Oktar, a prolific Turkish author who has written books specifically attacking evolution. His website at http://www.hyahya.org that makes it clear that his primary goal is to promote Islam:

> "Mr. Oktar became an "international hero" in communicating the fallacy of the theory of evolution and the fact of creation. The author has also produced various works on Zionist racism and Freemasonry and their negative effects on world history and politics. Besides these, Oktar has written more than a hundred books describing the morals of the Qur'an and faith related issues..."

> The target is to translate all books into English and many other languages in the near future, and thus to make them available for the benefit of all people...
>
> The common point in all the writer's works is that all the topics covered by his works are in full agreement with the Qur'an, and strongly affirmed by Qur'anic understanding...
>
> Each of the author's books on science-related topics stresses the might, sublimity, and majesty of God...A sub-group within this series are the 'Books Demolishing the Lie of Evolution'. The main purpose of these books is to demolish the materialistic and atheistic philosophy which has been put forward as an alternative and rival to religion and has been imposed on the whole world since the 19th century..."

Among his books are: *The Evolution Deceit*, which argues that recent developments in science completely disprove evolution, but that the idea is still being "foisted upon the public" through a worldwide "propaganda" campaign; *Disasters Darwinism Brought to Humanity*, which confuses Social Darwinism with biological evolution by natural selection; *Tell Me About the Creation*, which argues that evolution is wrong because living things did not come about by "chance" or "coincidence"; and *The Collapse of the Theory of Evolution*, which supposedly shows how new scientific findings and experiments prove that the theory of evolution is false.

Yahya has also written many articles. "The Fossil Record Refutes Evolution" merely combines the "missing links" argument with the "see, evolution isn't gradual" argument. When creationists say that evolution is not gradual, what they mean to say is that it does not happen at a gradual *and continuously steady rate*. This is a strawman because evolution does not require a continuously steady rate, and therefore, punctuated equilibrium can only *add* to the theory of evolution, *not* refute it. In other articles, he relies on the "irreducible complexity" argument.

In "A Special Animal In the Service of Mankind", Yahya argues that camels are well suited to their environment in the desert, saying they were especially designed to be "put into service for the comfort of man." He then argues that the camel could not have designed itself.

Yahya also claims that evolution has been supported by "forgeries" such as the Piltdown man, Nebraska man and Ramapithecus. But Piltdown man was revealed as a fraud after evidence from new fossils, improved dating technology, and new analytical tools showed that it was completely out of place in the fossil record. This was discovered by mainstream scientists, not creationists. Nebraska man was an honest mistake – taking a pig tooth to be hominid – that in fact was never widely accepted among scientists in the first place, and was quickly corrected even in the popular media. And Ramapithecus, once considered a hominid, is no longer accepted as such based on newer, more complete fossils. It was another honest mistake that was soon corrected. These three false leads do not compromise the hundreds of other hominid fossils.

Yahya also claims that all the transitional fossils between modern humans and ancient apes that have been found by scientists are either apes, or fully human. For instance, he claims that *Australopithecus* was fully an ape, because it was "later learned that it was not bipedal at all." However, no such discovery was ever made. Scientists agree that all evidence points to an Australopithecus that was upright and completely bipedal. Yahya gives other examples, but just like Christian creationists, nowhere does he explain what he *would* accept as a true transitional fossil.

One of the few Muslim sites that directly attacks science is the Witness-Pioneer website (http://www.witness-pioneer.org/vil/Articles/science/NK_islam_and_evolution.htm).

> "These considerations went through my mind at the University of Chicago during my 'logic of scientific explanation' days. They made me realize that my faith in scientism and evolutionism had something magical as its basis, the magic of an influential interpretation supported by a vast human enterprise. I do not propose that science should seriously try to comprehend itself, which it is not equipped to do anyway, but I have come to think that, for the sake of its consumers, it might have the epistemological modesty to 'get back,' from its current scientific pretentions to its true nature, as one area of human interpretation among others… I have hopes that science will someday get back to its true role, the production of technically exploitable knowledge for human life. That is, from pretentions to '*ilm* or 'knowledge,' to its true role as '**fann**' or 'technique.'"

Regarding evolution, it says that Islam and evolution are incompatible except for nonhuman evolution that does not include natural selection or random mutation. The author, Nuh Ha Mim Keller believes that all forms of evolution are "unscientific" but that natural selection and mutation in particular are *kufr*, unbelief in or infidelity to Islam, because they operate without the work of Allah, and therefore are against the Quran. This is especially true for any sort of evolution of humans since Keller argues that in the Quran, Allah set humans apart from the animals by giving people souls. Keller makes some of the usual creationist arguments, including "missing links" and the "see, evolution isn't gradual" argument. He writes:

> "From the point of view of **tawhid**, Islamic theism, nothing happens "at random," there is no "autonomous nature," and anyone who believes in either of these is necessarily beyond the pale of Islam.

> "Unfortunately, this seems to be exactly what most evolutionists think. In America and England, they are the ones who write the textbooks, which raises weighty moral questions about sending Muslim students to schools to be taught these atheistic premises as if they were 'givens of modern science.' Teaching unbelief (**kufr**) to Muslims as though it were a fact is unquestionably unlawful."

Keller also uses an argument similar to one favored by some Christian philosophers, saying that if "human consciousness itself is also governed by evolution," the theoretical conclusions we arrive at, including evolution, need not reflect external reality but only be useful to the extent they preserve the species. So, "By its own measure, it is not necessary that [evolution] be true, but only necessary that it be powerful in the struggle for survival. Presumably, any other theory – even if illusory – that had better implications for survival could displace evolution as a mode of explanation."

Of course, evolutionary theory does not demand that every evolved trait – such as being able to conceive of evolution – came about because this trait directly aided in survival. In science, we use our brains' evolved ability to imagine and test theories according to intellectual criteria other than whether they have a role in "the struggle for survival."

As this survey of the web indicates, Muslim creationism differs from Christian creationism in that it rarely attacks science as an activity or an institution, and young earth creationists are either a small minority among Muslims, or not connected to the Internet. An Islamic style of Intelligent Design seems to be popular among Muslims, although they don't usually call it that. Also, most of the Muslim arguments against evolution involve misunderstandings about the theory. Muslim apologists celebrate the quest for knowledge because they see it as central to, and as the path toward, Islam, and they therefore generally speak of science very highly. However, the lesson we can learn from this review of Muslim websites is that just because someone speaks highly of science doesn't necessarily mean he or she understands it.

[ABOUT THE AUTHOR]

Lynne H. Schultz is a freelance writer, book editor, ghostwriter, mother of two children, and contributor to the Darwin Day Program website. She is also a dues paying member of the National Center for Science Education, Americans United for Separation of Church and State, and the American Civil Liberties Union. She holds a B.A. in psychology.

[ADDITIONAL RESOURCES]

The Godlessheathen Home Page: http://www.atheism.org/~godlessheathen/

SECTION SEVEN

SCIENCE & SOCIETY:
AN INTIMATE RELATIONSHIP

> "Man with all his noble qualities, with sympathy which feels for the most debased, with benevolence which extends not only to other men but to the humblest living creature, with his god-like intellect which has penetrated into the movements and constitution of the solar system – with all these exalted powers – Man still bears in his bodily frame the indelible stamp of his lowly origin."
>
> – Charles Darwin in *The Descent of Man* (1871)

> "It is in the knowledge of the genuine conditions of our lives that we must draw our strength to live and our reasons for living."
>
> – Simone de Beauvoir in *All Said and Done* (1972)

The following essay is based on the William James Book Prize Lecture, presented by Steven Pinker to the Annual Meeting of the American Psychological Association in August, 1999. The essay appeared in the Annals of the New York Academy of Science and is republished here with permission from the author and the Academy.

Copyright © Steven Pinker. Copyright © 1999 by **New York Academy of Science***. All Rights Reserved.*

HOW THE MIND WORKS

by Steven Pinker

The human mind is a remarkable organ. It has allowed us to walk on the moon, to discover the physical basis of life and the universe, and to play chess almost as well as a computer. But the mind presents us with a paradox. On the one hand, many everyday tasks that we take for granted – walking around a room, picking up an object, recognizing a face, remembering information – are feats that scientists and engineers have been unable to duplicate in robots and computers. Nonetheless, these feats can be accomplished by any four-year-old, and we tend to be blasé about them.

On the other hand, for all its engineering excellence, the mind has many apparent quirks. For example, why is the thought of eating worms disgusting when worms are perfectly safe and nutritious? Why do men do insane things like challenge each other to duels and murder their ex-wives? Why do people believe in ghosts and spirits? Why do fools fall in love?

How the Mind Works is an attempt to answer those kinds of questions, using three key ideas: computation, evolution, and specialization.

The first idea, computation, is meant to explain how intelligence is possible in a physical system.

But what *is* intelligence? Few people today are satisfied with the traditional psychologist's definition, "whatever it is that IQ tests measure." A better definition comes from William James himself, who tried to put his finger on the difference between intelligent behavior and superficially similar behavior that we would not ascribe to intelligence:

> *Romeo wants Juliet as the filings want the magnet; and if no obstacles intervene he moves toward her by as straight a line as they. But Romeo and Juliet, if a wall be built between them, do not remain idiotically pressing their faces against the opposite sides like the magnet and filings with the card. Romeo soon finds a circuitous way, by scaling the wall or otherwise, of touching Juliet's lips directly. With the filings the path is fixed; whether it reaches the end depends on accidents. With the lover it is the end which is fixed; the path may be modified indefinitely."*

James identifies intelligence, then, with the pursuit of *goals* by means of *inference*, or the satisfaction of *desires* by *beliefs* about how the world works.

It is not just Romeo's behavior that we need to explain by invoking beliefs and desires, but virtually all human behavior. If I were to ask you, "Why did Bill just get on the bus?", to answer that question you wouldn't run a neural network simulation, and you wouldn't need to put Bill's head in a brain scanner. You could just *ask* him, and you might discover that the explanation for his behavior is that he wants to visit his grandmother, and he knows that the bus will take him to his grandmother's house. No science of the future is likely to provide an explanation with greater predictive power than that. If Bill hated the sight of his grandmother, or if he knew the route had changed, his body would not be on that bus.

But this excellent theory raises a puzzle. The beliefs and desires that cause Romeo's behavior, or Bill's behavior, are colorless, odorless, tasteless, and weightless. Nevertheless, they are as potent a cause of action as any billiard ball clacking into another billiard ball.

How do we explain this seeming paradox? The solution, I believe, is that beliefs and desires are *information*. Information is another commodity that is colorless, odorless, tasteless, and weightless yet can have physical effects without resorting to any occult or mysterious process. Information consists of patterns in matter or energy, namely symbols, that correlate with states of the world. That's what we mean when we say that something carries information. A second part of the solution is that beliefs and desires have their effects in computation-where computation is defined, roughly, as a process that takes place when a device is arranged so that information (namely, patterns in matter or energy inside the device) causes changes in the patterns of other bits of matter or energy, and the process mirrors the laws of logic, probability, or cause and effect in the world. The result is that if the old patterns are accurate or true, or correlate with some aspect of reality, the new arrangements of matter or energy will as well. The cascade gives the device an ability to deduce new truths from old truths in pursuit of a goal, which comes pretty close to William James' characterization of intelligence.

This idea, the computational theory of mind, is the only theory that I know of that can explain how it is that patterns of physical change in a device – be it a computer or a brain, or, for that matter, some extraterrestrial intelligent life – might accomplish something we would dignify with the term "thinking." It's the only explanation we have for how physical changes actually do something we would be willing to call intelligent.

A few comments must be added to this claim. One is that the computational theory of mind is very different from the computer *metaphor* of the mind. There are many ways in which commercially available computers are radically different from brains. Computers are serial; brains are parallel. Computers are fast; brains are slow. Computers have deterministic components; brains have noisy components. Computers are assembled by an external agent; brains have to assemble themselves. Computers display screen-savers with flying toasters; brains do not.

The claim is not that commercially available computers are a good model for the brain. Rather, the claim is that the answer to the question "What makes brains intelligent?" may overlap with the question "What makes computers intelligent?" The common feature, I suggest, is information-processing, or computation. An analogy is that when we want to understand how birds fly, we invoke principles of aerodynamics that also apply to airplanes. But that doesn't mean that we are committed to an airplane metaphor for birds and should ask whether birds have complimentary beverage service. It's a question of isolating the key component of the best explanation.

Another comment is that the computational theory of mind, explicitly or not, has set the agenda for brain science for decades. An old example from introductory neuroscience classes describes the naive person who asks, "Since the image on the retina is upside-down but we see the world right-side up, is there some part of the brain that turns the image right-side up?" We all realize that this question rests on a fallacy, that there is no such process in the brain, and that there doesn't need to be any such process. Why is it a fallacy? Because the orientation of the image on the retina makes no difference to how the brain processes information. Since information-processing is the relevant aspect of what goes on in the brain, the orientation on the retina-and, for that matter, on the visual cortex-is irrelevant; that is why the above is a pseudoquestion.

Similarly, the search for the neural basis of psychological functions is guided, from beginning to end, by invoking information-processing. One of the great frontiers of science is the search for the molecular basis of learning and memory. Well, of the hundreds or thousands of metabolic processes in the brain, how will we know when we've identified the one that corresponds to memory? We will know we have it when the process meets the requirements of the storage and retrieval of information. So again, it is information that sets the interesting questions in neuroscience.

A third comment is that the computational theory of mind is a radical challenge to our everyday way of thinking about the mind, because the theory says that the lifeblood of thought is information. That goes against our folk notion that the lifeblood of thought is energy or pressure. Why did the disgruntled postal worker shoot up the post office? Well, for many years, we say, pressure had been building up until he finally burst; if only he had had an alternative outlet to which to divert all of that energy, he could have released it in more constructive ways. The metaphor is that thought and emotion are animated by some superheated fluid or gas under pressure. Now, there is no doubt that this hydraulic metaphor captures something about our experience. But we know that it is not literally how the brain works: there is no container full of fluid and channels through which the fluid flows. And that raises an important scientific question: Why is the brain going to so much trouble to simulate energy and pressure, given that it doesn't literally work that way? I will return to that question later.

Let me continue with the second key idea: evolution. How do we understand a complex device? Imagine that you are rummaging through an antique store and you come across a contraption bristling with gears and springs and a handle and hinges and blades. You have no idea how to explain it until someone tells you what it's for – say, an olive-pitter. Once you realize what the device is for-what its function is – suddenly all the parts and their arrangements become clear in a satisfying rush of insight. This is an activity called "reverse engineering." In forward engineering, you start off with an idea for what you want a device to do and you go and build the device. In reverse engineering, you stumble across a device and try to figure out what it was designed to do. Reverse engineering is what the technicians at Panasonic do when Sony comes out with a new product. They go to the store, buy one, bring it back to the lab, take a screwdriver to it, and try to figure out what all the little widgets and gizmos are for.

For the last few hundred years, the science of physiology has been a kind of reverse engineering. Living bodies are complex devices and pose questions like "Why, in the eye, do we find the most transparent tissue in the body that just happens to be shaped like a lens, behind the lens an iris that expands and contracts in response to light, and a layer of light-sensitive tissue that happens to be at the focal plane of the lens?" Questions like these can be answered only by the idea that the eye was in some sense "designed" to form an image. We analyze it just as if it were a machine. For centuries, the complexity of the eye and other organs was taken as conclusive proof of the existence of God. If the eye shows signs of design, it must have a designer-namely, God. Darwin's great accomplishment was to explain signs of engineering in the natural world through a purely physical force, namely, the differential replication rates among replicators competing for resources in a finite environment, iterated over hundreds and thousands of generations.

Of course, the eye doesn't just sit by itself, isolated in the skull. Rather, the eye is connected to the brain. In fact, the eye can validly be considered to be an extension of the brain. And that naturally leads us to treat the mind as a complex natural device – in this case, a complex computational device – which makes the science of psychology a kind of reverse engineering. Just as in the case of the olive-pitter, we can understand the brain only once we have correctly identified its function. If we thought that the olive-pitter was a wrist-exerciser, we would have a very different explanation for what the parts are for. The crucial place to begin explaining the mind, therefore, is to understand its function. Since the mind is a product of natural selection, not of a conscious engineer, we have an answer to that question: the ultimate function of the mind is survival and reproduction in the environment in which the mind evolved-that is, the environment of hunting and gathering tribes in which we have spent more than 99% of our evolutionary history, before the recent invention of agriculture and civilizations only 10,000 years ago.

The third key idea is specialization. The mind is designed to solve many kinds of problems, such as seeing in three dimensions, moving arms and legs, understanding the physical world, finding and keeping mates, securing allies, and many others. These are very different kinds of problems, and the tools for solving them are bound to be different as well. We know that specialization is ubiquitous in biology. The body is not made of Spam, but is divided into systems and organs and tissues, each designed to perform a special function or functions. The heart has a different structure from the kidney because a device that pumps blood has to be different from a device that filters blood. This specialization continues all the way down: to the different tissues that the heart and the kidney ate made from, all the way down to differences in the molecules that they are made from. The mind, like the body is organized into mental systems, organs, and tissues. I doubt that the the mind will ever be explained in terms of some special essence or wonder tissue or almighty mathematical principle. Rather, the mind is a system of computational organs that allowed our ancestors to understand and outsmart objects, animals, plants, and each other.

I will try to give you a glimpse of how three of these organs of computation might be dissected, by presenting examples of seeing, thinking, and feeling.

Let's begin with seeing. The problem of vision can be made vivid by imagining what the world looks like from the brain's point of view. It is not what we whole, functioning human beings experience, namely, a showcase of three-dimensional objects arrayed in space. Rather, the brain "sees" a million activation levels corresponding to the brightnesses of tiny patches on the retina; the retinal image as a whole is a two-dimensional-projection of the three-dimensional world. The task for the visual system of the brain is to recover information about three-dimensional shapes and their arrangements from the pattern of intensities on the retinal image. The brain has evolved a number of tricks for solving this problem, and I am going to talk about one of them-sometimes called "shape-from-shading." Each of these tricks exploits a regularity of optics that is true by virtue of physical law, and the brain can, in a sense, run these laws "backwards" to try to make intelligent guesses about what is out there in the world based on the information that is coming in from the retina.

One important bit of physics is (roughly) that the steeper the angle formed by a surface with respect to a light source, the less light the surface reflects. So as I shine a flashlight perpendicularly to a card, it projects a concentrated, bright spot of light. But when I rotate the card, the beam is smeared across a large area, and any particular part of the area must be dimmer. Now, the shape-from-shading algorithms bit of psychology-more or less runs the law backwards and says that the dimmer a patch on the retina, the steeper the angle of the surface in the world. And with that algorithm, the brain can reconstruct the shape of an object by estimating the angles of the thousands of tiny facets or tangent planes that make up the surface.

This process works reasonably well, but it depends on a key assumption. Since it interprets differences in brightness as coming from differences in surface angle, it implicitly assumes a uniformly colored world, or at least a randomly colored world. That means that the process is vulnerable, because surfaces that are colored in clever ways should fool the shape-from-shading module and cause us to see things that aren't there. In fact, it does happen. One example is television. If alien anthropologists visited this planet, they would be puzzled by the fact that the average American spends four hours a day staring at a piece of glass on the front of a box. Why do we do this? Because the television set has been arranged to violate the assumption of uniform or random coloration. It has been engineered to display a highly nonrandom pattern that fools the shape-from-shading module of the brain into hallucinating a three-dimensional world behind the pane of glass.

Another example is makeup. A person who is skilled at applying makeup might put a little blush on the sides of the nose, because the eye of the beholder is attached to a shape-from-shading module that interprets darker surfaces as steeper angles, making the sides of the nose look more parallel and the nose smaller and more attractive. Conversely, if you put light powder on the upper lip, the brain says that lighter equals a flatter angle, which makes the lip took fuller, giving that desirable pouty look that models strive so hard to attain.

More generally, these examples offer an explanation for many of the seemingly inexplicable quirks of modern human thought and behavior. Many illusions, fallacies, and maladaptive behaviors may come not from some inherent defect or design flaw but from a *mismatch*: a mismatch between assumptions about an ancestral world that were built into our mental modules over millions of years and the structure of the current world (which we have tamed topsy-turvy by technology in our recent history). It has long been a puzzle for biologists why people do maladaptive things like eat junk food, use contraception (which, when you think of it, is a kind of Darwinian suicide), or gamble. But if you posit that our mental modules assume a world in which sweet foods are nutritious (namely, ripe fruit), in which sex leads to babies (as it tended to do until the invention of reliable contraceptives), and in which statistical patterns have underlying causes, then these activities no longer seem quite so mysterious.

Next, let me turn to the problem of thinking. There is an old puzzle that has worried philosophers and biologists ever since it was pointed out by Alfred Russel Wallace, the co-discoverer, with Darwin, of natural selection: What do illiterate, technologically primitive hunter-gatherers do with their capacity for abstract intelligence? In fact, this question might be more justly asked by hunter-gatherers about modem American couch potatoes. After all, life for hunters and gatherers was like a camping trip that never ended, but without Swiss army knives and tents and freeze-dried pasta. Our ancestors had to live by their wits and eke out a living from an eco-system in which most of the plants and animals whose bodies we consume as food would just as soon keep their bodies for themselves.

Our species succeeded by entering what a biologist might call the "cognitive niche": the ability to overtake the fixed defenses of other organisms by cause-and-effect reasoning. In all human societies, no matter how supposedly primitive, people use a variety of tools; traps; poisons; various ways of detoxifying plants by cooking, soaking, and leaching; methods of extracting medicines from plants to combat parasites and pathogens; and an ability to act cooperatively to accomplish what a single person acting alone could not achieve. These accomplishments show that the mind must be equipped with ways of grasping the causally significant parts of the world. The world is a heterogeneous place, and it is likely that we have several different intuitive theories or varieties of common sense that are adapted to figure out the causal structure of different aspects of the world. We can think of them as a kind of intuitive physics, intuitive biology, intuitive engineering, and intuitive psychology, each based on a core intuition.

The most basic is intuitive physics, an appreciation of how objects fall, roll, and bounce. The core intuition behind our intuitive physics is the existence of stable objects that obey some kind of physical laws. This is not a banal claim. William James said that the world of the infant is a "blooming, buzzing confusion'! — a kaleidoscope of shimmering pixels — and that knowledge of stable objects is an achievement only of late infancy. Yet one of the first things we learn in introductory courses in philosophy is that unless one has an assumption that the multitude of sensory impressions is caused by an -underlying stable object, one could experience the blooming and buzzing confusion all of one's life. Indeed, the more we know about the world of the infant, the more we see that William James, at least in this case, didn't have it quite right. The youngest infants that can be tested (about three months old) already are expecting a world that contains stable objects, and they are surprised when an experimenter rigs up a display in which an object vanishes, passes through another object, flies apart, or moves without an external push. As the psychologist David Geary summed up the literature: A "blooming, buzzing confusion" is a better description of the world of the *parents* of an infant than of the world of the infant.

But there are many objects that we encounter that seem to violate our intuitive physics. As the biologist Richard Dawkins has pointed out, if you throw a dead bird in the air, it will describe a graceful parabola and come to rest on the ground, just like the physics books say it should. But if you throw a live bird in the air, it won't describe a graceful parabola, and it might not touch land this side of the county boundary. In other words, we interpret living things such as birds not through our intuitive physics but through an intuitive biology. We do not assume that birds are some kind of weird, springy object that violates the laws of physics; we assume, rather, that birds follow a different kind of law altogether — the laws of biology. The core intuition of folk biology is that plants and animals have an internal essence that contains a renewable supply of energy or oomph, that gives the animal or plant its form, that drives its growth, and that orchestrates its bodily functions.

This deep-rooted intuition is found in all peoples and explains why hunter-gatherers are such excellent amateur biologists. Botanists and zoologists who do field work with hunter-gatherers are often astonished to learn that hunter-gatherers have remarkably detailed knowledge about local plants and animals and that their names for these plants and animals usually match the Linnaean genus or species of the professional biologists. These categorizations often involve lumping animals that, from surface appearance, look very different – for example, a caterpillar and a butterfly, or a male and a female bird with different plumage. Hunter-gatherers, using their intuitions about the hidden essences in animals or plants, predict their future behavior. They may, from a set of tracks, deduce the kind of animal and where it is likely to be heading so that they can surprise it at a resting place; or they might notice a flower in the spring and return to it in the fall to dig out a hidden tuber that the flower portends. They extract juices and powders of living things and try them out as medicines, poisons, and food additives.

The third kind of intuition, different from the first two, is an intuitive engineering. Our species is famous for exploiting and using tools or artifacts, and the core intuition behind tools is their function. If I ask you to define a "chair," you might say it is a stable horizontal surface supported by four legs. But that will not work for bean-bags, cubes, severed elephant's feet, and other objects that we can call chairs. The only thing that chairs have in common is that someone intended them to hold up a human behind. The core intuition behind our faculty to appreciate tools involves their function, or the intention of a designer. Young children, before they've entered school, sharply distinguish artifacts from living things. For example, in one experiment, children were told that doctors took a raccoon, spray-painted it black with a white stripe down its back, and implanted into it a sack of smelly stuff. The children were then shown a picture of a skunk and asked what it was. Most of them said that it was still a raccoon. But if they were told that doctors took a coffee pot, sawed off its handle, cut a hole through it, and filled it with birdseed, and then are shown a picture of a bird feeder and asked what it is, they say it's a bird feeder. This experiment shows that even young children appreciate that an artifact such as a bird feeder is anything that feeds birds, but a natural object such as a raccoon has an internal constitution that cannot be changed by superficial manipulations.

And finally, people have an intuitive version of psychology. I mentioned earlier that all of us explained Bill's behavior in getting on the bus not by assuming there is some kind of magnetic force that pulls him aboard or that he is a kind of artifact like a windup doll, but that he acts out of beliefs and desires, a kind of entity we cannot help but posit even though it is not directly observable. Again, this ability is displayed early by young children, who can, for example, deduce what an adult knows and wants just from observing what the adult is looking at.

There is evidence, apart from developmental psychology, that our reasoning ability really is divided into these intuitive theories or ways of thinking. For example, functional neuroimaging has shown that different parts of the brain are active when people think about tools or about living things. Moreover the presumably genetic syndrome of autism can be pretty well characterized by saying that it impairs a person's intuitive psychology: Autistic children really do interpret humans as if they were windup dolls, and have no concept that other people have beliefs and desires.

Misapplications of the four forms of thinking, or a shift from one way of thinking to another, can also explain certain puzzling behaviors and beliefs. One example is slapstick humor. We laugh when someone slips on a banana peel because of the sudden shift from thinking of the person in the usual way (using our intuitive psychology and thinking of him as a locus of beliefs and desires) to thinking of him as an object ignominiously obeying the laws of physics. Belief in souls and ghosts consists of taking our intuitive psychology and divorcing it from our intuitive biology, so that we think of minds that have an existence independent of bodies. And animistic beliefs do the opposite: They marry our intuitive psychology to our intuitive biology, physics, or engineering and allow us to think of trees, mountains, or idols as having minds.

I will now proceed to my final example: emotions elicited by other people. The main puzzle about our feelings toward other people is why they are often so *passionate* and seemingly *irrational*. Why do people pursue vengeance past the point of any value to themselves? Why do people defend their honor in crazy ways such as challenging each other to duels? Why do people fall head over heels in love?

The most common theory, among both scientists and lay people, is the "romantic theory" – the idea that the emotions come from a vestigial force (part of our heritage from nature), and that they are maladaptive and dangerous unless they are channeled into art and creativity. I'm going to explain a very different alternative, the "strategic theory," which proposes that passion is a "paradoxical tactic" wired into us. The basic idea is that a sacrifice of freedom and rationality can actually give one a strategic advantage when one is interacting with others whose interests are partly competing and partly overlapping with one's own. The theory applies particularly well to instances of promises, threats, and bargains. Just to show how unromantic this theory is, I am going to illustrate it by reverse-engineering romantic love.

Cynical social scientists and veterans of the dating scene agree on one thing: that love is a marketplace. There is a certain rationality to love-smart shopping. All of us at some point in our lives have to search for the nicest, smartest, richest, stablest, funniest, best-looking person who will settle for us. But that person is a needle in a haystack, and we might die single if we held out indefinitely for him or her. So we trade off value against time, and after a certain period set up house with the best person we have found up to that point. Good evidence for this sequence of events is the phenomenon called "assortative mating" by mate value: the overall desirabilities of a husband and a wife or a boyfriend and a girlfriend are approximately equally matched, as if each was trying to get the best partner he or she could.

Needless to say, that does not explain all there is to falling in love. There is an irrational part of love, an involuntariness and caprice to it. You cannot will yourself to fall in love. Many people can recall being fixed up with a person who looked perfect on paper, but when they met, they just didn't hit it off. Cupid's arrow didn't strike; the earth didn't move. It isn't a list of desirable traits that steals the heart; it's often something capricious like the way a person walks, talks, or laughs.

Is this any way to design a rational organism? As a matter of fact, it might be. Entering a partnership through totally "rational" shopping poses a problem. If you have set up house with the best person you have found up to a certain point, then by the law of averages, sooner or later someone even better will come along. At that point a rational agent would be tempted to drop a wife or husband like a hot potato. But now think of it from the spouse's point of view. Entering a partnership requires sacrifices – forgone opportunities with other potential partners and the time and energy put into child-rearing, among many other things. Rational spouses could anticipate that their partner would drop them when someone better came along, and they would be foolish to enter the relationship in the first place. Thus we would have the paradoxical situation in which what is in the interest of both parties – that they stick with each other – cannot be effected because neither one can trust the other if the other is acting as a rational, smart shopper.

Here is one solution to the problem. If we are wired so that we don't fall in love for rational reasons, perhaps we are less likely to decide to fall out of love for rational reasons. When Cupid strikes, it makes one's promise credible in the eyes of the object of desire. Romantic love is a guarantor of the implicit promise one makes in starting a romantic relationship, in the face of the problem that it may be rational to break that promise in the future.

Romantic love is an example of a concept from game theory called "paradoxical tactics," in which a lack of freedom and rationality can be an advantage. An analogy from a nonpsychological domain is the rationale for laws and contracts. When we apply for a mortgage from a bank, the law states that if we default on our payments, the bank has the power to foreclose on the mortgage and seize our house. It is only this law that makes it worth the bank's while to lend us the money, and therefore the law, paradoxically, works to the advantage of the borrower as well as the lender. Likewise, leases work to both the tenant's and the landlord's advantage by constraining the freedom of each. In this sense, many passions, such as romantic love, could be viewed as the neural equivalents of laws and contracts.

And by symmetrical logic, if passionate love and loyalty are guarantors that our promises are not double-crosses, so passionate vengeance and honor serve as guarantors that our threats are not bluffs. The problem with issuing a threat, such as "If you steal my goats, I will beat you up," is that carrying out a threat can be dangerous: you could get hurt beating someone up. The only value of the threat is as a deterrent; once it has to be carried out, it serves no one's purposes. Since the target of the threat is aware of that fact, he can threaten the threatener right back by calling his bluff and daring him to go through with the vengeance. How does one prevent one's bluff from being called? By being forced to carry out the threat. If we are wired to interpret defiance or trespass as an intolerable insult for which we demand vengeance regardless of the cost to ourselves, that emotion serves as a credible deterrent. One gets the reputation of being someone that people don't want to mess with.

Let me conclude. Is this a cynical view? Granted, most people don't like to think of themselves as as a system of computers "designed" by natural selection to promote survival and reproduction. On the other hand, the view is based on facts that I think can no longer be denied by any scientifically literate person. It is becoming increasingly clear, in particular, that the mind is a product of the brain; that the brain is a product of evolution, and that evolution is not guaranteed to produce niceness.

On the other hand, I personally do not think of it as a cynical view. Indeed, it may offer more grounds for optimism than some of the traditional ways of seeing man's place in nature. Recall the three key ideas of computation, evolution, and specialization. The idea of computation suggests that the mind is not a bundle of crude drives and reflexes, but is composed of intricate, ingenious, powerful software. The idea of evolution suggests that our legacy from natural selection is not just the nasty brutish emotions – greed, aggression, lust, a thirst for blood, a territorial imperative, and so on – but the kinder, gentler emotions as well, such as but love, friendship, sense of justice. Finally the idea of specialization – that the mind is a complex system composed of many parts – holds out the hope that some parts of the mind, those with the longest view of the future, can figure out ways to outsmart the other parts.

[ABOUT THE AUTHOR]

Steven Pinker is the Peter de Florez Professor in the Department of Brain and Cognitive Sciences, and Director of the Center for Cognitive Neuroscience at the Massachusetts Institute of Technology. He has published countless papers and has authored several books including, *How The Mind Works* (1998); *The Language Instinct: How the Mind Creates Language* (1999); *Words and Rules* (1999) and *The Blank Slate: The Modern Denial of Human Nature* (2002).

[ADDITIONAL RESOURCES]

Steven Pinker's Faculty Page: http://www.mit.edu/~pinker/

EDGE: Steven Pinker: http://www.edge.org/3rd_culture/bios/pinker.html

ECOVIEWS:
PATHOLOGY AND THE MEANING OF LIFE
by Ronald J. Brooks

We think of preservation of biodiversity as a natural behavior, perhaps evolved to ensure that we do not run out of important resources. Many people also assume that conservation of resources by placing long-term benefits ahead of short-term gains is widespread in the natural world, rather than just a cultural phenomenon of modern civilization. For example, we hear of prudent predators or parasites that restrict their own reproduction or virulence to protect a renewable resource base. Similarly, we embrace the view that native peoples or hunter-gatherers have an innate sense of conservation and preservation. So it is argued that modern civilizations have lost touch with nature and should turn to native peoples' wisdom to rediscover harmony with nature and a path to save our depleted planet.

These preservationist ideas are comforting in suggesting a return to nature as a clear solution to our current environmental woes, but this solution is not supported by evidence or by biological theory. All organisms have their rates of exploitation limited by external factors, usually their prey or competitors, not by self-restraint. Human sport hunters might eschew killing does or fawns because it isn't "fair", or because they know that this will help sustain the deer population in the future. Wolves have no such compunction and are subject to neither moral nor rational constraints. Similarly, it is egregious to argue that smallpox or tapeworms restrain themselves, consciously or otherwise, from exploiting hosts to the maximum. Survivors of such scourges are the most resistant individuals, just as the fastest, strongest deer are the ones that escape wolves.

A lack of long-term strategies in nature is what one would expect from Darwinian theory. Evolution proceeds by natural selection, which operates only on the current context, never with an eye to the future. Those individuals that reproduce most successfully leave the most genes for the future. If an organism committed suicide or remained celibate to ensure future supplies of limited resources, it would lose out. Lemmings do not jump off cliffs to relieve population pressure; otherwise only selfish lemmings would remain to pass on their selfish genes.

But if nature does not use restraint and conservation ethic to preserve biodiversity, surely our aboriginal ancestors did. Unfortunately, abundant evidence exists that stone-age peoples exterminated species at a rate to challenge even the most rapacious modern empire builders. Literally thousands of species were eliminated by ancient peoples who used only stone tools. These native peoples behaved naturally, taking all they could. Similarly, is any segment of our society more dedicated to erasing biodiversity than farmers and gardeners? Predators, parasites, competitors are all anathema to them. This destruction occurs precisely because these people are in touch with the land.

Despite the natural tendency to eradicate other life in support of our own, humans have developed an environmental conscience, an extension of our unique ability to worry about the future. But preservationism is largely confined to modern wealthy societies. Clearly, the less constrained we are by resources necessary for survival, the more we have options to plan for the future. Paradoxically, our overconsumption and access to huge amounts of energy have allowed us to see that this pace of exploitation may not be sustainable. We then try to slow the pace, but not enough that we would actually suffer.

The tenets of conservation are counterfactual and do not conform to prevailing biological theory. From nature's perspective, protecting other species at a cost to ourselves is, in fact, pathological. We must avoid the fallacy that what is natural is good; we must define and fight for our long-term environmental goals as if the weight of mother nature were against us, because it is. To plan successfully for the future of the planetary environment we must recognize that satisfying unrestrained short-term self-interest is normal but it guarantees calamity in the future. ∞

[ABOUT THE AUTHOR]

Ronald J. Brooks is a Professor of Zoology at the University of Guelph in Ontario, Canada. The major focus of his current research includes the life history of turtles, the changes in correlation among life history measures when these measures are examined among species, among populations, among individuals and within individuals over time and the social behavior of small mammals.

A modified version of this paper appears in the October 2002 issue of **GEOTIMES** *a journal published by the American Geological Institute.*

SUSTAINABILITY AND THE END OF HISTORY
by Ward Chesworth

Lawyers, economists, social scientists and politicians, the usual suspects, have enclosed the word sustainability in a semantic swamp. The morass becomes all the more impenetrable when sustainable is coupled with 'development'. In the middle of all the muskeg, is a simple idea trying to get out: a sustainable system is one that lasts. Simple though the concept is, problems begin when you try to decide how long a system must last in order for it to be labeled sustainable. Forever is not an option on a finite planet, governed by the laws of thermodynamics. Consequently a pragmatic limit is set.

In the long run, said Keynes, we're all dead. That goes for species too – extinction is the rule, not the exception. In the long run, human occupation of planet Earth is no more sustainable than a trilobite's. Natural Selection acts as the Grim Reaper, but a glance at the geological record shows that it has lots of help. The catastrophic impact of asteroid-sized meteorites, massive floods, volcanic eruptions and a climate swinging between greenhouse and icehouse, punctuate the history of the Earth like bursts from a cosmic Gatling gun. All of these events ensure that the biosphere is always in a state of adjustment, never completely stable. 'The balance of nature' does not exist in any real sense. At best, an ecosystem may have sufficient resilience (or inertia) to persist in at least a sort of quasi-equilibrium for a while, but geologically speaking, how long this might last – the effective sustainability of the system – can only be a short term phenomenon. But then, so is the history of Homo sapiens sapiens, a mere 200,000 years at most, on a planet four and a half billion years old.

For most of those 200,000 years and for all of the roughly 2,000,000 year lifespan of the genus Homo we functioned as hunters and gatherers, gradually evolving into a good Darwinian fit with respect to the environment of the African Savannah, learning to avoid big fierce animals, and consuming a diet rather different from the burgers, fries, donuts and caffeine of today. Then came the Neolithic Revolution, about 10 to 13 thousand years ago, and we developed a technology of genetic modification that enabled us to proceed from a population of perhaps a few million with a small ecological footprint, to a 6 billion strong super-species with a footprint that would cover four planet earths if the whole world enjoyed the standard of living of the average Western European or

North American. Our progression from being one of the extras in the Biosphere, to playing the starring role (hero or villain, as the case may be), is the unique and astounding characteristic of the geological epoch called the Holocene, the timespan since the last continental ice-sheets began to waste away. Throughout the Holocene, all the usual geological processes were at work, but they were joined by a new and hugely significant one, never before seen on the planet, and one without which the ascent of Homo sapiens to civilization would not have happened: agriculture, the technique of genetic modification already mentioned, in which a number of common grasses in particular, became the wheat, rice, corn, sorghum, oats and barley that we depend upon today.

It is legitimate to view agriculture as a geological process since it now involves the movement of earth materials on a scale to rival the effects that plate motions, mountain building, volcanic eruptions, earthquakes and other great planet-modifying events have on the surface of the planet. Globally, something like 1015 tonnes of soil per year are moved around by farmers in cultivating the land – an enormous, and totally new intervention in the Biosphere. Being totally new, the consequences are as yet poorly discerned and are therefore the occasion of copious argument, with much of it driven by the varied ideologies, Orwell's "smelly little orthodoxies", of the left and the right. Yet, from the 10,000 year history of arable agriculture a few clues may be obtained regarding the sustainability of our food-producing systems.

Using longevity or persistence as a proxy, the full spread in sustainability of farming systems capable of providing food or fibre to large populations, is from 5,000 years or more (Egypt, Northern China) to a couple of generations, say 50 years or less (the Midwest of the dustbowl, the Aral Sea region) – a range of two orders of magnitude. How long a given system may survive, is determined by a variety of factors including physical, biological and social ones. Our poor understanding of the variables involved, and especially of their interactions, largely accounts for the fact that we have not yet invented an agricultural system that is truly sustainable i.e. one that in principle leaves the ecosystem that contains it, continuously viable and recharged after each harvest. We seem to operate mostly by a form of crisis management in keeping a farming system going – the longevity of the system being a measure of a kind of band-aid persistence on the part of the farmer, rather than sustainability. Eventually, one or other of the determining factors is pushed to a breaking point or reaches such a point through natural planetary change. Human societies have a hard time remaining stable for as much as a few hundred years, and more often than not it is a failure of the food supply that promotes the breakdown.

The ultimate question regarding sustainability, as far as human society is concerned, is whether civilization itself is sustainable. Taking Felipe Fernandez-Armesto's definition of a civilization as a starting point – "a relationship to the natural environment, recrafted by the civilizing impulse, to meet human demands" – the question reduces to one of whether our demands have become so great, and our recrafting so extreme, that the natural environment in which we are embedded, breaks down as a life-support system, at least for Homo sapiens, once thought of as the Lord of Creation, but now brought down to earth as the culminating ape (H. G. Wells), the naked ape (Desmond Morris), or the third chimpanzee (Jared Diamond). Whatever kind of monkey we consider ourselves to be, the crucial resources in our struggle to survive are the supply of water and food. Undoubtedly, this supply is nowhere near as secure globally as might appear when viewed by the fortunate citizens of places as rich in both as the countries clustered around the North Atlantic. The anxious and continuing debate over "sustainable development" is a clear sign of this.

The basic question is: are there ways of coupling development to sustainability that might ensure an equitable supply of water and food for all, or is the only thing sustained by "sustainable development", development? If the latter is the case then we can soon expect to be "at one with Nineveh and Tyre". If recent figures of up to 50 calories being invested in food-production systems, for one calorie of food-energy produced, is any guide to the route that "development" is taking, we might as well leap onto the funeral pyre now.

No doubt in the industrialised world, we can enjoy our high material standard of living for a while longer by continuing to draw down the global capital of fossil fuel reserves, though it might mean a few more wars of the Gulf or Afghan variety to ensure the supply. And no doubt we can make, mend, and patch together, ad hoc "solutions" to see us through a decade or two, but the fact remains that we cannot, as the Bruntland Report of a few years ago proposed, raise less fortunate nations to our standard of living unless we can find another four planet earths.

So, how are we to avoid a terminal breakdown of society as we fight over resources in a Hobbesian-Darwinian "war of all against all"? Almost fifty years ago, a wise and now neglected geochemist, Harrison Brown, concluded that our high grade resources would eventually run out, but that we could continue to live well off low grade ones. He believed that in principle, population can be stabilised, and all of humanity adequately fed. The downside was that it would probably require a "completely controlled, collectivized industrial society" to make it happen. In other words "the end of history" that he foresaw was not the American style, liberal, capitalist democracy of Francis Fukuyama, but something more like Mao's China.

Is there anything we can do to be saved? Yes, said Harrison Brown, but we need to apply our considerable human intelligence, imagination and courage to the problem, make a prodigious effort of planning, and offer unselfish help to nations less fortunate. With each barrel of oil used, each additional mouth to feed, each centimetre of topsoil lost, the situation becomes ever more intractable. It is imperative we act now, he said.

That now, was half a century ago. ∞

[ABOUT THE AUTHOR]

Ward Chesworth is Professor of Geochemistry at the University of Guelph in Ontario, Canada. He was educated in England and Canada, and works on the chemical interactions between minerals and water in the terrestrial biosphere. For 10 years, he has taught a course that relates the history of civilization to the exploitation of geological resources, including soil. He is also an organizer of the Hammond Lectures, an annual lecture series on resource and environmental issues broadcast by the Canadian Broadcasting Corporation.

[ADDITIONAL RESOURCES]

GEOTIMES online: http://www.geotimes.org/current/

Darwin Course – Modes of Inquiry & Communication Across Disciplines:
    http://www.darwinday.org/education/guelph1.html

The Hammond Lectures: http://hammond.crle.uoguelph.ca/

Darwin Day 2002 Winning Essay
Strategy Paper on How to Increase the Public's Understanding and Support of Science

by David Aaronson

As I walked out of a test on evolution in freshman biology last year, I asked another student, "So, how'd you do?"

His reply was disappointing: "Not so well, but my family doesn't believe in evolution so I'll just get the teacher to discount that test."

I then debated whether to engage him in conversation or just mumble "oh" and move on. I chose the former and ended up convincing him to learn the material and retake the test rather than to try and discount it from his record. More importantly, though he did not say so outright, I suspect a wave of rationality was swaying him away from the incorrect beliefs that he held simply because his parents did, and towards truth. Unfortunately it is not always so easy.

I fear that in too many cases even the firmest evolutionists fail to do everything they can to promote the public understanding of evolution. Acceptance of evolution as fact – while necessary – is not sufficient for an adequate understanding of evolution. I found that in my high school biology class, class discussion focused more on the "evolutionary debate" than on the actual characteristics of evolution. While it is important to discuss in class why there is controversy over the subject – and completely unacceptable not to do so at all – it may be the case that as a result of this, students "believe" in evolution but do not truly understand it. And in classes where the "evolutionary debate" is even more prominent, students may actually believe that there exists a valid debate among scientists about the credibility of evolution, when of course in truth there is only a small but vocal minority of creationists.

A relatively small minority of those who "believe" in evolution actually understands some of its' most important aspects. These points include:

1. Evolution occurs at the level of genes, rather than the level of species or

organisms.

2. What we see as 'altruism' or 'cooperation' among individuals can actually evolve for selfish reasons – you cooperate because you expect the favor to be returned, or because the beneficiary is a family member who shares some of your genes.

3. Evolution (that life changed over time) is a separate idea from Darwinism or natural selection (the mechanism by which life changes).

4. Darwinism is not just a theory that explains in principle how complex life evolves from a simple beginning.

These are just the kinds of things that should be understood by every high school student in the country, but sadly are not.

The origin of the modern backlash against evolution can be traced back to post World War I America. After the war, many Americans took a fundamentalist view of Christianity, which in turn prompted a revolt against evolution since a literal interpretation of the Bible was in direct contradiction with evolution. The first targets naturally were schools, since they were the main source of information for soon-to-be adults.

In Tennessee, the Butler Law passed in early 1925. This law stated that evolution could not be taught in the classroom. The American Civil Liberties Union saw his law as unconstitutional, and set out to initiate a trial by which the law could be overturned. John T. Scopes was the science teacher that the ACLU found to actually initiate the court case. The trial turned into somewhat of a media circus. Scopes lost the trial, but this is just what he and his comrades wanted, in order to later appeal the decision to a higher court in the hopes of overturning the Butler Law. The media and public were in favor of Scopes, so the trial represented to the United States a moral victory for Scopes, despite the ruling against him. Cases like this appeared all over the country, but evolution was not firmly re-planted for another 30 years.

In the 1960's, evolution benefited from the Space Race. In response to suggestions that the Soviet Union had gained the upper hand in science, a revamped science curriculum included strong support for evolution, which consequently became prominent in American schools. However, this time period was also utilized by Fundamentalist and other Evangelical groups purporting creationism.

Several court cases since 1980 have had significant effects on the understanding of evolution. In McLean vs. Arkansas (1981), a law entitled "Balanced Treatment for Creation-Science and Evolution-Science Act" was overturned by the Supreme Court. The law had required that teachers give equal classroom time to creationism and evolution. A similar act was passed in Louisiana, requiring that both evolution and creationism or neither one could be taught in the public schools. The Act's constitutionality was tried in Federal District Court. Those opposing the law succeeded in overturning it; by a 7 to 2 vote, the act was found to violate the Establishment Clause of the First Amendment both in its illegitimate establishment of religion, and in it's barring of free speech. In 1999, the Kansas state school board voted to remove evolution from tests, thus effectively halting the teaching of evolution in that state. This action was met with a swift response from the scientific community, and was condemned across the nation. In February of 2001, a newly-elected school board reversed its previous decision, once again allowing the teaching of evolution.

The understanding of evolution should come as a result of improved standards in high school curricula. When its discussion is taken beyond the level of the controversy it creates, evolution can be understood as an integral part of science.

[ABOUT THE AUTHOR]

David Aaronson is a 12th grade student at New Hope Solebury High School.

Colin Tudge's article originally appeared in **The New Statesman** *on February 26, 2001. National Center for Science Education republished this piece in* **NCSE Reports** *and it is reprinted here with permission from the author.*

© *Colin Tudge* © **New Statesman Ltd** *2001. All rights reserved*

WHY SCIENCE SHOULD WARM OUR HEARTS
by Colin Tudge

I love science. It is what I have always done. I remember the warmth I nursed for weeks when, at age 13, I qualified for form Science 3A, already specializing at that tender age. I can still get the same thrill from some books and laboratories, when ideas are neat and properly decorated.

Science is not an innately arrogant pursuit. Newton said that science was for the glory of God – the God-given intellect dedicated to the glorification of God's works. We need not embrace the theological language of the 17th century, but the sentiment is precisely right. It is shared by many a modern scientist: that the true purpose of science is not to change the universe or to make it more comfortable, but to appreciate it more fully. Science has risen gloriously to the challenge: the universe that is now revealed, and the creatures within it, are infinitely more various and intricate than human beings ever conceived of without the help of science, and best of all is the realization that so much is still to be done.

Science, in short, should be heart-warming, encapsulating precisely that love of scholarship for its own sake (or, as Newton and many a rabbi and mullah would say, for God's sake) that runs through all civilization.

Other people do not see it like this. Science has a macho, gung-ho image. Understanding is not for its own sake, but is presented as the means to "conquest" – of the stars, of disease, of whatever. It comes across as a nuts-and-bolts pursuit: regrettably necessary, but posing various threats to the human spirit through its intemperate attacks on traditional beliefs and through its ruthless rationality. We are still locked in the battle of Dionysus v Apollo, with Apollo now cast as a blend of nerd and Strangelove. Schoolchildren turn away from science, and teachers must be bribed to take it up. For all this, scientists blame the media for their hype and general mischief (although the science correspondents are excellent); "the public" for its fecklessness and "ignorance"; and the subject itself, because it is too difficult and can properly be understood only by the officially initiated subsection of the intelligentsia.

What I want to suggest – in a spirit of friendliness – is that most of the fault lies with the scientists themselves and, in particular, with those who have striven hardest to be its advocates. Too often, they make it seem arrogant, macho, threatening, pompous but, in the end, naive: all those qualities that non-scientists say they find most repellent. Attempts to lighten it up frequently come across as clownishness – a dangerous quality to link to such obvious power. To some extent, this is just bad PR: there is no need for scientists to attack Christianity or Islam, for example. But the flaw runs deeper. It cannot be put right with a course in media training. The startling truth is that some of the most conspicuous advocates for science horribly misrepresent it: what it is, what it is like, what it can helpfully comment upon, and where it should be silent. They have, in fact, misconstrued the nature of their own craft.

The Nature Of Science

What science is was beautifully summarized by the philosopher Karl Popper. An idea can belong to science, he said, only if it is testable. Science is thus composed of testable hypotheses. He went on to say that hypotheses can, in principle, be shown to be false, but cannot be shown unequivocally to be true: so "testable hypothesis" became "falsifiable hypothesis". Various philosophers have taken him to task for this – pointing out that it can be just as hard to falsify as to verify. But "testability" wins through.

This idea is simple but far-reaching. It suggests immediately that science is not anchored, as many perceive it to be, in subject matter: it is not just the sum of chemistry, physics, and biology. Rather, it is a method, an approach, that can include the psychology and behavior of human beings or the policies of a government. Everything is within the compass of science, provided it is testable.

From Popper's notions, too, science emerges as an innately humble pursuit. Science is not an edifice of truth, built stone by stone. It is a landscape painting, never finished: each addition, each fresh handcart and bathing goddess, changes the balance of the whole, sometimes beyond rescue so the whole must be started again. Science's perceived arrogance is doubly unfortunate: it drives people away and it misrepresents the subject. Even if we reject Popper's strict principle of falsifiability, we see that the "truths" of science, its theories, must always be both partial and provisional. Every idea, no matter how satisfying and complete it seems, is waiting to be knocked off its perch, or at least improved upon. We can be certain at any one time only that there is more to know. All suggestions in the past that such-and-such a subject has been sewn up were invariably followed by the rudest of shocks. Michelson measured the speed of light in the late 19th century and declared that physics was over but for the dotting of is; in a decade or two came Einstein and then Planck, leading on to quantum mechanics, and then the whole universe was up for grabs, as it still is.

At any one time, it is logically impossible to know how much is not known – whether science has already lit up the universe like a football stadium, or merely laid a trail or two across the darkness. Non-scientists who fear that God's mystery has been forever compromised need have no fears; in the end, there is always mystery. Those who suggest that it is blasphemous to probe God's intentions are themselves guilty of blasphemy. God is not a conjuror, whose tricks seem tawdry when exposed. The more you see, the more wondrous it all becomes.

In short, as Newton and most of his contemporaries saw (including Galileo, who was a good Catholic), it is remarkably simple to reconcile excellent science with religion. Professor Richard Dawkins has made this very point: "If it is religious to perceive the universe with awe", he has said (although I paraphrase), "then I am religious." Much of the essence of religion is to experience first the awe, and then the sense of reverence that should follow from it. Science inspires in just this way.

ARE SCIENCE AND RELIGION INIMICAL?

Why, then, does science allow itself to be seen as the natural enemy of religion, and thus antagonize so many people for no good reason at all? Yes, there are some serious conflicts. The clash between Darwin and Genesis, for example, lies not in the details of geology, for Genesis can be seen as a good first draft, made in the virtual absence of data (or any inkling of "testable hypothesis"). The clash is as Daniel Dennett describes it in his book Darwin's Dangerous Idea (New York: Simon & Schuster, 1995). Orthodox Christians of the 19th century argued, as John Locke had done in the 17th, that intelligent beings could not be made except by an even more intelligent Creator already in place; but natural selection shows how, in principle, life and then intelligence can emerge from simple beginnings, with no overseer at all. But religion as a whole does not rest on that one piece of theology; and in general, given that religion is innately untestable, it remains outside the purview of science. There can be spats, but there is no mortal conflict in which to engage.

Why, then, has Dawkins, outstanding thinker and writer that he is within his own field, gone to such lengths to brandish his atheism, and so derisorily? His attacks have not been worthy of either his own scholarship or his victims'.

And why was Professor Lewis Wolpert so keen to emphasize the differences between religion and science in this year's Michael Faraday lecture (which might have made Faraday himself, a serious Christian, turn in his Sandemanian plot in Highgate Cemetery)? Wolpert is a Fellow of the Royal Society, former chairman of its Committee for the Public Understanding of Science, a prodigal broadcaster, and thus widely perceived as an official spokesperson. In prestigious lectures, what he says matters. And he told his audience that, whereas we have an evolved propensity for religion, with an innate tendency to believe in God, the scientific way of thinking is "unnatural", the antithesis of common sense. He has written a book on this: *The Unnatural Nature of Science* (Cambridge [MA]: Harvard University Press, 2000).

That human beings do have an evolved predilection for religion seems entirely plausible, and for the reasons Wolpert presented. We need to make sense of our environment, and "sense" in this context implies a feeling for cause and effect. Many religions are rooted in the entirely forgivable idea that nothing happens unless somebody makes it happen, and on the grand scale this "somebody" must be God. Furthermore, Wolpert might have added, societies cohere better if everyone subscribes publicly to a common belief, whatever that belief may be. Each needs to know what the others think, or they cannot trust each other.

Yet on Radio 4 a few days earlier, Wolpert spoke of religion as a "delusion". We are led to infer that belief in religion in general and God in particular is delusory because it is an evolved survival strategy. This "because" is a resounding non sequitur. What we are or are not evolved to believe in tells us nothing whatever about its reality. We are evolved to perceive light, but we do not conclude that light is delusory. Some theologians, quite independently of any Darwinian gloss, have argued that God must exist because otherwise we would not believe in Him. That argument is obviously fatuous, but so is its Wolpert-style antithesis.

Is science really unnatural? One can see that even Galileo's idea that light objects fall just as quickly as heavy ones has a counterintuitive quality, and quantum mechanics is off the scale of everyday conception. But the basic method of science as identified by Popper – make a guess and then test it – is the essence of all thinking. You do it, I do it, cats do it, even worms do it. For day-to-day purposes, there is no other way to get a feel for whatever is going on. Seen in this light, science emerges as the most natural process of all. The unnaturalness (if such it is) of science lies only in its explicitness: that it lays out problems for inspection, while our own commonsensical brains, bent on survival, draw lightning conclusions from fleeting impressions and are content with imperfection, provided it works.

Wolpert is also prone (and is far from alone in this) to emphasize the difficulty of science, and to conclude from this that it is best left to experts like, er, himself. At best, this view discourages, which is not a good thing for a teacher to do. At worst, it repels. It is an affront to democracy and, worse, to human dignity.

COMMUNICATING SCIENCE

Science can indeed be very hard – but for many different reasons, and it is important to distinguish them. It is hard because there is so much of it, and different bits depend on other bits, so it takes a long time to get into. But then, the same is true of any subject, from music to Spanish conversation. It is esoteric – meaning you have to know the background before you can get to grips with the matter in hand. Again, this is true of everything. Much of science, such as immunology, is complicated. But so is gardening – yet it is not innately difficult. Some science, such as quantum mechanics, is truly counterintuitive. But scientists, too, have difficulty with this: as Niels Bohr said, if you think it is easy, you haven't understood the problem. Or as a professor of physics once told me when I asked him how he pictured a nine-dimensional universe: "You don't. You just do the math." Math is always a problem, because the human brain is not geared to it. We are nature's wordsmiths. But some spectacularly good scientists have also been spectacularly bad mathematicians. Darwin regretted his own innumeracy. Faraday, a visionary physicist, pleaded forlornly for "plain words". There are very few Newtons around, able to invent a new form of math (calculus, in his case) when the traditional kinds prove inadequate.

In short, scientists also have trouble with the problems in science that are really hard. Most of them, like most of us, see only as far as the geniuses allow them to see. Indeed, take away the top 20 geniuses from the past 400 years and we would still be living in the 17th century, with the clever but stilted physics of Robert Boyle and John Ray's natural history. On the other hand, once the big ideas are explained, then some of them at least – including those of biology, which impact most directly on our lives – are actually rather easy. Natural selection can be explained in five minutes (although it has taken 140 years so far to work through the consequences), and Mendel's experiments with peas, the basis of all subsequent genetics, seem so simple that we may wonder what the fuss was about. In fact, Mendel's was the simplicity of genius. But we lesser mortals can wallow in his vision, just as we do in Mozart and Picasso. We do not have to belong to a special club to take part. Wolpert's insistence on the difficulty looks very like an attempt to protect the high priesthood. But those who build walls invite graffiti.

Scientists must loosen up. It is false, for example, to suggest, as they sometimes have, that people who do not practice science have no right to comment at all, and get it wrong when they do. The corollary, that scientists can be relied upon to get it right, is equally false. To be sure, there would be no science at all without scientists; but that does not mean that science belongs to them, any more than art belongs to artists, or politics to politicians. Science's greatest quality is that it does not rely upon authority, at least in principle. Its ideas are explicit, laid out for universal scrutiny. Only religion is arcane, and can make a virtue of this. To insist on the specialness of scientists, and to appeal to their authority, is to adopt the methods of religion at its most pristine, where all ideas must be filtered through the chosen few. If everyone comments on science, then many silly things will be said. But that is what it means for a subject truly to be part of culture.

When they are drawn into public debate, scientists, like all of us, should tell the truth, the whole truth, and nothing but the truth. Their presentations throughout the debates on "Mad Cow" Disease and genetically modified organisms have, on the whole, been woeful. We have been treated again and again to the stock phrase: "There is no evidence that…" I have never heard anyone add: "But absence of evidence does not mean evidence of absence." Without that codicil, we do not have the whole truth. I did not hear even one scientist explain in a public place why they took exception to the claim by the Aberdeen-based biologist Dr Arpad Pusztai that genetically modified potatoes had strange effects on rats. They had plenty of airtime, but they used it to complain that Pusztai had spoken to the press before apprising his peers. This was a fair complaint. But what really matters? People's well-being and enlightenment, or the dignity of scientists? When scientists ask me how to talk to the public, I ask them: "Have you ever tried behaving like a human being? Would you palm your Granny off with an unqualified, 'There is no evidence that…'?" It is not media-training that is needed, but a sense of citizenship.

Science needs a new image. Its Apollonian rationality is wonderful at its best, clear and pure. Beware, though, what has lately been called "the rationalistic fallacy". That it is rational does not make it right, or good, or necessarily better than some impassioned, if badly articulated, instinct. Besides, science has a romantic face, too. It is methodical, but it does not simply grind to its conclusions. Creativity matters at least as much as in the arts: huge leaps of imagination that come from nowhere. British students of English learn about Blake's antipathy to science and Thomas Gradgrind's obsession with "facts" ("A horse, Sir: a graminivorous quadruped"), but many English artists were inspired by science and technology: Turner, Ruskin, George Eliot, Gerard Manley Hopkins. Early 19th-century Germany gave us the buttoned-down end of modern biology, from cell theory through genetics (Mendel was German-speaking) to biochemistry. For much of that time, however, it was steeped in the literally "romantic" notions of Naturphilosophie and of vitalism, and in its turn the science inspired German Romanticism. All this seems to get written out of the act.

All in all, we need much more than committees and professors for the public understanding of science, lectures de haute en bas. We need a different kind of science education. Science should not be taught simply as an apprenticeship – which, more often than not, remains the case – but as a significant slice of cultural history and a way of looking at the world. ∞

[ABOUT THE AUTHOR]

Colin Tudge is a research fellow at the Centre for Philosophy of Natural and Social Sciences at the London School of Economics. He is the author of many popular books in biology, including *The Variety of Life: A Survey and Celebration of All the Creatures – that Have Ever Lived* (Oxford: Oxford University Press, 2000) and *The Impact of the Gene: From Mendel's Peas to Designer Babies* (New York: Hill and Wang, 2001).

[ADDITIONAL RESOURCES]

New Statesman Online: http://www.newstatesman.com/

EDGE: Colin Tudge: http://www.edge.org/3rd_culture/bios/tudge.html

IN CONCLUSION

...So Let's All Be Scientists!

> "We are at the very beginning of time for the human race. It is not unreasonable that we grapple with problems. But there are tens of thousands of years in the future. Our responsibility is to do what we can, learn what we can, improve the solutions, and pass them on."
>
> – Richard Feynman (1980)

> "Only a scientific people can survive in a scientific future."
>
> – Thomas H. Huxley (1896)

... So Let's All Be Scientists!
by Richard Carter

In his brief autobiography, completed less than a year before his death, Charles Darwin, with typical modesty, claimed to have had "no great quickness of apprehension or wit which is so remarkable in some clever men".

What's this? The genius who came up with the most important theory in biology (a theory, indeed, without which, one other illustrious biologist is forever being quoted as having remarked, nothing in biology makes sense); the man who worked out how coral reefs form before he had even seen one; the man whose noble bearded visage now graces the back of the Bank of England's £10 note; the man whose birthday we are urged to celebrate every February 12th: claiming that he wasn't particularly quick in the brain department? False modesty, surely, Mr Darwin!

But, no, Darwin knew where his real talent lay:

> *On the favourable side of the balance, I think that I am superior to the common run of men in noticing things which easily escape attention, and in observing them carefully. My industry has been nearly as great as it could have been in the observation and collection of facts. What is far more important, my love of natural science has been steady and ardent.*

Coming up with great theories, like other forms of invention, is typically 1% inspiration and 99% perspiration. It took Darwin a relatively short time following his return from his five-year voyage aboard HMS *Beagle* to piece together the basic ideas behind his theory of evolution by means of Natural Selection; he then spent the next 20 years amassing evidence in support of his theory before finally going to press. Indeed, it is debatable whether he would ever have published his theory during his lifetime, had he not been forced to do so to avoid being scooped by Alfred Russell Wallace.

Contrary to popular (and Darwin's own) belief, most major scientific advances do not come about by the careful, impartial observation of facts, which are gradually pieced together to form new and better theories. In the real world, most of the fact-gathering associated with major new theories occurs after the event: facts are gathered to test the new theories that scientists have concocted (sometimes almost out of the blue) in an attempt to explain anomalies associated with existing theories. In a process somewhat analogous to Darwinian Natural Selection, if the new theories are fundamentally inadequate, they will soon be discredited by observation and experiment and will die a quick death. If, however, the new theories are more robust, they will survive the initial tests, and will become worthy of further investigation. As the new theories pass more and more tests (possibly with a little adaptive fine-tuning), scientists become more and more convinced that there might be something in them (although they can never say categorically that they are "true"). Science, to extend the evolutionary analogy (although perhaps too far for some people), tends to be characterised by short bursts of revolution (where major shifts in scientific thinking take place), punctuated by much longer periods of "normal science" (where the accepted scientific theories of the day are tested, tinkered with, adapted, and generally fleshed-out).

So it was, albeit on a smaller, more personal scale, with Darwin's life in science: yes, he devised the (r)evolutionary theory that still underpins all the biological sciences, but most of Darwin's scientific life was spent carrying out good, occasionally brilliant, "normal science" to test his theory.

So, how did Darwin carry out this normal science? How did he exercise his great industry in the observation and collection of facts?

Darwin gathered his information in three ways: by talking and corresponding with other people, by reading, and by making observations and experiments of his own. His letters (which are still being compiled and will eventually be published in their entirety in the magnificently researched "Correspondence of Charles Darwin" [Cambridge University Press]) make fascinating reading for anyone interested in seeing the mind of a genius at work. They are jam-packed with references to books, papers and periodicals, requests for information, ideas and opinions, and descriptions of experiments (either carried out by Darwin himself, or to be carried out by the letters' recipients).

Darwin wrote to anyone he thought could help him with his research, from gardeners and pigeon fanciers to world-famous scientists and government representatives abroad. His requests for information ran from the mundane to the seriously weird. Here are just a few examples chosen at random from Darwin's correspondence of 1857:

- [To P. H. Gosse] Can you tell me, you who have so watched all sea-creatures, whether male Crustaceans ever fight for the females[?]

- [To W. B. Tegetmeier] I wonder whether Fowls when crossed throw odd & unexpected colours like Pigeons do. – Do you know of any such facts? For instance if you were to cross black Spanish with Black or Silver Polands, do you suppose ever red or other marked new colour would appear?

- [To Alfred Russel Wallace] Can you tell me positively that Black Jaguars or Leopards are believed generally always to pair with Black? ... Is the case of parrots fed on fat of fish turning colour, mentioned in your Travels?

- [To *Gardeners' Chronicle*] Will any reader of Gardeners' Chronicle be so kind as to take the trouble to inform me how Dun or Mouse-coloured Ponys (sic) with a dark stripe down their backs are bred? The breed is common in Norway on the banks of the Indus & in the Malayan archipelago, & is in some respects very interesting in relation to the origin of the domestic Horse. Is this peculiar colour thrown from Ponys of any other colour, or must one or both parents be Dun?

- [To T. C. Eyton] Do you know when owl or Hawk eats a little bird, how soon it throws up pellet? Can it throw up pellet whilst on wing? ... Could your gamekeepers find a roosting place, & collect a lot for me?

- [To J. D. Hooker] [D]o you remember, whether the introduced Sonchus in N. Zealand, was less, equally, or more common than the aboriginal stock of same species, where both occurred together[?]

- [To T. H. Huxley] Do you know whether the embryology of a Bat has ever been worked out?

Reading through Darwin's letters, you can't help wondering whether, on receiving the latest missive from Down House, some of his regular correspondents occasionally wondered "Oh good grief! What on earth does he want this time?". But such musings are both unfruitful and uncharitable: the truth of the matter is that Darwin was remarkably successful in enlisting the help of others in his research, and the help that he received was willingly and freely given – a remarkable testament to the spirit of cooperation that existed amongst individuals in pursuit of scientific knowledge during the mid-nineteenth century.

Darwin's other great external source of information was published documents in the form of books, periodicals, and scientific papers. He was a voracious reader, and regularly scanned scientific publications in search of evidence for or against his theories. He did not own copies of all the books he read, but borrowed many of them by post from the libraries of his friends, gentlemen's club, and various scientific bodies. [A modern bibliophile would shudder to see how Darwin treated the books in his own library, scribbling notes in the margins, and tearing some of the thicker books in half down the spine to make them easier to handle. But to Darwin, books were first and foremost a source of information: they were to be used, not cosseted.]

But Darwin didn't get all his information through other people's work. When it came to conducting his own experiments and making his own observations, he was certainly no slouch. Indeed, he was even prepared to carry out exhaustive experiments to verify (or sometimes refute) facts which everyone else deemed so obvious that checking them was unnecessary.

Nowhere was Darwin's willingness to put accepted truths to experimental test better illustrated than in his investigations into how various plant seeds could be transported across seas (a subject of great importance to his theory of evolution, one consequence of which was that related species on different islands must have descended from a common ancestor). The perceived wisdom of the day was that most seeds would not germinate after being exposed to salt water. Darwin decided to put the accepted dogma to the test. He filled dozens of small bottles with salt-water and placed different types of seeds in each, letting them soak for varying amounts of time before planting them in dishes in his study. To his delight, nearly all of the seeds grew into healthy plants – even after several days in salt-water. But, being Darwin, he didn't stop there: he wrote to one of his naturalist contacts and asked them to try leaving seeds in the sea; he got the British consul in Norway to send him exotic seeds that had washed up on the local beaches (J. D. Hooker identified them as Caribbean in origin, planted them, and was amazed to see them germinate); he wrote to his cousin to ask him to try similar experiments on lizards' eggs; and he carried out calculations to see just how far seeds could have been carried by ocean currents.

But, almost as an afterthought, Darwin then realised that there was an important problem with his hypothesis that seeds could be transported across the seas by ocean currents: most of the seeds in his experiments sank! So he began another series of weird experiments to determine alternative ways in which seeds might be carried over great distances: he floated fruit-covered branches in a tank of salt water (they rotted an sank); he tried feeding oats to fish (the fish spat them out); he inspected the feet of downed grouse and ducks for seed-carrying mud; he floated a dead pigeon whose crop was full of seeds in salt-water for a month, then successfully germinated the seeds; he retrieved more seeds from bird droppings and pellets and germinated those too.

∞

Charles Darwin was truly fortunate to be a man of independent means living in a golden age of science: an age when science had become sufficiently advanced to have separated into distinct disciplines, but when a virtual recluse working away in his home in the countryside could still make a revolutionary contribution to his chosen field.

As we progress through the early years of the twenty-first century, the world of modern science – with its industry-sponsored research grants, genetic patents, intellectual property rights, supercomputers, electron microscopes, satellite tracking systems, and rival genome projects – is very different from the scientific world so beloved of Darwin. Cutting-edge modern science consumes big bucks (and copious quids), and is usually carried out by whole teams of scientists. Sadly, there is no longer a place for dedicated amateurs like Darwin.

But hang on a minute! Why shouldn't there be a place for amateurs in the modern world of science? Darwin didn't need supercomputers or electron microscopes to carry out his work; all he needed was an enquiring mind, a few good friends to write to, and some (literally) common or garden species to observe and experiment on. Darwin's revolutionary theory might have been inspired by his round-the-world trip and the wildlife of the Galápagos, but what did he study for the rest of his life, when amassing the bulk of his data? Seeds, garden plants, barnacles, earthworms, etc. If a few thousand personal computer users can help search for extraterrestrial intelligence with nothing more than an internet connection and some screensaver software, what couldn't a few thousand amateur scientists achieve if they put their minds together?

Both the Darwin Day Program and the Friends of Charles Darwin were created in order to celebrate the life and works of the world's greatest amateur scientist. What better way to do this than by following in his footsteps? Not by dreaming up revolutionary new theories, but by observing and experimenting on whatever species are to hand.

For example, every summer my garden is inundated with slugs – thousands and thousands of slugs. What do I do when I see them? I spend many a satisfyingly mindless hour picking them up in a pooper-scooper and slinging them into the adjacent field. I know absolutely nothing about slugs (not even a half-way effective way of ridding my garden of them), but my slug-slinging activities have allowed me, quite unintentionally, to make a number of observations about slugs which might be worthy of further investigation. Here are a few examples:

- The slugs in my garden come in various sizes and colours, but exactly how many species am I dealing with? Are the brown slugs and black slugs different species (as

I suspect), or different varieties of the same species. Do the small, white slugs grow into large browns or large blacks or both (or do they stay forever small whites)?

- Am I just imagining it, or do some of the slugs actually feed other slugs?

- For all the thousands of slugs I have found, I have never come across a single snail in my garden. Why is that? Is it too cold (I live in the Pennines)? Do the slugs eat them (see previous point), or out-compete them? Am I just not looking hard enough? Or is there simply not enough calcium in the area to allow snails to make shells (possibly because the soil is too acidic)?

- Do the slugs in my garden differ from those in my parents' garden (separated, as they are, by 60 miles in distance and 220 metres in altitude)?

- Like many other gardeners, I half-suspect that the slugs I sling over the wall have a homing instinct. Do they really?

- The slugs seem to have favourite areas in the garden. Why do they favour these areas? Do they have favourite plants to eat or to shelter in, or are the clumpings imaginary?

- Is there any pattern in the meandering trails the slugs leave all over my patio?

- Are my slug-slinging activities exerting selective pressures on the slugs to grow wings?

I'm sure none of these questions is particularly new or insightful (apart, maybe, from the last one), and finding answers to them is hardly going to cause major rumblings in the professional scientific community, but maybe, just maybe, something useful might come out of my idle musings – such as a new strategy to stop the blighters from eating my potato plants, perhaps.

So why not give it a go? Build yourself a slug-arium; count the spots on ladybirds; look for peppered moths on tree trunks; try to create a blue sweet pea; breed pigeons; find out whether male crustaceans ever fight for the females; look for seeds in bird pellets; try floating seeds in salt-water; keep a notebook; involve your friends; e-mail people; read books; search the web; if you have a website, publish your findings (even if they're inconclusive).

Above all, exercise great industry in the observation and collection of facts.

Be a scientist.

[ABOUT THE AUTHOR]

Richard Carter, FCD, was born in England 57,027 days after Charles Darwin. He was one of the founders of The Friends of Charles Darwin, who successfully campaigned to have their hero celebrated on a Bank of England bank note. Despite possessing a complex brain evolved over several million years of natural selection, he is fighting a losing battle of wits against the molluscs in his garden.

[ADDITIONAL RESOURCES]

The Friends of Charles Darwin: http://www.gruts.demon.co.uk/darwin/